Topics in Information Systems

Editors:

Michael L. Brodie
John Mylopoulos
Joachim W. Schmidt

On Conceptual Modelling

Perspectives from Artificial Intelligence, Databases, and Programming Languages

Edited by

Michael L. Brodie
John Mylopoulos
Joachim W. Schmidt

With 25 Illustrations

Springer-Verlag
New York Berlin Heidelberg Tokyo

Michael L. Brodie
Computer Corporation of America
Four Cambridge Center
Cambridge, MA 02142
U.S.A.

Joachim W. Schmidt
Fachbereich Informatik
Universität Frankfurt
Dantestr. 9
6000 Frankfurt
Federal Republic of Germany

John Mylopoulos
Department of Computer Science
University of Toronto
Toronto, Ontario M5S 1A7
Canada

(C.R.) Computer Classification: I.6.0, I.2, H.2.0, D.3.0

Library of Congress Cataloging in Publication Data
Main entry under title:
On conceptual modelling.
Bibliography: p.
Includes index.
1. Digital computer simulation. 2. Artificial intelligence. 3. Database management. 4. Programming languages (Electronic computers) I. Brodie, Michael L. II. Mylopoulos, John. III. Schmidt, Joachim W., 1941–
QA76.9.C6505 1984 001.4'34 83-10552

Softcover reprint of the hardcover 1st edition 1984

ISBN-13: 978-1-4612-9732-1 e-ISBN-13: 978-1-4612-5196-5
DOI: 10.1007/978-1-4612-5196-5

9 8 7 6 5 4 3 2 1

Preface

The growing demand for systems of ever-increasing complexity and precision has stimulated the need for higher level concepts, tools, and techniques in every area of Computer Science. Some of these areas, in particular Artificial Intelligence, Databases, and Programming Languages, are attempting to meet this demand by defining a new, more abstract level of system description. We call this new level *conceptual* in recognition of its basic conceptual nature.

In Artificial Intelligence, the problem of designing an expert system is seen primarily as a problem of building a knowledge base that represents knowledge about an enterprise. Consequently, *Knowledge Representation* is viewed as a central issue in Artificial Intelligence research. Database design methodologies developed during the last five years are almost unanimous in offering *semantic data models* in terms of which the designer directly and naturally models an enterprise before proceeding to a detailed logical and physical database design. In Programming Languages, different forms of *abstraction* which allow implementation-independent specifications of data, functions, and control have been a major research theme for a decade. To emphasize the common goals of these three research efforts, we call this new activity *conceptual modelling.*

To date, Artificial Intelligence, Databases, and Programming Languages have contributed independently to the development of conceptual modelling. We believe that further advances in conceptual modelling require the integration of the concepts, tools, and techniques that were developed for system description. A prerequisite for integration is increased communication among researchers in the contributing areas. This volume is an outcome of a continuing effort directed at increasing such communication.

In our view, conceptual modelling needs can be met only by a leap to a higher, more abstract level of system descriptions. The required leap is analogous to the one that has been achieved in going from assembly languages to so-called high level programming languages in the tradition of Algol 60, PL/1, and Lisp. The move to high level languages resulted in developing high level mechanisms for algorithm specification in terms of such concepts as variable, function, data type, and control structure. The leap now needed for conceptual modelling requires high level mechanisms for the specification of large, complex models of an enterprise. It will involve identifying concepts and establishing techniques for conceptual modelling, and then developing tools (*e.g.*, languages) with which to support these concepts and techniques.

The fundamental characteristic of the new level of system description is that it is closer to the human conceptualization of a problem domain. Descriptions at this level can enhance communication between system designers, domain experts and, ultimately, system end-users. They can also serve as knowledge bases to be used by an expert system and as starting points for a system implementation. The features of the new level are not fixed yet, as the reader will soon learn, but they are beginning to take shape and form. They are expected to include facilities for modelling objects and their relationships, for expressing assertions that can be used in information retrieval, or as integrity constraints for modelling operations (*e.g.*, transactions and actions) and their relationships, and also as special facilities for modelling messages, exceptions, and defaults. Perhaps more importantly, the new level is expected to offer organizational principles for structuring a system description that has an *epistemological* basis, thus stressing the epistemological nature of system descriptions built at this level.

It is not new that the three research areas share research goals and could therefore share results and methodologies. In 1976, a joint SIGMOD/SIGPLAN conference on Data Abstraction, Definition, and Structure [ORGA76] attempted to promote communication between the areas of Databases and Programming Languages. A comparative survey of Knowledge Representation and Data Models published the following year [WONG77] attracted considerable attention. Likewise, a panel discussion on Data Models and Abstract Data Types at the 1978 VLDB Conference [BROD79] drew a large and enthusiastic audience. In 1979, a more ambitious effort was started with the goal of bringing together researchers from all three areas. The result, the Pingree Park Workshop on Data Abstraction, Databases, and Conceptual Modelling, was held in June 1980 with the sponsorship of SIGART, SIGMOD, and SIGPLAN. It was generally considered successful in creating among researchers a new awareness of concepts and achievements outside their own field that attempt to deal with conceptual modelling problems. The proceedings of the workshop [BZ80] included surveys of research on Knowledge Representation, Semantic Data Models, and Data Abstraction, position papers by the workshop participants, and edited manuscripts of the discussions that took place during the workshop sessions.

The events described above indicated that the process of communication among researches in Artificial Intelligence, Databases, and Programming Languages was underway. It was also clear that the process had already resulted in contributions to conceptual modelling. However, the process had only begun since a substantial portion of the discussion at Pingree Park dealt with definitions and basic goals. Hence, we felt that further specific efforts were required to stimulate fruitful communication. The efforts included a workshop that offered detailed discussions of specific research issues, as well as this book which elaborates the research issues and presents the technical discussions from the workshop.

The National Science Foundation was instrumental in encouraging and supporting both the workshop and the presentation of the technical discussions included in this book. The symposium took place in Intervale, New Hampshire, in June 1982. Attendance was limited to twenty, and each participant was asked to submit in advance research papers from the three areas on the general topic of Conceptual Modelling. The symposium program included one session per paper. To ensure participation of all three areas in each session, each paper was presented by someone who does not work in the research area treated by the paper. This decision resulted in lively discussions whose spirit, unfortunately, is only partially captured by the edited transcripts appearing in this volume. The symposium ended with three summary presentations, given by Carl Hewitt for Artificial Intelligence, Michael Stonebraker for Databases, and Stephen Zilles for Programming Languages.

The organization of the book is based on a somewhat contrived classification of the chapters into the three research areas. There is one chapter for each paper that was discussed at the symposium, along with an edited transcript of the discussion that followed each presentation. In an attempt to set the stage for the reader who is not familiar with the three areas, we included in the volume overviews of Knowledge Representation, Semantic Data Models, and Data Abstraction. Two late submissions, one related with Conceptual Office Modelling, and the other on Algebraic Data Specifications, are included with no discussions. The book ends with edited transcripts of the summaries presented by Hewitt, Stonebraker, and Zilles.

Bringing this project to a conclusion required great amounts of effort, time, and money and would not have been possible without the support of many individuals and organizations. We are particularly thankful for the financial support received from the National Science Foundation and Computer Corporation of America; also the Universities of Maryland, Toronto, and Hamburg. Dr. Michael McGill of the National Science Foundation provided valuable support to the project. Computer Corporation of America, in addition to providing strong encouragement and assistance, made a significant contribution in terms of text editing. In particular, it is a pleasure to acknowledge the contributions of David Darcy, Nancy Wolfe, and Bill Modlin. Winfried Lamersdorf, Michel Pilote, and Dzenan Ridjanovic volunteered their services to record and transcribe the symposium sessions. Special thanks are also due to all the participants for their contributions, both visible and invisible, to the success of this project. Finally, we would like to thank the Johnstons, the innkeepers at the New England Inn in Intervale, New Hampshire, for their hospitality, fine food, and beautiful mountain setting for the workshop.

Michael L. Brodie
John Mylopoulos
Joachim W. Schmidt

November, 1982

Contents

Part I

Artificial Intelligence, Database, and Programming Language Overviews

1
An Overview of Knowledge Representation

John Mylopoulos
Hector J. Levesque
University of Toronto

1. Introduction

This is a brief overview of terminology and issues related to Knowledge Representation (hereafter KR) research, intended primarily for researchers from the Database or Programming Language area.

Knowledge Representation is a central problem in Artificial Intelligence (AI) today. Its importance stems from the fact that the current design paradigm for "intelligent" systems stresses the need for the availability of expert knowledge in the system along with associated knowledge handling facilities. This paradigm is in sharp contrast to earlier ones which might be termed "power-oriented" [GP77] since they placed an emphasis on general purpose heuristic search techniques [NILS71].

The basic problem of KR is the development of a sufficiently precise notation with which to represent knowledge. Following [HAYE74] we shall refer to any such notation as a (knowledge) *representation scheme*. Using such a scheme one can specify a *knowledge base* consisting of *facts*. For the purposes of this paper, a knowledge base will be treated as a model of a world/enterprise/slice of reality.[1]

Hector Levesque is currently affiliated with Fairchild Laboratory for Artificial Intelligence Research, Palo Alto, California.

This is a revised and updated version of a paper that appeared in [BZ81].

[1] For other ways of viewing a knowledge base see [BS80] (p. 68).

A number of important papers on the subject already exist. [HAYE74] deals with central issues of KR theory, and [BC75] includes a fine collection of papers on KR theory and practice. More recently, [FIND79] [WH79] [GM78] have compiled important collections of papers on semantic network, production system, and logical representation schemes respectively. [BOBR77] contains an interesting collection of short presentations on a number of state-of-the-art schemes, and [GP77] relates KR to other important problems in AI. A recent SIGART Newsletter issue, [BS80], contains questionnaire results from more than 80 research groups working on or using a representation scheme. Finally, [WM77] examines KR issues and searches for counterparts in Data Modelling research.

2. A Taxonomy of Representation Schemes

When trying to classify representation schemes we consider the world as a collection of *individuals* and as a collection of *relationships* that exist between them. The collection of all individuals and relationships at any one time in any one world constitutes a *state*, and there can be *state transformations* that cause the creation/destruction of individuals or that can change the relationship among them. Depending on whether the starting point for a representation scheme is individuals/relationships, true assertions about states, or state transformations, we have a (semantic) *network, logical,* or *procedural* scheme respectively. A number of schemes proposed recently adapt more than one viewpoint and will be considered separately.

2.1 Logical Representation Schemes

Logical Representation Schemes employ the notions of constant, variable, function, predicate, logical connective, and quantifier in order to represent facts as logical formulas in some logic (first or higher order/multi-valued/modal/fuzzy, *etc.*). A knowledge base, according to this view, is a collection of logical formulas that provide a partial description of a state. Modifications to the knowledge base occur when the introduction or deletion of logical formulas occurs. In this sense, logical formulas serve as atomic units for knowledge base manipulation in such schemes.

An important advantage of logical schemes is the availability of inference rules in terms of which one can define proof procedures. Such procedures can be used for information retrieval [REIT78a], semantic constraint checking [NY78], and problem solving [GREE69].

[NILS71] presents a review of early results, applications, and promises of theorem-proving research, whereas [GM78] contains a representative sample of more recent work on logical schemes and theorem-proving and their applications to Databases.

Another strength of logical schemes is the availability of a clean, well understood and well accepted formal semantics [MEND64], at least for "pure" logical schemes that are quite close to first order logic. As one moves to representation schemes that try to deal with knowledge acquisition [MD78], beliefs [MOOR77], and defaults [REIT78b], the availability of a clean formal semantics becomes more problematic and is an area of active research. The chapter by Levesque dealing with the semantics of incomplete knowledge within a logical framework gives a good indication of what is and isn't provided by classical logic to the KR researcher.

A third strength of logical schemes is the simplicity of the notation employed, thus facilitating knowledge base descriptions that are understandable. Yet another strength is the conceptual economy encouraged by such schemes, allowing each fact to be represented once, independently of its different uses during the course of its presence in the knowledge base.

An important drawback of logical schemes is the lack of organizational principles for the facts that constitute a knowledge base. A large knowledge base, like a large program, needs organizational principles to be understandable as a unit. Without them, a knowledge base can be as unmanageable as a program written in a programming language that does not support abstraction facilities.

A second drawback is the difficulty in representing procedural and heuristic knowledge[2] such as:

"If you are trying to do A while condition B holds, try strategies C_1, C_2, ..., C_n."

An interesting departure from logical representation schemes has been proposed by Kowalski [KOWA74], who argues in favour of a dual semantics for logical formulas of the form:

"B_1 *and* B_2 *and* ... *and* B_m *implies* A"

The first is the traditional Tarskian semantics; the second is a procedural semantics that interprets the formula as:

"If you want to establish A, try to establish B_1 and B_2 and ... and B_m."

2 [HAYE77] argues against this point.

The language PROLOG [KOWA74] exemplifies this idea and has gained many supporters because it combines the advantages of logical and procedural representation schemes.

Another attempt to integrate logical and procedural representations has resulted in the representation language FOL [WEYH80]. Here procedures can be used as referents of logical expressions. Reasoning in FOL can be carried out either in terms of inference rules or procedures, thus combining the strengths of both approaches to KR.

Logical schemes are strongly related to Codd's Relational Model [CODD70], and it is fair to argue that such schemes have their counterparts in Database Management. The chapter by Reiter explores this relationship and argues for a proof-theoretic view of the Relational Model.

2.2 Network Representation Schemes

Semantic networks come in such a wide variety of forms and are used in so many ways that it is difficult to pinpoint what is common to all of them. To a large extent, this diversity is explained by the history of these networks that is summarized in the chapter by Israel and Brachman. In its most basic form, however, a semantic network represents knowledge in terms of a collection of objects (nodes) and binary associations (directed labelled edges), the former standing for individuals (or concepts of some sort), and the latter standing for binary relations over these. According to this view, a knowledge base is a collection of objects and relations defined over them, and modifications to the knowledge base occur through the insertion/deletion of objects and the manipulation of relations. Ever since they were originally proposed [QUIL68], most network schemes have favoured the use of binary relations as a means of representing binary or components of n-ary relationships. A network knowledge base has an obvious graphical representation where each node denotes an object and each labelled edge $(n_1, R, n_2,)$ indicates that $(n_1, n_2,) \in R$, R being one of the relations used in the knowledge base.

Early versions of network schemes tended to encourage a proliferation of relations that had little or no semantics when new kinds of knowledge were represented. Indeed, to some, semantic networks were nothing more than a (cute) notation in search of a semantics. This practice and other deficiencies of earlier network schemes are criticized in influential papers by Woods [WOOD75] and Schubert [SCHU76]. Such criticism has triggered a trend towards using network schemes that have formal semantics and are *descriptively adequate* (*i.e.*, can be used to represent any fact expressible in a logical scheme). Some of these schemes simply view network knowledge bases as convenient notations and/or implementations of logical knowledge bases ([SHAP79]

[SCHU76], *etc.*). Others, notably KL-ONE [BRAC79] view network schemes as tackling a different set of representational issues, and they propose a set of primitive relations accordingly.

A crucial issue of network schemes is the organizational axes they offer for structuring a knowledge base. Some of the axes that have been used are discussed briefly below.

Classification

According to classification, an object (*e.g.*, John Smith) should be associated with its generic type(s) (*e.g.*, STUDENT, MALE, PERSON). Including this organizational axis in a network scheme forces a distinction between *tokens* (*e.g.*, John Smith) and *types* (*e.g.*, PERSON). Some network schemes use classification recursively to define (meta) types with instances types, *etc.* (*e.g.*, PSN [LM79]).

Aggregation

This axis relates an object (*e.g.*, John Smith) to its components or parts. For example, the parts of John Smith, viewed as a physical object, are his head, arms *etc.* When viewed as a social object, they are his address, social insurance number, *etc.* As with classification, aggregation can be applied recursively so that one can represent the components of the components of an object, *etc.* Thus, aggregation defines a second organizational dimension for network schemes.

Generalization

Generalization relates a type (*e.g.*, STUDENT) to more generic ones (*e.g.*, PERSON). The generalization relation between types, often called is-a, is a partial order and organizes types into a *generalization* or *is-a hierarchy*. A common use of this hierarchy in semantic networks has been to minimize storage requirements by allowing properties associated with general object types to be inherited by more specialized ones. In addition, generalization and the other primitive association types provide the means for the overall organization and management of a large knowledge base.

Partitions

Another method of organizing network knowledge bases is proposed in [HEND75], and it involves grouping objects and elements of relations into *partitions* that are organized hierarchically, so that if partition A is below partition B, everything visible or present in B is also visible in A unless otherwise specified. Partitions have been found useful in representing time, hypothetical worlds, and belief spaces (*e.g.*, [COHE78]).

Not all network schemes treat the organizational principles mentioned above in the same way. For example, NETL [FAHL79] and others identify classification with generalization.

Due to their nature, network schemes directly address issues of information retrieval, since the associations between objects define access paths for traversing a network knowledge base. Another important feature of network schemes is the availability of organizational principles. A third is the graphical notation that can be used for network knowledge bases and that enhances their understandability.

A major drawback of network schemes has been the lack of formal semantics and standard terminology. The chapter by Israel and Brachman provides a brief history of semantic networks and a thorough account of their semantic deficiencies.

2.3 Procedural Representation Schemes

Such schemes view a knowledge base as a collection of active agents or processes. Most procedural schemes have been influenced quite heavily by LISP, which has been used almost exclusively as the implementation language for AI systems. Indeed, in the past, LISP itself was a favorite representation scheme due to, among other things, its basically symbolic nature and the dynamic run-time environment it offers its users.

Procedural schemes beyond LISP can be classified on the basis of the stand they take with respect to two issues. The first is concerned with the activation mechanism offered for processes. The second involves the control structures that are available.

On the first issue, PLANNER [HEWI71] [HEWI72] introduced the notion of *pattern directed procedure invocation.* A knowledge base is viewed in PLANNER as a global database of assertions and a collection of *theorems* (or *demons*) that watch over it and are activated whenever the database is modified or searched. Each theorem has an associated *pattern* which, upon the theorem's activation, is matched against the data about to be inserted/removed or retrieved from the database. If the match succeeds, the theorem is executed. Thus with theorems the usual procedure calling mechanism is replaced with one in which procedures are called whenever a condition is satisfied.

Production systems [WH79] offer a procedural scheme that is in many ways similar to PLANNER. A knowledge base is a collection of *production rules* and a global database. Production rules, like theorems, consist of a pattern and a body involving one or more *actions.* The database begins in some initial state, and rules are tried out in some prespecified order until one is found whose pattern matches the database. The body of that rule is then executed, and matching of other rules continues. This account is an idealization of production systems and most of them vary in the form of rules they follow and the order in which they are tried [DK75].

There are major differences between the activation mechanism of a PLANNER theorem and a production system rule as well. The order in which theorem patterns are matched is undetermined in PLANNER (although the user can define one for any particular situation in which he tries to tamper with the database). "Standard" production systems, like Markov algorithms, have a fixed ordering of rules that determine when each rule will be matched against the database. Another important difference is that theorems can directly call other theorems whereas productions can do so only indirectly by placing appropriate information in the database. Thus, a production system database can be viewed as a workspace or a bulletin board that provides the only means of communication between rules.

Turning to control structures, several proposals exist which extend or otherwise modify the usual hierarchical control structure of LISP or ALGOL. As indicated earlier, production systems offer one where there is no direct communication or control between rules. Thus a production system knowledge base consists of a collection of *loosely coupled* rules, and this feature renders such knowledge bases easy to understand and modify.

PLANNER's control structure for theorems uses *backtracking,* and when a theorem's body is executed and fails to achieve a predetermined goal, the side-effects of the unsuccessful theorem are erased and other theorems are tried until one is found that succeeds. It has been argued quite convincingly that backtracking is an unwieldy control structure [SM72] and it should be avoided at all costs.

An extreme proposal with regard to control structures is Hewitt's ACTOR formalism [HBS73] [HG74] which views *all* objects that are part of a knowledge base as *actors* (*i.e.,* active agents that play a role on cue according to a script). Actors are capable of sending and receiving *messages* which, naturally, are also actors. Thus, writing a program in the ACTOR formalism involves deciding on the objects in the domain, the messages each object should receive, and what each object should do when it receives each kind of message. The ACTOR formalism basically does not impose a preconceived control structure on its user. Instead, it provides him with control primitives so that he can define his own. The ACTOR formalism was inspired by the Smalltalk programming language [BYTE81] which has been under development at Xerox PARC for more than a decade.

Procedural schemes have, in principle, one major advantage and one major drawback compared with other types of schemes. They allow the specification of direct interactions between facts, thus eliminating the need for wasteful searching [WINO75]. On the other hand, a procedural knowledge base, like a program, is difficult to understand and modify. Each of the proposed schemes discussed in the previous paragraphs goes some distance toward eliminating the drawbacks of pure procedural schemes while maintaining their advantages.

2.4 Frame-Based Representation Schemes

Since 1975, when Minsky originally proposed it [MINS75], the notion of *frame* has played a key role in KR research. A frame is a complex data structure for representing a stereotypical situation, such as being in a certain kind of living room or going to a child's birthday party. The frame has slots for the objects that play a role in the stereotypical situation as well as relations between these slots. Attached to each frame are different kinds of information, such as how to use it, what to do if something unexpected happens, default values for its slots, *etc.* A knowledge base is now a collection of frames organized in terms of some of the organizational axes discussed earlier, but also other "looser" principles such as the notion of *similarity* between two frames.

Minsky's original frame proposal essentially provided a framework for developing representation schemes that combined ideas from semantic networks, procedural schemes, linguistics, *etc.* Several representation schemes proposed since then have further developed the frame proposal. Below we present brief descriptions of four of them.

FRL [GR77]

An FRL knowledge base consists of frames whose slots carry information such as comments on the source of a value bound to the slot, a default value, constraints, and procedures that are activated when a value is bound, unbound, or needed for a slot. All frames are organized into a hierarchy which appears to be a combination of classification and generalization as described in Section 2.2. The procedures attached to a slot are expressed in LISP.

KRL [BW77]

This is a more ambitious representation language than FRL. Like FRL, the basic units of a KRL knowledge base are frames that have slots and that have several kinds of information attached to each slot. Unlike FRL, where this information provides details about how to instantiate a frame, KRL is much more concerned with a matching operation for frames. All on-going processes are controlled by a multiprocessor agenda that can be scheduled by the designer of the knowledge base. KRL also supports belief contexts that can serve to define an attention focusing mechanism. "Self knowledge" can be included in a knowledge base by providing descriptions of other descriptions.

OWL [SHM77]

Unlike other frame-oriented schemes, OWL bases its features on the syntactic and semantic structure of English, taking as its founding principle the Whorfian Hypothesis that a person's language plays a key role in determining his model of the world and thus in structuring his thought. An OWL knowledge base can be viewed as a semantic network whose nodes are expressions representing the meaning of natural language sentences. Each node, called a concept, is defined by a pair (genus, specializer) where "genus" specifies the type or superconcept and "specializer" serves to distinguish this concept from all other concepts that have the same genus.

KL-ONE [BRAC79]

A KL-ONE knowledge base is a collection of concepts, and each concept is a highly structured object, having slots to which one can attach a variety of information (defaults, modalities, *etc.*). To a concept one can also attach structural descriptions that express constraints on the values that can be bound to the different slots of the concept. Concepts provide purely descriptional structure and make no assertions about existence of a referent or coreference of descriptions. A separate construct called a *nexus* is used to make assertions about the world being modelled. Also, KL-ONE offers procedural attachment as a means of associating procedural information (expressed at this time in LISP), with a concept. Another important feature of KL-ONE is the strong organization of concepts it encourages through a version of the generalization axis discussed in Section 2.2.

Two other important representation schemes are introduced in later chapters. Omega is a description-based scheme and is sketched briefly in the chapter by Hewitt and de Jong. The Plan Calculus, described by Rich, is a frame-based scheme intended for the representation of programming knowledge. The chapter by Borgida, Mylopoulos, and Wong derives many of its key ideas from PSN, yet another frame-oriented scheme described in [LM79].

3. Distinguishing Features of Representation Schemes

The reader who has a background in Databases and/or Programming Languages must have already noticed the similarity in basic goals between KR research as we have described it in this paper and research on Semantic Data Models or Program Specifications. In all three cases the aim is to provide tools for the development of descriptions of a world/enterprise/slice of reality which correspond *directly* and *naturally* to our own conceptualizations of the object of these descriptions. The tools under consideration involve a representation scheme/semantic data model/specification language that serves as the linguistic vehicle for such descriptions. Below we list some of the more technical (and less vague) characteristics of representation schemes whose qualities distinguish them from their semantic data model/program specification language cousins.

3.1 Multiple Uses of Facts

Unlike a database, whose facts are used exclusively for retrieval purposes, or a program, whose facts are used only during the execution of some procedure, a knowledge base contains facts that may have multiple uses. A representation scheme must take this into account in terms of the tools it offers. Below we list some possible uses [BOBR75].

Reasoning

Given a collection of facts, new facts may be deduced from them according to given rules of inference without interaction with the outside world. Some inferences have the flavour of inference techniques in logic. For knowledge bases, however, it is also sometimes useful to derive facts by means of specialized procedures that exploit given facts only in fixed ways. For example, a procedure that determines whether a pair is in the transitive closure of some binary relation can perform reasoning of a very specialized nature and is only applicable to facts associated with a transitive relation. Also, a knowledge base may be represented in such a way that there are "preferred inferences." The use of defaults is a good example of such a mechanism.

Deductive reasoning, which has a formal, special purpose or heuristic flavour, is not the only kind of reasoning. There are also inductive [BROW73] and abductive reasoning [POPL73], which have played a role in some knowledge bases.

Given this variety of reasoning mechanisms, the question for a designer of a representation scheme is not how he can include all of them in his scheme, but which one, if any, he is going to include. Logical schemes clearly have an advantage over other types of schemes when considered from the point of view of (general purpose) reasoning facilities.

Access

Access (and storage) of information in a knowledge base for question-answering purposes constitutes an all-important use of the knowledge base. The associationist viewpoint of network schemes, particularly their organizational axes, make them strong candidates for access-related uses.

Matching

Matching as a knowledge base operation can be used for a variety of purposes, including:

1. *classification* (*i.e.*, determining the type of an unknown input)
2. *confirmation* where a possible candidate to fit a description is matched against it for confirmation purposes
3. *decomposition* where a pattern with a substructure is matched against a structured unknown and the unknown is decomposed into subparts corresponding to thosę of the pattern
4. *correction* where the nature of a pattern match failure leads to error correction of the unknown input

The matching operation itself can be:

1. *syntactic* where the form of the unknown input is matched against another form
2. *parametric* in the tradition of Pattern Recognition research [DH73]
3. *semantic* where the function of the components of the pattern is specified and the matcher attempts to find elements of the input to serve this function
4. *forced matching* as in MERLIN [MN74] where a structure is viewed as though it were another and matches of corresponding items may be forced

KRL has paid special attention to matching as a knowledge base operation.

3.2 Incompleteness

Except for situations in which a knowledge base models artificial "microworlds" (*e.g.*, [WINO72]), it cannot be assumed that the knowledge base is a complete description of the world it is intended to model. This observation has important consequences for the operations defined over a knowledge base (inference, access, matching) as well as the design methodologies for knowledge bases.

Consider first the operations on a knowledge base. Incompleteness of the knowledge base can lead to very different answers to questions such as:

"Is there a person who lives in Toronto?"

and the answer will depend on whether it is assumed that the persons currently represented in the knowledge base are the only persons in the world being modelled. If the knowledge base is taken to be complete, it may be sufficient to search through the objects related in a certain way to the object representing Toronto. If the knowledge base is possibly incomplete, however, the answer can be "yes" without there being any corresponding object in the knowledge base. A second example is the question:

"How many children does Mary have?"

which might be answered, under the completeness assumption, by counting representational objects that satisfy some criteria. Without this assumption much more complex forms of reasoning (such as reasoning by cases, reductio ad absurdum and the like) might be required to determine the answer. Similarly, from the facts:

"Someone is married to Mary"
"John is not married to Mary"

one can draw different conclusions if George is the only other person represented in the knowledge base, depending on whether it is assumed that John, Mary and George are the only persons in the world being modelled. Similar remarks apply for matching.

Until recently much of the work on KR ignored the problem of incompleteness or dealt with it in an *ad hoc* way. The chapters in this volume by Levesque and Reiter can be seen as attempts to correct this situation. Reiter shows how different forms of incompleteness (and especially the null values of the Relational Model) can be explained in terms of the proof theory of first order logic. Levesque begins with the very general form of incompleteness allowed by first order logic and investigates a query language appropriate for knowledge bases that are radically incomplete.

Viewing a knowledge base as an incomplete and approximate model of a world that can always be improved but can never be quite complete, leads to design methodologies for knowledge bases that are drastically different from design methodologies that are designed for programs. Thus, in Programming Languages the leading design methodology encourages a "once and for all" process where the designer begins with a clear idea of the algorithm he wants to realize and proceeds to construct a complete design (*e.g.*, [WIRT81]). In AI, a knowledge base is developed over a period of time that can be as long as its lifetime by means of different *knowledge acquisition* processes that can range from interactive sessions with an expert (*e.g.*, [DAVI77]) to the automatic generation of new facts based on the system's "introspections" (*e.g.*, [LENA77]). Organizational principles underlying the structure of a knowledge base can play a crucial role in determining the direction of knowledge acquisition (*i.e.*, which facts should be acquired first and which facts should be acquired later).

3.3 Self Knowledge

There are many kinds of self knowledge, and some of them were described in the previous section. For instance, the statement:

"All students are known (to the knowledge base)"

says something about the state of the knowledge base, not the world. Facts that describe the form or allowable configurations of other facts (*e.g.*, type definitions) constitute an important class of self knowledge. Making such facts available for question answering and inference, by representing them the same way as other facts, is an important capability of *declarative* schemes (*i.e.*, logical and network schemes) generally not shared by procedural schemes. A good example of the use of such self-knowledge for knowledge acquisition is provided in TEIRESIAS [DAVI77].

A second kind of self-knowledge involves the ability of a system to answer elementary questions about its actions as in SHRDLU [WINO72], or about the strategies it uses to debug problem solving procedures as in HACKER [SUSS75].

A very general introspective architecture is proposed and investigated in [DOYL80]. It is shown that one's reasoning about what inferences to make can be used in making decisions and in taking action. All relevant aspects of the intentional state of the system (such as its goals, beliefs, *etc.*) are subject to scrutiny and are therefore explicitly represented.

[SMIT82] defines a new dialect of LISP in which programs can "reflect" on their own execution. At any stage of the computation, a program can jump to the level of its interpreter and examine what state it was in as encoded in the data structures of the interpreter. In particular, a program can look at what it has left to do on the stack and perhaps decide to do something completely different.

4. Current Issues

While there is perhaps no general agreement about the major unresolved issues in KR, there is a definite trend away from the more implementational issues and towards more formal and conceptual investigations of representation schemes. This has led, among other things, to a reappraisal of the role of formal logic in KR [NEWE81] [MOOR82]. The most apparent result of this is the recent trend towards hybrid schemes which incorporate both logical and nonlogical sublanguages [RICH82] [ISRA82] [BL82]. These hybrid schemes do not attempt to overlay features of a logical language on top of, for example, a semantic network, as was often done in the past, but instead partition the knowledge representation task so that the network and the logical languages are given separate responsibilities.

In [BL82], for example, a knowledge base is factored into a *terminological* component that maintains the technical vocabulary of a domain, and an *assertional* component that maintains a collection of facts about that domain. A terminological sublanguage in the style of KL-ONE is used to provide a set of term-forming facilities that allow new terms to be appropriately placed on a taxonomy relative to previously defined ones. A first order logical sublanguage is used to manage the assertional component and provides facilities for forming a theory and reasoning about the domain using a theorem prover. The point of contact between the two components is the predicate and function symbols of the logical language: these nonlogical symbols are, in fact, the technical terms of the terminological component. This means that deduction within the assertional component must treat the nonlogical symbols not as primitives (as in a standard logic), but as structured terms that have a complex meaning to be derived from the terminological component. The claimed advantage of the separation of the two areas, however, is that each component can be optimized independently and that neither has to suffer from the limitations of the other.

Another important issue in KR that recently has received considerable attention is the formalization of default reasoning. Standard logical deduction schemes are *monotonic* since new axioms never invalidate previous theorems. Common sense belief revision, on the other hand, is obviously *nonmonotonic* since the acquisition of knowledge can cause old beliefs (specifically, those that were held by default) to be discarded. The papers in [BOBR80] examine formal systems that have this nonmonotonicity property, and more recent developments are discussed in [ISRA80] [REIT81] [KONO82] [REIT82].

5. Acknowledgement

Alex Borgida read an earlier draft of this paper and offered many thoughtful suggestions for improvement.

6. References

[BOBR75] [BC75] [BOBR77] [BOBR80] [BW77] [BRAC79] [FIND79] [BS80] [BZ81] [BL82] [BROW73] [BYTE81] [CODD70] [COHE78] [DAVI77] [DK75] [DOYL80] [DH73] [FAHL79] [FEIG77] [FIND79] [GM78] [GP77] [GR77] [GREE69] [HAYE74] [HAYE77] [HEND75] [HEWI71] [HEWI72] [HBS73] [HG74] [ISRA80] [ISRA82] [KONO82] [KOWA74] [LENA77] [LM79] [MD78] [MEND64] [MINS75] [MOOR77] [MOOR82] [MN74] [NEWE81] [NY78] [NILS71] [POPL73] [QUIL68] [REIT78a] [REIT78b] [REIT81] [REIT82] [RICH82] [SCHU76] [SHAP79] [SMIT82] [SUSS75] [SM72] [SHM77] [WH79] [WEYH80] [WINO72] [WINO75] [WIRT71] [WM77] [WOOD75]

2
On the Development of Data Models

Michael L. Brodie
Computer Corporation of America

1. Data Modelling

This chapter presents a view of data models and their development. It outlines the basic problem of data modelling in the database context, data model concepts and terminology, a taxonomy of data models, research issues central to data models, and those issues of particular interest in current research.

Data models are central to information systems. The vast and growing majority of information systems are based on some form of data model. Data models provide the conceptual basis for thinking about data-intensive applications and they provide a formal basis for tools and techniques used in developing and using information systems. For many years there has been a rapid growth in information systems not only in sheer numbers but also in the scope of applications being developed. Whereas business information systems have been the largest application class, engineering and office systems may make even more extensive use of databases.

Data modelling with respect to *database design* can be described as follows. Given the information and processing requirements of a data intensive application (*e.g.,* an information system), construct a representation of the application that captures the static and dynamic properties needed to support the desired processes (*i.e.,* transitions and queries). In addition to capturing information requirements given at design time, the representation must be able to meet ever-changing requirements.

A *data model* is a collection of mathematically well defined concepts that help one to consider and express the static and dynamic properties of data intensive applications. (This definition is somewhat idealistic. Most data models have evolved intuitively and have not been formally defined.) It is generally assumed that an application can be characterized by:

- Static properties such as objects, object properties (sometimes called attributes), and relationships amongst objects (*i.e.*, a particular class of object properties)
- Dynamic properties such as operations on objects, operation properties, and relationships amongst operations (*e.g.*, to form transactions)
- Integrity rules over objects (*i.e.*, database states) and operations (*i.e.*, state transitions)

Hence, the constituent concepts of a data model fall into these three categories.

The result of data modelling is a representation that has two components. Static properties are defined in a schema, and dynamic properties are defined as specifications for transactions, queries, and reports. A *schema* consists of a definition of all application object types, including their attributes, relationships, and static constraints. Corresponding to the schema will be a data repository called a *database* which is an instance of the schema (*i.e.*, a collection of instances of the object types defined in the schema). A particular class of processes within an application (*e.g.*, paying benefits for an insurance company) need access only a predetermined subset of the objects defined in a schema. Further, the class of processes may require only some of the static properties. Hence, a subschema is designed for each class of processes that have similar information requirements. A *subschema* is some subset of the static properties defined in or derived from the schema. A *transaction* consists of several component operations or actions over objects in a schema or subschema. A transaction is used to define application events. A transaction is atomic in that if one component operation fails then the transaction fails and all of its (partial) effects are undone. A query can be expressed as a logical expression over the objects and relationships defined in the schema. A query results in identifying a logical subset of the database.

A data model provides a formal (notational and semantic) basis for tools and techniques used to support data modelling. Tools associated with data models are languages for defining, manipulating, querying, and supporting the evolution of databases. Most existing database management systems provide a *Data Definition Language* (DDL) for defining schemas and subschemas, a *Data Manipulation Language* (DML) for writing database programs, and a *Query Language* (QL) for writing queries. The partitioning of these functions into three languages is not necessary. Many database languages combine both query and manipulation. All three functions can be provided in one language. For example, mechanisms used to define queries also can be used to define schemas and subschemas. A *database management system* (DBMS) is a system that implements the tools associated with a data model (*e.g.*, the DDL, DML, and QL and the processors needed to implement schemas and execute transactions and queries).

Typically data models provide primitives to define, manipulate, and query databases. The primitives can be used as a low level language, embedded as call statements in a host language such as COBOL (these two cases are typical in commercial DBMSs), or designed directly into a high level programming language. The latter is a research direction which has produced languages such as PASCAL/R [SCHM77] [the chapter by Mall, Schmidt, and Riemer], Rigel [RS79], Plain [WASS79], ADAPLEX [SFL81], and TAXIS [MW80] [the chapter by Mylopoulos and Borgida].

To be useful, a data model must have associated techniques for using the model for the design of schemas, subschemas, transactions, and queries. Early data models were proposed without such techniques. Particularly motivated by the relational data model, techniques were developed for schema and subschema design (design of static properties). More recently, methodologies for transaction and event design have been proposed. To provide formal means for the design of dynamic properties, data models must be significantly extended and integrated with programming concepts. Three chapters in this book address data modelling methodologies for databases with an emphasis on modelling dynamic aspects. They are the chapters by Brodie and Ridjanovic, King and McLeod, and Mylopoulos and Borgida.

Typical database applications differ from typical AI or programming language applications. Databases generally are used to support the query and update of large amounts of regularly formatted data. Typical applications involve "real world" business and human situations. Often they are best considered in an object-oriented way. Such objects have significant and complex static and dynamic properties (*e.g.*, more real world properties than typical programming language applications but fewer than typical AI applications).

A database often serves a large community of users and a large number of distinct applications. This leads to a need for:

- A global logical model of the data (logical schema)
- A high level, problem oriented man-machine interface
- A stored data structure description (physical schema)

- Views particular to the needs of a class of users or processes (subschemas)
- Sharing data between user or process classes
- Data persistence (data persists whereas programs execute from time to time)

Due to the size and longevity of databases, they must be able to evolve piecewise while minimizing the harmful effects of change. Due to the many static interrelationships of objects and the fact that an application process may involve accessing and altering many objects, the concept of a transaction or atomic operation is essential to maintain database integrity with respect to the operation. A fundamental use of databases is to query large quantities of data. Ideally, these queries are expressed in the manner most appropriate for the user, either by content (*e.g.,* Is there a blue 1953 DeSoto with license number HEE 277?), or by context (*e.g.,* Find all the children and grandchildren of Edward VIII).

Data model research has focused on logical aspects of databases and on concepts, tools, and techniques for database design. The primary concerns have been for the logical representation of information objects. Data model research has not addressed implementation aspects such as performance, concurrency, physical integrity, and systems architectures. Early data model research was more closely related with physical representation aspects. However, for the past seven years, logical aspects of representation have been considered which, apart from a small amount of theoretical work, has been much more subjective and harder to evaluate than the previous work. Theoretical work has been done in the area of defining data model semantics [ABRI74] [BROD82] [MPBR82] [the chapter by Rieter], database design techniques based on the relational data model [BBG78], specification and verification of schemas and transactions [RB82a], analysis of query languages, query processing, query optimization, view update, (universal relation) interfaces, constraint analysis [BBC80], and applying logic to a variety of traditional database problems [JACO82] [GM78]. As in AI and programming languages, there is a constant striving for higher level data models. Two questions seldom addressed in data model research are "Why another data model?" and "What is the original contribution of the new data model?"

Many articles describe and compare specific data models that are mentioned only briefly in this chapter. The classical data models—hierarchic, network, and relational—are described and compared in [BS82b] [TL82] [DATE81] [DATE83] [TL76] [CHAM76] [TF80] [CODD70] [CODD82]. Discussions of advanced data models can be found in [KM82a] [ABRI74] [CODD79] [HM81] [CHEN76] [SS77a] [SS77b] [BROD80a]. Discussions of data model concepts and of data modelling can be found in [BZ81] [MS81] [WM77] [KENT78] [SS75] [MCGE76]

[TK78]. Discussions of data modelling tools and techniques can be found in [OSV82] [SW82].

2. Data Model Concepts

Most data models support the basic concepts of objects, operations, and constraints. However, they differ in the formalism provided for representing them and in the specific details associated with the basic concepts. This section presents a brief description of the basic data model concepts. The concepts form a framework within which to describe and compare data models. Section 3 uses the framework to compare several important data models.

Table 2.1 lists the basic data model concepts to be discussed in this section. The list will be used in the next section to compare some important data models.

Of the three basic data model concepts, objects and operations are either undefined terms or are obvious to the reader. Philosophers will always wonder what an entity is. Meanwhile there is some serious information processing to do! So we blithely define an object or entity as anything (concept, event, object, *etc.*) worth recording in the database that meets the information and processing requirements. However, it is useful to discuss the concept of (semantic integrity) constraints that apply to both objects and operations. They can be used to provide intuition into the differences between data models.

Constraints are rules used to define static and dynamic application properties that are not conveniently expressed using the object and operation features of a data model. A constraint often relates static and dynamic properties (*e.g.*, prevents an update that would produce an invalid database state). Hence, the concept of an integrity constraint is data model dependent. A data model independent definition is: A *semantic integrity constraint* is the representation of any property of an application. Each data model provides different means for representing constraints. There are three kinds of constraints:

- inherent
- explicit
- implicit

Some properties can be represented directly and indeed cannot be avoided in a data model. Relative to that data model, these are called *inherent constraints*. They constitute the basic semantic properties of a data model: rules that cannot be violated (*e.g.*, object relationships in

Table 2.1 *Basic Data Models: Concepts, Tools and Techniques*

1. CONCEPTS a. Statics simple object composite object object constraint object attribute relationship attribute attribute constraint attribute relationship object relationship relationship constraint b. Dynamics simple operation composite operation operation relationships exception handling c. Query facilities/constraints
2. TOOLS DDL DML QL data types variables automated design aids
3. TECHNIQUES schema design subschema design transaction design query design object/class concept

the hierarchical data model must be hierarchic, tuples in the relational model must be unique within a relation). Other properties can be defined explicitly by using some combination of the mechanisms provided by the data model. These are called *explicit constraints*. Their use is basic in database design. Examples of explicit constraints are: names, structure of objects, specific relationships, and assertions (*i.e.*, in first order logic) over objects and their properties. Finally, there are properties that are logical consequences of other constraints. These are called *implicit* constraints. Implicit constraints result from the interaction of other constraints (*e.g.*, logical inferences can be deduced from a set of assertions and a complete set of functional dependencies, FDs (relationships between attributes) can be deduced from a subset of FDs).

Data models differ primarily in what constraints are inherent, explicit, and implicit. Models are defined in terms of their inherent and explicit constraints. Without a formal definition of the semantics of a data model, it is difficult to identify or analyze implicit constraints. Sadly, far too many data models have been proposed without a precise definition of their semantics (see the chapter by Rieter and the related discussion).

Concepts for modelling static properties include objects, attributes, and relationships. Objects can be simple or composite. *Simple objects* are irreducible in that they cannot be decomposed into other objects. They are capable of an independent existence. In the relational data model they are called base relations. In other record based models they are represented by single records. The choice of which objects are simple is an important database design decision. *Composite objects* are composed from two or more objects; hence their existence depends on the existence of their constituent objects. A company would be a compound object if the database described it as consisting of various independently existing divisions. Using the relational data model, a compound object is represented by a derived relation (derived from two or more other relations). In the hierarchic or network models, a compound object would be represented by a record and an associated hierarchy or network of records. Objects can be constrained in a number of ways. For example, they can be constrained to having a unique existence in the database by ensuring that only one object of one type exists and that each object be uniquely identified by a non-null key. This constraint is called *entity integrity*.

An *attribute* describes a single, static property of an object and does not have an existence independently of the object. For example, an attribute may give an object's name, which is of no interest in the absence of the named object. Some advanced data models avoid the concept of an attribute by using simple, dependent objects to characterize objects, just as simple objects are used to characterize, via relationships, compound objects. Attributes also can be used to describe relationships (*e.g.*, a contract between two companies was created in 1979 in Kalamazoo).

Some early and most advanced data models use data types to represent attributes; hence attributes can be constrained accordingly. In addition, there are attribute constraints such as single- versus multi-valued, null versus non-null, modifiable or not, *etc.*

The ability to represent relationships has been essential to the development of data models. Primitive models did not explicitly support relationships. The hierarchic and network data models provided means for representing 1:1, 1:N, and restricted N:M relationships between objects. The relational data model provided direct means (the *n*-ary relation) for representing general N:M relationships. More advanced data models influenced by semantic networks attempt to model more application oriented relationships (*e.g.*, married-to, works-for, is-part-of, likes, *etc.*). Some data models provide a small fixed set of relationship types with which all application relationships must be represented (*e.g.*, using the hierarchic data model, all relationships must be hierarchic). Other data models provide general mechanisms for representing any application relationship (*e.g.*, a labelled edge in a semantic network). Some data models do not force a distinction between objects and relationships, but others do. When the distinction is not forced, the data model is said to support semantic relativism. (For a more detailed discussion see Section 4 of this chapter.)

Motivated by the relational data model there has been considerable interest in relationships between object attributes. One important attribute relationship basic to all record based data models is that of *functional dependency*. Attribute A is functionally dependent on attribute B in the relation R (denoted $B \rightarrow A$ which reads B functionally determines A), if a tuple in R contains value b for B and a for A then all tuples that contain b for B also have a for A. For instance if Michael has blue eyes in one tuple (NAME → EYE-COLOUR) then for consistency he better have blue eyes every time he is described.

Basic *relationship constraints* are those of mappings in mathematics (*e.g.*, 1:1, 1:N, N:M, onto, into, *etc.*). More advanced relationship constraints concern the existence of objects and the dependency of one object on other objects. For example, a compound object may be able to exist only if its constituents exist (a contract between two organizations requires that the two organizations exist). This relationship constraint, called *referential integrity*, requires that if object A is referred to by object B then B can exist only if A exists. Referential integrity first appeared as an inherent constraint of the hierarchic and network data models [CODA71]. Subsequently it was added as an explicit constraint to the relational data model [CODD79]. There are many other types of relationship constraints (*e.g.*, characteristic, designation, subtype, association, *etc.*). (See [ABRI74] [CODD79] [WE79] for further discussions of relationship types and constraints.) The above relationship types are not inherent in the relational data model, hence they are relationship constraints. They have now been integrated into most semantic data models as inherent constraints.

Concepts for modelling dynamic properties include simple and composite operations, operation relationships (control structures), dynamic constraints (*i.e.*, constraints on state transitions), and exception handling. All data models provide *simple operations* over objects such as insert, update, and delete. Insert and delete operations are used to insert and delete one (set of) object(s). An update is used to alter the value of attributes of one (set of) object(s). These primitive operations form the assembler language of database systems.

Seldom is one simple operation adequate to execute an application oriented operation. For example, when removing an item from a warehouse many objects are affected: the number of items in the warehouse, the stock slip, the delivery slip, the order level for the warehouse, the related summary and analytical data. Early data models provided no means for dealing with such groups of operations called *transactions.* Transactions are composed of elementary actions on individual objects. Research in this area is relatively recent, as chapters by Brodie and Ridjanovic, Mylopoulos and Borgida, and King and McLeod indicate. To represent transactions and actions, recent research draws on programming language concepts such as procedural abstractions, abstract data types, modules, and classes.

Relationships amongst operations are the control structures needed to represent control flow. Again, recent research has drawn from the programming language tool kit to use such control abstractions as sequence, choice (case), and repetition (for each). The choice of operation structure and control structure is strongly influenced by the static structure of objects (that is typically designed in advance of dynamic aspects).

Dynamic constraints are rules to ensure the appropriate execution of operations. Early data models used ON-conditions and triggers, but practical experience has found them to be inefficient for massive databases. More recent research has considered exception handling mechanisms from programming languages and AI research. The most popular means for representing dynamic constraints are pre- and postconditions that are placed around actions and transactions. *Preconditions* are used to verify that the database is in an acceptable state before the operation is allowed to proceed (*e.g.,* does the person have a name, salary, and manager before the person can be inserted as a new employee?). *Postconditions* ensure that everything happened correctly in the operation (*e.g.,* after the item was taken out of the warehouse did you remember to see if more items should be ordered?). The primary purpose of pre- and postconditions is to support communication between the constituent actions of a transaction. When violations of dynamic constraints are detected, exception handling is required. Apart from the database concepts of commit and undo (the results of actions in the transaction into the database), most mechanisms are drawn from programming languages and AI.

The final basic feature of a data model is a facility for stating *queries* (and constraints) over static aspects of a database. Early models provided record oriented operations used to "navigate" over the hierarchies and networks in the database. The relational model introduced both an algebra and an equivalent, high level calculus to query relational databases. Many high level query languages have been developed based on first order logic and on set theory. For example,

PROLOG has been applied to querying databases. Although there is no high level query language provided for many data models, this is not necessarily a consequence of the model itself. For example, high level languages akin to relational calculus have been proposed for the hierarchic and network data models [MP82]. Query language facilities can be used to define constraints. Constraints can be expressed as assertions in first order logics, hence query language facilities have been used to assert explicit constraints.

3. Taxonomy of Data Models

There have been three generations of data models. Current research is directed at developing a fourth generation. The four generations are:

1. Primitive data models
2. Classical data models
3. Semantic data models
4. Special purpose (application oriented) data models

In this section, important examples of each generation are described briefly. Early data modelling emphasized static properties of applications. Consequently, early data models provided concepts for statics, constraints, and queries with only primitive concepts for dynamics. Most data models can be broadly characterized by their concepts for representing objects and relationships. Hence, this section concentrates primarily on concepts for defining static properties.

3.1 Primitive (File) Model

Objects are represented in records that are grouped in files. Object relationships are those that can be represented using directories (*e.g.*, indexes and inverted lists). Operations provided are primitive read and write operations over records. An early hierarchic data model (*i.e.*, in the form of master and detail records) was used for some time on tape before DBMSs implemented hierarchies on direct access devices.

3.2 Classical Data Models

The classical data models are the *hierarchic* (a direct extension of the file model), the *network* (a superset of the hierarchic model) and the *relational* data models (a significant departure from both hierarchic and network models). Hierarchic and network data models represent objects in segments or records that are organized, using 1:N binary relationships, as nodes in trees and networks, respectively. These data models provided only primitive operations and primitive record-at-a-time navigational facilities. Unlike the relational languages, hierarchic and network languages were more representational (users must deal with more storage and implementation features), but they have a richer set of inherent constraints (*e.g.*, built-in relationship types).

The relational data model [CODD70] was based on the mathematical concept of a relation. A relation is a set of *n*-tuples. A tuple can be used to represent both objects and N:M, *n*-ary relationships. The relational algebra and calculus provide a set oriented query and access facility that also can be used to state constraints as assertions. (For a more detailed discussion of the relational data model see the chapter by Rieter.)

Most information systems today use a primitive data model such as a file system. Where the database approach has been adopted, a DBMS is used that supports some hybrid of the classical data models. In fact, there are almost no DBMSs that implement "pure" hierarchic, network, or relational data models. Implementors have adopted from different models what is logically appealing to users and efficient for executing database programs. The most widely used DBMSs for large database applications are primarily hierarchic and network in nature.

The concept of a data model was developed at the time the relational data model was proposed, which was after hierarchic and network DBMSs were in use. The hierarchic and network data models subsequently were defined independently of the languages and systems used to implement them. Before that they were collections of data structures and languages without a defined underlying theory. Relational DBMSs are growing rapidly in use. They have only recently become commercially available [BS82b] [CODD82]. Until recently, the relational data model had been used primarily for database design and education.

Table 3.1 lists some of the concepts and terms associated with the primitive and classical data models. The table is not complete. It is intended to illustrate similarities and difference between the data models, and the presence or absence of basic data model concepts.

3.3 Semantic Data Models

The primary driving force in data model design is to increase the modelling capability of the data model. That is, models are designed to provide richer, more expressive concepts with which to capture more meaning than was possible when using classical data models. Following the classical data models, a new generation of data models was

Table 3.1 *Primitive and Classical Data Models: Concepts, Tools, and Techniques*

		CLASSICAL MODELS		
	Primitive (files)	Hierarchic	Network	Relational
1. CONCEPTS				
a. Statics				
simple objects	records	segments	records	tuples
composite objects (abstract)	— segments	hierarchies of records	networks of	tuples
object constraints	—	existing parent	existing automatic owner	
object properties (attribute)	fields	fields	fields (items)	attributes
attribute constraints		keys, nonull, essential	keys	keys, tuple uniqueness assertions
attribute relationship	—	FDs	FDs	FDs, MVDs
object relationships	indexes (e.g., inverted lists)	hierarchic links 1:N	network links 1:N (owner-coupled set)	tuples, N:M
relationship constraints	—	deleting parent deletes children	deleting owner may delete member	referential integrity, assertions
b. Dynamics				
simple operations (I,U,D)	read/write record	segment oriented	record oriented	set oriented
composite operations (transactions)	—	—	—	—
operation relationships (control structures)	— hierarchy	(implicit) follows set members	(implicit) follows iteration	(implicit)
exception handling	—	completion codes	completion codes	—
c. Query facility/ constraints	—	qualified tree traversal	qualified set navigation	relational calculus, relational algebra
2. TOOLS				
DDL	file definition	yes	yes	yes
DML	—	segment oriented	record oriented	set oriented
QL	—	segment oriented	record oriented	algebra and calculus based
data types	record type	fields, segments	fields, records	attributes, tuples
variables	—	—	—	in algebra and calculus
automated design aids	—	yes	elementary	yes

Table 3.1 *Primitive and Classical Data Models: Concepts, Tools, and Techniques (continued)*

	Primitive (files)	CLASSICAL MODELS Hierarchic	Network	Relational
3. TECHNIQUES				
schema design	—	yes	yes	yes
subschema design	—	yes	—	yes
transaction design	—	—	—	—
query design	—	elementary	—	yes
object/class concept	—	—	—	—

developed called semantic data models. The name may be inappropriate since the next generation will also attempt semantic enhancements. Semantic data models can be classified into approximately five groups:

- Direct extensions of classical data models
- Mathematical data models
- Irreducible data models
- Static semantic hierarchy models
- Dynamic semantic hierarchy models

3.3.1 Direct Extensions of Classical Models

The *Structural model* [WE79] restricts relations in the relational data model to five specific types (or interpretations). For example, a relation between two objects must include a referent to each object. These restrictions guide database design choices and encourage precision in using the relational model. The Structural Model does not force a distinction between objects and relationships; hence, the resulting schemas are relational.

The *Object-Role model* [BACH77] extends the network model by adding the notion of role. One object may play many roles in an application and may have different properties for each role (*e.g.*, employee and manager roles). The Object-Role model reduces the redundancy of considering each role as a separate object and permits more application oriented modelling.

The *Entity-Relationship model* [CHEN76] combines features of the network and relational models. It makes a clear distinction between objects and relationships; hence, applications are represented as networks in which objects (entities) are nodes and relationships are edges. The E-R model provides a fairly unconstrained means for representing relationships, as opposed to a small set of relationship concepts. The popularity of the E-R model for high level database design is due to its economy of concepts and the widespread belief in entities and relationships as natural modelling concepts. The E-R model differs significantly from the classical models on which it is based.

3.3.2 Mathematical Models

Much of the appeal of the relational data model is due to its formal mathematical basis in set theory and predicate calculus. Several researchers have used this basis to formally define and extend the relational data model. Three such groups of mathematically defined models predominate: those based on set theory [CHIL77] [HARD80], those based on First Order Logic [the chapter by Rieter] [JACO82] [GM78], and those based on the universal instance assumption [ULLM80]. These models provide formal notations and definitions for concepts presented in other models and, most significantly, provide formal tools for analyzing (primarily structural) properties of applications and for solving related theoretical problems. Strictly speaking, these models do not introduce new data models. However, in defining other data models within a mathematical system, such as first order logic, the data model is extended by the associated mathematical tools and techniques (*e.g.,* means for proving consistency of assertions).

There is a major difference between the traditional view of a database and the database used in models that are based on first order logic. In the traditional view, objects are represented in a database as instances of object types defined in a corresponding schema. Typically there are a very large number of instances of each object type. Instances are added to and deleted from the database to reflect changes in the application environment. In the logical view, objects are represented as terms, and properties (attributes, relationships, constraints) are represented as logical sentences. There is a database of facts against which sentences are evaluated to answer queries. Changes in the application are reflected by adding logical sentences, but not necessarily by altering the database of facts. The efficiency of an implementation of the logical approach remains an open research issue, particularly for very large databases that have significant update activity.

3.3.3 Irreducible Data Models

A number of data models have been inspired by the desire to represent information as atomic facts rather than as complex groups of facts. These models are called irreducible since atomic facts cannot be further decomposed into other separate facts. It is felt that atomic facts simplify update since each fact can be altered independently. It is argued that atomic facts increase modelling precision since atomic facts can be combined in any appropriate way to form any reasonable higher level concept rather than having a fixed structure imposed on all facts.

The *Binary-Relationship model* [BPP76] is an irreducible data model that is a restriction of the relational model in which relationships are binary rather than *n*-ary. A binary relation represents a relationship between an object and a single attribute. It is considered to be an atomic fact. A binary relation is the smallest fact representable in the relational model.

In the *Irreducible Relational Model* [HOT76], relations need not be binary. They must have the property that that they cannot be non-loss decomposed into other relations. That is, information will be lost if an irreducible relation is decomposed into two or more relations. For example, information is lost in decomposing Inventory(Warehouse, Item, Quantity) into, say, I1(Warehouse, Item) and I2(Item, Quantity).

The most widely used irreducible data model is the *functional data model*. The functional data model combines aspects of the relational data model with functional programming. Objects are represented directly with object properties and relationships represented as functional mappings between objects. This is irreducible since each attribute is related to its associated object by a function. The most appealing property of the functional data model is the attractive and simple query facility based on functional composition (*e.g.*, age(student), name(manager(employee))). Three functional data models are: *DAPLEX* [SHIP81], *FQL* [BF79] [the chapter by Buneman and Nikhil], and *FDM* [HWY79].

3.3.4 Static Semantic Hierarchy Models

Many semantic data models have been influenced by semantic networks from AI. Static semantic hierarchy models integrate relational data model concepts with four important relationships from semantic nets, namely classification, aggregation, generalization, and association. Association is similar to partition as defined by Hendrix [HEND75]. These relationships are used to support data abstraction in which specific details are suppressed and those pertinent to the problem or view of information at hand are emphasized. Classification establishes a relationship between schema and database objects. Aggregation, generalization, and association establish relationships between object types in the schema, hence also between the corresponding object instances in the database. These relationships have well defined inherent constraints such as property inheritance. These relationships are fundamental to most semantic data models; thus they are defined here briefly.

Classification is a simple form of data abstraction in which an object type is defined as a set of instances. This establishes an instance-of relationship between an object type in a schema and its instances in the database.

Aggregation is a form of abstraction in which a relationship between objects is considered as a higher level aggregate object. When considering the aggregate, specific details of the constituent objects are suppressed. Every instance of an aggregate object can be decomposed into instances of the component objects. This establishes a part-of relationship between objects. For example, a person could be represented as an aggregate of person properties.

Generalization is a form of abstraction in which similar objects are related to a higher level generic object. The constituent objects are considered specializations of the generic object. At the level of the generic object, differences of the specializations are suppressed while the similarities are emphasized. Every instance of a generic object can be found as an instance of one or more of the specialized objects. This establishes an is-a relationship between objects. For example, a university and high school are specializations of the generic concept of educational institution.

Association [BROD81a] is a form of abstraction in which a relationship between similar objects is considered as a higher level set object. The details of a member object are suppressed and properties of the set object are emphasized. An instance of a set object can be decomposed into a set of instances of the member object. This establishes a member-of relationship between a member object and a set object. For example, the set object "dogs" is defined over the member object "dog." Note that a member object dog might have as attributes number of legs, tail, head, whereas the set object dogs would not. Association also has been called grouping and partitioning.

Using semantic hierarchy models, schemas are represented as aggregation, generalization, and association hierarchies of objects. Each object is either simple (defined on its own) or composite (defined as an aggregate, generic, or association of other objects). Each abstraction can be applied repeatedly to form aggregation hierarchies, generalization hierarchies, *etc.* One object can have a hierarchic decomposition according to each of aggregation, generalization, and association. Static semantic hierarchy models include *SHM* [SS77a] [SS77b] *ADD* [ROUS77], *LGDM* [BROD78] [BROD82], *RM/T* [CODD79], *SAM* [SL79], and *SDM* [HM81].

3.3.5 Dynamic Semantic Hierarchy Models

Extensions of static semantic hierarchy models were developed to integrate concepts for modelling dynamics with those for modelling statics. These models integrate a number of programming language concepts with database concepts. These models include many of the dynamic features described in the previous section. They also make strong use of advanced data type concepts such as abstract data types, classes, strong typing, and polymorphic types. Dynamic semantic hierarchy models include: *SHM+* [BROD81b] [RB82a] [the chapter by Brodie and Ridjanovic], *TAXIS* [MBW80] [the chapter by Mylopoulos and Borgida], and the *Event Model* described in the chapter by King and McLeod.

3.4 Special Purpose Semantic Data Models

The next generation of semantic data models appears to be devoted to special purpose applications. Semantic modelling theory is now being applied to particular applications. Previous models have provided general purpose concepts for modelling most databases, just as general purpose programming languages provide general concepts for most programming. The desire to have high level languages and models has led to the development of data models for specific applications such as office procedures, VLSI, CAD/CAM, cartography, *etc.*, as well as for the traditional applications such as inventory, billing, and insurance.

Table 3.2 lists some of the concepts associated with some semantic data models. As with Table 3.1, the table is not complete. It is intended to illustrate similarities and differences.

Choosing a data model for a particular application is similar to choosing a programming language, a knowledge representation scheme, or a mathematical notation. It is very subjective. When the classical data models were first introduced, there was great debate over the relative merits of the models. It now appears that the models do not differ significantly in their expressive power. Not only are there high level languages that apply to all three models [MP82], the associated database design rules lead to similar schemas. The primary difference (in addition to notational) is in whether specific constraints are inherent, explicit, or implicit.

Some work [MPBR82] has demonstrated that the three classical data models have a common core of concepts (see Figure 3.1). The hierarchic and network data models have, in addition to the core concepts, other concepts common to both and then concepts unique to each of them. Similarly, the relational data model can be expressed as some uniquely relational concepts added to the core data model concepts.

A similar argument has been proposed in [DATE81] in which the relational model is contained by the hierarchic data model which is contained by the network data model.

Table 3.2 *Semantic Data Models: Concepts, Tools, and Techniques*

Key:

A = aggregation
G = generalization
C = classification

	SEMANTIC MODELS					
	Entity-Relationship	Functional	SHM+	SDM/ Event Model	TAXIS	RM/T
1. CONCEPTS						
a. Statics						
simple objects	entity	object	object	class/object, event	object	entity (various kinds)
composite objects (abstract)	entity (network)	object (hierarchy)	object (hierarchy)	class/event (hierarchy)	object (hierarchy)	entity (hierarchy)
object constraints	existence dependency		existence dependency	(non)base, duplicates	—	entity integrity
object properties (attribute)	attributes	object function	attributes	attributes	property (single valued attributes)	single valued attributes
attribute constraints	keys	in function	abstract data type	attribute definition language	assertions (restricted FOL)	property integrity
attribute relationship (intra-relation)	FDs	in function, FDs	FDs, nonull, etc		—	FDs, surrogates
object relationships (inter-relation)	relationship, N:M etc.	functions (A,G)	C,A,G, Association	A,G,C characteristic,	C,A,G	G,A,
relationship constraints	bounded, quantified, relationship key	in function	(in)dependent, (in)essential, inherent in C,A,G, Assn	onto, total/partial	inherent in C,A,G	referential integrity, etc.
b. Dynamics						
simple operations (I,U,D)	—	yes	yes	yes	yes	yes
composite operations (transactions)	—	—	actions, transactions	yes	hierarchies	—
operation relationships (control structures)	—	functional composition	A,G, Association hierarchies	yes	A,G hierarchies	event precedence
exception handling	—	—	yes		hierarchies	—
c. Query facilities/ constraints	in development	functions	—	predicate language	procedural query language	relational calculus

Table 3.2 Semantic Data Models: Concepts, Tools, and Techniques (continued)

	SEMANTIC MODELS					
	Entity-Relationship	Functional	SHM+	SDM/ Event Model	TAXIS	RM/T
2. TOOLS						
DDL	yes	yes	yes	yes	yes	yes
DML	—	yes	yes	yes	yes	yes
QL	yes	yes	—	yes	yes	yes
data types	attributes, entities, relationships	all statics	yes (throughout SHM+)	yes	classes, metaclasses	yes
variables	—	yes	yes	—/yes	in transactions	—
automated design aids	in development	—	—	—/yes	editor, interpreter, compiler	—
3. TECHNIQUES						
schema design	yes	—	yes	yes	yes	—
subschema design	—	—	yes	—	—	—
transaction design	—	—	yes	yes	yes	—
query design	—	yes	—	yes	yes	—
object/class concept	— metaclass	yes	yes	yes	class,	yes

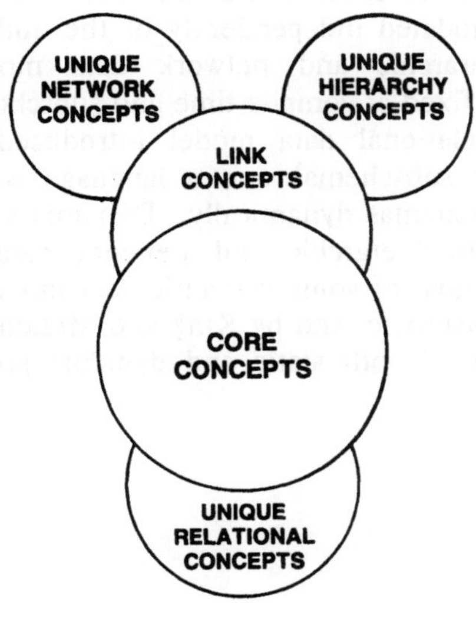

Figure 3.1 *Relating the Classical Data Models*

4. The Development of Data Models

Several themes that are related to the purposes of data models stand out. This section gives a brief presentation of the predominant themes. The themes suggest research directions, not all of which can be achieved mutually.

4.1 Data Independence

Data independence is a principal goal of database technology. It involves the separation of logical and physical (implementation) properties in order to facilitate evolution. For example, it involves the immunity of applications to changes in storage structure and access strategy. *Logical data independence* encourages addressing individual and community requirements separately. It involves the isolation of logical changes from other aspects of an application (*e.g.*, ability to add, delete, or modify objects, relationships, queries, and whole applications) with as little impact as possible. *Physical data independence* encourages addressing functional and performance requirements separately. It involves the isolation of physical changes (*e.g.*, alter access paths, reorganize storage, and alter the storage devices) with as little impact as possible.

Data independence is never fully achieved. Primitive models offer little to support data independence. The classical data models introduced the concepts of schema and subschema so that logical changes could be accommodated independently of the underlying implementations. With hierarchic and network data models, schemas and subschemas were fixed at compile time and subschemas were subsets of schemas. The relational data model introduced the concept of a derived view (or subschema) and a language with which to define schemas and subschemas dynamically. Dynamic views have now been proposed for both hierarchic and network data models [MPBR82] [DB82]. It is the goal of some semantic data models (see the chapters by Brodie and Ridjanovic, and by King and McLeod) to provide means for the evolution of both static and dynamic properties of database applications.

4.2 Semantic Relativism

Semantic relativism concerns the ability to view and manipulate data in the way most appropriate for the viewer (*e.g.*, potentially view the same information as an object, attribute, relationship, or function). The viewer is not forced to interpret information in a particular way (*e.g.*, a marriage could be considered to be: an object consisting of two people, an attribute of one or both of the two people, a relationship between two people, or a function mapping between two people). A particular view could be determined at any time by the information and operational requirements.

Semantic relativism permits differing views to coexist and evolve. It also permits relationships and entities to take part in further relationships and entities (a powerful form of closure). Semantic relativism supports logical data independence since it supports the design of views, the evolution of schemas and subschemas, and the design of interfaces tailored to specific user needs. Forcing a distinction causes problems for database design, specifically for subschema derivation (or integration to form a global schema), since information viewed as an object in one subschema may be viewed as a relationship in another — and never the twain shall meet.

Semantic relativism was introduced by the relational data model in which all objects and relationships are represented in *n*-ary relations. One is allowed to interpret a relation as an entity with *n* attributes, or as a relationship amongst *n* objects or as some combination of these (*e.g.*, a relationship amongst *k* objects with $n-k$ attributes describing the relationship which itself might be viewed as an entity). The network and hierarchic models and their variants, including the Entity-Relationship model, do not support semantic relativism; however, most semantic data models based on the relational data model do.

4.3 Integrating Structure and Behaviour

The complete specification of the semantics of a database application includes both the static and dynamic properties of the application objects. The traditional approach emphasized static properties. Database design typically involved: extracting all structural properties from all programs that would access the database, designing a schema to represent those properties, and writing programs and queries as needed against the schema or a subschema. It was felt that static properties were stable and could be defined abstractly in a schema which would be used by any programs and queries that were developed. This differs sharply with the programming language view that emphasizes dynamics and that views data structure design as more representational.

It is now clear that both static and dynamic properties can be treated abstractly and that both aspects are required to completely define the semantics of an object. Hence, it is now a research goal to integrate data model and programming language concepts, tools, and techniques to support the complete specification of object oriented databases. For more details on these points, see the chapter by Brodie and Ridjanovic and the related discussion.

4.4 Support of Data and Procedural Abstraction

Abstraction involves the ability to emphasize details essential to the problem at hand and to suppress all irrelevant details. Abstraction is essential in database applications due to their inherent complexity which must be managed. Typically, a database application consists of a very large number of objects that have many relationships between them. Data abstraction concerns abstraction applied to static properties. Procedural abstraction concerns abstraction applied to dynamic properties.

The first approach to data abstraction was data independence, which was aimed at separating logical and representational concerns. This separated data modelling into logical and physical components. As a result, logical data modelling was raised from a representational record orientation to a logical object orientation. The network model contributed the concept of a schema which mediates between logical and physical descriptions. The relational data model contributed by providing a high level logical view of the database with very few physical details. Semantic data models contributed further to data abstraction by adopting a strong object orientation and abstraction concepts such as classification, aggregation, generalization, and association.

A major modelling goal of abstraction is called *localization*. Localization encourages the design properties of objects in isolation from others and then the integration of the designs into a coherent database design. Localization was motivated by programming language concepts, such as modularity, which until recently have not been applied to database design.

In the past, data models did not include mechanisms for modelling operations. Now, procedural abstractions and concepts such as abstract data types and classes are being adopted from programming languages for modelling dynamic properties of databases. Following the integration of data and procedural abstraction, database modelling will addressed at a higher, more conceptual level called conceptual modelling.

4.5 Modelling Support

Another goal of data models is to provide modelling concepts that are natural for or familiar to designers. There are several ways of supporting modelling.

Modelling directness requires data model concepts that directly represent application properties. Ideally, the properties inherent in the application are also the inherent constraints of the data model. It is more error prone and more awkward to use several concepts in combination to represent a property.

Modelling uniqueness is achieved if there is only one way in which a property is represented. This is aimed at reducing the number of design choices presented by the model or the methodology. Modelling directness and modelling uniqueness attempt to reduce complexity but may also reduce modelling flexibility.

A clear goal for a data model is that it be expressive. Using the data model, one should be able to represent any static or dynamic property of interest to the desired degree of precision in order to capture the intended meaning. As an example, consider the expressiveness of a data model for object relationships. Primitive data models had no such concepts. Hierarchic and network data models offered means for representing binary, 1:N relationships in trees and networks that were determined at compile time. The relational data model provided direct means for representing N:M relationships which can be defined dynamically. However, there is no direct means for ensuring that such relationships are meaningful. A goal for semantic data models is to provide means to represent application oriented relationships (*e.g.*, as frequently used in semantic networks) and to ensure that they are meaningful. One method is to provide a small number of constructs with which to represent all relationships (*e.g.*, aggregation, generalization, association, partition). Another is to provide a general means for defining any relationship (*e.g.*, a first order language).

4.6 Precise Definition

Concepts that constitute a particular data model must be precisely defined. Precise definitions aid people in understanding the data model, ensuring the soundness of the data model concepts and their interaction, developing analytical tools, and implementing related languages and techniques. Typically, data models have not been formally defined (see the chapter by Rieter and the related discussion). Consequently, data models are difficult to understand, apply, compare, and analyze.

Major goals of data model design include providing means to prove consistency (*i.e.*, of constraints in a schema), completeness (with respect to other descriptions), and the existence of desirable properties (*e.g.*, nonredundancy and absence of anomalous results under update).

4.7 Understandability

Some data models bear similarity to baroque cathedrals. They are remarkably ornate, sometimes beautiful, sometimes not, but always, *un peu de trop.* This issue is related to precise definition. Two objectives for conceptualization, understanding, documentation, and use are simplicity and picturability. Simplicity can be achieved by providing an economy and independence of concepts, along with a simple notation. The relational data model is a paragon in this regard. Due to the complexity of objects and their relationships, it is desirable to graphically represent schemas and subschemas for design and documentation.

4.8 Languages and Methodologies

A data model should provide a base for high level tools (*e.g.*, languages) and techniques (*e.g.*, modelling methodologies) with which to realize and use the data model concepts. The various languages and methodologies should interact in clearly defined ways.

4.9 Implementability

A data model should be realizable using safe and efficient implementation techniques. The goal of data independence has been to separate these concerns from the logical aspects concerning data models. Most database research has been devoted to the implementation of the primitive and classical data models. Very few semantic data models have been considered for implementation. The largest semantic data model implementation project concerns DAPLEX [SHIP81] which is being implemented as a database facility for ADA in the ADAPLEX project [SFL81].

4.10 Representing Data Model Constituents

A major research topic in data model design is the representation of data model constituents (see Table 2.1). This research has drawn primarily from programming languages and to a lesser extent from AI.

One major concept is that of data type. Primitive data models used simple data types to define fields. Hierarchic and network data models used simple data types for fields, as well as for segment, record, and relationship (link) types. The relational data model used data types for attributes and relations. Starting with LGDM [BROD78], there was an attempt to formulate all semantic data model concepts in terms of data types. Strong typing (*e.g.*, abstract data types and classes) is used for semantic integrity and defining update semantics precisely. One trend in data model development is the decreasing ratio between data types and the corresponding instances in the database. Early data models had few data types in the schema and vast numbers of instances. The most recent data models have many more data types in the schemas (*i.e.*, complex objects are represented in a type hierarchy composed of many individual data types).

Another major representation issue concerns constraints. Since early data models did not provide means for representing all constraints (*e.g.*, no dynamics, only simple relationships), it was necessary to use means outside the data model for representing constraints. Many mechanisms were used (*e.g.*, ON conditions, triggers, first order predicates) but the primary means was to incorporate constraints in application programs. Due to the lack of uniformity, constraints (hence any database application) were difficult to define, analyze, control, and modify consistently. In addition, the implementation means were inefficient, hence constraints often were not defined or enforced.

Data model research has attempted to develop means for expressing constraints in a uniform way that will support definition, analysis, and modification. There is considerable effort directed at doing as much type (semantic integrity) checking as possible with as little run time cost as possible. One means of achieving this goal has been to make as many constraints as possible inherent in the data model. A second approach has been to integrate data and procedural concepts in uniform mechanisms using existing programming language and AI results.

4.11 Using AI and Programming Language Concepts

Research in AI, programming languages, and databases share many common goals such as high level concepts, tools, and techniques; abstraction, modelling, *etc.* But there are also significant differences in the problem scope, nature of solution, and intended audience.

The development of data models has drawn on results from AI, programming languages, and software engineering. Many constituents of data models have been drawn from knowledge representation schemes, particularly semantic networks. AI also has contributed to interface concepts used in high level languages. As the chapters by Rieter and by Levesque indicate, logic has been used in defining data models, database languages, and as a notation for addressing database problems. So far in database research there has been little or no deduction, the closed-world assumption has been made, and expert systems have not been used. However, researchers are now beginning to apply these concepts. Database model research has drawn heavily from the programming language tool kit. Extensive use has been made of: the data type concept, abstract data types, the class concept, strong typing, variables, data and procedural abstractions, control structures, high level languages, language design, specification and verification concepts, functional programming, exception handling, and database language design, to mention only a few. Software engineering concepts have been applied to databases in the development of data model tools and techniques (*e.g.*, programming methodologies, programming environments, software life cycle).

5. Current Issues

The research goals given in the previous section continue to motivate data model research. The topics listed in this section are currently of particular interest.

5.1 Extending the Scope of Database Applications

Most database applications involve traditional business situations in which data is uniform and formatted. These applications involve less than 15 percent of all data used by large organizations. However, databases are useful for storing, manipulating, and accessing all kinds of information. There is now considerable motivation to support applications in which data is less structured, less formatted, and that may involve data types that are much more complex than the simple integers and strings currently supported. Examples of these applications come from VLSI, office and factory automation, all engineering databases (specifically CAD/CAM), cartography, databases of photographs and other images, geometric figures and shapes, scientific applications, economics, intelligence (command, control, communications, and intelligence), text applications, statistical databases, *etc.*, in fact any application that involves large amounts of data. These applications will require means for modelling the associated application semantics. This is leading to the next generation of data models called special purpose or application oriented data models.

5.2 Database Environments

Typically the development of a database application involves an extensive life cycle that would benefit from considerable automated support. For example, it would be useful to have tools to support: requirements definition, specification, verification (pre-run time checking), validation (run time checking), exception handling, logical design and evolution (schema languages), semantic data modelling (*e.g.*, application definition, transaction and query programming), higher level programming (*e.g.*, end user scenarios, scripts), embedding database functionality into conventional programming languages, man-machine interfaces (*e.g.*, screen interactions, 2D and 3D pictorial languages), and multiple data models and schemas.

One goal is a database environment (or workbench) which is a programming or software engineering environment dedicated to support data modelling using data model based tools and techniques throughout the life cycle.

5.3 Extending Data Model and Languages

A few key semantic aspects of data models are still open problems. Some that are of particular interest are: modelling time, modelling events, handling anomalous information, incomplete knowledge, and exception handling. One challenging language problem involves achieving a cleaner integration between the relational data model and the semantic hierarchy concepts. The relational model had the powerful and useful property of closure. Applying relational operations to relations always produces relations. In adding semantic hierarchies to relations closure was lost. Currently, there is no query or access language over semantic hierarchies that supports data abstraction and that has the appealing properties of the relational data model. A second language problem involves integrating the abstract data type (or class) concept (used to deal with update semantics) with high level query languages.

Two related trends in the development of data models are: reducing the sharp distinction between data and meta-data (*e.g.*, schemas), and increasing the number of object types in the schema relative to the number of instances in the database. Reducing the data/meta-data distinction is intended to permit the same language concepts to be used in querying and updating both the schema and the database. Reducing the type to instance ratio is a consequence of more precise modelling (*e.g.*, by using type hierarchies rather than a single type to represent complex objects).

5.4 Practical Modelling Methodologies

To be useful, a data model must have associated methodologies for designing database applications [OSV82]. Few data models have provided such methodologies. This area, perhaps more so than the rest of data model research, is rather vague due to its basic (human) problem solving nature.

5.5 Integrating Technologies

As discussed at the end of the previous section, database research has drawn heavily from AI, programming languages, and software engineering. The challenges lie in integrating the ideas in clean, well defined, and effective ways. The extension of the scope of database applications will require such integration. The potential application areas involve communications, expert knowledge, special purpose interfaces, complex semantics, high level (special purpose) languages, strong type checking, and will require considerable software engineering throughout the system life cycle.

5.6 Conceptual Modelling

There clearly has been a trend away from modelling only specific application properties (*e.g.,* statics in databases and dynamics in programming languages) and toward modelling all properties of an application. This includes modelling communications (see the chapter by Hewitt and De Jong), man-machine interface, and systems environment, as well as statics and dynamics. Abstraction mechanisms will be needed more than ever to manage the added complexity of the extra details and their interaction. These observations have led many researchers (a subset of which are represented in the chapters of this book) to the conclusion that there is a need for a higher level modelling called conceptual modelling. Many data models are now being developed with conceptual modelling as an ultimate goal.

6. Acknowedgements

The author is grateful to Dzenan Ridjanovic, John Mylopoulos, Frank Manola, and Dennis McLeod for their comments and suggestions on this chapter, and to David Darcy for his help in editing the chapter.

7. References

[ABRI74] [BACH77] [BBC80] [BBG78] [BF79] [BPP76] [BROD78] [BROD80a] [BROD81b] [BROD82] [BS82b] [BZ81] [CHAM76] [CHEN76] [CHIL77] [CODD70] [CODD79] [CODD82] [DATE81] [DATE83] [DB82] [GM78] [HARD80] [HEND75] [HM81] [HOT76] [HWY79] [JACO82] [KENT78] [KM82a] [MBW80] [MCGE76] [MP82] [MPBR82] [MS81] [MW80] [OSV82] [RB82a] [ROUS77] [RS79] [SFL81] [SHIP81] [SL79] [SS75] [SS77] [SS77a] [SS77b] [SW82] [TF80] [TK78] [TL76] [TL82] [ULLM80] [WASS79] [WE79] [WM77]

3
The Impact of Modelling and Abstraction Concerns on Modern Programming Languages

Mary Shaw
Carnegie-Mellon University

ABSTRACT *The major issues of modern software are its size and complexity, and its major problems involve finding effective techniques and tools for organization and maintenance. This chapter traces the important ideas of modern programming languages to their roots in the problems and languages of the past decade and shows how these modern languages respond to contemporary problems in software development. Modern programming's key concept for controlling complexity is* abstraction — *that is, selective emphasis on detail. New developments in programming languages provide ways to support and exploit abstraction techniques.*

1. Issues of Modern Software

The major issues of modern software development stem from the costs of software development, use, and maintenance — which are too high — and the quality of the resulting systems — which is too low.

This paper is an update and revision of "The Impact of Abstraction Concerns on Modern Programming Languages," which appeared in *Proceedings of the IEEE*, Vol. 68, No. 9, September 1980, pages 1119-1130.

This research was sponsored by the National Science Foundation under Grant MCS77-03883 and by the Defense Advanced Research Projects Agency (DOD), ARPA Order No. 3597, monitored by the Air Force Avionics Laboratory under Contract F33615-78-C-1551. The views and conclusions contained in this document are those of the author and should not be interpreted as representing the official policies, either expressed or implied, of the National Science Foundation, the Defense Advanced Research Projects Agency, or the U.S. Government.

These problems are particularly severe for the large complex programs that have long useful lifetimes and that characterize modern software. Such programs typically involve many programmers, not only during their development but also for maintenance and enhancement after they are initially released. As a result, the cost and quality of software are influenced by both management and software engineering considerations [BROO75] [GOLD73].

This chapter examines one theme that runs through the history of the attempts to solve the problems of high cost and low quality: the effects of modelling and abstraction techniques and of their associated specification and verification issues on the evolution of modern programming languages and methods. This theme places a strong emphasis on engineering concerns, including design, specification, correctness, and reliability.

The modelling theme has influenced areas other than programming languages. Programs certainly are not the only complex systems that people deal with. Other systems, such as the national economy and the motion of atoms in a simple physical object, are far more complex. No human understands these systems in fine detail. Instead, they deal with such systems by ignoring details; they develop *models* that reflect only macroscopic behavioral properties which they believe to be important. This chapter deals with the way that the modelling paradigm is applied to programming languages. Other chapters in this volume explore some of the ways modelling is used in the fields of artificial intelligence and databases.

The chapter begins with a review of the ideas about program development and analysis that heavily influenced the development of current programming language techniques (Section 2). Many of these ideas are of current interest as well as of historical importance. This review provides a setting for a survey of the ideas from current research projects that are influencing modern language design and software methodology (Section 3). Section 4 illustrates the changes in program organization this work has stimulated by developing an example in three different languages intended for production use: Fortran, Ada, and Pascal. Although Sections 2 and 3 present a certain amount of technical detail, Section 4 gives examples of the concepts that should be accessible to all readers. An assessment of the current status and the potential of current abstraction techniques (Section 5) concludes the chapter.

2. Historical Review of Abstraction Techniques

Controlling software development and maintenance has always involved managing the intellectual complexity of programs and systems of programs. Not only must the systems be created, they must be tested, maintained, and extended. As a result, many different people must understand and modify them at various times during their lifetimes. This section identifies one set of ideas about managing program complexity and shows how those ideas have shaped programming languages and methodologies during the past ten to fifteen years.

A dominant theme in the evolution of methodologies and languages is the development of tools for dealing with abstractions. An *abstraction* is a simplified description, or *specification,* of a system that emphasizes some of the system's details or properties while suppressing others. A *good* abstraction is one in which information that is significant to the reader (*i.e.,* the user) is emphasized, and details that are immaterial or diversionary, at least for the moment, are suppressed.

What we call "abstraction" in programming systems corresponds closely to what is called "analytic modelling" in many other fields. Construction of a model usually starts with observations (measurements) and hypothesizes a set of principles or axioms to explain the observations. These axioms are used to derive or construct models of observable systems. The parameters or variables of these models may be derived from the axioms, or they may be estimated from observation. The model is then used to make new predictions about properties (metrics) of the observed system. The final step is to perform experiments (observations in controlled or understood environments) to determine the accuracy and robustness of models and of the statements of principles. The cycle of hypothesizing and validating models is then continued with the additional observations.

In software development, the requirements or intended functionality of a system play the role of the observations to be explained. The abstraction process is thus very similar to the general modelling paradigm; the process includes deciding which characteristics of the system are important, what variability (*i.e.,* parameters) should be included, which descriptive formalism to use, how the model can be validated, and so on. As in many other fields, we often define hierarchies of models in which lower level models provide more detailed explanations for the phenomena that appear in higher-level models. Our models also share the property that the description is sufficiently different from the underlying system to require explicit validation. We refer to the abstract description of a model as its *specification* and to the next lower level model in the hierarchy as its *implementation.* The validation that the specification is consistent with the implementation is called *verification.* The abstractions we use for software tend to emphasize functional properties of the software, emphasizing *what* results are to be obtained and suppressing details about *how* this is to be achieved.

Many important techniques for program and language organization have been based on the principle of abstraction. These techniques have evolved in step not only with our understanding of programming issues, but also with our ability to use the abstractions as *formal specifications* of the systems they describe. In the 1960s, for example, the important developments in methodology and languages were centered around functions and procedures, which summarize a program segment in terms of a name and a parameter list. At that time, we only knew how to perform syntactic validity checks, and specification techniques reflected this; "specification" meant little more than "procedure header" until late in the decade. By the late 1970s, developments were centered on the design of data structures, specification techniques drew on quite sophisticated techniques of mathematical logic, and programming language semantics were well enough understood to permit formal verification that these programs and specifications were consistent.

Programming languages and methodologies often develop in response to new ideas about how to cope with complexity in programs and systems of programs. As languages evolve to meet these ideas, we reshape our perceptions of the problems and solutions in response to the new experiences. Our sharpened perceptions in turn generate new ideas which feed the evolutionary cycle. This chapter explores the routes by which these cyclic advances in methodology and specification have led to current concepts and principles of programming languages.

2.1 Early Abstraction Techniques

Before the late 1960s, the set of programming topics regarded as important was dominated by the syntax of programming languages, translation techniques, and solutions to specific implementation problems. Thus we saw many papers about solutions to specific problems such as parsing, storage allocation, and data representation. Procedures were well understood, and libraries of procedures were set up. These libraries met with mixed success, often because the documentation (informal specification) was inadequate or because the parameterization of the procedures did not support the cases of interest. Basic data structures such as stacks and linked lists were just beginning to be understood, but they were sufficiently unfamiliar to make it difficult to separate the concepts from the particular implementations. Perhaps it was too early in the history of the field for generalization and synthesis to take place, but in any event abstraction played only a minor role.

Abstraction was first treated consciously as a program organization technique in the late 1960s. Earlier languages supported built-in data types including at least integers, real numbers, and arrays, and sometimes booleans, high precision reals, *etc.* Data structures were first treated systematically in 1968 (the first edition of [KNUT73]), and the notion that a programmer might define data types tailored to a particular problem first appeared in 1967 (*e.g.,* [STAN67]). Although discussions of programming techniques date back to the beginning of the field, the notion that programming is an activity that should be studied and subjected to some sort of discipline dates to the NATO Software Engineering conferences of 1968 [NR69] and 1969 [BR70].

2.2 Extensible Languages

The late 1960s also saw efforts to abstract from the built-in notations of programming languages in such a way that any programmer could add new notation and new data types to a base language. The objectives of the extensible language work included allowing individual programmers to extend the syntax of the programming language, to define new data structures, to add new operators (including infix operators as well as ordinary functions) for both old and new data structures, and to add new control structures to the base language. This work on extensibility [SCHU71] died out, in part because it underestimated the difficulty of defining interesting extensions. The problems included difficulty with keeping independent extensions compatible when all of them modify the syntax of the base language, with organizing definitions so that related information was grouped in common locations, and with finding techniques for describing an extension accurately (other than by exhibiting the code for the extension). However, it left a legacy in its influence on the abstract data types and generic definitions of the 1970s.

2.3 Structured Programming

By the early 1970s, a methodology emerged for constructing programs by progressing from a statement of the objective through successively more precise intermediate stages to final code [DIJK72] [WIRT71]. Called "stepwise refinement" or "top-down programming," this methodology involves approaching a problem by writing a program that is free to assume the existence of any data structures and operations that can be directly applied to the problem at hand, even if those structures and operations are quite sophisticated and difficult to implement. Thus the initial program is presumably small, clear, directly problem related, and "obviously" correct. Although the assumed structures and operations may be specified only informally, the programmer's intuitions about them should make it possible to concentrate on the overall organization of the program and to defer concerns about the implementations of the assumed definitions. When each of the latter definitions is addressed, the same technique is applied again, and the implementations of the high level operations are substituted for the corresponding invocations. The result is a new, more detailed program that is convincingly like the previous one, but that depends on fewer or simpler definitions (and hence is closer to being compilable). Successive steps of the program development add details of the sort more relevant to the programming language than to the problem domain until the program is completely expressed using the operations and data types of the base language, for which a compiler is available.

This separation of concerns between the structures that are used to solve a problem and the way those structures are implemented provides a methodology for decomposing complex problems into smaller, fairly independent segments. The key to the success of the methodology is the degree of abstraction imposed by selecting high level data structures and operations. The chief limitation of the methodology, which was not appreciated until the methodology had been in use for some time, is that the final program does not preserve the series of abstractions through which it was created, and so the task of modifying the program after it is completed is not necessarily simpler than it would be for a program developed in any other way. Another limitation of the methodology is that informal descriptions of operations do not convey precise information. Misunderstandings about exactly what an operation is supposed to do can complicate the program development process, and informal descriptions of procedures may not be adequate to assure true independence of modules. The development of techniques for formal program specification helps to alleviate this set of problems.

At about the same time this methodology was emerging, we also began to be concerned about how people understand programs and how programs can be organized to make them easier to understand, and hence to modify. We realized that it is of primary importance to be able to determine what assumptions about the program state are being made at any point in the program. Further, arbitrary transfers of control that span large amounts of program text interfere with this goal. The control flow patterns that lend themselves to understandable programs are the ones that have a single entry point (at the beginning of the text) and, at least conceptually, a single exit point (at the end of the text). Examples of statements that satisfy this rule are the **if... then... else** and the **for** and **while** loops. The chief violator of the rule is the **go to** statement.

The first discussion of this question appeared in 1968 [DIJK68], and we converged on a common set of "ideal" control constructs a few years later [DIJK72] [HW73]. Although a true consensus on this set of constructs still has not been achieved, the question is no longer regarded as an issue.

2.4 Program Verification

In parallel with the development of "ideal" control constructs—in fact, as part of their motivation—computer scientists became interested in finding ways to make precise, mathematically manipulatable statements about what a program computes. The ability to make such statements is essential to the development of techniques for reasoning about programs, particularly for techniques that rely on abstract specifications of effects. New techniques were required because procedure headers, even accompanied by prose commentary, provide inadequate information for reasoning precisely about programs, and imprecise statements lead to ambiguities about responsibilities and inadequate separation of modules.

The notion that it is possible to make formal statements about values of variables (a set of values for the variables of a program is called the *program state*) and to reason rigorously about the effect of executing a statement on the program's state first appeared in the late 1960s [FLOY67] [HOAR69]. The formal statements are expressed as formulas in the predicate calculus, such as

$$y > x \wedge (x > 0 \supset z = x^2).$$

A programming language is described by a set of rules that define the effect each statement has on the logical formula that describes the program state. The rules for the language are applied to the assertions in the program in order to obtain theorems whose proofs assure that the program matches the specification.[1] By the early 1970s the basic concepts of verifying assertions about simple programs and describing a language in such a way that this is possible were under control [HW73] [LGHL78]. When applied by hand, verification techniques tend to be error prone, and formal specifications, like informal ones, are susceptible to errors of omission [GY76]. In response to this problem, systems for performing the verification steps automatically have been developed [GW79]. Verification requires converting a program annotated with logical assertions to logical theorems with the property that the program is correct if and only if the theorems are true. This conversion process, called *verification condition generation*, is well understood, but considerable work remains to be done on the problem of proving those theorems.

When the emphasis in programming methodology shifted to using data structures as a basis for program organization, corresponding problems arose for specification and verification techniques. The initial

---

[1] A survey of these ideas appears in [LOND75]; introductions to the methods appear in Chapter 3 of [MANN74] and Chapter 5 of [WSHF81].

efforts addressed the question of what information is useful in a specification [PARN72a]. Subsequent attention concentrated on making those specifications more formal and dealing with the verification problems [HOAR72a]. From this basis, work on verification for abstract data types proceeded as described in Section 3.

2.5 Abstract Data Types

In the 1970s we recognized the importance of organizing programs into modules in such a way that knowledge about implementation details was localized as much as possible. This led to language support for data types [HOAR72b], for specifications that are organized using the same structure as data [GHM78] [LHLM77] [WLS76], and for generic definitions [SCHU76b]. The language facilities are based on the **class** construct of Simula [DMN68] [DH72], ideas about strategies for defining modules [PARN71] [PARN72b], and concerns over the impact of locality on program organization [WS73]. The corresponding specification techniques include strong typing and verification of assertions about functional correctness.

During the late 1970s, most research activity in abstraction techniques was focused on the language and specification issues raised by these considerations; much of the work is identified with the concept of *abstract data types*. Like structured programming, the methodology of abstract data types emphasizes locality of related collections of information. In this case, attention is focused on data rather than on control, and the strategy is to form modules consisting of a data structure and its associated operations. The objective is to treat these modules the same way as ordinary types such as integers and reals are treated; this requires support for declarations, infix operators, specification of routine parameters, and so on. The result, called an *abstract data type*, effectively extends the set of types available to a program — it explains the properties of a new group of variables by specifying the values one of these variables may have, and it explains the operations that will be permitted on the variables of the new type by giving the effects these operations have on the values of the variables.

In a data type abstraction, we specify the functional properties of a data structure and its operations, then we implement them in terms of existing language constructs (and other data types) and show that the specification is accurate. When we subsequently use the abstraction, we deal with the new type solely in terms of its specification. (This technique is discussed in detail in Section 3.) This philosophy was developed in several recent language research and development projects, including Ada [IKWL80], Alphard [WLS76], CLU [LSAS77], Concurrent Pascal [BRIN75], Euclid [LHLM77], Gypsy [AGBB77], Mesa [GMS77], and Modula [WIRT77].

The specification techniques used for abstract data types evolved from the predicates used in simple sequential programs. Additional expressive power was incorporated to deal with the way information is packaged into modules and with the problem of abstracting from an implementation to a data type [GUTT80]. One class of specification techniques draws on the similarity between a data type and the mathematical structure called an algebra [GHM78] [LZ75]. Another class of techniques explicitly models a newly defined type by defining its properties in terms of the properties of common, well understood types [WLS76].

In conjunction with the work on abstract data types and formal specifications, the generic definitions that originated in extensible languages have been developed to a level of expressiveness and precision far beyond the anticipation of their originators. These definitions, discussed in detail in Section 3.3, are parameterized not only in terms of variables that can be manipulated during program execution, but also in terms of data types. They can now describe restrictions on which types are acceptable parameters in considerable detail, as in [BS79].

2.6 Interactions Between Abstraction and Specification Techniques

As this review shows, programming languages and methodologies evolve in response to the needs that are perceived by software designers and implementors. However, these perceived needs themselves evolve in response to experience gained from past solutions. The original abstraction techniques of structured programming were procedures or macros;[2] these have evolved to abstract types and generic definitions. Methodologies for program development emerge when we find common useful patterns and try to use them as models; languages evolve to support these methodologies when the models become so common and stable that they are regarded as standard. A more extensive review of the development of software abstractions appears in [GUAR78]. As abstraction techniques have become capable of addressing a wider range of program organizations, formal specification techniques have become more precise and have played a more crucial role in the programming process.

For an abstraction to be used effectively, its specification must express all the information needed by the programmer who uses it. Initial attempts at specification used the notation of the programming language to express things that could be checked by the compiler: the

---

2 Although procedures were originally viewed as devices to save code space, they soon came to be regarded, like macros, as abstraction tools.

name of a routine and the number and types of its parameters. Other facts, such as the description of what the routine computed and under what conditions it should be used, were expressed informally [YZ80]. We have now progressed to the point that we can write precise descriptions of many important relations among routines, including their assumptions about the values of their inputs and the effects they have on the program state. However, many other properties of abstractions are still specified only informally. These include time and space consumption, interactions with special purpose devices, very complex aggregate behavior, reliability in the face of hardware malfunctions, and many aspects of concurrent processing. It is reasonable to expect future developments in specification techniques and programming languages to respond to those issues.

The history of programming languages shows a balance between language ideas and formal techniques; in each methodology, the properties we specify are matched to our current ability to validate (verify) the consistency of a specification and its implementation. Thus, since we can rely on formal specifications only to the extent that we are certain that they match their implementations, the development of abstraction techniques, specification techniques, and methods of verifying the consistency of a specification and an implementation must surely proceed hand in hand. In the future, we should expect to see more diversity in the programs that are used as a basis for modularization; we should also expect to see specifications that are concerned with aspects of programs other than the purely functional properties we now consider.

3. Abstraction Facilities in Modern Programming Languages

With the historical background of Section 2, we now turn to the abstraction methodologies and specification techniques that are currently under development in the programming language research community. Some of the ideas are well enough worked out to be ready for transfer to practical languages, but others are still under development.

Although the ideas behind modern abstraction techniques can be explored independently of programming languages, the instantiation of these ideas in actual languages is also important. Programming languages are our primary notational vehicle for expressing a class of very complex ideas; the concepts we must deal with include not only the functional relations of mathematics, but also constructs that deal with relations over time, such as sequentiality and synchronization. Language designs influence the ways we think about algorithms by making some program structures easier to describe than others. In addition, programming languages are used for communication among people as well as for controlling machines. This role is particularly important in long-lived programs, because a program is in many ways the most practical medium for expressing the structure imposed by the designer and for maintaining the accuracy of this documentation over time. Thus, even though most programming languages technically have the same expressive power, differences among languages can significantly affect their practical utility.

3.1 The New Ideas

Current activity in programming languages is motivated by three sets of global concerns: simplicity of design, the potential for applying precise analytic techniques to formal specifications, and the need to control costs over the entire lifetime of a long-lived program.

Simplicity has emerged as a major criterion for evaluating programming language designs. We see a certain tension between the need for "just the right construct" for a task and the need for a language small enough to understand thoroughly. This is an example of a tradeoff between specialization and generality: if highly specialized constructs are provided, individual programs will be smaller, but at the expense of complexity (and feature-by-feature interactions) in the system as a whole. The current trend is to provide a relatively small base language that provides facilities for defining special facilities in a regular way [SW80]. An emphasis on simplicity underlies a number of design criteria that are now commonly used. When programs are organized to localize information, for example, assumptions shared among program parts and module interfaces can be significantly simplified. The introduction of support for abstract data types in programming languages allows programmers to design special-purpose structures and deal with them in a simple way; it does so by providing a definition facility that allows the extensions to be made in a regular, predictable fashion. The regularity introduced by using these facilities can substantially reduce maintenance problems by making it easier for a programmer who is unfamiliar with the code to understand the assumptions about the program state that are made at a given point in the program, thereby increasing the odds that he or she can make a change without introducing new errors.

Our understanding of the principles underlying programming languages has improved to the point that *formal and quantitative techniques* are both feasible and useful. Current methods for specifying properties of abstract data types and for verifying that those specifications are consistent with the implementation are discussed in Section 3.2. Critical studies of testing methods are being performed [HOWD79], and interest in quantitative methods for evaluating programs is increasing [IEEE79a].

It is interesting to note that there seems to be a strong correlation between the ease with which proof rules for language constructs can be written and the ease with which programmers can use those constructs correctly and understand programs that use them.

The 1970s mark the beginning of a real appreciation that the cost of software includes the *costs over the lifetime of the program*, not just the costs of initial development or of execution. For large, long-lived programs, the costs of enhancement and maintenance usually dominate design, development, and execution costs, often by large factors. Two classes of issues arise [DK76]. First, in order to modify a program successfully, a programmer must be able to determine what other portions of the program depend on the section about to be modified. The problem of making this determination is simplified if the information is localized and if the design structure is retained in the structure of the program. Off-line design notes or other documents are not an adequate substitute except in the unlikely case that they are meticulously (and correctly) updated. Second, large programs rarely exist in only one version. The major issues concerning the control of large scale program development are problems of management, not of programming. Nevertheless, language-related tools can significantly ease the problems. Tools are becoming available for managing the interactions among many versions of a program.

3.2 Language Support for Abstract Data Types

During the 1970s, the major thrust of research activity in programming languages and methodology was to explore the issues related to abstract data types. The current state has emerged directly from the historical roots described in Section 2.5. The methodological concerns included the need for information hiding [PARN71] [PARN72b] and locality of data access [WS73], a systematic view of data structures [HOAR72b], a program organization strategy exemplified by the Simula **class** construct [DMN68] [DH72], and the notion of generic definition [SCHU76b]. The formal roots included a proposal for separating abstract properties from implementation [HOAR72a] and a debate on the philosophy of types, which finally led to the view that types share the formal characteristics of abstract algebras [GHM78] [GUTT77] [LZ75] [MORR73a].

Whereas structured programming involves progressive development of a program by adding detail to its control structure, programming with abstract data types involves partitioning the program *in advance* into modules that correspond to the major data structures of the final system. The two methodologies are complementary, because the techniques of structured programming may be used within type definition modules, and conversely. An example of the interaction of the two design styles appears in [BROW80].

In most languages that provide the facility, the definition of an abstract data type consists of a program unit that includes the following information:

1. *Visible outside the type definition.* The name of the type and the names and routine headers of all operations (procedures and functions) that are permitted to use the representation of the type. Some languages also include formal specifications of the values that variables of this type may assume and of the properties of the operations.

2. *Not visible outside the type definition.* The representation of the type in terms of built-in data types or other defined types, the bodies of the visible routines, and hidden routines that may be called only from within the module.

An example of a module that defines an abstract data type appears in Figure 4.5.

The general question of abstract data types has been addressed in a number of research projects. These include Alphard [WLS76], CLU [LSAS77], Gypsy [AGBB77], Russell [DD80], Concurrent Pascal [BRIN75], and Modula [WIRT77]. Although they differ in detail, they share the goal of providing language support adequate to the task of abstracting from data structures to abstract data types and allowing those abstract definitions to hold the same status as built-in data types. Detailed descriptions of the differences among these projects are best obtained by studying them in more detail than is appropriate here. As with many research projects, the impact they have is likely to take the form of influence on other languages (rather than their complete adoption). Indeed, the influence of several of the research projects on Ada [IKWL80] and Euclid [LHLM77] is apparent.

Programming with abstract data types requires support from the programming language, not simply managerial exhortations about program organization. Suitable language support requires solutions to a number of technical issues involving both design and implementation. These include:

1. *Naming.* Scope rules are required to ensure the appropriate visibility of names. In addition, protection mechanisms [JL76] [MORR73b] should be considered in order to guarantee that hidden information remains private. Further, programmers must be prevented from naming the same data in more than one way ("aliasing") if current verification technology is to be relied upon.

2. *Type checking.* It is necessary to check actual parameters to routines, preferably during compilation, to be sure they will be acceptable to the routines. The problem is more complex than the type checking problem for conventional languages because new types may be added during the compilation process and the parameterization of types

requires subtle decisions in the definition of a useful type checking rule.

3. *Specification notation.* The formal specifications of an abstract data type should convey all information needed by the programmer. This is not yet possible, but current progress is described below. As for any specification formalism, it is also necessary to develop a method for verifying that a specification is consistent with its implementation.

4. *Distributed properties.* In addition to providing operations that are called as routines or infix operators, abstract data types must often supply definitions to support type-specific interpretation of various constructs of the programming language. These constructs include storage allocation, loops that operate on the elements of a data structure without knowledge of the representation, and synchronization. Some of these have been explored, but many open questions remain [LSAS77] [SWL77] [SW80].

5. *Separate compilation.* Abstract data types introduce two new problems to the process of separate compilation. First, type checking should be done across compilation units as well as within units. Second, generic definitions offer significant potential for optimization (or for inefficient implementation).

Specification techniques for abstract data types are the topic of a number of current research projects. Techniques that have been proposed include informal but precise and stylized English [HENI79], models that relate the new type to previously defined types [WLS76], and algebraic axioms that specify new types independently of other types [GUTT77]. Many problems remain. The emphasis to date has been on the specification of properties of the code; the correspondence of these specifications to informally understood requirements is also important [DR79]. Further, the work to date has concentrated almost exclusively on the functional properties of the definition without attending, for example, to performance or reliability.

Not all the language developments include formal specifications as part of the code. For example, Alphard includes language constructs that associate a specification with the implementation of a module; Ada and Mesa expect interface definitions that contain at least enough information to support separate compilation. All the work, however, is based on the premise that the specification must include all information that should be available to a user of the abstract data type. When it has been verified that the implementation performs in accordance with its public specification [HOAR72a], the abstract specification may safely be used as the definitive source of information about how higher level programs may correctly use the module. In one sense we build up "bigger" definitions out of "smaller" ones; but because a specification alone suffices for understanding, the new definition is in another sense no bigger than the preexisting components. It is this regimentation of detail that gives the technique its power.

3.3 Generic Definitions

A particularly rich kind of abstract data type definition allows one abstraction to take another abstraction (*e.g.*, a data type) as a parameter. These *generic* definitions provide a dimension of modelling flexibility that conventionally parameterized definitions lack.

For example, consider the problem of defining data types for an application that uses three kinds of unordered sets: sets of integers, sets of reals, and sets of a user defined type for points in three-dimensional space. One alternative would be to write a separate definition for each of these three types. However, that would involve a great deal of duplicated text, since both the specifications and the code will be very similar for all the definitions. In fact, the programs would probably differ only where specific references to the types of set elements are made, and the machine code would probably differ only where operations on set elements (such as the assignment used to store a new value into the data structure) are performed. The obvious drawbacks of this situation include duplicated code, redundant programming effort, and complicated maintenance (since bugs must be fixed and improvements must be made in all versions).

Another alternative would be to separate the properties of unordered sets from the properties of their elements. This is possible because the definition of the sets relies on very few specific properties of the elements. It probably assumes only that ordinary assignment and equality operations for the element type are defined. Making that assumption, it is possible to write a single definition, say

```
type UnOrderedSet(T: type) is ...
```

that can be used to declare sets that have several different types of elements, as in

```
var
        Counters: UnOrderedSet(integer);
        Timers:   UnOrderedSet(integer);
        Sizes:    UnOrderedSet(real);
        Places:   UnOrderedSet(PointIn3Space);
```

using a syntax appropriate to the language that supports the generic definition facility. The definition of `UnOrderedSet` would provide operations such as `Insert`, `TestMembership`, and so on; the declarations of the variables would instantiate versions of these operations for all relevant element types, and the compiler would determine which of the operations to use at any particular time by inspecting the parameters to the routines.

The flexibility provided by generic definitions is demonstrated by the algorithmic transformation of [BS79], which automatically converts any solution of one class of problems to a solution of the corresponding problem in a somewhat larger class. This generic definition is notable for the detail and precision with which the assumptions about the generic parameter can be specified.

4. Practical Realizations

A number of programming languages provide some or all of the facilities required to support abstract data types. In addition to implementations of research projects, several language efforts have been directed primarily at providing practical implementations. These include Ada [IKWL80], Mesa [GMS77], Pascal [JW74], and Simula [DMN68]. Of these, Pascal currently has the largest user community, and the objective of the Ada development has been to make available a language to support most of the modern ideas about programming. Because of the major roles they play in the programming language community, Pascal and Ada will be discussed in some detail.

The evolution of programming languages through the introduction of abstraction techniques will be illustrated with a small program. The program is presented in Fortran IV to illustrate the state of our understanding in the late 1960s. Revised versions of the program in Pascal and Ada show how abstraction techniques for Ada have evolved.

4.1 A Small Example Program

In order to illustrate the effects that modern languages have on program organization and programming style, we will carry a small example through the discussion. This section presents a Fortran program for the example; Pascal and Ada versions are developed in Section 4.2 and 4.3.

The purpose of the program is to produce the data needed to print an internal telephone list for a division of a small company. A database containing information about all employees, including their names, divisions, telephone numbers, and salaries is assumed to be available. The program must produce a data structure containing a sorted list of the employees in a selected division and their telephone extensions.

Suitable declarations of the employee database and the divisional telephone list for the Fortran implementation are given in Figure 4.1. A program fragment for constructing the telephone list is given in Figure 4.2.

```
C     Vectors that contain Employee information
C     Name is in EmpNam (24 chars), Phone is in EmpFon (integer)
C     Salary is in EmpSal (real), Division is in EmpDiv (4 chars)
      integer EmpFon(1000), EmpDiv(1000)
      real EmpSal(1000)
      double precision EmpNam(3,1000)

C     Vectors that contain Phone list information
C     Name is in DivNam (24 chars), Phone is in DivFon (integer)
      integer DivFon(1000)
      double precision DivNam(3,1000)

C     declarations of scalars used in program
      integer StafSz, DivSz, i, j
      integer WhichD
      double precision q
```

Figure 4.1 *Declarations for Fortran Version of Telephone List Program*

The employee database is represented as a set of vectors, one for each unit of information about the employee. The vectors are used "in parallel" as a single data structure — that is, part of the information about the *i*th employee is stored in the *i*th element of each vector. Similarly, the telephone list is constructed in two arrays, `DivNam` for names and `DivFon` for telephone numbers.

The telephone list is constructed in two stages. First, the database is scanned for employees whose division (`EmpDiv(i)`) matches the division desired (`WhichD`). When a match is found, the name and phone number of the employee are added to the telephone list. Second, the telephone list is sorted using an insertion sort.[3]

There are several important things to notice about this program. First, the data about employees is stored in four arrays, and the relation among these arrays is shown only by the similar naming and the comment with their declarations. Second, the character string for each employee's name must be handled in eight-character segments, and there is no clear indication in either the declarations or the code that character strings are involved.[4] The six-line test that determines

[3] This selection is not an endorsement of insertion sorting in general. However,most readers will recognize the algorithm, and the topic of this chapter is the evolution of programming languages, not sorting techniques.

[4] Indeed, the implementations of floating point in some versions of Fortran interfere with this type violation. Character strings are dealt with more appropriately in the Fortran77 standard.

whether DivNam(*,i) < DivNam(*,j) could be reduced to three tests if it were changed to a test for less-than-or-equal, but this would make the sort unstable. Third, all the data about employees, including salaries, is easily accessible and modifiable. This is undesirable from an administrative standpoint.

```
C    Get data for division WhichD only

     DivSz = 0
     do 200 i = 1,StafSz
         if (EmpDiv(i) .ne. WhichD) go to 200
         DivSz = DivSz + 1
         DivNam(1,DivSz) = EmpNam(1,i)
         DivNam(2,DivSz) = EmpNam(2,i)
         DivNam(3,DivSz) = EmpNam(3,i)
         DivFon(DivSz) = EmpFon(i)
200      continue

C    Sort telephone list

     if (DivSz .eq. 0) go to 210
     do 220 i = 1,DivSz
         do 230 j = i+1,DivSz
            if (DivNam(1,i) .gt. DivNam(1,j)) go to 240
            if (DivNam(1,i) .lt. DivNam(1,j)) go to 230
            if (DivNam(2,i) .gt. DivNam(2,j)) go to 240
            if (DivNam(2,i) .lt. DivNam(2,j)) go to 230
            if (DivNam(3,i) .gt. DivNam(3,j)) go to 240
            go to 230
240         do 250 k = 1,3
               q = DivNam(k,i)
               DivNam(k,i) = Divnam(k,j)
250            DivNam(k,j) = q
            k = DivFon(i)
            DivFon(i) = DivFon(j)
            DivFon(j) = k
230         continue
220      continue
210   continue
```

Figure 4.2 Code for Fortran Version of Telephone List Program

4.2 Pascal

Pascal [JW74] is a simple algebraic language that was designed to achieve three primary objectives. It was to support modern programming development methodology; it was to be a simple enough language to teach to students; and it was to be easy to implement reliably, even on small computers. It has, in general, succeeded in all three respects.

Pascal provides a number of facilities for supporting structured programming. It provides the standard control constructs of structured programming, and a formal definition [HW73] facilitates verification of Pascal programs. It supports a set of data organization constructs that are suitable for defining abstractions. These include the ability to define a list of arbitrary constants as an *enumerated type*, the ability to define heterogeneous **records** with individually named fields, data types that can be dynamically allocated and referred to by pointers, and the ability to name a data structure as a **type** (though not to bundle up the data structure with a set of operations).

The language has become quite widely used. In addition to serving as a teaching language for undergraduates, it is used as an implementation language for microcomputers [BOWL77], and it has been extended to deal with parallel programming [BRIN75]. An international standardization effort is currently under way [IOS79].

Pascal is not without its disadvantages. It provides limited support for large programs, lacking separate compilation facilities and block structure other than nested procedures. Type checking does not provide quite as much control over parameter passing as one might wish, and there is no support for the encapsulation of related definitions in such a way that they can be isolated from the remainder of the program. Many of the disadvantages are addressed in extensions, derivative languages, and the standardization effort.

We can illustrate some of Pascal's characteristics by returning to the program for creating telephone lists. Suitable data structures, including both type definitions and data declarations, are shown in Figure 4.3. A program fragment for constructing the telephone list is given in Figure 4.4.

The declarations open with definitions of four types that are not predefined in Pascal. Two (`String` and `ShortString`) are generally useful, and the other two (`EmpRec` and `PhoneRec`) were designed for this particular problem.

The definition of `String` and `ShortString` as types permits named variables to be treated as single units; operations are performed on an entire string variable, not on individual groups of characters. This abstraction simplifies the program, but, more importantly, it allows the programmer to concentrate on the algorithm that uses the strings as names, rather than on keeping track of the individual fragments of a name. The difference in the complexity of the code in Figures 4.2 and 4.4 may not seem great, but when it is compounded over many individual composite structures with different representations, the difference can be large indeed. If Pascal allowed programmer-defined types to accept parameters, a single definition of strings that took the string length as a parameter could replace `String` and `ShortString`;

Ada does allow this, and the change is made in the Ada program of Section 4.3.

```
type
  String = packed array [1..24] of char;
  ShortString = packed array [1..8] of char;
  EmpRec = record
      Name:String;
      Phone:integer;
      Salary:real;
      Division:ShortString;
      end;
  PhoneRec = record Name:String; Phone:integer; end;

var
  Staff: array [1..1000] of EmpRec;
  Phones: array [1..1000] of PhoneRec;
  StaffSize, DivSize,i,j: integer;
  WhichDiv: char;
  q: PhoneRec;
```

Figure 4.3 *Declarations for Pascal Version of Telephone List Program*

```
    { Get data for division WhichDiv only }

    DivSize := 0;
    for i := 1 to StaffSize do
        if Staff[i].Division = WhichDiv then
            begin
            DivSize := DivSize + 1;
            Phones[DivSize].Name := Staff[i].Name;
            Phones[DivSize].Phone := Staff[i].Phone;
            end;

    { Sort telephone list }

    for i := 1 to DivSize - 1 do
        for j := i+1 to DivSize do
            if Phones[i].Name > Phones[j].Name then
                begin
                q := Phones[i];
                Phones[i] := Phones[j];
                Phones[j] := q;
                end;
```

Figure 4.4 *Code for Pascal Version of Telephone List Program*

The type definitions for `EmpRec` and `PhoneRec` abstract from specific data items to the notions "record of information about an employee" and "record of information for a telephone list." Both the employee database and the telephone list can thus be represented as vectors whose elements are records of the appropriate types.

The declarations of `Staff` and `Phones` have the effect of indicating that all the components are related to the same information structure. In addition, the definition is organized as a collection of records, one for each employee—so the primary organization of the data structure is by employee. On the other hand, the data organization of the Fortran program was dominated by the arrays that correspond to the fields, and the employees were secondary.

Just as in the Fortran program, the telephone list is constructed in two stages (Figure 4.4). Note that Pascal's ability to operate on strings and records as single units has substantially simplified the manipulation of names and the interchange step of the sort. Another notable difference between the two programs is in the use of conditional statements. In the Pascal program, the use of **if** ... **then** statements emphasizes the conditions that will cause the bodies of the **if** statements to be executed. The Fortran **if** statements with **go to**'s, however, describe conditions in which code is *not* to be executed, leaving the reader of the program to compute the conditions that actually correspond to the actions.

It is also worth mentioning that the Pascal program will not execute the body of the sort loop at all if no employees work in division `WhichDiv` (that is, if `DivSize` is 0). The body of the corresponding Fortran loop would be executed once in that situation if the loop had not been protected by an explicit test for an empty list. While it would do no harm to execute this particular loop once on an empty list, in general it is necessary to guard Fortran loops against the possibility that the upper bound is less than the lower bound.

4.3 Ada

The Ada language is currently being developed under the auspices of the Department of Defense in an attempt to reduce the software costs of embedded computer systems. The project includes components for both a language and a programming support environment. The specific objectives of the Ada development include significantly reducing the number of programming languages that must be learned, supported, and maintained within the Department of Defense. The language design emphasized the goals of high program reliability, low maintenance costs, support for modern programming methodology, and efficiency of compilers and object programs [IKWL80] [IBHK79].

The Ada language was developed through competitive designs constrained by a set of requirements [DoD78]. Revisions to the language were completed in the summer of 1980 and the initial language reference manual was published in November 1980. Revisions to the manual were made in 1981 and 1982, and a proposed ANSI standard was circulated in July 1982. Development of the programming environment will continue over the next several years [DoD80]. Since compilers for the language are not yet widely available, it is too soon to evaluate how well the language meets its goals. However, it is possible to describe the way various features of the language are intended to respond to the abstraction issues raised here.

Although Ada grew out of the Pascal language philosophy, extensive syntactic changes and semantic extensions make it a very different language from Pascal. The major additions include module structures and interface specifications for large program organizations and separate compilation, encapsulation facilities and generic definitions to support abstract data types, support for parallel processing, and control over low-level implementation issues related to the architecture of object machines.

There are three major abstraction tools in Ada. The **package** is used for encapsulating a set of related definitions and isolating them from the rest of the program. The **type** determines the values a variable (or data structure) may take on and how it can be manipulated. The **generic** definition allows many similar abstractions to be generated from a single template, as described in Section 3.3.

The incorporation of many of these ideas into Ada is illustrated in the example of Section 4.1. The data organization of the Pascal program (Figures 4.3 and 4.4) could be carried over almost directly to the Ada program, and the result could be made to take advantage of Ada reasonably well. However, Ada provides additional facilities that can be applied to this problem. Recall that neither the Fortran program nor the Pascal program can allow a programmer to access names, telephone numbers, and divisions without also allowing him to access private information, here illustrated by salaries. Ada programs can provide such selected access, and we will extend the previous example to do so.

We now organize the program in three components: a definition of the record for each employee (Figure 4.5), declarations of the data needed by the program (Figure 4.6), and code for construction of the telephone list (Figure 4.7).

The **package** of information about employees whose specification is shown in Figure 4.5 illustrates one of Ada's major additions to our tool kit of abstraction facilities. This definition establishes `EmpRec` as a data type with a small set of privileged operations. Only the specification of the package is presented here. Ada does not require the package body to accompany the specification (though it must be defined before the program can be executed); moreover, programmers are permitted to rely only on the specifications, not on the body of a package. The specification itself is divided into a visible part (everything from **package** to **private**) and a private part (from **private** to **end**). The private part is intended only to provide information for separate compilation.

```
package Employee is
   type PrivStuff is limited private;
   type EmpRec is
         record
             Name: string(1..24);
             Phone: integer;
             PrivPart: PrivStuff;
         end record;
   procedure SetSalary(Who: in out EmpRec; Sal: float);
   function GetSalary(Who: EmpRec) return float;
   procedure SetDiv(Who: in out EmpRec; Div: string(1..8));
   function GetDiv(Who: EmpRec) return string(1..8);
private
   type PrivStuff is
         record
             Salary: float;
             Division: string(1..8);
         end record;
end Employee;
```

Figure 4.5 *Ada Package Definition for Employee Records*

```
    declare
         use Employee;

         type PhoneRec is
              record
                   Name: string(1..24);
                   Phone: integer;
              end record;

         Staff: array (1..1000) of EmpRec;
         Phones: array (1..1000) of PhoneRec;
         StaffSize, DivSize: integer range 1..1000;
         WhichDiv: string(1..8);
         q: PhoneRec;
```

Figure 4.6 *Declarations for Ada Version of Telephone List Program*

Assume that the policy for using `EmpRecs` is that the `Name` and `Phone` fields are accessible to anyone, that it is permissible for anyone to read but not to write the `Division` field, and that access to the `Salary` field and modification of the `Division` field are supposed to be done only by authorized programs. Two characteristics of Ada make it possible to establish this policy. First, the scope rules prevent any portion of the program outside a package from accessing any names except the ones listed in the visible part of the specification. Thus, in the particular case of the `Employee` package, the `Salary` and `Division` fields of an `EmpRec` cannot be directly read or written outside the package. Therefore the integrity of the data can be controlled by verifying that the routines that are exported from the package are correct. Presumably the routines `SetSalary`, `GetSalary`, `SetDiv`, and `GetDiv` perform reads and writes as their names suggest; they might also keep records showing who made changes and when. Second, Ada provides ways to control the visibility of each routine and variable name.

```
-- Get data for division WhichDiv only

    DivSize := 0;
    for i in 1..StaffSize loop
          if GetDiv(Staff(i)) = WhichDiv then
              DivSize := DivSize + 1;
              Phones(DivSize) := (Staff(i).Name, Staff(i).Phone);
          end if;
    end loop;

-- Sort telephone list

    for i in 1..DivSize - 1 loop
          for j in i+1..DivSize loop
              if Phones(i).Name > Phones(j).Name then
                   q := Phones(i);
                   Phones(i) := Phones(j);
                   Phones(j) := q;
              end if;
          end loop;
    end loop;
```

Figure 4.7 *Code for Ada Version of Telephone List Program*

Although the field name `PrivPart` is exported from the `Employee` package along with `Name` and `Phone`, there is no danger in doing so. An auxiliary type was defined to protect the salary and division information;. the declaration

```
    type PrivStuff is limited private;
```

indicates not only that the content and organization of the data structure are hidden from the user (**private**), but also that all operations on data of type `PrivStuff` are forbidden except for calls on the routines exported from the package. For **limited private** types, even assignment and comparison for equality are forbidden. Naturally, the code inside the body of the `Employee` package may manipulate these hidden fields; the purpose of the packaging is to guarantee that *only* the code inside the package body can do so.

The ability to force manipulation of a data structure to be carried out only through a known set of routines is central to the support of abstract data types. It is useful not only in examples such as the one given here, but also for cases in which the representation may change radically from time to time and for cases in which some kind of internal consistency among fields, such as checksums, must be maintained. Support for *secure* computation is not among Ada's goals. It can be achieved in this case, but only through a combination of an extra level of packaging and some management control performed in the subprograms. Even without guarantees about security, however, the packaging of information about how employee data is handled provides a useful structure for the development and maintenance of the program.

The declarations of Figure 4.6 are much like the declarations of the Pascal program. The `Employee` package is used instead of a simple record, and there are minor syntactic differences between the languages. The clause

```
use Employee;
```

says that all the visible names of the `Employee` package are available in the current block. Since Ada, unlike Pascal, allows nonprimitive types to take parameters, `Names` and `Divisions` are declared as `Strings` of specified length.

In the code of the Ada program itself (Figure 4.7), we assume that visibility rules allow the non-**private** field names of `EmpRecs` and the `GetDiv` function to be used. Ada provides a way to create a complete record value and assign it with a single statement; thus the assignment

```
Phones(DivSize) := (Staff(i).Name, Staff(i).Phone);
```

sets both fields of the `PhoneRec` at once. Aside from this and minor syntactic distinctions, this program fragment is very much like to the Pascal fragment of Figure 4.4.

5. Status and Potential

It is clear that methodologies and analytic techniques based on the principle of abstraction have played a major role in the development of software engineering and that they will continue to do so. In this section we describe the ways our current programming habits are changing to respond to those ideas. We also note some of the limitations of current techniques and how future work may deal with them, and we conclude with some suggestions for further reading on abstraction techniques.

5.1 How New Ideas Affect Programming

As techniques such as abstract data types have emerged, they have affected both the overall organization of programs and the style of writing small segments of code.

The new languages will have the most sweeping effects on the techniques we use for the high level organization of program systems, and hence on the management of design and implementation projects. Modularization features that impose controls on the distribution of variable, routine, and type names can profoundly shape the strategies for decomposing a program into modules. Further, the availability of precise (and enforceable) specifications for module interfaces will influence management of software projects [YZ80]. For example, the requirements document for a large avionics system has already been converted to a precise, if informal, specification [HENI79]. Project organization also will be influenced by the growing availability of support tools for managing multiple modules in multiple versions [MILL79].

The organization and style of the code within modules will also be affected. Section 4 shows how the treatment of both control and data changes within a module as the same problem is solved in languages that have increasingly powerful abstraction techniques.

The ideas behind the abstract data type methodology are still not entirely validated. Projects using various portions of the methodology — such as design based on data types, but no formal specification, or conversely specification and verification without modularity — have been successful, but a complete demonstration on a large project has not yet been completed [SFFH78]. Although complete validation experiments have not been done, some of the initial trials are encouraging. A large, interesting program using data-type organization in a language without encapsulation facilities has been written and largely verified [GW79], and abstract data types specified via algebraic axioms have proved useful as a design tool [GH80].

5.2 Limitations of Current Programming Language Abstraction Techniques

Efforts to use abstract data types have also revealed some limitations of the technique. In some cases problems are not comfortably cast as data types, or the necessary functionality is not readily expressed using the specification techniques now available. In other cases, the problem requires a set of definitions that are clearly very similar but cannot be expressed by systematic instantiation or invocation of a data type definition, even using generic definitions.

A number of familiar, well structured program organizations do not fit well into precisely the abstract data type paradigm. These include, for example, filters and shells in the Unix spirit [KP76] and interactive programs in which the command syntax dominates the specification. These organizations are unquestionably useful and potentially as well understood as abstract data types, and there is every reason to believe that similarly precise formal models can be developed. Some of these alternative points of view are already represented in high level design systems for software [GM80] [PETE80].

Although facilities for defining routines and modules whose parameters may be generic (*i.e.*, of types that cannot be manipulated in the language) have been developed during the past five years, there has been little exploration of the *generality of generic definitions*. Part of the problem has been lack of facilities for specifying the precise dependence of the definition on its generic parameters. A specific example of a complex generic definition, giving an algorithmic transformation that can be applied to a wide variety of problems, has been written and verified [BS79].

The language investigations described above, together with other research projects [GW79] [GHM78] [GH80] [HOAR72a] [LZ75] [PARN72b] have addressed questions of functional specification in considerable detail. That is, they provide formal notations such as input-output predicates, abstract models, and algebraic axioms for making assertions about the effects that operators have on program values. In many cases, the specifications of a system cannot be reduced to formal assertions; in these cases we resort to testing in order to increase our confidence in the program [GM80]. In other situations, moreover, a programmer is concerned with properties other than pure functional correctness. Such properties include time and space requirements, memory access patterns, reliability, synchronization, and process independence; these have not been addressed by the data type research. A specification methodology that addresses these properties must have two important characteristics. First, it must be possible for the programmer to make and verify assertions about the properties rather than simply analyzing the program text to derive exact values or complete specifications. This is analogous to our approach to functional specifications—we don't attempt to formally derive the mathematical function defined by a program; rather, we specify certain properties of the computation that are important and must be preserved. Further, it is important to avoid adding a new conceptual framework for each new class of properties. This implies that mechanisms for dealing with new properties should be compatible with the mechanisms already used for functional correctness.

A certain amount of work on formal specifications and verification of extra-functional properties has already been done. Most of it is directed at specific properties rather than at techniques that can be applied to a variety of properties; the results are, nonetheless, interesting. The need to address a variety of requirements in practical real-time systems was vividly demonstrated at the Conference on Specifications of Reliable Software [IEEE79b], most notably by Heninger [HENI79]. Other work includes specifications of security properties [FN79] [MILL76] [WKP80], reliability [WLGL78], performance [RAMS79] [SHAW79], and communication protocols [GOOD77].

5.3 The Interface with Databases and Artificial Intelligence

This volume was instigated by a workshop that addressed the issues of conceptual modelling techniques in the areas of programming languages, databases, and artificial intelligence. That meeting revealed considerable common ground among the areas; it also highlighted some differences of attitude and usage.

Many of the apparent philosophical differences among these three areas may arise from differences in emphasis. For example, data sharing and a dominance of data over computation receive more attention in artificial intelligence and particularly in databases than in programming languages. Implicit computation performed as a side effect of data access or modification follows the same pattern. On the other hand, formal techniques—particularly for specification—play a much larger role in programming languages than in the other two areas. There are also differences in the degree of regularity assumed for an *ordinary* data structure; large, irregular heterogeneous structures appear much more often in artificial intelligence than in programming languages, but much less often in databases.

These differences of emphasis among the areas highlight a number of issues that deserve more attention from the programming language community. It would be useful to find ways to specify and control

- implicit computation as a side effect of data access or modification,
- long-lived data—in particular, data that outlives the programs that manipulate it,
- inconsistent, partially correct, or incomplete systems,
- data sharing, particularly when several processes are cooperatively updating a structure, and
- richer (for example, non-hierarchical) type systems,

without adding excess cost or complexity to programming languages.

5.4 Further Reading

This paper has included extensive citations in order to make further information about briefly-discussed topics easy to obtain. The purpose of this section is to identify the books and papers that will be most helpful for general or background reading.

General issues of software development, including both management and implementation issues, are discussed in Brook's very readable book [BROO75]. The philosophy of structured programming and the principles of data organization that underlie the representation issues of abstract data types receive careful technical treatment in [DH72] [DIJK72] [HOAR72b]. The proceedings of the Conference on Specifications of Reliable Software [IEEE79b] contain papers on both prose descriptions of requirements and mathematical specification of abstractions.

More specific (and more deeply technical) readings include Parnas's seminal paper on information hiding [PARN72b], Guttag and Horning's discussion of the use of algebraic axioms as a design tool [GH80], London's survey of verification techniques [LOND75], and papers on specification techniques including algebraic axioms [GUTT77], and abstract models [WLS76].

6. References

[AGBB77] [BOWL77] [BR70] [BRIN75] [BROO75] [BROW80] [BS79] [DD80] [DH72] [DIJK68] [DIJK72] [DK76] [DMN68] [DoD78] [DoD80] [DR79] [FLOY67] [FN79] [GH80] [GHM78] [GM80] [GMS77] [GOLD73] [GOOD77] [GUAR78] [GUTT77] [GUTT80] [GW79] [GY76] [HENI79] [HOAR69] [HOAR72a] [HOAR72b] [HOWD79] [HW73] [IBHK79] [IEEE79a] [IEEE79b] [IKWL80] [IOS79] [JL76] [JW74] [KNUT73] [KP76]

[LGHL78] [LHLM77] [LOND75] [LSAS77] [LZ75] [MANN74] [MILL76] [MILL79] [MORR73a] [MORR73b] [NR69] [PARN71] [PARN72a] [PARN72b] [PETE80] [RAMS79] [SCHU71] [SCHU76b] [SFFH78] [SHAW79] [STAN67] [SW80] [SWL77] [WIRT71] [WIRT77] [WKP80] [WLGL78] [WLS76] [WS73] [WSHF81] [YZ80]

Discussion

Currently, data abstraction in programming languages arises in two contexts: abstract data types (ADT), and object oriented programming (OOP). Although the two approaches have much in common, there are also claimed differences.

Object Oriented Programming

In OOP systems, notions of message passing are central, whereas in ADT systems, no such concepts play a role. Still, for all OOP systems that are not truly multi-processor-based ("actor" type systems), the talk about "message passing" is misleading. The crucial feature is that in order to identify (call) a function in OOP, one must also identify the type of (at least) one of its arguments. So the name of a function is not simply an identifier, it is a *n*-tuple of a function identifier and some type identifiers. That is, in fact, very similar to what happens in ADT systems. In OOP, the "properties," including function definitions (methods), are conceived of as belonging to a class or type of objects. SMALLTALK is a typical example of this approach. In David Moon's system FLAVORS at MIT, an object type can be created more dynamically from "all the little bits of FLAVOR that are lying around." So FLAVORS is more concerned with how to group sets of properties associated with different types (classes). In SMALLTALK, the properties reside "physically" with a single class (modulo their susceptibility to "downwards inheritance"). In a sense every operator is unary ("curried"), since one operand, the first, is distinguished as the object, and its type is dispatched on, the others being treated as a sort of parameter. (If objects exist on different machines, then one of them must be informed of the whereabouts of the others in order to interact.) In ADT languages, such as CLU and ALPHARD, all operands are created equal. In either case, the languages are seen as providing operations on classes of objects, thus supporting an "algebraic style" of programming in which an algebra is a collection of objects (or types of objects) and operations and relations defined on them.

Rebuttal by Carl Hewitt: "This is missing an important point: the control structure of message passing is not necessarily that of a procedure call. While it is true that the content of a message is often similar to the arguments of a procedure, the *control structure* is different."

Abstract Data Types

ADT emphasizes the separation between specification and implementation, while OOP does not. In ADT, one gets the picture of many different levels, one level being an implementation of another, while the second may, in turn, be at the implementation level relative to a third. Although OOP people do not tend to use "specification-implementation" dichotomy so much, aren't they in fact applying a similar paradigm? If the "specification-implementation" subdivision of ADT is extended by a notion of "substitutability," ADT provides the ability to substitute one implementation of a specification for another without crossing a given set of specification boundaries. FORTRAN subroutines, for example, already provide a kind of "substitutability interface" which works, however, only for code substitution, not for data structures. Both OOP and ADT systems are attempts to achieve substitutability at more and more abstract and general levels. (However, there are doubts whether "substitutability" is capable of implementing actor message passing. See the chapter by Hewitt and DeJong.)

Rebuttal by Mary Shaw: "I am afraid that the point is being missed. The issue is not 'substitutability' but appropriateness. The specification contains information appropriate for the user of the component (for example, a description of computational properties in the user's frame of reference). The implementation, on the other hand, contains information pertinent only to the maintainer of the module (for example, the code for accessing fields of packed representations)."

Historically, however, OOP people and ADT people seem to come from different backgrounds. On the one hand, OOP, with its largely AI background, is more concerned with irregular, nonhomogeneous objects (data structures), while ADT, being more directly an offspring of programming language research, concentrates on more regular, canonicalized structures. Examples of the latter are stacks, queues, and symbol tables which are relatively well understood theoretically, in some cases forming a well defined algebra.

One gets the impression from ADT literature that the great advantage of the specification-implementation dichotomy is that the specification is stable and therefore provides a good basis for proofs (*e.g.*, of correctness and completeness). The implementation, on the other hand, can vary. But in many AI applications, data structure design (the specification of the objects) is more a matter of "invention" and typically involves modifying the definition more or less wholesale (and not just the implementation). Under these conditions of continual change the ADT dichotomy is not necessarily very useful.

Rebuttal by Carl Hewitt: "I believe that the interface description-implementation spectrum is fundamental even in AI applications. Just because interfaces continually evolve doesn't mean that they are not important. Because they are changing it is even more crucial to describe and track them."

Mary Shaw: "If we were to redesign ALPHARD we would not make the close association anymore between a type and the encapsulation mechanism."

First Order Languages

There are related issues concerning the appropriateness of different representational languages that are use for different purposes. All programming languages may have the same expressive (functional) power; however, some are more appropriate than others for given purposes, but not one is best for all possible purposes. Standard first order languages (FOLs) are arguably universal; that is, they can express everything that is expressible. One characteristic of FOL that makes it universal is that anything can be a value of its individual variables. Its variables are universal.

This characteristic leads to a certain "flatness" in standard first order languages. For instance, if one treats time and tense in a standard FOL, variables can be bound to both time instances and people. This approach does not respect the fact that time is usually conceived in a very special way. A different approach to dealing with time in FOL is to change monadic predicates to two place predicates. Thus a previously monadic predicate, "Teacher(x)," gets changed to a two-place predicate, "Teacher(t,x)," understood to mean "at time t, x is a teacher."

Rebuttal by Carl Hewitt: "Where is the argument that first order languages are universal? In higher order logics, predicates such as equality can be defined:

$$x=y <-> (\forall x\, P(x) <=> P(y)).$$

How do we know that FOL is not leaving out something crucial?"

FOL Extensions

Another way to go is to introduce, instead, (intentional—non-truthfunctional) temporal operators such as: P(Teacher(x)) means that in the past, x was a teacher. P is not a standard FOL sentential operator, and you can prove that, with some small number of these, you can say everything that you can say quantifying over instants (though not also over sets of instants). Other examples include dynamic logics for programming languages that use intentional (modal) operators explicitly. It may well be that these (mildly) nonstandard formalisms are closer to the phenomena of interest — as one thinks about them — than the corresponding FOL expressions.

Take, for example, all the work on formal semantics of natural language. All of it uses formal languages that deviate from FOL. The methodological reason is the complicated syntactic and semantic structure of natural languages. If one had stipulated that the formal language used had to be FOL, one would have to be very inventive indeed about the translation from the natural language into the formalism. But it is very hard to be precise and formal about this translation. This is where ad hoc heuristics come into play. Whereas, if one starts with FOL, one can be inventive and creative and at the same time precise and simplify the translation procedures considerably. That is the great advantage.

Ray Reiter: "Is FOL really flat? We can always formalize a meta language and then use that formalization to talk about object level things."

David Israel: "It's a matter of intuition. One can do the meta theory of a first order language in FOL, but the result is still 'flat.' That is the glory and the pitfall of FOLs, the universality of the range of the one kind of variables (modulo syntactic sugaring via sorting). Again, for example, note that temporal logic treats the time parameter in a distinctive way just as dynamic logic does with the program parameter. Different things get treated differently."

Ray Reiter: "I think that the 'flatness' objection is really a red herring, which fails to take into account different levels of representation. If you have a 'bumpy' account of, say, time as some modal logic with a semantics which captures our intuitions about time, then I can provide a 'flat' first order representation, probably by ascending to the meta level of FOL, within which to represent your modal logic. Mine would be an equivalent representation, but in a different language, although I grant that yours might be more perspicuous."

The real problem with theories granting first class status to things like belief, time, *etc.,* is that they are nonadditive. Suppose you have a modal logic for belief, a different one for knowledge, and another for time. How do you combine them, as would be required, for example, for the correct representation of "John believes that Mary knows that Maureen was a teacher"? The beauty of first order representation for things like belief, time, *etc.,* is that they are additive; just throw all the axioms into one pot.

David Israel: "If you did the encoding of the non-truthfunctional (intentional) operators the way that Bob Moore does for 'believe' and 'knowledge' in a standard FOL, then you may find yourself talking about things you did not think you were talking about (or you did not want to talk about), things like sentences and terms as well as possible worlds and possible objects, *etc.*"

Abstraction Mechanisms in Programming Languages

Mary Shaw: "I see modelling and abstraction concerns raising several as yet unresolved issues.

- Techniques are required to support ways of specifying fragments dependently rather than monolithically.
- State transition specifications appear repeatedly and better notations for specifying them are needed.
- Strong typing is too strong.
- Operators for program definition are required that are richer than composition, substitution, and parameter binding.
- Implicit computation becomes more and more important, that is, computation via side effects and demons.
- Finally, the scope of formal specifications should be extended to include time/space requirements, reliability issues, *etc.* A major shortcoming of all the ADT work has been that it focuses exclusively on computational functionality and does not address efficiency considerations at all."

In conclusion, one can say that abstraction mechanisms are only as sophisticated or as general as the formal analysis techniques allow. Vice versa, the formal analysis techniques grow only when required to support mechanisms of current interest.

Mary Shaw: "For example, take the ALPHARD symbol table. There is an instantiation parameter determining the size of the hash table representation that appears nowhere in the specification. This parameter is a piece of the specification that is missing. Moreover, we took the wrong thing into the visible part. Now, I would try to put in the size parameter position a value that expresses something interpretable to a human being, such as a specification of the time-space-tradeoff. In the implementation I would then reinterpret that parameter to an integer governing the size of the hash-table."

Furthermore, there is the general question of trade-off between power and specialization. Knowing, for example, that programmers spend less time using a programming language than struggling with, say, text formatters, editors, command languages ("languages"!), *etc.*, raise the question of how these systems can best be improved by applying language design principles.

Part II

Perspectives from Artificial Intelligence

4
Generalization/Specialization as a Basis for Software Specification

Alexander Borgida, John Mylopoulos
and Harry K.T. Wong
University of Toronto

ABSTRACT *This paper describes a software specification methodology based on the notion of concept specialization. The methodology, which is particularly useful for Information Systems, applies uniformly to the various components of such systems, such as data classes, transactions, exceptions, and user interfaces (scripts), and its goal is the systematic and structured description of highly detailed world models, where concepts occur in many variations. An example from the domain of university information systems is used to illustrate and motivate the approach.*

1. Introduction

Complaints about the high cost of software development and maintenance are now commonplace. Research in Programming Languages, Software Engineering, and Database Management attempts to deal with this problem by proposing tools and techniques for managing the ever increasing complexity of software. Many of these techniques are based on *abstraction mechanisms* that advocate the development of software in a stepwise fashion, each step involving only some of the details of the

---

Alexander Borgida's current address: Dept. of Computer Science, Rutgers University, New Brunswick, NJ 08903.

Harry K.T. Wong's current address: Lawrence Berkeley Labs, Berkeley, CA 94720.

whole problem while others, hopefully the less relevant ones, are suppressed until some later step.[1]

For example, some current methodologies advocate the creation of a sequence of *models* ranging from the initial "real-world problem" to the final machine-executable program. This abstraction, called *Representation* in [SS79], involves implementation details and is supported by a number of languages and methodologies (*e.g.*, [PARN72] and [WLS76], among others). A second abstraction that has been advocated involves grouping a collection of units into a new conceptual unit (*Aggregation*). Software development through stepwise refinement [WIRT71] is based on this abstraction and offers decomposition as a methodological tool for building complex systems. This chapter focuses on *conceptual modelling*, *i.e.*, the specification of models that are closer to the human's conception of reality than to the machine's representation, and proposes a stepwise methodology based on *concept specialization*. In this case, the abstraction involves factoring out the commonalities in the description of several concepts into the description of a more general concept, and the refinement process reintroduces these details by specifying the ways in which a more specialized concept differs from the more general one. This methodology, which we call *taxonomic specification*, is complementary to stepwise refinement and methodologies based on Representation, and we feel that it is particularly appropriate when there are a large number of relatively simple, but interrelated, facts to be captured.

Section 2 elaborates on the notions of "model" and "abstraction," and Section 3 discusses Generalization as an abstraction mechanism and compares our version to others that have been proposed in the literature. In Section 4 we present a long example using a language along the lines of TAXIS[2] [MBW80] [WONG81] to illustrate the nature and the virtues of taxonomic specification. Section 5 sketches scripts that facilitate the description of the user dialogues that need to be supported by the system under design, and Section 6 discusses exceptions and an exception-handling mechanism that can be used as a tool in cases of over-abstraction. Finally, Section 7 presents conclusions and directions for further research.

---

[1] The term "abstraction" is used here in a more general sense than usual in the field of Programming Languages, where its meaning is usually that of "representation abstraction," as that notion is defined below.

[2] TAXIS is a programming language for the design of interactive information systems, such as on-line inventory control and airline reservations, which supports taxonomic programming and offers many of the features discussed in the rest of the chapter.

2. Models and Abstractions

The observation that a computer system constitutes a model of a "world" or "slice of reality" about which it contains information has been made repeatedly in the literature (*e.g.*, [ABRI74] [BC75] [WILS75]), and is most obvious in the case of information systems. This observation motivates our first axiom: in a substantial number of cases, the process of software specification can be viewed as the process of building an accurate model of some enterprise. In order to facilitate the task of the modeler, as well as communication with the eventual users, we also assume that these models should reflect naturally and directly the users' conceptualization of the universe of discourse.

Unfortunately, the term "model" has several different technical meanings and it seems appropriate to contrast them with the sense used in this chapter.

The term receives its most precise and technical sense in the field of mathematical logic where, given a set of axioms and their deductive consequences, one interprets them in terms of a "model" (*i.e.*, a set of mathematical entities and relations which satisfy the axioms). This notion underlies in one way or another all other uses of the term, but in this technical sense its use is restricted to the theory of mathematical logic.

Two other uses of the term, namely as an analogue device (*e.g.*, a wind-tunnel model of an airplane) and as a mathematical model (*e.g.*, Maxwell's equations as a model of electricity) are common in science and engineering, but they are quite distinct from the term as used in this chapter.

From the cognitive sciences we obtain the notion of "conceptual model," which is much closer to what we want. Such a model consists of a number of symbol structures and symbol structure manipulators which, according to a rather naive mentalistic philosophy, are supposed to correspond to the conceptualizations of the world by human observers. This view appears to underlie work on "semantic data models" (*e.g.*, survey in [BORG82b]) and "knowledge representation" (*e.g.*, overviews in [BD81] and [MYLO81]).

Another sense of the term "model" is current in the area of Data Base Management Systems under the guise of "data model." A *data model* (see [TL82] for example) specifies the rules according to which data are structured and what associated operations are permitted on them. The traditional data models underlying commercial Database Management Systems consider as data only strings and numbers, and they are concerned primarily with the manner in which data is accessed by the user (in some cases reflecting how data is stored in the computer), and have little or no regard for the *interpretation* process required to make *information* out of *data*.

Since our concern here is with human oriented models of a world, we adopt the "conceptual model" sense of the term rather than one of the others.

If one accepts the need for conceptual models he is immediately faced with the problem of identifying the constructs that facilitate their creation. Not surprisingly, many of the proposed constructs have their roots in epistemological methods for organizing knowledge.

Abstraction is a fundamental conceptual tool used for organizing information. The following are just a few aspects of abstraction that are useful in describing complex conceptual models:

- *Classification.* Grouping entities that share common characteristics into a *class* over which uniform conditions hold. The class `PERSON`, for example, can be derived from the entities `john smith`, `mary brown`, *etc.*, through classification. The inverse of Classification, *Instantiation*, can be used to obtain other entities that conform to the constraints associated with the definition of the class `person`.

- *Aggregation.* Treating a collection of concepts as a single concept. For example, `person` could be thought of, rather naively, as an aggregation of its `name`, `address`, and `profession`. *Decomposition* is the opposite of Aggregation since it decomposes a class into its constituent parts.

- *Generalization.* Extracting from one or more given classes the description of a more general class that captures the commonalities but suppresses some of the detailed differences in the descriptions of the given classes. `Employee`, for instance, is a generalization of the classes `secretary`, `trucker`, and `accountant`. The process that has the opposite effect to Generalization (*i.e.*, creates a new class by introducing additional detail to the description of an existing one) is called *Specialization*.

There are other abstraction mechanisms, such as "normalization" (suppression of details that deal with deviations from the norm and emphasis of details that deal only with the normal or ordinary circumstances [BORG82a]) but the three above have received the most attention. Conceptual models of complex worlds are bound to be large if they are to account for sufficiently many properties of their subjects. The abstraction mechanisms discussed above offer both *organizational principles* and *design methodologies* for conceptual models.

Not surprisingly, each of these mechanisms, as well as the representation abstraction noted in the introduction, has led to proposals for software development methodologies. For example, Representation has led to abstract data type-related methodologies and important programming languages such as Simula [DH72], CLU [LSAS77], Alphard [WLS76], *etc.* (See the chapter by Shaw.) These have been defined to support the development of software through the gradual introduction of implementation detail. Similarly, aggregation has led to proposals for the design of software through stepwise refinement (by decomposition) (*e.g.*, [WIRT71] [DIJK72]), and languages such as Pascal have been found suitable for supporting this abstraction. Object-oriented programming is based on classification and is supported by Simula and some of its successors, notably Smalltalk [INGA78] and Actors [HBS73]. Finally, generalization leads to methodologies that organize the collection of classes constituting a model into hierarchies (taxonomies). Simula (again!) and in a different context [SS77] follow this route.

Of course, a successful software development methodology has to employ as many of the above mentioned abstraction mechanisms as possible. For the purposes of research strategy, however, it seems fruitful to focus on one mechanism and to formalize it, examine its applicability, and study its usefulness; hence, this chapter concentrates on the notion of Generalization/Specialization.

3. Generalization/Specialization

We are interested in formulating a methodology for building conceptual models based on Generalization/Specialization. The key idea of such a methodology is that a model can be constructed by modelling first, in terms of classes, the most general concepts and tasks in the application area, and then proceeding to deal with sub-cases through more specialized classes. Models constructed through such a process have their classes structured into a *taxonomy* or so-called *IS-A hierarchy*. For example, when building a student enrollment system for a university, one might consider first the concepts of student and course and the task of enrolling a student for a course. Later, the designer can consider graduate and undergraduate students and courses, full- and part-time students, day and evening courses, and the rules and regulations that apply to these classes. Indeed, we believe that most situations of application programming, such as ones for student enrollment, inventory control, airline or hotel reservations, inherently involve *large* amounts of *simple* detail, and that taxonomies offer a fundamental tool for coping with such situations.

Taxonomies of classes have been used in one form or another in artificial intelligence, programming languages and databases for over a decade (*e.g.*, [QUIL68] [DH72]). However, each author formulates them differently. The rest of this section outlines the main points of view and contrasts them to the one adopted in the chapter.

One of the advantages of organizing descriptions into taxonomies is the notion of *inheritance*. Since instances of a subclass are generally also instances of its superclasses, there is no need to repeat the information specified in the description of a class for each of its subclasses, and their own subclasses, *etc.* As a result, taxonomic descriptions can be abbreviated, and some clerical errors can be avoided by reducing the amount of repetition in descriptions.

There are two basic ways to view the description one associates with a class such as **PERSON** (intended to model the concept of person). The first is that the description simply characterizes a prototypical instance of the concept, *i.e.*, a prototypical person. It follows from this view that some of the assertions of the description (*e.g.*, that a person has a telephone number) might be contradicted by a particular instance of the class (*e.g.*, `bill brown` who doesn't have a telephone number because he doesn't have a telephone). Much of the Knowledge Representation research within Artificial Intelligence views classes (concepts/frames/units/ . . .) in those terms. The second view treats the description associated with a class as asserting necessary conditions that must be satisfied by all of its instances. Simula and the semantic data models adopt this view. The consequences of this choice on the nature of taxonomies (IS-A hierarchies) are immediate.

1. *Class as prototype.* If class C *IS-A* class B (*i.e.*, C is a specialization of B and therefore lower down on the hierarchy) and B has some properties, these properties can be over-ridden in the definition of C. Thus even though "All birds fly" and "Penguins are birds," penguins do not necessarily fly (in fact they don't!). Inheriting properties from a more general class is done by default here (*default inheritance*), *i.e.*, only if the description of the more specialized class does not assert otherwise. The assertions associated with a class have an "unless-otherwise-told" or default nature.

2. *Class as template.* If C *IS-A* B and B has some properties, then necessarily C must have the same properties. Asserting that every bird flies implies, with this view, that penguins *can't* be birds since they don't fly. Thus inheritance of properties from a class to its specializations is now strict (*strict inheritance*).

We adopt the second view of what a class is, and, as we will see in Sections 5 and 6, treat exceptions through a separate exception-handling mechanism rather than by weakening the assertional force of a class definition.

There is still another choice to consider once one has made this decision. Neither Simula, nor the semantic data models that have been proposed, with the exception of TAXIS, allow a property to be "refined" as one specializes a class. For instance, if we have asserted that every person has an age between 0 and 120 (years) in the description of the class **PERSON**, we would like to refine this property to "every student has an age between 12 and 80 when **PERSON** is specialized to obtain **STUDENT**. With strict inheritance a new class inherits all the properties of its generalizations and it can also have new properties of its own. However, it cannot refine any of the properties of its generalizations along the lines suggested above.

We consider that an important modelling tool is the ability to refine properties of a class as one generates its specializations.

We would like to emphasize even at this stage that the utility of generalization hierarchies for software engineering is not limited to the use of inheritance, although this feature is often the most visible. In particular, the *construction* of the hierarchies systematizes and structures the *process of information/requirements gathering*, and since the hierarchies persist even after the system is designed, they provide an *organization* of the information that facilitates the *location of information* and the *estimation of the effect of changes* (*e.g.*, changes to a class description will affect all subclasses of that class) during program maintenance. Furthermore, the development of procedures through stepwise refinement by specialization down the IS-A hierarchy permits an incremental testing of such programs, in contrast to programs developed through stepwise refinement by decomposition [WIRT71], where only the final stage of the refinement is an executable program. In this chapter, we shall concentrate on the use of Generalization hierarchies in the description of Information Systems; we describe elsewhere the application of these ideas to requirements specification [GBM82] and verification [WONG81] [BORG81], among others.

4. Taxonomic Specification

As argued earlier, we view our task as having to describe the conceptual data objects and activities that occur in the domain of discourse, and their associated constraints. Throughout this section our ideas will be illustrated with examples from the student enrollment process at the University of Toronto. In order not to distract from the methodological aspects of this chapter, we have chosen to present the examples in a semiformal way, preferring a skeletal language augmented with English descriptions of programming language code; the interested reader is referred to [WONG81] and [MBW80] for details of a programming language into which these descriptions can be immediately translated. Better known languages such as Simula [DH72] and Smalltalk [INGA78], and recent systems such as Pie [BG80a], also support versions of the abstractions involved in our methodology.

Aggregation is supported by the notion of *property*—a function which, when evaluated for an entity, returns one of its components or, more vaguely, a related entity. For example, if "cs100" was some particular course, then *title*("cs100"), *limit*("cs100"), *size*("cs100") and *class-list*("cs100") might represent respectively the title of this course, 'Introduction to Programming,' the maximum and current enrollment in the course, say 800 and 647 respectively, and the list of students currently enrolled in "cs100." In the case of aggregation as applied to an activity, some properties would have as value those activities that would result from one step of decomposition as suggested by stepwise refinement. Other properties of an activity would indicate the participants in the activity, as well as possibly other "meta-information" such as its beginning time, deadline for completion, *etc.* For example, if "e" is the activity of enrolling the student "bilbo" into the course "cs100," then we might have *student*("e") = "bilbo," *course*("e") = "cs100" as the participants, and one of the component activities, say *p2*("e"), would add *student*("e") to the *class-list* of *course*("e").

Clearly, describing a model in terms of such specific "factual" information is hardly satisfactory for the purposes of software specification. In fact, the information required is of a "generic" nature, and this imposes limitations on the facts that the computer system might record. These are known as semantic constraints [HM75].

Classification provides one important means for introducing such generic information by allowing us to present both the properties applicable to all of the instances of a class and the constraints that restrict the possible values of these properties. For example, the definition of the class COURSE might include as properties *title, limit, size, class-list, instructor*, *etc.* Constraints on these would include at the very least an indication of the range classes of these functions, as well as possibly more complex limitations. For example, *size* might have 0 to 2000 as range, as well as the additional constraint that the *size* of the course must be no greater than its *limit* (constraint *course-limit* of COURSE). This kind of information is obviously closely related to the notions of type declaration in Programming Languages and to schema definition in Databases. The diagram in Figure 4.1 describes two classes of objects, STUDENT and COURSE, which will play a central role in our enrollment system.

Whereas classification of objects yields data class definitions, classification of activities yields transaction class definitions, similar to procedure declarations in Programming Languages. The participants in the activity play the role of formal parameters in procedure declarations; the constraints on the values of these properties include type information and initial, final, and invariant conditions, which act as 'well-formedness' constraints on the transaction invocation and execution. As suggested above, other properties indicate the subactions comprising the definition of the procedure. Figure 4.2 is a schematic description of the ENROL transaction class in our proposed student record system.

```
data class STUDENT with
  attributes
    name: PERSON_NAME;
    age: 12..80;
    home-address: ADDRESS;
    univ-address: ADDRESS;
    faculty: {Arts&Science, GradSchool, Medicine};
    status: {Full-time, Part-time}
    courses-taken: set of COURSE;
    taking-courses: set of COURSE;
end STUDENT;

data class COURSE with
  attributes
    title: STRING;
    dept: DEPARTMENT;
    limit: 0..2000;
    size: 0..2000;
    enrollment: set of STUDENT;
    level: {1st-year,...,4th-year,intro-grad,adv-grad};
    instructor: PROFESSOR;
  invariants
    course limit: (size ≤ limit);
end COURSE;
```

Figure 4.1 *Definition of STUDENT and COURSE Classes*

```
transaction ENROL with
  parameters
     s: STUDENT;
     c: COURSE;
  prerequisites
     Not-full?:  (c.size<c.limit);
  actions
     a1: add c to the list taking-courses of s;
     a2: add s to the enrollment-list of c;
     a3: increment size of c by 1;
end ENROL;
```

Figure 4.2. *The ENROL Transaction Definition*

Since defining the appropriate classes is an important aspect of our methodology we offer two heuristics for designers.

1. In general, properties, regarded as functions, are undefined everywhere except over the instances of the class they have been associated with, and usually every new class definition introduces several new properties; hence a new class ought to be introduced whenever

we desire a property whose domain of definition is not an already existing class.

2. Secondly, almost all semantic constraints are stated through quantification over the instances of classes (*e.g.*, all instances of STUDENT must have as *age* an instance of INTEGER in the range 12 to 80).

Additional expressive machinery occasionally may be needed but we feel that these heuristics are adequate for a large number of modelling situations.

Our methodology so far has only systematized and slightly extended normal practices in software specification. As stated above, we are particularly interested in extending this methodology to deal with situations where there are a multitude of minute details relating to many classes that share common characteristics. Specialization allows us to describe each *subclass* of a more general class by specifying only the additional details necessary for its definition, through the notion of inheritance described in Section 3. As discussed there, in specializing a class we can 1) "strengthen" any of the constraints stated for the parent class (*i.e.*, replace a constraint of the parent class, say A, with a stronger one B such that B implies A); 2) provide additional constraints; and/or 3) introduce new properties and related constraints. Figure 4.3 is a description of the subclass GRAD_STUDENT of STUDENT.

```
data class GRAD_STUDENT is a STUDENT with
  attributes
    faculty: {GradSchool};
    dept: DEPARTMENT;
    advisor:PROFESSOR;
    level: {MSc, PhD};
end GRAD_STUDENT;
```

Figure 4.3 *A Specialized Subclass of STUDENT*

Note that the *faculty* property of STUDENT was (consistently) refined in GRAD_STUDENT so that it admits only one value, GradSchool. Also, three new properties, *dept, advisor,* and *level* were introduced; these only apply to graduate students while all other properties of STUDENT are of course inherited by GRAD_STUDENT. It may be worth contrasting our notion of inheritance with that used in Simula or Smalltalk. Simula allows only complete textual inheritance in the sense that in describing subclasses one cannot alter the code described for the superclass, but must inherit it completely (strict inheritance). Smalltalk on the other hand uses default inheritance. Our description of Specialization above requires that the refined version of a constraint must not contradict the original one; this ensures that all instances of subclasses are also legal instances of all the classes higher up in the hierarchy. Finally, it appears that neither Simula nor Smalltalk allows multiple inheritance (*i.e.*, inheritance from several distinct classes), a feature that we shall find quite useful in describing transactions.

In the case of transactions, the specialization of parameters proceeds in the same way as that of properties for data classes. As far as component properties are concerned, one can either specialize the transaction class of which a property must be an instance, or provide additional properties. The example in Figure 4.4 illustrates the specialization of the transaction class ENROL whose instances have graduate students as the student *s* participant.

```
specialize ENROL (s : GRAD_STUDENT, c : COURSE)
  add
    prerequisite
      Advanced? (c.level ≥ 4th-year);
    action
      a4:  inform School of Graduate Studies
                about the enrollment;
end;
```

Figure 4.4 *Specializing the ENROL Transaction*

Here an additional prerequisite is added to ENROL for graduate students to ensure that they are not allowed to take courses that are below Fourth Year. There is also an extra action that will be carried out only during the enrollment of graduate students. We will henceforth use ENROL (*s* : C1, *c* : C2) to denote the subclass of ENROL whose instances have the student *s* in C1 and the course *c* in C2.

In order to provide a more convincing demonstration of the utility of specialization as a specification methodology, we present next a partial list of conditions on the enrollment of students in Computer Science courses. Many of these were actually required until recently at the University of Toronto, although some were not checked until the students were told that they had not taken the appropriate program and would have to take one or more additional courses! It would clearly be beneficial if these conditions were incorporated into any computerized student information system, and hence modelling these constraints becomes an important goal. For ease of reference, we have labeled each with a mnemonic name followed by a question mark, indicating that each of these will be a constraint predicate. The list in Figure 4.5 is clearly haphazardly drawn up and it is exactly our point that such restrictions should be gathered in a more systematic way by system designers, and hence our software development methodology should support such systematization. In this case, we have chosen to encode most, although not all, of these constraints as prerequisites of the

ENROL transaction. The understanding is that if any of these prerequisites is false, an *exception* will be raised and execution of the transaction will be suspended. (We leave unspecified for the moment what action should be taken to handle such exceptions.) As the first step in our description, we present in Figure 4.6 the prerequisites and actions of ENROL that apply to all students and all courses. This is in accord with our proposal that one ought to describe first the more general classes, and hence the constraints which apply to most objects.

Not-taken-before?	A student cannot take the same course more than once.
Permission?	An undergraduate student requires the permission of the instructor before taking a graduate course.
Part-time-min.?	Part-time students need not take any courses in any particular year.
At-least-4th-year?	Graduate students cannot take first, second, or third year courses.
Not-full?	A student cannot enroll in a course whose enrollment limit has been reached.
Undergrad-min.?	A full-time undergraduate must take at least 5 courses each year.
Undergrad-max.?	A full-time undergraduate may not take more than 6 courses in one year.
Not-excluded?	There exist groups of mutually exclusive undergraduate courses and an undergraduate may take at most one course from such a group.
Before-deadline?	Undergraduates must register in courses by October 13th.
Offered?	A student cannot take a course that is not offered at the time requested.
Has-preparation?	An undergraduate course may have prerequisites that an undergraduate student must have taken in previous terms.
Part-time-max.?	Part-time students may not take more than 3 courses a year.
Areas-OK?	A graduate Computer Science student must have taken courses in each of three major areas.
Another-1st-year?	At most 6 First Year courses may be counted toward the 22 required for a B.Sc. degree.

Specialist?	Arts & Science students desiring a specialist's degree must have taken the appropriate selection of courses.
Has-coreqs?	Certain undergraduate courses may require undergraduates to take other courses at the same time (*e.g.*, in mathematics).
Probation-max.?	An undergraduate student on probation may take no more than 5 courses a year.
Grad-max?	Graduate students should not take more than 6 half-courses a year.

Figure 4.5 *Restrictions on Enrolling in Computer Science Courses*

```
ENROL (s: STUDENT, c: COURSE);
  prerequisites
    Offered?;
    Not-full?;
    Not-taken-before?;
  actions
    a1: add c to the list taking-courses of s;
    a2: add s to the enrollment-list of c;
    a3: increment size of c by 1;
end ENROL;
```

Figure 4.6 *Most General Definition of ENROL*

In order to introduce further details about ENROL, we can first describe two subclasses of STUDENT, namely GRAD_STUDENT and UNDERGRAD_STUDENT. Since one of the properties of ENROL is the parameter *s*, supposedly an instance of STUDENT, we can describe two subclasses of ENROL: one for which *s* is restricted to be an instance of GRAD_STUDENT, another for which *s* is an instance of UNDERGRAD_STUDENT. In each case, we can introduce further constraints that must be checked before enrolling a student in a course (see Figure 4.7).

Similarly, we can distinguish subclass GRAD_COURSE and UNDERGRAD_COURSE of COURSE, and in the case of graduate courses we have a number of additional actions to be done in ENROL, as illustrated in Figure 4.8.

There are two important points to note here about the interpretation of ENROL ("bilbo," "cs100"), assuming "bilbo" is an instance of UNDERGRAD_STUDENT and "cs100" is an instance of GRAD_COURSE: by inheritance, this activity will have all the properties of ENROL(*s*: STUDENT, *c*: COURSE), ENROL(*s*: UNDERGRAD_STUDENT, *c*: COURSE), and ENROL(*s*: STUDENT, *c*: GRAD_COURSE), and by an obviously useful convention, all inherited prerequisites will be checked before any of the inherited actions will be executed. In this example multiple inheritance is obviously a useful tool for the designer of a system.

```
specialize ENROL(s: UNDERGRAD_STUDENT, c: COURSE);
   add
      prerequisites
         Before-deadline?;
         Not-too-many: Undergrad-max?;
end;

specialize ENROL (s: GRAD_STUDENT, c: COURSE);
   add
      prerequisites
         At-least-4th-year?;
         Areas-OK?;
         Not-too-many: Grad-max?;
      actions
         a4: inform School of Graduate Studies
                about the enrollment;
end;
```

Figure 4.7 *Some Specializations of ENROL*

```
specialize ENROL (s: STUDENT, c: GRAD_COURSE);
   add
      actions
         a6: issue to s a key to the library;
         a7: give s an unlimited $ computer account;
end;
```

Figure 4.8 *Another Specialization of ENROL*

Resuming the task of introducing the constraints in Figure 4.5, we can now consider specialization of ENROL where more than one parameter is specialized. As a result, we add additional constraints on ENROL(*s*: UNDERGRAD_STUDENT, *c*: UNDERGRAD_COURSE), ENROL(*s*: UNDERGRAD_STUDENT, *c*: GRAD_COURSE) and ENROL (*s*: GRAD_STUDENT, *c*: UNDERGRAD_COURSE), as in Figure 4.9.

Finally, by creating additional subclasses PART_TIME_STUDENT and STUDENT_ON_PROBATION of UNDERGRAD_STUDENT, we specialize the *Not-too-many?* prerequisite to *Part-time-max?* and *Probation-max?* respectively.

```
specialize ENROL(s: UNDERGRAD_STUDENT, c: GRAD_COURSE);
 add
    prerequisites
       Permission?;
end;

specialize ENROL(s: UNDERGRAD_STUDENT, c: UNDERGRAD_COURSE);
 add
    prerequisites
       Has-preparation?;
       Not-excluded?;
       Another-1st-year?;
end;

specialize ENROL(s: GRAD_STUDENT, c: UNDERGRAD_COURSE);
 add
    prerequisites
       At-least-4th-year?;
end;
```

Figure 4.9 *Further Specializations of ENROL*

A number of remarks are in order at this point. First, note that some restrictions, such as the minimum number of courses that a student must take, cannot be checked until a student has enrolled in all the courses he or she was going to take, and hence these restrictions should not be placed in the ENROL transaction. Instead, one may have a REGISTER transaction which requires as a parameter the list of courses that the student intends to take in that year, and the above conditions would then be prerequisites on this list of courses. Alternatively, after a certain date has passed, a transaction could be run automatically to check such constraints on the list of courses each student is taking. Secondly, note that since we treat data and transactions in a uniform manner, there is no reason why the conditions in Figure 4.5 could not be considered as invariant assertions for the classes of objects STUDENT and COURSE. In particular, they could be grouped around the *class-list* property of COURSE and properties *taking-courses* and *courses-taken* of STUDENT, and they could be introduced in a manner similar to the one used by describing the appropriate subclasses of STUDENT and COURSE. In this case however, violations of the constraints would be detected when the ENROL procedure attempts to insert a new element in the *taking-courses* list of a student, rather than at the time ENROL is originally invoked.

5. Scripts

As we have remarked in the previous section, not all conditions in Figure 4.5 can be accounted for as prerequisites of the ENROL transaction (for example: checking for co-requisites or for conditions involving a minimum number of courses where one needs to know what other courses the student is or will be enrolling in this year). Furthermore, a central attribute of many systems is the ability to communicate interactively with its users in order to obtain the data which "drives" the transactions. We must therefore be able to specify the communication protocols that make up the user interfaces.

For the above purposes we propose *scripts* (generalized processes that have elaborate communication and synchronization mechanisms for the system designer). The script formalism used is an adaptation of Zisman's Augmented Petri Nets [ZISM78] proposed for office automation systems and it is described in more detail in [BARR80]. Each script is essentially a Petri net that has parameters, local variables, and state transitions. In turn, each transition consists of conditions that must be true in order for the transition to fire, and actions that are to be carried out if the transition does fire. In order to enable communication, scripts can employ operators for *message passing* between a script and a terminal, or, more generally, between any two scripts. These operators are based on Hoare's primitives *give* and *take* [HOAR78], and they provide further ability for synchronization, especially when the clock is allowed to send "wake up" messages at desired times. Although much more elaborate communication mechanisms are being currently developed, we will consider here a message as simply a *form* that has text and slots that can be filled by the user (or some other script) and then sent off. (See [TSIC82] for a detailed discussion of the utility of forms as communication means in an office environment.)

To illustrate the use of scripts let us place *enrolling into courses* into a wider context. At our university, students register first with the university. This includes paying fees, selecting a program of studies that is "correct," *etc.* However, students take courses directly from the departments offering them, thus allowing the departments to have direct contact with students in order, for example, to sell them required lecture notes, lab materials, *etc.* Consider therefore the TAKE_COURSE script which describes the protocol for taking a course (see Figure 5.1).

The script is parameterized by the department *d*, which is supposedly offering the course, and it includes five states represented by circles and five state transitions represented by vertical bars. Each transition has associated conditions and actions, and these are separated by => on the diagrams. An instance of the TAKE_COURSE script is created by the secretary of the appropriate department whenever a student enrolls in a course. The initial transition on the script requests a description of the student *s* and the course *c*, which are properties of the script. Once this information has been received, the script proceeds with the process of enrolling the student for the course, and this includes expecting a grade from the instructor of the course. At the same time, the script is set up to expect and act on a "drop the course" request at any time while the student is taking the course. Following normal procedures for enrolling, once the student and the course are identified the script invokes the ENROL transaction and then awaits the message indicating the grade that the student has received in the course. We remark that this script "lives" until the final state is reached, which may be several months later, and that every student would have several such scripts, one for each course he is taking, thus requiring sophisticated use of the database for maintaining all this information.

```
parameters
  d : department;
locals
  s : student;
  c : course;
```

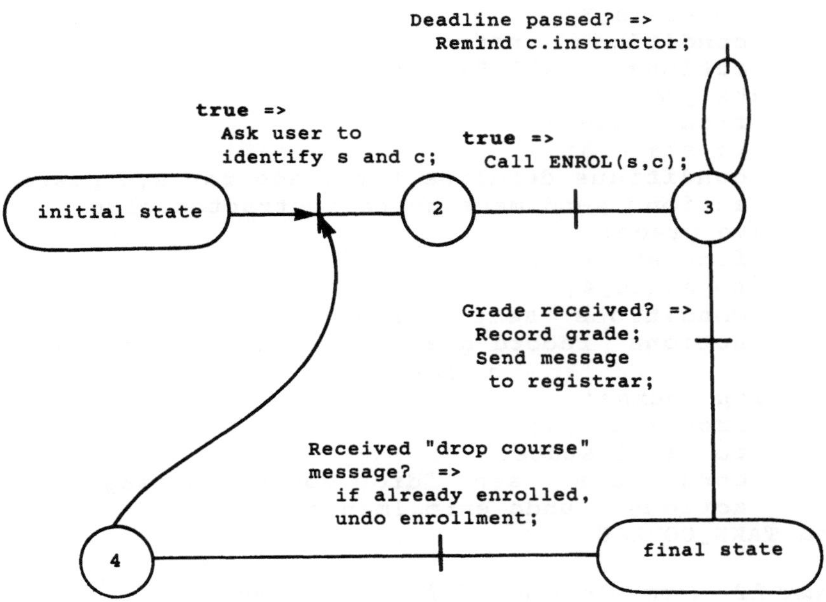

Figure 5.1 *Diagram of the TAKE_COURSE Script*

Scripts, like all other constructs, are treated as classes in our methodology. Thus their bodies (*i.e.*, their states and transitions), and also all other information associated with their definition is specified through properties that link a script to other classes. (Figure 5.2 shows the definition of the TAKE_COURSE script.)

```
script class TAKE_COURSE(d)
  parameters
    d:  DEPARTMENT;
  locals
    s:  STUDENT;
    c:  COURSE;
    grade:  {0..100};

  states
    initial:  initial_state;
    final:  final_state;
    others:  state_2, state_3, state_4;

  transitions
    obtain information:
      from initial state;
      to state_2, state_4;
      conditions   none
      actions   get s and c from user;
    enrollment:
      from state_2;
      to state_3;
      conditions   none;
      actions   call ENROL(s,c);
    late-grade:
      from state_3;
      to state_3;
      conditions deadline for grade for s,c passed?
      actions send message to instructor of c
    have-grade:
      from state_3;
      to state_4;
      conditions  sent a grade?
      actions  record grade and send message to
                    registrar;
    drop course:
      from state_4;
      to final state;
      conditions   sent "drop course" message?;
      actions   undo enrollment;
end TAKE_COURSE
```

Figure 5.2 *Textual Description of TAKE_COURSE Script*

It follows that transitions can be specialized in a manner similar to transactions, and more generally one can add new states and transitions in order to create a script that applies in more restricted circumstances than a given script. For example, the Engineering departments may require a mid-term mark to be recorded and mailed to each student;

this could be accomplished by specializing TAKE_COURSE (*d*: DEPARTMENT) to TAKE_COURSE (*d*: ENGINEERING_DEPT) by adding the script in Figure 5.3.

```
                true => call ENROL(s,c);

. . . 2                                            3

                      5
                           Received mid-term grade? =>
                             Record mid-term grade;

    Deadline for mid-term passed?  =>
      Remind c.instructor;
```

Figure 5.3 *Additions for TAKE_COURSE(d:ENGINEERING_DEPT)*

Before leaving this section we present a second example of a script that models the sequence of events from the time an undergraduate student registers for his *n*th ($1 \leqslant n \leqslant 4$) year of (university) study until the time he completes it (Figure 5.4). The basic protocol described by the script involves accepting information about the student, followed by the courses he proposes to take, then waiting for the grades he/she is assigned in these courses, and finally determining that the student has completed the year satisfactorily. Secondary protocols are also defined to take care of such contingencies as withdrawal from the program or late arrival of grades.

To summarize, scripts are useful in enforcing dynamic integrity constraints on transaction call sequences (*e.g.*, one can't receive grades until enrolled in a course), and in defining the format and the protocol of interactions with users. They are a natural place for exception-handling, including exceptions arising because of time delays, as will be seen in the next section.

For simple examples, the introduction of scripts as modelling tools may seem heavy-handed and perhaps unnecessary. There is evidence, however, that designing the environment within which a system will run, including its user interfaces, is one of the thorniest problems facing a system designer [CM79]. We consider this observation a sufficient justification of the introduction and use of scripts within our modelling framework.

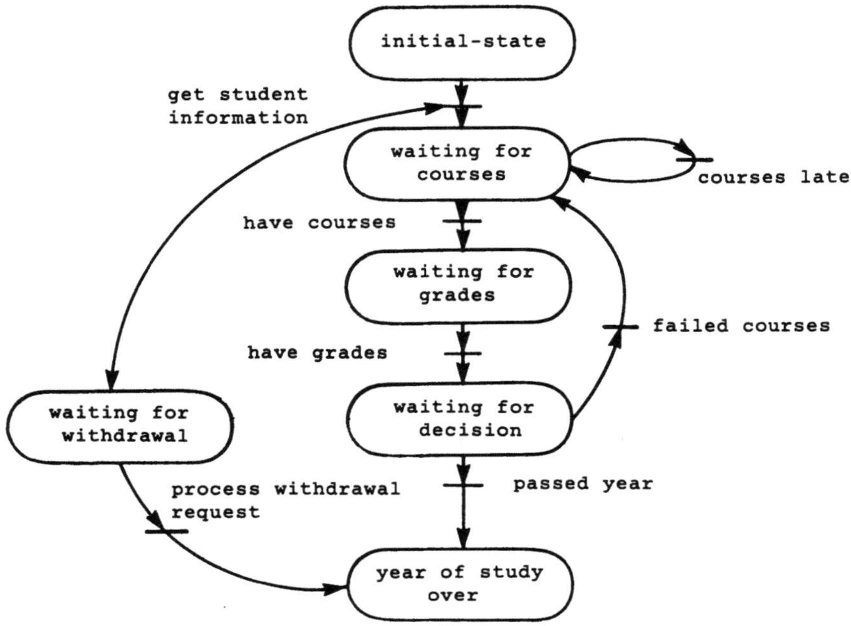

Figure 5.4 *The YEAR_OF_STUDY Script*

6. Exceptions

The ability to *manage exceptions* (*i.e.,* deal with over-abstraction) is characteristic of human behaviour and, we believe, of central importance in managing a multitude of details. Until recently this ability has been noticeably absent from computer application software. In our case, the traditional view dictates that a transaction such as ENROL should be aborted, hopefully with at least an error message, if any of its constraints (*e.g.,* prerequisites or restrictions on parameters) were not met. Alternatively, one might replace the prerequisites by successive IF-THEN conditionals, specifying in each case the course of action to be taken if the constraint were false. In addition to the limitation that this imposes on handling exceptions (see [LEVI77]), it appears to run counter to the "natural" flow of description: one has to constantly take detours from describing how students usually enroll in courses in order to say what is to be done in rare special cases. A more palatable alternative appears to be to adopt the convention that whenever a constraint (such as a prerequisite) evaluates to false, an *exception object* is raised (*i.e.,* is inserted as an instance of a special class). One can then describe in a separate pass the ways in which exceptions are to be handled. Furthermore, exceptions and exception-handlers can be described using the same methodology of concept specialization.

In order to simplify the discussion, we assume in our example that whenever a prerequisite is not satisfied, an instance of the exception labelled by the negation of the condition is raised (*e.g.,* if *Not-full?* is false then the exception *Full* is raised).

One possibility in specifying exceptions is to proceed methodically down the specialization hierarchy of ENROLs and specify which exceptions are raised when different conditions are violated. Alternatively, we may want to organize exceptions, including those raised by conditions that could not be checked in ENROL, into a specialization hierarchy organized along different lines than that of ENROL.[3] Figure 6.1 illustrates a hierarchy of exception classes constructed by answering the question "What can go wrong with enrolling in a course?" at various levels of generality.

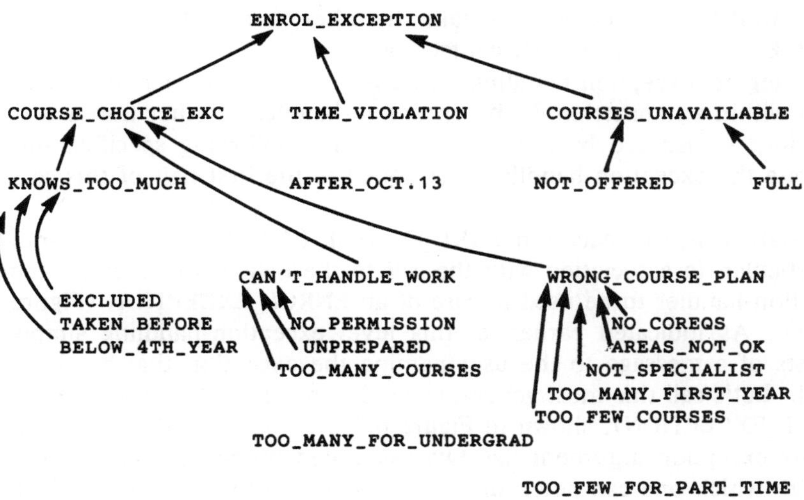

Figure 6.1 *Specialization Hierarchy for Exceptions*

The topmost exception class on the hierarchy, ENROL_EXCEPTION is intended simply to signal that an exception was raised during the execution of an ENROL transaction. Turning to its immediate subclasses, COURSES_UNAVAILABLE indicates that the course cannot be accommodated at the university, so one must abort the ENROL that caused the exception. Alternatively, the system may give the student

[3] Clearly, in doing this type design, computer aids are imperative when one checks to see whether all prerequisites have been accounted for.

information about when the course will next be given, and it might put the student on a waiting list before aborting. For TIMING_ VIOLATIONS, students can petition to a special committee in order to be allowed to register late. In an automated office environment this might result in the ENROL being suspended while a PETITION is taking place. As far as COURSE_CHOICE_EX is concerned, there is nothing we can say that is applicable in all cases; one of the advantages of our methodology over more traditional approaches such as decision tables is that we do not have to say anything if we have no new information to add. However, considering subclasses of COURSE_CHOICE_EX, we note that instances of KNOW_TOO_MUCH should always be handled by "abort," since students should not be allowed to pick up credits gratis, while instances of CAN'T_HANDLE_WORK require petitioning again. In neither case need we say anything more about the subclasses of these two types of exceptions. Finally, the WRONG_COURSE_PLAN exceptions require distinctive individual treatment. For NO_ COREQUISITE, the student must take the other course. For TOO_FEW_ COURSES, he must take other courses, *etc.*

Turning to exception-handling, we assume that for each exception raised within a transaction *T*, the exception-handler, another transaction or script, is specified by the caller of *T*. The following specifications illustrate the exception-handling mentioned in the first half of this section.

To start with, we specify in TAKE_COURSE (*d*: DEPARTMENT), and, in particular, in association with the call to the ENROL transaction, the exception-handler to be used in case of an ENROL_EXCEPTION (Figure 6.2(a)). As indicated earlier, at this level exception-handling simply consists of a message to the user naming the exception that has been raised. Let's call this most general exception-handler EX_HANDLER (*e*: ENROL_EXCEPTION), shown in Figure 6.2(b). EX_HANDLER assumes that its exception argument has two associated properties, *std* and *crs*, through which one can determine the student and the course for which the exception was raised.

Dealing with some of the more specialized exceptions involves the adding of actions to be carried out by EX_HANDLER. For example, EX_HANDLER (*e*: COURSE_UNAVAILABLE) may output, in addition to the exception message, another message that specifies when the course is given in the future, and then abort the attempted enrollment (see Figure 6.3).

Other exceptions require additional states and transitions in EX_HANDLER. Thus TIMING_VIOLATION exceptions involve petitioning a committee and may eventually result in an enrollment (see Figure 6.4).

```
script class TAKE_COURSE(d:  DEPARTMENT)
  ....
  enrollment:
   ....
   actions call ENROL(s,c)
     for exception e∈ENROL_EXCEPTION with std←s, crs←c
     use EX_HANDLER(e)
     ....
```

Modified enrollment transition in TAKE_COURSE

(a)

```
script class EX_HANDLER(e)
  parameters
    e:  ENROL_EXCEPTION;
  states
    initial:  initial_state;
    final:  final_state;
    others:  none;
  transitions
      send message;
        from initial state;
        to final state;
        conditions   none
        actions   send Class_of(e).message
  end EX_HANDLER;
```

Class_of(e) evaluates to the most specialized class **e** is an instance of, say C, and C.message evaluates to a(n error) message associated with that class as an attribute.

(b)

Figure 6.2 Raising and Handling Exceptions

```
specialize EX_HANDLER (e: COURSE_UNAVAILABLE);
 transitions
  send message:
   actions
     inform user when the course is given next;
     send "drop course" message to TAKE_COURSE
          (std,crs);
end;
```

Figure 6.3 Specialization of an Exception-Handler

```
specialize EX_HANDLER (e:  TIMING_VIOLATION);
  locals
    reply:  {YES,NO};
  states
    others:  awaiting_reply;
  transitions
    send message;
      from initial_state;
      to awaiting_reply;
      conditions none;
      actions
           send type (e).message;
           send petition (e.std, e.crs) to committee script;
    positive reply;
      from awaiting_reply;
      to final_state;
      conditions sent reply = YES?
      actions
           inform user;
           call ENROL(e.std,e.crs);
    negative reply;
      from awaiting_reply;
      to final_state;
      conditions sent reply = NO?
      actions
           inform user;
           send "drop course" message to TAKE_COURSE(std, crs);
end;
```

Figure 6.4 *Another Specialization of EX_HANDLER*

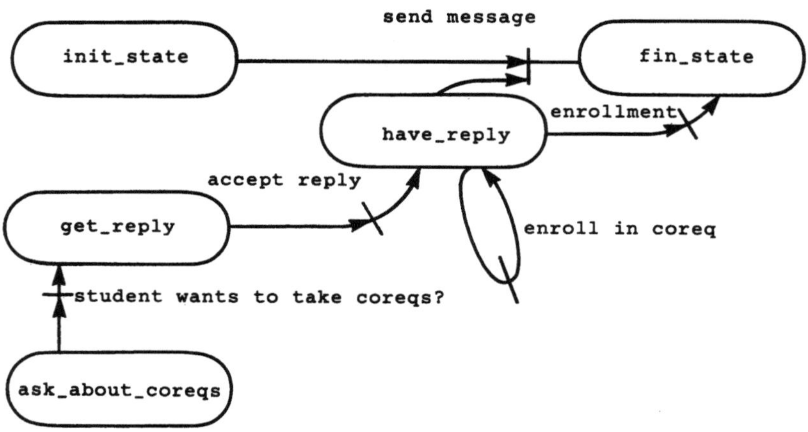

Ask_about_coreqs is also an initial state. Transition send message only fires if the reply has been negative; otherwise, enrollment fires.

Figure 6.5 *Exception Handler for Course Corequisites*

Among COURSE_CHOICE_EX exceptions, only WRONG_COURSE_PLAN requires special exception-handling facilities. For NO_COREQS exceptions, for example, EX_HANDLER must communicate with the user to determine whether the student is willing to enroll in all these courses. If he is, EX_HANDLER carries out all such enrollments and then proceeds with the enrollment originally requested. This specialization of EX_HANDLER is shown graphically in Figure 6.5.

We conclude this section by noting that the ability to describe scripts, exceptions, and exception-handlers within the same framework as provided for the normal data and transaction classes gives a pleasing uniformity and conceptual parsimony to the proposed methodology.

7. Conclusions

We have outlined and illustrated the principal elements of a software specification methodology that combines stepwise refinement by decomposition with concept specialization in order to introduce the multitude of details typically associated with large interactive systems. To recapitulate, the methodology suggests that the designer should start by defining the most general naturally occurring classes of objects and events in the domain. This is to be accomplished by the use of named properties that connect related concepts, and by the use of assertions that restrict the potential relationships. Further details of the proposed system are then introduced in successive iterations by describing subclasses of already presented classes and specializing transactions in order to deal with the objects in these classes.[4] The result is a hierarchy (taxonomy) of data, transaction, and script classes on which inheritance operates to abbreviate natural redundancy without losing the benefit of being able to check consistency. Once the usual/normal aspects of the system are described to some level of detail, the designer can describe, using the same methodology, the exceptions raised by the failure of assertions and their handling mechanism.

In evaluating the methodology, we feel that it is conducive to a natural style of description because it is oriented toward the *conceptual object* and *activities* occurring in the user's world. Our heuristics for identifying classes, and the suggestion of describing first general classes and then more specialized subclasses, provide some needed guidance to the designer. Similarly, the virtual specialization hierarchy that results

---

[4] Of course, this does not prevent one from introducing at any stage new classes, transactions, and scripts as they are needed.

when considering the possible specializations of each parameter for a transaction is a convenient conceptual rack on which to hang the details of the problem domain. In addition to its role of abridging descriptions, multiple inheritance, as illustrated in our example, allows one to think separately about independent aspects of the world (*e.g.*, undergraduate students and graduate courses) with inheritance taking care of their interaction. Finally, we feel that the systematic treatment of exceptions and exception-handlers within the same framework of data, transaction, and script classes supports another important abstraction principle: the ability to disregard the exceptional or unusual situations during the first pass in the design.

By developing program specifications according to the above methodology, one also gains some advantage in verifying the correctness of the final system. For example, having verified that a "general" transaction (*i.e.*, one high in the generalization hierarchy) maintains an invariant, one can often (because of inheritance) reuse this proof in demonstrating that the various specializations of the transaction also maintain the invariant (see [WONG81] [BORG81]).

Two other chapters in this book, those by King and McLeod and Brodie and Ridjanovic, also address the problem of designing complete database systems; hence a brief comparison of the three approaches is in order.

To begin with, there are a number of striking similarities in the general philosophy of the approaches taken, similarities due in no small part to the principles expressed in the title of this book: "conceptual modelling." Thus all three chapters start the design process with a conceptual model of the enterprise as seen by the system's eventual users. This model is meant to capture as much of the *semantics* of the real world as possible, certainly more than in traditional database design; in other words, all three chapters would be classified as work in "semantic/conceptual data models." Among others, this leads to an emphasis on modelling entities and their semantic relationships rather than on pure data organization. In a departure from most other semantic data models, all three emphasize the importance of modelling the *dynamic/behavioural*, not just the static parts of an enterprise, and the need to *integrate* these two facets of the description. Furthermore, all three chapters recognize the difficulties that arise in designing large, complex systems, and hence they emphasize the importance of a *methodology of design* that is inseparably linked to the modelling features offered. As a natural extension to this concern, the three research groups also offer a variety of computer tools that are meant to assist the designer in achieving a complete and accurate design.

Among the notable general differences are the fact that TAXIS, at least as presented here, focuses on design at one level only, while both the others consider design at several levels of detail. Thus in ACM/

PCM (see the chapter by Brodie and Ridjanovic), there is a general graphical schema, a more precise predicate-based technique for specification, and finally a functional technique for full details, wherever desired, while the "event model" of King and McLeod has an initial design schema, which drives the building of a conceptual schema, which in turn forms the basis of a physical design. On the other hand, through the notions of scripts, messages, exceptions, and exception-handlers, TAXIS probably addresses in detail a wider variety of aspects of an information system, though we should point out that the event model does model at least part of what scripts are intended to accomplish.

Although both this chapter and that of Brodie and Ridjanovic look for *uniformity* in the way objects and activities are modeled, they come up with different answers. ACM/PCM sees association of objects as paralleling iteration, and specialization of concepts corresponding to choice, while TAXIS's notion of iteration is not related to the abstraction principles, and specialization of transactions is quite similar in spirit to specialization of entities. A different attempt at uniformity shows up in the chapter of King and McLeod, in their novel attempt at incorporating the *modelling events* themselves into the model, thus bringing program maintenance into the same uniform framework.

Finally, the chapters can be distinguished by the basic metaphors which in some sense "drive" the design process. In the event model, the design schema describes mostly events and their interactions, and this drives the process of describing entities, *etc.* In contrast, the other chapters use the structure of the data descriptions to "drive" the description of the activities. In ACM/PCM, this is evident from the way that the actions associated with an application object are determined by its structure — the "context" (*e.g.*, in the Hotel-reservation actions). In TAXIS, on the other hand, the hierarchy of data classes "drives" the specialization of transactions, while the hierarchy of exceptions drives that of exception-handlers.

There are, of course, many other comparisons that could be drawn, but space limits us to those which we feel are most significant.

To conclude, we reiterate our belief that taxonomic organization is an essential human activity that allows us to cope with multitudes of detail. Our goal is to propose linguistic and computer tools that would support precisely such an organization during the development of a software system. Evidence of such tools can be seen in [BMW82] and in forthcoming MSc theses by B. Nixon and P. O'Brien. Since, in the end, the only demonstration of the importance of an idea is its successful practical use, our group has attempted to model in significant detail a number of applications in the university and hospital environments, with results presented in [WONG81] and in forthcoming theses by C. Di Marco and I. Buchan. Finally, research is still in progress on the use of these ideas for general requirements specification and for designing the language of interaction between users and a specific system.

The authors gratefully acknowledge the permission of North Holland Publishing Company to reproduce portions of an earlier version of this paper.

8. References

[ABRI74] [BD81] [BARR80] [BG80a] [BC75] [BORG81] [BORG82a] [BORG82b] [BW81] [BMW82] [CM79] [DH72] [DIJK72] [GBM82] [HM75] [HBS73] [HOAR78] [INGA78] [LEVI77] [LSAS77] [MS81] [MYLO81] [MBW80] [PARN72] [QUIL68] [SS79] [TSIC82] [TL82] [WASS77] [WILS75] [WIRT71] [WONG81] [WLS76] [ZISM78]

Discussion

The key point made in this chapter is that generalization should be used as a cornerstone in designing data-intensive applications. Generalization hierarchies help the designer organize the process of gathering detail and integrating it into a coherent information system.

Classes

One can think of a class as a collection of attributes, which in general can be complex, and a collection of integrity constraints. The latter are similar to tuple constraints (*i.e.*, predicates that take single instances of the class as arguments). A key point about TAXIS classes is that they inherit everything from their superclasses in the generalization hierarchy. Classes are similar to types as used in Programming Languages, except that types usually don't have associated integrity constraints.

Class invariants are checked every time one does an operation on an instance of a class. The purpose of prerequisites is to detect possible future violations of invariants early. For example, instead of trying to enroll a student for a course only to find that a constraint on course size is violated, you check the constraint ahead of time through a prerequisite of the transaction that does the enrollment. Some integrity constraints cannot be expressed easily in the TAXIS framework. Suppose, for example that the average grade for all university students must be 3.1/4.0. It is unclear where one can attach this information. It should be added, however, that the problem with the representation of this constraint is not particular to TAXIS. Other modelling frameworks would probably have it as well.

Inheritance

Multiple inheritance is allowed in TAXIS. For example, one can define the class STUDENT-EMPLOYEE to be directly below both STUDENT and EMPLOYEE in the generalization hierarchy. It follows that attributes may be inherited from different directions, and a cute example is given in the chapter of how this inheritance can be of use. As classes are specialized by moving down a hierarchy, new attributes are introduced and existing ones are revised, provided that the revisions don't contradict information specified higher up.

Transactions

One is allowed to use IF-THEN-ELSE, CASE, *etc.*, when specifying an action inside a transaction. Execution of a transaction proceeds by first evaluating all prerequisites of the transaction. If they return "true," actions are executed in an unspecified order. Here, there is no control flow between the actions of a transaction. Each transaction models a database operation. If the designer wants to model complex processes that involve user dialogue or communication with other processes, he should use scripts instead of transactions. Although none of the examples in the chapter show it, transactions can have postconditions that are checked after the execution of all actions. If a postcondition is found to be false, an exception is raised and an exception handling transaction takes over.

Scripts

Scripts are basically extended Petri nets. Each node of a script represents a state, and each transition represents an event that can change the state of the process being represented. As indicated earlier, scripts are intended to model long-term events in the world such as studying at a university or engaging a user in a clarification dialogue.

Unlike action schemata (chapter by Brodie and Ridjanovic) and process events (chapter by King and McLeod), scripts are treated as an integral part of a TAXIS program; action schemata and process events, on the other hand, are used as gross descriptions that serve as blueprints for the design of real programs.

More than one state of a script instance may be active at any one time. For example, after firing the first transition of the TAKE_COURSE script (shown in Figure 5.1 of this chapter), the script has two active states. The first, state 2 on the figure, is the state in which the system is ready to do an enrollment. The second, state 4 on the figure, is the state in which the system is ready to abort a particular TAKE_COURSE process when notified to do so. It might be simpler to think of each script instance as an object that is in one state at any one time (as in Smalltalk or Actors) and that can handle messages accordingly. Thus, an instance of the TAKE_COURSE script would be in a state that corresponds to states 2 *and* 4, from which it would leave either by doing an enrollment or by aborting the script instance. TAXIS does not support this second view. A script is expected to describe all possible execution histories that an object can go through. Thus TAXIS provides facilities for specifying what messages are acceptable when a certain state is active, and what new states should be activated when a certain message is received.

Petri nets are offered as a tool for modelling processes such as the following. A user shows up at the terminal and puts a message on the screen: "Hi! I am Superfriend! There are three things I can do for you. Type r to raise someone's salary; type e to enroll a student for a course; and type c to get someone a computer account." The script that drives this dialogue has a three-way branch at this point which depends on the message received from the user. Note that the same effect can be achieved with an IF-THEN-ELSE control structure. The Petri net formalism seems rather cumbersome for handling such simple situations.

Another issue about scripts arises when a script instance receives an unexpected message such as a drop-course message from a student who hasn't yet enrolled for the course. Such situations are dealt with through exceptions, and they are in general difficult to handle in an information system. Since prerequisites associated with a transition are used to enable or disable paths within the script, they cannot be used to mark unexpected situations (*i.e.*, raise exceptions). Instead, exceptions are raised within a script when an invariant associated with a state is found to be false while the state is active.

Conclusions

TAXIS is the result of an attempt to integrate tools for the design of information systems, such as data classes, transactions, scripts, and exceptions into a tight conceptual framework based on generalization. In some ways it goes farthest in achieving this goal as compared with other proposals. It is fair to add that until now no real application has used generalization as proposed in the paper, and some predict that no real application ever will.

There are a large number of proposals for languages intended to help the designer of application programs, including those by King and McLeod and Brodie and Ridjanovic presented in this volume, as well as DeJong's SBA, Rowe's FADS and Tsichritzis's OFL. Many of these proposals offer design frameworks based on forms and messages. TAXIS is quite different in the fundamental ideas it utilizes in proposing a design framework because it emphasizes the organization rather than the nature of the units that constitute a conceptual schema.

5
Some Remarks on the Semantics of Representation Languages

David J. Israel
Bolt Beranek & Newman, Inc.

Ronald J. Brachman
Fairchild Laboratory for Artificial Intelligence Research

ABSTRACT *It has been said many times that semantic nets are mere notational variants of predicate calculus. But before we lay down our nets, we ought at least to be clear about what predicate calculus is. We will attempt to make some clarifications in this regard. We also devote some attention to the notions of semantic nets. In the end, we simply plead for an open mind.*

Introductory Remarks

This chapter takes the form of an exploration over some hotly contested territory in the area of Knowledge Representation Formalisms in Artificial Intelligence. It was originally intended for those who had been in the trenches; hence, a good deal of familiarity with the issues was taken for granted. We have done some rewriting; but it soon became apparent that it would require extensive changes to render the piece suitable for an audience composed largely of people outside that sub-field within AI. *This* we have not attempted. But a few words are both in order and possible.

This research was supported in part by the Defense Advanced Research Projects Agency, monitored by ONR under Contract No. N00014-77-C-0378.

This chapter is based on: Israel, D. J., and R. J. Brachman, "Distinctions and Confusions: A Catalogue Raisonne," *Proc. 7th International Joint Conference on Artificial Intelligence*, Vancouver, B.C., Canada, August 1981.

First, with respect to issues in programming language design: we feel that one of our main points is fully in line with at least one major trend in the theory and design of programming languages, the line both discussed and represented in Mary Shaw's chapter on Modelling and Abstraction in Programming Languages. A representational formalism should include constructs that allow a user to capture intuitions about the structure of the domain(s) of application—for example, intuitions about the appropriate conceptualization of the objects, properties, and relations of the domain. Surely this requirement, among others, has motivated much of the research on incorporating abstract data typing facilities into programming languages.[1] Indeed, in the most general sense, it was this motivation that led to the development of high level programming languages.

So, too, one informal (not necessarily "uninformed") complaint about formalizations of domains of knowledge using standard first-order languages is that they are too flat. One can, of course, specify a domain which includes, for example, both individuals of some type, say natural numbers, and functions over such individuals. But, to put it informally, neither the syntax nor the "general" semantics of first order languages will take cognizance of the distinction between the two types of thing. Things of both types will simply be values of individual variables, and arguments—indiscriminately—of predicates (and function-symbols). Of course, to some extent the analogue of the particular "semantic flatness" in programming languages, which is meant to be handled by the introduction of data types and typing facilities, *can* be treated within first-order languages by introducing sortal quantification and, correlatively, sorted individual terms, *etc.* This may still leave one with the feeling of treating very dissimilar kinds of things in too uniform a way. For a particular example of this, with a tendentious analogy with respect to the semantics of programming languages, see our discussion of modal constructions in Section 4.5.[2]

---

[1] We do not mean to claim, in the case of representational formalisms, that this requirement rules out certain formalisms, but simply that the ease and naturalness with which the requirement, in a given case, can be met is a criterion of choice among competing systems.

[2] The analogy concerns the use of modal constructs in dynamic logic. The tendentiousness resides, among other places, in the implied claim that the formalism of first-order dynamic logic is better suited for its job than the associated purely extensional (nonmodal) multi-sorted first-order theory. The crucial point, though, is that quite apart from proofs of equivalence or nonequivalence of various logics for programming languages, a first test of a formal scheme is surely the extent to which it is faithful to and captures considered, "expert," intuitions about appropriate conceptualizations. (Not that the experts are likely to agree about their intuitions.)

There is one more point that we should make about the connection to programming languages; or, at least, one more place in the chapter to point to. At the very end, we suggest that a closer interaction between those working on the semantics of programming languages and those concerned with the semantics of representational formalisms might be mutually beneficial. That suggestion is by way of making up for the otherwise negative tone of the chapter.

As for database theory, one of the most striking features of the current explorations in databases, at least as it is represented by the chapters in this volume, is the attempt to deploy concepts and techniques from the field of Knowledge Representation, and especially from work on semantic networks, in combination with relational databases. (See especially the chapters by Borgida, Mylopoulos, and Wong; by Brodie and Ridjanovic; and by King and McLeod.) There is, however, something of a paradox in the focus on network-type formalisms. The backbone of most such formalisms is a taxonomic (or ISA) hierarchy, sometimes generalized to deal with multiple inheritance. A governing design requirement is to capture semantic interdependencies (both inclusions and exclusions) among the various kinds of things ("concepts") dealt with. But the explicit embodiment of such interdependencies seems to be ruled out by the relational model, which requires that domain names be treated in the way that monadic predicate-letters (and/or function symbols) are handled in standard treatments of first-order logic. Just as it is assumed, in the latter case, that there are no semantic dependencies among atomic wffs, so too, it is assumed in the former case that there are no such dependencies between tuples, or between a value's appearing in one tuple and its appearing, within the same or another domain, in another. All constraints between domains must be kept firmly in the eye of the beholder.

Given the above (or at least our limited understanding of it), it is hard to see how such notions as type hierarchies, inheritance, and exclusion can be imported within the boundaries of the relational model. Note that Reiter's proposed handling of hierarchies and inheritance is part of a reconstruction, from within the theory of first-order logic, of database theory. (See his chapter *Towards a Logical Reconstruction of Relational Database Theory*). It is not meant to be part of a proposed extension of the relational model. Indeed, what Reiter claims is that "the kinds of real world knowledge which extended data models (especially those involving hierarchies and inheritance) attempt to capture have natural representations as first order formulae." (Naturally, we might quibble about the "naturalness.") In our view, though, it is not clear whether the "extensions to the relational model" Reiter mentions are really extensions at all. Rather, they may be attempts to incorporate a standard relational database (unsullied) within a larger, more semantically rich and differentiated system (*e.g.*, a system based on a semantic network-type representational formalism, or one whose language is that of first-order quantification theory). Or perhaps they are really proposals to jettison the relational model altogether and to incorporate powerful database facilities and operations into one or another Knowledge Representation system. About this, and about much else besides, we await enlightenment.

A final word on databases. We should note that we accept almost every letter of Reiter's chapter, but not necessarily its spirit. To give only the most weird reason for our demurral, it seems to us more natural to think about relational databases (especially as conceived of originally) as *models* of the kinds of first order theories Reiter describes. Indeed, if one sticks to the original conception — in which no attempt was made to accommodate incomplete information — it's almost natural to think of relational databases as "analog" devices, and not as symbolic representations at all. Analog because they can only convey indeterminate (incomplete) information derivatively, by conveying completely determinate information within which the indeterminate is implicitly nested. (For instance, a thermometer can convey that the temperature is somewhere between 80 and 90 degrees, but only because this information is "automatically carried along with" the calibration-dependent fully determinate information that the thermometer conveys, *e.g.*, that the temperature is 87.) More particularly, we find it illuminating to think about even extended relational databases in terms of locally finite dimensional cylindrical algebras, algebras whose elements are sets of finite sequences of objects, rather than in terms of first-order theories. Again, this seems to indicate that we are more drawn to the relational algebra than to the relational calculus; that is, we are more drawn to an algebraic and semantic than to a syntactic, proof-theoretic, account of the relational model. There are, of course, intimate connections between algebra and calculus; so too, there are intimate connections between (locally finite) cylindrical algebras and standard quantification theory, in both its syntax and semantics. In fact, Tarski's original definition of truth for quantificational languages was given in terms of cylindrical algebras, although not then so named.

1. Introduction

With "knowledge representation" being a hot topic in Artificial Intelligence, many a discussion at an AI conference has turned to the relationship between logic and AI representation languages. Sitting across the table from one another we might find a hard-core semantic nets aficionado and a born-again logician debating the relative merits of nodes and links, predicates and variables. The discussion is likely to get heated. Somehow, despite an inability to prove that his network scheme has greater expressive power than first-order logic,[3] the networker "knows" that there is something more to his nets than is dreamed of in the logician's philosophy.

Whom shall we believe in this tangled dialectic? We will contend here that it's not even really clear what the competing positions are. We will first take a brief look at the ancestry of semantic nets, only to discover a tangled family tree. Sad to say, the greatest clarity concerning the meaning of semantic nets has been bestowed by those who view them as mere notational variants of traditional logical notations; thus, we examine some of the positions adopted by these "net-logicians." Unfortunately, we find even these to be a bit hazy as well. Lest our doubts about the logicians' position be taken for a defense of semantic nets, we turn back to the network hackers for some critical comments. In particular, we cast a sidelong glance at prototypes, illustrating how their primacy in networks has caused perhaps unnecessary confusion. In the end, we throw our own hat into the ring, advocating, like the logicians, a strong formal-semantical approach. Yet we refuse to be forced into the strait jacket of classical logic. We conclude by offering some extremely brief suggestions of alternative ways of looking at representation. These are at best programmatic, and may not do much to counteract the overall negative tone of the chapter. Still, we do feel that the field needs a critical overview.

2. A Brief Tendentious History of Semantic Nets

Semantic networks are the point of contention in our debate, and in an attempt to shed some light on these creatures of darkness, we should consider a little history. Even a brief study of their ancestry will indicate traits inherited from a succession of apparently very mixed marriages.[4]

First, of course, there was Quillian's work on Semantic Memory [QUIL68]. Quillian used a network structure to model human verbal memory. His intent was to get "humanlike use" by processing the

[3] Indeed, despite an inability to specify clearly the expressive power of his formalism at all....

[4] This is of necessity a rough-and-tumble trip. See [BRAC79] for a more comprehensive survey with references. Also, see [BZ81] (pp. 14-18) especially the comments by Goldstein, for more about the confusing hand that history has dealt to semantic nets.

network of associations with a spreading activation search. Many of the main features of current network representations were present in that first venture, including descriptions in the class-plus-modifier tradition.

Collins and Quillian followed up the original work with a series of psychological plausibility tests for network models, using reaction times to test how many "levels" intervened between stored facts. After a couple of years of work with this strictly psychological motivation, semantic nets were off and running.

The next big move on network notations came from a natural language processing point of view. (Quillian had this in mind from the very start, it should be noted.) In particular, nodes came to be looked at as surrogates for verbs and nouns, with links standing for semantic "case" relations. For the most part, the nets were still intended to be psychologically plausible models, although some formal semantic considerations were starting to creep in.

More or less simultaneously with the "linguisticizing" [*sic*] of networks, though largely independently of it, nodes began to be used to denote (physical) objects in the (blocks) world, and links began to be used to represent relations among those objects. This in fact represented a significant departure in the interpretation of the network notation. Nodes were now supposed to stand for structured objects in virtue of their own semantically significant structure.[5] The connection with verbal memory was being severed. While the nets were still strictly *notations*, and not *languages*, in this "representational" use, they began to be thought of as akin to more familiar formalisms, notably formal quantificational languages.

Two papers from the middle 1970s constitute critical chapters in this history. Minsky's "Frames" paper [MINS75] focused tremendous attention on default-oriented reasoning with large-scale chunks of information. In many network notations, nodes came to resemble "frames." The prominent feature of these notations was that the nodes stood principally for "prototypes" (*e.g.*, THE TYPICAL-ELEPHANT). Once again, psychological concerns were reasserted as the primary motivation for much of the work on principles of network organization and on reasoning.

The other influential paper was Woods's "What's in a Link" paper [WOOD75], a first attempt to examine the "semantics" of semantic nets. Woods showed that often net-workers had been vague, and their network "languages," semantics-less. But perhaps the paper's most significant contribution to the field was the subtle shift in perspective it induced. In essence, it granted semantic networks full-fledged

---

[5] Not that there was any explicit account of how they did this (*i.e.*, of the principles of semantic composition involved).

"representation language" status. The consequence of Woods's stipulation that semantic nets were languages was that a great number of people took seriously the challenge of providing their network formalisms with an appropriate well specified semantics. In particular, one line of development that followed almost immediately was a series of network notations modelled directly on the language of first-order logic (*e.g.*, [SCHU76a]). Other efforts took Woods seriously in other ways, providing us with an interesting diversity of interpretations of the "semantics of semantic nets" (for example, see KL-ONE, KRL, NETL, and PSNs).[6]

3. Drawing the Battle Lines

The variegated background of semantic nets has left most people seeing them as "representation languages," despite the fact that they were initially intended primarily as (parts of) psychologically testable memory models and not as languages at all. For some, the expressive power of the nets is to be psychologically unconstrained and perchance universal. Some see nets as peculiarly tied to verbal comprehension; others, though unmindful of this latter connection, remain faithful to the original psychological motivation, typically by taking prototypes as their central focus. And almost everyone now takes Woods's dictum — "specify your semantics" — as gospel. Indeed, some zealous net-workers feel that the only way to answer that challenge is to base networks directly on well understood formal languages. Some (usually non-net-workers) go even further, and claim that semantic nets are (and can be) nothing other than notational variants of standard first-order languages.[7]

Just for argument's sake, let's divide the field as it currently stands into four factions:

1. *Logicians.* Former net-workers who have now accepted Logic, as well as those who never were net-workers and have always known The One True Logic [*sic*].

---

[6] Hence the occasional bemusement on the part of those who are familiar with the tangled web net-workers have woven, at the presupposition, subscribed to by many "innocents," that there is a significant shared body of theory of semantic networks on which to build. Would that it were so.

[7] For more about this see [ISRA82].

2. *Net-logicians.* Those who claim their networks are simply notational variants of standard first-order languages, perhaps with special indexing considerations.

3. *Extended-net-logicians.* Those whose nets are variant notations for more or less standard formal languages, with extensions.

4. *Net-workers.* Those whose nets are not claimed to be variants of standard quantificational formalisms, or are explicitly claimed not to be. This group breaks down into two sub-factions:

   - *Psycho-net-workers.* Those whose networks are mainly psychologically motivated.
   - *Non-psycho-net-workers.* Those whose nets are oriented towards psychologically unconstrained universal expressive power.

As we hinted above, perhaps the clearest response to Woods's concern about the semantics of semantic nets has come from the first three of these groups. In the following section we analyze in some depth the concerns and assumptions of these "logical" types.

4. On Semantic Nets and First-Order Logic

Imagine believing that "semantic net notation, *i.e.*, the graphical symbolism used by semantic net theorists, is a variant of traditional logical notation" [SGC79] (p. 122). Why then go to the trouble of being a semantic net theorist?[8] Far and away the most commonly cited reason has to do with access and retrieval features. Witness Shapiro, as cited in [SGC79] (p. 122): "All the information about a given conceptual entity should be reachable from a common place." In a network, knowledge about a given entity (or a given kind) is "directly attached" to the node for that entity (kind). Indeed, Schubert, *et al.*, enunciate a fundamental assumption that motivates the deployment of semantic nets: "... the knowledge required to perform an intellectual task generally lies in the semantic vicinity of the concepts involved in the task." [SGC79] (p. 123).

This bundling feature is quite distinct, say such net-logicians, from the networks considered purely as representational formalisms; that is, the access and retrieval features do not distinguish network formalisms

---

[8] We assume that by "traditional logical notation" the authors mean languages of the standard quantificational variety. This assumption seems well warranted.

from their "traditional" counterparts with respect to expressive power.[9] Indeed, we are reminded to keep quite distinct the following aspects of a representational system:

1. The purely representational or expressive features of the formalism involved.
2. The deductive apparatus (*calculus*) defined over the formalism (or more broadly, any set of syntactically-specified rules of transformation).
3. An algorithm implementing (2), which might involve (4).
4. Access and retrieval procedures defined over the formalism.

(We will soon add another distinction: that between a language and a logic.) In sum, our logical friends aver that networks and "predicate calculus formalisms"[10] are equivalent on (1), but not necessarily on any of (2) through (4).

4.1 On Standard Quantificational Formalisms

Now that we've been told, at least with respect to representational issues, to boil everything down to (standard) quantificational formalisms, all would be peachy if only it were agreed on all sides what the residue was. In particular, what *does* one embrace when one accepts a "standard" quantificational *formalism*? Well, it's not absolutely clear (see Section 4.3). But it is pretty clear what you get when you buy a standard quantificational *language*: essentially, some syntactic equipment. First, some sentential connectives, but just the connectives, not their usual (standard or classical) interpretations. They need not (all) even be truth-functional. (On this last point, ask your favorite intuitionist for further exciting details.) You also get:

1. A countable number of enumerable sets of variables of different types. For example:

---

[9] Note that it is one thing to treat a formalism as a mere notational variant of a standard language; it is quite another to treat it as a different language equivalent in expressive power to such a language.

[10] A minor point of terminology. The use of the phrase "predicate calculus" (or "predicate calculus formalisms") can be confusing. It would be best, we think, to reserve the word "calculus" for talk about the inferential relationships defined over a language, and not for the language itself.

- individual variables only in the case of first-order quantificational languages.
- function variables, sentence variables, and predicate variables in higher-order languages.

2. One or two variable-binding operators that take formulae into formulae. (Again, just these, not their standard interpretation. On this point, if you didn't believe the intuitionist, ask a substitutionalist.)
3. Optionally, (infinite) stocks of nonlogical constants of various sorts.
4. Typically, two delimiters, one for each end.
5. The standard recursive definition of a well formed formula.

In other words, when you buy a formal language, a language is all you get. Of course it must also be said that there *is* a standard and classical recipe for concocting a semantics for any language of the standard quantificational variety. The recipe is provided by Tarski in "The Concept of Truth in Formalized Languages" [TARK56]. But, as we will note in Section 4.3, to say that there is *a* theory of interpretation for such languages that can be considered standard is not to say that there is only *one* such scheme available.

4.2 The Logic of Natural Language

Let us assume that much of the work in AI that exploits either logical formalisms or graph-theoretic transcriptions of these is directed toward the representation of the meaning of sentences of a natural language. This assumption introduces an interesting complication. Little current work in the formal semantics of natural languages is being done within the framework of standard quantificational languages. All (both?) programs for formulating formal semantic accounts for significant fragments of natural languages (fragments containing interesting semantic constructions) exploit formal languages that are quite different from that of first-order logic. (We have in mind Montague-style semantics and Barwise and Perry's Situation Semantics.) Moreover, no significant fragment of any natural language has ever been semantically analyzed by way of a (systematic) translation into a standard first-order language. Indeed, to our knowledge, no one has ever seriously attempted it.

There do seem to be good methodological reasons for the above facts. Any account of the semantics of natural languages that exploits a formal language has a choice of where to take on the risks of innovation and inventiveness. (Such choices go with the territory of deep and general unsolved problems.) It can be inventive in the specification of the formal language and its semantics, and this is the route taken by

Montague and Barwise/Perry. Montague's language (the language IL [MONT74]) is a "throw in everything but the kitchen sink" omega-order intensional logic that freely uses lambda-abstraction and intensional operators of all degrees. Its semantics is, in a sense, standard. It consists of extending Tarski-style treatments of quantificational languages of arbitrary order to modal and intensional languages, an extension pioneered by, *inter alia*, Montague. Barwise and Perry's formal language ALIASS is much closer in syntax to the surface syntax of English. Though they have not yet gone fully public with their semantic account, in some thoroughly uninteresting sense, it too will be more of the same (that is, more set theory). But this may be quite misleading. The guiding intuitions argue that special constraints are to be put on the kinds of sets, and operations thereon, to be allowed. (Classical or standard Tarski-style semantics places no such constraints.)[11]

To return to our theme, the route taken by Montague and Barwise and Perry has the advantage that the inventiveness is confined to an area susceptible to precise mathematico-logical treatment. It also allows (or seems to allow) for simple (recursive) translation procedures between English and the target formal language. The other (standard first-order) route focuses its "creativity" on the procedures for paraphrase (translation) from the natural to the formal language. However, it leaves such procedures in precisely the state that they assume in introductory logic texts: imprecise, nonformalizable rules-of-thumb—heuristics based on appeals to intuition. The contrast is illuminating and, on grounds of good scientific methodology, highly unfavorable to the "conservative" route.

4.3 On Equivalence of Expressive Power

We now want to take a brief look at an extension of the standard form of first-order languages to allow for the formation, via a form of lambda-abstraction, of complex predicates. Remember that the standard equipment includes no operation for forming complex predicates from atomic ones. To see this, one must bear in mind the distinction between (a) compound open formulae, formed from atomic open formulae by, say, *conjunction* (as in "Fx & Gx"), and (b) complex predicates, formed by *abstraction*, which can be predicated of individual terms (as in "lambda x. (Fx & Gx)"). It is only (a) above that we get for nothing in a standard first-order language.

---

[11] The relevant literature is still mostly underground manuscripts circulating in odd places. Still, soon there will be two books, and there already is a small handful of published articles. See [BP81a] [BP81b] [BP80].

So let us imagine that we do have complex-predicate forming operators. What does this extension do? Given the *standard* semantics for first-order languages and the semantics for the new language gotten by minimum mutilation therefrom, one can show that the two languages are equivalent in expressive power *in one sense.* But *perhaps* not in other, at least equally important, senses. The two languages, call them FOL and FOL+, are equivalent in the following way: for every closed sentence of one, there is a sentence of the other (its translation), which has the same truth-value relative to any given model (and assignment function). But do the two languages have the same power of expressing distinct thoughts in distinct ways? Do they have the same power to discern shades of meaning by distinguishing among the logical forms of sentences that might be used to express those meanings? It can be argued that only as long as one stays strictly within the confines of standard first-order logic are the two systems equally powerful in this respect. In particular, if one simply adds definite descriptions as complex singular terms to the two languages, FOL+ can be shown to be capable of making finer distinctions of logical form than FOL. The same situation prevails if one adds modal operators, and even more so if one adds both.[12]

In fact, even without these additions, one can see some possibilities for distinctions within FOL+ that get lost in FOL. For example, consider (1) "Fa & Ga" vs. (2) "(lambda x.(Fx & Gx))(a)." Both these sentences of FOL+ get translated into the same sentence of FOL—the one that looks just like (1). There might be some good reasons, however, for wanting to distinguish between (1) and (2). In our discussion of prototype-nets, we shall indicate at least one such reason.

There is one general point about expressive power that we would like to make here, a point similar to one often made about equivalence results in the theory of computability. The point is that such results don't (can't), by themselves, constitute arguments for choosing any one computational system or representational formalism over another. Nor do they by themselves constitute arguments for the overriding importance of that dimension on which the various systems are, in fact, proved equivalent. Thus, when faced with a choice between systems equivalent in a certain respect, one must look to other (perhaps task-specific) factors that distinguish them.

---

[12] For a quick peek at the first and simplest case, fix your attention on those old favorites: "The king of France is not bald" vs. "It is not the case that the King of France is bald." Remember that in the standard formalism there is no way of distinguishing the negation of an atomic predicational wff from the predication of the negation of an atomic predicate. Indeed, there is no such animal as the latter. That is, there is no straightforward, simple way to capture the distinction between "((lambda x. [Not[Bald(x)]])(ix.King-of-France(x)))" and "[Not[Bald(ix.King-of-France(x))]]."

Compare, for instance, the situation for representational formalisms with the situation for programming languages. Almost all programming languages are equivalent in expressive (functional) power; almost all of them can be said to determine virtual machines equivalent in power to a universal Turing machine. But surely no one thinks that all programming languages are equally "good"—not even along some one dimension. And, surely no one but religious devotees would claim for any given language that it was better than all others for all plausible intents and purposes. As Mary Shaw notes in her chapter:

> Language designs influence the ways we think about algorithms by making some program structures easier to describe than others... Thus, even though most programming languages have the same expressive power, differences among languages can significantly affect their practical utility.

Remember as well that there can be different conceptions of equality in expressive power.[13] The standard conception is of the truth of paired sentences under paired interpretations. As we have seen, this conception abstracts from differences that might arise within the sentences, differences among subsentential structures and their modes of combination. Just so, different algorithms for one and the same function can differ dramatically along a host of important dimensions (both within one programming language, and even more so across different languages).

4.4 On Nonequivalence of Expressive Power

It is often argued in favor of the language of first-order logic that it is universal in a certain sense. Roughly speaking the claim is that anything sayable in any language is sayable in a standard first-order language. (A more radical view is that anything thinkable is expressible in a first-order language.) This, of course, is a thesis like Church's Thesis—not up for proof but always subject to refutation. It is also, of course, a lot more informal than Church's Thesis (compare "sayable" with "effective").

Now imagine you are considering two languages for use; and one can be proven stronger in expressive power, as standardly conceived, than the other. Does this fact obviate the need for thought? Can it ever be rational to choose the weaker of the two? Surely the answer is *yes.*[14] To

---

[13] See our example of FOL vs. FOL+.

[14] Note: If you said to yourself, "Well, it all depends...," then you agree that surely the answer is yes.

take first a slightly odd case: imagine that the choice is between the typed and the untyped lambda calculus. The first has the nice properties that every expression can be reduced to normal form and every sequence of reductions halts with a normal form as output. The second has neither of these. Still, the second is more powerful than the first. There are functions definable in it that are not definable in the typed lambda calculus. If one is prepared to live without those functions definable in the untyped lambda calculus, as certainly one may reasonably be, then there are a host of reasons for opting for the weaker system.[15]

Our second case is more to the point, perhaps. It has been argued that an extensional first-order encoding of quantified modal logic is superior to quantified modal logic on account of the greater expressive power of the former. Suppose we grant that the claim of greater expressive power is true.[16] Is the difference in expressive power worthwhile? That is, are the kinds of things one can say in the extensional first-order version and not in the quantified modal logic worth saying? To this question there can be no all-or-nothing, application-independent answer. It is difficult to give a general characterization of the things sayable in the one but not the other. But put very roughly: If one wants to talk explicitly about possible individuals, possible worlds, and the interrelationships between "things" of those two kinds, then one's best bet is a first-order theory about just such things. If, on the other hand, you find talk of nonactual possibilia bizarre or unnecessary, especially in one's object language; or if you think it forces you to think about making distinctions (*e.g.*, between different possible worlds or about identity and/or distinctness of possible individuals across possible worlds) that you don't feel you have to worry about making, then, by all means, go unrepentantly modal. For more about this, see [LEWI68].

---

[15] Happily, this is not the place for further discussion of the relevance of this case to real programming languages. For a discussion of types in programming languages, see the chapters by Shaw and Krieg-Brueckner. We should note, though, that there is much room for confusion in all this talk about types. Within the programming languages community, there has been debate about what types are. Are they sets, or sets together with (relations and) operations thereon? If the latter, how are they best represented or conceptualized (as continuous lattices, category-theoretically, in terms of sets of equations, *etc.*)? Just to confuse matters further, what is the relation between programming language notions of abstract data types and the notions of class or type as these arise in semantic networks? Fortunately, we must, in the interests of space, sanity, inability, *etc.*, refrain from attempting to sort out the various notions of type that are buzzing around.

[16] As it is for standard quantified modal logics; but where there is a standard, there are deviations. Sure enough, there are modal logics which are "expressively complete." For such, see [BRES72] [HAZE76].

4.5 What's in a Logic?

It's time to make another distinction, the distinction between a *language* and a *logic*, in particular, say, between first-order languages and "first-order logics." The notion of a first-order language (or, if you like, of a standard first-order language) is *a purely syntactic notion*. A language is a standard first-order language just in case it meets certain syntactic specs. The notion of a first-order logic is that of an account of the property of validity defined over sentences of a first-order language.

A given language can have many logics defined over it. Often, when folks talk of first-order logic, it can be assumed they have in mind the standard, classical accounts due mainly to Tarski (*et al.*). Sadly, often it can also be presumed that they are either unaware of other accounts or that they are insensitive to the distinction between languages and logics. For as noted, there can be (yea, verily, there are) different brands of first-order logics. Other accounts include the intuitionist account, the so-called truth-value or substitutional account, probabilistic accounts, the various and sundry Relevance accounts, Hintikka's game-theoretic semantics, the sundry many-valued accounts, and Zadeh's fuzzy logic account (not to be confused with the probabilistic account). And there are others.

It is, of course, possible to identify a logic for a language with the set of logical truths (according to that logic) of the language. If, moreover, there is a provably complete axiomatization of the valid wffs of the language (for that logic) then one can "represent" the logic with the system of axioms plus derivation rules or rules of inference. Still, distinct things must be distinguished, right?

While we're at it, there is yet another general distinction to be made—or, if you prefer, another nit to be picked, the one between a *language with a given logic* (theory of interpretation) and *theories* expressed or expressible in that language (with that logic). No one would confuse a first-order formulation of, for example, classical mechanics, with "first-order logic"; but people are prone to incorporate other, more abstract and general theories in *their* various first-order guises, into (standard) first-order logic itself. It's been done to set-theory, though in this case, at least, a great and longstanding controversy about the relationship between set theory and quantification theory provides a plausible excuse. It may have been done to modal logic, for instance in the following passage from Newell's "Physical Symbol Systems":

> Modal notions, such as *possibility* and *necessity*, long handled axiomatically in a way that made their relationship to standard logic (hence universal symbol systems) obscure, now appear to have an appropriate formulation within what is called *possible*

world semantics, which again brings them back within standard logic. [NEWE80] (p. 177)

Here, Newell *seems* to be confusing: (a) the result of extending the classical semantics of Tarski (*et al.*) as found in Kripke and Montague (*et al.*) to handle the new extended languages (*e.g.*, FOL with modal operators treated as logical operators on a par with the quantifiers and connectives) with (b), a first-order theory (in a standardly interpreted first-order language) of possible worlds and possible individuals (see [LEWI68]). And perhaps, but only perhaps, he is assuming the incorporation of theory (b) into first-order logic itself.

4.6 A Word In Defense of FOL

No doubt some criticisms of "logic" or of "the predicate calculus" have been, at least in part, criticisms of some particular way of formally representing some domain in an interpreted or applied first-order language. These are best understood as objections to the effect that the objects, properties, and relations of the domain have been wrongly conceived (or wrongly represented). Instead, they seem to have been understood as objections to the language of logic itself, as if adopting, for example, the language of first-order logic involved adopting some one particular way of "cutting the world (or any part of it) at its joints," a way that was arguably inappropriate to many domains and for many purposes. But of course, as a representational formalism, a logical language is (just) a tool. Given a certain task, this tool can be used more or less well. For instance, Pat Hayes has argued persuasively that if the task at hand is to represent in a first-order language what an intelligent person must know about liquids, then one should opt to include 4-dimensional space-time volumes in one's ontology histories (see [HAYE78]). This move represents a very different way of carving up the world than one that recognizes only 3-dimensional objects and instants (or intervals) of time. Both options, and others yet more weird, are realizable within a first-order language. To repeat: a commitment to standard quantificational formalisms does not carry along with it a commitment to a particular metaphysics or ontology, let alone to a particularly wrong-headed one.

Of course, given what we say elsewhere in this chapter the reader must realize that we feel that the language of first-order logic might not always be the best scheme to use, that its universal applicability does not guarantee universal optimality. Indeed the features in virtue of which it can lay a claim to universal expressive power might be precisely those that make it less than optimal for some applications. If one keeps in mind that the language of first order logic is a tool, surely just this is to be expected. The most generally applicable tool is unlikely to be the best for every application.

4.7 A Word about Natural Language

We might as well address, though briefly, a controversial issue we have so far deliberately been skirting, the relationship between work on artificial (formal) representational languages and work in the area of natural language. At various points in this chapter we may seem to assume that the task at hand (for all hands) is that of formally encoding the logical form of sentences of natural language, and then of providing a semantics for such sentences by way of providing a semantics for their formal surrogates. This is a deceptive appearance. We are interested in "non-natural" representational formalisms in their own right. We have no particular applications in mind; hence, we have no particular natural language applications in mind either. We do assume here that, to be of significant use, a representational formalism must have the expressive power of a significant fragment of a natural language (any one will do—say, English). There are lots of interesting thoughts (propositions, if you like) that, unless appearances are wildly deceiving, can be expressed in natural language. They can, one must hope, also be expressed in one's favorite representational formalism, even if, compositionally speaking, quite differently. (And one needn't really care about those differences.) However we are by no means assuming that the one and only (or even the most crucial) use of representation formalisms is to encode the meanings of natural language sentences.

5. On Proto-Formalisms

5.1 Logical Implications of Prototypes

We now turn our attention, as promised, to net work in a less logical vein. In particular, we examine the current work that is most faithful to the psychological origins of network schemes. Arguably the most important legacy handed down from psychologists to network-theorists has been the notion of *prototypes* and of stereotypical and plausible reasoning. (See the work of Rosch and associates [ROSC75].) It matters not whether the AI researchers in question knew of the relevant psychological literature directly; merely that their work was, at least in part, informed by a common-sense prototype-type theory. Fahlman puts the relevant point as follows:

I should also point out that a *TYPE node of the normal sort describes the typical member of a set, but does not define that set. It is not the case that any individual fitting the *TYPE-node's description must be placed in the set. The recognition system is allowed to examine *TYPE-node descriptions and to suggest which type-set a new individual fits into best, but this works by a sort of weighted average over the available features, not by satisfying a formal definition. The *TYPE-node sets are very similar in spirit to the exemplar-based sets that, according to Rosch, dominate much of human recognition and thinking. [FAHL79] (p. 92)

Now Fahlman is surely not presenting NETL as a mere two-dimensional notational variant of FOL or of any standard quantificational formalism. NETL is a representational scheme in its own right.[17] Even some logicians (see [HAYE79] [REIT78c]) seem to believe that if there is one "representational" feature of most semantic network schemes not easily or directly accommodatable within the standard formalisms, it involves prototypes and defaults.[18]

It is not clear, however, that this distinguishing feature of proto-nets is an aspect of their representational, expressive power at all. (Recall the distinctions of Section 4). It is at least arguable that, if one wants to realize the "logic of default reasoning" one need not tamper with (the syntax or) the semantics of the representational formalism. Rather, one can tamper a whole lot with the inferential apparatus. (See articles by Reiter and McCarthy in [AI80]. See also [ISRA80].)

On the other hand, one *may* choose to fool around with the "language" itself, and thence with the logic. In particular one may take as one's base a standard first-order language and add a special intensional (modal) "typically" operator to it (see [MCDE80] regarding the problem of specifying a semantics for this operator). Indeed, one can even think of Fahlman's *TYPE-nodes as follows. Take a Doyle-McDermott-type sentence-forming operator (one applicable to sentences both open and closed) and transform it (Voila!) into a complex predicate-forming operator, taking predicates into predicates. Or, given

---

17 Needless to say there are "fragments" of NETL that correspond quite directly to bits and pieces of more standard systems; but even here appearances can be deceiving. For instance, an *EVERY node, it seems, can only govern a compound open sentence. Once one has fixed an (intuitive) interpretation for the primitive *TYPE nodes, one is debarred from linking a single *TYPE-node up to an *EVERY-node. So don't confuse an *EVERY-node with the universal quantifier. (We are not implying that Fahlman himself makes this misidentification).

18 Notice that this feature has nothing to do with the network structure. It merely has to do with the primacy of prototypes.

that the typical operands are, syntactically speaking, common nouns (that is, in the context of representing the content of sentences of a natural language), the operator acts like a determiner which, when combined with a common noun, yields a generalized quantifier. In other cases, as when applied to a verb-phrase, it plays the role of an adverb, in particular, an adverb of quantification. Exactly what its semantics should be is another and thoroughly open question.

At this point, we must admit to the following qualm: we are at a loss to take sides in a debate about the adequacy of FOL for prototypes and defaults, since it isn't clear what the sides are. Maybe prototype/default notions are representational (*semantic*) notions having to do with the interpretations of monadic predicates, and maybe they're not. Maybe they are notions to be treated by generalizing the concept of a rule of inference (as in McCarthy and Reiter), maybe not. Much of the discussion about these matters has mixed together semantic issues with epistemological and psychological issues, concerns about plausible reasoning and inconclusively justified belief. Perhaps this mixing has been principled and self-conscious; but then again, perhaps not. In such a situation, silence from someone is probably golden.

5.2 Prototypes and Complex Concepts

Regardless of their relation to standard logics, prototype representations are a fact of life in most AI representation frameworks. Here we take a quick look at how prototype representations seem to rule out the possibility of compound concepts, thereby, and despite illusions to the contrary, limiting themselves to primitive, atomic concepts.[19]

The principal quantificational import of a prototype is simply this: unless otherwise told, assume that all properties of the prototype hold of each and every "instance" of the type. So, if we know CLYDE to be, say, a CAMEL, then we assume that all properties of the TYPICAL-CAMEL hold of him, too. At some point we may learn about some special feature of Clyde that distinguishes him from the prototype (say, for instance, that he talks to his owner). We simply notate this by cancelling the normally inherited property (*e.g.*, that camels don't talk) and substituting the new one. Prototype notations usually carry some explicit cancelling mechanism that allows them to accommodate the fact that rarely do real camels match their prototypes exactly.

Thus, properties of prototypes are always *default* properties.[20]

[19] This section briefly recapitulates a more detailed discussion that can be found in [BRAC80a].

[20] At least this is the most reasonable interpretation. Sometimes it is totally unclear what is meant by prototype.

Properties are almost universally represented by "slots" of frames, and the attribution of properties of the prototype to any individual is achieved by "inheritance of properties." In more logical notation, the meaning of a frame representing the concept C, with slot-relationships R1,...,Rn becomes the following [HAYE79]:

```
    (x) Cx -> R1(x, f1(x))
&   (x) Cx -> R2(x, f2(x))
&   .
    .
    .
```

This logical notation expresses the inheritance, but not the default nature of it. The default rules can be expressed as in Reiter's "Logic for Default Reasoning" [AI80], leaving the object language as is.

Now, what does that leave us with as the import of the frames, units, *etc.*? First and foremost we have the universal quantification over instances, with embedded existentials for the slots. If Clyde is known to be a CAMEL, then he inherits all of the properties associated with the TYPICAL-CAMEL. Second, we know that since TYPICAL-CAMEL is a prototype, Clyde, as an individual camel, has the right to have properties incompatible with those of the typical camel. All this seems quite reasonable from a psychological point of view (again, see [ROSC75]).

Given that the properties of the prototype can be violated by instances of it, these properties are clearly nondefinitional. This conclusion is reinforced by the "outward" nature of the slots of the frames. If Clyde is (known to be) a camel, then he has typical-camel-properties, not the other way around (*i.e.*, the connective in the above logical reformulation is the conditional, not the biconditional). Again, this seems well and good, since there are certainly no defining properties for camelhood; the camel is a "natural kind." And, you might add, so are most, if not all of the concepts that an AI system will have to deal with. Leave abstract and defined concepts like "rhombus" to the mathematicians, and leave the philosophers to argue about whether "bachelor" can be defined.

This intuitively appealing and pervasive line is predicated on an interesting, though unargued and plausibly erroneous assumption: as the camel goes, so go all other kinds. The unwarranted belief that, with a few technical exceptions, every concept is a natural kind has had at least one significant consequence. There has been no felt need to provide a facility for expressing analytic or definitional connections. This raises no problems with the conceptual counterparts of lexical items like "camel." But just as we can create the English phrase, "camel that talks to the sheik of the burning sand," we should expect to be able to create the node for the composite concept that it expresses. Two things are certain: a camel that talks to its owner can't fail to be a camel, and it can't help but talk to its owner! That is, the composite concept certainly stands in an analytic relationship to its "head" concept, even if that concept is associated with a natural kind.

Since the "Frames" paper, defaults have been almost universally adopted at the expense of definitions or other analytic connections. But this has left network representations in a funny state. Inheritance of properties works okay, and one can represent exceptions (three-legged elephants and the like); but one can't represent even the simplest of conceptual composites. It follows from the lack of composites that every single node (or frame or whatever) in the network is in fact semantically simple. In other words, it's a primitive. (But see the Note on Fahlman's *EVERY-nodes, above.) An AI system certainly can use such a network as a database repository for such classificatory facts as the user sees fit to tell it (*e.g.*, that CLYDE is a TYPICAL-CAMEL), but it cannot draw any such conclusions itself. Without being told *explicitly*, the system cannot even tell that an elephant that has three legs is an elephant!

5.3 On Simplicity and Definability: Lexical vs. Structural Semantics

With respect to the points made above about lexical items and (non)definability, we have noted a nasty rumor going around to the effect that if one embraces the paradigm of formal (model-theoretic) semantics for natural languages, one thereby, and ineluctably, finds oneself stuck with "analytic definitions" for everything in sight. This rumor is completely unfounded; worse, it is just plain false. Moreover, given what we've said elsewhere in this chapter, we feel it incumbent on ourselves to defend the honor, at least in this regard, of formal semantics—even of a fairly orthodox form.

Let's do a "worst case" analysis, namely, the application of a rich model-theoretic analysis of higher-order intensional logic to a natural language (English), by a logician, Richard Montague, who couldn't have cared less about psychological reality or computational issues. In Montague's semantics, every lexical item in a natural language is associated with a primitive of (some one of a certain family of) higher-order intensional logics. For such items there is no lexical decomposition; there are no definable lexical items. Of course, *syntactically composite items* (*e.g.*, "camel that talks to its owner") can have analytic definitions associated with them. But Montague absolutely rejects the line that assigns to lexical items some analysis in terms of "features" or that posits an analysis into some composition of allegedly universal, innate, and ultimate conceptual primitives. Mind you, it is easy to take care of those relatively rare lexical items of English (*e.g.*, "rhombus" and "bachelor") that do seem to be analytically definable by way of what

Montague, following Carnap, calls "meaning postulates," which, canonically at least, take the form of universalized conditionals (not, typically, biconditionals) with the necessity operator standing guard in front. In sum, there is no necessary connection between formal-semantical analyses of language and the multiplication of (analytic) definitions beyond necessity.

6. Concluding Remarks — An End to This FOL-ishness

To be skeptical of the claims made for standard first-order languages and their standard logics is not, ipso facto, to be anti-logical. Though *they* may think, With friends like us, who needs enemies?, we in fact intend to be taken as allies of those researchers in AI who have stressed the need for the kind of conceptual clarity that the theoretically self-conscious use of formal languages enforces. But as we shall duly note, we also align ourselves with those philosophers and logicians who look at least a little askance at efforts to force everything and anything into the procrustean bed of first-order languages and their classical logic.

With respect to the above, a little intellectual history might be in order yet again. From the very beginnings of AI, there has been a debate about the relevance and usefulness of work in formal (but nonprogramming) languages done by philosophers and logicians, in particular about the relevance and applicability of work done in and on the fairly standard quantificational formalisms. (We gather that this disagreement was in the open at the founding 1956 Dartmouth Conference, with McCarthy on the side of the angels, and Minsky and Newell and Simon on the other side.) The debate has taken on various forms: procedural vs. declarative encodings of knowledge, general theorem-proving techniques vs. domain-specific heuristics and ad hoc procedures, *etc.* Now, imagine yourself having fought and having to continue to fight this battle, often against people who seem to be laboring under significant misconceptions about the nature of formal languages and formal semantics (see [HAYE77], which is directed explicitly against some such misunderstandings). To imagine this is to imagine a particular brand of opponent, not one who wishes to counterpose to standard first-order formalisms, for example, full omega-order type theory with lambda-abstraction, intensional operators, and various other bells and whistles. Rather, the "enemy" doesn't see the point at all of precisely specifying a general formalism for which a well defined semantics can be given. In this situation, it makes perfect sense to stress the considerable virtues of standard first-order formalisms and their standard Tarski-type semantics, not least among which is that such systems have been studied to a fare-thee-well. We might be accused, then, of systematically misreading and distorting the arguments of the "logicians," distorting them by reading them as if they were directed against a very different type of opponent than that toward which they were in fact addressed. We plead guilty, sort of, but our intentions are honorable. Moreover, it is at least possible that some of the researchers in question have been trapped by the tactics and strategy of their arguments with the anti-logicians into a too ready accommodation to the familiar, the tried and (lest it be forgotten), as far as it goes, the true.

It will also doubtless be objected that the present discussion has been merely negative, or at best admonitory, in character. What constructive proposals have we to make? First, we advocate pursuit of alternative styles of formal systems, with careful attention paid to semantics for any non-classical constructs. Our views on this type of research program are elaborated in [BRAC79] [BRAC80b] [BL82] [ISRA82].

We do have one vague and open-ended suggestion to make. (In fact, it's so purely programmatic that it's best expressed in the form of a fond wish.) One thing we would like to see is a unification of programming language and representation language research, a unification plausibly less artificial than that proposed by PROLOG proponents, and one in which more of the "give" is from the representational side of the great divide. There are straws in the wind. First, of course, is the fact that much of the work on the formal semantics of natural languages within and around the Montague tradition is done within the framework of Church-Henkin type-theoretic (lambda-categorial) languages [CHUR40] [HENK50]. These are higher-order representational formalisms that bear an absolutely uncanny resemblance to the (typed) lambda calculus. The latter can itself be thought of as a programming language and (especially in its untyped embodiment) was long in use (albeit informally) as a kind of universal metalanguage with which to describe the semantics of "real" programming languages. This use has since been validated with the provision, by Dana Scott (and others), of a coherent and intuitively-grounded denotational semantics for both the typed and untyped lambda calculus. In this regard, we might note the attempt by Ray Turner to apply Dana Scott's work on models of the untyped lambda calculus to Montague-style type-theoretic languages (see [TURN81b].) The work of Brian Smith on the general issue of conditions of adequacy for semantic accounts of programming languages and the relation of these to declarative, representational formalisms, should also be mentioned here (see [SMIT82]). Finally, the already alluded to program of Situation Semantics of Barwise and Perry constitutes perhaps the heaviest straw now afloat; indeed, one can think of this work as, among other things, an attempt to give serious mathematical content to a computability constraint on the semantic functions deployed in natural language. One of (especially) Barwise's complaints against Montague's framework is that it is "computationally intractable." Whatever this complaint comes to exactly, we can't help noting that the general recursion-theoretic framework suggested by Barwise is connected to the framework of Scott-style denotational semantics of programming languages alluded to above.

That anything would come of such a unification is highly speculative, of course. But now is no time to be a stick-in-the-mud. Witness Jon Barwise:

> One of my own motivations was to use the insights of generalized recursion theory to find a computationally plausible alternative to Montague grammar... [Mine] is a mathematical theory of linguistic meaning, one that replaces the view of the connection between language and the world at the heart of Tarski-style semantics... [It] rejects a level of "logical form" that has anything to do with first-order logic. [BARW81]

An even more radical view of standard logic is espoused by the logician, Richard Routley:

> On the whole there has been far too much effort expended on trying to accommodate philosophical clarifications to going logical systems and strait jackets... rather than trying to develop logical systems to handle the evident data and to deal with going philosophical problems. Classical logic, although once and briefly an instrument of liberation and clarification in philosophy and mathematics, has, in becoming entrenched, become rigid, resistant to change and highly conservative, and so has become an oppressive and stultifying influence.... Classical logic is, as now enforced, a reactionary doctrine. [ROUT79]

Finally, and in summary, a word from Mao Ze Dong: "Let at least a few flowers bloom."

7. References

[AI80] [BARW81] [BP80] [BP81a] [BP81b] [BRAC79] [BRAC80a] [BRAC80b] [BL82] [BRES72] [BZ81] [CHUR40] [FAHL79] [HAYE77] [HAYE78] [HAYE79] [HAZE76] [HENK50] [ISRA80] [ISRA82] [LEWI68] [MCDE80] [MINS75] [MONT74] [NEWE80] [QUIL68] [REIT78c] [ROSC75] [ROUT79] [SCHU76a] [SGC79] [SMIT82] [TARK56] [TURN81b] [WOOD75]

Discussion

Much discussion has been generated within AI on the relative merits and expressive power of representation languages based on Logic on one hand and semantic networks on the other. This chapter presents a critical examination of the positions advocated by the two camps and finds them both lacking in rigor with respect to the claims they make. From a brief historical survey of semantic network literature it becomes apparent that they often have been used as a notation rather than as (a basis for) a representation language. Logic, on the other hand, has enjoyed a well accepted semantics, but its support as a knowledge representation scheme often has left unclear which aspects of Logic it proposes to use, and indeed, as this chapter argues, which Logic it is referring to.

No comparable discussion seems to have taken place in Databases or Programming Languages, although the notion of relational completeness and the debates on the relative merits of the relational, network, and hierarchical models are somewhat relevant.

Semantic Networks and Data Models

In reading the brief history of semantic networks presented in the chapter, it is interesting to note that there has been considerable migration of techniques from semantic networks to data models. The list of techniques that have migrated includes inheritance, higher order types, IS-A hierarchies, and to some extent PART-OF hierarchies. However, Database researchers are only now beginning to talk about multiple inheritance, whereas AI researchers have been talking about it for quite some time. One feature of semantic networks that hasn't been considered yet by any data model is inheritance suppression where inheritance of a property of a class (say, flying for birds) is suppressed for one of its subclasses (say, penguins).

One may wonder why semantic networks haven't been used directly for database purposes. First, as indicated by the historical review in the chapter, it isn't clear what it would mean to adapt semantic networks since they come in many strikingly different forms. Another and more pragmatic response is that although semantic networks and semantic data models are in a sense equally powerful, they are intended for applications that have very different characteristics. Databases generally deal with relatively few types and very large numbers of instances for each type, whereas semantic networks assume situations in which one is dealing with many types and only a few instances per type. However, there is a trend in databases to deal with applications that involve an ever increasing number of types, and this means that the gap in intended applications between data models and semantic networks seems to be narrowing.

New vs. Old Technologies

Database researchers have to consider many possible uses for a database, only some of which would be of relevance to AI. Their approach has been to find the least common denominator of all these applications and then implement it so that it works. Although requirements for databases have changed during the last few years, it is not obvious that the least common denominator for a framework that handles forms, visual and speech data, messages *etc.*, is semantic networks. Nor is it clear that a general proposal along the lines suggested by semantic networks is appropriate or even feasible for large scale use.

Database Applications to AI

Interaction between Database and AI research is not a one-way street with results always migrating from AI to Databases. One could argue that in order to introduce efficiency into an expert system using large amounts of data one should use Database technology. For instance, one could implement KL-ONE using a relational database management system to get efficiency without having to deal with the inner workings of a LISP implementation. An experiment along those lines was conducted at Berkeley, where a natural language understanding system was implemented on a relational database management system. The resulting system wasn't faster than its LISP counterpart, but it did deliver for free services such as transactions, error recovery, views, and general searching algorithms which would not have been available otherwise. One could also argue, however, that efficiency might be obtained for expert systems in terms of new technologies unrelated to Databases. It should be noted here that expert systems were developed in the past almost exclusively as experimental prototypes, and that neither efficiency nor other engineering features were important during this stage of development. This seems to be changing today as knowledge bases continue to grow and consideration is given to exporting expert systems to users other than their designers.

Designers of expert systems have generally chosen their tools keeping in mind that their systems are prototypes and that their attitude towards efficiency, exportability, and robustness has generally been that these are important concerns only after one has a satisfactory prototype. A counterargument to this "worry-about-it-later" attitude is that engineering considerations should play a role in the selection of design tools at the beginning of a design project, not later on. Programming Language research, for example, has developed sophisticated languages, but it didn't worry about programs that deal with large amounts of data until recently. Now that they do, in some ways they are reinventing the (database) wheel. Perhaps something similar will happen with AI when the designers of expert systems move from research to development.

On LISP

One may argue that systems implemented in LISP can be very efficient because of the many kinds of optimization and the new specialized machine architectures they utilize. It is questionable, however, that new hardware and LISP-based optimization can introduce the kind of efficiency provided in Databases which, after all, required many man-years of effort for its development from many very capable researchers. But, then again, one wonders whether the technology developed by Database research applies to the new office-related applications whose primary feature is that databases and computing are distributed.

The database technology is based on a particular generation of hardware and software. Today we are dealing with a new situation that has to do with semantic networks, new hardware, and new applications. The technology that will deal best with this situation may be something other than Database technology as we know it.

Finding a Solution vs. Making It Run Efficiently

The problems being worked on by the Database and AI communities are different. The AI community is interested in finding solutions to problems; the Database community tries to find efficient solutions, and as a result it needs to tackle simpler, more focused problems. Any comparison of research from the two areas should distinguish between what features are appropriate for a new conceptual model on the one hand, and which engineering considerations for the systems support it on the other.

The End-User View

There are two ways to help an office manager specify his application domain. The first is to give him SBA or TAXIS (see chapter by Borgida, *et al.*), or any one of a dozen other representation languages. The other approach is to provide him with a toolkit that includes a text editor, a database management system, a graphics package, *etc.* Some feel that the toolkit approach is wrong; the end-user should be presented with an integrated environment. Others feel that the system offered to an office manager has to be viewed in terms of subsystems due to its size, although it may be helpful to have an interface that does project a uniform point of view to the end-user. In either case, everyone seems to agree that it would be helpful to provide the user of such a system with functions that assist him in his modelling activity.

Conclusions

From a Database point of view, conceptual modelling appears to require a multitude of functions that Database technology provides today, and this has resulted in some scepticism towards new proposals such as those presented in this volume. This point of view also insists that existing technologies for database management will be essential for the development of new technologies that are attempting to deal with office and/or expert systems. AI research concentrates on the development of techniques for building expert systems that are adequate from a competence point of view. It is not constrained by existing technologies.

6
Open Systems

Carl Hewitt and Peter de Jong
Massachusetts Institute of Technology

ABSTRACT *This chapter describes some problems and opportunities associated with conceptual modelling for the kind of "open systems" we foresee developing in the future. Computer applications will be based on communication between subsystems that will have been developed separately and independently. Some of the reasons for independent development are: competition, economics, geographical distribution, and diverse goals and responsibilities. We must deal with all the problems that arise from* conceptual *disparities. Subsystems will be open-ended and incremental—undergoing continual evolution. There are no global objects. The only thing that all the various subsystems hold in common is the ability to communicate with each other. Message Passing Semantics is a methodology that we are developing to deal with highly parallel, distributed, open systems. Various aspects of this methodology deal with communication, description, transaction management, problem solving, change, completeness, and self-knowledge.*

1. Introduction

A goal of conceptual modelling is to aid in the implementation of next generation computing systems by applying and unifying results from the fields of programming languages, data bases, and artificial intelligence. A central theme is to have the computer systems understand the application as well as the environment in which it will operate. Our approach to a conceptual modelling system reflects the authors' views of the way computer systems are developing now and of the ways we expect them to evolve. We expect that the standard use of

---

This chapter describes research done at the Artificial Intelligence Laboratory of the Massachusetts Institute of Technology. Major support for the research reported in this chapter was provided by the System Development Foundation. Support for the Artificial Intelligence Laboratory as a whole is provided by the Advanced Research Projects Agency of the Department of Defense under Office of Naval Research contract N0014-80-C-0505.

computer applications will involve the interaction of subsystems that have been independently developed at disparate geographical locations [DEJO80]. Thus we regard the design, implementation, and analysis of the semantics of communication as a central theme of conceptual modelling. Thus far, work on communication semantics has not been sufficiently emphasized in conceptual modelling. We regard this lack as one of the most significant limitations in the current state of the art. In part the lack stems from the fact that in the basic areas that contribute to conceptual modelling (*viz.*, programming languages, data bases, and artificial intelligence), research on distributed systems is in its infancy. Unfortunately each of these contributing areas has for the most part tried to make a simple extrapolation of the methodology and technology of single computer systems to a distributed environment. These simple extrapolations are inadequate when dealing with the systems of the future. In this chapter we discuss how message-passing semantics applies to the conceptual modelling of Open Systems. In particular we discuss a number of technologies that we are developing in order to address the problems of modelling Open Systems.

2. Open Systems

The kind of systems we envisage will be open-ended and incremental—undergoing continual evolution. In an open system it becomes very difficult to determine what objects exist at any point in time. For example, a query might never finish looking for possible answers. A query to find a bargain priced used refrigerator in good condition would reference information stored in any of a number of personal and organizational computers. Enormous amounts of effort and time can be expended processing the query to find such refrigerators without being certain that the best buy has been located. This example illustrates how the "closed world assumption" is intrinsically contrary to the nature of Open Systems. We understand the "closed world assumption" to be one in which information about the world being modeled is complete, in the sense that *all and only* the relationships that can possibly hold among objects are those implied by the given information at hand. See the chapter by Ray Reiter for a more detailed discussion of the closed world assumption.

Similarly, if a system is asked to find all the passengers serviced by a particular airline, it might have a hard time answering. It can give all the passengers it has found so far, but there is no guarantee that another passenger won't be found a few seconds later. To solve this problem, we use a kind of resource called a repository. A repository maintains a complete list of all the objects sent to it. Repositories provide definite answers to questions about the membership of an object in a repository as of the time when the query is received by the repository. For example, a repository could be used to maintain a complete roster of the employees of a branch office. Of course, the use of repositories has certain associated costs, and it is not desirable to attempt to store everything possible in them.

Once a piece of knowledge is disseminated, other knowledge in the system might be affected. When an airline guide is disseminated, travel plans can include the scheduled flights. When the guide is revised on a certain date, some travel plans might use the old schedule, and some might use the new schedule. Because of the distributed nature of Open Systems, when a piece of information is disseminated, in general the version disseminated cannot be accessed. Instead of accessing the original information, mechanisms such as disseminating errata, updates, and revisions must be used to correct it.

There are no global objects in Open Systems. The only thing that all the various subsystems hold in common is the ability to communicate with each other. We believe that negotiation will be a fundamentally important mode of communication in the operation of Open Systems. Similar concepts and capabilities will develop and evolve in many different locations in Open Systems. For example, each bank will offer similar services that differ in detail from the services of its competitors. Systems will need to negotiate the terms and conditions of their transactions.

To function effectively in an Open System, self-knowledge is necessary if a subsystem is to understand its own abilities as well as the limits of its knowledge and power. As knowledge is added incrementally to a subsystem, it must relate the new knowledge to its existing knowledge. Any subsystem can have only partial knowledge of the overall system, and partial power to affect other subsystems. A travel agency has the power to make plane reservations but in general does not have the power to cancel flights. Means for distributed problem solving and negotiation are necessary in order to combine the knowledge and powers of various subsystems that accomplish application goals. Accommodating the above characteristics of Open Systems will be necessary in order for conceptual modelling to be relevant in the future.

3. Travel Example

A simple example will clarify some of the above points. The application is a vacation trip. The agents involved are a traveler, a travel agent, and a banker. To make the example more modern, the traveler is at home using a computer to communicate with a travel agency and a bank. The trip will be planned interactively with extensive support from the computer systems. The people in the scenario have their own conceptual models that describe the objects they deal with, the organization and subsystems within which they work, and the applications they can perform. In general, each conceptual model has been constructed independently of the others at different times and places. The personal computer system in the home must deal with many travel agents and many banks, each with its own view of how it should run its own business. These business computer systems are geographically distributed, each running its own computers. For the most part they run in a parallel nonstop mode, always ready to interact with their customers. They are united by their ability to communicate with each other. Each workstation user's knowledge is partial. The travel agent does not know about the traveler's dealings with the bank. Each agent's power is limited. The travel agent can arrange the trip, but he will not finance it. The travel agent compiles more information about travel and changes in travel possibilities. New trips are continually being planned. Each conceptual modelling system needs to have extensive knowledge of its own capabilities and partial knowledge of other system's capabilities. The travel agent uses his self-knowledge to help guide its interactions with customers.

Now assume that the traveler wants to take a vacation in Europe. The traveler's desire to travel to Europe must be communicated to the travel agent. The process of communication would have to go on at different levels in a dialogue in order to negotiate a European trip. The arranging of the trip can be broken up into many sub-problems. The travel agent must book flights, ground transportation, and hotels. This requires the interfacing with multiple computer systems and conceptual models. The traveler must arrange financing. This might require a negotiating process with the banker or with multiple bankers in order to get the best loan rate. At any step in the problem-solving activity, a problem might arise that would require an approach different from the one currently being pursued. If the traveler has a limit of $4000, and the current trip plan is $5000, an adjustment must be made. Perhaps some four star hotels can be replaced by two star hotels. A festival in one country could be missed, which would allow a train trip to be substituted for an airplane trip. Since the conceptual modelling systems have only partial knowledge, they must use multiple strategies in planning the trip. Some parts of a model used might completely describe part of the trip planning process—perhaps the part that makes the airline reservations. The first time an airline reservation is made it will have to be stated as a problem to be solved. If the system can remember how it first solved the problem it would then run in a more algorithmic way; that is, there would be fewer hypotheses generated, and thus fewer unsuccessful attempts. Whenever the reservation attempt fails, new hypotheses would be generated and new subgoals tried. Open Systems must address the central issue of "coherence" of behavior (*i.e.,* convergence in a set of negotiations [BRAD82]). Starting negotiations is only the beginning; we must develop mechanisms for bringing them to successful conclusions.

4. Problem Solving Procedures

On the basis of the above discussion, we conclude that interaction with workstation users and negotiation with other systems necessitate the introduction and analysis of problem solving procedures into Conceptual Modelling. Algorithmic procedures are those for which definite properties (*e.g.,* termination, certain outputs always produced, *etc.*) are known to hold. The *stronger* the known properties the *more algorithmic* the procedure. In contrast, problem solving procedures are those about which fewer and weaker properties are known. Thus we have a spectrum of possible procedures that range from problem solving to algorithms that have proven properties.

```
PROBLEM SOLVING <------------------> ALGORITHMIC
```

Subsystems of workstation procedures can move in both directions along this spectrum. They can be moved in the algorithmic direction by mechanizing more cases, by analysis to ameliorate their shortcomings, *etc.* We would like to move the human interface more in the direction of teaching computers how to perform tasks, in contrast to the current technology which necessitates programming them to perform tasks. Procedures can be moved further into the problem-solving realm by unanticipated external changes that result in anomalous results, by the discovery that their range of applicability is not as great as previously believed, *etc.* Movement along the spectrum between problem solving procedures and algorithms should be one of the central concerns of conceptual modelling.

5. Concurrent Systems

To build a conceptual modelling system that has the above properties, we need to develop a coherent understanding of the semantics of concurrent message-passing systems. The semantics of concurrent message-passing systems involves important aspects of parallelism and serialization beyond the sequential coroutine message-passing developed in systems like Simula and SmallTalk.

An actor system is composed of abstract objects called *actors*. Actors communicate with each other by using messages. Control structures can be characterized in terms of patterns of message passing [HEWI77]. When a message is received an actor can change its local state, *create* new actors, and *transmit* messages [HB77]. If an actor can change its local state, it is called a *serialized* actor. A serialized actor accepts for processing only one message at a time. A serialized actor will not accept another message for processing until it has dealt with the one it is processing in at least a preliminary fashion. All messages received when a serialized actor is processing a message are queued in order of arrival until they can be examined. An important special case occurs when an actor never changes its local state. Such an actor is called *unserialized* and is treated specially so that conceptually it is able to process arbitrarily many messages at the same time. Actors such as the square root function and the text of Lincoln's Gettysburg Address are unserialized.

An airline seat reservation system needs to handle a high transaction rate. Many changes can occur in the minutes just before the plane takes off. To implement this type of resource we use serialized actors. A reservation results in a change of the local state of the actor for the flight. Inquiries about the flight are implemented by sending messages to the actor for the flight. Traditional properties of transactions (*e.g.*, the all or nothing property) can be implemented by having actors follow the appropriate message protocols. These actors are called transaction managers. Flight actors can be implemented as specializations of transaction managers and thereby inherit the proper message protocol.

The Actor Model unifies the conceptual basis of both the lambda calculus and the object-oriented schools of programming languages. The object-oriented programming languages (*e.g.*, [BDMN73] [LSAS77] [SWL77] [IKWL80]) are built of objects (sometimes called "data abstractions") that are completely separate from the procedures in the language. Similarly the lambda calculus programming languages (*e.g.*, [MCCA62] [LAND65] [FW76b] [BACK78] [SS78c]) are built on functions and data structures (*viz.*, lists, arrays, *etc.*) that are separate. SmallTalk [INGA78] is somewhat a special case since it simplified Simula by leaving out the procedures entirely (*i.e.*, it has only classes). The Simula-like languages provide effective support for coroutines but not for concurrency. In contrast, the Actor Model is designed to aid in conceptual modelling of shared objects in a highly parallel open systems. Actors provide a unified conceptual basis for functions, data structures, classes, suspensions, futures, objects, procedures, processes, *etc.*, in all of the above programming languages [BH77] [LIEB81a] [HAL79]. *The Actor Model is mathematically defined and thus independent of all programming languages.*

In general, each actor is independent and can run in parallel. A system consisting of multiple processors (called the APIARY) is being developed in order to use the inherent parallelism of actor systems to increase the speed of computation [HEWI80]. Message Passing Semantics builds on Actor Theory as a foundation for the conceptual modelling of Open Systems. The modelling proceeds by the development of *description* actors, general purpose *resource* actors, and *sprites.* Each of these is discussed below in the context of their relationship to conceptual modelling.

6. Descriptions

The attempt by practitioners in the field of Artificial Intelligence to construct "knowledge representation systems" has led to a morass of confusion and poor terminology. In contrast we advocate the use of *descriptions* to model the relationship of objects in Open Systems [HAS80] [AS81]. Descriptions are implemented using several different kinds of actors: atomic descriptions, instance descriptions, *etc.* For example, `FRANCE` is an actor that is an atomic description, and `(a COUNTRY)` is an actor that is an instance description. A user can hypothesize that the two descriptions are related using the following inheritance statement (in which key words having a special technical meaning are set in bold faced type):

```
(FRANCE is (a COUNTRY))
```

which states that `FRANCE` is a specialization of `(a COUNTRY)`. The effect is to send a message to the actor `FRANCE` informing it that it is a specialization of the actor `(a COUNTRY)`, and in parallel to send a message to the actor `(a COUNTRY)` informing it that it is a generalization of the actor `FRANCE`. The operational import of the above statement is that France inherits all the properties of a country.

Instance descriptions can be specialized using attributions. For example:

```
(a COUNTRY with CAPITAL PARIS))
```

is a specialization of (a COUNTRY). The following expresses the statement that **FRANCE** is a **COUNTRY** with capital Paris:

```
(FRANCE is (a COUNTRY (with CAPITAL PARIS)))
```

and hence France inherits all the properties of a country with capital Paris. Multiple partial incremental descriptions form the basis of expressing complicated relationships between objects. For example the system can subsequently be told:

```
(FRANCE is (a EURAIL-PASS-MEMBER))
```

which says that France is a specialization of a Eurail Pass Member so that in addition France inherits all the properties of Eurail Pass Members. In this way later descriptions are related to earlier ones in a lattice structure.

Our rules for *descriptions* are designed to facilitate the conceptual modelling of the objects and properties of Open Systems. Descriptions are defined by a rigorous mathematical semantics that have an epistemological basis compatible with the realities of Open Systems, both of which have been missing in previous systems. For example, systems based on the "closed world hypothesis" have attempted to leverage themselves on their own ignorance (*e.g.*, by always assuming that all the instances of a concept that they happened to know were the only ones that existed). On the other hand "knowledge representation," "frame," "schema," *etc.*, systems have suffered from a lack of mathematical semantics and from being based instead on low level sequential programming languages (*e.g.*, Lisp). *Since description lattices are implemented using actors, they can be distributed over multiple computers and can operate in parallel, thus facilitating communication and sharing in Open Systems.*

7. Resources

The modelling of shared resources is fundamental to Open Systems. In this section we discuss how Message Passing Semantics can help clear up some of the vast confusion that surrounds the conceptual modelling of shared resources in Open Systems. Actor systems aim to provide a clean way to implement *effects*, not "side-effects." The term "side-effect" is pejorative (*e.g.*, it has been used as a kind of curse by proponents of purely applicative programming in the lambda calculus) and fuzzy (since it is not rigorously defined). By an *effect* we mean a local state change in a shared actor that causes a change in behavior visible to other users. For example, sending a deposit to an account shared by multiple users should have the effect of increasing the balance in the account. In this section we present a simple example that illustrates our approach to implementing shared resources in Open Systems. A `PersonalAccount` is a resource that protects against timing errors when concurrent attempts by multiple users are made to deposit or withdraw money in the same account. To a given user, a shared `PersonalAccount` will exhibit indeterminacy in the balance, depending on the deposits and withdrawals made by other users. The indeterminacy arises from the indeterminacy in the arrival order of messages at the `PersonalAccount`. A `PersonalAccount` maintains the constraint that the balance is not allowed to become negative when it processes withdrawal and deposit messages. A `PersonalAccount` inherits its balance attribute and message protocol for deposit and withdrawal messages from Accounts in general:

```
(a PersonalAccount) is  (an Account (with balance (> 0)))
```

In addition to being an `Account`, a `PersonalAccount` is a `Possession`:

```
(a PersonalAccount) is  (a Possession (with owner (a Person)))
```

From the description of a `Possession`, each `PersonalAccount` inherits the owner attribute and the message protocols for ownership.

A `PersonalAccount` inherits attributes and behavior from *both* the description of an `Account` *and* the description of a `Possession`. Dealing with the issues raised by the above kind of possibility has become known as the "Multiple Inheritance Problem." A number of approaches have been developed in the last few years including: [WM81] [CBLL82] [BI82] [BS82a], and the chapter by Borgida, Mylopoulos, and Wong. Our approach differs since it builds on the theory of an underlying description system [AS81] and because it is designed for a parallel message passing environment, in contrast to the sequential coroutine object-oriented programming languages derived from Simula.

Below we present part of the implementation of `PersonalAccounts`. This implementation is written out in "parenthesized English" [KAHN79] [HAS80] [LIEB81b] [THER82], which we are gradually developing into a technical language. The words set in bold faced type have special technical meanings.

```
(Each new PersonalAccount (with Account Balance b)
                        and (with Possession Owner o))
has the following implementation
 (After acceptance
  select one of the following handlers for the communication
    (If it is (an Account Balance) query
       then do (reply b))
    (If it is (a Withdrawal with Amount w) request
       then do (select one of the following cases for w
        (If it is (less than or equal to b)
          then do
           (reply (a Completion Report)) as well as
           (become (new PersonalAccount
                              (with Account Balance (b - w)))))
        (If it is (greater than b)
          then do (complain an Overdraft Complaint))))
    (If it is (a Possession Owner) query
       then do (reply o)))
```

At this point we would like to take note of several unusual aspects of the above implementation. By default, commands are executed concurrently. For example, in the communication handler for `Withdrawal` requests above, the following two commands are executed concurrently:

```
(reply (a Completion Report))
(become (new PersonalAccount (with Account Balance (b - w))))
```

The principle of maximizing concurrency is fundamental to the design of actor programming languages. It accounts for many of the differences in conventional languages based on communicating sequential processes. Another example of maximizing concurrency is that the processing of messages by a serialized actor can be pipelined. Serialized actors can be pipelined since processing on a subsequent message can commence once processing on the message accepted has proceeded to the point of executing the **`become`** command. For example, after accepting a `Withdrawal` message, then executing the following **`become`** command

```
(become (new PersonalAccount (with Account Balance (b - w))))
```

a `PersonalAccount` can then *concurrently* **`accept`** an `Account Balance` query and **`reply`** with the Completion Report for the `Withdrawal` request. Of course, an actor that is unserialized (never changes its local state) has even more parallelism since there is no limit on the number of messages that it can process concurrently.

Another unusual aspect is that there are *no* assignment commands. Effects are implemented by an actor changing its *own local state* using a `become` command [HAL79]. We model change by actors that change their own local state, as opposed to the usual model in which assignment commands cause side effects on a universal global state. The absence of a well defined global state is a fundamental difference between the actor model and classical sequential models of computation (*viz.*, [TURI37] [CHUR41] [ROSS82], *etc.*). *Actor systems can perform nondeterministic computations for which there is no equivalent nondeterministic Turing Machine.* The nonequivalence points up the limitations of attempting to model parallel systems as nondeterministic sequential machines. Will Clinger has developed an elegant mathematical theory that accounts for capabilities of actor systems that *go beyond* those of nondeterministic Turing Machines [CLIN81].

The limitations of the nondeterministic sequential model have practical consequences in terms of the properties we can prove about useful concurrent systems. It is a consequence of the Actor Model [HAL79] that a `PersonalAccount` will respond to each message that it is sent. This property cannot be proved in the nondeterministic sequential model. Suppose we are attempting to withdraw money from a `PersonalAccount` that we share with others. In the nondeterministic sequential model the oracle (malicious demon) might always choose to have the `PersonalAccount` accept a message from someone else and *never* choose to have it accept the message we sent [HOAR78].

It is a consequence of the Actor Model that purely functional programming languages based on the lambda calculus cannot implement shared accounts in Open Systems. The technique promoted by Strachey and Milne [MILN78] for simulating some kinds of parallelism in the lambda calculus using continuations does not apply to Open Systems. The lambda calculus simulation is sequential whereas Open Systems are inherently parallel. Concurrency in the lambda calculus stems from the concurrent reduction/evaluation of various parts of a *single* lambda expression. *In Open Systems concurrency stems from the parallel operation of a incrementally growing number of multiple, independent, communicating sites.* Furthermore, sites join the Open System dynamically in the course of its normal operation, sometimes even affecting the results of computations initiated before they joined. *Actor Theory has been designed to accurately model the computational properties of Open Systems.*

Therefore we take issue with the common thesis that the primary advantage of applicative programming is referential transparency (*i.e.*, the absence of effects). Rather, the primary advantage of applicative programming is the very attractive way in which actions and the results of actions can be composed. We [HAL79] are *extending* the applicative style of programming and its elegant proof theory [SCOT72] to a more general programming methodology capable of causing and describing effects.

8. Hypothesis Formation

Hypothesis formation is a key problem solving activity in Conceptual Modelling. For example, from the hypothesis that Mike uses his credit card properly in 1955, we would like to be able to hypothesize that Mike uses his credit card properly in 1956.

A sprite is an actor attached to a description in a description network in order to process *disseminated* messages [KH81] [KORN82] [BARB82]. Sprites are used in problem solving to reason about hypotheses and goals. Each sprite has access to the material disseminated in a single description network that can be distributed over many computers.

The reasoning about Mike's use of his credit card can easily be performed by the following sprite.

```
(when (hypothesis (USE-PROPERLY MIKE 1955) do
     (hypothesize (USE-PROPERLY MIKE 1956))
```

Note that the reasoning expressed by the above sprite is not the same as the following implication:

```
(USE-PROPERLY MIKE 1955) implies (USE-PROPERLY MIKE 1956)
```

The bug in the above implication manifests itself under the circumstance in which Mike doesn't use his credit card properly in 1956 even though he did use it properly in 1955. Using the rules of first order logic from `(not (USE-PROPERLY MIKE 1956))` and the above implication, we can logically infer `(not (USE-PROPERLY MIKE 1955))`, which is a mistake. For want of a better name we will call this mistake the Contrapositive Bug in first order logic. *Hypothesis formation that goes beyond the use of first order logical reasoning within a single theory is necessary for Conceptual Modelling.*

9. Due Process

Due Process is the problem solving method of gathering evidence on all sides of a question in parallel, weighing the evidence, and then making a decision. *Understanding Due Process Reasoning is central to modelling the reasoning processes that go on in Open Systems.* In this section we consider a concrete example of Due Process reasoning. Note that the hypothesis that Mike didn't use his credit card properly before 1984 is evidence for the hypothesis that he will not use his credit card properly in 1984. This reasoning is expressed by the sprite below:

```
(when (hypothesis ((not (USE-PROPERLY MIKE y))
                   and (y PRECEDES 1984)))) do
    (hypothesize (not (USE-PROPERLY MIKE 1984)))
```

Using Due Process reasoning, a goal cannot be established by looking for evidence *only* in favor of the goal. In order to decide whether Mike uses his credit card properly in 1984, proponent activities must be established to gather evidence in favor and skeptic activities to gather evidence against [KH81]. After the expenditure of an amount of resources to gather the evidence which has been programmed as being appropriate for the question, the evidence is weighed and if possible a decision is made. For example, suppose we have information that Mike did not use his credit card properly in 1956, but that he did use it properly in 1982 and 1983. Then the sprite given above together with the following:

```
(when (hypothesis (USE-PROPERLY MIKE 1983) do
      (hypothesize (USE-PROPERLY MIKE 1984))
```

can be invoked in parallel to produce evidence both for and against the hypothesis that Mike uses his card properly in 1984. Due Process can proceed by sprites that have been programmed to hypothesize that a card will be used properly in a year if has been used properly recent previous years, even though it was used improperly in the distant past.

Note that the reasoning expressed by the above sprite for gathering evidence that a card is not used properly differs from the following implication:

```
((not (USE-PROPERLY MIKE y)) and (y PRECEDES 1984)) implies)
                  (not (USE-PROPERLY MIKE 1984)))
```

A problem with the above implication manifests itself under the circumstance in which Mike uses his credit card properly in 1984 even though he didn't use it properly in 1956. Using the rules of first order logic from `(not (USE-PROPERLY MIKE 1956))` and the above implication, we can logically infer `(not (USE-PROPERLY MIKE 1984))`, which is not a reasonable overall conclusion in the circumstances discussed above. The above implication in first order logic makes use of reasoning that is far more rigid than we would like.

In fact, the following first order sentences that attempt to summarize the situation we are describing

```
(USE-PROPERLY MIKE 1982)
(USE-PROPERLY MIKE 1983)
((not (USE-PROPERLY MIKE y)) and (y PRECEDES 1984)) implies
                (not (USE-PROPERLY MIKE 1984)))
(not (USE-PROPERLY MIKE 1956)
(USE-PROPERLY MIKE 1983) implies (USE-PROPERLY MIKE 1984)
(1956 PRECEDES 1984)
```

are *inconsistent.* By the rules of first order logic, from the above inconsistency any arbitrary conclusion can be drawn no matter how ridiculous. For the want of a better name we will call this mistake the Inconsistency Bug in first order logic.

We conjecture that any set of axioms that purports to describe the expert knowledge of a complicated, real system (viz., *human kidneys, the Japanese economy, the US Supreme Court,* etc.) *will be inconsistent. From this we conclude that the Inconsistency Bug of first order logic can represent a danger to the user* [HEWI75] [DISE77] [MINS75].

The existence of bugs has not gone unnoticed by advocates of the use of first order logic for the mechanization of reasoning. They have prompted the development of "nonmonotonic logic" [AI80]. The development of nonmonotonic logic is currently in a state of rapid flux [KOLA82]. Ray Reiter pointed out that one of the approaches (called circumscription) as presently formulated does not deal at all well with the problem of inconsistent evidence. Some advocates of first order logic concerned with the problems discussed above are attempting to use *multiple* first order logical theories and their meta-theories (*viz.,* [MCCA80] [WEYH80] [HAYE77] [MOOR82], *etc.*). It will be interesting to see the extent to which the use of multiple theories and their meta theories can help ameliorate the problems with first order logic. *It is impossible to implement Due Process Reasoning for Open Systems in first order logic because it lacks the necessary communication capabilities.*

Due Process is central to the operation of most community decision making (*viz.,* trial courts, legislatures, appeal courts, regulatory agencies, scientific communities, *etc.*). We must address the problem of making computer systems apply Due Process with something approaching the subtlety and sophistication of human communities.

10. Doing and/or Describing

One of the most challenging problems in Conceptual Modelling is sorting out the relationship between *doing* and *describing.* The difference between doing and describing can be seen clearly, in the clerical work in offices of large corporations. Policies and procedures manuals, memos, guidelines, *etc.*, provide a description, whereas the office workers themselves perform the clerical work. Currently, the discrepancies between the available descriptions and the realities of the actual work are huge (*cf.* [SUCH79] and [WYNN77]). Modern office work is learned mainly by apprenticeship.

The distinction between doing and describing is different from the separation made in Artificial Intelligence [MH69] [HAYE77] between the *epistemological adequacy* of a system (its well-formedness with respect to truth-theoretic semantics [TARS44]) and the *heuristic adequacy* (the ability of its inferential procedures to arrive at desired conclusions in a reasonable amount of time). First order logic can thought of as *inference rules* that lay out the first order rules of inference, and a *sentence structure* that lays out the syntax of first order sentences. The truth-theoretic semantics formalized by Tarski provides a connection between the inference rules and sentence structure of first order logic. The Contrapositive Bug, Inconsistency Bug, and the inability to perform Due Process Reasoning are examples of the limitations of the inference rules of first order logic. Sprites can perform logical inferences in contexts where this is appropriate. For example, the following sprite

```
(when (hypothesis (and sentence1 sentence2)) do
      (hypothesize sentence1) as well as
      (hypothesize sentence2))
```

will concurrently hypothesize individual sentences (call them `sentence1` and `sentence2`) whenever the conjunction of the two sentences is hypothesized. Note that Actor Semantics takes a different perspective on the meaning of a sentence from that of truth-theoretic semantics. In truth-theoretic semantics, the meaning of a sentence is determined by the models that make it true. For example, the conjunction of two sentence is true exactly when both of its conjuncts are true. *Actor Semantics takes the meaning of a message to be the effect it can have on the future behavior of the system.*

An important limitation of truth-theoretic semantics is that it provides for hypotheses but not goals. The distinction between *hypothesis invoked* reasoning (*i.e.*, sprites of the form `(when (hypothesis ...) ...)` and *goal invoked* reasoning (*i.e.*, sprites of the form `(when (goal...) ...)` is central to process based reasoning such as Due Process. For example, from the following sprite considered earlier which performs hypothesis formation

```
(when (hypothesis (USE-PROPERLY MIKE 1983)) do
      (hypothesize (USE-PROPERLY MIKE 1984))
```

we can *derive* the following sprite

```
(when (goal (USE-PROPERLY MIKE 1984)) do
      (show (USE-PROPERLY MIKE 1983)))
```

which, when invoked with the goal that Mike uses his card properly in 1984, attempts to show that he uses his card properly in 1983. Making the distinction between hypothesis-invoked and goal-invoked reasoning, a key component of a language for problem solving was proposed by [HEWI69] and implemented by [SWC70], which built on earlier work by Minsky and Papert, as well as work by Newell, Shaw, and Simon [NEWE62]. *The separation of hypotheses and goals and explicitly reasoning about both is an important advantage of process-based reasoning over truth-theoretic based reasoning* (cf. [HEWI75] [DDSS77]). Winograd made excellent use of this work [WINO71] and further developed these ideas [WINO80]. The rules for sprites [KH81] extend this work to Open Systems.

11. Self-Reference, Self-Knowledge, and Self-Development

Self-reference, self-knowledge, and self-development will be important capabilities for the effective utilization of Open Systems. Therefore understanding these capabilities is central to Conceptual Modelling. Unfortunately, the analysis of the communication semantics of these capabilities is still quite rudimentary. However, we feel that the prospects for deeper analysis are excellent. Note that both negotiation and Due Process are inherently self-referential activities in which reference and appeal to the nature of the ongoing process is often made from within.

Many of the advantages of self-reference stem from the ability to analyze the meaning of past communications. Such an analysis can indicate that the system is in a rut or (alternatively) that it is making good progress toward some goal. Analysis of recent communications can provide valuable information about how certain negotiations are proceeding. Historical analysis provides leverage by giving a subsystem a handle on the semantics of the communications between itself and the external environment. In general, knowledge of the nature of this interaction cannot be derived solely from general theories independently of the historical context.

Of course analysis of its own mechanisms can sometimes help. For example, a subsystem may find that it has a mechanism by which a paycheck received each month is deposited in an account in a certain bank, and another mechanism by which a mortgage payment is made each month to another bank. Analysis may indicate that the benefit of additional float can be obtained by requesting that the employer deposit the money directly in a high interest bearing account, and then using electronic funds transfer to pay the mortgage.

Additional leverage is provided by the capability for a subsystem to have explicit knowledge of its own goals. Such knowledge enables a system to relate its goals to one another so that in some cases it can detect partial conflicts and overlaps. In addition it can aid in focusing effort by providing information that can potentially be used to help judge whether or not it is spreading its resources too thin.

12. Conclusion

In this chapter we have discussed a number of technologies we are developing to address the problems of Open Systems. We have described the properties that a conceptual modelling system must have to properly model the kind of highly parallel, incrementally growing, distributed, open systems we foresee developing in the future. Together with our colleagues, we have implemented many *separate* systems to deal with different aspects of the issues involved: Act 1 [LIEB81b], Omega [BARB82], Ether [KORN82], SBA [BSD82], *etc.* Currently the Message Passing Semantics Group is constructing a system that *unifies* these technologies in order to support the conceptual modelling of Open Systems as described in this chapter. Message Passing Semantics is in an active research phase. As a result, the examples presented in this chapter represent our current thoughts about what is needed for future conceptual modelling systems, rather than our final system.

13. Acknowledgments

We would like to thank Michael Brodie for many long discussions concerning conceptual modelling. We would also like to thank the other participants of the Conceptual Modelling Workshop for sharpening our ideas about this subject. Subsequent to the workshop, conversations with several of our colleagues provided additional valuable insights which have been incorporated: Discussions with David Israel, John McCarthy, and Ray Reiter helped us to sharpen our critique of first order logic. Fanya Montalvo helped to develop the section on self knowledge and suggested how to make the chapter more coherent. A discussion with Allen Newell suggested that Due Process Reasoning is even more fundamental than first supposed and can be used to derive what he calls "weak methods." A conversation with John Wheeler established some fascinating connections with developments in modern physics which will be a topic in a forthcoming paper. Jonathan Amsterdam, Mike Brady, Toni Cohen, Randy Davis, Charles Smith, and Daniel Weld provided valuable comments.

This report describes research done at the Artificial Intelligence Laboratory of the Massachusetts Institute of Technology. Major support for the research reported in this chapter was provided by the System Development Foundation. Support for the Artificial Intelligence Laboratory as a whole is provided by the Advanced Research Projects Agency of the Department of Defense under Office of Naval Research contract N0014-80-C-0505. We would like to thank Charles Smith and Patrick Winston for their support and encouragement.

Much of the work underlying our ideas was conducted by members of the Message Passing Semantics group at MIT. We especially would like to thank Giuseppe Attardi, Jerry Barber, Bill Kornfeld, Henry Lieberman, Dan Theriault, and Maria Simi. The development of the Actor Model has benefited from extensive interaction with the work of Jack Dennis, Bert Halstead, Tony Hoare, Gilles Kahn, Dave MacQueen, Robin Milner, Gordon Plotkin, and Steve Ward during the past half decade. The work on Simula and its successors SmallTalk, CLU, Alphard, *etc.*, has profoundly influenced our work. We are particularly grateful to Alan Kay, Peter Deutsch, and the other members of the Learning Research group for interactions and useful suggestions.

14. References

[AI80] [AS81] [BACK78] [BARB82] [BDMN73] [BH77] [BI82] [BRAD82] [BS82a] [BSD82] [CBLL82] [CHUR41] [CLIN81] [DDSS77] [DEJO77] [DISE77] [FW76b] [HAL79] [HAS80] [HAYE77] [HB77] [HEWI69] [HEWI75] [HEWI77] [HEWI80] [HOAR78] [IKWL80] [INGA78] [KAHN79] [KH81] [KOLA81] [KORN82] [LAND65] [LIEB81a] [LIEB81b] [LSAS77] [MH69] [MCCA62] [MCCA80] [MILN78] [MINS75] [MOOR82] [NEWE62] [ROSS82] [SCOT72] [SS78c] [SUCH79] [SWC70] [SWL77] [TARS44] [THER82] [TURI37] [WEYH80] [WINO77] [WINO80] [WM81] [WYNN79]

7
The Logic of Incomplete Knowledge Bases

Hector J. Levesque
University of Toronto

ABSTRACT *Some formal representation issues underlying the use of incomplete knowledge bases are discussed. An incomplete knowledge base is one that has only partial knowledge of the application domain. It is argued that a language that can refer to both the application domain and to the state of the knowledge base is required to specify and to question an incomplete knowledge base. A formal logical language with this expressive ability is presented and its semantics and proof theory are defined. It is also shown how different the use of the language must be, depending on whether the interaction involves querying or defining the knowledge base.*

1. Introduction

An important characteristic of any knowledge based system is its interaction with a *knowledge base* (KB) that provides and maintains information about the application domain. In general, there are two distinct modes of interaction between an expert system and its KB: the system will want to *ask* and to *tell* the KB about the application area. The assumption here is that a KB is interesting only as a repository for information about the domain and that the questions and assertions of interest are about the domain and not about the structure of the KB itself. In this chapter, I will examine what special expressive requirements are placed on the language(s) of interaction when a system must deal with a KB that is *incomplete.*

Generally speaking, a KB is incomplete when it does not have all the information necessary to answer a question of interest to the system. In this case, the user of the KB (man or machine) must distinguish between what is *known* by the KB and what is *true* in the intended application area. For example, a KB may know that someone is married without knowing to whom; it may know that one person is younger than another without knowing either person's age. In situations such as these, any interaction with the KB must be based on the understanding that the KB may have only partial knowledge of certain relevant aspects of the application. Specifically, the KB cannot be treated simply as a direct model or analogue of the domain. For instance, with an incomplete KB, one cannot establish how many people there are in the domain by simply counting representational objects of a certain type. Only when a KB is sufficiently complete will there be a structural similarity between the domain and the KB.

The reason incomplete KBs are so important is that, in many applications, the KB undergoes a continual evolution. At each stage, information can be acquired that is potentially very vague or indefinite in nature. More important, a problem solving system cannot simply wait for the KB to stabilize in some final and complete form since this may *never* happen.

When a knowledge based system is forced to depend on an incomplete KB, its ability to make decisions or solve problems is seriously compromised. In some cases, the lack of knowledge can be circumvented by using general defaults [REIT78c], while in other situations, special heuristics are required [CWAM75]. However, no matter how a system plans to deal with incompleteness, it must first be able to determine where this incompleteness lies. In other words, *a system has to find out exactly where knowledge is lacking before it can decide what to do about it.* This suggests that a KB must be capable of providing information not only about the application area, but about itself as well. Thus, the language used to interact with a KB must allow a user to define and inquire about what the KB does and does not know. The major issue of this chapter, then, is what impact this capability will have on the language of interaction.

The approach taken in my work focuses primarily on the formal aspects of this issue. As described in Section 2, I will be dealing with KBs consisting of formulas of the first order predicate calculus. In Section 3, I examine what questions one would like to be able to ask such a KB and conclude that these questions are best phrased in a superset of the predicate calculus I call KL. In Section 4, I examine the language KL in detail and provide a semantics and proof theory. Given this analysis of KL, I then consider it as a language used to interact with a KB. In Section 5, the formulas of KL are used to *query* a KB, and I show that this involves a nonmonotonic version of the language. In Section 6, the formulas of KL are used to *define* a KB, and I indicate why this requires converting the formulas into the language of the KB. In Section 7, I briefly survey how incompleteness has been handled in Database Management and, in Section 8, I discuss how my work could relate to traditional Knowledge Representation.

Three areas of related research should be noted. First of all, my formalization of KL owes much to the work on the logic of knowledge and belief pioneered in [HINT62] and continued in [MOOR80] and [MSHI78] (though my application is somewhat different). Secondly, there has been research on incompleteness from the database area (*e.g.*, [VASS80] [LIPS78]) concentrating primarily on efficient query evaluation. Finally, although the research here does not deal with defaults or assumptions, the work on nonmonotonic reasoning [MD78] [MCDE80] [MCCA80] [REIT80] has provided technical inspiration. Despite the inherent formality of the subject matter, the tone of this chapter is somewhat informal. In particular, three nontrivial results are announced without proof. In each case, the length of the proof would have severely restricted the space available for motivation and discussion of the framework. The interested reader is invited to consult [LEVE81a] for the technical details of these results. This chapter itself is an extension and refinement of [LEVE81b].

2. First Order Knowledge Bases

As described in [GM78], a first order KB is a finite set of closed formulas of first order logic (FOL). I will restrict my attention to formulas that do not contain function symbols other than a (possibly infinite) set of 0-ary symbols called constants. Moreover, it is assumed that there are as many constants as there are entities in the domain of discourse.

A query in this framework is any formula of FOL and is answered by consulting the provability relation $\vdash$ to determine what does and does not follow from the KB. In this chapter, I will consider only closed queries which correspond to yes/no questions. For each query α there are three possible replies:

- *yes*, when KB $\vdash \alpha$
- *no*, when KB $\vdash \neg\alpha$
- *unknown*, when neither KB $\vdash \alpha$ nor KB $\vdash \neg\alpha$

If we allow for inconsistent KBs, there is a fourth possibility which is:

- *both*, when KB $\vdash \alpha$ and KB $\vdash \neg\alpha$

Typically, a first order KB can be factored into two parts, one containing particular facts of the application domain such as

Student(bill), Student(joe), Teaches(john,bill)

and the other containing general rules regarding the usage of predicate symbols such as

$$(\forall x) \neg \text{Teaches}(x,x)$$

or

$$(\forall x)[\text{Teacher}(x) \equiv (\exists y)\ \text{Teaches}(x,y)].$$

The first rule above might be used as an integrity constraint, and the second can be used to deduce who the teachers are.

To avoid having to include within a KB all the "negative" facts about the application such as

$$\neg\,\text{Student(john)},\ \neg\,\text{Teaches(bill,john)},$$

$$\neg\,\text{Teaches(joe,john)},\ \neg\,\text{Teaches(john,joe)},$$

$$\neg\,\text{Teaches(joe,bill)},\ \neg\,\text{Teaches(bill,joe)},$$

an assumption is usually made (once and for all) that the negation of any atomic formula can be inferred from the inability to infer the atomic formula. This is the *closed world assumption* (CWA) [REIT78b] and results in a new view of query evaluation. In this case, a query is answered in terms of

$$\text{KB} \vdash_{cwa} \alpha$$

where $\vdash_{cwa}$ is a provability relation that takes the assumption into account. Letting

$$\overline{\text{KB}} = \{\neg\, p \mid \text{p is atomic and } \neg\ \text{KB} \vdash p\}$$

then we have

$$\text{KB} \vdash_{cwa} \alpha \text{ iff KB} \cup \overline{\text{KB}} \vdash \alpha.$$

If the CWA is used along with the assumption that the constants correspond to the entities in the domain,[1] we have the property that for any closed formula α either

$$\text{KB} \vdash_{cwa} \alpha \text{ or KB} \vdash_{cwa} \neg\,\alpha.$$

---

[1] What this assumption amounts to is that $\vdash$ is such that any set of sentences containing $\exists\, x\alpha$ and $\neg\alpha^x_c$ for every constant c is inconsistent. The set of constants need not be finite and there could be other function symbols including additional 0-ary ones.

I will call a KB where no closed query has an unknown answer *complete* since it provides a complete picture of the domain it is intended to model relative to the query language.

In an *incomplete* KB, on the other hand, there are relevant queries having *unknown* as an answer. Consider, for example, a KB that contains

$$[\text{Student(mary)} \vee \text{Student(susan)}]$$

but neither

$$\text{Student(mary)}$$

nor

$$\text{Student(susan)}.$$

In this case, $KB \cup \overline{KB}$ is inconsistent so the CWA cannot be used. This KB only partially describes a world since it specifies that Mary or Susan is a student but does not particularize. Thus, there is a query that is true in the intended application but whose truth cannot be determined on the basis of what is available in the KB.

To say that a KB is incomplete is quite different from the somewhat trivial observation that a KB can never completely capture all aspects of some domain and that therefore unknowns exist. To allow the CWA to be used, queries are normally constrained to deal only with the KB's area of expertise (for example, by restricting the predicate symbols that can be used). Within this narrow area, the KB may indeed be complete. The key point regarding the above KB is that even within its domain of expertise it is incomplete because it does specify that Mary or Susan is a student. So there is, in fact, a *relevant* query (*i.e.*, whether or not Mary is a student), that cannot be answered with certainty.

For the rest of this chapter, I will say that a KB *knows* a formula if it answers *yes* to the query and, for any predicate *p* and constant *c*, that *c* is a *known p* when the formula $p(c)$ is known.

3. The Knowledge Base Query Language

Even though a KB is incomplete and the CWA cannot be used, there may be completeness in certain areas. For example, suppose that

$$\text{KB} \vdash (\forall x)[\text{Teacher}(x) \equiv (x = \text{john} \vee x = \text{george})].$$

In this case, not only are John and George teachers, but the KB knows that they are the only teachers. It therefore has a complete picture of the teachers. On the other hand, it may be the case that

$$KB \vdash (\exists x)Teacher(x)$$

without there being any known teachers. In this situation, the KB knows that there is a teacher but does not know who, indicating, therefore, that is does not have a complete list of teachers. There is, moreover, a third possibility, where it cannot be determined whether or not the KB has complete knowledge of the teachers. For example, suppose that the only thing the KB knows about the teachers is that John is one of them. In this case, it is neither true that

$$KB \vdash (\exists x)[Teacher(x) \wedge (x \neq john)]$$

nor

$$KB \vdash \neg(\exists x)[Teacher(x) \wedge (x \neq john)].$$

In other words, the KB may or may not already know all of the teachers. So just as the question

Is John a teacher?

may be answered *yes*, *no*, or *unknown*, the question

Are all the teachers known?

may also be *yes*, *no*, or *unknown*, depending only on what is in the KB.

If the purpose of a query language is to provide an accurate picture of what is and is not available in the KB, we should be able to formulate queries that ask the KB about its incompleteness. The query

$$(\exists x)[Teacher(x) \wedge (x \neq john)]$$

does not suffice since it asks only if there is a teacher other than John. It may turn out, for example, that

$$KB \vdash Teacher(george)$$

in which case the query is answered *yes* without telling us whether all the teachers are known. What is really required is the query

$$(\exists x)[Teacher(x) \wedge x \neq c_1 \wedge x \neq c_2 \wedge \ldots \wedge x \neq c_k)]$$

where the c's are constants ranging over all the teachers known to the KB.

There are a couple of problems with this method of asking whether all the teachers are known. First of all, there could be a very large number of known teachers. In some applications and for some predicates, there may even be an *infinite* number. Secondly, to be able to formulate the query we have to know what these constants are. For a large and complex KB, it could happen that only the KB has this information. One can also imagine situations in which the KB will not divulge this information for security reasons while still being able to answer questions about its incompleteness.

This suggests that the KB itself should keep track of its incompleteness in the same way it maintains knowledge of the application area. One possibility, for example, is to have a predicate

$$\textit{Known-teacher}\ (\mathrm{x})$$

and to allow a KB containing the following:

Teacher(john), *Known-teacher* (john),
[Teacher(george) $\vee$ Teacher(dan)],
$\neg$ *Known-teacher* (george), $\neg$ *Known-teacher* (dan).

Granted this arrangement, we can ask whether the KB has a complete list of teachers by the query

$$(\exists \mathrm{x})[\mathrm{Teacher(x)} \wedge \neg\, \textit{Known-teacher}\ (\mathrm{x})]$$

for which the answer here is *yes*, confirming the fact that the KB is incomplete.

The problem with this approach (and any other that involves a direct encoding into FOL) is the management of this extended language. There is a very definite relationship between "Teacher" and "*Known-teacher*" that must be captured somehow. Among other things, we intend that whenever

$$\mathrm{Teacher}(c)$$

is in the KB, then

$$\textit{Known-teacher(c)}$$

is in the KB as well. The closest we can come to expressing this is by an axiom stating that

$$(\forall \mathrm{x})[\mathrm{Teacher(x)} \supset \textit{Known-teacher}(\mathrm{x})].$$

However, this does not work since, for the above KB, it implies that

$$[\textit{Known-teacher}(\mathrm{george}) \vee \textit{Known-teacher}\ (\mathrm{dan})]$$

which is inconsistent with what is already known. Moreover, once we admit that "*Known-teacher*" is a predicate, there is a new source of potential incompleteness for the KB, and thus we will want to be able to ask if the KB has all instances of this predicate:

$$(\exists x)[\textit{Known-teacher}(x) \land \neg \textit{Known-Known-teacher}(x)].$$

This, of course, leads to an infinite regression of predicates, none of which are very relevant to the application area. In a nutshell, "*Known-teacher*" should not be a predicate for the simple reason that its truth or falsity does not depend on the domain being modelled but on the model, the KB itself.

The solution, then, is to leave the KB as is but to extend the query language in order to allow questions that refer to the current state of knowledge of the KB. The query language I propose, called KL, contains all of FOL, and in addition has formulas of the form $K\alpha$ read as

The KB knows that α.

This leaves us with a first order KB while still allowing us to query the KB regarding its incompleteness. In particular, we have a new form of query evaluation

$$KB \Vdash \alpha$$

where $\Vdash$ is some (as yet to be specified) provability relation and α is any formula of KL possibly containing K's.

For example, to find out whether the KB had a incomplete list of teachers, we must find out whether

$$KB \Vdash (\exists x)[\text{Teacher}(x) \land \neg K[\text{Teacher}(x)]].$$

Similarly, while the query

$$(\exists x)\text{Teacher}(x)$$

can be used to find out whether there are any teachers, the query

$$(\exists x)K[\text{Teacher}(x)]$$

asks whether the KB knows who any of them are. To be able to define the $\Vdash$ relation, we must first look at the semantics of the language KL itself.

4. The Language KL

The query language KL has the same formation rules as FOL but also includes the rule

$$\text{If } \alpha \in \text{KL then K } \alpha \in \text{KL.}$$

Consequently there are two kinds of formulas in KL. The first, like

$$p(c) \wedge (\exists x)q(x)$$

will be true or false depending only on the interpretation of the constant and predicate symbols. The second, like

$$K[p(c) \wedge (\exists x)q(x)]$$

will be true or false depending only on the KB and on what is known or not known. I will call the latter formulas *pure*. There are also formulas in KL that are mixtures of the two types and whose truth value depends both on the interpretation and the KB. KL also allows for *meta-knowledge* in formulas such as

$$K[(\exists x)Kp(x)]$$

which talk about the KB's knowledge of its own knowledge.

The semantic interpretation of a closed formula of KL will depend on both a world description (or interpretation, in the Tarskian sense) and a description of a KB. In general, a KB can be viewed as a partial description of a world and can thus be characterized by a set of world descriptions. If we characterize a KB by a set of world descriptions *m*, we have

> K α is true in the KB described by *m* iff α is true in every world described by an element of *m*.

To make all this more precise, first note that because of the correspondence between constants and entities in the domain, a world description need only assign a truth value to the atomic sentences in order to determine the truth value of all sentences of FOL. Thus, we can define

$$\text{the set of world descriptions, } \mathcal{W} = [\text{ATOMS} \rightarrow \text{T,F}].$$

A KB description is, then, just a nonempty set of world descriptions

$$\text{the set of KB descriptions, } \mathcal{M} = \{\, m \subseteq \mathcal{W} \mid m \neq \emptyset \}.$$

The interpretation of any closed formula α is provided by the function Φ.

$$\Phi \in [\mathrm{KL} \times \mathcal{W} \times \mathcal{M} \rightarrow \{T,F\}] \text{ is defined by}$$
$$\Phi(\alpha,w,m) = w(\alpha) \text{ when } \alpha \text{ is atomic.}$$
$$\Phi(\neg\alpha,w,m) = T \text{ iff } \Phi(\alpha,w,m) = F.$$
$$\Phi([\alpha \vee \beta],w,m) = T \text{ iff } \Phi(\alpha,w,m) = T \text{ or } \Phi(\beta,w,m) = T.$$
$$\Phi((\exists x)\,\alpha,w,m) = T \text{ iff for some } c,\ \Phi(\alpha_c^x,w,m) = T.$$
$$\Phi(K\alpha,w,m) = T \text{ iff for every } w' \in m,\ \Phi(\alpha,w',m) = T.$$

A formula is *valid* when it is true on every world and KB description. In the case where α is pure, I will use $\Phi(\alpha,m)$ to refer to the truth value of α on the KB described by m.

Turning now to the proof theory for KL, since the language includes FOL as a subset, we will need the two inference rules of FOL: *modus ponens* and *universal generalization.* In fact, these are the only two rules required. As for axioms, we need the axioms of FOL in order to guarantee that negation, implication, and quantification behave properly.

To account for the K operator, we have to realize that it behaves like a provability relation because something is known when it "follows" from what is available in the KB. We will, therefore, insist that the axioms of FOL are known and that the KB is able to perform modus ponens and universal generalization[2] based on what is known. This might be called the assumption of *competence.* As for meta-knowledge, it is convenient to assume that the KB knows the correct truth value of any pure formula. In other words, there is never any reason to tell the KB about itself nor is there any reason to doubt what the KB knows about itself. No matter how incomplete or inaccurate a KB can be about the world, it is assumed to be the final authority on itself. This might be called the assumption of *closure.* Note that this assumption applies only to pure sentences. Fortunately, these can be given a syntactic characterization:

> A formula is *pure* iff every occurrence of a predicate symbol appears within the scope of a K operator.

We therefore have the following axiomatization of the language KL:

---

[2] The actual form of universal generalization needed here is somewhat special since, among other things, we have to be able to infer a universal sentence from a (possibly infinite) set of positive instances. A finitary version of this inference rule that has this property is presented in [LEVE81a].

Axiom Schemata

- The axioms of FOL
- $K\alpha$ where α is an axiom of FOL
- $K(\alpha \supset \beta) \supset (K\alpha \supset K\beta)$
- $(\forall x)K\alpha \supset K(\forall x)\alpha$
- $\alpha \equiv K\alpha$ where α is pure

Rules of Inference

- Modus ponens and Universal Generalization

If we let $\vdash$ denote the provability relation for this axiomatization, then the key result here is that the proof theory is both sound and complete with respect to the semantics given earlier:

Proposition 1. $\vdash \alpha$ *iff* α *is valid.*

Given this equivalence between the proof theory and the semantics, certain properties of KL are easily verified. For example, we have

$$\vdash K\alpha \supset \neg K\neg\alpha$$

which says that a KB is always *consistent* since it contains no contradictory information. This is easily verified by noting that no element of $\mathcal{M}$ is empty. One thing to notice is that by the closure property, we have that for any pure α

$$\vdash K\alpha \supset \alpha.$$

This is, however, not the case for arbitrary α since, for example, the set

$$\{\neg p(c), Kp(c)\}$$

is satisfiable and, hence, logically consistent. This is a situation in which the KB is behaving properly but just happens to be mistaken about the world. So, in some sense, the K operator should be read as "believe" rather than "know." On the other hand, the kind of belief involved here is very special since a KB will always think it is dealing with knowledge because

$$\vdash K(K\alpha \supset \alpha)$$

for any formula α. In other words, a KB will always believe that what it believes is true. So there is an aspect of *commitment* to what is believed because a KB will never believe it has mistaken beliefs.

5. Queries Revisited

Having examined the semantics and proof theory of KL, we are still faced with the problem of specifying what is meant by

$$\text{KB} \Vdash \alpha \text{ where KB} \subseteq \text{FOL and } \alpha \in \text{KL}.$$

The idea here is that this should mean

If all I know is what is in KB, then I know that α.

The tricky part is characterizing the "all" in the above sentence, what Konolige calls "circumscriptive ignorance" [KONO82]. Semantically, this means that $K\alpha$ is true with respect to the knowledge base that has the *least amount* of world knowledge consistent with knowing everything in KB. Thinking of a knowledge base as described by a set of world descriptions, we want the least amount of world knowledge and, thus, the largest possible set.

$$\text{Let } \mathcal{M}(\text{KB}) = \{w \mid w \text{ satisfies the KB}\}.$$

Any knowledge base that knows what is in the KB is described by a subset of $\mathcal{M}$ (KB) and therefore has a more refined view of the world. For example, if the KB is empty then $\mathcal{M}$ (KB) is the set of all possible world descriptions. This suggests how query evaluation can be defined semantically:

$$\text{Let KB} \Vdash \alpha \text{ iff } \Phi(K\alpha, \mathcal{M}(\text{KB})) = T.$$

Thus, the answer to a question is *yes* exactly when the question is known to be true in $\mathcal{M}$ (KB). For example, if

$$\text{KB1} = \{\text{Teacher(john)}\}$$

then

$$\begin{aligned}
&\text{KB1} \Vdash \text{Teacher(john)},\\
&\text{KB1} \Vdash \neg K[\text{Student(bill)}],\\
&\text{KB1} \Vdash (\exists x)K[\text{Teacher}(x)],\\
&\text{KB1} \Vdash K \neg K[\text{Student(bill)}],\\
&\text{KB1} \Vdash \neg K[(\exists x)[\text{Teacher}(x) \wedge \neg K\, \text{Teacher}(x)]].
\end{aligned}$$

The last statement above confirms that KB1 knows that it does not know whether or not it has a complete list of teachers.

Note that for any pure α we have that either

$$\text{KB} \Vdash \alpha \text{ or KB} \Vdash \neg\alpha$$

since the KB has complete knowledge about itself. Also worth noting is that $\Vdash$ is a nonmonotonic operator because it is not the case that

$$\text{KB1} + \text{Student(bill)} \Vdash \neg\, \text{K[Student(bill)]}.$$

However, unlike a fully general nonmonotonic operator like the one presented in [MD78] or [MCDE80], the $\Vdash$ operator here has been given a simple and natural semantic characterization. Below I will present a theoretic proof analogue of this operator and claim a soundness and completeness type result, but before doing so it is necessary to examine how KL can be used to specify a KB.

6. The Knowledge Base Definition Language

Since, for incomplete KBs, the CWA is not used uniformly, it would be extremely convenient to be able to tell the KB when (if ever) the assumption could be used for special cases. Conversely, we should also be able to tell the KB when the CWA cannot be used. If we let

$$\pi = (\exists x)[\text{Teacher}(x) \wedge \neg \text{KTeacher}(x)]$$

then $\neg\pi$ states that if someone is not currently known to be a teacher then he is not a teacher. So $\neg\pi$ is the CWA relativized to teachers, while π itself is a statement that this assumption cannot be used (because there are teachers other than the currently known ones). The question immediately arises as to whether or not we can add formulas such as π or $\neg\pi$ to a KB, thus generalizing a KB to be any consistent set of formulas from KL instead of FOL.

There are a number of problems with this generalization, but I will address only one that relates to the formula π. The idea here is that we would start off with a KB such as KB1 defined earlier. Since KB1 does not know whether or not John is the only teacher, it is not the case that either

$$\text{KB1} \Vdash \pi \text{ or KB1} \Vdash \neg\pi.$$

Suppose we consider telling it that it does not have all the teachers and get

$$\text{KB2} = \text{KB1} + \pi$$

If we now want to tell the KB that George is a teacher, we get

$$\text{KB3} = \text{KB2} + \text{Teacher(george)}$$

The problem here is that KB3 still contains π and, consequently, still thinks it is missing a teacher. In fact, no matter how many teachers we tell the KB about, it will still think it is missing at least one. Moreover, if we try to tell it that it finally has all of them by adding $\neg\pi$, then we arrive at an inconsistent KB since it also contains π.

What *should* have happened here is somewhat different. Once we arrived at KB2, the KB should know that it is missing a teacher and hence believe π. However, once a new teacher is added to the KB producing KB3, the KB has no way to decide if this is the last teacher it was missing. So it should be the case (as with KB1) that neither

$$\text{KB3} \Vdash \pi \text{ nor } \text{KB3} \Vdash \neg\pi.$$

In other words, after the introduction of George, the KB should no longer know whether or not it has all the teachers. In fact, the knowledge it had as KB2 is lost when it becomes KB3.

This is a strange kind of nonmonotonicity. The usual symptom of a nonmonotonic logic is that the addition of a new axiom invalidates a previous *theorem*. In our case, the addition of the new axiom invalidated a previous *axiom*. The curious puzzle here is that there is no "belief revision" going on in the sense of a realization that an axiom was incorrectly added to the KB. Similarly, there is no admission of the world having changed in the sense of someone becoming or ceasing to be a teacher. In fact, the only change that has taken place is a change in what is known about the world. But this is enough since π does make reference to the *current* state of the KB. So without admitting that the world has changed or that some previous statement about the world needs revision, we can still maintain that the truth value of π can change by noting that the state of the KB has changed. Thus, π cannot be part of the KB since the state of knowledge it refers to disappears as information is acquired.

The solution to the problem of the addition of π to a KB is, therefore, to treat the formula as ordinary world knowledge where the K operator is used to refer to the current state of the KB. This is only natural since a KB is assumed to have complete knowledge of itself. Consequently, any mention of what is known in a new piece of information must be "referential" and not "attributive." Thus, the addition to the KB must be understood by first resolving these references. In other words, the solution to the problem is not to prohibit additions like π, but rather to allow π in the KB definition language but not the KB itself. For example, KB2 now becomes

$$\text{KB2} = \text{KB1} + \pi = \{\text{Teacher(john)}, (\exists x)[\text{Teacher}(x) \wedge (x \neq \text{john})]\}$$

where we have replaced the open formula

$$\text{K[Teacher}(x)]$$

by a first order formula that resolves this reference with respect to KB1:

$$(x = \text{john}).$$

This produces the property that

$$\text{KB2} \Vdash \pi$$

and neither

$$\text{KB3} \Vdash \pi \text{ nor } \text{KB3} \Vdash \neg \pi$$

as desired. Similarly, if we start with KB1 and wish to tell it that it has all the teachers, then we add

$$(\forall x)[\neg K[\text{Teacher}(x)] \supset \neg \text{Teacher}(x)]$$

which for KB1 resolves to

$$(\forall x)[\text{Teacher}(x) \supset (x = \text{john})]$$

again a formula of FOL. Note that if we start with a KB that is missing a teacher such as

$$\{\text{Teacher}(\text{john}), [\text{Teacher}(\text{george}) \vee \text{Teacher}(\text{dan})]\}$$

then the attempt to add the CWA for teachers will correctly result in an inconsistency.

The solution I have proposed above presupposes that there always will be a formula of FOL that can be used to resolve any reference to what is known. It is worth noting that this cannot be done independently of a KB since there is no formula α of FOL such that

$$\vdash K\pi \equiv K\alpha.$$

In this sense, the language KL is more expressive than FOL. Of course, all we really need is a formula for each KB and not a formula that works for every KB. Fortunately, if we assume the availability of an equality predicate and restrict ourselves to *finite* KBs, this can always be done.

Proposition 2. *Assume* $KB \subseteq FOL$ *finite and* $\alpha(x_1, \ldots x_k) \in KL$. *There exists a formula* $/\alpha/ \in FOL$ *(with equality) such that* $KB \Vdash (\forall x_1) \ldots (\forall x_k) [K\alpha \equiv K/\alpha/]$.

The method of allowing all of KL to specify a KB is thus to let

$$\text{KB} + \alpha = \text{KB} \cup \{/\alpha/\} \text{ for any } \alpha \in \text{KL}.$$

Viewed more semantically in terms of world descriptions, we have that

$$\mathcal{M}(\text{KB}) \cap \{w \mid \Phi(\alpha, w, \mathcal{M}(\text{KB})) = T\} = \mathcal{M}(\text{KB} \cup \{/\alpha/\}).$$

For any formula $\alpha \in KL$, a formula $/\alpha/ \in FOL$ that satisfies the above proposition can be defined by

$$/\alpha/ = \alpha \text{ when } \alpha \in \text{FOL},\ /\neg\alpha/ = \neg/\alpha/,\ /(\alpha \supset \beta)/ = (/\alpha/ \supset /\beta/)$$
$$/(\forall x)\alpha/ = (\forall x)/\alpha/ \text{ and } /K\alpha/ = \text{RESOLVE}\ [/\alpha/].$$

RESOLVE[α] = **If** α *has no free variables*
then if KB $\vdash \alpha$ **then** $(\forall x)(x = x)$ **else** $\neg\ (\forall x)(x = x)$
else /* *Assume x is a free variable of* α and
$c_1, \ldots, c_k$ *are all the constants in* α or KB */
$[(x = c_1 \wedge \text{RESOLVE}[\alpha^x_{c_1}]) \vee \ldots \vee (x = c_k \wedge \text{RESOLVE}[\alpha^x_{c_k}]) \vee$
/* *Assume c is any constant not in* α or KB */
$(x \neq c_1 \wedge \ldots \wedge x \neq c_k \wedge \text{RESOLVE}[\alpha^x_c]^c_x)]$

The point of this definition is to show a formula that works but obviously not the *shortest* one. Note that although the function RESOLVE is not recursive, it is strictly proof-theoretic. Moreover, it can be shown that

Proposition 3. *KB* $\Vdash \alpha$ *iff KB* $\vdash /\alpha/$ *for any* $\alpha \in KL$.

In other words, for any query α in KL, the answer is *yes* exactly when $/\alpha/$ is a (first order) consequence of the sentences in the KB. This defines a purely first order syntactic version of query evaluation that is exactly equivalent to the semantic one defined earlier. Of course, the proof theory is not axiomatic but this is to be expected given that

$$\{\alpha \in KL \mid \Vdash \alpha\}$$

is not recursively enumerable. So, to summarize, although the interaction with a first order KB should allow the language KL to be used, this interaction can be understood in first order terms when the KB is finite.

7. Incompleteness in Database Management

It is perhaps worthwhile at this stage to compare my approach to three other proposals in Database Management that have made special provisions for dealing with incompleteness: the relational model as presented in [CODD79] and [VASS80], the TAXIS model [MW80], and the model advocated by Lipski [LIPS78]. While the three models attempt to deal with a wide variety of issues, my only concern here is the extent to which incompleteness is allowed in the information system (KB, database).

A common feature of the three models is the ability to represent information such as

Mary's supervisor is *unknown.*

over and above specific information like

Bill's supervisor is George.

The supervisor of Mary, in this case, is represented by a *null value* [CODD70] indicating that its exact value is not (yet) known. The intent appears to be the same as knowing that

$$(\exists x)\ \mathrm{Supervisor}\ (x,\mathrm{mary})$$

where, perhaps, it is also known that every student has at most one supervisor:

$$(\forall x)\ (\exists y)\ (\forall z)\ [\mathrm{Student}(x) \wedge \mathrm{Supervisor}(z,x) \supset y{=}z].$$

A serious limitation of the relational and TAXIS models is that they do not allow information about a null value to be accumulated. If Mary's supervisor is not known, all that can be known about it is that it falls within the domain of supervisors. For example, an assertion such as

$$[\mathrm{Supervisor}(\mathrm{joe},\mathrm{mary}) \vee \mathrm{Supervisor}(\mathrm{jim},\mathrm{mary})]$$

which would severely constrain Mary's (unknown) supervisor, cannot be represented even though each disjunct can be. Similarly, a very weak constraint on the null value, such as

$$\neg\ \mathrm{Supervisor}(\mathrm{george},\mathrm{mary})$$

cannot be handled by either data model.

This particular limitation is not shared by Lipski's model since it allows one to specify a set for each attribute (*e.g.,* supervisor) of each object (*e.g.,* Mary). If the set contains one element, then the value is known; otherwise, the value is only known to be a member of the set. However, the Lipski model is limited in other ways. Like the TAXIS model, it is "object-centered" because everything that is known about the world is expressed in terms of properties of specific objects. There is, consequently, no provision for uncertainty regarding which object is being characterized. For example, statements such as

$$[\mathrm{Supervisor}(\mathrm{joe},\mathrm{mary}) \vee \mathrm{Supervisor}(\mathrm{joe},\mathrm{john})]$$

or

$$(\exists x)[\mathrm{Student}(x) \wedge \mathrm{Supervisor}(\mathrm{jim},x)]$$

cannot be accommodated since, in each case, the student claiming to have a certain supervisor is not known.

Apart from their limited ability to relate null values to known values, none of the three models allow null values to be related to each other. Suppose, for example, that the supervisor of Mary is not known. There is no way of representing the fact that John's (unknown) supervisor is distinct from Mary's,

$$(\exists x)[\text{Supervisor}(x,\text{john}) \wedge \neg\, \text{Supervisor}(x,\text{mary})]$$

or that Bill's is identical to hers,

$$(\exists x)[\text{Supervisor}(x,\text{bill}) \wedge \text{Supervisor}(x,\text{mary})].$$

The implicit assumption is that null values *independently* represent known values. This assumption, when applied to unknown truth values, leads to rules such as

If α and β are *unknown*, then so is $(\alpha \vee \beta)$.

which is quite inappropriate when β is the negation of α .

The limitations of the relational, TAXIS and Lipski models are nicely summarized in a passage from [MOOR80] (p. 137):

> Any system adequate for representing the knowledge of an intelligent being must surely be able to:
>
> - Say that something has a certain property without saying what thing has that property.
> - Say that everything in a certain class has a certain property without saying what everything in that class is.
> - Say that at least one of two statements is true without saying which statement is true.
> - Explicitly say that something is false.
> - Either settle or leave open to doubt whether two nonidentical expressions name the same object.

Note that I made reference to all but the second requirement in my examination of the three models.[3] The crucial point here, however, is that *all* these requirements are based on provisions for various kinds of incompleteness. As the chapter by Reiter points out, the incompleteness admitted by the three models can be accommodated within a FOL framework. In other words, the reason for wanting the expressive

[3] That requirement will be dealt with in the next section.

power of FOL is not to be able to represent detailed knowledge of a complex domain, but rather to be able to represent very shallow and incomplete knowledge of the domain. It is important to realize that the choice is not so much between a "logical" or a "nonlogical" representation language, but more a decision about what kinds of incompleteness will be tolerated.

My approach differs from these three data models primarily because it allows a much wider variety of incompleteness. The main argument of this chapter is that, given this incompleteness, a more expressive language is required to interact with the KB. It should be noted that Lipski does allow his query language to distinguish between, in my terminology,

$$\text{Supervisor}(\text{joe}, x) \text{ and } K[\text{Supervisor}(\text{joe}, x)].$$

The fact that the usefulness of this is questioned in [VASS80] is perhaps explained by the limited forms of incompleteness under consideration. It must be remembered, of course, that the concerns that gave rise to these limitations may be perfectly valid from a database viewpoint (even if they do not coincide with those of knowledge based systems).

8. Incompleteness in Knowledge Representation

Arguments presented in the last section should not be taken to imply that representation languages in Artificial Intelligence do not share the limitations of those in Database Management. Indeed, the "nonlogical" representation schemes (such as KL-ONE [BRAC76], PSN [LM79], NETL [FAHL79], or KRL [BW77]) appear to suffer from the same assertional poverty induced by object centeredness. For these languages and others, reasoning depends upon having a close correspondence between the objects and relationships in the domain and their representational counterparts in a system. In this section, I will briefly suggest a possible unification of the "logical" and "nonlogical" approaches to Knowledge Representation that preserves the advantages of each by completely separating their concerns. The suggestion should be taken as preliminary and in need of much research.[4]

Suppose we are interested in using a predicate "FlyingBird." We would certainly want any KB using this predicate to know that

$$\text{A. } (\forall x)[\text{FlyingBird}(x) \equiv \text{Bird}(x) \wedge \text{Fly}(x)].$$

[4] See also [BL82] for a further refinement of these ideas.

If we are interested in modelling a world where penguins are the only birds that do not fly, we should be able to tell the KB that

B. $(\forall x)[\text{FlyingBird}(x) \equiv \text{Bird}(x) \wedge \neg\, \text{Penguin}(x)]$.

Note that because of possible incomplete knowledge about the world, we should be able to assert (B) and intend it to apply to *all* birds (in that world) and not just the currently known ones. This is again the kind of partial knowledge usually not representable in an object-centered scheme. The main point here, however, is that the import of (B) is quite distinct from that of (A) even though the KB should know that both are true. Specifically, (B) need not be true in a different world, and thus its truth conveys information about the world. The intent of (A), on the other hand, is that it cannot fail to be true and thus conveys no information about the world. If these two statements are to coexist in a KB, they must be distinguished somehow. An important characteristic of both (A) and (B) is that the predicate "FlyingBird" can, in some sense, be eliminated.

A′. $(\forall x)[\text{Bird}(x) \wedge \text{Fly}(x) \equiv \text{Bird}(x) \wedge \text{Fly}(x)]$

B′. $(\forall x)[\text{Bird}(x) \wedge \text{Fly}(x) \equiv \text{Bird}(x) \wedge \neg\, \text{Penguin}(x)]$.

Once again, (B′) but not (A′) could be false and says something about the world. Moreover, (B′) appears to say the same thing about the world that (B) does. But if (A′) says the same thing as (A), then (A) is not really asserting anything at all.

My claim here is that (A) is best understood not as an assertion (about some world) but as an addition to terminology used when talking about a world. In other words, (A) is best paraphrased by something like

D. $\text{FlyingBird} \leftarrow \lambda\, x.\ [\text{Bird}(x) \wedge \text{Fly}(x)]$

which defines a predicate in terms of two other predicates. The question of whether (D) is true or false simply does not arise since it is not the kind of linguistic expression that can take a truth value. If we insist on talking about the truth value of (A), we can take the position that it is true in the same way (A′) is true—vacuously and by virtue of the way the language is intended to be used. In its present form, (A) is quite misleading, however, because it looks like (B). Following a distinction made in [WOOD75], I will call statements like (A) that introduce terminology *definitional,* and those like (B) that convey information about a world *assertional.*

Why should a representation scheme that is interested only in expressing knowledge about a world have to deal with statements that carry no information? The answer, I believe, is that definitional mechanisms facilitate the interaction between a user (man or machine) and the KB. The addition of terminology is not a matter of truth or falsity but a matter of convenience to the user. In particular, the definitional mechanisms of a language should help structure and should organize what eventually will be said or asked about the world.

In the previous section, I argued that a "logical" language like KL was essential to allow sufficiently weak assertions to be made about a world. Indeed, the traditional concern of logical languages is precisely to provide adequate assertional facilities of various kinds. The "nonlogical" representation languages (and most semantic data models), on the other hand, while weak at the assertional level, do attempt to provide adequate facilities for organizing and structuring the set of terms (predicates, types, classes, concepts, units) being used. For example, the ubiquitous IS-A hierarchy is perhaps best viewed as a mechanism for introducing new terms by specializing or generalizing existing ones rather than as a facility for asserting restricted universal generalizations. The goal need not (and should not) be to supplant or extend the assertional features of the language, any more than the abstraction mechanisms of high level programming languages extend the computational power of lower level languages. Conversely, as Israel and Brachman argue in their chapter, the fact that definitions can be explained away, to a certain extent, at the assertional level cannot be taken as an argument that they are not needed. The assertional and definitional levels each has its own purpose, methodology, and standards of adequacy. It is this separation of concerns that might permit the "logical" and "nonlogical" approaches to be profitably unified within a single representation scheme.

The research reported here deals only with the expressive adequacy of the assertional level but could also have repercussions at the definitional level. For example, new terms are often required for which no necessary and sufficient conditions seem appropriate (*e.g.,* natural kinds). These are sometimes best characterized at the definitional level in terms of prototypes and defaults. In this case, the definitional level has to be able to refer not only to the the world being modelled, but to the state of the KB as well. This, of course, is the original motivation behind my language KL. At any rate, the best way to proceed in this regard remains to be seen.

9. Conclusion

In this chapter, I have considered from a formal standpoint the problem of interacting with an incomplete KB. The motivation behind the research is that, to effectively deal with partial knowledge, a system first must be able to determine the exact limits of what is known. This, in turn, places certain requirements on the language used to interact with a KB. In particular, the language has to be able to refer to the state of the KB as well as to the state of the application domain.

To this effect, I proposed a language KL for interacting with a first order KB and presented a proof theory and semantics which were direct extensions of their FOL counterparts. KL was then applied to query evaluation and I showed that this required a nonmonotonic operator. Semantic and syntactic interpretations of this operator were provided. Finally, KL was applied to KB definition and I demonstrated why this required reducing KL into the language of the KB, FOL. In fact, the net result was that the KB remained first order, but that interaction with it took place in a more expressive language.

Apart from the more practical implications of this work, there remain open questions even within the formal framework. I have not mentioned, for example, what impact the presence of an equality relation or nonconstant terms would have on KL. Also, a method of handling defaults (and exceptions) is a reasonable goal granted that the framework allows one to determine where its application is needed. In summary, the framework provides not only a formal standard against which to measure representation languages, but also a basis for further exploration.

10. References

[BW77] [BRAC76] [BL82] [CODD70] [CODD79] [CWAM75] [FAHL79] [GM78] [HINT62] [KONO82] [LEVE81a] [LEVE81b] [LM79] [LIPS78] [MCCA80] [MSHI78] [MCDE80] [MD78] [MOOR81] [MW80] [REIT78b] [REIT78c] [REIT80] [VASS80] [WOOD75]

Discussion

This chapter presents a very general account of incomplete knowledge, and it should be of interest to knowledge base and database system designers. The account applies to systems whose knowledge base can be expressed in terms of a set of first order formulas. The range of things that can be expressed in this way goes well beyond current Database practice (see also the chapter by Reiter). One way to distinguish between a database and a knowledge base is in terms of the things it is perceived to contain. A (relational) database contains tuples and a query such as: "Is there a tuple e in the EMPLOYEE relation such that e.name = bill will always return true or false." With a knowledge base, on the other hand, one is interpreting the data and reasoning about them so that the answer to a query may be neither true nor false.

The Closed World Assumption (CWA)

All forms of the CWA can be expressed in English as "Anything not known to be true is false." The divergence between different accounts arises in the formulation of "not known." An early proposal that links knowledge (on the part of the database) to provability has problems in dealing with disjunction and null values (see Section 6 of the chapter by Reiter). A different formulation is proposed in this chapter. Another very general formulation called circumscription is due to McCarthy.

The K Operator

In cases where the CWA is not (or cannot be) used, a new kind of query suggests itself. Suppose that we are dealing with a knowledge base about teachers which knows only that John and Bill are teachers. A possible query to this knowledge base is:

1. "Is there a teacher who is not known to the knowledge base"

or, alternatively for this particular knowledge base,

2. "Is there a teacher who isn't John or Bill"

Note that this query is about the knowledge base, not the world. The second formulation of the query is clearly unsatisfactory when there are many known teachers. To represent "known" in the first formulation we might consider introducing a predicate Known-teacher so (1) is reformulated as:

3. "Is there someone who is a teacher and not a known-teacher"

The problem now is that the representation treats the predicates Teacher and Known-teacher as distinct even though they are intimately related. Also, this solution creates a need for other predicates such as Known-known-teacher, *etc.*, for queries that involve nested knowledge statements. Instead of these unsatisfactory solutions, the chapter proposes a *modal operator* K such that K&& is read as:

"The knowledge base knows that &&"

In providing a formal semantics for K we view the knowledge base as an (incomplete) description that fits a set of possible worlds. To evaluate a query such as "K&&" amounts to checking that && is satisfied by all possible worlds described by the knowledge base.

The framework presented in the chapter allows only first order formulas in the knowledge base, although updates and queries are expressed in a modal language, called KL, which includes the operator K. A provability theory has been developed for this language and has been shown to be sound and complete. Without the K operator the theory reduces to first order provability theory.

It is important to note that the designer of the knowledge base does not specify explicitly possible worlds. Instead he tells the knowledge base that, for example, a sentence, FOO, is true, and as a result the set of possible worlds described by the knowledge base is reduced by leaving out worlds that do not satisfy FOO.

Deductive Capabilities

The proposed framework is mainly intended as a way of correctly *understanding incomplete knowledge bases in general and not as a method of implementing specific application problems.* There are, for example, a family of puzzles that deal with constraint satisfaction (given an apparently incomplete description of the solution). We might be given separate lists of first and last names, and also information about where people with these names reside, as well as other information such as: "Smith and Jones drink together," "Bill and Paul live in different cities," *etc.* The problem is to find correspondences between first and last names. However, the use of KL to solve such problems would be somewhat of an overkill. These problems are finite and it is possible to solve them by simply making a table and trying out possibilities until one is found that satisfies all constraints. It should also be noted that use of the framework demands a full-fledged first order theorem prover, which means that the process of finding a solution may be slow and inefficient when compared with other possibilities for solving the problem.

In trying to generate a solution to such puzzles or answers to arbitrary queries expressed in KL, the theorem prover will not necessarily have to replace existential quantifiers with null values.

Concluding Remarks

Once you raise the question of incompleteness for a wide variety of knowledge bases, it is natural to ask such questions as: What is the logic of the situations that may arise? What can be proven about these situations? What would you want to be able to tell and not to tell about the knowledge base? What should updates look like and what should queries return. These are the issues dealt with in this chapter.

In his chapter, Reiter builds (from the bottom up) a closed world and the conditions it must satisfy. This chapter, on the other hand, lays down criteria once and for all in a broad brush stroke for dealing with incomplete knowledge. The broad brush approach exposes technical problems for a very general class of incomplete knowledge bases.

8
Towards a Logical Reconstruction of Relational Database Theory

Raymond Reiter
University of British Columbia

ABSTRACT *Insofar as database theory can be said to owe a debt to logic, the currency on loan is* model theoretic *in the sense that a database can be viewed as a particular kind of first order interpretation, and query evaluation is a process of truth functional evaluation of first order formulae with respect to this interpretation. It is this model theoretic paradigm which leads, for example, to many valued propositional logics for databases with null values.*

In this chapter I argue that a proof theoretic *view of databases is possible, and indeed much more fruitful. Specifically, I show how relational databases can be seen as special theories of first order logic, namely theories incorporating the following assumptions:*

1. *The domain closure assumption. The individuals occurring in the database are all and only the existing individuals.*

2. *The unique name assumption. Individuals with distinct names are distinct.*

3. *The closed world assumption. The only possible instances of a relation are those implied by the database.*

It will follow that a proof theoretic paradigm for relational databases provides a correct treatment of:

1. *Query evaluation for databases that have incomplete information, including null values.*

2. *Integrity constraints and their enforcement.*

3. *Conceptual modelling and the extension of the relational model to incorporate more real world semantics.*

1. Introduction

There is in our midst a small group of researchers whose devotion to logic and databases[1] is viewed with some perplexity by the majority of database theoreticians and practitioners. Their literature is peppered with obscure logical notation and theorems. As befits logicians, they claim privileged sovereignty over the Truth about databases. Can this cabal possibly be saying anything of interest to the database community?

Of course, everyone is at least dimly conscious of some logical debt owed by database theory, if only because the relational calculus relies on a first order language. What other outstanding logical loans are generally acknowledged? Well, a relational calculus query is a first order formula that is *evaluated* with respect to a database of facts. Since logic dictates that formulae have values (truth values) only with respect to *interpretations,* a database is commonly viewed as just that — a first order interpretation in the standard Tarskian sense. The value of a relational calculus query is determined by those instances of its free variables that make the query true with respect to the interpretation specified by the underlying database. This view of a database as a first order interpretation also neatly accommodates the concept of an integrity constraint. Insofar as one can view an integrity constraint as a first order formula, a database can be said to satisfy this constraint iff the constraint is true with respect to the database as interpretation. That is, given a set of integrity constraints, one cannot admit just any interpretation as a correct representation of one's domain of application; the interpretation must be a *model* (again, in the standard Tarskian sense) of the integrity constraints.

I think it is fair to say that, as far as database theoreticians conceive the field in logical terms, it is this *model theoretic* point of view that prevails. A database is a model of some set of integrity constraints, and a query is some formula to be evaluated with respect to this model. Now I invite you to survey the literature of the database logicians. You will, for the most part, find little mention of models and interpretations. Poor Tarski gets short shift here. And the relational algebra at best is granted footnote status. Instead, you will find most theoretical constructs couched in proof theoretic terms. A database is viewed as a set of first order formulae, not as a model. Queries are formulae to be proven, given the database as premises. Satisfaction of integrity constraints is defined in terms of consistency.[2] Considerable

---

[1] See, for example, [GM78].

[2] I shall provide a different definition in this chapter, but one which nevertheless is proof theoretic.

energy is invested in obtaining algorithms for efficiently finding proofs. In short, the logicians adopt a *proof theoretic* view of database theory.

What, then, is the preferred formal perspective on database theory—the model theoretic or the proof theoretic? Without a careful analysis, of course, one cannot say. This chapter presumes to provide such an analysis. My conclusion will be that both paradigms are reconcilable, but that the proof theoretic view is richer and more fruitful. More precisely, I shall show how, when given a model theoretic database *DB* *without null values*, one can transform *DB* into a suitable set of first order axioms, such that the resulting first order theory provides a proof theoretic characterization of query evaluation and integrity constraints. By itself this would not be a very exciting result. Curious perhaps, but not exciting. The idea bears fruit only in its capacity for generalization. For now that databases can be perceived as special kinds of first order theories, one can generalize these theories in order to provide answers to a variety of outstanding questions about databases:

1. How can the relational model be extended in order to incorporate more real world knowledge?
2. A number of null values have been proposed. What is their semantics?
3. What really are databases that have incomplete information?
4. What is the correct notion of an answer to a query in the presence of semantically rich databases such as those incorporating the features mentioned in 1-3 above?
5. For such semantically rich databases, what is an appropriate notion of an integrity constraint and what does it mean to satisfy a constraint?

My purpose in this chapter is to show how answers to these questions emerge in a very natural way from a proof theoretic characterization of database theory.

2. Databases and Logic: The Model Theoretic Perspective

This section outlines in some detail what I take to be the model theoretic paradigm in relational database theory.[3] To that end we require some formal preliminaries.

---

[3] Many of the ideas of this section, in particular the concept of a database as a first order model of a set of integrity constraints, derive from [NG78]. In effect, Sections 2.1-2.3 below formalize this concept.

2.1 First Order Languages

A first order language F is specified by a pair $(\mathcal{A}, \mathcal{W})$ where $\mathcal{A}$ is an alphabet of symbols and $\mathcal{W}$ is a set of syntactically well formed expressions called well formed formulae constructed using the symbols of $\mathcal{A}$. The rules for constructing the formulae of $\mathcal{W}$ are the same for all first order languages F; only the alphabet $\mathcal{A}$ may vary. $\mathcal{A}$ must contain symbols of the following kind, and only such symbols:

Variables: $x, y, z, x_1, y_1, z_1, \ldots,$
There must be infinitely many of these.

Constants: a, b, c, part17, acme, . . . ,
There may be 0 or more of these, possibly infinitely many.

Predicates: P, Q, R, *SUPPLIES*, *EMPLOYEE*, . . . ,
There must be at least one of these, possibly infinitely many. With each is associated an integer $n \geqslant 0$, its *arity*, denoting the number of arguments it takes.

Punctuation Signs: (,) ,,

Logical Constants: $\supset$ (implies), $\wedge$ (and), $\vee$ (or), $\sim$ (not), $\equiv$ (iff).

Notice that function symbols are not included in this alphabet. I omit them because their introduction leads to severe difficulties for database theory [REIT78a] (pp. 173-175). Fortunately, they are not required for a formal treatment of current ideas in databases.

With such an alphabet $\mathcal{A}$ in hand, we can construct a set of syntactically well formed expressions, culminating in a definition of the set $\mathcal{W}$ of well formed formulae, as follows:

Terms

A variable or a constant of $\mathcal{A}$ is a *term*.

Atomic Formulae

If P is an n-ary predicate of $\mathcal{A}$ and $t_1, \ldots, t_n$ are terms, then $P(t_1, \ldots, t_n)$ is an *atomic formula*. $P(t_1, \ldots, t_n)$ is a *ground* atomic formula iff $t_1, \ldots, t_n$ are all constants.

Well Formed Formulae

$\mathcal{W}$ is the smallest set such that:

1. An atomic formula is a well formed formula (wff).
2. If W_1 and W_2 are wffs, so also are $(W_1 \wedge W_2)$, $(W_1 \vee W_2)$, $(W_1 \supset W_2)$, $(W_1 \equiv W_2)$, $\sim W_1$.
3. If x is a variable and W is a wff, then $(x)(W)$ and $(Ex)(W)$ are wffs. Here (x) is a *universal quantifier* and (Ex) an *existential quantifier.*

For the purposes of formally defining a relational database, we won't require arbitrary first order languages; a suitable proper subset of these will do. Accordingly, define a first order language $F = (\mathcal{A}, \mathcal{W})$ to be a *relational language* iff $\mathcal{A}$ has the following properties:

1. There are only finitely many constants in $\mathcal{A}$, but at least one.
2. There are only finitely many predicates in $\mathcal{A}$.
3. Among the predicates of $\mathcal{A}$ there is a distinguished binary predicate $=$ which will function for us as equality.
4. Among the predicates of $\mathcal{A}$ there is a distinguished subset, possibly empty, of unary predicates. Such unary predicates are called *simple types.* Not all unary predicates of $\mathcal{A}$ need be simple types. Such simple types, together with boolean combinations of simple types, will, in part, model the concept of the domain of a relation as it arises in standard database theory.

Given a relational language $R = (\mathcal{A}, \mathcal{W})$ we can define the set of *types* of R as the smallest set such that:

1. A simple type of $\mathcal{A}$ is a type.
2. If τ_1 and τ_2 are types, so also are $(\tau_1 \wedge \tau_2)$, $(\tau_1 \vee \tau_2)$, $\sim\tau_1$.

For a relational language $R = (\mathcal{A}, \mathcal{W})$ it is convenient to define appropriate syntactically sugared *abbreviations* for certain of the wffs of $\mathcal{W}$, as follows:

If τ is a type, then

$$(x/\tau)(W) \text{ abbreviates } (x)(\tau(x) \supset W)$$
$$(Ex/\tau)(W) \text{ abbreviates } (Ex)(\tau(x) \wedge W)$$

where

1. If τ is $(\tau_1 \wedge \tau_2)$ then $\tau(x)$ is $(\tau_1(x) \wedge \tau_2(x))$.
2. If τ is $(\tau_1 \vee \tau_2)$ then $\tau(x)$ is $(\tau_1(x) \vee \tau_2(x))$.
3. If τ is $\sim\tau_1$ then $\tau(x)$ is $\sim\tau_1(x)$.

Here $(x/\tau)(W)$ should be read as: "For all x which are τ, W is the case," and $(Ex/\tau)(W)$ as: "there is an x, which is a τ, such that W is the case." Thus these *type restricted quantifiers* are meant to restrict the possible x's to just those which belong to the class τ. Notice that quantifiers may be restricted only by types, not by arbitrary predicates.

Example 2.1

If *MALE, EMPLOYEE, MANAGER, SUPPLIER,* and *PART* are simple types, the following are type restricted quantified wffs;

$$(x/SUPPLIER)\ (Ey/PART)SUPPLIES(x,y)$$

which abbreviates the ordinary wff

$$(x)[SUPPLIER(x) \supset (Ey)(PART(y) \wedge SUPPLIES(x,y))]$$

i.e., "Every supplier supplies at least one part."

$$(x/MALE \wedge EMPLOYEE \wedge \sim MANAGER)[DEPT(x,13) \supset PENSION-PLAN(x)]$$

which abbreviates the ordinary wff

$$(x)[MALE(x) \wedge EMPLOYEE(x) \wedge \sim MANAGER(x) \supset [DEPT(x,13) \supset PENSION-PLAN(x)]]$$

i.e., "All male employees of department 13 who are not managers belong to the pension plan."

In this example I have omitted a lot of parentheses on the assumption (correct, I hope) that you all know what these formulae *mean.* I shall continue this practice whenever no ambiguity will result.

2.2 The Semantics of First Order Languages

The objective here is to assign a precise meaning to each of the symbols of the alphabet $\mathcal{A}$ of a first order language $F = (\mathcal{A}, \mathcal{W})$ and, using this assignment as a basis, to define the truth values of arbitrary wffs in $\mathcal{W}$ constructed from these symbols. The required definitions are by now standard (see, for example, [MEND64]).

An *interpretation I for the first order language* $F = (\mathcal{A}, \mathcal{W})$ is a triple (D,K,E) where

1. D is a non empty set, called the *domain* of I, over which the variables of $\mathcal{A}$ are meant to range.

2. K is mapping from the constants of $\mathcal{A}$ into D (*i.e.,* for each constant c, $K(c) \in D$).

3. E is a mapping from the predicates of $\mathcal{A}$ into sets of tuples of elements of D (*i.e.,* for each n-ary predicate symbol P, $E(P) \subseteq D^n$). $E(P)$ is called the *extension* of P in the interpretation I.

Example 2.2

Consider a relational language $R = (\mathcal{A}, \mathcal{W})$ where the only predicates and constants of $\mathcal{A}$ are the following:

Predicates: $TEACHER(\cdot)$, $COURSE(\cdot)$, $STUDENT(\cdot)$, $TEACH(\cdot,\cdot)$, $ENROLLED(\cdot,\cdot)$, $=(\cdot,\cdot)$.

Simple Types: $TEACHER(\cdot)$, $COURSE(\cdot)$, $STUDENT(\cdot)$.

Constants: A, B, C, a, b, c, d, $CS100$, $CS200$, $P100$, $P200$.

Then the following defines an interpretation for R, with domain $\{A, B, C, a, b, c, d, CS100, CS200, P100, P200\}$:

TEACHER	COURSE	STUDENT	TEACH	ENROLLED	=	
A	CS100	a	A CS100	a CS100	A	A
B	CS200	b	A CS200	a P100	B	B
C	P100	c	B P100	b CS100	C	C
	P200	d	C P200	c P100	a	a
				d CS200	b	b
				d P200	c	c
					d	d
					CS100	CS100
					CS200	CS200
					P100	P100
					P200	P200

Here the tables define the extensions of the predicate symbols *TEACHER*, *COURSE*, *etc.* Notice that, strictly speaking, the domain elements A, B, C, *etc.*, are *not* the same as the constant symbols A, B, C, *etc.*, which are part of our alphabet of symbols. In effect, I have chosen to name the domain elements by the constant symbols. So think of the domain elements in the tables as coloured red, and the constant symbols as coloured black. In subsequent examples I shall freely name domain elements by constant symbols.

Now given an interpretation $I = (D,K,E)$ for a first order language $F = (\mathcal{A}, \mathcal{W})$, let ρ be a mapping from the variables of $\mathcal{A}$ into D (*i.e.*, for each variable $x \in \mathcal{A}$, $\rho(x) \in D$). ρ is called an *environment* for the variables of $\mathcal{A}$. For a given environment ρ, define a mapping:

$\|\cdot\|^{\rho}_{I}$: terms $\rightarrow D$ as follows:

$$\|c\|^{\rho}_{I} = K(c) \text{ for each constant symbol } c \in \mathcal{A}.$$
$$\|x\|^{\rho}_{I} = \rho(x) \text{ for each variable } x \in \mathcal{A}.$$

Next define a relation $\models_{I,\rho}$ by:

1. $\models_{I,\rho} P(t_1, \ldots, t_n)$ iff $(\|t_1\|^{\rho}_{I}, \ldots, \|t_n\|^{\rho}_{I}) \in E(P)$ for each atomic formula $P(t_1, \ldots, t_n) \in \mathcal{W}$.
2. $\models_{I,\rho} W_1 \wedge W_2$ iff $\models_{I,\rho} W_1$ and $\models_{I,\rho} W_2$.
3. $\models_{I,\rho} W_1 \vee W_2$ iff $\models_{I,\rho} W_1$ or $\models_{I,\rho} W_2$.
4. $\models_{I,\rho} \sim W$ iff not $\models_{I,\rho} W$.
5. $\models_{I,\rho} W_1 \supset W_2$ iff $\models_{I,\rho} \sim W_1 \vee W_2$.
6. $\models_{I,\rho} W_1 \equiv W_2$ iff $\models_{I,\rho} (W_1 \supset W_2) \wedge (W_2 \supset W_1)$.
7. $\models_{I,\rho} (x)W$ iff for all $d \in D$, $\models_{I,\rho[x \rightarrow d]} W$ where $\rho[x \rightarrow d]$ denotes an environment identical to ρ except that this new environment maps the variable x to the domain element d.
8. $\models_{I,\rho} (Ex)W$ iff $\models_{I,\rho} \sim(x)\sim W$.

Finally, define $\models_I W$ iff $\models_{I,\rho} W$ for all environments ρ, in which case W is said to be *true in the interpretation I*. W is *false in the interpretation I* iff for no environment ρ is it the case that $\models_{I,\rho} W$. An interpretation I is a *model* of the wff W iff W is true in I. I is a *model* of a set S of wffs iff W is true in I for each $W \in S$.

Example 2.2 (continued)

The previous interpretation is a model for each of the following formulae:

$$(x)(y)[TEACH(x,y) \supset TEACHER(x) \wedge COURSE(y)] \quad (2.1)$$

$$(x)(y)[ENROLLED(x,y) \supset STUDENT(x) \wedge COURSE(y)] \quad (2.2)$$

$$(x/COURSE)(Ey/TEACHER)\,TEACH(y,x) \quad (2.3)$$

$$(x/TEACHER)(Ey/COURSE)\,TEACH(x,y) \quad (2.4)$$

Notice that, on the view that types formalize the concept of "domain of a relation," then (2.1) and (2.2) specify the domains of the relations *TEACH* and *ENROLLED*.[4] Formulae (2.1)-(2.4) can be viewed as integrity constraints that happen to be true in the given interpretation.

Notice also that the logician's fancy definition of truth in an interpretation, involving as it does the notion of an environment ρ for variables, is motivated by the requirement of maintaining the distinction between the objects of the interpretation and the purely syntactic symbols of the first order language. Of course, no one really thinks of

[4] Notice that I have not yet defined the concept of a relation. It should be clear from Example 2.2, however, that *TEACH* and *ENROLLED* will be examples of relations by whatever definition I eventually come up with.

interpretations in this way, at least not in the database setting. Rather, one thinks of the tables of an interpretation as defining a set of propositions. In Example 2.2, the true propositions are *TEACHER* (A), *TEACHER* (B) , . . . , *ENROLLED* $(d,P200)$, $=(a,a)$, . . . , $=(P200, P200)$. Those propositions not included in this set are treated as false. For example, *TEACHER* (d), *TEACH* $(B,CS100)$ and $=(A,B)$ are false. Then a wff $(x)\ W(x)$ is true in an interpretation iff for every d in the domain of the interpretation, $W(d)$ is true. $(Ex)\ W(x)$ is true iff for some d, $W(d)$ is true. Of course the logical constants $\wedge$, $\vee$, $\sim$, $\supset$ and $\equiv$ are given their usual truth table definitions. Thus, in the case of finite interpretations, determining the truth of an arbitrary wff reduces to purely propositional truth table evaluations.

2.3 Relational Databases Defined

Recall that a relational language $R = (\mathcal{A}, \mathcal{W})$ is a first order language for which $\mathcal{A}$ contains finitely many constants and finitely many predicates, among which is a distinguished equality predicate and possibly some distinguished unary predicates called simple types. Among all of the possible interpretations for a relational language R, we can single out the class of relational interpretations as follows:

Let $R = (\mathcal{A}, \mathcal{W})$ be a relational language. An interpretation $I = (D,K,E)$ for R is a *relational interpretation* for R iff

1. K: constants of $\mathcal{A} \xrightarrow[onto]{1-1} D$ (so that D must be finite).

2. $E(=) = \{ (d,d) \mid d \in D \}$.

The interpretation of Example 2.2 is a relational interpretation.

A *relational database* is a triple (R,I,IC) where:

1. R is a relational language.

2. I is a relational interpretation for R.

3. IC is a set of wffs of R, called *integrity constraints.* In particular, it is required that for each n-ary predicate P distinct from $=$ and the simple types, IC must contain a wff of the form

$$(x_1) \ldots (x_n)[P(x_1, \ldots, x_n) \supset \tau_1(x_1) \wedge \ldots \wedge \tau_n(x_n)]$$

where the τ_i are types. $\tau_1, \ldots, \tau_n$ are called the *domains* of P.

For each predicate P distinct from the simple types, the extension $E(P)$ is called a *relation.* When the context is clear, I shall often refer to a relation by the name of the corresponding predicate P. Thus I will speak of "the relation P" in referring to P's extension.

The integrity constraints *IC* of a relational database (*R,I,IC*) are said to be *satisfied* iff *I* is a model for *IC*. Wffs (2.1)-(2.4) of Example 2.2 (continued) might well be taken to define a set of integrity constraints in which case Example 2.2, together with its continuation, defines a relational database. The wffs (2.1) and (2.2) then define the domains of the predicates *TEACH* and *ENROLLED*. For this example, the relational database satisfies its integrity constraints.

A few remarks are in order.

1. Since the extension of the equality predicate is the set of all pairs (*d,d*) of domain elements, =(*d,d'*) is false for all distinct domain elements *d,d'*. This is in keeping with the universally adopted assumption in database theory that distinctly named individuals are in fact distinct. From our model theoretic perspective, this means that different domain elements denote different individuals, so that in Example 2.2, the proposition =(*P*100,*P*200) is false, whereas =(*P*100,*P*100) is true.

2. Relational database theory generally incorporates a set of arithmetic comparison operators like $<$, $=$, $>$ *etc.*, as needed. I have chosen only to represent the equality "operator," primarily because it will play a prominent role in the subsequent theory. It would be a simple matter to modify my definition of a relational database to include the binary predicates $<$, $>$, and indeed any set of desired binary "operators." The basic difference between my approach and the conventional one is that I treat these operators as predicates that are extensionally defined within the theory, whereas conventionally these operators are viewed as procedures whose formal properties are understood by everyone and therefore are not defined within the theory. They are, so to speak, "external operators."

3. The concept of an integrity constraint as defined above corresponds to the so-called *static* integrity constraints or *state laws* of [NY78]. Such constraints are meant to be satisfied by any state of the database. In contrast there is also the concept of a *dynamic* integrity constraint or *transition law* [NY78]. Satisfaction of a dynamic constraint is a function of not just the current state of the database but also of its successor state. I do not, in this chapter, address this latter class of integrity constraints, except to point out their intimate connection with the well known "frame problem" in Artificial Intelligence [RAPH71].

2.4 A First Order Query Language

The query language I will appeal to is one first defined in [REIT77] and used subsequently in [REIT78a] and [REIT80a]. It is obviously a close relative of that used in the domain calculus of [ULLM80] (pp. 116-117).

Queries are defined relative to a given relational language $R = (\mathcal{A}, \mathcal{W})$. Specifically, a *query for R* is any expression of the form $<\vec{x}/\vec{\tau} \mid W(\vec{x})>$ where:

1. $\vec{x}/\vec{\tau}$ denotes the sequence $x_1/\tau_1, \ldots, x_n/\tau_n$, and the x_i are variables of $\mathcal{A}$.

2. Each τ_i is a type composed of simple types of $\mathcal{A}$.

3. $W(\vec{x}) \in \mathcal{W}$ and the only free variables of $W(\vec{x})$ are among $\vec{x} = x_1, \ldots, x_n$. Moreover, all of the quantifiers occurring in $W(\vec{x})$ are type restricted quantifiers.

If $DB = (R, I, IC)$ is a relational database then a query for R is said to be *applicable* to DB. The intention here is that information may be retrieved from a relational database only by posing queries that are applicable to that database.

Intuitively, the query $<\vec{x}/\vec{\tau} \mid W(\vec{x})>$ is meant to denote the set of all tuples of constants $\vec{c} = c_1, \ldots, c_n$ such that each c_i satisfies the type τ_i, and such that the database satisfies $W(\vec{c})$. A formal definition will follow the next example.

Example 2.3

The following are sample queries applicable to the education database of Example 2.2:

Who teaches $P100$?

$$<x/TEACHER \mid TEACH(x, P100)>$$

Who are all of A's students?

$$<x/STUDENT \mid (Ey/COURSE)\, TEACH(A, y) \wedge ENROLLED(x, y)>$$

What courses does a take, and who teaches them?

$$<x/COURSE,\ y/TEACHER \mid ENROLLED(a, x) \wedge TEACH(y, x)>$$

Who teaches all of the students?

$$<x/TEACHER \mid (y/STUDENT)\,(Ez/COURSE)\, TEACH(x, z) \wedge ENROLLED(y, z)>$$

The following queries are not applicable to this database because they involve constants or predicates that are not part of the alphabet of the relational language for the database:

$$<x/TEACHER \mid TEACH(x,MATH100)>$$

$$<x/SUPPLIER \mid (y/PART)SUPPLIES\ (x,y)>$$

Formally, let $DB = (R,I,IC)$ and let $Q = <\vec{x}/\vec{\tau} \mid W(\vec{x})>$ be a query applicable to DB. A tuple $\vec{c}$ of constants of R's alphabet is an *answer* to Q *with respect to* DB iff

1. $\tau_i(c_i)$ is true in I, $i = 1, \ldots, n$.
2. $W(\vec{c})$ is true in I.

Notice that the concept of an answer is defined only for queries applicable to DB. A query not applicable to DB must involve predicates not contained in R's alphabet and which therefore have no extensions in I, or constants not contained in R's alphabet and which thus have no corresponding domain elements in I. In other words, DB *does not know* about these predicates or constants, in which case the query must be viewed as meaningless.

Finally, notice that there is no correlate in my definition of a query to the notion of a safe [ULLM80] or definite [KUHN67] or range separable [CODD72] query. Essentially these latter restrictions on queries are deemed necessary in order to avoid ever computing the unrestricted complement of a relation; this because such complements are seen as either infinite or undefined. But notice that when a relational database is a triple (R,I,IC), the complement of a type or a relation is finite and perfectly well defined since there are but finitely many individuals in the domain of I. These are the only individuals the database *knows* about; as far as it is concerned *these are all and only the existing individuals.* There is no need for the concept of a safe query.

The source of the safe query constraint in conventional database theory can be traced to the concept of a domain for a relation as the totality of all individuals of a certain kind. Thus, the totality of all parts might be a domain for an inventory database, or the totality of all suppliers. Domains might be infinite, as is the set of all integers. Whether these domains are conceived as being finite or infinite, it is the *completed totality* of such individuals that is somehow seen to be part of the database, despite the fact that in any state of the database only a finite subset of this totality will be explicitly represented. Unrestricted complements of relations are understood to be defined with respect to the completed totality of database individuals, not with respect to the finitely many explicitly present representatives of this totality. Hence the requirement of safe queries.

Now I must confess to a certain discomfort over this notion of complementation with respect to completed totalities. For this totality is never explicitly represented in the database; rather, it is a conceptualization that we, as humans, entertain. There is no way that the database can be said to know about, say, the set of all integers, at least not without some representation of Peano arithmetic. It knows only about some finitely many integers, and precious little about them. It seems to me that queries are about things the database *knows about* (suppliers, integers, *etc.*, that it has explicit representations for). A query $<\vec{x}/\vec{\tau} \mid W(\vec{x})>$ asks for all tuples $\vec{x}$ *known to the database,* satisfying $\vec{\tau}$ and W. In this view, complementation is perfectly respectable. $<x/INTEGER \mid \sim P(x)>$ denotes the set of all integers known to the database for which $\sim P(x)$ is known to be true.

2.5 Some Problems with the Model Theoretic Perspective

The model theoretic paradigm has an elegance and simplicity that accounts, in large measure, for the overwhelming success of Codd's original proposal for a relational model of data [CODD70]. Yet it is not without its difficulties, some of which (*e.g.,* null values) Codd had foreseen, others of which have subsequently emerged. I shall here focus on two such problems with the model theoretic world view.

2.5.1 Databases with Incomplete Information

A variety of phenomena fall under this rubric. I shall consider two of these: disjunctive information and the need for null values.

2.5.1.1 Disjunctive Information

One encounters this problem whenever there is the need to represent a fact of the kind "*P* is the case, or *Q* is the case, or . . . " but it is not known which of *P,Q,* . . . , actually is the case. [LIPS79] proposes a treatment of this situation under certain simplifying assumptions. For the education database of Example 2.2, we face this problem in an attempt to represent the fact "*a* is enrolled in *P*200 or in *CS*200, but I don't know which." The obvious (and indeed only) approach within the model theoretic framework is to split the given interpretation into three interpretations I_1, I_2 and I_3, each identical to the given one, except that, in I_1, the relation *ENROLLED* contains the additional tuple (*a,P*200). In I_2 it contains (*a,CS*200), while in I_3 it contains both (*a,P*200) and (*a,CS*200). Then $\vec{c}$ will be defined to be an answer to the query $<\vec{x}/\vec{\tau} \mid W(\vec{x})>$ iff $\tau_i(c_i)$ and $W(\vec{c})$ are all true in all three interpretations I_1, I_2 and I_3. This idea generalizes in the obvious way to the concept of a database involving many interpretations, and the concept of query evaluation requiring truth in all these interpretations.

Anyone familiar with the completeness theorem for first order logic will immediately detect proof theory in this observation.

Notice that we cannot avoid the problem of multiple interpretations by treating the formula *ENROLLED*$(a,P200) \vee$ *ENROLLED* $(a,CS200)$ as an integrity constraint. For to do so would require that at least one of $(a,P200)$ and $(a,CS200)$ be included in the relation *ENROLLED* in order for this constraint to be satisfied, and we don't know which of these tuples is the case.

2.5.1.2 Null Values

This terminology embraces a multitude of necessary evils in database theory. I shall focus here on just one such null, namely "value at present unknown." In fact this null value has two distinct manifestations: "value at present unknown, but one of some finite set of known possible values," and "value at present unknown, yet *not necessarily* one of some finite set of known possible values." As an example of the former, suppose that in our education database we wish to represent the fact that e is a student who is enrolled in some course, but we don't know which course that is. Suppose further that we know that the only existing courses are the ones mentioned in the database, so that a priori, whichever course that e is taking, it is one of $CS100$, $CS200$, . . . , $P200$. Then our task is to represent the disjunctive fact:

$$ENROLLED(e,CS100) \vee ENROLLED(e,CS200)$$
$$\vee \ldots \vee ENROLLED(e,P200)$$

which is just the problem of disjunctive information discussed above.

As an example of the latter "value unknown" null, consider the ubiquitous "supplier and parts" database which contains a relation *SUPPLIES* (.,.) whose domains are specified by:

$$(x)(y)\,[SUPPLIES(x,y) \supset SUPPLIER(x) \wedge PART(y)]$$

Now suppose that p is a part with no known supplier, but we do know that someone, perhaps one of the known suppliers, perhaps not, does supply it. How shall we represent this fact? The standard approach (see, for example, [CODD79]) is to postulate a new unknown but existing entity ω, a *null value,* then add the tuple (ω,p) to the *SUPPLIES* table, add ω to the *SUPPLIER* table and p to the *PART* table. But ω is an individual with quite a different character from the other known individuals of the database, so it is deemed necessary to augment the conventional truth values {true, false} with a third truth value "unknown" in order to correctly evaluate queries over databases containing such null values. The effect of this third truth value is then an extension of the relational algebra so that, for example, equality and the join operator suitably reflect the intended meaning of this null value.

Notice that *the multiple truth valued approach to null values is a direct and natural consequence of the model theoretic paradigm of relational database theory.* Models are concerned with truth. Since two truth values suffice for the evaluation of wffs in an interpretation without nulls, it is only natural to try inventing new truth values in order to evaluate queries in an interpretation with nulls. Notice also that a correct treatment of nulls is predicated on a prior notion of what these null values *mean.* Without a correct *semantics,* no correct extended relational algebra is possible. On this view, multi-valued logics provide one possible framework within which a semantics for values may be defined. Alas, within this framework it is by no means clear how to extend the relational model to correctly represent null values. Although several approaches exist in the literature (*e.g.,* [BISK81] [CODD79] [WALK80] [VASS79] [ZANI77]), there is no general agreement about which of these, if any, provides a correct semantics for nulls. This difficulty is compounded in the presence of additional kinds of null values (*e.g.,* "no value permitted").

2.5.2 Extending the Relational Model to Incorporate More World Knowledge

It is becoming increasingly evident that the relational model provides limited expressive power, and that extensions to the formalism are required in order to incorporate more real world meaning [CODD79] [BZ81]. The following are typical examples of the kinds of real world knowledge that an extended relational model might accommodate:

1. General facts about the world such as "The subpart relation is transitive" and "All men are mortal."
2. Events: Their sequencing and times of occurrence.
3. Generalization hierarchies (IS-A hierarchies) with property inheritance.

It is true that certain kinds of knowledge can be represented within the model theoretic paradigm by treating this knowledge as an integrity constraint. For example, the fact that the subpart relation is transitive

$$(x/PART)\,(y/PART)\,(z/PART)\,[SUBPART(x,y) \wedge SUBPART(y,z) \supset SUBPART(x,z)]$$

could be an integrity constraint, thereby forcing the extension of *SUBPART* to be closed under transitivity. But other kinds of information, for example disjunctive information, cannot be treated as integrity constraints, as observed in Section 2.5.1.1. Because of this, and because there are settings in which various forms of inference seem necessary (for example, property inheritance in hierarchies), other approaches to the strict model theoretic have been proposed. I shall return to these issues in Section 4.2 in the context of a proof theoretic view of databases.

3. Databases and Logic: the Proof Theoretic Perspective

My objective in this section is to show how the model theoretic perspective on databases can be reinterpreted in purely proof theoretic terms. Specifically, I shall define a class of first order theories, called relational theories, and prove an equivalence result relating relational theories to relational interpretations. From this it will follow that a definition of a relational database, equivalent to the one presented in Section 2.3, is as a triple (R,T,IC) where T is a relational theory. Then, all prior definitions, involving as they do truth in a relational interpretation, can be reformulated in terms of provability in the theory T. The point of this result, namely its capacity for generalization, will be taken up in Section 4.

3.1 Relational Theories

Imagine given a database (R,I,IC). I shall assume, as I have assumed all along, that the domain elements of I are named using constant symbols of R's alphabet.[5] In addition, instead of viewing the relational interpretation I as a set of tables, think of it as a set of ground atomic formulae. Thus, in Example 2.2, think of the interpretation as being specified by the ground atomic formulae

$$\{TEACHER(A),\ TEACHER(B),\ TEACHER(C),\ \ldots,$$
$$ENROLLED(d,P100), ENROLLED(d,P200),$$
$$=(A,A),\ =(B,B),\ \ldots,\ =(P200,P200)\}.$$

I now propose viewing this set as a first order theory (*i.e.*, as a set of wffs of the underlying relational language).[6] Currently, these wffs are simply ground atomic formulae, but I shall shortly have occasion to modify this set using other kinds of formulae.

---

[5] See the comments of Example 2.2.

[6] In general if $(\mathcal{A}, \mathcal{W})$ is a first order language, then any subset of $\mathcal{W}$ is called a *first order theory* of the language.

Given such a relational interpretation, reinterpreted as a first order theory T, there are various formulae that can be proven, given T as premises. Thus, with reference to Example 2.2 we have the following:

$$T \vdash ENROLLED(c,P100)$$ [7]

$$T \vdash ENROLLED(a,P100) \wedge TEACH(B,P100)$$

$$T \vdash (Ey/COURSE)\, TEACH(A,y) \wedge ENROLLED(a,y)$$

Notice that all of these provable formulae also happen to be true in the original interpretation. However, there are formulae that are true in the interpretation but that are not provable from the corresponding first order theory. For example:

$$(x)[TEACHER(x) \vee COURSE(x) \vee STUDENT(x)]$$

is such a formula. This is not provable because the first order theory T does not know that $A,B, \ldots ,P100,P200$ are all and only the existing individuals. As far as T is concerned, there might be other existing individuals in the world. So augment T with the following domain closure axiom:

$$(x)[=(x,A) \vee =(x,B) \vee \ldots \vee =(x,P100) \vee =(x,P200)]$$

In general, if I is a relational interpretation with domain $c_1, \ldots ,c_n$, then the *domain closure axiom* for I [REIT80a] is

$$(x)[=(x,c_1) \vee =(x,c_2) \vee \ldots \vee =(x,c_n)]$$

We can also simplify the representation of the equality relation by replacing all of its instances $=(A,A)$, $=(B,B)$, $\ldots$, $=(P200,P200)$ by the single formula $(x)=(x,x)$. Our transformed first order theory T now consists of the following wffs:

$$(x)=(x,x)$$

$$(x)[=(x,A) \vee =(x,B) \vee \ldots \vee =(x,P100) \vee =(x,P200)]$$

$$TEACHER(A),\ TEACHER(B),\ \ldots,\ ENROLLED(d,CS200),$$

$$ENROLLED(d,P200).$$

Unfortunately, there still remain wffs true in the original interpretation I but unprovable from T, for example all of the inequalities $\sim\!=(A,B)$, $\sim\!=(A,C)$, *etc.* So for each pair of distinct constants c,c' of the domain, augment T with the *unique name axioms* $\sim\!=(c,c')$ [REIT80a]. Since I am proposing to treat equality proof theoretically, we shall also require the standard axioms specifying the intuitive

---

[7] If W is a set of first order formulae and if w is a first order formula, then $W \vdash w$ means that there is a first order proof of w from premises W.

properties that equality should have, namely commutativity, transitivity, and substitution of one term for another term that is equal to it. These axioms will be given below.

Our theory T now contains unique name axioms, together with axioms for equality. The only remaining problem with T is that it fails to treat negation properly. For example, the wff $\sim TEACHER(a)$, while true in I, is not provable from T. The reason is clear enough; T has models in which $TEACHER(a)$ is true. To avoid this, we need a first order wff which says that the only individuals $TEACHER$ can be predicated of are A, B, and C. This can be done using the *completion* of the predicate $TEACHER$:

$$(x)[TEACHER(x) \supset =(x,A) \vee =(x,B) \vee =(x,C)]$$

Similarly, the completion of the predicate $TEACH$ for our education database is

$$\begin{aligned}(x)\,(y)[TEACH(x,y) \supset\ & =(x,A) \wedge =(y,CS100)\\ & \vee =(x,A) \wedge =(y,CS200) \vee =(x,B) \wedge =(y,P100)\\ & \vee =(x,C) \wedge =(y,P200)]\end{aligned}$$

We can now augment the theory T for the education example with the completions of each of the predicates of that database. The first order theory that we finally end up with consists of the following formulae:

1. Domain closure axiom:

$$(x)[=(x,A) \vee =(x,B) \vee \ldots \vee =(x,P100) \vee =(x,P200)]$$

2. Unique name axioms:

$$\sim=(A,B),\ \sim=(B,C),\ \sim=(A,a),\ \ldots,$$

3. Equality axioms specifying the reflexivity, commutativity and transitivity of equality, and the principle of substitution of equal terms.

4. The ground atomic facts:

$$TEACHER(A),\ TEACHER(B),\ \ldots,\ ENROLLED(d,P200).$$

5. Completion axioms for each predicate:

$$(x)[TEACHER(x) \supset =(x,A) \vee =(x,B) \vee =(x,C)]$$

$$\begin{aligned}(x)\,(y)[ENROLLED(x,y) \supset\ & =(x,a) \wedge =(y,CS100) \vee \ldots \vee\\ & =(x,d) \wedge =(y,P200)]\end{aligned}$$

etc.

Notice that *the only model of this theory is the original interpretation* of Example 2.2. Thus, whenever we had occasion to speak of *truth in this interpretation,* we can instead speak of *provability in the theory.* All of which motivates the following definition:

Let $R = (\mathcal{A}, \mathcal{W})$ be a relational language. A first order theory $T \subseteq \mathcal{W}$ is a *relational theory* of R iff it satisfies the following properties:

1. If $c_1, \ldots, c_n$ are all of the constants of $\mathcal{A}$, T contains the domain closure axiom

$$(x)[=(x,c_1) \vee \ldots \vee =(x,c_n)]$$

   T contains the unique name axioms

$$\sim=(c_i,c_j) \quad i, j = 1, \ldots, n \; i < j$$

2. T contains each of the following equality axioms:

   (i) Reflexivity
   $(x)=(x,x)$

   (ii) Commutativity
   $(x)[=(x,y) \supset =(y,x)]$

   (iii) Transitivity
   $(x)\ (y)\ (z)[=(x,y) \wedge =(y,z) \supset =(x,z)]$

   (iv) Leibnitz' principle of substitution of equal terms:

   For each m-ary predicate symbol P of $\mathcal{A}$,

$$(x_1) \ldots (x_m)\ (y_1) \ldots (y_m)[P(x_1, \ldots, x_m) \wedge =(x_1,y_1) \wedge \ldots \wedge =(x_m,y_m) \supset P(y_1, \ldots, y_m)]$$

3. For some set $\Delta \subseteq \mathcal{W}$ of ground atomic formulae, none of whose predicates is the equality predicate, $\Delta \subseteq T$.
   For each m-ary predicate P of $\mathcal{A}$ distinct from the equality predicate define a set C_P of m-tuples of constants by

$$C_P = \{\vec{c} \mid P(\vec{c}) \in \Delta\}.$$

   The set $\{P(\vec{c}) \mid \vec{c} \in C_P\}$ is called the *extension of P in T*.[8]

---

[8] Not to be confused with the concept of the extension of a predicate P in an interpretation.

Suppose $C_P = \{(c_1^{(1)}, \ldots, c_m^{(1)}), \ldots, (c_1^{(r)}, \ldots, c_m^{(r)})\}$. Then in addition to the wffs of Δ, T contains the following *completion axiom* for P:

$$(x_1) \ldots (x_m)[P(x_1, \ldots, x_m) \supset =(x_1, c_1^{(1)}) \wedge \ldots \wedge =(x_m, c_m^{(1)})$$
$$\vee \ldots \vee =(x_1, c_1^{(r)}) \wedge \ldots \wedge =(x_m, c_m^{(r)})]$$

If $C_P = \{\ \}$, then P's extension in T is empty, and T's completion axiom is

$$(x_1) \ldots (x_m) \sim P(x_1, \ldots, x_m).$$

4. The only wffs of T are those sanctioned by conditions 1-3 above.

Notice that in a relational theory T the extension of P in T together with P's completion axiom is logically equivalent to the wff

$$(x_1) \ldots (x_m)[P(x_1, \ldots, x_m) \equiv =(x_1, c_1^{(1)}) \wedge \ldots \wedge =(x_m, c_m^{(1)})$$
$$\vee \ldots \vee =(x_1, c_1^{(r)}) \wedge \ldots \wedge =(x_m, c_m^{(r)})]$$

This is the "if and only if form" of the predicate P as defined in [CLAR78]. The idea of using a completion axiom in the above definition derives from Clark's paper.

The following theorem establishes an equivalence between relational theories and relational interpretations.

Theorem 3.1. *Suppose $R = (\mathcal{A}, \mathcal{W})$ is a relational language. Then:*

1. *If T is a relational theory of R, then T has a unique model I which is a relational interpretation for R.*
2. *If I is a relational interpretation for R then there is a relational theory T of R such that I is the only model of T.*

Proof.

1. Let $I = (D,K,E)$ be the following relational interpretation for R:

   (i) $D = \{c_1, \ldots, c_n\}$ where $c_1, \ldots, c_n$ are all of the constants of $\mathcal{A}$.

   (ii) $K(c_i) = c_i,\ i = 1, \ldots, n.$

   (iii) $E(=) = \{(c,c) \mid c \in D\}$

   If P is a m-ary predicate of $\mathcal{A}$ whose completion axiom in T has the form

   $$(x_1), \ldots (x_m) \sim P(x_1, \ldots, x_m) \tag{3.1}$$

   (so that P's extension in T is empty), $E(P) = \{\ \}$. Otherwise P's completion axiom in T has the form

$$(x_1) \ldots (x_m)[P(x_1, \ldots, x_m) \supset =(x_1, c_1^{(1)}) \wedge \ldots \wedge =(x_m, c_m^{(1)}) \vee \ldots \vee =(x_1, c_1^{(r)}) \wedge \ldots \wedge =(x_m, c_m^{(r)})] \quad (3.2)$$

where the $c_i^{(j)}$ are all constants of $\mathcal{A}$. In this case P's extension in T is $\{P(c_1^{(1)}, \ldots, c_m^{(1)}), \ldots, P(c_1^{(r)}, \ldots, c_m^{(r)})\}$ and $E(P) = \{(c_1^{(1)}, \ldots, c_m^{(1)}), \ldots, (c_1^{(r)}, \ldots, c_m^{(r)})\}$.

I is clearly a model of T. To see that I is T's only model notice first that T's domain closure and unique name axioms force any model M of T to have the same domain as I (up to renaming of I's domain elements). Secondly, T's reflexivity axiom forces the extension in M of the equality predicate to be the same as in I. Finally, the extension and completion axiom, in T, of a predicate P together with T's unique name axioms force P's extension in M to be the same as its extension in I.

2. The proof here involves constructing, from I, a relational theory T in the same fashion as in the educational database of Example 2.2. So, given a relational interpretation $I = (D,K,E)$ for R, define a first order theory $T \subseteq \mathcal{W}$ as follows:

(i) If $D = \{c_1, \ldots, c_n\}$ then T contains the wffs

$$(x)[=(x,c_1) \vee \ldots \vee =(x,c_n)]$$

$$\sim=(c_i,c_j) \quad i, j = 1, \ldots, n, \ i<j.$$

(ii) T contains axioms for the reflexivity, commutativity and transitivity of the equality predicate, together with axioms for the principle of substitution of equal terms for each predicate P of $\mathcal{A}$.

(iii) For each m-ary predicate P of $\mathcal{A}$ distinct from the equality predicate:

If $E(P) = \{\ \}$ then T contains the wff (3.1).

If $E(P) = \{(c_1^{(1)}, \ldots, c_m^{(1)}), \ldots, (c_1^{(r)}, \ldots, c_m^{(r)})\}$ then T contains the wff (3.2), together with each of the wffs $P(c_1^{(i)}, \ldots, c_m^{(i)})$ $i = 1, \ldots, r$.

(iv) The only wffs in T are those sanctioned by (i)-(iii) above.

Then T is a relational theory of R and it is not hard to see, as in the proof of 1 above, that I is a unique model of T.

QED

Corollary 3.2. *Suppose T is a relational theory of a relational language R, and that I is a model of T. Then for any wff w of R, w is true in I iff* $T \vdash w$.

Proof. The proof follows from the fact that I must be a unique model of T and the completeness theorem for first order logic.

3.2 A Proof Theoretic Reconstruction of Relational Database Theory

Theorem 3.1 and Corollary 3.2 form the basis for a proof theoretic reconstruction of all the model theoretic concepts and definitions of Section 2. For if (R,I,IC) is a relational database, then we can construct, as in the proof of 2. of Theorem 3.1, a relational theory T of R for which I is T's only model. By Corollary 3.2, the concepts of truth in I and provability from T are equivalent. Conversely, by 1. of Theorem 3.1, any relational theory T defines a unique relational interpretation I, and again, by Corollary 3.2, truth in I is equivalent to provability from T.

Accordingly, we can equivalently define a *relational database* to be a triple (R, T, IC) where R and IC are as before, and T is a relational theory of R. The integrity constraints IC are said to be *satisfied* iff for each $w \in IC$, $T \vdash w$. If $Q = \langle \vec{x}/\vec{\tau} \mid W(\vec{x}) \rangle$ is a query applicable to this database, then an n-tuple $\vec{c}$ of constants of R's alphabet is an *answer* to *Q with respect to this database* iff

1. $T \vdash \tau_i(c_i) \quad i = 1, \ldots, n$ and
2. $T \vdash W(\vec{c})$

4. Generalizing the Proof Theoretic Perspective

In this section I shall show how the proof theoretic view of a relational database as a triple (R,T,IC) admits a variety of generalizations, through modification of the first order theory T.

4.1 Databases That Contain Incomplete Information

Recall that in Section 2.5.1 I discussed two manifestations of the problem of representing incomplete information within the model theoretic paradigm of database theory, namely disjunctive information and null values. Let us return to these problems and determine the sense in which the proof theoretic view provides clarification and solutions.

4.1.1 Disjunctive Information

This was the problem of representing disjunctive facts of the form: "*P* is the case, or *Q* is, or ... , but I don't know which," and of using such incomplete information in deriving answers to database queries.

Example 4.1

Consider the following relational theory for a supplier and parts world:

PART	*SUPPLIER*	*SUPPLIES*	*SUBPART*
p_1	Acme	Acme p_1	p_1 p_2
p_2	Foo	Foo p_2	
p_3			

where for brevity I use tables to specify the predicate extensions in the theory instead of the ground atomic formulae $PART(p_1)$, $PART(p_2), \ldots, SUBPART(p_1,p_2)$.

Domain Closure Axiom:

$$(x)[=(x,p_1) \vee =(x,p_2) \vee =(x,p_3) \vee =(x,Acme) \vee =(x,Foo)]$$

Unique Name Axioms:

$$\sim=(p_1,p_2),\ \sim=(p_2,p_3),\ etc.$$

Equality Axioms: as usual

Completion Axioms:

1. $(x)[PART(x) \supset =(x,p_1) \vee =(x,p_2) \vee =(x,p_3)]$
2. $(x)[SUPPLIER(x) \supset =(x,Acme) \vee =(x,Foo)]$
3. $(x)(y)[SUPPLIES(x,y) \supset =(x,Acme) \wedge =(y,p_1) \vee =(x,Foo) \wedge =(y,p_2)]$
4. $(x)(y)[SUBPART(x,y) \supset =(x,p_1) \wedge =(y,p_2)]$

Now suppose that we also wish to represent the disjunctive fact: "Foo supplies p_1 or Foo supplies p_3 but I don't know which." This item of information can be represented by the wff:

$$SUPPLIES(Foo,p_1) \vee SUPPLIES(Foo,p_3) \tag{4.1}$$

Now one must resist the natural temptation to simply add this wff to the above theory, thinking that one has thereby provided a correct representation of this world. To see why, consider the contrapositive of 3, the completion axiom for *SUPPLIES*:

$$(x)\,(y)\,[[\sim=(x,Acme) \vee \sim=(y,p_1)] \wedge [\sim=(x,Foo) \vee \sim=(y,p_2)]$$
$$\supset \sim SUPPLIES(x,y)]$$

From this and from the unique name axioms we can prove, taking $x = Foo$ and $y = p_1$, the wff $\sim SUPPLIES(Foo,p_1)$. Similarly we can prove $\sim SUPPLIES(Foo,p_3)$. But these two facts are inconsistent with the disjunctive wff (4.1).

The reason for this "anomaly" is clear enough; the completion axiom 3 was designed to say that, of the original theory, the *only possible instances* of *SUPPLIES* are $(Acme,p_1)$ and (Foo,p_2). But the disjunctive wff (4.1) says that *there are other possible instances* of *SUPPLIES*, namely (Foo,p_1) and (Foo,p_3). To accommodate these new possible instances replace the completion axiom 3 by:

3′. $(x)\,(y)\,[SUPPLIES(x,y) \supset =(x,Acme) \wedge =(y,p_1)$
$\vee =(x,Foo) \wedge =(y,p_2) \vee =(x,Foo) \wedge =(y,p_1)$
$\vee =(x,Foo) \wedge =(y,p_3)]$

Notice that we can, with 3′, still prove $\sim SUPPLIES(Acme,p_2)$ as before, but we can no longer, as we could before, prove $\sim SUPPLIES(Foo,p_1)$ or $\sim SUPPLIES(Foo,p_3)$. This is precisely what one's intuition about disjunctive facts such as (4.1) would demand.

Now consider representing, in addition to (4.1), the fact

> "If Acme does not supply p_2 then p_2 must be a subpart of p_3."

This can also be represented as a disjunctive wff

$$SUPPLIES(Acme,\ p_2) \vee SUBPART(p_2,p_3) \qquad (4.2)$$

Again we want to include this wff in the theory, but the completion axioms 3′ and 4 must both be modified to accommodate the new possible instances $(Acme,\ p_2)$ and (p_2,p_3) of *SUPPLIES* and *SUBPART*. So replace 3′ and 4 by

3″. $(x)\,(y)\,[SUPPLIES(x,y) \supset =(x,Acme) \wedge =(y,p_1)$
$\vee =(x,Foo) \wedge =(y,p_2) \vee =(x,Foo) \wedge =(y,p_1)$
$\vee =(x,Foo) \wedge =(y,p_2) \vee =(x,Acme) \wedge =(y,p_2)]$

4′. $(x)\,(y)\,[SUBPART(x,y) \supset =(x,p_1) \wedge =(y,p_2) \vee =(x,p_2) \wedge =(y,p_3)]$

All of which leads to a new theory consisting of:

1. The extensions defined by the tables.
2. The domain closure, unique name, and equality axioms.

3. The completion axioms 1, 2, 3″ and 4′.

4. The disjunctive wffs (4.1) and (4.2).

This theory provides an intuitively correct representation for this incompletely specified world.

These considerations lead to a natural generalization of the concept of a relational database to incorporate disjunctive information, as follows.

Let $R = (\mathcal{A}, \mathcal{W})$ be a relational theory. A wff of $\mathcal{W}$ is called a *positive ground clause* of R iff it has the form $A_1 \vee \ldots \vee A_r$ where each A_i is a ground atomic formula whose predicate is distinct from the equality predicate. The case $r = 1$ is permitted, in which case the clause is simply a ground nonequality atomic formula. A first order theory $T \subseteq \mathcal{W}$ is a *generalized relational theory* of T iff it satisfies the following properties:

1. If $c_1, \ldots, c_n$ are all of the constants of $\mathcal{A}$, T contains the domain closure axiom

$$(x)[=(x,c_1) \vee \ldots \vee =(x,c_n)].$$

T contains the unique name axioms

$$\sim=(c_i,c_j) \quad i,j = 1, \ldots, n \quad i < j$$

2. T contains axioms for the reflexivity, commutativity and transitivity of equality, together with an axiom for the substitution of equal terms for each predicate P of $\mathcal{A}$.

3. For some set $\Delta \subseteq \mathcal{W}$ of positive ground clauses of R, $\Delta \subseteq T$. For each m-ary predicate P of $\mathcal{A}$ distinct from the equality predicate, define a set C_P of m-tuples of constants by

$C_P = \{\vec{c} \mid$ for some positive ground clause $A_1 \vee \ldots \vee A_r$ of Δ and some i, $1 \leqslant i \leqslant r$, A_i *is* $P(\vec{c})\}$

Suppose $C_P = \{(c_1^{(1)}, \ldots, c_m^{(1)}), \ldots, (c_1^{(r)}, \ldots, c_m^{(r)})\}$. Then in addition to the wffs of Δ, T contains the following *completion axiom* for P:

$$(x_1) \ldots (x_m)[P(x_1, \ldots, x_m) \supset =(x_1,c_1^{(1)}) \wedge \ldots \wedge =(x_m,c_m^{(1)}) \vee \ldots \vee =(x_1,c_1^{(r)}) \wedge \ldots \wedge =(x_m,c_m^{(r)})]$$

If $C_P = \{\ \}$, then T's completion axiom is

$$(x_1) \ldots (x_m) \sim P(x_1, \ldots, x_m).$$

4. The only wffs of T are those sanctioned by conditions 1-3 above.

Notice that the definition of a relational theory of Section 3.1 is a special case of the above definition, in which Δ is a set of ground nonequality atomic formulae. It is natural to define a *generalized relational database* to be a triple (R,T,IC) where T is a generalized relational theory, and R and IC are as before. Similarly, the definition of IC being *satisfied* and the definition of an *answer* to a query are as in Section 3.2.

Generalized relational theories are sufficiently complicated to cause concern about their consistency. Not to worry.

Theorem 4.1. *Every generalized relational theory T is consistent.*

Proof: This is proven by constructing a model of T. Suppose $R = (\mathcal{A}, \mathcal{W})$ and $T \subseteq \mathcal{W}$ is a generalized relational theory. Define an interpretation $I = (D,K,E)$ for R with domain $D = \{c_1, \ldots, c_n\}$ where these are all of the constants of $\mathcal{A}$. Define $E(=) = \{(c,c) \mid c \in D\}$. Then I satisfies the domain closure, unique name, and equality axioms of T. Finally, for each nonequality predicate P of $\mathcal{A}$ define $E(P) = \{\vec{c} \mid \vec{c} \in C_P\}$. Then I satisfies each wff of Δ as well as the completion axioms for each nonequality predicate of $\mathcal{A}$. Hence I is a model of T.

QED

4.1.2 The Semantics of Null Values

The concept of a relational database as developed in Sections 2 and 3 or as generalized in Section 4.1.1 did not accommodate null values. Indeed, as I remarked in Section 2.5.1.2, it is by no means clear what some of these null values even *mean*. My purpose now is to show in some detail how one particular null (namely "value at present unknown, but not necessarily one of some finite set of known possible values")[9] may be defined within the proof theoretic paradigm for database theory.[10]

To focus the discussion, consider the relational theory defined at the beginning of Example 4.1. Suppose we wish to represent the fact:

[9] See the discussion of Section 2.5.1.2.

[10] The other most common null value, namely "no value permitted," also has a simple first order representation. For example, suppose *EMP(p,m,s)* denoted that person *p* whose marital status is *m* (*M*arried or *S*ingle) has spouse *s*. Then if John-Doe is single, no value for *s* is permitted. This can be represented by *(s/PERSON)* $\sim$*EMP (John-Doe,S,s)*. I shall not consider such nulls in this chapter.

"Some supplier supplies part p_3 but I don't know who it is. Moreover, this supplier may or may not be one of the known suppliers Acme and Foo."

This fact may be represented by the first order wff

$$(Ex)SUPPLIER(x) \wedge SUPPLIES(x,p_3) \tag{4.3}$$

which asserts the existence of an individual x with the desired properties. Now we can choose to name this existing individual (call it ω) and instead of (4.3), ascribe these properties to ω directly:

$$SUPPLIER(\omega) \wedge SUPPLIES(\omega,p_3) \tag{4.4}$$

In database terminology, ω is a *null value*. It is called a *Skolem constant* by logicians. Skolem constants, or more generally Skolem functions, provide a technical device for the elimination of existential quantifiers in proof theory (see, for example, [CL73]).

The problem at hand is how to correctly integrate the facts (4.4) into our supplier and parts relational theory. Notice first that ω is a new constant, perhaps denoting the same individual as some known constant, perhaps not. So the unique name axioms remain untouched. The domain closure axiom, however, must be expanded to accommodate this new constant:

$$(x)[=(x,p_1) \vee =(x,p_2) \vee =(x,p_3) \vee =(x,Acme) \vee =(x,Foo) \vee =(x,\omega)] \tag{4.5}$$

Moreover, the completion axioms for *SUPPLIER* and *SUPPLIES* must likewise be expanded:

$$(x)[SUPPLIER(x) \supset =(x,Acme) \vee =(x,Foo) \vee =(x,\omega)] \tag{4.6}$$

$$(x)(y)[SUPPLIES(x,y) \supset =(x,Acme) \wedge =(y,p_1) \vee =(x,Foo) \wedge =(y,p_2) \vee =(x,\omega) \wedge =(y,p_3)] \tag{4.7}$$

If now we add the facts $SUPPLIER(\omega)$ and $SUPPLIES(\omega,p_3)$ to this modified theory we end up with an intuitively correct representation. Notice that in this resulting theory, *the only thing that distinguishes the Skolem constant ω from the "ordinary" constants Acme, Foo, etc., is the absence of unique name axioms for ω.*

Notice also that in this theory we can prove things like $\sim SUPPLIES(Acme,p_2)$, and $\sim SUPPLIES(Foo,p_1)$, but *not* $\sim SUPPLIES(Acme,p_3)$ or $\sim SUPPLIES(Foo,p_3)$. Intuitively, this is precisely what we want. For we know $SUPPLIES(\omega,p_3)$. Moreover, we *don't know* whether ω is the same as, or different than, Acme or Foo.[11]

[11] Remember that there are no unique name axioms for ω.

So if we could prove, say $\sim SUPPLIES(Acme,p_3)$, we could also prove $\sim =(\omega,Acme)$, contradicting our presumed ignorance about the identity of ω. What we really have here is a correct formalization of the closed world assumption [REIT78b] in the presence of null values. I shall return to this issue in Section 4.2.4.

One last observation is in order. If we wanted, in addition, to represent the fact:

> "Some supplier (possibly the same as Acme or Foo, possibly not) supplies p_2"

$$(Ex)SUPPLIER(x) \wedge SUPPLIES(x,p_2)$$

we must choose a name for this supplier, say ω', which must be distinct from the name of the previous unknown supplier ω. This is for obvious reasons. Moreover, the domain closure axiom (4.5) and the completion axioms (4.6) and (4.7) must be expanded to take ω' into account. In general, each time a new null value is introduced into the theory, the null must be denoted by a fresh name, distinct from all other names of the theory, and the domain closure and completion axioms must be expanded.

These ideas now can be formalized as follows: Let $R = (\mathcal{A}, \mathcal{W})$ be a relational theory, where the constants of $\mathcal{A}$ are partitioned into two disjoint sets of constants $C = \{c_1, \ldots, c_n\}$ and $\Omega = \{\omega_1, \ldots, \omega_r\}$. Here Ω may be empty, but C may not be. Each ω_i is called a *null value*. As before, a wff of $\mathcal{W}$ is called a *positive ground clause* of R iff it has the form $A_1 \vee \ldots \vee A_m$ where each A_i is a nonequality ground atomic formula. The case $m = 1$ is permitted. A first order theory $T \subseteq \mathcal{W}$ is a *generalized relational theory of R with null values* iff it satisfies the following properties:

1. T contains the domain closure axiom:

$$(x)[=(x,c_1) \vee \ldots \vee =(x,c_n) \vee =(x,\omega_1) \vee \ldots \vee =(x,\omega_r)].$$

Moreover, T contains the unique name axioms:

$$\sim =(c_i,c_j) \quad i < j, \ i, \ j = 1, \ldots, n.$$

In addition, T *may* contain one or more inequalitites of the following forms:

$$\sim =(\omega_i,c_j) \text{ for some } 1 \leqslant i \leqslant r, \ \ 1 \leqslant j \leqslant n.$$

$$\sim =(\omega_i,\omega_j) \text{ for some } 1 \leqslant i, \ \ j \leqslant r, \ \ i < j.$$

2. T contains the usual equality axioms.

3. For some set $\Delta \subseteq \mathcal{W}$ of positive ground clauses of R, $\Delta \subseteq T$. For each m-ary predicate P of $\mathcal{A}$ distinct from the equality predicate define a set K_P of m-tuples of constants from $C \cup \Omega$ by

   $K_P = \{\vec{k} \mid$ for some positive ground clause $A_1 \vee \ldots \vee A_m$ of Δ and some i, $1 \leqslant i \leqslant m$, A_i is $P(\vec{k})\}$.

   Suppose $K_P = \{(k_1^{(1)}, \ldots, k_m^{(1)}), \ldots, (k_1^{(s)}, \ldots, k_m^{(s)})\}$. Then in addition to the wffs of Δ, T contains the following *completion axiom* for P:

$$(x_1) \ldots (x_m)[P(x_1, \ldots, x_m) \supset =(x_1,k_1^{(1)}) \wedge \ldots \wedge =(x_m,k_m^{(1)}) \vee \ldots \vee =(x_1,k_1^{(s)}) \wedge \ldots \wedge =(x_m,k_m^{(s)})]$$

   If $K_P = \{\ \}$, then T's completion axiom is

$$(x_1) \ldots (x_m) \sim P(x_1, \ldots, x_m)$$

4. The only wffs of T are those sanctioned by conditions 1-3 above.

The definition of a generalized relational theory of Section 4.1.1 is a special case of the above definition, in which $\Omega = \{\ \}$.

A *generalized relational database with null values* is a triple (R,T,IC) where R and T are as above, and $IC \subseteq \mathcal{W}$ is a set of integrity constraints. The definitions of an *answer* to a query, and of *satisfaction* of the integrity constraints remain the same as before.

Having formalized a class of first order theories that accommodate null values, we can now observe that *the only formal distinction between a null value $\omega \in \Omega$ and an "ordinary" constant $c \in C$ is that some of the possible unique name axioms for ω are absent from the theory.* If in fact all of the unique name axioms for ω were present (the definition does allow this), then ω would be indistinguishable from an "ordinary" constant.

Notice also that generalized relational theories with null values provide for disjunctive information as well, and permit some quite subtle distinctions to be represented. For example:

> "Someone supplies p_3 but I don't know who. Whoever it is, it is neither A nor B."

$$(Ex/SUPPLIER)SUPPLIES(x,p_3) \wedge \sim=(x,A) \wedge \sim=(x,B)$$

which, after elimination of the existential quantifier becomes

$$SUPPLIER(\omega) \wedge SUPPLIES(\omega,p_3) \wedge \sim=(\omega,A) \wedge \sim=(\omega,B)$$

"Someone supplies p_2 and someone supplies p_3. I don't know who they are but I do know they are not the same suppliers."

$$(Ex/SUPPLIER)\,(Ey/SUPPLIER)\,SUPPLIES(x,p_2) \wedge SUPPLIES(y,p_3) \wedge \sim=(x,y)$$

which becomes

$$SUPPLIER(\omega_1) \wedge SUPPLIER(\omega_2) \wedge SUPPLIES(\omega_1,p_2) \wedge SUPPLIES(\omega_2,p_3) \wedge \sim=(\omega_1,\omega_2)$$

"Someone supplies p_2 or p_3 but I don't know who. I do know it is not A."

$$(Ex/SUPPLIER)\,[SUPPLIES(x,p_2) \vee SUPPLIES(x,p_3)] \wedge \sim=(x,A)$$

which becomes

$$SUPPLIER(\omega) \wedge [SUPPLIES(\omega,p_2) \vee SUPPLIES(\omega,p_3)] \wedge \sim=(\omega,A)$$

The following result is comforting.

Theorem 4.2. *Every generalized relational theory T with null values is consistent.*

Proof: The proof is constructed by adding enough inequalities to T to yield a generalized relational theory. By Theorem 4.1, this enlarged theory will be consistent in which case so will any subset of it, in particular T itself.

To suitably enlarge T add to it every inequality $\sim=(c_i,\omega_j)$ such that neither this inequality nor the inequality $\sim=(\omega_j,c_i)$ is already present in T. Similarly, add to T every inequality $\sim=(\omega_i,\omega_j)$ for $i \neq j$ such that neither this nor the inequality $\sim=(\omega_j,\omega_i)$ is already present in T. The resulting theory is a generalized relational theory.

QED

One final observation: any generalized relational theory with null values is decidable, basically because the domain closure axiom restricts the class of its models to those whose domains are no larger than the finite set of constants of the theory. Of course testing a wff for theoremhood by testing it for truth in all these models is hardly an exemplary procedure. A theorem proving approach would certainly be preferable. Better still would be a suitable generalization of the relational algebra, but whether this is even possible remains to be seen.

4.2 Conceptual Modelling: Incorporating More World Knowledge

As I remarked in Section 2.5.2, there is a perceived need within the database community to extend the relational model to accommodate more real world knowledge, and many of the required extensions cannot be accommodated by the model theoretic paradigm for relational databases. A bewildering variety of proposals have been advanced in response to this need. Representative examples include the "Tasmanian" relational model [CODD79], TAXIS, an object oriented programming language [MBW80], class oriented data models [HM78], and semantic networks [SOWA76]. Now there are two problems with this embarrassing number of proposals:

1. How can one begin to compare them? In what formal sense could one claim that two such proposals have the same representational "powers," or that one is a generalization of another? Most such proposals involve different representation languages and different (and in some cases underspecified) semantics, making mappings between them virtually impossible.
2. Insofar as the concept of an answer to a query is defined at all, it is defined operationally, for example by a generalization of the relational algebra, or by some set of retrieval routines which may or may not perform inferences. Now these data models are complicated. Therefore these operational definitions for answers to queries are also complicated. Why should one believe that these definitions are *correct* (*i.e.*, that any answer returned will be intuitively appropriate)? Why should one believe that these definitions are *complete* (*i.e.*, that anything that intuitively should be an answer will be returned)?

My purpose in this section is to indicate how a logical framework can alleviate these problems. Specifically, I shall argue that the kinds of real world knowledge that these extended data models attempt to capture have natural representations as first order formulae. If you grant me this claim for the moment, it follows that such non logical data models can be equivalently formalized by suitably restricted classes of first order theories, much as Section 4.1.2 formalized the relational model with disjunctive information and null values as the class of generalized relational theories with null values. Provided this mapping from a non logical data model to a logical one can be done, we would enjoy a number of immediate benefits [REIT80b]:

1. The semantics of the non logical data model would be precisely defined by its logical translation.

2. Two different non logical data models could be compared (say, with respect to their representational "power"), by comparing their translations.

3. The definition of an answer to a query remains the same as in Section 3.2. This is a central point: no matter how one extends one's data models to incorporate more real world meaning, *the definition of an answer to a query remains the same, as long as this extension is first order definable.* This is not to say that one's query evaluation algorithms must resemble the logician's proof procedures. The relational algebra is such an algorithm, and it looks nothing like proof theory. Nevertheless, logic is the final arbiter of the correctness of proposed query evaluation mechanism for any first order definable data model. Thus *we can prove the correctness of proposed query evaluation algorithms.*

4. Similar remarks hold for integrity constraints. The definition of satisfaction of an integrity constraint remains as it was expressed in Section 3.2 for any first order data model. Thus *we can prove the correctness of proposed integrity maintenance algorithms.*

It remains for me to argue that the kinds of real world knowledge that various semantic data models attempt to capture are representable within first order logic. Space limitations prevent an exhaustive or detailed survey of the kinds of knowledge modelled in the database literature, so I shall focus instead on some of the more prominent semantic requirements.

4.2.1 The Representation of Events

First order event based representations have been used extensively in Artificial Intelligence for modelling verbs and their associated case frames for natural language understanding systems [BRUC75]. These ideas translate very naturally into the database setting. The idea is to extend one's ontology to include a new class of individuals of type *EVENT*, and then to postulate various properties that these individuals may possess. For example, in an inventory database, one may want to represent the fact that an order has been received on June 12, 1981, to be filled by Sept. 1, 1981, and which is to be shipped to Acme. The order is for 12 pipewrenches, catalogue number 1376, and for 24 doors, catalogue number 2001, colour brown. This has as its event-based first order representation:

$$\begin{aligned}&(Ex/ORDER-EVENT)[DATE-RECEIVED(x,\ June\ 12\ 1981)\\&\quad \wedge DATE-TO-BE-FILLED(x,\ Sept\ 1\ 1981) \wedge SHIP-TO(x, Acme)\\&\quad \wedge GOODS-ORDERED(x, pipewrench)\\&\quad \wedge CATALOGUE-NO(x, pipewrench,\ 1376)\end{aligned}$$

$\wedge$ *QUANTITY*(*x*,*pipewrench*, 12) $\wedge$ *GOODS*−*ORDERED*(*x*,*door*)

$\wedge$ *CATALOGUE*−*NO*(*x*,*door*, 2001) $\wedge$ *QUANTITY*(*x*,*door*, 24)

$\wedge$ *COLOUR*(*x*,*door*,*brown*)]

Associated with any individual of type *ORDER*−*EVENT* might be an integrity constraint specifying that there must be someone to whom the goods are to be shipped, that there are some goods on order, and that the date the order is received must precede the date it is to be filled.

(*x*/*ORDER*−*EVENT*) (*Ey*/*DATE*) (*Ez*/*DATE*) (*Eu*/*BUYER*)

(*Ew*/*INVENTORY*−*ITEM*) [*DATE*−*RECEIVED*(*x*,*y*)

$\wedge$ *DATE*−*TO*−*BE*−*FILLED*(*x*,*z*) $\wedge$ $y<z$

$\wedge$ *SHIP*−*TO*(*x*,*u*) $\wedge$ *GOODS*−*ORDERED*(*x*,*w*)]

4.2.2 Hierarchies and the Inheritance of Properties

The modelling task here is to provide a first order representation of generalization (IS-A) hierarchies, the properties associated with "classes" in the hierarchy, and how these properties are inherited by classes "lower down" in the hierarchy. These features are common to virtually every attempt in the literature to define data models with more "meaning" (*e.g.*, [CODD79] [HM78] [MBW80] [SS77b]).

For example, consider an educational domain with the hierarchy of simple types (classes) of Figure 4.1. The semantics of this hierarchy can be specified by the following first order wffs:

(*x*)[*UNDERGRADUATE*(*x*) ⊃ *STUDENT*(*x*)]

(*x*)[*GRADUATE*(*x*) ⊃ *STUDENT*(*x*)]

(*x*)[*FRESHMAN*(*x*) ⊃ *UNDERGRADUATE*(*x*)]

(*x*)[*JUNIOR*(*x*) ⊃ *UNDERGRADUATE*(*x*)]

etc.,

together with wffs specifying the disjointness of these types, namely:

(*x*)∼[*UNDERGRADUATE*(*x*) $\wedge$ *GRADUATE*(*x*)]

(*x*)∼[*FRESHMAN*(*x*) $\wedge$ *JUNIOR*(*x*)]

(*x*)∼[*FRESHMAN*(*x*) $\wedge$ *SOPHOMORE*(*x*)]

etc.

In addition to this hierarchy, there might be properties that generally hold for simple types "high up" in the hierarchy and that are inherited by any instances of simple types "lower down." For example, it will likely be the case that every student should have a student number:

$$(x/STUDENT)\ (Ey/INTEGER)STUDENT-NO(x,y)$$

This is an example of a *property* associated with the type *STUDENT*. In general a property of the simple type τ is a wff of the form $(x/\tau)\ (Ey/\theta)P(x,y)$ where θ is some type and P is a binary predicate.

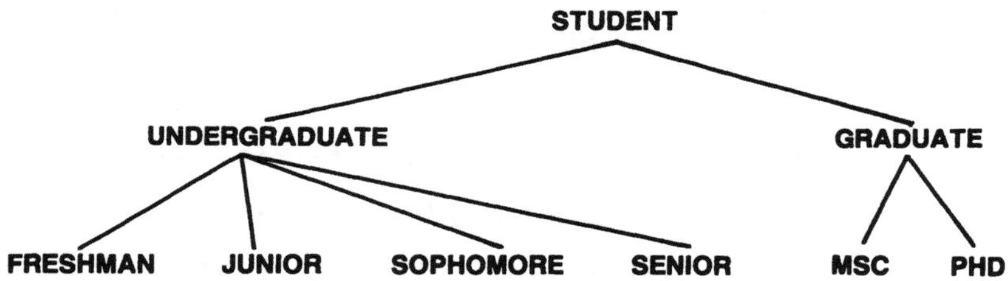

Figure 4.1 *A Hierarchy of Simple Types*

For the example at hand it is easy to see that the following wffs are all *deducible* from the wffs defining the hierarchy, and the student number property:

$$(x/GRADUATE)\ (Ey/INTEGER)STUDENT-NO(x,y)$$

$$(x/FRESHMAN)\ (Ey/INTEGER)STUDENT-NO(x,y)$$

etc.

This is an example of the *inheritance of properties* applying to superclasses down the hierarchy to subclasses. Properties only inherit "downwards." If every freshman must be enrolled in English 100

$$(x/FRESHMAN)ENROLLED(x,E100)$$

it does not follow, either intuitively or logically from our representation, that every undergraduate must be enrolled in English 100.

The transitivity of "IS-A" is a simple consequence of the transitivity of "implies." Thus the following is provable:

$$(x)[MSC(x) \supset STUDENT(x)]$$

Finally, the concept of a token t of a class C translates into the logical ground atomic formula $C(t)$. Thus John Doe as a token of the class *GRADUATE* is represented by *GRADUATE*(*John*−*Doe*).

4.2.3 Aggregations

This modelling notion was introduced in [HM78] and is also treated in [CODD79] [MBW80]. An aggregation is a set of some kind to which one wishes to ascribe various properties. I shall indicate how to represent aggregations in first order logic by modelling certain aspects of professional societies. The simple type *SET* takes sets as its argument. To improve readability, I use upper case symbols for set variables and constants.

Subset defined:

$$(X/SET)\,(Y/SET)[SUBSET(X,Y) \equiv (z)[MEMBER(z,X) \supset MEMBER(z,Y)]]$$

A professional society is a set of people representing a field. Any member of the society is interested in at least one subfield of this field.

$$(X)[PROF\text{-}SOC(X) \supset SET(X)]$$

$$(X)[PROF\text{-}SOC(X) \supset (y)[MEMBER(y,X) \supset PERSON(y)]]$$

$$(X)[PROF\text{-}SOC(X) \supset (Ex/FIELD\text{-}TYPE)[FIELD(X,x) \wedge (y)[MEMBER(y,X) \supset (Ez/FIELD\text{-}TYPE)SUBFIELD(z,x) \wedge INTERESTS(y,z)]]]$$

Notice that this is not a definition of a professional society. The wffs merely define various properties that anything called a professional society must possess.

ACM is a professional society of computer scientists.

$$PROF\text{-}SOC(ACM)$$

$$FIELD\text{-}TYPE(cs)$$

$$FIELD(ACM,cs)$$

The executive board of a professional society is a subset of the members of the society and always has a president, a secretary, a treasurer, and members-at-large. Neither the president, treasurer nor secretary may be members-at-large.

$$(X)\,(Y/PROF\text{-}SOC)[EX\text{-}BOARD(X,Y) \supset SET(X) \wedge SUBSET(X,Y)]$$

$$(X/SET)\,(Y/PROF\text{-}SOC)[EX\text{-}BOARD(X,Y) \supset [(Eu/PERSON)MEMBER(u,X) \wedge PRESIDENT(u,Y)] \wedge [(Ev/PERSON)MEMBER(v,X) \wedge SECRETARY(v,Y)] \wedge [(Ew/PERSON)MEMBER(w,X) \wedge TREASURER(w,Y)]]$$

$$(X/SET)\ (Y/PROF-SOC)[EX-BOARD(X,Y) \supset$$
$$(EZ/SET)[SUBSET(Z,X) \wedge MEMBERS-AT-LARGE(Z,Y)$$
$$\wedge\ (x/PERSON)[MEMBER(x,Z) \supset \sim PRESIDENT(x) \wedge$$
$$\sim SECRETARY(x) \wedge \sim TREASURER(x)]]]$$

Lady Lovelace is a member of ACM's executive board.

$$(EX)EXECUTIVE-BOARD(X,ACM) \wedge MEMBER(Lady-Lovelace,X)$$

If one replaces the existentially quantified variable X by a Skolem constant Ω (*i.e.*, a null value) this latter wff becomes

$$EXECUTIVE-BOARD(\Omega,ACM) \wedge MEMBER(Lady-Lovelace,\Omega)$$

Using these wffs together with some of the earlier ones we can deduce, among other things

$$PERSON(Lady-Lovelace)$$
$$MEMBER(Lady-Lovelace,ACM)$$

A special interest group of a professional society is a set of individuals interested in some subfield of the society.

$$(X)\ (Y/PROF-SOC)[SIG(X,Y) \supset SET(X)]$$
$$(X/SET)\ (Y/PROF-SOC)\ [SIG(X,Y) \supset$$
$$(z)\ [MEMBER(z,X) \supset PERSON(z)]]$$
$$(X/SET)\ (Y/PROF-SOC)\ (u/FIELD-TYPE)\ (v/FIELD-TYPE)$$
$$[SIG(X,Y) \wedge FIELD(X,u) \wedge FIELD(Y,v) \supset$$
$$SUBFIELD(u,v) \wedge (z/PERSON)[MEMBER(z,X) \supset$$
$$INTERESTS(z,u)]]$$

Notice that one may be a member of a special interest group without being a member of the professional society.

SIGART is a special interest group of ACM for Artificial Intelligence.

$$SIG(SIGART,ACM)$$
$$FIELD(SIGART,ai)$$

Using the wffs on hand we can deduce:

$$SUBFIELD(ai,cs)$$

Suppose *rr* is a member of SIGART.

$$MEMBER(rr,SIGART)$$

We can deduce:

PERSON (*rr*)

INTERESTS (*rr*,*ai*)

4.2.4 Discussion

I have indicated how a variety of data modelling concepts can be naturally represented as first order formulae. Now my earlier conclusions (Section 4.1) were that various species of relational databases are all formalizable by suitable triples (R,T,IC). It is natural, then, to persevere with this notion and to further generalize relational databases to accommodate these new data modelling concepts. More precisely, insofar as a semantic data model admits first order formulae of a certain kind (*e.g.*, formulae for aggregations), then some of these formulae normally will be viewed as integrity constraints. Put them in IC. The remaining formulae then serve as general world knowledge for the inferential retrieval of answers. Put them in T.

Now this leaves us with the mildly uncomfortable view that, in order to do arbitrary conceptual modelling, we must accept databases (R,T,IC) where T and IC are arbitrary first order theories of the relational language R. While this is essentially true, there are certain constraints that one is likely to impose upon T:

1. It should contain a domain closure axiom.

2. It should contain unique name axioms for the known constants of R (but not necessarily for its null values).

3. T should represent the closed world assumption.

This latter point requires amplification. In [REIT78b] I studied the problem of representing negative information in first order databases without null values. My point of departure was the observation that in conventional relational databases, a negative fact like $\sim$*SUPPLIES* (*s*,*p*), is held to be true provided its positive part (*i.e.*, *SUPPLIES* (*s*,*p*)), is not in the database. In other words, a tuple satisfies the negation of a relation iff the tuple is absent from the relation's table. In keeping with my proof theoretic bias, I generalized this notion to first order theories T as follows:

$$\text{Infer } \sim R(\vec{c}) \text{ iff } T \not\vdash R(\vec{c}).$$

This characterization of negation in database theory I termed the *closed world assumption.* For a number of reasons, this particular version of the closed world assumption is unsuitable:

1. It treats null values incorrectly.
2. In the presence of disjunctive information it leads to inconsistencies.
3. Since it is a rule of inference, and not a wff or set of wffs, it is not, strictly speaking, first order representable. It is a meta-notion.

Now there is a different way of viewing the closed world assumption, one which provides a strong clue for its first order representability. For it assumes that the given information about the world being modelled is complete in the sense that *all and only* the relationships that can possibly hold among the known individuals are those implied by the given information. It is this point of view that led to the completion axioms for generalized relational theories with null values (Section 4.1.2). These axioms permit the derivation of negative facts from the theory, but only such facts as do not conflict with the unknown individual property of null values, and which do not lead to inconsistencies with the disjunctive information. In this limited setting, the completion axioms provide a correct first order representation of the closed world assumption.

I do not know whether suitable completion axioms can be formulated for more general first order settings, for example settings representing hierarchies and/or aggregations. Whether this is possible or not, some representation of the closed world assumption is necessary. Moreover, this is not a problem peculiar to a logical view of database theory. Any formalism for extended conceptual modelling must provide for the representation of negative information and its use in query evaluation, although this problem is rarely addressed in the literature.

It is of some interest to observe that variants of the closed world assumption arise in contexts other than database theory, for example in providing a semantics for negation in PROLOG and PLANNER-like programming languages [CLAR78] [AV80], and for Artificial Intelligence applications [MCCA80] [REIT80c]. In particular, Clark and McCarthy provide different but extremely interesting first order approaches to the closed world assumption, approaches well worth investigating for their potential impact on database theory. In this connection [REIT82] shows how, for certain classes of databases viewed as first order theories, McCarthy's formalization of the closed world assumption is a generalization of Clark's.

5. Conclusions

I have, in some detail, carried out a logical reconstruction of various aspects of conventional relational database theory. The value of this logical embedding is, in my view, primarily *semantic;* a number of central concepts in database theory have been given precise definitions. Among these are: databases that have incomplete information, including null values; integrity constraints and what it means for them to be satisfied; queries and their answers; and conceptual modelling and what it might mean to represent more real world knowledge.

As I see it, the major *conceptual* advantage of this logical reconstruction is its uniformity:

1. Representational uniformity. Queries, integrity constraints and facts in the database are all represented in the same first order language.
2. Operational uniformity. First order proof theory is the sole mechanism for query evaluation and the satisfaction of integrity constraints.

This uniformity provides a number of practical advantages:

1. Nonlogical data models can be given precise semantics by translating them into logical terms.
2. Different data models may be compared.
3. Non proof theoretic query evaluation algorithms may be proven correct with respect to the logical semantics of queries.
4. Integrity maintenance algorithms may be proven correct with respect to the proof theoretic definition of constraint satisfaction.

A wide variety of questions have not been explored in the chapter, and they require further research.

1. Can the relational algebra be generalized to deal correctly with null values? With disjunctive information?
2. What is an appropriate formalization of the closed world assumption for arbitrary first order theories?
3. Which first order theories admit efficient query evaluation procedures? In this connection, notice that so-called Horn theories accommodate efficient theorem proving techniques [KOWA79] that can be directly applied to query evaluation.
4. What are some criteria for deciding whether a given wff should be treated as an integrity constraint or as knowledge to be used in deriving answers?

5. Suppose we restrict attention to relational databases as defined in Section 3.2. Determine natural classes of integrity constraints for which efficient and provably correct integrity maintenance algorithms can be found. Contrast this approach to correctness proofs with that of [BBC80].

6. Discussion: Why Logic?

In this chapter I have made some arguments favouring a logical (specifically proof theoretic) perspective for relational database theory. While this logical perspective was couched in the first order predicate calculus, other logics are certainly possible, perhaps even desirable in certain settings. (See, for example, Levesque's chapter on incomplete knowledge bases, or [JACO82].) Exactly which logic as appropriate for conceptual modelling can be a contentious issue, as the chapter by Israel and Brachman indicates, and I do not wish here to take sides in this dispute. But there is a prior issue which I do wish to address, and that is whether logic, whatever its species, is even a suitable formalism for conceptual modelling.

The standard opposing view to the logical paradigm has it that data models are definable by a choice of data representation together with suitable *operations* on the data representation (*i.e.,* by the database operations performed for retrieval, updates, deletions, *etc.,* [TL82]). It is the total constellation of these operations that defines the "meaning" of one's representation. But surely this confuses *implementation* with *specification,* for whatever else it might be, a database is a representation of various things which are *known* (or better, *believed*) *about some aspect of the real world.* Logic provides an abstract *specification* language for expressing this knowledge. The logical formulae which presume to specify this knowledge are things which are either true or false in the real world. Of course, they are intended to be true. Nevertheless, they are open for inspection by the sceptical as well as the curious. For example, in Section 4.2.3, I proposed a collection of formulae specifying what I mean by a professional society. You, in turn, are free to decide whether these formulae are true of the world, and whether there are important features (for your application) of a professional society which I failed to specify. If you agree with my formulae, well and good. If not, then at least we have a solid basis for dispute. Either way, the logical formulae are completely up front; they unambiguously specify exactly what I mean by a professional society, no more, no less. In this sense, logic provides a rigorous specification of meaning. Moreover, it does so at a very high level of abstraction, in the sense that the specification is entirely nonprocedural. It tells us *what* knowledge is being represented. It tells us *what* is meant, for example, by an answer to a query, namely, any tuple of constants which make the query true in all models of the formulae. Similarly, a logic suitable for representing state changes would tell us *what* should be the result of a database update. In no sense does a logical specification include procedures detailing *how* to perform database operations; hence its nonprocedural character.

Of course this emphasis on logic as a specification language ignores a crucial aspect of conceptual modelling, the *implementation* problem. How do we computationally *realize* the abstract logical specification? It is at this implementation level that database operations assume their proper role. A wide variety of options are possible. One extreme is literally to encode the formulae as themselves, and define the database operation for retrieval, say, to be a theorem prover. This approach is advocated by the PROLOG community whenever the formulae are Horn clauses [VANE78]. Another possibility is to represent formulae by a semantic network of some kind, and define the database operation of retrieval by some sort of network interpreter. Usually, such network representations are strongly oriented towards hierarchies and property inheritance, and the associated network interpreter is designed to search up hierarchies for inherited properties [MBW80]. (See Section 4.2.2 for a sketch of a logical specification of such hierarchies. See also [SCHU76a].) Conventional relational database theory encodes ground atomic formulae as themselves (*i.e.,* as a set of relational instances), and the relational algebra supplies the operations for retrieval. Whatever one's choice of data model for realizing a logical specification, this choice will provide a lower level of abstraction, reflecting a concern for implementing the specification, hence a preoccupation with database operations. While necessary, this emphasis on database operations has unpleasant semantic consequences. The semantic effects of certain formulae in the logical specifications are buried in the operations. For example, the effects of the domain closure axiom in the logical specification of a relational database (Section 3.1) are realized in the relational data model by the division operator. The completion axioms are realized by the operation of set difference. *Such axioms are not encoded as part of the data representation, but as data model operations.* The more complex data models become, the more we can expect such operational encodings of specification axioms (not to mention the operational encoding of logical deduction). Provided there is a logical specification to begin with, this makes for good computer science; one can prove that one's data model is a correct realization of the specification.

But what if, as is current practice, a data model is served up without benefit of an abstract specification of the assumptions made by that data model about the world being modelled? Whatever these assumptions might be, they are likely to be buried deeply within the data model's operations. When these are complex operations, how is one to know what the assumptions are? Are they correctly and completely realized by the operations? For that matter, what can "correct" and "complete" even mean in this setting? Without a specification of the "knowledge content" of the database, one which provides a direct connection to the real world being modelled, there can be no concept of the correctness and completeness of a data model's operations. A mature theory of databases will provide for this distinction between a logical specification and its realization by a procedurally oriented data model, and it will require that the operations and data representations of this data model be proven correct and complete with respect to a given specification.

In summary, I have argued the following advantages of logically defined data models for conceptual modelling:

1. Logic is precise and unambiguous. It has a well defined semantics that provides the crucial connection between its formulae and the real world being modelled.

2. Logical data models provide a very high level of abstraction because there are no database operations. They are entirely nonprocedural. They act as specifications of those aspects of the real world being modelled, and of the assumptions one is making about that world.

3. A logical data model is transparent. All and only the knowledge being represented is open for inspection, including assumptions that might otherwise be buried in procedurally oriented data models.

4. Because they are specifications, logical data models can be realized in a variety of ways by procedurally oriented data models. Such data models can be proven correct and complete with respect to the logical specifications that they realize. Since a logical specification provides a connection with the world being modelled (See 1. above), this notion of correctness and completeness is probably the best that one can hope for.

7. Acknowledgments

The bulk of this research was supported by the National Science and Engineering Research Council of Canada under grant A7642. Additional support was provided by NSF Grant MCS-8203954.

I am grateful to David Etherington, Hervé Gallaire, Randy Goebel, Jean Marie Nicolas, Moshe Vardi and K. Yazdanian, all of whom read an earlier draft of this chapter and provided valuable comments and corrections.

8. References

[AV80] [BBC80] [BISK81] [BRUC75] [BZ81] [CL73] [CLAR78] [CODD70] [CODD72] [CODD79] [HM78] [JACO82] [KOWA79] [KUHN67] [LIPS79] [MBW80] [MCCA80] [MEND64] [RAPH71] [REIT77] [REIT78a] [REIT78b] [REIT80a] [REIT80b] [REIT80c] [REIT82] [SCHU76a] [SOWA76] [SS77b] [TL82] [ULLM80] [VANE78] [VASS79] [WALK80] [ZANI77]

Discussion

This chapter uses first order logic (FOL) to express popular DB concepts such as events, hierarchies, and integrity constraints to illustrate the utility of FOL in dealing with issues surrounding the relational data model (RDM).

Current relational database theory is based on model theoretic (MT) notions. The chapter attempts to show that the proof theoretic (PT) approach is better. MT definitions are generalized to PT definitions to provide a good basis for extending RDM theory and to talk precisely about the semantics of extensions, such as those needed for incomplete knowledge (disjunctive information and null values), integrity constraints, and conceptual modelling extensions (events, hierarchies, inheritance, aggregation, and association). The resulting theories are all decidable since the domain of a database (DB) is finite.

Domains

There are at least two different domain notions, one from MT and the other from the RDM. The MT view is that a domain is a set of constants. The DB approach presumes to enumerate all possible values of a domain (like a type in programming language (PL) without the related operations). For example, an *address* domain is the set of *all* possible addresses. Some people attempt to embed as much semantics as possible in the data type of an object (*e.g.,* address and its operations, salary and its operations). In that case, a type such as a string is only a representation of the address object.

Reiter's notion of domain does not make a distinction between type and variable, although such a distinction is generally useful for semantic integrity checking. Reiter claims that such benefits can be gained through axioms (*e.g.,* manager is a subtype of employee). However, the issue here may not be expressibility, but convenience.

Ray Reiter: "This comment implies a misunderstanding of the chapter that addresses *semantic* issues, *not* convenience, efficiency, or implementation. It should be clear that knowledge representation (viewed as an abstract formalism) and database representation (viewed as an implementation) are two different issues."

Extending the RDM Using PT

There are many problems for which the RDM must be extended (*e.g.*, incomplete information, events, and hierarchies). Many of the approaches proposed for these extensions are ad hoc and pose new problems. The RDM can be considered, at a logical level, as a special kind of theory of FOL. The MT approach, the most direct representation for the RDM, cannot deal adequately with the desired extensions. When defining the RDM in the PT approach and one gets not only the RDM but also all the other machinery of FOL with which to resolve other RDM problems. The PT approach provides a proof theory for databases. Using PT, integrity constraints are satisfied if they can be derived from the theory given by the axioms, and queries are answered via proof theory. FOL also can be used to provide a clear semantics for the RDM and its problems and a convenient framework within which to attack the problems.

Reiter proposes that the RDM be extended by using new axioms to handle problems such as disjunctive information and nulls. An example of disjunctive information is "Foo supplies P1 or Foo supplies P3 but I don't know which." The RDM does not permit the information in this statement to be stored or returned. Although there are other such proposed extensions in the literature, their semantics often are not clear. What is meant by the answer to a query in the presence of incomplete information? To understand disjunctive information, you should build a suitable first order theory (in your mind at least) and then use proofs to determine the answer to the query on incomplete information. Having so defined a correct semantics, implement efficient mechanisms to support the semantics, and prove that the implementation corresponds to the given semantics. If one is unhappy with the semantics, then define another. *It is not wise to add a new concept without knowing its semantics.*

It is extremely important that precise specifications be given for any new data model or model extension. If the semantics are not clear, the models or languages are hard to use. In the future, we should not accept a new model or feature without a precise specification that is complete, formal, and unambiguously communicable to its users.

When using a logical formalism to express new models, some things come for free (*e.g.*, means of answering or resolving queries). Papers proposing new models usually give complex ways of retrieving information without demonstrating their correctness. If a data model is specified using FOL, the correct notion of an answer is free. The logic definition correctly characterizes an intuition of how the answer is to be derived, and every answer for which there is an intuition can be retrieved by the same mechanism.

Null Values

In the chapter, null values are special constants about which questions can be asked. There is a recognition problem involving different null values in the RDM literature. For example, if null-x supplies P1 and null-y supplies P3, are null-x and null-y the same? In the PT approach, special constant symbols (W1, W2, ...) are introduced that may or may not be equal to any existing DB constant. If two null values are the same, one must explicitly state this fact. Contrary to some DB proposals, null values are not an issue for three value logic. The issue is what is provable and what is not. If we can neither prove nor disapprove something it means that we have incompletely specified knowledge. The literature is full of conditions of the form: T *or not*(T) evaluates to unknown if T happens to be unknown, but T *or not*(T) is a tautology and so is always true.

State Versus State Transitions

The chapter considers database theory that has not addressed dynamic aspects of databases. Data structures have received considerable emphasis in DB. Now that many structural problems are solved, there is a growing emphasis on behaviour, the semantics and representation of operations over databases. Being able to express the semantics of events is very important—what actually happens when an event takes place. The chapter avoids state changes because of the frame problem, an open problem in AI. The frame problem is that of stating all the invariants for each state change. For example, if you change the state of a room by opening a window, there are unbelievably many invariants (*e.g.*, people in the room remain seated). A complementary problem is to state all changes for an event. What is to be ignored and what is to be emphasized? For a finite domain (*e.g.*, a DB) one can list all the changes and invariants. But, even if one could state all the invariants and changes there is an inference problem; a change can have many side effects. Some of these issues can be addressed using type hierarchies.

Hierarchies and Property Inheritance

In data models, there are higher-level (higher than 1st order) axioms (or model inherent constraints) stating that all hierarchies of the same type have the same properties. This saves writing the same axioms for every application. The same effect can be achieved in FOL through notational convention rather than resorting to a higher order logic.

To deal adequately with hierarchies in PT, completion axioms are needed which allow you to ask questions about elements that are not part of the hierarchy. These axioms are not well understood. Although they may turn out to be simple, they currently appear to be very difficult.

Logical Modelling and Efficiency

Some first order theories permit more efficient query evaluation than others. This fact is used in the PROLOG community (*e.g.,* Horn clauses provide efficient computation and a PROLOG program can be annotated to improve efficiency). There are two issues here. First, there are many ways to ask the same question. Second, is the efficiency of the system measured by how well it performs on the most efficient representation of a query? In this regard, input for efficient implementation should not be sought at the logical description level but in meta-knowledge (*e.g.,* query optimizers should look for hints in the dictionary, not in the database). Efficiency in the RDM is a different problem. It is hard to define predicates that will help in evaluating optimal search paths.

What is the relationship between FOL and implementation efficiency? How does one theory relate to another on the basis of efficiency, assuming that the theories have equivalent interpretations? There is no known answer to these questions. If one happens to know how PROLOG works, then annotations can be used to take advantage of it. Annotation was used long ago for FORTRAN II but annotated programs were found to be less efficient than the standard compiled programs. The RDM is a subset of FOL that is reasonably efficient to process; maybe other "theories" are even more efficient.

Efficiency concerns representation and not logic. There are several ways of improving representations. One approach is to have the compiler collect data from programs (to be kept as a meta-knowledge) and from users (in exceptional cases). Another approach would be to automatically and incrementally map from one representation, say pure PROLOG, to equivalent and more efficient representations.

Concluding Remarks

There are four main benefits of mapping nonlogical models to logical models.

1. Precise definitions of nonlogical data models.

2. Possibility to compare the representational powers of nonlogical models.

3. Defines precisely the concept of an answer to a query. Hence to prove the correctness of proposed evaluation algorithms for a query.

4. Defines satisfiability of an integrity constraint. Hence, to prove the correctness of proposed integrity maintenance algorithms.

The emphasis in using FOL should be on mental hygiene, rather than on theorem proving. FOL should be used if there are doubts about the clear semantics of new database concepts (*e.g.,* incomplete information). When the semantics of a construct is clear, go back to a level that is convenient for data modelling.

Reiter's chapter, which draws examples from DB literature, makes several questionable assumptions about databases. Examples used in the DB literature do not reflect the size or complexity of real databases. A database is a large collection of data, and database applications form large systems. Toy examples do not illustrate the real problems of designing large database applications. For example, census databases are very complex and have several hundred record types, each with several thousand attributes. Database design and definition become extremely complex. The large number of axioms needed to handle the complexity of database applications, coupled with the size of databases, raises serious questions about the practicality of using FOL for real database applications.

Ray Reiter: "The above comment misses the point of the chapter, which provides a framework for defining the semantics of data models. Implementation issues are not addressed nor is the complexity of actual applications except insofar as this complexity has to do with *representational* issues. If you are trying to capture complex *semantic* properties of the real world in a *data model* then use FOL to define that data model. That is all the chapter says."

The following characterization was proposed from the PL point of view: The essence of database is captured by sets and set oriented operations, and the whole database problem is really just an efficiency problem. The response: The characterization ignores many important aspects. Capturing structural properties by sets is a reasonable thing to do, but much of the semantics cannot be captured by using sets. The concept of transactions is ignored. DB has been in the set oriented framework for a long time. Now more difficult problems are being addressed (*i.e.,* many basic problems faced in PL embedded in data intensive applications).

In conclusion, it is fair to say that some formal system is better than no formal system. Model theory and proof theory have been discussed, but other formal systems are also candidates.

9
A Formal Representation For Plans In The Programmer's Apprentice

Charles Rich
Massachusetts Institute of Technology

ABSTRACT *A plan calculus is presented that is used to represent programs as well as a library of standard data and control abstractions in the Programmer's Apprentice. Important features of this formalism include programming language independence, additivity, verifiability, and multiple points of view. The logical foundations of the representation are specified formally by using a situational calculus in which side effects and overlapping mutable data structures are accounted for. The plan calculus is compared with other formalisms such as program schemas, and its advantages are pointed out.*

Foreword

Conceptual modelling is at the heart of building knowledge-based artificial intelligence systems. The goal of the Programmer's Apprentice work, from which the following chapter is drawn, is to build an interactive knowledge-based system to assist expert programmers in the tasks of analyzing, synthesizing, modifying, explaining, verifying, and documenting programs. In the knowledge-based approach to this goal,

---

This chapter describes research done at the Artificial Intelligence Laboratory of the Massachusetts Institute of Technology. Support for the laboratory's artificial intelligence research has been provided in part by the Advanced Research Projects Agency of the Department of Defense under Office of Naval Research contracts N00014-75-C-0643 and N00014-80-C-0505, and in part by National Science Foundation grant MCS-7912179. The views and conclusions contained in this chapter are those of the author, and should not be interpreted as necessarily representing the official policies, either expressed or implied, of the Department of Defense, the National Science Foundation, or the United States Government. This chapter is reprinted with permission from the Proceedings of the Seventh International Joint Conference on Artificial Intelligence, Vancouver, BC, Canada, August 24-28, 1981.

we begin by asking the question, What overall conceptual framework and specific concepts do programmers currently use in these tasks? By modelling this conceptual framework in the computer we can begin to automate these tasks with a kind of man-machine interaction that current programmers will find natural.

It is interesting from the standpoint of this volume that the two most basic features of the overall conceptual framework of programming tasks, namely the notions of procedure and state, are also basic to many other modelling domains. There are therefore a number of issues in common between this chapter and many other chapters in this book.

Beginning with the notion of procedure, we see a number of chapters in the database area (Brodie and Ridjanovic, King and McLeod, and Reimer *et al.*) concerned with modelling compound database operations, variously called "action schemes," "events," or "transaction procedures." All of these are kinds of procedures, with the special case in the database area that the primitive actions are database transactions (*i.e.*, addition, deletion, or modification of records). Borgida *et al.*, and Shaw also describe various kinds of generic procedures. Two major issues that arise in all of these papers are the methods of composition (*i.e.*, how the primitive actions are combined to form procedures), and the methods of abstraction (*i.e.*, how procedures are generalized to cover a wide range of specific behaviors).

The database procedures in the Brodie and Ridjanovic and the King and McLeod chapters are composed of primitive actions by essentially the same methods used in conventional sequential programming languages, namely sequencing, alternation, conditionals, and iteration (as control constructs), and program variables to carry data. The *plan calculus* described in this paper is also essentially a sequential framework. However, it is a variable-free formalism that uses port-to-port equality to specify the flow of data. The plan calculus also does not require the actions in a schema to be totally ordered. For example, the order of actions that have no side effects and no data flow interdependency may be left unconstrained. The conceptual frameworks introduced by Hewitt and de Jong, Reimer *et al.*, and Borgida *et al.*, go beyond sequential procedures in order to deal with parallel processes and synchronization.

Methods of abstraction are an important theme of many chapters in this book. All of the formalisms mentioned above, and notably that of Borgida *et al.*, include methods for constructing very general procedures. The two most commonly used methods used are data abstraction (separating the physical representation of data from its abstract properties, especially the operations that may be performed on it), and various kinds of parameterization beyond the usual input parameters of a subroutine. Shaw traces the history and influence of these ideas in modern programming languages. Not surprisingly, the plan calculus also supports these abstraction methods. However, compared with the usual approaches to abstract data types (*e.g.,* Zilles), *data plans* in the plan calculus model objects with state. The plan calculus also provides a special mechanism, called an *overlay*, for constructing multiple views of a concept. One of the main uses of overlays is to specify the relationship between abstract and concrete views of data and procedures.

On the topic of modelling state there is some divergence of approach in this book. In the plan calculus, a formal distinction is made between the identity of an object and its behavior at different points in time. A set of index variables, called *situations*, are then introduced to distinguish between the different behaviors (states) of a given object. An important feature of this approach is that the same index variables are used in both the state descriptions and in the procedural schemas (*temporal plans*). In the standard database framework (*e.g.,* Reimer *et al.*) all state changes are ultimately modelled as updates of records or tuples in a relation. In contrast, the point of the work of Brodie and Ridjanovic, and of King and McLeod, is to hide the relational view by constructing a more natural, object oriented model of the application domain. Finally, Buneman and Nikhil depart entirely from the notion of state and argue for a purely functional data model.

In addition to the overall conceptual framework of procedure and state models, the following chapter also briefly addresses the issue of how to organize a large body of specific concepts. This issue is a major concern of all knowledge-based artificial intelligence systems, since a very large body of knowledge is typically required to achieve expert levels of performance. The most common technique used for this purpose is generalization (or specialization) hierarchies. For example, this technique is in the title of the chapter by Borgida *et al.* Similarly, type hierarchies are now a familiar idea in programming languages (Krieg-Brueckner, Shaw).

An important direction I see in this area is the development of a more refined vocabulary of taxonomic concepts. Currently, "generalization" is taken to mean too many different things. I have taken a step in the direction of a more refined vocabulary in this chapter by distinguishing what I call *specialization*, which formally induces a subset relation on instances of the relevant concepts, from *extension*, which involves adding a component to a concept. In a similar vein, although in the context of much more regularly structured data, the calculus of relational databases (Stonebraker) distinguishes several ways in which relations may be derived from one another. The natural relations between algebraic theories (Zilles) also provide a kind of taxonomic vocabulary.

I would like to close this foreword by dwelling on some methodological issues. Although these are the most vague connections to be made between the chapters in this book, I feel they are the most important to attempt.

The main methodological point I wish to bring up is one that was very prominent in the symposium discussions, namely the proper role of formal logic (*e.g.*, predicate calculus) in the whole endeavor of conceptual modelling and the implementation of knowledge-based systems. The thrust of the following chapter, as reflected in the title, is certainly that formal logic has an important place in the semantic foundations of modelling procedures. I take the thrust of the chapters in this book by Israel and Brachman, Levesque, and Reiter to be essentially in agreement with this point. However, what is much more mysterious to me is the relationship between the logical foundations of a modelling formalism like the plan calculus and its intuitive roots. In the case of the plan calculus, the logical foundations were an afterthought. The essence of the formalism (*i.e.*, the box and arrow diagrams) came from my own and others' intuitions about program structure and from our observations of the typical programmer's informal jottings on blackboards and scratch pads. Now that the formal semantics has been defined, however, what is the proper status of the original plan diagrams?

Regarding the relevance of formal logic to the implementation of a system like the Programmer's Apprentice, I have had an interesting change of viewpoint. When I wrote the following chapter, the major benefit I expected to gain from the formal semantics was to clarify some grey areas in the meaning of plan diagrams. As a corollary, I also expected to use the formal semantics as a kind of specification against which manipulations of plan diagrams could be validated. I did not, however, expect the predicate calculus to show up in any direct way in the system implementation. It turns out that I was wrong! The predicate calculus formalization was directly usable as the basis for a practical implementation in which predicate calculus and plan diagrams coexist. (I elaborate on this point in a recent paper [RICH82]. Brachman and Levesque seem to be moving in a similar direction in another paper in the same proceedings.)

Finally, it is interesting to note in passing that almost all of the chapters that deal with modelling procedures in this book have found it useful to introduce some form of diagrammatic notation, at least for expositional purposes. Furthermore, all of these diagrams suppress some of the detail that is ultimately present in the corresponding internal representations in favor of highlighting some particular aspect of structure, such as the hierarchy of subprocedures, data flow, or control flow. Perhaps this also tells us something important about conceptual modelling in general.

1. Introduction

This chapter reports on recent developments in a formalism called the *plan calculus* which is being used in the Programmer's Apprentice [RSW79] to represent and reason about programs. The plan calculus was originally developed by Rich and Shrobe [RS76] and was subsequently elaborated on by Shrobe [SHRO79] and Waters [WATE78]. Most recently the author has extended the plan calculus by adding data abstraction and multiple points of view, as well as by providing a formal semantics.

The goal of the Programmer's Apprentice project is to develop a knowledge-based tool for program development. The Programmer's Apprentice attacks the complexity barrier [WINO73] in programming in several ways:

1. By providing an on-line database of design decisions, documentation, and descriptions of a program's design at various levels of detail.

2. By reasoning about these descriptions to detect inconsistencies and to predict the influence of incremental changes.

3. By providing a library of standard forms for use in program construction and analysis.

This paper focuses on the representation used in building the library of standard forms. Reasoning about plans will not be discussed in detail (see [SHRO79]), other than to describe the formal system in which such reasoning takes place, nor will the detailed contents of the library be discussed except to show some examples.

The utility of a library of standard forms in program development is motivated by the observation that expert programmers (like experts in many other fields) are distinguished from novices by their use of a richer vocabulary of intermediate level programming concepts. The novice programmer thinks of constructing a program from assignments, tests, arrays, DO loops, *etc.,* whereas the expert programmer works with larger, less language-specific concepts, such as searching, accumulation, hashing, *etc.* There are deep reasons for this having to do with managing the complexity of the design process [RSWS78]. To the extent that the Programmer's Apprentice can provide a library of such standard building blocks, the programmer benefits by a reduction in the amount he needs to say in order to construct a program.

The idea of developing libraries of standard software components in order to gain the same benefits that the use of standard components has provided in other areas of engineering is not new [SCHW75]. I believe that part of the reason that efforts in this direction have not been more successful is because of deficiencies in the formalisms used. The plan calculus is an attempt to remedy these deficiencies.

2. The Plan Calculus

To a first approximation, the plan calculus may be thought of as unifying in one formalism ideas from flowchart schemas [MANN74], data flow schemas [DENN75], program transformations [CHEA81] [BALZ81] [BD77], and abstract data types [LZ77]. An example of a *plan* is shown in Figure 2.1. The details of the notation used in this figure can wait until later. For now the reader may note that a plan is basically a hierarchical structure made up of different kinds of boxes and arrows. The inner rectangular boxes denote operations and tests, while the arrows between boxes denote data flow (solid arrows) and control flow (hatched arrows). The chief features of this representation, as compared with previous formalisms, are as follows.

1. *Language Independence.* To achieve some measure of canonical form, the plan calculus suppresses features of a program that stem solely from the way an algorithm must be expressed in a particular programming language.

2. *Additivity.* For a library to be easy to use, the rules for combining forms must be straightforward and explicit. Combining forms in the plan calculus has the same formal properties as the union of axiom systems (*i.e.,* the result of combining two non-contradictory forms is always a form that satisfies the constraints of both of the original forms).

3. *Verifiability.* Simply having a library of standard forms addresses only the low productivity part of the software crisis. The plan calculus also provides leverage on the software reliability problem by providing a methodology (in this case, an axiomatic semantics) for verification of library components. Furthermore, this methodology provides a framework in which inconsistencies between uses of standard forms can be detected.

4. *Multiple Points Of View.* Multiple and overlapping points of view are represented in the plan calculus by *overlays* between plans. An example of an overlay is shown in Figure 2.2 (discussed further in the next section). Overlays are used to express the relationship between levels of implementation, to describe overlapping module hierarchies, and to decompose data and control structures in ways that make their relationship to the library more explicit.

An additional desideratum we set for representing the library of standard forms in the Programmer's Apprentice is that the formalism must be neutral between analysis, synthesis, and verification of programs. This turns out to be of great practical importance for building an interactive programming aid, since in real program design situations all three of these activities are intermingled. A neutral representation of standard forms is also theoretically more interesting since it is more likely *a priori* to capture significant features of human understanding of these forms than a representation tailored specifically for analysis, synthesis, or verification only.

2.1 Comparison With Other Formalisms

Past efforts to construct knowledge bases for automatic or partially automated programming have used one of the following formalisms: program schemas [GERH75], program transformations [CHEA81] [BALZ81] [BD77], program refinement rules [BARS77], or formal grammars [RUTH73]. Although each of these representations has been found useful in certain applications, none combine all of the important features of the plan calculus listed above. This section will serve both to contrast the plan calculus with these other formalisms, and as the preliminary to a more careful definition of the plan calculus to follow.

For example, program schemas (incomplete program texts with constraints on the unfilled parts) have been used by Wirth [WIRT73] to catalog programs based on recurrence relations, by Basu and Misra [BM76] to represent typical loops for which the loop invariant is already known, and by Gerhart [GERH75] and Misra [MISR78] to represent and prove the properties of various other common forms. Unfortunately, the syntax of conventional programming languages is not well suited for the kind of generalization needed in this endeavor. For example, the idea of a search loop (a standard programming form) expressed informally in English should be something like the following.

A *search loop* is a loop that has two exits in which a given predicate (the same one each time) is applied to a succession of objects until either the predicate is satisfied (in which case that object is made available for use outside the loop), or the objects to be searched are exhausted.

In Lisp, as in other languages, this kind of loop can be written in innumerable forms, many of which are syntactically (and structurally) very different. For example:

```
(PROG ()
   LP (COND (exhausted (RETURN NIL)))
       ...
       (COND ((predicate current)(RETURN current)))
       ...
       (GO LP))
```

or with only one RETURN instead of two,

```
(PROG ()
   LP (COND (exhausted NIL)
            (T ...
               (COND ((predicate current)
                      (RETURN current)))
               ...
               (GO LP))))
```

or even recursively, *e.g.*,

```
(DEFINE SEARCH ()
   (COND (exhausted NIL)
         (T ...
            (COND ((predicate current) current)
                  (T ...
                     (SEARCH)))))))
```

The problem here is that conventional programming languages are oriented toward specifying computations in enough detail so that a simple local interpreter can carry them out. Unfortunately a lot of this detail is often arbitrary and conceptually unimportant. In the plan calculus, all three of the schemas above (and many other such variations) are expressed by the single plan shown in Figure 2.1.

A new generation of programming languages descended from Simula [DN66], such as CLU [LISK77] and Alphard [SWL77], provide a syntax for specifying standard forms (such as the search loop) in a more canonical way. However, there are two more fundamental difficulties with using program schemas to represent standard program forms, which Simula and its descendants do not solve. First, programs (and therefore program schemas) generally are not easy to combine, nor are they additive. Thus, when you combine two program schemas, the resulting schema is not guaranteed to satisfy the constraints of both of the original schemas, due to such factors as destructive interactions between variable assignments. Second, existing programming languages do not allow multiple views of the same program or overlapping module hierarchies. I believe the reason is that a program is still basically thought of, from the standpoint of these languages, as a set of instructions to be executed, rather than as a set of descriptions (*e.g.*, blueprints) which together specify a computation.

Currently the most common way to represent relationships between standard forms (typically implementation/abstraction relationships) is via program transformations or program refinement rules [BARS77]. Compared with overlays, these formalisms have two serious problems that stem from their lack of neutralness between analysis and synthesis. An overlay in the plan calculus, as in Figure 2.2, is made up of two

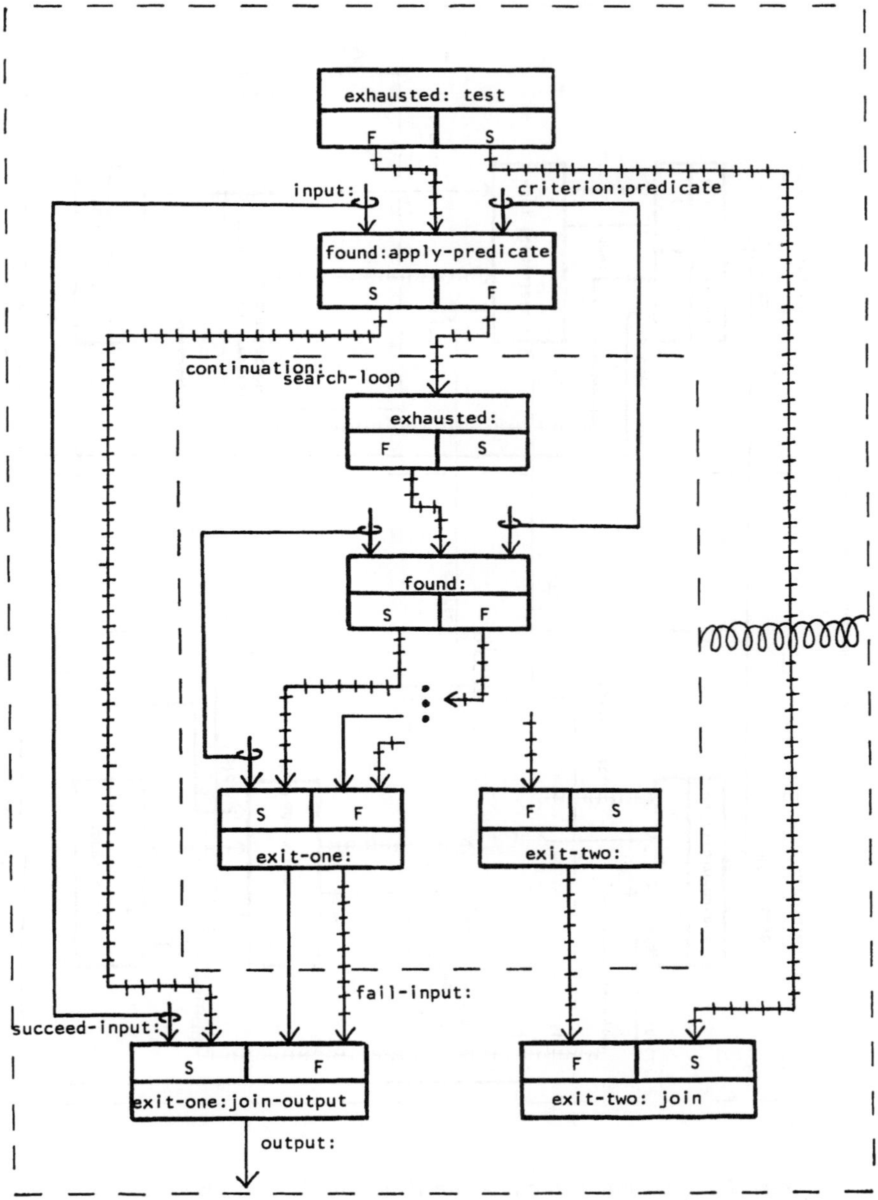

Figure 2.1 Plan for a Search Loop

plans and a set of *correspondences* between the parts of the two plans. Each plan represents a point of view, and the correspondences express the relationship between the points of view. For example, in an

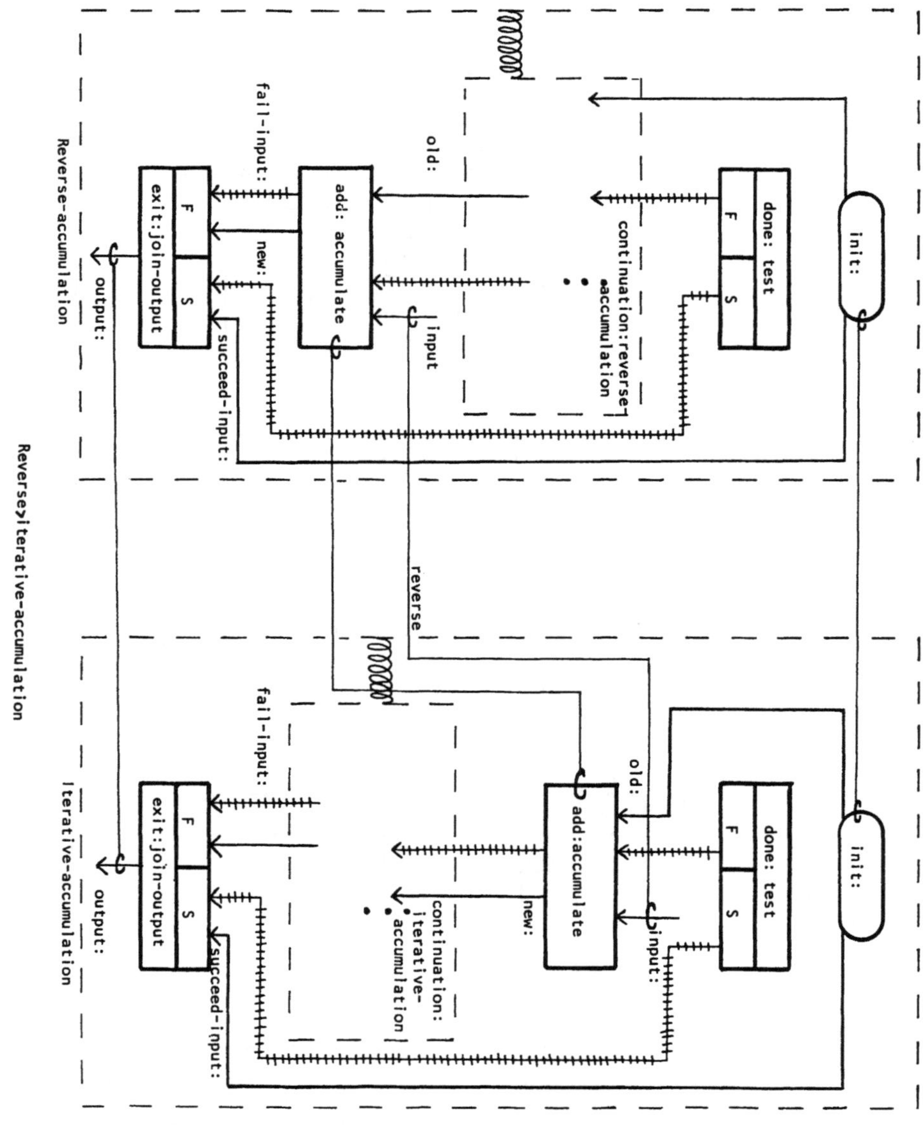

Figure 2.2 Overlay Between Accumulation on the Way Down vs. Up

implementation overlay the plan on the right hand side is the abstract description and the plan on the left hand side is an implementation. It is important, however, that either plan can be used as the "pattern." In a typical program synthesis step using overlays, the right hand plan is used as the pattern and the left hand plan is instantiated as a further implementation. Conversely, in a typical analysis step, the left hand plan serves as the pattern and the right hand plan is instantiated as a more abstract description. With both program refinement rules and knowledge-based[1] program transformations, this sort of symmetric use is not possible since the right hand side of a transformation or refinement rule is typically a sequence of substitutions or modifications to be performed rather than a pattern.

A second problem stemming from the asymmetry of program transformations and refinement rules is their lack of verifiability. The correctness of an overlay in the plan calculus is verified by proving essentially that the constraints of the plan on the left hand side, together with the correspondences (which are formally a set of equalities between terms on the left and terms on the right), imply the constraints of the plan on the right hand side. Neither Balzer's transformation language nor Green and Barstow's refinement tree notation has been adequately formalized to permit the question of correctness to be addressed. The recent work of Broy and Pepper [BP81c] is an improvement, since their transformations have program forms on both the left and right hand sides, with associated proof rules. Unfortunately, they use program schemas as the representation of the standard forms which have the difficulties discussed above.

Another formalism that some people have found attractive for codifying programming knowledge is formal grammars. For example, Ruth [RUTH73] constructed a grammar (that has global switches to control conditional expansions) that represented the class of programs expected to be handed in as exercises in an introductory PL/1 programming class. This grammar was used in a combination of top-down, bottom-up and heuristic parsing techniques in order to recognize correct and near-correct programs. Miller and Goldstein [MG77] also used a grammar formalism (implemented as an augmented transition network) to represent classes of programs in a domain of graphical programming using stick figures. The major shortcoming of these grammars from the point of view of the Programmer's Apprentice is their lack of a clear semantics upon which a verification methodology can be based.

---

1 As opposed to the folding-unfolding and similar transformations of Burstall and Darlington [BD77] which are intended to be a small set of very general transformations that are formally adequate but which must be composed appropriately to construct intuitively meaningful implementation steps.

3. A Situational Calculus

Before defining the plan calculus more formally, we first need to introduce the underlying logical foundations using a *situational calculus* similar to the one developed by Green [GREE69b] and used by McCarthy and Hayes [MH69]. A situational calculus is a variant of predicate calculus in which certain variables and constants are interpreted as denoting *situations*. Situations can be thought of informally as "instants in time" or "states of the world."

3.1 Side Effects

One basic issue to be addressed in the logical foundations of the plan calculus is the description of *mutable objects*. In programming, as in the everyday world of physical objects, objects can change their behavior (or properties) over time without changing their identity. The approach taken by Green to this problem was to add an extra situational variable to the various function and relation symbols which described the time-dependent aspects of objects. So for example, for a mutable set A he would write $member(x,A,s)$ to assert that x is a member of A at time s. At some other time $t \neq s$, it then might be the case that $\neg\, member\,(x,A,t)$. We then say that A has been *modified* or that a *side effect* has occurred.

This situational notation becomes awkward, however, when one introduces defined relationships between objects. For example, suppose we wish to assert that between situations s and t some elements may have been removed from set A, but none have been added. The appropriate relation to use here is subset. In Green's approach we are forced to define subset as follows, adding two situational arguments:

$$subset\,(A,B,s,t) \equiv \forall x\,[member\,(x,A,s) \supset member\,(x,B,t)].$$

We then would then assert $subset\,(A,A,t,s)$ to specify the side effect discussed above.

This chapter proposes an alternative situational calculus that allows us to preserve the standard algebra of set relations. Mutable objects are treated formally here as functions from situations to *behaviors*. Behaviors are mathematical domains, such as sets, in which there are no side effects (*i.e.*, in which the usual axioms of extensionality apply).[2] A mutable set, such as A, is then formally a function from situations to sets. So for example we could write

---

[2] The axiom of extensionality for sets states that two sets are equal if and only if they have exactly the same members.

$A(s) = \{1,2,3\}$

$A(t) = \{1,2\}$ where $s \neq t$.

and $A(t) \subseteq A(s)$ to specify the side effect discussed above.

This is the most straightforward example of specifying side effects. Additional complexity enters in when side effects are combined with hierarchical objects (objects that have objects as parts) and multiple points of view. The representation of such side effects in the situational calculus in these more complex cases will be touched upon slightly in the sections on data plans and overlays. These topics are treated in detail in [RICH80]. Shrobe [SHRO79] also discusses some techniques for reasoning about such complex side effects.

3.2 Control Flow

Besides distinguishing the different behavior states of mutable objects, situations can be used to represent control information. This is achieved formally by introducing a primitive partial order on situations (called *precedes*). Intuitively, this relation captures the notion of states that occur before or after other states. This relation also makes it possible to talk about cyclic computations in which all objects return to the same state as at some earlier time.

Another basic feature of control flow that we need to deal with in the situational calculus is conditionals. To do so formally, we introduce a distinguished constant $\perp$ into the domain of situations, such that $\forall s$ *precedes* $(s, \perp)$.

Intuitively, $\perp$ represents a situation that is never reached. As we shall see in the following section, $\perp$ appears in the axioms for tests as a way of saying that the two branches of a test are mutually exclusive. $\perp$ also gives us the power to talk about the termination of a loop.

3.3 Computations

Given objects and situations, we can by induction construct a domain of n-tuples (and n-tuples of n-tuples) in which the base components are objects and situations. We call each such n-tuple a *computation*. So for example, the 3-tuple $\langle A,s,t \rangle$ is a computation involving the object A and situations s and t. If the assertions given in the example above for A, s and t hold, then this computation involves a side effect to the mutable set A.

As we shall see in the next section, a plan is formally a *predicate* on computations (with the syntactic variation of referring to the components of an n-tuple by selector functions rather than by numerical index).

4. Plans

We are now in a position to give a formal definition of the plan calculus. In doing so, it is important to distinguish three levels of definition:

1. *Plan Diagrams.* This is the diagrammatic notation illustrated in Figure 2.1 and Figure 2.2. Historically this was the first level of the plan calculus to be developed and is still the notation used most by the author for intuition and explanation. It is also the abstract "mental language" of the Programmer's Apprentice, *i.e.*, the most natural language in which to describe its operations and strategies. (Of course there also has to be a concrete implementation of this language in computer memory, as discussed below.)

2. *Formal Semantics.* A systematic method is given to translate each form of plan diagram into the axiomatization of a predicate in the situational calculus. This axiomatization provides the rules of inference on plans, verifiability and additivity. Note also that for presentation purposes the actual formulae associated with some constraints in plans will often be omitted from plan diagrams, and the existence of a constraint just indicated by an arc between the constrained parts.

3. *Implementation.* Several different representations of the plan calculus as Lisp data structures have been implemented and used by the author, Shrobe, and Waters. Two early versions of the implementation used a general purpose fully inverted assertional database with pattern matching (similar to the one used in Conniver [MS73]), in which a separate assertion was stored in order to represent each feature (box, arrow, *etc.*) of a plan diagram. A subsequent re-implementation by Waters optimized this database by providing specific access paths tailored to the specific assertion types and pattern matching that was required by the current Programmer's Apprentice system. Most recently a third version was implemented using McAllester's truth maintenance system [MCAL80] in which the logical axioms are represented explicitly with additional extra-logical annotation that encodes the diagram level information. The implementation level will not be discussed further in this chapter, other than to show the external Lisp form in which plan definitions are entered in the most recent version.

The basic idea of a plan, as used in the Programmer's Apprentice, comes from an analogy between programming and other engineering activities [RSWS78]. "Plans" of various kinds are used by many different kinds of engineers. For example, an electrical engineer uses circuit diagrams and block diagrams at various levels of abstraction. A structural engineer uses large-scale and detailed blue prints that show both the architectural framework of a building and also various subsystems such as heating, wiring and plumbing. A mechanical engineer uses overlapping hierarchical descriptions of the interconnections between mechanical parts and assemblies.

Programming is viewed here as a process involving the construction and manipulation of specifications at various levels of abstraction. In this view, there is no fundamental distinction between specifications and programs. A program (*e.g.*, in Lisp) is merely a specification detailed enough to be carried out by some particular interpreter. This view is consistent with the current trend in computer science toward wide spectrum languages. The advantage of this approach is that various parts of a program design can be refined to different degrees without intervening shifts of formalism.

The current plan calculus is based on a very simple model of computation (some limitations of this model and possible future extensions are discussed in the final remarks). In this model all computations are composed of three types of primitives: operations, tests, and primitive data objects. Corresponding to each primitive type, there is a primitive specification form in the plan calculus. Operations are specified by input-output specifications (preconditions and postconditions). Tests are specified by a condition on the inputs that determines whether the test succeeds or fails. Primitive data objects are specified in an appropriate mathematical theory, such as numbers, sets, or functions.

Plans are composite specifications constructed by the uniform mechanism of defining parts (called *roles*) and *constraints*. Two kinds of plans are distinguished according to the types of the roles. *Data plans* specify data structures whose roles are primitive data objects or other data structures. Data plans thus embody a kind of data abstraction.

Temporal plans specify computations whose parts are operations, tests, data structures or other composite computations. The plan for a search loop in Figure 2.1 is an example of a temporal plan. In addition to arbitrary logical constraints between roles, temporal plans also include data flow and control flow constraints. Temporal plans thus embody a kind of control abstraction. Since temporal plans can have embedded data plans, and the same compositional mechanism is used for both, control and data abstraction are unified in the plan calculus. The following sections describe the diagrams and formal semantics for each kind of plan in detail.

4.1 Input-Output Specifications

In plan diagrams an input-output specification is drawn as a solid rectangular box that has solid arrows entering at the top and leaving at the bottom, as shown in Figure 4.1. Each arrow entering at the top represents an input; each arrow leaving at the bottom represents an output.

$$
\begin{aligned}
&\mathit{Set\text{-}add}\,(\alpha)\equiv\\
&\qquad [\mathit{precedes}\,(\mathit{in}\,(\alpha),\mathit{out}\,(\alpha))\wedge \mathit{co\text{-}occur}(\mathit{in}\,(\alpha),\mathit{out}\,(\alpha))\\
&\qquad \wedge \mathit{set}\,(\mathit{old}\,(\alpha)\,(\mathit{in}\,(\alpha)))\wedge \mathit{set}\,(\mathit{new}\,(\alpha)\,(\mathit{out}\,(\alpha)))\\
&\qquad \wedge\, \mathit{member}\,(\mathit{input}\,(\alpha),\mathit{new}\,(\alpha)\,(\mathit{out}\,(\alpha)))\\
&\qquad \wedge \forall x\,[\mathit{member}\,(x,\mathit{old}\,(\alpha)\,(\mathit{in}\,(\alpha)))\\
&\qquad\qquad\qquad \supset \mathit{member}\,(x,\mathit{new}\,(\alpha)\,(\mathit{out}\,(\alpha)))]\\
&\qquad \wedge \forall x\,[\mathit{member}\,(x,\mathit{new}\,(\alpha)\,(\mathit{out}\,(\alpha)))\wedge x\neq \mathit{input}\\
&\qquad\qquad\qquad \supset \mathit{member}\,(x,\mathit{old}\,(\alpha)\,(\mathit{in}\,(\alpha)))]]
\end{aligned}
$$

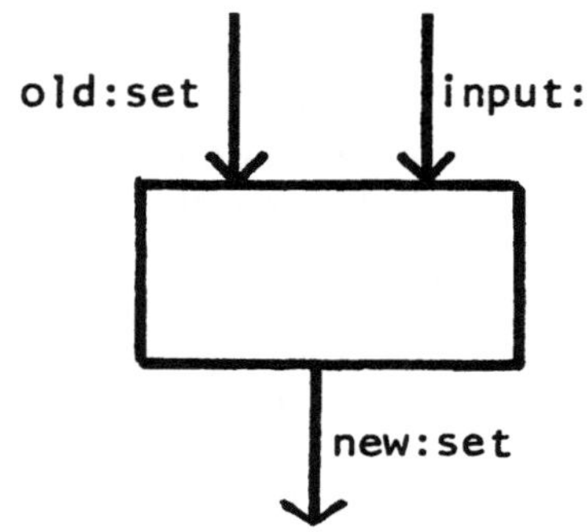


```
(DEFIOSPEC SET-ADD
   ((OLD SET) INPUT)                    ;inputs
   ((NEW SET))                          ;outputs
   ()                                   ;preconditions
   ((MEMBER INPUT (NEW))                ;postconditions
    (FORALL X (IMPLIES (MEMBER X (OLD))
                       (MEMBER X (NEW))))
    (FORALL X (IMPLIES (AND (MEMBER X (NEW))
                            (NOT (= X INPUT)))
                       (MEMBER X (OLD))))))
```

Figure 4.1 *Input-output Specification for Adding to a Set*

Constraints between inputs (preconditions) and between outputs and inputs (postconditions) are usually omitted in plan diagrams.

The definition of Set-add in the external format of the current database implementation is shown in Figure 4.1 next to the diagram. Set-add has two inputs: Old (constrained to be a set), and Input (which may be an object of any type), and no other preconditions. The only output of Set-add is named New (a set). The postconditions of Set-add specify that the New set has exactly the same members as the Old set, with the sole addition of the Input. In terms of its semantics, this input-output specification is translated into a type predicate on computations, Set-add, defined as shown below.[3]

Note that each input and output name becomes a function symbol that is the selector function for a component of a computation. Such functions are called *role functions.* Thus input-output specifications (and also tests), although introduced as primitive above, are in fact composite from the standpoint of the formal semantics. Input and output names are treated as role names in other composite plans.

Note that two role functions in the definition above, In and Out, were implicit in the DEFIOSPEC form. These are situational roles that correspond intuitively to the situations immediately preceding and immediately following the execution of the specified operation. The constraint between them is that the In situation precedes the Out situation, and that they co-occur. Co-occur is an equivalence on situations which is defined as follows.

$$Co\text{-}occur(s,t) \equiv [s=\bot \vee t=\bot]$$

This means that if the In situation is reached, it follows that the Out situation is reached (*i.e.,* the operation terminates). Conversely, if the In situation does not occur (*i.e.,* $s=\bot$), then the Out situation does not occur. This converse implication, together with the axiomatization of tests shown in the next section, guarantees that none of the situations that follow in control flow from the failure side of a test occur.

Finally, note the terms $old(\alpha)(in(\alpha))$ and $new(\alpha)(out(\alpha))$ in the definition of Set-add. Input and output role functions return *objects* that must be applied to the appropriate situational arguments in order to talk about their behavior. Thus Old and New are mutable sets. However this specification makes no commitment about whether or not the Input object is added by side effect. (Note that we don't care about the behavior of the Input object here, only its identity.) Whether or not a side effect is allowed depends on the larger plan in which a particular use of Set-add appears, specifically on whether the Old set is used again after the operation. Formally, the specification of the side effect comes down to the question of equality between the Old and New objects. For example, a specialized form (the specialization mechanism used here will be explained further below) of Set-add can be defined by adding one more simple postcondition that stipulates that the addition be achieved by side effect.

---

[3] The axioms in this paper are slightly simplified by ignoring the fact that certain functions are partial. An axiom of extensionality for each plan type (*i.e.,* equality of instances follows from equality of all the parts) is also being omitted here. The complete axioms are given in [RICH80].

```
(DEFIOSPEC IMPURE-SET-ADD
           SPECIALIZATION SET-ADD
   (OLD INPUT)
   (NEW)
   ()
   ((= OLD NEW)))
```

The meaning of this definition is shown below. Note that whether or not the role function is to be applied to a situational argument is encoded in the database input notation by the presence or absence of parentheses around the role name in the constraint expression.

$$\textit{Impure-set-add}\ (\alpha) \equiv [\textit{set-add}(\alpha) \wedge \textit{old}\ (\alpha) = \textit{new}\ (\alpha)]$$

4.2 Test Specifications

In plan diagrams a test specification is drawn as a solid rectangular box that has a divided bottom part, as shown in Figure 4.2. The inputs and outputs of a test specification and their types are indicated in the same way that the inputs and outputs of an input-output specification are indicated. A test also has preconditions and postconditions, just like an input-output specification. A test specification differs from an input-output specification because two distinct output situations, named Succeed and Fail, are implicitly specified. Which one occurs depends on whether a given relation (called the *condition* of the test) holds true between the inputs. Control flow arcs originating from either the part of the test box marked S (for succeed), or the part marked F (for fail), are then used to indicate which other parts of a plan are executed, depending on the test.[4]

The definition of the test specification Apply-predicate, written in the format of the current database implementation, is also shown in Figure 4.2. Note that this is the test specification used in the Found role of the Search-loop plan of Figure 2.1. The two exit roles of Figure 2.1 illustrate *joins* that are the mirror images of tests in the plan calculus. Joins are required in conditional plans to specify what the output is in each case.

Apply-predicate has two inputs: Criterion (a predicate) and Input (any object to which the predicate is applicable), but it has no outputs. The test succeeds when the Criterion is true of the Input; otherwise it fails. In terms of its semantics, this test specification is translated into a type predicate on computations with three situational roles, In, Succeed, and Fail, as shown below.

[4] More complicated tests using more than two cases can be represented by composing binary tests. Alternatively, the test notation may be generalized to more than two cases.

$$
\begin{aligned}
&\textit{Apply-predicate}(\alpha) \equiv \\
&\quad [\textit{precedes}(\textit{in}(\alpha), \textit{succeed}(\alpha)) \land \textit{precedes}(\textit{in}(\alpha), \textit{fail}(\alpha)) \\
&\quad \land \textit{mutex}(\textit{succeed}(\alpha), \textit{fail}(\alpha)) \\
&\quad \land \textit{predicate}(\textit{criterion}(\alpha)(\textit{in}(\alpha))) \\
&\quad \land \textit{member}(\textit{input}(\alpha), \textit{domain}(\textit{criterion}(\alpha)(\textit{in}(\alpha)))) \\
&\quad \land [\textit{apply}(\textit{criterion}(\alpha)(\textit{in}(\alpha)), \textit{input}(\alpha)) \\
&\qquad \supset \textit{co-occur}(\textit{in}(\alpha), \textit{succeed}(\alpha))] \\
&\quad \land [\neg \textit{apply}(\textit{criterion}(\alpha)(\textit{in}(\alpha)), \textit{input}(\alpha)) \\
&\qquad \supset \textit{co-occur}(\textit{in}(\alpha), \textit{fail}(\alpha))]]
\end{aligned}
$$

$$\textit{Mutex}(s,t) \equiv [s = \bot \lor t = \bot]$$

From this way of defining tests it is possible to reason both backward and forward in time. For example, if the In situation is reached (*i.e.*, $in(\alpha) \neq \bot$) and the Criterion is true, it follows that the Succeed situation is reached. Conversely, if we know that the either the Succeed or Fail situation is reached, it follows that the In situation must have been reached.

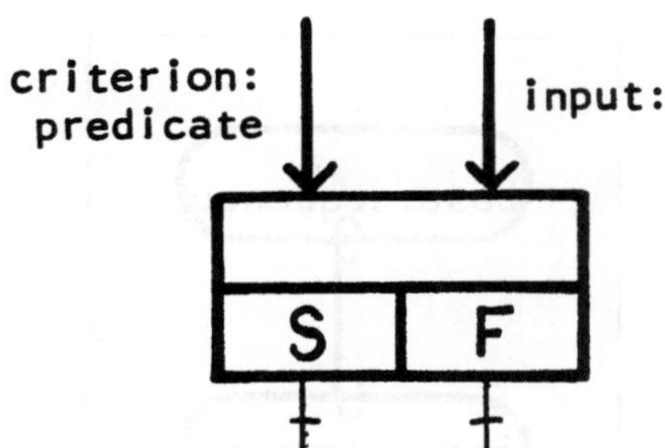


```
(DEFTEST APPLY-PREDICATE
  ((CRITERION PREDICATE) INPUT)             ;inputs
  ()                                        ;outputs
  ((MEMBER INPUT (DOMAIN (CRITERION))))     ;precondns
  ()                                        ;postcondns
  (APPLY (CRITERION) INPUT))                ;test condn
```

Figure 4.2 *Test Specification for Applying a Predicate*

4.3 Data Plans

Data plans are plans whose roles are primitive data objects or other data plans. In plan diagrams primitive data objects are drawn as solid ovals. Data plans are drawn as dashed boxes. Data plans are used to represent standard data structure configurations that may be used in the implementation of more abstract data types. For example, the data plan Indexed-Sequence, shown in Figure 4.3, represents the common cliche of a sequence (typically implemented more concretely as an array) with an associated index pointer. This configuration is typically used to implement such things as buffers, queues, and stacks. (Implementation relationships are represented using overlays, discussed further in another section.)

The plan Indexed-sequence has two roles, Base (a sequence) and Index (an integer). There is the constraint that the Index is between zero and the length of the sequence. The definition of Indexed-sequence in the external format of the database is also shown in Figure 4.3.

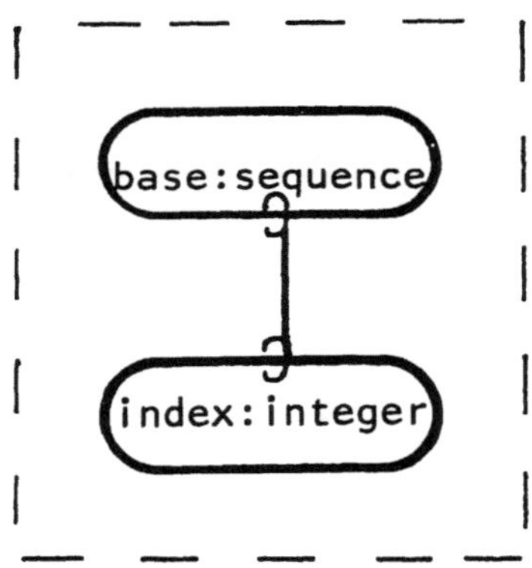


```
(DEFDATAPLAN INDEXED-SEQUENCE
   ((BASE SEQUENCE) (INDEX INTEGER)) ;roles
   ((GT (INDEX) 0)                   ;constraints
    (LE (INDEX) (LENGTH (BASE)))))
```

Figure 4.3 *Data Plan for an Indexed Sequence*

Data plans used as a mechanism for data abstraction are similar in certain ways to to algebraic axioms [GUTT77] [GTW78] and abstract data types [LZ77]. The constraints between roles of a data plan are similar to what is called the *invariant* in other formalisms. From this point of view, the semantic translation of a data plan can be thought of as a data type predicate. For example, Indexed-sequence is defined below.

$$
\begin{aligned}
&\textit{Indexed-sequence}(\delta) \equiv \\
&\qquad \forall s\,[\textit{sequence}(\textit{base}(\delta)(s)) \wedge \textit{integer}(\textit{index}(\delta)(s)) \\
&\qquad\qquad \wedge \textit{gt}(\textit{index}(\delta)(s), 0) \\
&\qquad\qquad \wedge \textit{le}(\textit{index}(\delta)(s), \textit{length}(\textit{base}(\delta)(s)))]
\end{aligned}
$$

Algebraic axioms and abstract data types, however, do not allow one to specify side effects on data structures. All operations are purely functional. In the plan calculus, we single out the primitive selector operations of the data abstraction, which become the role functions. Side effects are then specified in terms of changes to the roles of a data structure. Note that Indexed-sequence is defined as a predicate on behaviors not objects (*i.e.*, δ above is meant to denote a 2-tuple with components named Base and Index). A mutable indexed sequence is an object D such that, for example, $D(s)=\delta$. Aspects of this formalization of mutable data structures are similar to the approaches taken by Earley [EARL71], by Reynolds [REYN79] for reasoning about arrays, and by Guttag and Horning [GH80].

The plan calculus also represents sharing (*i.e.*, aliasing) in composite data objects, which is not the case with algebraic axioms or abstract data types. Space does not allow a full treatment of this topic here (see [RICH80]); the basic idea is that the parts of a composite data object can themselves be data objects (*e.g.*, $\textit{base}(D(s))$ above is a mutable sequence). In this formalization a side effect to $\textit{base}(D(s))$ logically propagates to $D(s)$.

4.4 Temporal Plans

Temporal plans are the most general form of plan in which both data and control abstraction can be expressed. The roles of a temporal plan may be either primitive data objects, data plans, input-output specifications, or test specifications. The most typical constraints between input-output and test specification roles are data flow and control flow constraints. An example of the diagram for a temporal plan is shown in Figure 4.4 (note that Figure 2.1 also illustrates a temporal plan).

The Bump+update plan in Figure 4.4 has four roles: Bump, a subtract one operation; Update, an operation to change one term in a sequence; and Old and New, which are indexed sequence data structures. This plan captures the cliched pattern of operations on an indexed sequence in which the index is decremented and a new term is stored. (Among other things, this is the implementation of a Push operation if the Old and New indexed sequences are viewed as stacks. See the section on overlays.)

Solid arrows in a temporal plan diagram, such as between the Output of the Bump step and the Index input of the Update step, denote data flow (*i.e.*, the Output of Bump becomes the Index input of Update).

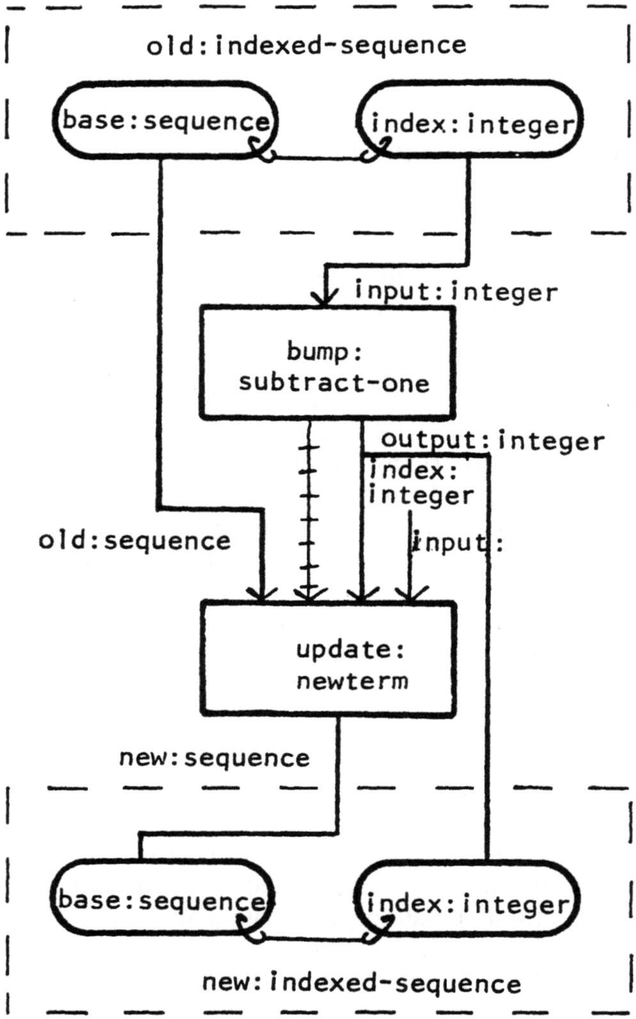


```
(DEFPLAN BUMP+UPDATE
   ;roles
   ((OLD INDEXED-SEQUENCE)(NEW INDEXED-SEQUENCE)
    (BUMP SUBTRACT-ONE)(UPDATE NEWTERM))
   ;constraints
   ((CFLOW (OUT (BUMP)) (IN (UPDATE)))
    (= ((INDEX (OLD))) ((INPUT (BUMP))))
    (= ((BASE (OLD))) ((OLD (UPDATE))))
    (= ((OUTPUT (BUMP))) ((INDEX (UPDATE))))
    (= ((OUTPUT (UPDATE))) ((BASE (NEW))))
    (= ((OUTPUT (BUMP))) ((INDEX (NEW))))))
```

Figure 4.4 *Temporal Plan for Updating an Indexed Sequence*

This notion of data flow is intuitively one of the main sources of additivity in the plan calculus. An arbitrary amount of other computation may be added between Bump and Update as long as the stipulated data flow is not disturbed. As we shall see below, data flow constraints are formalized logically as equalities between terms that denote the respective input and output ports. The additional solid lines in Figure 4.4 denote equality constraints between parts other than the input and output ports of input-output specifications. For example, the Base of the Old indexed sequence becomes the Old sequence input to the Update step. The Base of the New indexed sequence is the New sequence output of the Update step.

A second feature of temporal plan diagrams introduced in Figure 4.4 is control flow (cross-hatched) arrows. The control flow arrow between Bump and Update means that the termination of the Bump step precedes (and implies) the initiation of the Update step. The external plan definition form for Bump+Update given in Figure 4.4 summarizes all of these features. Also shown below are the input-output specifications of the Subtract-one and Newterm, which are straightforward.

```
(DEFIOSPEC SUBTRACT-ONE
   ((INPUT INTEGER))
   ((OUTPUT INTEGER))
   ()
   ((= (OUTPUT)(- (INPUT) 1))))

(DEFIOSPEC NEWTERM
   ((OLD SEQUENCE)(INDEX INTEGER) INPUT)
   ((NEW SEQUENCE))
   ((GT (INDEX) 0)(LE (INDEX)(LENGTH (OLD))))
   ((= (LENGTH (NEW))(LENGTH (OLD)))
    (= (TERM (NEW)(INDEX)) INPUT)
    (FORALL I
     (IMPLIES (NOT (= I (INDEX)))
       (= (TERM (OLD) I)(TERM (NEW) I))))))
```

There are two further features of the Bump+update plan to note before looking at the semantic translation. First, like Set-add this plan makes no commitment to whether or not a side effect is involved. A specialized version of Bump+update can be specified in which the Update step is specialized to an impure Newterm specification, and in which the Old and New indexed sequences are constrained to be identical. Also note that the Input to Newterm (the value of the new term) is not constrained in this plan. Temporal plans are typically combined by providing data flow from and to such ports.

Shown below are the semantics of the temporal plan Bump+update which is defined, similar to input-output and test specifications, as a predicate on computations.

$$
\begin{aligned}
&\mathit{Bump{+}update}(\alpha) \equiv \\
&\quad [\mathit{subtract{-}one}(\mathit{bump}(\alpha)) \wedge \mathit{newterm}(\mathit{update}(\alpha)) \\
&\quad \wedge \mathit{cflow}(\mathit{out}(\mathit{bump}(\alpha)), \mathit{in}(\mathit{update}(\alpha))) \\
&\quad \wedge \mathit{output}(\mathit{bump}(\alpha))(\mathit{out}(\mathit{bump}(\alpha))) \\
&\qquad = \mathit{index}(\mathit{update}(\alpha))(\mathit{in}(\mathit{update}(\alpha))) \\
&\quad \wedge \exists s\, [\mathit{indexed{-}sequence}(\mathit{old}(\alpha)(s)) \\
&\qquad \wedge \mathit{index}(\mathit{old}(\alpha)(s))(s) = \mathit{input}(\mathit{bump}(\alpha))(\mathit{in}(\mathit{bump}(\alpha))) \\
&\qquad \wedge \mathit{base}(\mathit{old}(\alpha)(s))(s) = \mathit{old}(\mathit{update}(\alpha))(\mathit{in}(\mathit{update}(\alpha)))] \\
&\quad \wedge \exists t\, [\mathit{indexed{-}sequence}(\mathit{new}(\alpha)(t)) \\
&\qquad \wedge \mathit{index}(\mathit{new}(\alpha)(t))(t) = \mathit{output}(\mathit{bump}(\alpha))(\mathit{out}(\mathit{bump}(\alpha))) \\
&\qquad \wedge \mathit{base}(\mathit{new}(\alpha)(t))(t) = \mathit{output}(\mathit{update}(\alpha))(\mathit{out}(\mathit{update}(\alpha)))]]
\end{aligned}
$$

$$\mathit{Cflow}(s,t) \equiv [\mathit{precedes}(s,t) \wedge \mathit{co\text{-}occur}(s,t)]$$

The interpretation of this formal definition is left largely to the reader. The major complexity of translating temporal plans into their logical equivalent is in providing the appropriate situational arguments. In particular, for roles that are data plans, such as Old and New above, we posit the existence of some situation (*e.g.*, s and t above) in which the constraints of the data plan hold, and then assert constraints between the behavior of the parts in that situation and the input and output ports to which they are connected in the plan diagram. The default situational arguments for input and output ports here are assigned in the same way as the corresponding input-output specifications, namely In for input objects and Out for output objects.

The Bump+update plan does not illustrate an additional important feature of temporal plans, namely the use of recursion to represent loops. Recent work on Lisp interpreters [SS78b] and compilers [STEE78] suggests that the distinction between loops and singly recursive programs in which the recursive call is the last step of the program (so called "tail recursions") should be considered only a superficial syntactic variation. The plan calculus takes this point of view. Recursion in plan diagrams (data plans may also be recursively defined) is indicated by a spiral line as shown in Figure 2.1, the plan for a search loop, introduced earlier.

4.5 Programming Languages

The plan calculus makes it possible to build a Programmer's Apprentice which is concerned with the syntactic details of different programming languages only at its most superficial interface. In order to translate back and forth between a given programming language and the plan calculus, the primitives of the programming language are divided into two categories:

1. The primitive *actions* and *tests* of the language, such as CAR, CDR, CONS, NULL, and EQ in Lisp, are represented as input-output specifications and test specifications.

2. The primitive *connectives*, such as PROG, COND, SETQ, GO, and RETURN in Lisp, are represented as patterns of control and data flow constraints between operations and tests.

The translation from standard program text to an equivalent plan representation has been implemented for reasonable subsets of Lisp [RS76], Fortran [WATE79], and Cobol [FAUS81]. The translation from suitably restricted plans to Lisp code has also been implemented by Waters [WATE81].

5. Relations Between Plans

Figure 5.1 is a small excerpt from the current plan library that illustrates the the taxonomic structure of the library. An initial observation to make about the nodes of the library shown in this example is that they are a mixture of both data abstractions (*e.g.*, set, predicate, directed graph) and control abstractions. (Find and Thread-find are input-output specifications, and in general there are also temporal plans in the library, but none are shown here.)

The four types of relations that relate nodes of the library are named in the upper right hand corner of the figure next to an example of the type of line or arrow used to represent each relation in the body of the figure. The first relation, *component*, simply indexes which plans are used in the definition of other plans, as for example Indexed-sequence was used in the definition of Bump+update above. The next two relations are simple inheritance relationships by which a plan inherits the roles and constraints of another plan and then adds its own additional roles or constraints or both. *Specialization* is the relation in which only constraints are added; *extension* involves adding roles (and usually, constraints between new roles and inherited ones).

Overlays are the most important type of relation between plans in the library because overlays represent significant additional knowledge, such as the details of how one abstraction may be implemented in terms of another. The diagram notation and semantics for overlays are explained in the following section.

Starting with Set in Figure 5.1, a typical question we might want to ask in the course of program analysis or synthesis is, What plans (*e.g.*, input-output specifications) in the library use sets? This type of question is answered in general by looking up the composition relation (in this example from Set to Find). Find is an input-output specification

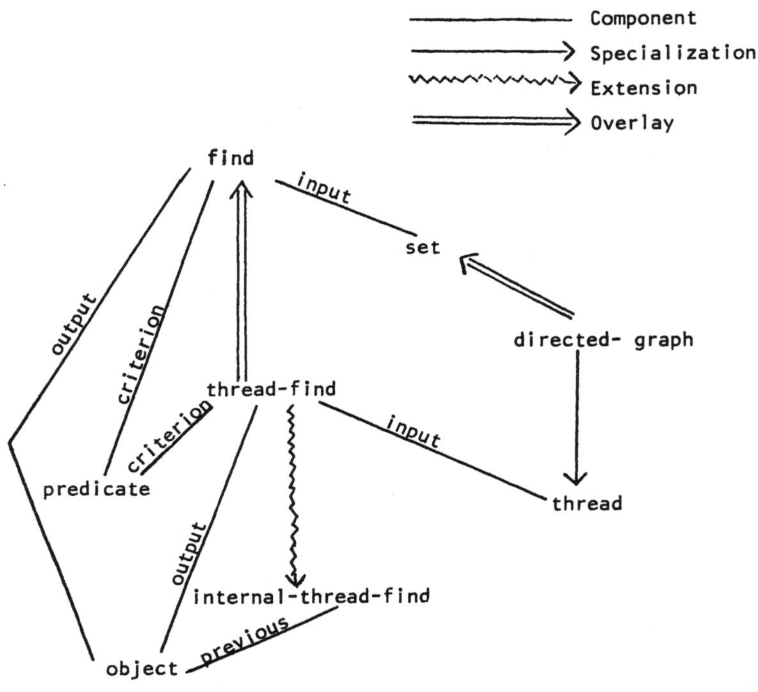

Figure 5.1 Excerpt from Plan Library Illustrating Taxonomic Relations

that has three roles, an Input set, a Criterion predicate, and an Output object. Its precondition is that an element of the Input set exists that satisfies the Criterion. Its postcondition is that the Output is such an element.

Overlays pointing to a node answer questions of the form, What implementations are available for Find operations? In this example, one answer is that Find may be implemented as Thread-find, where the Input set is implemented as a thread. (Note that Thread is a specialization of Directed-graph in which each node has at most one predecessor or successor and there are no cycles.) The input-output specifications of Thread-find are shown below. It has three roles similar to Find: an Input thread, a Criterion predicate, and an Output object. Its precondition is that a node of the Input thread exists that satisfies the Criterion. Its postcondition is that the Output is such a node.

```
(DEFIOSPEC THREAD-FIND
   ((INPUT THREAD)(CRITERION PREDICATE))
   (OUTPUT)
   ((EXISTS X (AND (NODE (INPUT) X)
                   (APPLY (CRITERION) X))))
   ((NODE (INPUT) OUTPUT)
    (APPLY (CRITERION) OUTPUT)))
```

Finally, extension is a relation between plans that can be used to access useful variations of a plan. For example, in the figure an extension of Thread-find is Internal-thread-find. The input-output specifications of Internal-thread-find are shown below.

```
(DEFIOSPEC INTERNAL-THREAD-FIND
           EXTENSION THREAD-FIND
   (INPUT CRITERION)
   (OUTPUT PREVIOUS)
   ((NOT (APPLY (CRITERION)(ROOT (INPUT)))))
   ((SUCCESSOR (INPUT) PREVIOUS OUTPUT)))
```

Note that an additional output role, Previous, has been added with the constraint that it be the predecessor of the Output node in the Input thread. This is a very common kind of operation on directed graphs when splicing of nodes in and out is being performed. In order to be used properly, Internal-thread-find must also have the additional precondition (from which its name is suggested) that the Criterion is false for the root node of the Input thread.

5.1 Overlays

Overlays provide a mechanism in the plan calculus for representing the relationship between two different points of view, each of which is represented by a plan. Overlays are similar to Sussman's "slices" [SUSS78], which he uses to represent equivalences in electronic circuit analysis and synthesis. Formally, an overlay is a mapping from instances of one plan to instances of another. Such mappings are a very general mechanism. The intuitive import of various overlays depends on what kind of plans are involved, whether the mapping is many-to-one or one-to-one, and how the mapping is defined.

An example of an overlay between a temporal plan and an input-output specification is shown in Figure 5.2. Intuitively, this overlay expresses how a Push operation can be implemented by the Bump+update plan discussed above, given that the stack is implemented as an indexed sequence.

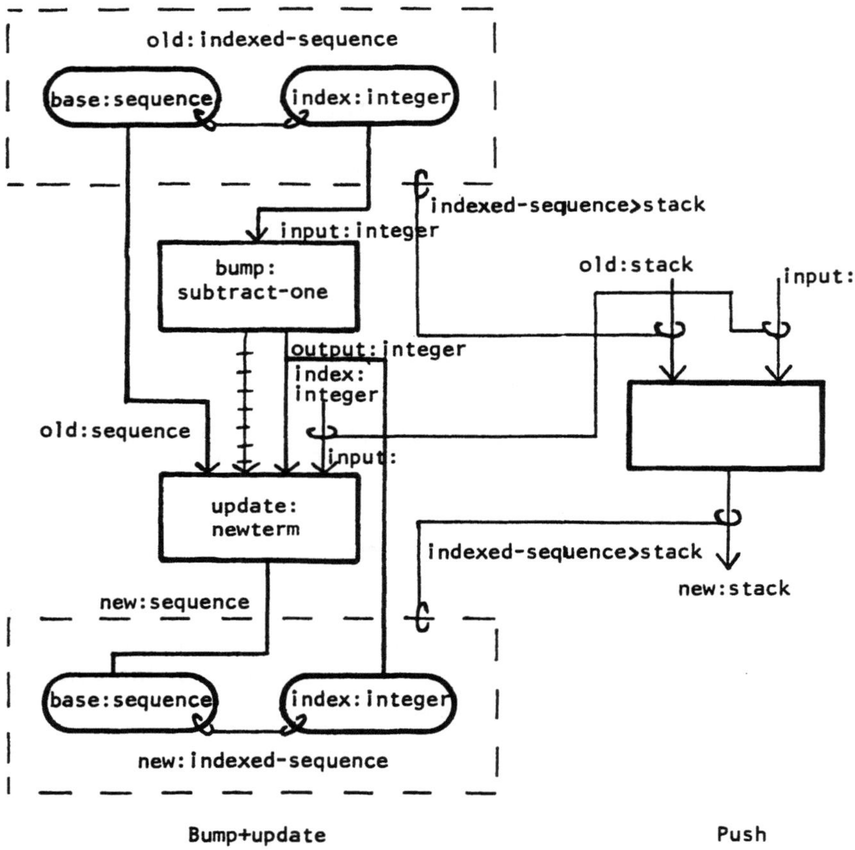

Figure 5.2 Implementation Overlay for Push on Indexed Sequence

Note that the diagram for an overlay is composed of a plan on the left hand side (which is the domain of the mapping), a plan on the right hand side (which is the range of the mapping), and a set of hooked lines showing a set of *correspondences* between roles of the two plans (which defines the mapping). In the external format of the current database, an overlay is defined as follows.

```
(DEFOVERLAY BUMP+UPDATE>PUSH (BUMP+UPDATE PUSH)
   (= (OLD PUSH)
      (INDEXED-SEQUENCE>STACK (OLD BUMP+UPDATE)))
   (= (NEW PUSH)
      (INDEXED-SEQUENCE>STACK (NEW BUMP+UPDATE)))
   (= (INPUT PUSH) (INPUT (UPDATE BUMP+UPDATE)))
   (= (IN PUSH) (IN (BUMP BUMP+UPDATE)))
   (= (OUT PUSH) (OUT (UPDATE BUMP+UPDATE))))
```

Notice that each overlay has a name (*e.g.*, Bump+update>push)[5] that will become a function symbol in the formal semantics. Correspondences between roles are either simple equalities, as in

```
(= (INPUT PUSH) (INPUT (UPDATE BUMP+UPDATE))),
```

which says that the Input to Push (the object which becomes the head of the new stack) corresponds to the Input of the Update step in the Bump+update plan, or correspondences defined in terms of other overlays, as in

```
(= (OLD PUSH)
   (INDEXED-SEQUENCE>STACK (OLD BUMP+UPDATE))).
```

The overlay Indexed-sequence>stack is an example of a many-to-one overlay between data plans. The basic idea of this overlay is that an indexed sequence may be viewed as the implementation of a stack in which the head is the term of the sequence indexed by the current index, and the tail is, recursively, the sequence with index value one greater. The formal definition of this overlay will not be shown here because it is very similar to what is called an abstraction function in abstract data types. The formal semantics of the Bump+update>push overlay is the following function definition.

$$
\begin{aligned}
\beta = \mathit{Bump+update>push}(\alpha) \equiv \\
&[\mathit{old}(\beta) = \mathit{indexed\text{-}sequence>stack}(\mathit{old}(\alpha)) \\
&\wedge \mathit{new}(\beta) = \mathit{indexed\text{-}sequence>stack}(\mathit{new}(\alpha)) \\
&\wedge \mathit{input}(\beta) = \mathit{input}(\mathit{update}(\alpha)) \\
&\wedge \mathit{in}(\beta) = \mathit{in}(\mathit{bump}(\alpha)) \\
&\wedge \mathit{out}(\beta) = \mathit{out}(\mathit{update}(\alpha))]
\end{aligned}
$$

Implementation overlays such as Bump+update>push and Indexed-sequence>stack are typically many-to-one. There are also one-to-one overlays in the library, which are naturally thought of as providing alternative points of view or transformations of data or control structure. For example, a Lisp list can be viewed alternatively as a stack (*i.e.*, a

---

[5] This symbol is intended to be read "Bump and Update as Push".

recursively defined data structure), as a labelled directed graph (in particular a thread) wherein the nodes are Cons cells connected by the Cdr relation and labelled by the Car relation, or as a sequence wherein the *i*th term is the Car of (*i*−1)th Cdr. Each of these data plans provides its own vocabulary for specifying properties of a data structure and a standard set of manipulations on it. There are one-to-one overlays in the library between them so that the appropriate point of view can be used depending on the properties and manipulations of interest. There are also one-to-one overlays in the library between temporal plans, such the overlay introduced earlier in Figure 2.2 that captures the relationship in general between singly recursive programs that accumulate "on the way down" (*e.g.*, reverse copying a list), and those that accumulate "on the way up" (*e.g.*, copying a list).

Other overlays of particular interest are those that map from temporal plans to data plans, in particular from recursive temporal plans to lists. These latter are called *stream* overlays and embody a kind of abstraction in which the objects filling a given role at all levels in a recursive plan are viewed as a single data structure. For example, there is a stream overlay in the library by means of which the succession of Inputs to the Found test in the Search-loop plan are viewed as a list. And if that overlay is composed with the overlay to view a list as the implementation of a set, then Search-loop can be viewed as the implementation of the Find specification discussed above. This method of abstraction provides a very powerful means of decomposing loops and recursions in a way that makes their behavior easier to understand than the standard invariant assertion method. For a further discussion of this idea see Waters [WATE79].

A final note regarding the use of overlays is that they are not only part of the taxonomic structure of the plan library, they are also used to construct the refinement tree of a particular program. This tree encodes the design history of a program at many levels of detail. A way in which overlays differ from other refinement tree notations is that overlays permit *overlapping* implementations [RICH81], and components that are distinct at one level of abstraction share parts at lower levels. This is a feature of good engineering design and is an important way in which overlays are an improvement over previous notations.

6. Final Remarks

The emphasis in this paper on representation rather than reasoning should not obscure an important dimension of the plan calculus. In the Programmer's Apprentice, reasoning about plans takes place within a system [MCAL80] that maintains explicit dependencies between each assertion in the data base. These dependencies are crucial for supporting evolutionary design and debugging programs. Each overlay in the library has a precompiled network of dependencies between the specifications on the left and right hand sides (called its *teleological* structure) which is instantiated along with the parts, constraints, and correspondences when it is used.

There are several areas in which we have found the current plan calculus deficient, and we hope to extend it further in the future. Important among these are the following:

1. *Performance Considerations.* A way of formalizing time and space trade-offs is needed both for the library and for reasoning about particular programs.

2. *Error Handling.* The non-local flow of control typically involved in error handling code is not well represented in the current plan calculus.

3. *Global Shared Data.* Programs that communicate primarily by inserting and retrieving information in a global shared database are not well decomposed by the data flow ideas in the current calculus.

Finally, we intend to investigate the usefulness of the plan calculus in other planning contexts. In particular, I believe there is potential for a fruitful flow of ideas between program understanding (analysis, synthesis, and verification) and robot planning (*e.g.,* Abstrips [SACE74]). Many of the insights underlying the plan calculus originate from work in robot planning. I also believe that some of the techniques developed in the plan calculus for representing and reasoning about overlapping data structures and side effects have bearing on aspects of the classical "frame problem" [MH69] in robot planning.

7. References

[BALZ81] [BARS77] [BD77] [BM76] [BP81c] [CHEA81] [DENN74] [DN66] [EARL71] [FAUS81] [GERH75] [GH80] [GREE69c] [GTW78] [GUTT77] [LISK77] [LZ77] [MANN74] [MCAL80] [MG77] [MH69] [MISR78] [MS73] [REYN79] [RS76] [RSW79] [RSWS78] [RICH80] [RICH81] [RUTH73] [SACE74] [SCHW75] [SHRO79] [SS78b] [STEE78] [SUSS78] [SWL79] [WATE78] [WATE79] [WATE81] [WINO73] [WIRT73]

Discussion

The basic insight of this chapter is that programmers conceptualize in larger chunks than:

```
if ... then ... else ... fi
while ... do ... od, etc.
```

The question raised is how to take advantage of this insight in order to provide better tools for managing the complexity of program development. The solution proposed in this chapter is the Plan Calculus which unifies in one formalism ideas from flowchart and data flow schemata, program transformations, and abstract data types. The key features of the Plan Calculus are:

- Language independence. Ordinary programming language syntax does not support the right kinds of generalization.
- Additivity. Well formed composition rules are needed to put together program chunks meaningfully.
- Verifiability. Elements Being combined are large enough that correctness is not obvious and needs to be taken into account in the development of the Plan Calculus.
- Multiple points of view. "Overlays" support overlapping definitions and other interactions.

Language Independence

A "loop" has several different syntactic forms such as:

```
for ... do ... od
while ... do ... od
L: (COND (done NIL)
   (T (... L)))
```

When none of these is appropriate for a particular situation, the programmer has to improvise. The idea behind the Plan Calculus is to capture all the different flavors of a loop in terms of a single plan.

Additivity

In order for any "calculus" to be effective, it must offer composition rules that yield elements suitable for further composition. Programming languages do this, but only weakly: syntactically through the use of grammar nonterminals, and semantically through parameter binding. Programmers exploit a much richer space of relations in order to take advantage of similarity, overlap, or redundancy among program objects. Traditional structured programming techniques emphasize program decomposition. The Plan Calculus equally stresses composition and decomposition. As a result, it can be used both for program analysis and synthesis, unlike other work such as David Burstow's Ph.D. thesis on knowledge-based program synthesis. One can think of a Plan Calculus knowledge base as a library of programming "cliches" that are represented declaratively and can be used generatively, to produce a program, or as a parser, to analyze a program. The key idea here is that you need to represent your algorithms in terms of loosely coupled subsystems. Among other things, this idea suggests that one way to maintain a large program is to describe it in terms of the Plan Calculus, and then maintain that description in order to avoid maintenance at the code level.

This work assumes that the system will help an expert programmer with his task—much like an apprentice, never taking the programmer away from something he could have done previously. The apprentice metaphor implies that if we build an editor that can handle logical structure, it should not take away from the user the ability to operate either at a syntax or text structure level. It was a mistake to develop syntax editors that do not let their users touch text. Instead, it makes much more sense to allow the users to operate on the text and then have the system reanalyze its syntactic structure.

Verifiability

Any time a component is used on the basis of its specification (alone), it is critical that the specification be correct. Hence the importance of verification and the attention paid here to formal semantics for situations and plans.

There are two potential contributions that a formal semantics can make to a programming language. It could be a useful tool for programmers who use the language and who wish to find out what things mean. Denotational semantics, as a case in point, is not useful in this sense today, although a derivative system might be in the future. A formal semantics can also call one's attention to specific features of a programming language that require care. With denotational semantics, for example, there is a strong emphasis on understanding the distinction between syntax and semantics.

Something similar can be said about verification. Verification is not at this point a tool for practical programming, although some day it will be. On the other hand, teaching programmers verification permits them to think about their programs in a new way, and they can construct programs keeping verifiability in mind as a design criterion.

Multiple Points of View

It is frequently helpful to view a single entity in different ways at different times (*e.g.*, at different abstraction levels, as data or control, or as an instance of several different types). The Plan Calculus supports this idea through the notion of "overlay."

It is not true that in the Plan Calculus an object can be an instance of many types at the same time. Rather, projection functions are provided which project an object of type A onto another one of type B. Unlike a system like FLAVORS, you cannot have an object that is at the same time an instance of type A and B. So, for example, you couldn't build an object that is an instance of TREE and LIST and call it a threaded tree. It is interesting to note that the use of projection functions sidesteps the view update problem encountered in Databases research.

Implementation

A special knowledge-based editor has been implemented by Richard Waters that can operate at a textual, syntactic, and logical level. The editor was implemented as an extension of EMACS, a LISP editor that can handle both text and syntax for LISP. The editor maintains a library of plans in the background to analyze a piece of code that might be typed in by a programmer. The library is also used to put together plans in terms of composition rules and code can be generated for composite plans.

The long term goal for this project is to extend the editor so that it can reason about the programs under construction and can use default designs appropriately.

Programming Practice

The Programmer's Apprentice project in its current state is not intended to help the programmer or manager who is responsible for maintaining a very large existing program. The tools that might be helpful in such a situation include a version control system, a performance assistant that can identify places where the program can be improved through macro expansion or other simple means, and a reference index that will help whenever the code needs to undergo change. On the other hand, if one were to start developing a large program from scratch, the knowledge-based editor could help in the creation of a conceptual description of what the program does. This description could then be of great value in maintaining the program or understanding the difference between versions.

Automatic programming is totally unrealistic for a general setting. It may be feasible for a very narrow domain such as data management programs, but for more general problem areas we can only hope to achieve a partial automation mode. This is why the project stresses so much the programming apprentice metaphor. The programmer gets help from the system in doing simple things, he gets bits and pieces of code, and he also has his code criticized and documented.

Conclusions

The results on multiple viewpoints presented in this work reinforce the argument that strict type hierarchies are too rigid. The Plan Calculus also illustrates the importance of rigorous program composition techniques that include general operators that map programs onto other programs.

One question that remains open concerns the graphical techniques used and how difficult it will be to make them rigorous.

Part III

Perspectives from Databases

10
On the Design and Specification of Database Transactions

Michael L. Brodie
Computer Corporation of America

Dzenan Ridjanovic
University of Minnesota

ABSTRACT *A complete design and specification of database transactions must include both structural and behavioural properties. Structure deals with states and static properties while behaviour concerns state transitions and dynamic properties. Database design techniques emphasize the importance of behaviour but seldom provide for modelling and integrating behaviour* and *structure.*

This chapter presents concepts, tools, and techniques for the design and specification of behavioural and structural properties of database transactions. The concepts, tools, and techniques result from the integration of programming language (PL) and database (DB) technologies. Design principles from PLs (e.g., *abstraction and refinement), are applied to DB design and a new DB design principle, called localization, is proposed. PL concepts such as procedural abstractions, abstract data types, control structures, and specification techniques are integrated with DB concepts such as data abstractions, integrity constraints, data structures, and data models to produce a semantic data model for the conceptual design of databases and their associated transactions. The integration is based on the correspondence between the structure of complex databases and the structure of the associated transactions. In the proposed methodology, hierarchies of transactions and their constituent actions are designed in correspondence with the hierarchies designed to relate objects. As proposed in both artificial intelligence and PLs, design and specification are leveled. Gross design is done using graphic notation while detailed design is done using a conventional predicate based specification language. Appropriate concepts, tools, and techniques are presented for each level. The methodology is adequate for most database applications. However, complex and critical database applications* (e.g., *critical patient care, nuclear power plants) require precise, structured specifications. An appropriate formal specification technique, based on functional programming, is introduced. Formal specifications support increased precision and permit automated analysis and verification. The motivation for this work is similar to that for precise specifications in PLs. However, the existence of a database changes the nature of the problem and the required solution.*

The relationship between this chapter and other chapters is presented in a concluding Epilogue.

1. Motivation

Database applications have both structural and behavioural properties. *Structure* refers to states and static properties (*i.e.*, entities and their relationships). *Behaviour* refers to state transitions and dynamic properties (*i.e.*, operations and their relationships). A complete design and specification of a database application must include both structure and behaviour. For example, only part of the semantics of *hotel-reservation* is given in the structural properties represented by the relation *hotel-reservation (reservation#, hotel, room, person, arrival-date, departure-date)* represented in Figure 1.1. The semantics of actions that alter *hotel-reservation,* such as *insert-hotel-reservation, delete-hotel-reservation,* and *update-hotel-reservation,* is needed to complete the definition. The actions can then be used to design more complex operations such as *cancel-reservation, make-group-reservation,* and *convert-reservation-to-registration.* Database design requires concepts, tools, and techniques for modelling both structure and behaviour.

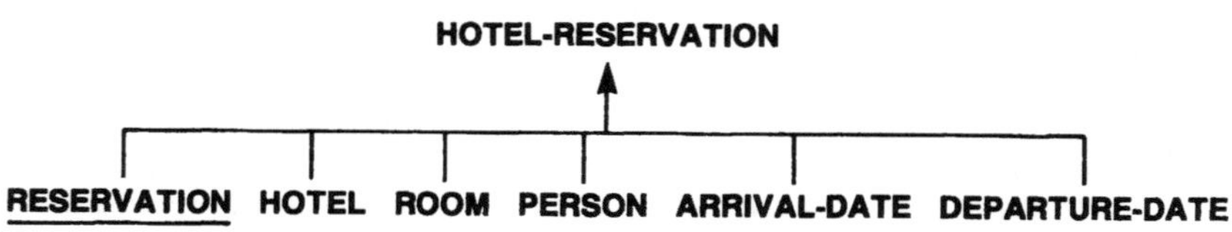

Figure 1.1 *Hotel-Reservation Object Scheme*

A principal objective of database design has been to extract as many structural properties as possible from programs that will access the database in order to define conceptual and external schemas. Consequently, many excellent concepts, such as semantic data models, were developed to deal with structure explicitly and abstractly (see the database overview by Ridjanovic, Brodie, and McLeod). Some behavioural properties are defined implicitly by structural properties. The remaining behavioural properties are defined using insert, update, and delete primitives and procedural abstractions not included in data models. The separate treatment of structure and behaviour complicates design, specification, modification, and semantic integrity analysis. Increasingly, the database emphasis on structure is shifting to include behaviour [SUNA78] (and the chapters by Borgida, Mylopoulos and Wong and by King and McLeod).

In the programming language area, behavioural properties are considered to be more abstract (*i.e.*, representation-free) than structural properties. As a result many excellent concepts, such as procedural and control abstractions, have been developed to deal explicitly and abstractly with behaviour. Some structural properties are specified implicitly by behavioural properties (*e.g.*, abstract data types). The emphasis on behaviour is currently shifting in light of recent interest in data abstractions (see the chapter by Shaw) and object-oriented programming.

2. Active and Passive Component Modelling

This chapter presents concepts, tools, and techniques for the design and specification of database applications and an associated design methodology called Active and Passive Component Modelling (ACM/PCM) [BROD81a] [BS82c] [RB82a] [RB82b] [RB82d].

Two principles are used in ACM/PCM to manage the complexity of database design: the principle of abstraction and the principle of localization. The *principle of abstraction* is the suppression of some detail in order to emphasize more appropriate detail (see the chapter by Shaw). ACM/PCM integrates behaviour and structure by means of data abstractions and abstract data types. Data abstraction here refers to composition rules used to compose higher level data objects from its constituents. Both structural and behavioural properties of each application object are defined completely in an integration of data abstraction and abstract data type. The *principle of localization* leads a designer to model each property of an application object independently (localized) and then to integrate the properties to produce a complete design. Concepts and tools are presented for the design and specification of data and procedural abstractions using the principle of localization.

Behaviour modelling concepts are presented as extensions of the semantic hierarchy model [SS77b]. The additions are a structural abstraction and forms of control and procedural abstraction with which to compose abstract operations. These behavioural abstractions are similar to the structural abstractions used to compose abstract objects from primitive objects.

In ACM/PCM, three levels are distinguished: the transaction level, the conceptual level, and the database level. The levels are similar to those in the ANSI/SPARC architecture. The transaction level, like the external schema level, is designed for specific application and end user needs. *Transaction modelling* involves the design and specification of structural and behavioural properties of transactions, queries, and reports. The conceptual level, like the conceptual schema level, is designed to meet the common needs of all known transactions. *Conceptual modelling* involves the design and specification using data abstraction of an abstract data type (*i.e.*, structure and actions) for each application object. The database level, like the internal schema level, involves the implementation and maintenance of the properties specified at the other levels using existing software (*e.g.*, DBMSs and programming languages). Modelling at all three levels involves behaviour and structure. This chapter focuses on behaviour modelling at the conceptual and transaction levels. The design and specification of database structure is described in more detail elsewhere [BROD80a] [BROD81a] [BROD82] [RB82a] [RB82b] [RB82c].

The result of applying ACM/PCM to an application is not only a deep structure (hierarchy) of objects but also a corresponding deep structure (hierarchy) of procedures. A procedure hierarchy, called a transaction-action hierarchy, goes across the three levels and defines the invocation hierarchy of the transaction. The concept of procedure hierarchies is used extensively in the chapter by Borgida, Mylopoulos, and Wong.

ACM/PCM integrates operation (action and transaction) modelling with event modelling. An action is a behavioural property of one object and can be invoked to produce a state transition for the object. A transaction is composed of actions and produces a collection of logically related state transitions called an event. Hence, a class of events is designed by modelling a transaction. This approach to event modelling has several advantages. First, behavioural relationships among actions are used explicitly to define legal event classes. As the chapter will show, behavioural relationships (composition rules) among actions can be deduced directly from the structural relationships among the corresponding objects. Second, time can be modelled to the extent that actions and transactions can be invoked to run in sequence or in parallel.

Modelling in ACM/PCM proceeds in two steps. First, properties are designed at a gross level of detail. Then, the properties are specified precisely in an incremental way. The design levels are intended to support abstraction through incremental design as is intended for the design and conceptual schema approach presented in the chapter by King and McLeod. This chapter presents object schemes and behaviour schemes as design aids for gross design and semi-formal and formal behaviour specifications for precise design.

3. Structure Modelling

3.1 Extended Semantic Hierarchy Model (SHM+)

For the design and specification of structural properties of database applications, SHM+ provides one structural concept, the object, and four forms of data abstraction for relating objects: classification, aggregation, generalization, and association. The data abstractions are fundamental for most semantic data models. Classification, aggregation, and generalization are being used in various forms [SS77b] (and the chapters by Borgida, Mylopoulos and Wong and by McLeod and King) whereas association has only recently been formalized [BROD81a] [RB82a] [RB82c].

Classification is a form of abstraction in which a collection of objects is considered as a higher level object class. An *object class* is a precise characterization of all properties shared by each object in the collection. An *object* is an instance of an object class if it has the properties defined in the class. Classification represents an ***instance-of*** relationship between an object class in a schema and an object in a database. For example, an object class *employee* that has properties *employee-name, employee-number,* and *salary* may have as an instance the object with property values "John Smith," 402, and $50,000. Classification is used in conceptual modelling to identify, classify, and describe objects in terms of object classes. In the remainder of the chapter, "object" is used to refer to object classes and the associated objects except when the two concepts must be distinguished.

Aggregation, generalization, and association are used to relate objects. Some properties of an object are determined through inheritance by the role it plays in one or more of these relationships. *Aggregation* is a form of abstraction in which a relationship between *component objects* is considered as a higher level *aggregate object.* This is the ***part-of*** relationship. For example, an *employee* may be an aggregate of components *employee-number, employee-name,* and *salary. Generalization* is a form of abstraction in which a relationship between *category objects* is considered as a higher level *generic object.* This is the ***is-a*** relationship. For example, the generic *employee* may be a generalization of categories *secretary* and *manager* (*i.e., secretary* ***is-a*** *employee* and *manager* ***is-a*** *employee*). *Association* is a form of abstraction in which a relationship between *member objects* is considered as a higher level *set object.* This is the ***member-of*** relationship. For example, the set *trade-union* is an association of *employee* members and the set *management* is an association of *employee* members.

The important features of aggregation, generalization, and association are expressed in the following predicate calculus and set theoretic expressions: (when P is a predicate, let the set of P_s denote $\{x|P(x)\}$).
Aggregation: Let A be the aggregate with components P_i.

$$A(x) <=> \exists y_1, \ldots, y_n P_1(x,y_1) \,\&\, \ldots \,\&\, P_n(x,y_n)$$

$$x \in A_s <=> x \in \{z | \exists y_1 P_1(z,y_1)\} \,\&\, \ldots \,\&\, x \in \{z | \exists y_n P_n(z,y_n)\}$$

Generalization: Let G be the generic with categories C_i.

$$C_i(x) => G(x)$$

$$x \in C_{i_s} => x \in G_s \text{ or } C_{i_s} \subset G_s$$

Association: Let S be the set type and M be the member type.

$$S(x) <=> \forall y (y \in x => M(y))$$

$$x \in S_s <=> x \in P(M) \text{ where } P(x) \text{ is the power set over } x.$$

The predicate calculus and set theoretic expressions are intended to give intuition into the concepts. The expressions, however, do lose some of the richness of the concepts such as abstraction (suppression of details) and property inheritance. It is essential to completely define the semantics of these concepts (see the chapter by Reiter). The concepts presented in this chapter are defined precisely in [BROD82] by means of predicate axioms and in [RB82a] [RB82c] by means of sets and functions.

Aggregation bears some similarity to the artificial intelligence (AI) concept of frames (see the Knowledge Representation Overview by Mylopoulos and Levesque). A component of an aggregate corresponds to a slot in a frame. Like slots, components, as defined in this chapter, have both static (data structure) and dynamic (operation) properties. Defaults, such as exist in frames, have not been addressed in aggregation with the exception of identifying essential components. Defaults would be an excellent concept to integrate into aggregation hierarchies. Frames and aggregation, as defined here, differ, just as prototypes differ from types. An "instance" of a prototype need not have all properties given in the frame, whereas a type instance must have all the properties defined in the aggregate. (For a further discussion of this distinction see Hewitt's conclusion at the end of the book.) Hence, SHM+ provides not only a frame-like knowledge representation mechanism, it also provides generalization and association for structuring frame-like representations.

The three forms of abstraction provide techniques for structure modelling: composition/decomposition, association/membership (which emphasizes set oriented design as a special case of composition/

decomposition), and generalization/specialization which all take advantage of property inheritance. The use of generalization is discussed in detail in the chapter by Borgida, Mylopoulos, and Wong. Aggregation and association support upward inheritance in which properties of the components or members are inherited by the aggregate or set. For example, the properties of the components *employee-name, employee-number,* and *salary* are inherited as properties of the aggregate *employee.* Aggregates and sets are designed by *decomposition* into, or *composition* from, components or members without concern for their properties. Generalization supports downward inheritance in which all properties of a generic object are inherited by each of its category objects. For example, the categories *secretary* and *manager* inherit all properties of the generic *employee.* Categories are designed by *specialization* in which only those properties that distinguish the category object from the generic object are defined. For example, a *secretary* is defined as an *employee* who has the distinguishing property of *typing-speed.* Alternatively, a generic object can be generalized from the common properties of distinct objects. Property inheritance supports abstraction, modularity, and consistency, since essential properties of an object are defined once and are inherited in all relationships in which it takes part.

Structure modelling at the conceptual level involves the identification and relationship of all objects required for an application. Aggregation, generalization, and association can be applied to compose objects to form aggregates, generics, and sets, and to decompose objects into components, categories, and members. Repeated application of composition/decomposition results in aggregation and association hierarchies. The repeated applications of generalization/specialization results in generalization hierarchies. An object can simultaneously take part in all three kinds of hierarchies provided by the orthogonal nature of the abstractions.

The design of the abstraction hierarchies for complex database applications is a complex process. The principle of localization is used to design these hierarchies step by step. Only one application object and objects immediately related by aggregation, generalization, and association are considered at one time. The combined result of structure modelling is a conceptual model of the application that reflects the complexity of the application being modelled. The complexity can be reduced by reapplying localization to ignore particular details and to consider each object independently as an aggregate, component, generic, category, set, or member.

Structure modelling at the transaction level involves identifying objects and relationships in the conceptual model that need to be accessed by a transaction. Objects and relationships not in the conceptual model but needed by the transaction may be introduced as local to the transaction. These local objects, relationships, and associated actions are called virtual and explained in detail in [RB82a] [RB82d].

3.2 Object Schemes

In structure modelling, a semantic data model aids in identifying and relating structural properties and in specifying those properties precisely. These two roles are at different levels of precision and form the basis of a two step modelling process. First, the gross structural properties (*e.g.*, objects and their relationships) are designed. Second, the fine details of those properties are specified. SHM+ provides design tools for both steps. Object schemes are used for gross structure design. A structure specification language, Beta [BROD80a] [BROD81a] [BROD82] [BS82c], is used for structure specification. Similarly, the chapter by King and McLeod proposes two kinds of schema.

An object scheme, like a data structure diagram and an E-R diagram, graphically represents the objects and structural relationships of a database application. An *object scheme* is a directed graph in which nodes are strings denoting objects, and edges identify aggregation, generalization, and association relationships between objects. The graphic notation for the three forms of abstraction is given in Figure 3.1.

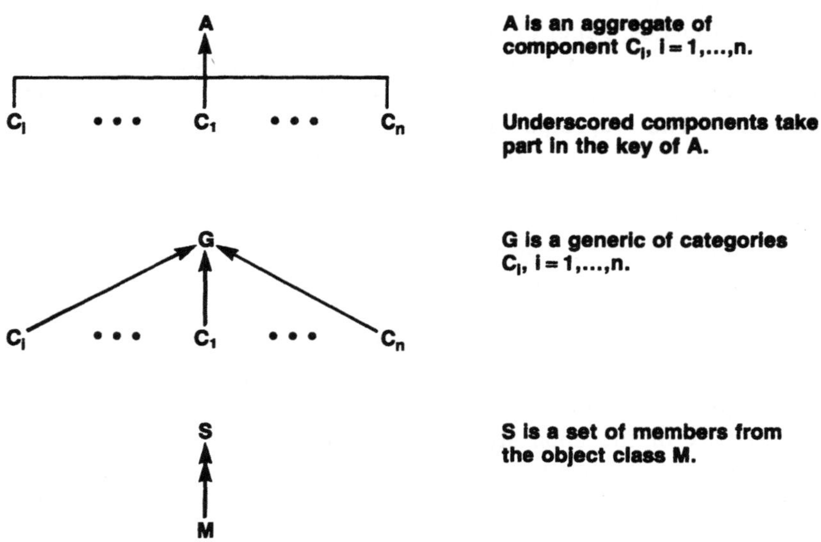

Figure 3.1 *Object Scheme Notational Conventions*

The result of applying composition/decomposition and generalization/specialization to a single object can be represented, according to the principle of localization, in one or more object schemes. Figure 3.2 contains two object schemes for *employee.*

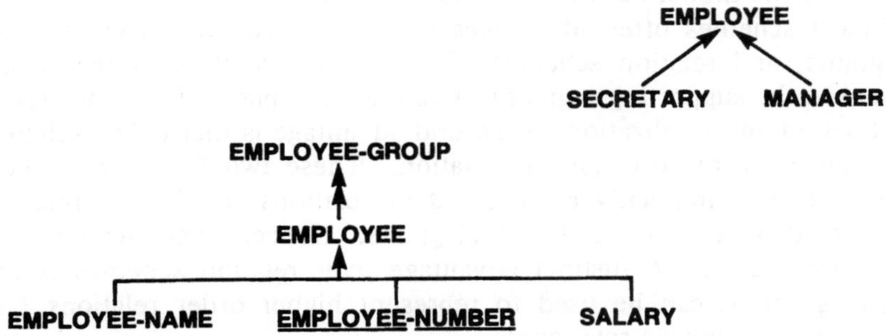

Figure 3.2 *Employee Object Schemes*

Using the principle of localization, additional properties of objects in an object scheme can be modelled by extending the object scheme or by designing independent object schemes. Object schemes can be composed/decomposed and generalized/specialized. In transaction modelling, object schemes for each object involved in a transaction can be combined to form a transaction object scheme. In conceptual modelling, an object scheme containing all objects and relationships can be created by combining the object schemes of either all transactions or of each independent object (*e.g.,* these alternatives correspond to view integration and conceptual schema design). Subsequently, object schemes for new transactions can be abstracted from the object scheme of the conceptual model and by introducing, if necessary, virtual objects.

Using object schemes, the gross design of structure takes advantage of abstraction and modularity. Detailed information about constituent objects can be ignored when designing an object. Many structural properties can be assumed through property inheritance.

Object schemes have been presented as a design aid for SHM+ databases. However, they also can be used with most other data models. Effective techniques exist [RB82a] for mapping SHM+ object schemes to each of the "classical" data models. Due to the fundamental nature of SHM+, object schemes also can be used as a graphic design aid for most semantic data models. Specifically, object schemes can be used with the semantic data models that support semantic relativism [MS81] such as SHM [SS77b], TAXIS [MBW80], SDM [HM81], and RM/T [CODD79]. According to semantic relativism, an object can be considered both independently and in terms of any relationship in which it takes part. In turn, a relationship can be considered as an object. Depending on one's point of view, properties of objects can be considered as attributes, entities, or relationships; a distinction is not forced by the model but can be made by the observer.

Object schemes offer advantages over data structure diagrams, E-R diagrams, and relation schemes. The major advantage is that object schemes, in supporting semantic relativism, support the principles of abstraction and localization. A second advantage is that object schemes distinguish aggregation and association. These two fundamental concepts are only implicitly represented in relations and in 1:N relationships of data structure and E-R diagrams. Hence, object schemes can be more precise. A distinct advantage over relation schemes is that object schemes can be used to represent higher order relations (*i.e.*, relationships between relations).

4. Behaviour Modelling

For the design and specification of behavioural properties of database applications, SHM+ provides primitive database operations on objects, three forms of control abstraction with which to compose application-oriented operations, and two forms of procedural abstraction: *actions* for conceptual modelling and *transactions* for transaction modelling. The three forms of control abstraction are direct analogs to the three forms of data abstraction (aggregation, generalization, and association). They are fundamental to function theory, hence, to all programming languages.

Each database operation is either an altering or a retrieval operation over a single instance of an object class. The altering operations are ***INSERT, DELETE, UPDATE*** (*e.g.*, ***INSERT*** *employee*, ***UPDATE*** *employee-salary*, and ***DELETE*** *employee-group*). Altering operations ensure SHM+ semantics for each role an object plays (*e.g.*, aggregates can be inserted only if their essential components exist; deleting a generic causes its dependent categories to be deleted). Retrieval operations for object values are: ***FIND*** an object in the database, ***CREATE*** an object using a defined procedure, and ***REQUEST*** an object (interactively) from the user.

Control abstractions are used to relate operations to form higher-level, composite operations. The three forms of control abstraction sequence, choice, and repetition are *behavioural analogs* of the three forms of data abstraction. Aggregation corresponds to either *sequence* or *parallel* relationship of operations. An operation on an aggregate is composed of either a sequence or parallel of operations, one for each component. The essence here is that there is a fixed number of possibly different operations. For example, an action *insert-hotel-reservation* on *hotel-reservation* (Figure 1.1) for a given hotel over given dates might be composed of a sequence of operations to create a *reservation#*, request a *person,* reserve a *room,* plus ***INSERT*** the *hotel-reservation.* Generalization corresponds to *choice* (*e.g.,* if-then or case control structures). An operation on a generic is composed of a choice of operations, one for each category (case is used for nonoverlapping categories; sequence or parallel of if-then control structures is used for overlapping categories). For example, a *hire-employee* action on *employee* (Figure 3.2) consists of a choice of two insert operations, one for *secretary* and one for *manager*, plus ***INSERT*** the *employee.* Association corresponds to *repetition* (*e.g.,* do-while or for-each control structures used in the framework of either sequence or parallel control structures). An operation on a set is composed of an operation that is applied in sequence or parallel to each member of the set. The essence here is that there is an undetermined (at compile time) number of identical operations. For example, an action *dissolve-employee-group* on the object *employee-group* (Figure 3.2) is composed of a delete operation for each *employee*, plus ***DELETE*** the *employee-group.* The three forms of control abstraction can be used to define all partial recursive (*i.e.,* computable) functions [DAVI58]. Hence, they are sufficient for all application-oriented operations. Although the above data structure-control structure correspondence is only an analogy, it gives considerable insight into the relationship between data and its related operations, hence between structure modelling and behaviour modelling.

Behaviour modelling at the conceptual level involves the identification, design, and specification of actions for each object. Many of the modelling concepts here are based on abstract data types. An *action* is a conceptual level, application-oriented operation designed, using the principle of localization, for *one* object to ensure that all properties of the object are satisfied. An action is designed from a single database altering operation by providing the necessary invocation context. Before invoking the database operation, certain preconditions must be met, and actions on other objects may be necessary. After the actions are invoked, a postcondition must be checked and the database operation is executed. For both pre- and postconditions, exception handling must be designed. The *insert-hotel-reservation* operation described earlier has as a precondition that the *hotel* exists and that an appropriate *room* be available on the desired dates. If the precondition is true then the room must be reserved by invoking other operations. The postcondition ensures that the room is reserved and that the *hotel-reservation* can be ***INSERT***ed.

Actions provide the only means of altering an object. This ensures the semantic integrity of an object since all constraints on the object must be satisfied by all attempts to alter it. An *action local scope* includes the object of interest and all objects immediately related by aggregation, generalization, and association. An *action complete scope* is inferred from the hierarchy of invoked actions. The database operation can alter only the object of interest. All other objects are accessed by means of actions. Actions provide a degree of modularity that aids design and redesign. For example, redefining *insert-hotel-reservation* effectively and consistently redefines all operations that invoke it.

The behaviour of an object is completely defined by its actions. Typically, an object has one insert, one delete, and zero or more update actions. The *hotel-reservation* object has one insert, one delete, and two update actions (one update to alter *hotel* and *room,* and another to alter the *dates*). The purpose of designing actions for an object is that they may be used to construct any legal, application-oriented operation at the transaction level that would access it.

The behavioural and structural properties of an object constitute an abstraction that completely defines the semantics of the object. The result of conceptual modelling, the conceptual model of the application, is a network of abstractions related by the three forms of abstraction. In terms of structure there is a hierarchy of objects. In terms of behaviour there is a hierarchy of actions. The purpose of conceptual modelling is to provide an adequate basis for the design of all application-oriented objects and operations at the transaction level.

Behaviour modelling at the transaction level involves the identification, design, and specification of transactions. A *transaction* is an application-oriented operation at the transaction level that alters *one* or *more* objects. A *transaction scope* includes all objects accessed in the transaction. A transaction is designed from actions on objects in the scope by providing an appropriate invocation context. The invocation context of a transaction provides a particular *behavioural view* of the underlying conceptual model just as derivation rules and constraints provide particular *structural views.* Preconditions, action invocations, postconditions, and exception-handling are required, as is the case with actions. However, unlike actions there is no database operation.

Transactions are designed to fulfill specific user requirements. Consider two transactions for use by clerks at a hotel's front desk. The first, *cancel-reservation,* checks that the *reservation* exists, invokes the *delete-hotel-reservation* action, and ensures that the *reservation* was deleted. The second transaction, *convert-reservation-to-registration* is used to create a *hotel-registration* from an arriving guest's *hotel-reservation.* The precondition checks that the *hotel-reservation* exists, verifies the reservation information, and ensures that the room is available. The transaction then creates, finds, or requests registration information and invokes the actions *insert-hotel-registration* and *delete-hotel-reservation*. The postcondition checks the success of the actions. Both transactions provide different invocation contexts for the *delete-hotel-reservation* action, thereby ensuring the same constraints on *hotel-reservation*. Both transactions were designed abstractly (*i.e.*, without concern for the details of the actions involved, exception handling, *etc.*).

To ensure the semantic integrity of database applications there is a strict invocation hierarchy. Transactions are the only means for end users to alter the database. Transactions invoke actions that are the only means of altering objects. Each action invokes a single database operation to alter a single object. Both actions and transactions are well-defined logical units that have well-defined scopes, pre- and postconditions, and effects on the database. Typically, transactions have been used as a unit of physical integrity (*e.g.*, concurrency [BHR80]). Design using the SHM+ and ACM/PCM treats actions and transactions as units of semantic integrity.

Behaviour modelling is done, together with structure modelling, in a two step process that reduces the amount of detail to be considered at one time (incremental or refinement design). First the gross behavioural properties are designed. Actions and transactions are identified and related to objects. Then, aided by the gross designs, the fine details of actions and transactions are specified. As a result of this process the structure of the resulting invocation hierarchy, called the transaction-action hierarchy, corresponds directly to the structure of the object hierarchy.

SHM+ provides design and documentation aids for both behaviour design and behaviour specification. Behaviour schemes are used for the design of gross behavioural properties. Behavioural specifications are used to specify those properties precisely. Behaviour schemes and specifications provide designer, user, and implementor guidance and form a basis for semantic integrity analysis.

5. Behaviour Schemes

A behaviour scheme is an explicit graphical representation of the gross properties of a single action or transaction. Schemes provide graphical means for designing behavioural properties of database applications, as do paths in the chapter by King and McLeod and scripts in the chapter by Borgida, Mylopoulos, and Wong. Three forms of control abstraction, (*i.e.*, sequence or parallel, choice, and repetition) are used to represent the behavioural relationships between an action (or transaction) and its constituent operations. There is a constituent operation for each object in the action local scope or transaction scope. Constituent operations and their relationships are represented by adding behavioural information to an object scheme. This facilitates the explicit modelling of behaviour at a gross level of detail. Behaviour schemes integrate structural and behavioural properties in one representation.

A *behaviour scheme* for an action (transaction) is an object scheme that includes each object in the local scope (transaction scope), plus an operation label on each edge, one label for each constituent operation. An operation label indicates the nature of a constituent operation by naming the database operation(s) on which it is based and by giving an invocation context by means of an arrow (→). The arrow points to the object on which the operation is invoked and points from the object that invoked it. A double arrow (=>) is used to distinguish the action or transaction from the constituent operations. The relationship between operations is given by the forms of abstractions.

Figure 5.1 gives the notation for behavioural relationships and invocation contexts for behaviour schemes by adding operation edge notation to the object scheme notation given in Figure 3.1. In Figure 5.1, T_1, T_2, and T_3 name actions or transactions; $O_1, O_2, \cdots, O_n$ and O name constituent operations.

Although most constituent operations are based on one action, they can be composed by sequence or parallel, choice, and repetition of one or more actions. Operation edges name the database operations on which the action is based. The syntax for operation names is given by the grammar,

```
OP ::= insert|update|delete|find|request|create|noop

       |OP  V  OP|OP  &  OP|OP*
```

where "&" indicates *and* (for sequence or parallel); "V" indicates *or* (for choice); and "*" indicates zero or more repetitions.

To construct behaviour schemes (Figures 5.2 and 5.3) for the insert and delete from *hotel-reservation* object scheme (Figure 1.1), some details must be known about the component objects. *Reservation#* is generated automatically by the system. *Hotel* and *room* objects exist independently of the *reservation*. *Person, departure-date,* and *arrival-date* exist only in the context of a *reservation.*

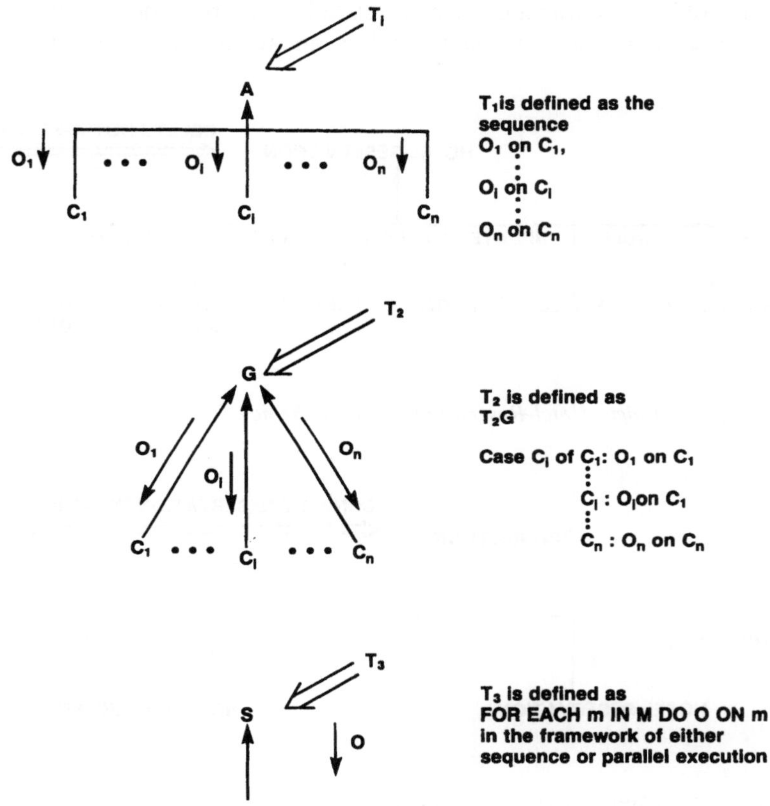

Figure 5.1 *Behavioural Relationships in Behaviour Schemes*

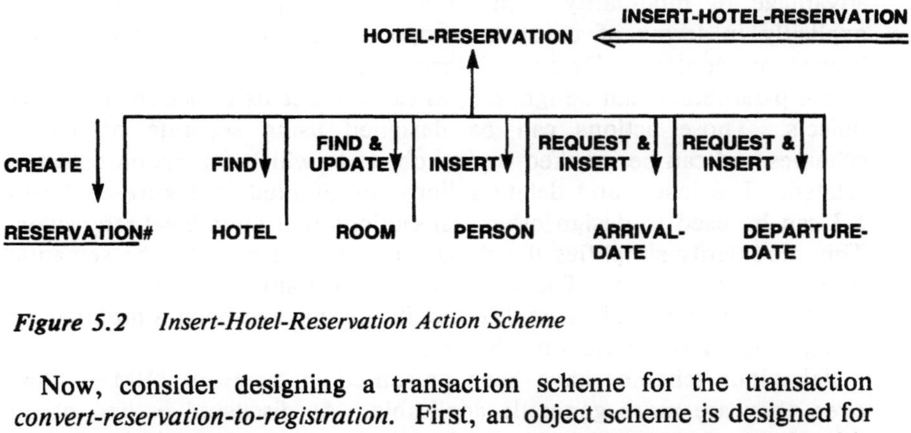

Figure 5.2 *Insert-Hotel-Reservation Action Scheme*

Now, consider designing a transaction scheme for the transaction *convert-reservation-to-registration.* First, an object scheme is designed for the transaction scope. To represent the behavioural relationship between a transaction and its constituent actions, a transaction object (virtual object) is introduced and related to each object in the scope. The *transaction* object in Figure 5.4 is an aggregate of objects in the scope.

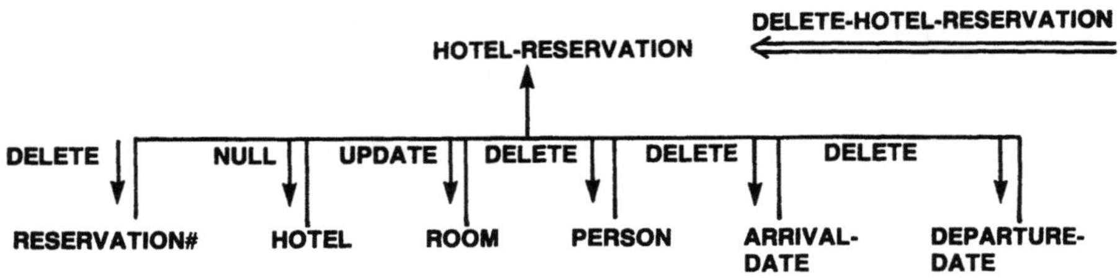

Figure 5.3 *Delete-Hotel-Reservation Action Scheme*

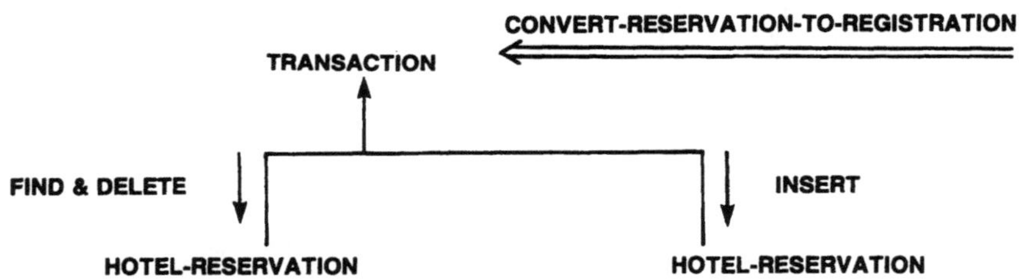

Figure 5.4 *Convert-Reservation-to-Registration Transaction Scheme*

Using behaviour schemes, the design of gross behavioural properties of actions and transactions can be done explicitly and abstractly taking advantage of modularity. The effect of an operation is considered explicitly in terms of constituent operations, their relationship, and invocation context. Detailed information about constituent objects, hence parameters, can be ignored, as can the details of actions on those objects. Those actions can be designed using separate behaviour schemes and can be invoked by any object to which the action object is related. The insert and delete actions represented in Figures 5.2 and 5.3 can be used to design other transactions that alter *hotel-reservation*. This modularity simplifies the design process and ensures the semantic integrity of the object. The semantics of the transaction represented in Figure 5.4 is relatively complex but its design has been simplified by using action and transaction schemes.

Behaviour schemes have been presented in terms of SHM+; however, they are more generally applicable. As discussed earlier, object schemes can be used in conjunction with many data models.

Correspondingly, behaviour schemes can be used for the gross design of actions and transactions over those models as long as the data model rules are satisfied (*e.g.*, triggered delete for hierarchies, storage and removal constraints for networks, referential integrity for relations [RB83], and structure invariants for models based on the semantic hierarchy model) [BROD81a].

Behaviour schemes and SHM+ provide control and procedural abstractions for behaviour modelling not provided for in data structure and E-R diagrams, relation schemes, and the semantic data models mentioned earlier. Behaviour schemes provide explicit means for the design and representation of behavioural properties at a gross level of detail. More important, behaviour schemes can be used to design and represent both structural *and* behavioural properties of database applications.

Due to abstraction and modularity inherent in object and behaviour schemes, gross conceptual modelling can precede or follow gross transaction modelling. If transaction modelling is done first, the resulting object schemes can be integrated by identifying common objects in transaction scopes and applying composition/decomposition and generalization/specialization. Then, action schemes can be designed for objects in the conceptual model and compared with the transaction schemes for completeness. When conceptual modelling is done first, and when new transactions are being designed, a transaction scope can be derived from the conceptual model and virtual objects, and transaction schemes can be designed using existing actions and virtual actions [RB82a] [RB82d]. Experience with SHM+ has shown that neither transaction nor conceptual modelling should be completed independently, but that design is an iterative process. Generally, a preliminary design of transaction schemes aids substantially in conceptual modelling, which is then followed by complete transaction modelling.

6. Behaviour Specifications

To complete behaviour modelling, the fine details of actions and transactions designed using behaviour schemes must be specified. This is done in a behaviour specification that is a complete definition of the behavioural properties of an action or transaction. Such specifications should be precise, abstract, formal, and easy to use and modify. To be complete, all properties must be defined precisely and explicitly. Typically this means many constraints on each operation. A specification is abstract if it gives a minimum amount of detail to define the operation (*e.g.*, implementation detail should be excluded). Formal (possibly automated) techniques can be applied for semantic integrity analysis of formal specifications and for database transaction verification. Finally, due to the size, complexity, and evolutionary nature of database applications, specifications should be easily constructed, understood, and modified. This requires that specifications be structured. Structured specifications enable (among other things) abstraction to be applied during the specification of complex applications, specifying partial functions (constraints), and the manipulation (*e.g.*, modification and composition) of specifications.

Many techniques have been proposed for the specification of behaviour. In the programming language area the principal techniques include axiomatics [HW73], predicate transformers [DIJK76], algebra [GH78], functions [LMW79], and the Vienna Development Method (VDM) [BJ78]. With the exception of VDM, these techniques treat structural properties implicitly, hence they are inappropriate for structural properties of databases. All techniques require mathematical sophistication, making them somewhat difficult to use. With the exception of the functional approach, constraints are difficult to specify and modify. None of these techniques permit the specification structuring and modification essential for complex database applications. Consequently, these techniques have not proved practical for large scale systems.

Object and behaviour schemes are abstract and easy to use and modify, but they are neither precise nor do they have associated analysis techniques. Formal techniques that support analysis and verification are precise but are often difficult to use. The gap between graphical and mathematically formal techniques is large. This chapter proposes an intermediate step between graphical object and behaviour schemes and a formal technique for analysis and verification. The intermediate step involves specifying behaviour using the axiomatic and predicate transformer techniques. These predicate behaviour specifications can be used for semantic integrity analysis of database transactions. They are adequate for most database applications. However, particularly complex applications, with many objects, relationships, and constraints, require the precision and analysis that only advanced formal approaches have so far been able to provide [BG80b] [WIRS82] [WB81] [WPPD83]. Specifically, structuring and modification of specifications, not supported by axiomatic and predicate transformer techniques, are essential for complex database applications. For critical database applications (*e.g.*, critical patient care, nuclear power plant operation) verification techniques are essential. The extension of the functional technique [LMW79] is proposed here as a promising candidate for structuring and modifying transaction specifications and for verifying transaction specifications and their corresponding programs [RB82a] [RB82e].

6.1 Predicate Specifications

The form of the behaviour specifications proposed here is based on the axiomatic and predicate transformer techniques. Databases are treated explicitly since behaviour specifications refer to objects for which a structure specification is given. Axioms and inference rules for the structure specification language are given elsewhere [BROD82]. A behaviour specification is given in terms of constraints expressed as predicates; hence, they can be both abstract and precise. For most database applications, constraints are readily constructed and modified by adding and deleting predicates.

Actions and transactions have similar components based on the form:

$$N\ (V)\ I, O, L : P\ \{A\}\ Q, D$$

N is the operation name and V is a parameter list. I, O, L defines the operation's scope (local scope for an action, transaction scope for a transaction) by naming: I, the objects accessed through actions and retrieval operations; O, the object altered through the database operation, D; and L, the objects local to the operation. The effect of the operation is specified in terms of a precondition, P; an active role, A; a postcondition, Q; and possibly a database operation D. P and Q are lists of predicates and A is composed of zero or more action invocations.

An action alters one object, O, directly by means of an SHM+ primitive ***INSERT***, ***UPDATE***, or ***DELETE*** operation, D, and can access objects, I, that are immediately related to O by means of actions in A. $P\{A\}Q$ constitutes the precondition to be satisfied to ensure the successful execution of D. $P\{A\}Q$ must check or establish every relationship between O and objects in I. The potential complexity of $P\{A\}Q$ warrants its being considered in three parts. P ensures that A can be invoked. The actions in A appropriately alter the objects in I to ensure the desired relationships. Q checks the success of A.

A transaction can access any collection of objects only by means of their actions, hence, O and D are empty. I and L define the transaction scope. P is the precondition that determines whether A can proceed. A is composed of actions that achieve the desired effects of the transaction which are checked by the postcondition Q.

A predicate behaviour specification has the form:

$$N\ (V)\ I, O, L : P\{\,\}Q, D$$

The effect of an action or transaction (*i.e.*, exactly *what* it does), is completely defined by $P\{\,\}Q,D$. The active role A defines *how* the effect is achieved and is therefore excluded as inappropriate detail for a specification. The effect of an operation is specified in terms of simple predicates (these predicates are simple for most databases) in P and Q

that can be precise, abstract, semi-formal, and easy to specify and modify.

As an example, consider the specification of the *insert-hotel-reservation* action (Figure 6.1) guided by the action scheme in Figure 5.2.

```
ACTION insert-hotel-reservation (h,p)
IN (n: reservation#, h: hotel, r: room, p: person
    a: arrival-date, d: departure-date)
OUT (hotel-reservation)
PRECONDITION: hotel-exists (h)?
              legal-person (p)?
POSTCONDITION: room-reserved (n,h,r,a,d)?
DB-OPERATION: INSERT hotel-reservation (n,h,r,p,a,d)
```

Figure 6.1 *Insert-Hotel-Reservation Action Specification*

First, the scope *I* and *O* is determined directly from the object scheme. *O* is *hotel-reservation* and *I* includes all of its components. Second, the parameter list *V* is determined by considering how objects are to be retrieved. The action scheme indicates that *reservation#* is to be created and that *arrival-date* and *departure-date* are to be requested interactively from the user within the active role. *Person* is to be inserted, hence, is input via a parameter. *Hotel* and *room* are to be found in the database. As a design decision, it is stated that reservations be made by giving a hotel name and that rooms can be reserved automatically by giving the *hotel, arrival-date,* and *departure-date.* Hence, *hotel* and *person* are the parameters. The precondition checks the validity of the input parameters. The only requirement for the success of the database operation, ***INSERT*** *hotel-reservation,* is that the active role ensures that an appropriate room is found and reserved. The postcondition is expressed as a predicate that checks this requirement.

The action specification for *delete-hotel-reservation* (Figure 6.2) and the transaction specification for *convert-reservation-to-registration* (Figure 6.3) can be similarly designed from their respective behaviour schemes (Figures 5.3 and 5.4).

6.2 Specifying Predicates and Exception Handling

Predicates in the pre- and postconditions, *P* and *Q*, are used to detect and handle errors and exceptional conditions. The failure of any predicate in *P* and *Q* causes the operation to be terminated. The failure of *Q* additionally requires that the effects of the active role be undone. Exception handling in this approach, unlike that using triggers

```
ACTION delete-hotel-reservation (n)
IN (n: reservation#, r: room)
OUT (hotel-reservation)
PRECONDITION: hotel-reservation-exists (n)?
POSTCONDITION: room-freed (h,r,a,d)?
DB-OPERATION: DELETE hotel-reservation (n)
```

Figure 6.2 Delete-Hotel-Reservation Action Specification

```
TRANSACTION convert-reservation-to-registration (n1)
SCOPE (n1: hotel-reservation, n2: hotel-registration)
PRECONDITION: reservation-verifies (n1)?
              room-available (n1)?
POSTCONDITION: hotel-reservation-cancelled (n1)?
               hotel-registration-exists (n2)?
```

Figure 6.3 Convert-Reservation-to-Registration Transaction Specification

and database procedures, is used only to undo the effects of an incomplete or unsuccessful active role. This approach is based on the small, limited scope (local scope) of actions that are units of logical integrity.

Due to the principle of localization, exception handling for the pre- and postconditions is ignored in action and transaction specifications. It is specified separately using predicates and procedures, combined with action and transaction specifications, to complete them.

Predicates are specified using predicate calculus (based on PASCAL/R syntax [SCHM77]) over objects in the scope. In addition, each predicate also can have exception handling specified for the failure of the predicate. For example, the predicate *hotel-reservation-exists (r)* used in the precondition of the *delete-hotel-reservation* specification (Figure 6.2) is specified as:

```
hotel-reservation-exists (R) :=
   some h in hotel-reservation (h.reservation# = R)
```

Additionally, exception handling could be specified for the predicate's failure. For example, there could be an interaction with the hotel clerk to retrieve other identifying information for the desired *hotel* or an alternative *hotel.*

6.3 Object Class Specifications

Generally, structure and behaviour modelling are quite separate. Structural properties of an object are designed and defined in schemas and subschemas. Behavioural properties are defined by all programs that alter the object. New programs are defined using primitive altering operations that extend, and possibly alter or conflict with, existing properties. While each program should not be concerned with all properties of the objects they alter, these properties must be maintained consistently.

Typically, to relate structural and behavioural properties, new constraints are defined independently of programs and schemas. The constraints are implemented using assertions, triggers, database procedures, on conditions, check clauses, *etc.* These techniques implement constraints as side effects of operations. Hence, the properties of objects are defined implicitly and explicitly, in three different forms, and in different places throughout an application definition. This complicates design, definition, modification, and semantic integrity analysis.

Using SHM+, structure and behaviour specifications of an object are integrated to form an object class (integration using data abstractions to form abstract data types). An object class is a complete definition of the properties of an object. It consists of a structure specification and an action specification for each action available on objects of the class. An action specification refers to structure specifications by naming the object in its local scope. All properties to be altered by an action are stated explicitly in $P\{\,\}Q,D$. Abstraction (*i.e.*, the suppression of irrelevant detail) is applied in designing and specifying object classes. The modular nature of abstractions aids in semantic integrity and modification. The integration using data abstraction to form abstract data types borrows the good features of abstract data types but still allows database retrieval by a query language.

7. Action and Transaction Programs

An action or transaction program is constructed by adding an active role to the associated behaviour specification. The design of an active role is guided by both the behaviour specification and the behaviour scheme.

The following syntax is used to illustrate action program design:

```
ACTION  <action name>(<parameter list>)
IN  (<object list>)
OUT  (<object list>)

if  <precondition>
then  <active role>
{else  terminate action}

if  <postcondition>
then  <database operation>
{else  undo active role and terminate action}
```

The backout actions given in the *else* clauses are handled in the pre- and postcondition predicates. The database operations are denoted ":+" for *INSERT*, ":&" for *UPDATE* and ":-" for *DELETE* following the syntax of PASCAL/R.

The active role is a number of action invocations related by some control constructs. The actions can be deduced from operation labels on behaviour schemes. Control structures can be determined from the forms of abstraction relating to the objects (Figure 5.1) and from details given by the operation label.

```
ACTION insert-hotel-reservation (h,p)
IN (n: reservation#, h: hotel, r: room, p: person,
    a: arrival-date, d: departure-date)
OUT (hotel-reservation)
 if hotel-exists (h) and
    legal-person (p)
 then request-arrival-date (a)
      request-departure-date (d)
      create-reservation# (n)
      reserve-room (n,h,r,a,d)
 if room-reserved (n,h,r,a,d)
 then hotel-reservation :+ (n,h,r,p,a,d)
```

Figure 7.1 *Insert-Hotel-Reservation Action*

For example, the *insert-hotel-reservation* program (Figure 7.1) can be designed by adding to its specification (Figure 6.1) active role details expressed in its action scheme (Figure 5.2). Aggregation results, in this example, in a sequence of action invocations. Inserts of *arrival-date, departure-date,* and *person* occur directly in the database operation. *Hotel* is found in the precondition. The remaining operations are achieved through four action invocations. Abstraction aids in the design of active roles. Designers need know only *what* actions do, not *how* they do it. In the design of *insert-hotel-reservation* it is necessary to know that given *n, h, a*, and *d*, *reserve-room* reserves a room and returns a reference to it in the result parameter *r*. It is not necessary to know the algorithm or human interaction needed to reserve the room. *Delete-hotel-reservation* (Figure 7.2) and *convert-reservation-to-registration* (Figure 7.3) were designed similarly.

```
ACTION delete-hotel-reservation (n)
IN (n: reservation#, r: room)
OUT (hotel-reservation)
 if hotel-reservation-exists (n)
 then delete-room-reservation (n,h,r,a,d)
 if room-freed (h,r,a,d)
 then hotel-reservation :- n
```

Figure 7.2 *Delete-Hotel-Reservation Action*

```
TRANSACTION convert-reservation-to-registration (n1)
SCOPE (n1: hotel-reservation,
       n2: hotel-registration)
 if reservation-verifies (n1) and
    room-available (n1)
 then delete-hotel-reservation (n1)
      insert-hotel-registration (n2)
 check hotel-reservation-cancelled (n1)
       hotel-registration-exists (n2)
```

Figure 7.3 *Convert-Reservation-to-Registration Transaction*

8. Functional Specifications

This section is intended to give intuition into the formal specification and verification technique underlying SHM+ and ACM/PCM. For very complex database applications, side-effects of actions, expressed through their active roles, can refer to a large portion of a database. The associated chain of action invocations can be represented as a hierarchy of actions that is invoked by the transaction. For these transaction-action hierarchies, predicate behaviour specifications can become complex and very detailed, hence difficult to manage and modify. Predicate specifications are not structured. Functional specifications, however, can be easily structured in a hierarchy of functions that specifies a corresponding transaction-action hierarchy. Regardless of the hierarchy's size, every function is of manageable size and its place in the hierarchy is precisely defined. The structuring and modifying of behaviour specifications is based on the principle of localization and the algebraic nature of the functional technique.

A specification of a database program (transaction or action) is a given function, called the *intended database program function.* A function domain is represented by a sequence of application objects called the *input state vector.* A function range is represented by an identically ordered sequence of the same objects (possibly altered), called the *output state vector.* Using the principle of localization and defining, in every state vector, only the object of interest and its related input data, the size of intended database program functions becomes manageable. In general, an intended database program function f, with state vector sv, is given in the form illustrated in Figure 8.1. The output state vector (sv') indicates that some objects in the input state vector (sv) are altered.

$$f(sv) = \begin{cases} (sv') & \textit{if} \text{ objects in (sv) satisfy certain properties} \\ & \textit{and} \text{ active role is successful} \\ (sv) & \textit{else.} \end{cases}$$

Figure 8.1 *Database Program Function Specification*

The meaning of a database program is a computed database program function that completely determines a mapping from the input state vector to the output state vector. More precisely, given a database program *DP* (*DP* denotes a program syntax) its semantics is the function [*DP*] computed by the program *DP*. [*DP*] is the functional composition of the computed functions of the database programs, SHM+ primitives, and the control abstractions used in *DP*. Computed functions of the primitives and control abstractions are given by definition [RB82a] [RB82e].

A database program *DP* is correct with respect to its specification (the intended program function) f if and only if

$$f = [DP]$$

where

1. The number of arguments in state vectors must agree
2. Domains must agree (*i.e., f* and [*DP*] are defined on exactly the same objects)

Due to the principle of localization, each function (or database program) in a hierarchy of transactions and actions is of manageable size. However, the hierarchy can be very deep when it is used for very complex database applications. The associated verification method [LMW79], which is convenient for a small number of relatively small programs, can be time- and space-consuming for large transaction-action hierarchies. Hence, there is a need for the new verification method that takes advantage of the hierarchical structure and the principle of localization. Such a technique is being developed [RB82a] [RB82e].

9. Conclusions

Due to the complex, evolutionary nature of database applications and to the growing need for precision and semantic integrity, database designers are faced with increasingly more complex requirements. They face such problems as "where to start," "how to proceed," "what representations to use," and "model correctness and completeness." Database research has provided semantic data models and design methodologies for modelling structure but little guidance for modelling behaviour. Since database design and specification is incomplete without a definition of its behaviour, note that concepts, tools, and techniques are required for behaviour modelling and should be integrated with their structural counterparts for structure modelling.

This chapter presents and illustrates concepts, tools, and techniques for behaviour modelling of database applications. The primary goals are the integration of control and procedural abstractions with data abstractions, and the development of tools to aid designers in applying the forms of abstraction. Sequence or parallel, choice, and repetition are control abstractions that are the behavioural analogs of the forms of data abstraction: aggregation, generalization, and association. Control abstractions are used to compose abstract operations from primitive operations, just as forms of data abstraction are used to compose abstract objects from primitive objects. Actions and transactions are procedural abstractions used to represent abstract operations. Procedural abstractions permit modularity in behaviour modelling just as data abstractions provide modularity in structure modelling. Also, data abstraction object properties (aggregation, generalization and association) and abstract data type object properties (actions and transactions) are integrated to form an object class that is an abstract, complete, and precise characterization both of the structural and behavioural properties of the object. SHM+ is a storage model that attempts to integrate the fundamental concepts of (semantic) data models and programming languages.

This chapter also introduces three specification techniques: a graphical technique for gross design, a semiformal predicate based technique for a detailed specification of most database applications, and a formal, functional technique for applications where precision and analysis with verification are critical. All three techniques are based on SHM+. The more informal techniques were derived from the functional technique, with the goal of providing techniques that are easy to use and understand while maintaining precision and soundness. It is shown that behaviour schemes and predicate behaviour specifications can be used to design and specify behavioural properties explicitly, abstractly, and in a modular fashion. Although the concepts, tools, and techniques are presented in the context of ACM/PCM and SHM+, they are more generally applicable due to the fundamental concepts on which SHM+ is based [RB82c] [RB82f].

Finally, the chapter presents ACM/PCM, a design methodology that incorporates the above results for the design and specification of database applications. A distinctive contribution of ACM/PCM is that it provides a database transaction design and specification techniques that are fully integrated with structure design. There is a cost associated with the precise specification of database applications and the adopting of the principle of localization. ACM/PCM leads to a large number of small procedures. Since more properties are being modelled there is a possibility of over-specification and undesirable rigidity. These problems have ramifications for design and redesign. However, a disciplined database application development process significantly increases project success in terms of time, cost, and customer satisfaction. ACM/PCM does not resolve a number of important problems. For example, the decomposition of an application into the appropriate data abstractions is not resolved, but design aids are provided to support it. Also, the design and specification of queries and reports are not addressed.

ACM/PCM has been used by novices and by experts to design and specify a number of database applications: a university registration system, a hotel reservation system, soccer team management, a real estate sales management system, and a criminal court scheduling system. The criminal court system has been implemented many times following ACM/PCM. Although the main implementation tool was PASCAL/R (each version entailing approximately 10,000 lines of code), COBOL and the CODASYL system DMS1100 were also used. This experience has been used to refine and test the concepts, tools, and techniques. The greatest benefit of the approach is the guidance provided to manage the complexity of the application semantics on one hand and of the design and development process on the other hand.

10. Epilogue

This chapter discusses several concepts that are fundamental to other chapters in the book.

Abstraction. Both data abstraction (aggregation, generalization and association) from DBs and abstract data types (object class specifications) from PLs are used to design and specify structure and behaviour of database applications. Aggregation and generalization are used in the chapters by Borgida, Mylopoulos and Wong; King and McLeod; and Reiter. Generalization/specialization hierarchies and property inheritance are used for both objects and operations. This chapter provides a user with hierarchies that are based on all three data abstractions. Association hierarchies are used to emphasize a set oriented design of database transactions. King and McLeod use the simple form of generalization hierarchies where the properties are inherited only by attribute restrictions. Abstract data types are used in the chapters by Krieg-Brueckner; Reimer, Schmidt and Mall; Shaw; Stonebraker; and Zilles. Stonebraker uses abstract data types in a simplified way to represent properties of relation attributes. This chapter uses abstract data types to represent more complex objects and integrates the notions of data abstraction and abstract data types that provide an important communication path between DBs and PLs. The property inheritance concept from AI is not fully used in the behavioural design.

Localization. Localization is a concept addressed for the first time in this chapter. It is used to design properties separately and then to combine them to obtain the complete design. One of the consequences of applying the principle of localization is that the action local scopes are precisely defined by the underlying object and its relationship with immediately related objects. In part, the principle resembles the notion related to partitioning and focusing from AI used in the chapter by Rich.

Incremental design. Incremental design from AI and stepwise refinement from PLs are used in several chapters. The chapters by King and McLeod; Rich; and this chapter go from the level of gross design (informal text, diagrams, schemes, syntactical cliches) toward the more detailed and formal designs. King and McLeod present two levels (design and conceptual schemas) that are not essentially different by the level of details. This chapter provides more levels (object and behaviour schemes, semi-formal predicates, formal functions, programs), thus providing a smooth transition between levels. Beside the different levels of precision, the chapter presents three different levels of modelling (transaction, conceptual, and database), thus partitioning the levels of precision.

Kinds of modelling. It is obvious from the book that there are shifts in research directions in the three areas. Behavioural aspects (events, transactions, actions) are becoming more important in DBs, and structural aspects (persistent and more complex objects) are becoming more important in PLs. This chapter uses control structures from PLs to design database behaviour. Integration is done using the concepts of data abstraction and abstract data types. The same control structures are used to design both behaviour and structure. In the chapter by Borgida, Mylopoulos and Wong, separate mechanisms are used to design composition of more complex structures and operations. Constraints, exceptions, incomplete knowledge, and side-effects are the other kinds of modelling that are considered more often. Procedural abstractions from PLs are used to design events, transactions, and actions. In the chapter by King and McLeod, events from DBs and procedures from PLs appear to be similar. In this chapter, an event is described as an instance of a transaction concept. Transactions and actions are shown to be special kinds of procedures that have precisely defined constituents. An action is an application-oriented operation at the conceptual level designed for one object (only one database operation is invoked) in order to ensure that all properties of the object are satisfied (preconditions are checked, the other actions are invoked, and postconditions are checked). A transaction is an application-oriented operation at the transaction level (view-oriented procedure) that alters one or more objects by using actions and not database operations.

Integration of different concepts, tools, and techniques. There are many useful existing concepts, tools, and techniques from AI, DBs, and PLs. It seems that we do not need the new concepts, but we need to combine them into an integrated whole (see Zilles' conclusion at the end of the book) in order to develop new tools, techniques, and systems that are capable of solving current problems in conceptual modelling. This chapter attempts to integrate abstract data types from PLs, data abstractions from DBs, aspects of property inheritance from AI, and view oriented objects and operations (useful abstractions that are not so rigid as abstract data types) from DBs. Our impression is that the successful integration of these concepts will provide useful systems for conceptual modelling of real-world applications.

This chapter is based on Brodie, M.L., "On Modelling Behavioural Semantics of Databases," *Proc. 7th International Conference on Very Large Databases*, Cannes, France, September 1981.

11. References

[BG80b] [BHR80] [BJ78] [BROD80a] [BROD81a] [BROD82] [BS82c] [CODD79] [DAVI58] [DIJK76] [GH78] [HM81] [HW73] [LMW79] [MBW80] [MS81] [RB82a] [RB82b] [RB82c] [RB82d] [RB82e] [RB82f] [RB83] [SCHM77] [SS77b] [SUNA78] [WB81] [WIRS82] [WPPD83]

Discussion

What is impressive about this work is the completeness of the whole process of design, specification, and implementation, and the fact that both structural and behavioural properties of applications are not only designed but also integrated.

The chapter describes a strict application of divide and conquer to logical database design. The authors isolate concepts for abstraction and design, and provide a methodology with which to apply these concepts in order to come up with a uniform design. They provide concepts, tools, and techniques in an integrated approach for the database transaction design, specification, modification, integrity analysis, and documentation.

Database applications have both structural and behavioural properties. In the past, structural properties were emphasized. However, structural properties capture only a part of the semantics of database applications. Behavioural properties must also be specified. The approach places equal emphasis on database (structure) design and transaction (behaviour) design in order to achieve an integrated result.

Traditional DB models provide structural abstractions and primitive operations, but no means for designing complex operations. One contribution of the chapter is that it provides procedural abstractions appropriate for modelling database transactions from primitive operations. Operations are divided into three types: transactions, actions, and primitive operations. The different types are used to design strict operation invocation hierarchies that mirror the corresponding object hierarchies. Transactions invoke actions, and actions invoke primitive operations. Each type of operation is used at a different modelling level. Transactions are used at the transaction (application) level, actions are used at the conceptual level, and DB primitive operations are used at the database (implementation) level. An action is the behavioural property of *one* object. An object can have more than one action. A transaction is a controlled collection of actions on *several* objects.

The Approach

The approach is based on three principles: abstraction (for structural and behavioural properties), localization (design properties separately, then combine them to get the desired result), and refinement (gross design followed by detailed design, specification, and implementation).

Since the design of database applications is not yet well understood (*i.e.*, cannot be expressed algorithmically), the authors took an empirical approach. Several large, complex database applications were designed. Using existing semantic modelling concepts, they developed and refined a methodology. The target specification and implementation vehicle was the relational data model plus PASCAL (*i.e.*, PASCAL/R) although the methodology applies to any DBMS (a CODASYL DBMS was also used). The goal was to develop a high level semantic model for data and procedures. The model was to be object oriented and was to include transaction concepts, hence it had to be at a higher level than the relational model. Methodological concepts that were proven to be effective in practice were embedded into the model. Hence, the research paradigm was to go from methodology to model to implementation. This covers the complete spectrum in the development of database applications.

The major concern is the integration of structural and behavioural modelling. The authors provide a technique to control action and transaction design using rules analogous to those for object composition. The design of behavioural properties is guided by structural properties.

SHM+: A Semantic Data Model

The approach is based on an object oriented semantic data model, called SHM+, rather than on a record oriented data model such as that of the relational data model. SHM+ uses the traditional structuring concepts of classification, aggregation, and generalization and introduces a new concept called association. These concepts are referred to as forms of abstraction since they are used to combine objects into higher level (*i.e.*, more abstract) objects.

Classification is used to define an object class from the instances of the class. Aggregation is used to define compound objects from its parts. Generalization is used to define generic objects from their categories. Association is used to determine a set of objects from its members.

Classification is a relationship between a type and its instances, whereas aggregation, generalization, and association are relationships between types. The type relationships are the important ones for modelling. Any one type can simultaneously have aggregation, generalization, and association relationships with other types. An object can be viewed simultaneously as an aggregate of parts, as a generic of categories, and as a set of members. Alternatively, an object can be a part, a category, and a member in other types.

Defining Data Model Concepts

The notions of aggregation, generalization, and association may be clear to those in the DB community who developed them; however, they may not be clear to others, such as those in the AI and PL communities. The concepts must be defined precisely for those who will use them for modelling. Precision aids not only our understanding of the concepts but also our investigations of the properties of the concepts. For example, the authors claim that their concepts support disjoint types, multiple hierarchies, multiple inheritance, and nonhierarchical structures.

A framework is required to define and use new, complex semantic data models concepts. English does not appear to be adequate. A formal framework such as axiomatics or FOL appears to be more appropriate. In a previous paper, Brodie defined the concepts axiomatically. Developing the axiomization was a valuable process in formulating the concepts, but the result was formidable. Over 150 axioms were required to define the static properties alone. Intuition can be lost due to the large amount of detail.

Mary Shaw: "Some day we will come to understand that specifications, just like code, must be organized carefully if they are to be readable or maintainable."

The chapter presents single sentence definitions of each of the concepts in FOL and in set theory. The definitions do not capture all of the properties. They are intended to avoid the problems of jargon and to provide intuition and a basis for understanding and communicating. A major disadvantage of FOL, set theory, and axiomatics is their inability to handle dynamic properties. Not only must procedurality be defined for database applications, it must be integrated with the definition of the static properties. In any case, any semantic data model must be precisely defined for the community that will use it. The ideal framework or formalism has yet to be determined.

Structure Design

Structure design proceeds in three steps: gross design, detailed design (specification), and type definition. A graphical notation, called object schemes, is used to characterize gross structural properties. An object scheme is a directed graph in which nodes represent objects and edges represent the relationship between objects. There are three kinds of edge, one for each form of abstraction. Object schemes are used to document database designs and to guide the detailed design, which is expressed using the specification language for SHM+ databases. If the type specification is not implemented directly on the target DBMS, then an appropriate type or schema definition must be generated. There is an algorithm for generating relational schemes from SHM+ specifications. Roughly speaking, one object corresponds to one relation. Primary and foreign keys are used to represent the relationships that must be maintained by all operations accessing the relations. For this reason, relation types (relations and their operations) are implemented as abstract data types. The chapter describes structure design briefly and refers to the authors' detailed methodology called Active and Passive Component Modelling (ACM/PCM).

Behaviour Modelling Concepts

For behavioural modelling, three kinds of concepts are provided: primitive DB operations, two forms of procedural abstraction (actions and transactions), and three forms of control abstraction. The DB primitive operations are those of the target DBMS, typically insert, delete, and update. An action consists of a single DB operation and an appropriate invocation context. Transactions are application or user oriented operations and can be defined over any collection of objects. Transactions are designed or composed from actions (the modules or building blocks for transactions) together with an appropriate invocation context. An invocation context is specified by means of preconditions, postconditions, and exceptions. Integrity of objects is always maintained since only actions (which are predefined, meaningful operations) can be used to access objects.

Events and Generalized Schemas

An event is something that happens in time. A procedure represents a class of events just as a data type represents a class of data values. Hence, a class of events in a database application is represented by an action or transaction. In that sense, the concept of schema is generalized in this work to include action and transaction definitions as well as data definitions.

Behaviour Modelling

Following the authors' goal of integrating structure and behaviour, behaviour design follows structural design closely. Gross behaviour design involves designing behaviour schemes from the already designed object schemes. A behaviour scheme is used to represent the properties of an action on an object or a transaction over a collection of objects related by aggregation, generalization, and association. A behaviour scheme is an object scheme with edges added to indicate the constituent operations of an action or transaction and the objects they act on.

Detailed behaviour design, which is guided by behaviour schemes, results in high level action and transaction specifications. There are two levels of behaviour specification, a semiformal, predicate specification and a formal, functional specification. In each case, the same format is used for both actions and transactions. Transactions differ from action specifications because transactions have larger scopes and they cannot invoke DB primitives. The final step in behaviour design is the generation of programs for actions and transactions. Specifications are used systematically for program generation. As with specifications, action and transaction programs follow the same pattern. For uniformity, the authors attempt to use the same syntax and design concepts for actions and transactions wherever possible.

Analogies Between Structure and Behaviour

The authors develop an appealing analogy between structural and behavioural concepts in order to integrate structure and behaviour. The analogy is based on the assumption that the structure of objects mirrors that of the associated operations, and vice versa. The claim is that control structures (used for organizing programs) are the behavioural counterparts of data structures (used for organizing data). More specifically, the claim is that aggregation, generalization, and association are adequate and necessary for relating or structuring objects as well as operations, at least in database applications. The authors point out that it is an analogy and cannot be pushed too far.

The analogy can be explained as follows. Aggregation applied to objects (components) produces an aggregate or record type data structure. An operation over an aggregate consists of a fixed number of possibly different operations in sequence or in parallel, one for each component. Hence, aggregation relates the aggregate data structure and the sequence or parallel control structure. Generalization applied to objects (categories) produces a generic data structure or type hierarchy. An operation over a type hierarchy consists of an operation on the generic followed by a choice of operations, one for each category in the hierarchy. Hence, generalization relates type hierarchies and choice (case or if..then) control structure. Finally, association applied to objects (members) produces a set data structure. An operation over a set consists of one operation repeated for each member of the set. Hence, association relates the set data structure and iteration or the "do while" control structure.

There are several appealing features of the analogy. The first is elegance. Only three concepts are necessary for modelling both structure and behaviour. The second is integration. The analogy establishes a strong relationship between structure and behaviour. Data structure can be used to determine transaction structure, and vice versa. On this basis, structure and behaviour modelling can be integrated. The third is a possible completeness argument. Since sequence, choice, and iteration are necessary and sufficient to express all computable functions, database transaction can be expressed by using them. The hope is that any data structure also can be expressed using them.

Intuition gained by means of the proposed correspondence between structure and behaviour has been useful in understanding database transactions. The fact that complex objects naturally decompose into rather deep aggregation, generalization, and association hierarchies led to the discovery that the associated transactions naturally decompose into a similar deep structure. The authors therefore developed the concept of transaction-action hierarchies and the associated strict invocation hierarchies in which transactions invoke actions that invoke DB operations.

11
A Unified Model and Methodology for Conceptual Database Design

Roger King and Dennis McLeod
University of Southern California

ABSTRACT *The* event model *integrates a set of data structuring and manipulation primitives with a database schema design and evolution methodology. A number of database research efforts have concentrated on expanding the expressiveness of database modelling mechanisms in order to increase the understandability and usability of database conceptual schemas. The event model includes a simple set of such high-level "semantic" modelling constructs; an associated methodology provides prescriptive assistance in the task of specifying and maintaining a conceptual schema. A primary goal of this approach is to reduce the expertise required to design, evolve, and access databases. An interactive database design and evolution system based upon the event model has been implemented and is in use on an experimental basis.*

1. Introduction

This chapter presents a methodology for conceptual database design and evolution. It addresses the "middle third" of database design: the phase that occurs after software requirements have been formulated and before physical design is performed. Typical database design methodologies provide techniques for either gathering data and processing requirements, or for translating a conceptual specification (schema) into a physical database. A major goal of the methodology presented here is to provide prescriptive assistance during the important design phase in

This research was supported, in part, by the Joint Services Electronics Program through the Air Force Office of Scientific Research under contract F44620-76-C-0061. The assistance of the Information Sciences Institute of USC and the Lockheed California Company is gratefully acknowledged.

which the conceptual schema of a database is derived. In sum, the methodology guides a designer in the process of translating data and processing requirements into a database conceptual schema. The conceptual schema describes the manner in which information is structured and manipulated in the application environment from the point of view of the users.

A number of database research efforts have concentrated on expanding the expressiveness of database modelling mechanisms, in order to increase the understandability and usability of conceptual schemas. These so-called "semantic models" are complex, and they present a database designer with many degrees of freedom for modelling. The technique described in this chapter provides a simple set of semantic modelling constructs, along with methodological facilities that guide a designer during the processes of constructing and evolving a conceptual database schema.

The modelling constructs upon which the methodology is based, together with the design and evolution methodology itself, constitute the *event model.* The unifying concept of the event model is the *event.* The start of an event marks its initiation. Database transactions, known as "application events," are formed from high-level data operations and basic control constructs. The event concept is also used to represent a manipulation of a conceptual schema; such an event, called a "modelling event," consists of database design operations whose selection is governed by the design methodology of the event model.

A typical event database life-cycle begins with a modelling event that maps an application environment into a *design schema*, which is intended to serve as a simple medium for specifying the activities involved in the application environment.

A design schema represents the environment as a set of "process events" (modelling database application functions), which are interrelated according to the manner in which they exchange information. After the design schema for a given application environment is complete, it is mapped into a *conceptual schema.* The process events of the design schema become (with a few exceptions) application events, and the information flow among the process events characterizes database objects types and interrelationships. This design step of mapping a design schema into a conceptual schema is performed via modelling events that algorithmically translate the design schema into the core of a conceptual schema, and then interactively collect from the user the information required to complete the detailed description of the application events and objects.

To evolve a conceptual design, the designer may initiate a modelling event to reconfigure the design schema. The designer then initiates modelling events that alter the conceptual schema. During these latter events, the methodology interactively gathers from the designer detailed information necessary to transform the conceptual schema into a form that corresponds to the new design schema. If only minor changes are necessary (*viz.*, those that do not alter the design schema), the designer directly uses modelling events that alter the conceptual schema.

Throughout this chapter, a simple office system example is used to illustrate the structure and use of the event model. Design and conceptual schemas representing forms preparation and distribution are described. Although the example is simple, it is hoped that it will illustrate a typical application of the model. In Section 2 of this chapter, related research is surveyed. Section 3 describes the design schema, while Section 4 examines the conceptual schema. Section 5 presents the conceptual design methodology. Section 6 then describes the event database specification system, an interactive database design tool based on the event model. Finally, Section 7 concludes with a discussion of future research. Rather than presenting a detailed description, this chapter focuses on the motivation and underlying principles of the event model. For details the reader is referred to [KING82] [KM82b] [KM82c].

2. Background

Typically, end-users of databases have a good understanding of their application environment, but they have little familiarity with database technology. Moreover, the individuals who have the knowledge necessary to specify the data and processing requirements of a database system are application specialists, not database designers. Thus, there are two (possibly overlapping) groups of non-database specialists who must interact with database systems: users and conceptual designers. To provide a mechanism whereby users and logical designers can communicate directly with database systems, semantic database models have been developed. A semantic database model provides high-level data structuring and manipulation primitives that are oriented to improving the expressiveness of database conceptual schemas, and thus to increasing database accessibility.

Semantic database models attempt to embed the semantics of an application environment in the database schema in order to make the database generally useful and evolvable. Thus, rather than having modelling constructs based on the concept of the logical record (as in the relational, hierarchical, and network models), semantic models typically represent the application environment as a collection of objects (entities). Objects are typically interrelated via attributes (inter-object mappings), and are classified according to types (classes) and subtypes (subclasses). A summary of the essential techniques and recent research in semantic database models is provided in [KM82a]. Examples of recently developed semantic modelling mechanisms include [BROD81b] [BF79] [CHEN76] [CODD79] [FALK80] [HM81] [HWY79] [MBW80] [SHIP81] [SS77b] [SL79] [WE79] and the chapters by Borgida, Mylopolous, and Wong, and by Buneman and Nikhil.

To specifically support the process of database design, several researchers have concentrated on simplifying the process of specifying a database schema (*e.g.*, [CHEN78] [HWY79] [SS79] [TF80]). While these techniques significantly aid in applying high-level database models, they focus exclusively on the statics (objects, relationships among objects, and object classifications) of an application environment. A notable exception is the approach described in [BROD81b] and the chapter by Brodie and Ridjanovic, which directly employs behavior modelling to specify the dynamic aspects of an application environment; the application event concept of the event model is analogously intended to support the specification of dynamics. Further, semantic database models provide quite limited guidance to the designer. For example, the designer may be required to identify and distinguish "entities," "relationships," and the like, with little prescriptive guidance.

In research areas related to conceptual database design, software requirements specification tools have been devised that have languages to support the top-down specification of software system requirements [BBD77] [DV77] [GANE80] [ROSS77] [TH77]. These languages are intended to accommodate users who are not necessarily experienced software engineers. These tools provide structured design methodologies and typically include automated requirements integration and analysis mechanisms. Significantly, these tools use such concepts as top-down, multi-phased design and information flow modelling to support the software engineering process. These concepts are applicable, in an adapted form, to conceptual database design and evolution.

3. The Design Schema

The most abstract level of specification of a database described with the event model is a design schema. A design schema consists of two kinds of information that describe application environment structure and activities, respectively. *Process events* and *function links* are used to model an application environment's structure. Process events model application functions (units of processing), while function links model the structural hierarchy (tree) of the process events. A (directed) function link is established from one process to another if the same authorities (individuals or programs) are responsible for both processes, and if the second process is logically embedded within the first.

The activities of an application environment are modelled in a design schema by means of directed *communication links*, which indicate the flow of information among process events. Selected sequences of communication links are formed into *communication paths*, which indicate specific invocation sequences of process events. Communication path names are associated with communication paths. Each communication path has an ordering, which establishes a partial order of the communication links in a path. In this way, communication paths are used to relate the activities that occur among the processes that model an application environment.

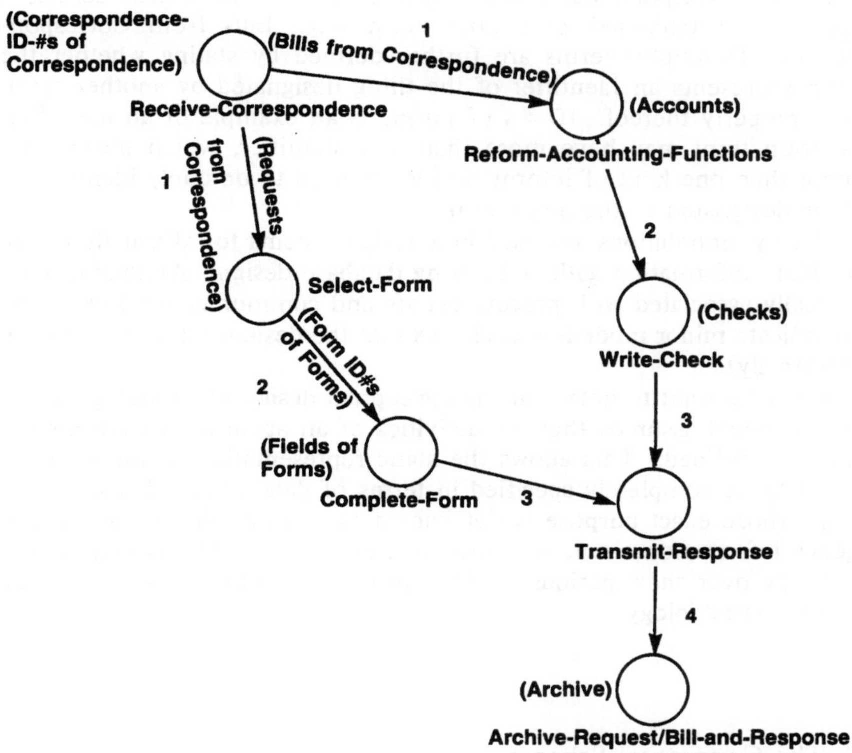

Figure 3.1 The Path "Process-Correspondence"

Figure 3.1 illustrates the communication path Process-Correspondence, which is part of the design schema of the office system example. In Process-Correspondence, an item of correspondence is first received. If the correspondence is a bill, some accounting functions are performed, and a check is written. If the correspondence is a request for information, the proper form for the response is selected and completed. In either case, the response is then transmitted, and a copy of the response is archived along with a copy of the incoming correspondence. Note that two links that have the same ordering (*e.g.*, the two links emanating from Receive-Correspondence) indicate a decision. For simplicity, no function links or annotations are shown.

Terms are associated with communication links and process events in order to identify the general nature of information flow. In Figure 3.1, terms are enclosed in parentheses. There are three kinds of terms: a noun term, which represents an atomic kind of information (*e.g.*, Correspondence); a descriptor term, which describes another term (*e.g.*, Kind of Correspondence); and a specialization term, which defines a special case (subtype) of a noun term (*e.g.*, Bills from Correspondence). Descriptor terms are further defined by stating whether the term represents an identifier of the thing designated by another term, or a property thereof. ID-#s of Forms is an example of an identifier. A noun term may have more than one identifier, which means that more than one kind of information is required to uniquely identify the thing designated by the noun term.

Finally, annotations are used in a design schema to informally record ancillary information gathered during database design. Annotations are typically associated with process events and communication links (*e.g.*, to indicate minor modelling decisions that the designer desires to record informally).

It is important to note that the conceptual design methodology of the event model assumes that the activities of an application environment are well defined. This allows the static representation of the environment to be completely specified in terms of data usage. Thus, a database whose exact purpose is not known (scientific information, intelligence information, *etc.*), or whose processing requirements may change radically over short periods of time, probably would not be well suited to the methodology.

4. The Conceptual Schema

The output of the conceptual design methodology of the event model is a conceptual schema: a specification of a database's static and dynamic structure. The constructs available to specify an event model conceptual schema arise from unifying and simplifying those found in various semantic database models. In particular, an event model conceptual schema consists of *objects* and *application events* (transactions). Both objects and application events are classified by *type*.

There are two varieties of objects: *descriptor objects* and *abstract objects*. Descriptor objects are atomic alphanumeric strings that generally serve as symbolic identifiers. Abstract objects are nonatomic entities that are defined in terms of their relationships with other objects through *attributes*. An attribute is a mapping from one type of object to another, and it is associated with a type. At a given time, an object of a given type (attribute domain) has a specific attribute value that is a subset of the *value type* of the attribute (attribute range). An attribute may optionally be defined as being a unique identifier, single-valued (the default is multi-valued), or non-null. An attribute (A) of an object type (T) may also be required to "exhaust" its value type (V), meaning that every instance of V is a value of attribute A for some instance of type T. Also, two attributes may be defined as being inverses (or more precisely, reverses) of each other. A type that is designed to represent a unique object is defined to have no "multiplicity," while a type that represents a set of similar objects is defined as having multiplicity.

Subtypes of descriptor and abstract object types can be defined by specifying predicates on the values of attributes. A predicate is specified by forming a composite of some number of attributes of one type and comparing it with a constant or a composite of attributes of a second type. The result is a subtype of the first object type. Complex predicates may be formed by defining a series of subtypes. The subtype relationships form a tree in which a subtype inherits all the attributes of the parent type (supertype), and may have additional attributes. Attribute constraints (as defined above) and multiplicity are also inherited.

Figure 4.1 presents the object type definitions for the office system application environment. The Process-Correspondence communication path shown in Figure 3.1 has been translated into the more detailed form of a conceptual schema by using the conceptual design methodology of the event model. ID-# s is an example descriptor object subtype that is a subtype of Strings. Correspondence is an example abstract object type, with the attribute ID-# s serving as a unique identifier. Bills is an example subtype that consists of all instances of Correspondence for which the attribute Kind has value "bill."

As stated above, an application event models a database transaction; it is a "packaged" manipulation designed using the event model. Each application event definition specifies a particular transaction type in terms of: a collection of *parameters*, whose types are descriptor or abstract objects; a collection of *working subtypes*, which define those object subtypes the application event manipulates; and a collection of *actions*. An action is either an invocation of another application event or an invocation of a primitive data operation (*e.g.*, add instance to type, remove instance from type, update attribute). The actions of an application event are structured using sequencing, selection/conditional, and iteration control structures (as in the chapter by Brodie and Ridjanovic).

```
Type: Correspondence
  primary attributes: ID from Correspondence-ID-#s
                       (singled-valued, non-null)
  dependent attributes: Kind from
                         Correspondence-Kinds (singled-valued)

Subtype: Bills
           all Correspondence where Kind = "bill"

Subtype: Requests
           all Correspondence where Kind = "request"

Type: Forms
  primary attributes: ID from Form-ID-#s
                       (single-valued, non-null)
  dependent attributes: Fields from
                         Form-Fields (singled-valued)


Other object types:
Accounts
Correspondence-ID-#s
Correspondence-Kinds
Form-ID-#s
Checks
Fields
Archive

Other object subtypes:
Bills-to-Audit
```

Figure 4.1 *Object Type Definitions*

Application events are organized in a type/subtype tree. An application event is a subtype of another if the value types of the parameters of the former are subtypes of the parameters of the latter, and if the actions of the former are a special case of the actions of the latter. A restricted form of an application event is a *perusal event*, which accommodates unplanned queries of databases defined with the event model.

Figure 4.2 presents the application event type definitions for the office system example. Process-Correspondence is an example of an application event type, with parameter Correspondence-# (the identifier needed to identify an instance of Correspondence). The working subtype identifies the item of correspondence to process. The actions of the application event are: to invoke either Select-Form and Complete-Form or to Perform-Accounting-Function and Write-Check; then, in either case, to invoke Transmit-Response and Archive-Correspondence-and-Response. Process-Correspondence has the event subtypes Process-Bill and Process-Request. These two event subtypes are defined since it is possible to identify which items of correspondence are bills and which are requests before processing begins (by examining the Kind attribute of the instance of Correspondence), and since the two types of processing differ.

```
Type: Process-Correspondence
       parameters: Item from Correspondence-ID-#s
       working subtypes: P is
                         Correspondence where Correspondence.ID
                         =Item
       actions: if P.Kind = "request" then
                  (Select-Form (P), Complete-Form(P))

               else if P.Kind ="bill" then
                  (Perform-Accounting-Functions (P),
                   Write-Check (P))

               Transmit-Response (P),
               Archive-Request/Bill-and-Response


Other application event types:
Perform-Accounting-Functions
Write-Check
Select-Form
Complete-Form
Transmit-Response
Archive-Request/Bill-and-Response

Other application event subtypes:
Process-Bill
Process-Request
```

Figure 4.2 *Application Event Definitions*

5. The Conceptual Design Process

As described above, the conceptual design methodology of the event model employs a two-step approach. First, the designer follows a prescriptive methodology that assists in specifying user requirements in terms of a process and information flow model, thereby producing a design schema. This first step is also referred to as phase one of the methodology. During the second design step, the design schema is mapped into a detailed conceptual schema. This second step consists of two phases: during phase two of design, the definitions of object types and subtypes are derived; during phase three, the definitions of application event types and subtypes are derived. Phases two and three are largely automatic, requiring limited additional information from the designer.

The three design phases correspond to three *modelling events*, each of which consists of a series of *modelling operations.* The three design phases are summarized below. A complete specification of the individual modelling operations and the associated methodology appears in [KING82] [KM82c].

5.1 Phase One

Phase one modelling operations are termed *design operations* and they are selected by the designer in order to construct a design schema. Design operations may be categorized in five major groups. The first group consists of those used to create and delete process events and function links during the development of a function hierarchy. The second group includes those that are used to build paths link-by-link, and to assign terms to both the constituent links and process events. The third group of design operations consists of those that are used to coordinate ambiguous and redundant vocabulary (among terms and process event names). The fourth group of design operations includes those used to annotate communication links and process events. The fifth and final group includes those operations that are used to correct design errors.

Phase one of the conceptual design methodology of the event model specifically guides the designer through the following substeps.

1. A process of step-wise refinement is used to model the functional organization of the application environment as a hierarchy of process events and function links. This is accomplished using the first group of design operations. Typically, the function hierarchy will correspond to information processing units and loci of control in the application environment.

2. After building a complete function hierarchy, the designer adds communication links and terms in parallel, in a top-down manner. While communication paths are being constructed using the second group of design operations, the various types of terms are used to distinguish different forms of communication. Identifier terms indicate information used to identify data that is to be manipulated on a path; *e.g.*, a correspondence ID is needed to identify an item of correspondence. A specialization term indicates a divergence of a path into two or more subpaths. For example, Requests and Bills mark the divergence of the path on the links emanating from Receive-Correspondence. Lastly, noun and property terms indicate data that is used during processing and data that is created.

3. As a fundamental purpose of phase one is to isolate a unique vocabulary and top-level structure for modelling the processes and information flow in an application environment, it may be necessary to refine a design schema and the terminology associated with it. The designer therefore must examine the design schema in order to identify processes and terms that are identical but that are defined separately, and to identify processes and terms that need to be further differentiated. Ambiguities in terminology are also eliminated at this point. These functions are accomplished by means of the third group of design operations.

Upon completion of the above substeps, a design schema is complete. It is significant to note that in some cases a "quick prototype" design schema is beneficial. A complete phase one design can then be generated to gain an understanding of the design problem. This design schema may be discarded before the actual design process commences. The designer may intersperse operations from the fourth group (of design operations) during the substeps of phase one in order to annotate a developing design schema. Annotating processes and terms with informal specifications of detail that may support phases two and three is particularly beneficial. Further, errors in the design schema development process can be rectified with the fifth group of design operations (used during phase one as appropriate).

5.2 Phases Two and Three

During phases two and three, the conceptual design process is completed by mapping a design schema into a conceptual schema. This mapping process is largely automatic, the designer providing the details necessary to complete the conceptual schema. The methodology guides the designer through phase two, which involves using statics operations to define the objects in the conceptual schema. During this process, the methodology automatically maps terms into object definitions, obtaining from the designer the additional information necessary to complete the definitions. Analogously, the methodology guides the designer through phase three of the design process, which involves using dynamics operations to map processes into application events.

To further illustrate phase two of the design process, note that the first statics operation automatically maps all noun terms to object types, all specialization terms to subtypes, and all descriptor terms to attributes. Other statics operations then complete attribute value types, attribute constraints, and subtype predicates. The specifications generated in phase two are checked dynamically for consistency. An analogous process is followed in phase three in order to complete application event definitions.

6. The Event Database Specification System

The *event database specification system* (EDSS) is an interactive software system that guides a database designer through the conceptual design methodology of the event model. EDSS provides instructional material concerning the use of the methodology, and steps the designer through the three modelling phases (events). EDSS utilizes a menu-based interface to allow a designer to select various modelling operations, and to obtain details needed to support the partially automatic phases two and three. A prototype EDSS has been designed and implemented, and is in use on an experimental basis. The prototype implementation is written in Pascal, consists of approximately seven thousand lines of code, and presently runs under the TOPS-20 operating system.

An important design consideration in constructing the EDSS prototype was ease-of-use. In consequence, EDSS should include a graphics interface. During phase one, the designer would then manipulate a design schema utilizing graphic images, rather than a linear syntax or menu-based interface. However, at the time the initial EDSS prototype was constructed, appropriate graphics facilities were not readily available, and research in the area of graphics interfaces for design support was beyond the scope of the initial prototype effort. A graphics interface was therefore not actually implemented. Rather, for phase one, an extensive set of formatted windows is used to organize the information a designer must supply at the various stages in the design process. This same interface is used to organize information that the system requests of the designer during phases two and three.

The EDSS prototype consists of three functional components:

1. A user interface supports designer system dialogue, manages a developing design schema, provides menu facilities, and handles terminal input and output.

2. An event model compiler manages a developing conceptual schema, maintains a parse tree of the conceptual schema, and may decompile the parse tree at any time during phases two and three so that the designer may view the developing conceptual schema.

3. A guide prescribes the three design phases.

7. Discussion

The event model has been developed to provide prescriptive support for conceptual database design, a simple set of design and modelling constructs, and mechanisms to support graceful database evolution. (A discussion of database evolution using the event model appears in [KM82c].) Within the methodology, a prescriptive approach is used whenever possible; only during phase one is the designer asked to make significantly creative decisions.

The event model provides multi-level design specification. A design schema is intended to be conceptually simple and to omit design details. As such, a goal of the design schema is to provide a model of an application environment that is easier for a nonspecialist in database technology to understand and manipulate than one produced with a typical data definition language.

The event model leads to an essentially top-down design methodology. A designer is able to focus on the most significant design issues during phase one, while detailed design issues are resolved separately in an automatic or semiautomatic manner during phases two and three. For example, the methodology automatically dictates what objects and application events are needed in the conceptual schema, based upon the types of communication specified on the paths in the design schema. As a significant part of the translation from design to conceptual schema is automatic, the methodology controls a number of design decisions that do not effect central design issues (as these have been resolved in the design schema). For example, the methodology specifies application event parameters.

The event methodology and experimental prototype system have been used to develop a claims processing insurance database specification [KM82b]. A "meta" example has also been defined, which consists of design and conceptual schemas that represent the structure and use of the event model itself [KM82c]. Also, computer-aided design (CAD) and VLSI design conceptual schemas were produced first without using the methodology (mapping directly from user requirements into objects and events), and then using the methodology. During the second design attempts, several errors and design problems introduced in the first design attempts were discovered. This suggests that the methodology, even for simple examples, might be beneficial in increasing accuracy and consistency in conceptual database design.

The EDSS prototype is currently in use on an experimental basis, to provide feedback on the design of the event model itself. Several extensions are planned, including extending the event model and the notion of prescriptive design methodologies to accommodate physical database design. The event model is also being extended to include the design of user interfaces to event databases. Efforts are also currently underway to employ a version of the event model in an experimental personal information management environment. These extensions are discussed briefly below.

In extending the event methodology to include physical design, a central goal of the physical design methodology is to provide for the implementation of a conceptual schema in a manner that makes data manipulation efficient, and that accommodates the process of evolving the implementation when changes in processing requirements occur. One possible approach to physical design is to map a conceptual schema into a conventional schema (*e.g.*, relational), and then implement the conventional database as usual. However, a good deal of information on data semantics captured by the conceptual design methodology would be lost by translating a conceptual schema into a conventional schema. This information is potentially quite useful as a basis for physical design decisions. Another approach, which preserves semantic information, is to map a conceptual schema directly into a physical implementation. This approach is currently being pursued as an extension of the event model.

An automated database life-cycle support tool could be formed by incorporating the conceptual design methodology, the physical design methodology, and an interactive interface to event databases in one software system. Such a system would guide a designer and user in every phase of the database life-cycle. The window to the database would in all cases be the graphic design schema, with the support tool automatically maintaining and organizing the corresponding components of the conceptual schema, physical design, and database.

Efforts are currently underway to employ a version of the event model in an experimental personal information management environment called INFOBASE (for INFOrmation BAse Support Environment). INFOBASE attempts to serve in effect as a lens on a user's information space, allowing the user to view at various levels of abstraction a variety of owned and shared information objects. INFOBASE will provide facilities that allow the user to define, classify, interrelate, and manipulate information objects of various modalities. It will also support controlled sharing among collections of information ("information bases"), and it must provide access to a large network of databases and services.

An experimental INFOBASE prototype is currently being designed, and an implementation is underway on a powerful personal workstation computer. Its intended applications include managing the information required to support the day-to-day activities of a professional, office worker, or home computer user. Specialized information management is also well suited to INFOBASE, including data management for software engineering and engineering design-support systems (*e.g.*, CAD,

VLSI). The event model provides a semantic information model and guidance design methodologies, which should prove directly useful in INFOBASE.

8. Acknowledgments

The authors gratefully acknowledge the assistance and helpful criticisms of: Dennis Heimbigner (of the University of Colorado), Hamideh Afsarmanesh, Rafiul Ahad, Tim Connors, Alex Hwang, Peter Lyngbaek, and Bapa Rao (all of the University of Southern California). The careful review and valuable comments provided by Michael Brodie are sincerely appreciated.

9. References

[BBD77] [BROD81b] [BF79] [CHEN76] [CHEN78] [CODD79] [DV77] [FALK80] [GANE80] [HM81] [HWY79] [KING82] [KM82a] [KM82b] [KM82c] [MBW80] [ROSS77] [SHIP81] [SS77b] [SS78a] [SL79] [TH77] [TF80] [WE79]

Discussion

Until recently, database design concerned modelling data, the design of database structures. Now emphasis is being placed on modelling activities, the design of database procedures. The chapter presents concepts for tools that support the design of objects and their associated operations.

General purpose specification, design, and implementation techniques, as well as general purpose programming languages, database management systems, and general purpose data models are too general for specific problems such as office procedures. Specialized techniques, languages, and models are required. At least syntactical support is needed to address special purpose problems. High level, problem-oriented tools can be designed after understanding both the problem and the steps people use to deal with it.

The goal of this work is to reduce the expertise required to design, evolve, and access databases by means of a unified model and methodology. The authors believe that more nonspecialists will deal directly with databases. Hence, the model and methodology are intended for nonspecialists. The chapter presents a set of ideas for conceptual design and evolution, and computer tools to support them. Physical design is not discussed. The intended applications are detailed, predetermined activities (*e.g.*, office procedures), as opposed to much less predefined applications such as intelligence gathering. Presumably a different conceptual framework is needed to design databases for which exact requirements are not know in advance.

Conceptual Framework

Three different kinds of concepts are used: objects, events, and taxonomy. Examples of objects are items of correspondence, bills, checks, and forms. Each object is treated as an abstract type that has attributes. Objects flow between events. Events are either primitive or composite (events with subevents) actions. Finally, hierarchies are used to organize objects and events.

Objects

Objects are seen conventionally as having attributes. Each object has a single primary attribute that uniquely identifies it along with any number of dependent attributes. An attribute can be optional, single-valued or multi-valued. Object hierarchies are defined by attribute restriction. For example, a bill is a subtype of correspondence (*i.e.,* all bills constitute a subset of all correspondence).

The following questions arise concerning type hierarchies. How does simple attribute restriction for constructing type hierarchies compare with more complicated taxonomic systems such as TAXIS and SHM+ which provide multiple inheritance? When are the more complicated systems needed?

Events

The purpose of an event is to give to a nonspecialized person a concept with which to model. Eventually, events implemented on relational systems will free designers and users from lower level details. Currently, events aid in clarifying the meaning of operations. The names "event" and "object" are intended to give the designer intuition about what goes into a description (*e.g.,* don't use one procedure to both send correspondence and validate a check). One particular kind of event, called an application event, is basically a transaction.

Events are represented by parameterized (data manipulations) programs. Primitive events are of three kinds: create/destroy object, update attribute values of an object, and perusal events (no state changes). Composite events are made by combining other events using sequencing, conditional, and iteration. The structure of the objects (*i.e.,* the type-subtype hierarchies), determines the program structure. There is a certain internal data flow within procedures; however, the mechanism is not clear.

Computer Tools for Nonspecialists

Fully half of the chapter is based on the observation that nonspecialists will require software tools to deal with complex office procedures. Three basic ideas for tools are presented: structured, specialized syntax editors for the conceptual language that are used to assist evolution, interactive window interfaces (that have menus, prompting, and defaults) to aid design, and a tool used for constructing diagrams.

Two primary goals are proposed for computer tools: informality and incremental development. Interactions between a person and a computer should not be formal and pedantic. In the past, formality (*e.g.*, complete detail) was required when writing a program. Recently there has been some emphasis on informal software specifications. In the proposed methodology, English input is used, together with knowledge of the domain, to go incrementally toward specifications and programs. Many modules of the proposed system deal only with the issue of informality (*e.g.*, a diagram construction tool). The diagrams are intended to provide informality. Diagrams are to be converted to programs. The conversion starts with a basic program skeleton and the rest is filled in through menu interactions.

The goal of incremental development is to make the amount of work appropriate to the amount of change. Although the authors discuss evolution, no specific techniques are presented. Perhaps truth maintenance techniques from AI [MCAL80] could be used here. The idea is to have a general metaphor for building a database that maintains references not only to data, but also to the data from which it was derived. This provides a facility for determining the scope of a change.

One means for incremental development is to support leveled specifications. The goal is to provide an informal means for nonspecialists to go incrementally through designs. Although natural language is proposed for the first level, it is an unrealistic choice. A second level is called a design schema and it is refined by using an interactive and incremental methodology into a third level called a conceptual schema. The design and conceptual schemas do not really appear as two different levels of specification; they appear as two different representations of the same thing that have no fundamental difference. The difference between design schemas (basically flow diagrams) and conceptual schemas (basically programs) is a matter of the user interface and detail. It is important to realize that there are different levels and kinds of details. Some details, such as exception conditions, sequencing, and efficiency can be ignored in the early design phase, so that one can concentrate on the main cases.

It may not be realistic to expect nonspecialists to design their own systems using only their knowledge of the application and without the benefits of computer related knowledge. Perhaps nonspecialists who use the systems should provide the input to the design process and specialists should do the design.

Formality and Precision

Something that is formal lends itself to mathematical and mechanical manipulation (*i.e.*, is precise for a machine). Something that is precise (for human understanding) provides all the needed details accurately.

"Formal" means that there is a form for it; there may be no content. A common misconception is that formality implies precision. Precision does not require completeness; this is where the issue of abstraction detail comes in. Abstraction can be precise even if there is not enough detail for execution. Precise means that one understands all the details as much as one needs to. Although one cannot say that a description is totally precise (it may be precise for me but not precise for a machine), one can say that it is totally imprecise or more precise than another.

Something can be formal and imprecise or informal and precise; all combinations exist. Generally, we reject descriptions that are both informal and imprecise. We call them sloppy. Many system description mechanisms are both formal and precise, since they are best for mathematical and computer manipulation. There is considerable potential for mechanisms that are informal yet precise (*e.g.*, natural language). Euclid's algorithms were written precisely in natural language. The final combination, formal and imprecise, is also interesting; the whole field of AI could be characterized as trying to deal formally with imprecisely defined problems.

Experience with graphical tools suggests that graphics are good for simple descriptions, but too cumbersome for detailed descriptions. The switch to text is needed for understandability. The text of a twenty line program is easier to read than a graphical representation. Graphical representation versus textual description has to do more with what one is trying to do and not with differences in concepts. Another issue is the universe of discourse. An office system and office procedures are relatively simple. Specialized graphical notation languages are highly appropriate. Here, graphics are useful to describe major structures and not details. It is fundamental to design to get a perception of what is actually going on at a very high level. Graphics are helpful for that.

12
Adding Semantic Knowledge to a Relational Database System

Michael Stonebraker
University of California

ABSTRACT *This chapter suggests two mechanisms for adding semantic knowledge to a data manager, namely inclusion of an AI oriented rules system and a particular use of abstract data types. Both topics are explored in the context of the INGRES relational database system.*

1. Introduction

There have been numerous proposals for extending the relational model to contain additional semantic knowledge. A few examples are:

- classes [HM81]
- generalization and aggregation [SS77b]
- relations as an abstract data type [RS79] [SCHM78]
- entities and relationships [CODD79] [and many others]
- is-a hierarchies [MBW78]
- ordered relations [STON82a]

Any extension entails a substantial amount of effort to implement and an added construct for a user to understand. Hence, the focus should be on extensions that have a high value compared to their implementation effort.

This research was supported by the Naval Electronics Systems Command under Contract N00039-76-C-0022.

In this chapter we propose two such extensions, namely:

1. Columns of a relation as an abstract data type.
2. An AI oriented rules system.

2. The Use of Abstract Data Types

2.1 Introduction

Abstract data types (ADTs) [LZ74] [GUTT77] have been extensively investigated in a programming language context. Basically, an ADT is an encapsulation of a data structure (so that its implementation details are not visible to an outside client procedure) along with a collection of related operations on this encapsulated structure. The canonical example of an ADT is a stack with related operations: new, push, pop, and empty.

ADTs have been considered extensively in the context of semantic data modelling (see the chapter by Brodie and Ridjanovic) and as a central theme in database system implementation [LOCK79]. Moreover, the use of ADTs in a relational database context has been discussed in [RS79] [SCHM78] [WASS79]. In these proposals a relation would be an abstract data type whose implementation details would be hidden from application level software. Thus allowable operations would be defined by procedures written in a programming language that supported both database access and ADTs.

One use of this kind of abstract data type is suggested in [RS79] and involves an EMPLOYEE abstract data type with its related operations hire_employee, fire_employee and change_salary. This use of ADTs can limit access to a relation in prespecified ways, thereby guaranteeing a higher level of data security and data integrity. Also, a view [STON75] can be defined as an ADT. Consequently, the algorithm that transforms updates on views into updates on relations actually stored in the database can be encapsulated in the ADT, thereby providing a high degree of data independence.

This section presents a different use of ADTs. We will explore using ADTs for individual columns of a relation. The goal is to extend the semantic power of a relational data base system by defining new data types and related operators on these data types using user defined procedures that obey a specialized protocol. This use of ADTs is a generalization of database experts [SK80b].

We begin with a motivational example in Section 2.2. Then Section 2.3 defines our particular use of abstract data types. Lastly, Sections 2.4 and 2.5 close with an implementation proposal and some possible window extensions of our ADTs.

2.2 Time as an ADT

One would like to be able to define a column of a relation to have the data type "time." For example, one might define an event relation as follows:

```
create event (ename = c20,
              p-cancel = f4,
              type = c6
              date = time)
```

Here, the event relation has four fields: the name of the event as a character string, its probability of cancellation as a floating point number, its event type as a character string, and the date of the event as a time field.

Event tuples can be added to this relation using QUEL [STON76] [STON80] as follows:

```
append to event (ename = "lunch",
                 p-cancel = 0,
                 type = "food",
                 date = "12:00 - 1:00")
```

Clearly, all fields can be correctly converted to an internal representation and stored in a database system, with the exception of the string "12:00 — 1:00." In order to be interpreted as a time, special recognition code is required.

Moreover, one would like to use standard DBMS operators on the time domain. For example:

```
range of E is event
replace E ( date = E.date + "1 hour")
        where E.ename = "lunch"
```

The intended effect of this command is to move lunch forward one hour. Somehow, a data manager must be instructed how to interpret the addition of two times.

In addition, one would like to define new functions on the time column. Numerical columns have sin, cos, log, *etc.*, defined as built-in functions. Each of these accepts an integer or floating point number as input and returns another floating point number. Similarly, one might want to define the length of a time interval and use it in data manipulation commands. For example:

```
retrieve (E.ename)
where length(E.date) < "1 hour"
```

The problems here are twofold. First, one must actually define for the database manager the function "length," which accepts a time as input and returns a time. Second, one must define chronological order (*i.e.,* the meaning of "<" for the data type "time"). Without this added semantic knowledge, a DBMS cannot know that "59 minutes" is less than "1 hour."

In addition, one might like to define new comparison operations. For example, one might wish to define the concept "contained in," and to have a corresponding operator, "¦=", defined for this purpose. The containment operator could then be used to ask if there was any event contained within the lunch period as follows:

```
range of E is event
range of F is event
retrieve (F.ename) where F.date ¦= E.date
                   and E.ename = "lunch"
```

Lastly, one would like to be able to define aggregate functions for the time column. For example, one would like to be able to find the first future event as follows:

```
retrieve (E.ename) where
E.date = min (E.date where E.date > "today")
```

Again, extra semantic knowledge is required to to define the "min" function for this new data type.

Consequently, a mechanism is required to allow a new data type to be defined with its own particular internal representation. In addition, normal comparison, arithmetic and aggregate operators may be defined for this new type. To complete the definition of the type, new operators that obey the syntactic conventions of built-in functions, comparison operators, arithmetic operators, and aggregate functions are required. The next section proposes a simple mechanism to support the above capabilities.

2.3 ADTs

ADTs are mechanisms used for adding to a data manager procedural knowledge associated with a column. Basically, the definition of an

ADT consists of a registration process and the specification of a collection of functions. These are discussed in turn.

An ADT is registered with a data manager by giving the length of its internal representation along with a collection of optional fields. For example:

```
define ADT name
(length = value{, optional-field = value})
```

Thus,

```
define ADT time (length = 32)
```

will register a time ADT with a 32 byte internal representation.

One implementation of time [OVER81] uses the first 16 bytes as the lower bound of a time range and the other 16 bytes as the upper bound. The coding would be:

```
year:         4 bytes
month:        2 bytes
day:          2 bytes
day-of-week:  1 byte
am/pm:        1 byte
hour:         2 bytes
minute:       2 bytes
second:       2 bytes
```

The optional fields are used in query processing heuristics. For example, suppose one wants to find the names of events occuring at 9:30 by using the expression:

```
retrieve (E.ename) where E.date = "9:30"
```

Once the string "9:30" is converted to a 32 byte internal representation, a data manager such as INGRES can find qualifying tuples. If the event relation is stored by indexing or hashing on the name of the event, then the above command will require a sequential search of all tuples in the relation. However, if the relation is organized using date as a key, then the above command should be performed quickly. INGRES can use the fast access path to find all tuples that have a data field that matches the 32 byte representation for "9:30." However, INGRES must know that no other values for the date field can possibly match "9:30." Without this knowledge, a complete sequential scan of the events relation is required. Hence, the first optional field is set to true if normal equality can be used by INGRES to limit the search space for qualifying tuples.

The second optional field is set to true if the normal meaning of "<" and ">" can be use to limit the search for qualifying tuples. If additional query processing information is useful, more optional fields may be required.

These hints allow fast access paths to be built for new data types and used in the normal way by INGRES query processing heuristics. Hence, an ADT does not need to become involved in query processing. However, using this approach, only ADTs that have a particular semantics for equality and comparison can be optimized. It is probably useful to define a notion of an "abstract index" so that the query processing engine in a relational DBMS can handle indexes on more general ADT fields. Optimized query processing in such an environment is an open problem.

Once an ADT has been registered, one can define various operations on it by using one of two formats:

```
define procedure-type operator-name (adt-name)
                      as procedure-name
                      returning adt-name
```

for functions and

```
define procedure-type adt-name operator adt-name
                      as procedure-name
                      returning adt-name
```

for binary operations. The various types of procedures are now described.

A. *Conversion Routines*

In order to process time columns, routines must be provided that will convert between character string representation and 32 byte internal representation. For example:

```
define conversion input (character)
                  as my-proc-1
                  returning time

define conversion output (time)
                  as my-proc-2
                  returning character
```

These routines would be called as needed to convert the time of lunch between its 32 byte internal format and the string "12:00 — 1:00." A user can define any collection of conversion routines to allow transformations of an ADT field into different data types. These conversion routines are automatically called to perform necessary type conversions, as will be noted in Section 2.4.

B. *Comparison Routines*

Since the 32 byte internal representation for time may use a peculiar coding convention, it is necessary to provide procedures that will interpret the standard INGRES comparison operators {<, <=, =, >=, != }. One can also define new comparison operators that obey the syntactic conventions of the normal comparison operators. The syntax is:

```
define comparison adt-name operator adt-name
                  as procedure-name
                  returning adt-name
```

For example, one could define "<" and "¦=" as follows:

```
define comparison time < time
                  as my-proc-3
                  returning boolean

define comparison time ¦= time
                  as my-proc-4
                  returning boolean
```

Notice that operators can be defined that return types other than their operands. Moreover, one can define routines that have operands that are of different types.

C. *Arithmetic Operators*

In order to use DBMS arithmetic for a new data type, one must define the arithmetic operators {+, -, *, **, /, mod} procedurally. Also, one might want to define new operators that obey the syntactic conventions of arithmetic operators for the data type "time." The syntax would be:

```
define arithmetic adt-name operator adt-name
                  as procedure-name
                  returning adt-name
```

For example one can define the operator "+" and a new operator "/=\", which finds the intersection of two time ranges as follows:

```
define arithmetic time + time
                  as my-proc-5
                  returning time
```

```
define arithmetic time /=\ time
                  as my-proc-6
                  returning time
```

D. *Functions*

The syntax used to specify user defined functions on new data types is as follows:

```
define function function-name (adt-name)
                as procedure-name
                returning adt-name
```

For example, one can define the length of a time interval as follows:

```
define function length (time)
                as my-proc-7
                returning time
```

We can also use this facility to expand the collection of allowable operations on normal data types.

E. *Aggregate Functions*

Currently INGRES supports aggregate functions such as:

```
avg (E.p-cancel where E.type = "food")
min (E.p-cancel by E.type)
min (E.p-cancel by E.type where E.date > "today")
```

The first computes the average cancellation probability while the second computes the minimum cancellation probability for each class of events. The last aggregate computes the minimum cancellation probability by type for future events. We require a mechanism to define such aggregates for user defined types, as well as the ability to define new aggregate operators for user defined and normal types. The syntax would be:

```
define aggregate agg-name (adt-name)
                 as procedure-name
                 returning adt-name
```

The following examples define the aggregate "min" and a new aggregate "third from the smallest."

```
define aggregate min (time)
                 as my-proc-8
                 returning time
```

```
define aggregate third-low (time)
                 as my-proc-9
                 returning time
```

Using the last aggregate, we can find the third food event in the future as:

```
retrieve (E.ename) where
E.date = third-low (E.date where E.type = "food")
```

Consequently, an ADT is a registration process followed by a collection of procedure specifications of the above form. A user needs to know only the calling conventions used by the data manager in order to define an ADT. In the next section we turn to the impact of these ADTs on a DBMS.

2.4 Implementation Considerations

Each define command would cause entry of a new tuple in the following relation.

```
ADT( adt-name = c12,
     operator-type = c12,
     operator-name = c12,
     token-value = i2,
     first-operand = c12,
     second-operand = c12,
     result-type = c12,
     procedure-name = c12)
```

For simplicity we assume that the names of ADTs are unique. Each defined operator must be assigned a token for use by the parser when representing user commands as a tree structure. The registration information concerning the internal length and processing hints can be stored in the relation that contains column information. In INGRES this is the ATTRIBUTE relation.

There are two kinds of implementation difficulties, parsing and query processing. We illustrate each by use of the command:

```
range of E is event
retrieve (E.ename)
where E.time + "1 hour" < "9:15"
and E.time > avg (length (E.time) by E.type)
```

This command finds all events whose time plus 1 hour is less than 9:15 and whose length is greater than the average event length for the same type of event. First, one must build a parse tree for this command using standard parsing techniques. Then type incompatibilities must be resolved. For example, the expression e.time + "1 hour" requires adding a character string to a time. If there is an entry in the ADT relation that has input operands of type time and character string, and an operator name of "+", then the associated procedure can be used to evaluate the expression. If no such entry exists, a data conversion must be attempted. If a conversion routine exists from character string to time, "1 hour" can be changed to a time. Presupposing that procedures exist for evaluating "+" and "<" for two time operands, one can replace the original command with a parsed version of:

```
range of E is event
retrieve (E.name) where
E.date + input ("1 hour") < input ("9:15")
and length (E.date) >
    avg (length (E.date) by E.type)
```

This command has all operands of the same type and is ready for evaluation.

On the other hand, suppose there is no routine for converting between times and character strings. In this case, one must look for some data type for which there exists conversion routines from both time and character string fields. If a unique data type exists, it is chosen as the target type and appropriate conversions are performed. If either none or more than one is found, an ambiguity exists and an error message must be issued.

This analysis of types may be very costly. Optimizing the procedure by caching portions of the ADT relation in primary memory may be useful. Also, built-in rules for the standard types are probably desirable.

Query processing entails evaluating the parse tree for database tuples by either generating code for the tree or interpreting it at run time. In the former case one must simply generate code in order to call the various system and user provided routines at the appropriate times during tree evaluation, pass arguments from descendent nodes, and send the result of the procedure call up the tree. Aggregate operators must be passed both the partial result being accumulated and the data element in the current tuple. The routine must then return a new partial result. The query processing algorithms in [LW76] appear to have no difficulty with this added generality.

If the parse tree is interpreted, then the DBMS must hold a procedure library of all possible ADT routines. This may lead to a large run time system, which would discourage supporting user defined types. An alternative approach is to dynamically link procedures from the library as necessary.

2.5 Extensions

In this section we sketch a few possible extensions to the above mechanism.

2.5.1 Inheritance

It is useful to specify that a new type inherits all the operations of an existing type. This concept has been used in generalization [SS77b], classes [HM81], and is-a hierarchies [MWB78]. Inheritance can be specified as:

```
define adt-name-1 is-a adt-name-2
```

For example, one might specify:

```
define future-time is-a time
```

Note that all procedures defined for the time data type must work correctly for future-time.

2.5.2 Functions That Have Multiple Arguments

Certain ADTs may require functions to be defined that have multiple arguments. For example, one might want to create a new time interval between two other times. For example:

```
make-interval( "lunch", "5:00")
```

Current relational query languages do not support any functions that have multiple arguments. Hence, there are no query processing heuristics or parser templates for this sort of operation. It would be a useful extension if relational systems supported such functions.

2.5.3 New Types of Aggregates

One would also like certain kinds of generalized aggregates. For example, suppose one wanted the food event that was closest to lunch. For example:

```
retrieve (E.ename) where E.date =
min (abs(E.date - F.date) where E.type = "food"
and F.date = "lunch")
```

Although this is currently a legal aggregate, assuming that "abs", "-", and "min" are defined for times, it is clearly an awkward notation. A preferable notation would be:

```
retrieve (E.ename) where E.date =
closest(E.date TO "lunch" where E.type = "food")
```

Syntactically "closest" is similar to an aggregate function. The scope of the column being evaluated is limited by a "where" clause. Also, "closest" must keep a running tabulation of its answer. The only difference between normal aggregates and this one is the presence of a "TO" clause. The specification of more general aggregate operators and their associated query processing heuristics has yet to be investigated.

3. Rules Systems

3.1 Introduction

Many services of a database management system (DBMS) can be interpreted as rules systems. For example, integrity constraints [STON75] [HM76] specify conditions that must be guaranteed by a data manager. One such constraint for the relation

```
EMP(name, age, salary, dept, manager)
```

is that employee salaries be greater than 1000. It can be expressed in the current INGRES DBMS [STON76] [STON80] as:

```
range of E is EMP
define integrity E.salary > 1000
```

This condition is automatically enforced by modifying each incoming salary update to one which is guaranteed not to violate the constraint. For example, the command

```
range of E is EMP
replace E(salary = .8 * E.salary) where
E.name = "Smith"
```

is changed to

```
range of E is EMP
replace E(salary = .8 * E.salary) where
E.name = "Smith" and .8 * E.salary > 1000.
```

The last clause ensures that Smith's updated salary cannot violate the constraint.

This modification procedure is triggered by an incoming command and performs a collection of actions which alter the command. Hence, it is of the form

```
On condition
Then action
```

As such, it is a special purpose rules system. In addition, alerters [BC79], triggers [ESWA76], protection services [GW76] [SW74], and support systems for views [CHAM75] [STON75] follow the same paradigm. Consequently, they are also rules systems.

Many DBMSs implement such database services individually. For example, INGRES implements integrity control, protection, and views with three independent modules, each of which is a special purpose rules system. The purpose of this section is to propose a single rules system that will provide all these database services. In this way, only one mechanism need be implemented, and an economy of database code may result. Moreover, many rules not possible with existing DBMS services also can be formulated. In fact, our proposal even can be thought of as a special purpose programming language.

3.2 RAISIN

The language by which a database administrator or user specifies rules is called RAISIN (Rules from AI Specified for INGRES). Its basic structure is a sequence of ON-THEN clauses. That is,

```
ON (condition) THEN (action)
ON (condition) THEN (action)
               :
               :
```

For example,

```
ON replace, append, delete
THEN CANCEL
```

is a rule that will abort all update operations, guaranteeing a read-only database.

For each ON-THEN clause, the condition specifies constraints to be met by an incoming data manipulation command before applying the specified action. Moreover, the condition can depend on existing data in the database system. The action consists of a set of operations to be performed on the command as well as other possibly new operations to be performed on the database.

In this subsection we specify the allowable conditions and actions in RAISIN. The general form of a condition is:

```
ON          command(s)
TO          relations(s)
AFFECTING   field(s)
QUALIFYING  field(s)
BY          user-name(s)
DURING      time-range
FOR         day-range
WHERE       qualification
```

Hence, a condition is a collection of terms, each of which is a keyword followed by a parameter. The following are examples of conditions:

```
ON         replace
TO         EMP

ON         replace
TO         EMP
AFFECTING  salary
WHERE      EMP.name = "Smith"


ON         append, replace
TO         *
BY         Jones
DURING     8:00-17:00
FOR        mon-fri
```

The first condition applies to all replace operations to the EMP relation, and the second applies to a salary update for an employee named Smith. The third condition applies to all database modifications made by Jones during normal working hours.

Note that all terms in a condition except the first are optional and the wild card "*" is a valid parameter standing for "always." The TO clause specifies a list of relations in the current database to which this rule applies, and the AFFECTING term indicates what fields must be updated by the command in order that the condition apply. For example, the first condition above applies to all replace operations to the EMP relation, whereas the second applies only to updates that change an employee's salary. Moreover, the QUALIFYING clause indicates what fields must be present in the qualification of a user command for the condition to apply. For example, the command that gave a 20 percent salary decrease to Smith uses name in the qualification. Hence, a rule which included the term

```
QUALIFYING name
```

would apply to this update.

The day-range, time-range, and user-name constructs are self-explanatory. Lastly, the WHERE clause qualifies data to which the rule applies. Hence, it should be a valid qualification in a data manipulation language. In RAISIN the qualification is a QUEL WHERE clause modified in one important way. In QUEL, all field names must have an attached range variable. In the above QUEL example, E is declared to range over EMP and fields are designated by E.name and E.salary. In RAISIN qualifications we assume that a relation name is prefixed to a field name instead of a range variable. Hence, EMP.name and EMP.salary would be valid field names.

For any incoming data manipulation command, the first condition of any rule is either true or false. If the condition is false, the rule does not apply. If, on the other hand, the condition is true, the action part of the rule is executed and the remainder of the ON-THEN statements (if any) are checked for applicability. We now turn to the legal actions that can appear in a RAISIN statement.

The action portion of an ON-THEN statement is an ordered collection of commands from the following list.

1. *EXECUTE*

The user command is performed automatically at the end of a rule. Hence, the user does not need to explicitly call for the execution of his command. However, if a user wants the command to be run before the end of a rule, he must use an EXECUTE statement. Two EXECUTE statements in a row would cause the user command to be run twice.

2. *CANCEL*

This action cancels the execution of the user's command.

3. *UNDO*

This action undoes all changes to the database that occurred since the triggering of the rule. By including this action one implicitly assumes that transactions are supported by the database management system.

4. *CHANGE relation-1 TO relation-2, ...,relation-N*

This action will change the scope of the user command from relation-1 to relation-2, ..., relation-N. More precisely, whenever one has

```
range of var-1 is relation-1
```

this is changed to

```
range of var-2 is relation-2
   .
   .
   .
range of var-N is relation-N
```

Var-2, ..., var-N are internally assigned by a RAISIN implementation. Moreover, for any given field name, F, in relation-1, it is assumed that only one relation, say relation-j, has a field of the same name. Hence,

```
var-1.F
```

is changed to

```
var-j.F
```

For example, one can deflect all operations on the EMP relation to the NEW-EMP relation by means of the following rule.

```
ON      *
TO      EMP
THEN
CHANGE  EMP to NEW-EMP
```

5. *RENAME field-1 TO field-2*

This action causes all references to field-1 to be changed to field-2. If, for example, NEW-EMP has a salary field named dollars, the action statements of the above rule should be extended to:

```
RENAME salary TO dollars
CHANGE EMP TO NEW-EMP
```

6. *MESSAGE { TO user-name} "message text"*

A message is returned to the person who issued the command that activated the rule. If the optional clause TO user-name is included, the message is directed to the named user. The MESSAGE action is useful when a command must be cancelled and an error message returned.

7. *ILLEGAL "message text"*

This action inspects the current command to see if it is syntactically valid. If not, it will perform a CANCEL and generate a message. Consequently, it has the following effect:

```
ON        syntax error
THEN
CANCEL
MESSAGE "message text"
```

In this way a syntax error can be caught before the execution of the user command and an appropriate error message generated.

8. *QUEL command*

Any QUEL command is a legal action. For example, suppose RULES is a relation that has two fields, a rule number, and a count field indicating how many times any given rule has been executed. The action statement needed to correctly update this relation for rule number 16 would be:

```
range of R is RULES
replace R (count = R.count + 1) where
R.number = 16
```

One extension is needed to QUEL commands in the RAISIN context. Portions of the user command that activate the rule can be substituted in a QUEL statement that is applied as an action. The following keywords indicate the needed portions.

qualification	a keyword for the qualification in the users command
command	a keyword for the whole user command
new.field-name	a keyword for the value being assigned to field-name by the user command

These can appear where they are semantically valid in a QUEL command. For example, in the command that gave a 20 percent pay decrease to Smith, qualification has the value

```
E.name = "Smith"
```

while new.salary has the value

```
.8 * E.salary
```

9. *ADDQUAL qualification*

This action will perform query modification [STON75] on the current command, adding the indicated qualification to that specified by the user. This extra qualification follows the syntax of QUEL WHERE clauses except that each field name has a relation name prefixed instead of a range variable. Since the user's command will have a range variable in front of each field name, the qualification must be preprocessed to find each field name, remove the prefixed relation name, and substitute the user's range variable.

For example, we can restrict Jones to the subset of employees under 30 by the following rule:

```
ON        *
TO        EMP
BY        Jones
THEN
ADDQUAL   EMP.age < 30
```

If Jones issues a query such as

```
range of E is EMP
retrieve (E.salary) where E.name = "Smith"
```

then it will be modified to

```
retrieve (E.salary) where E.name = "Smith"
                                      and
                              E.age < 30
```

Notice that EMP.age is preprocessed to E.age before being added to the command. One other processing step must take place. The keywords noted in command (8) are also valid here, and the appropriate substitutions must be made.

3.3 Examples

We indicate the use of RAISIN to accomplish integrity constraints and protection statements. Additional examples are presented in [STON82a] to support alerters [BC79], nonstandard updating of views, and general triggers [ESWA76]. The following integrity constraint in QUEL expresses the constraint that employees earn more than 1000.

```
range of E is EMP
define integrity E.salary > 1000
```

This rule can be expressed in RAISIN as:

```
ON       replace, append
TO       EMP
THEN
ADDQUAL new.salary > 1000
```

Note that new.salary refers to the value assigned to salary by the user command.

A protection constraint might be that Jones can only update salaries of employees, for whom he is the manager, between 8 A.M. and 5 P.M. This can be expressed in QUEL as:

```
range of E is EMP
define permit replace of E(salary) to Jones
FROM 800 to 1700 WHERE E.manager = "Jones"
```

This can also be specified in RAISIN as:

```
ON          replace
TO          EMP
AFFECTING   salary
BY          Jones
DURING      8:00-17:00
THEN
ADDQUAL     EMP.manager = "Jones"
```

3.4 Summary

The above section has outlined a rules system that can be used to obtain all popular database services. It is anticipated that this system can be made as efficient as the same database services produced by special purpose code. Moreover, a single rules system is easier to implement than the same collection of individually implemented services.

Three questions remain unresolved. First, storage of rules in a relational DBMS is not appealing. A storage structure for RAISIN rules is suggested in [STON82b]; however, it is neither particularly efficient nor easy to understand. It is an open question about how to extend a relational DBMS to be a more attractive storage system for rules. The same sort of deficiencies arise in attempting to use a relational DBMS to store the parsed representation of a program in a general purpose programming language [POWE82].

The second question concerns the specification of rules. In general, integrity constraints, protection statements, and view specifications are easier to understand than the comparable RAISIN statements. Of course, it is a simple matter to internally map these classes of statements to RAISIN rules. However, the design of a more appealing syntax for RAISIN triggers and alerters should be studied.

Moreover, in the RAISIN context it is possible to design applications with a large collection of triggers. In fact, some applications can be primarily specified by triggers. An application specified in this manner will not be particularly easy for a person to understand, debug, or maintain. Office automation languages containing messages (*e.g.*, [ROWE82]) have the same readability problem. Another open question concerns how to design a specification system for triggers that is easy to understand. Unless a friendly notation can be developed, the viability of triggers in such environments is suspect.

The third issue concerns commands containing a join of a relation to itself. For example, one can give a 10 percent pay cut to all employees who earn more than their managers as follows:

```
range of E is EMP
range of M is EMP
replace E (salary = 0.9 * E.salary) WHERE
       E.salary > M.salary AND
       E.manager = M.name
```

The RENAME action can be applied to this command; however, it will change the command so that no employee can possibly qualify. Moreover, the statement

```
ADDQUAL EMP.salary > 1000
```

is ambiguous. One is uncertain whether this qualification applies to employee salaries or to manager salaries. Consequently, the application of rules to reflexive joins is an open issue.

4. Conclusions

This chapter has suggested the inclusion of a rules system in a relational data manager and the use of ADTs at the column level of a relation. With a rules facility one can imagine a sophisticated user being able to extend his application environment with more elaborate integrity constraints, triggers, alerters, protection statements, and view update algorithms than is possible with current relational systems.

One can also envision libraries of column ADTs and an individual installation using a subset of them in its run time system. One can also envision a sophisticated user writing his own ADTs, thereby extending a relational database system with knowledge specific to his domain of discourse.

Using these two facilities a data manager can be tailored to the needs of an individual application. It is hoped that other mechanisms can be discovered that will serve to further augment the power of contemporary data managers.

At this time (September 1982) column ADTs are operational [FOGG82] [ONG82]. The only restriction is that aggregates are not available on user defined types. An implementation of RAISIN has not yet been attempted. Although the code to support rules is not overly taxing, work on it has not started because it it is felt that there may be a more user friendly way to get the same level of functionality.

5. References

[BUNE79] [CHAM75] [CODD79] [ESWA76] [FOGG82] [GRIF76] [GUTT77] [HM76] [HM81] [LOCK79] [LW76] [LZ74] [MBW78] [ONG82] [OVER81] [POWE82] [ROWE82] [RS79] [SCHM78] [SK80b] [SS77b] [STON75] [STON76] [STON80] [STON82a] [STON82b] [SW74] [WASS79]

Discussion

The chapter makes two proposals: one for a uniform production rule representation (a la AI expert systems) for integrity control, protection, and views, and another for abstract data types (ADTs) in order to extend the semantics of columns in relations.

Production Rules

A production rule is treated as a command, or sequence of commands, which alters some relation or set of relations (*i.e.,* a field or a set of fields). The main idea is to identify special purpose actions and conditions that support protection, access control, integrity control, and views, and to treat them as production systems.

Command Modification

The database update "Give a 10% pay cut to all employees earning more than their managers" involves a reflexive join that leads to ambiguity. The update can be expressed in the database language QUEL as:

```
range of E is EMP
range of M is EMP
replace E (salary = 0.9 * E.salary) WHERE
    E.salary > M.salary AND
    E.manager = M.name
```

Does the constraint:

```
ADDQUAL EMP.salary>1000
```

apply to employee salaries or to manager salaries? It is not clear whether to bind ADDQUAL to E or to M. It may be obvious, but one can bind to both. The chapter claims that this is a problem when using the production rules approach. Is it not really a problem when command modification is used to add ADDQUAL to the system? The problem concerns qualification, and it leads to the question of "How general is command modification?" Is it simply that reflexive joins are problematic? How can the user be assured that integrity is maintained? Are there any formal results on these issues?

Michael Stonebraker: "Reflexive joins are the only case that I can think of. There are no formal results."

Abstract Data Types

Databases do not have extensible type systems. These benefits can be gained by adding ADTs, which this chapter proposes for defining the semantics of individual columns of a relation. Columns or attributes of relations have been very simple. Attributes can be extended to act as roles by appropriate naming and by adding role oriented operations. For example, one can associate a "time" ADT with a relation called EVENT which has attributes event-name, type, date, and probability-of-cancellation. For instance, "lunch" is a "food" event that takes place at "12:00 p.m.-1:00 p.m." with a zero probability of cancellation. Attributes can be represented using standard string, integer, or floating point data types. Although the standard data types do not pose representation problems, they may not be adequate for the operations one wants to perform. One may want to add an hour to a particular time, to compare times, to talk about time intervals (containment or overlap), *etc.* There are many time related operations that are not supported by standard data type or database operations.

Database support for Computer Aided Design (CAD) poses problems of representation and operation. No general purpose database system handles the right kind of objects such as points, lines, and polygons. One wants operators that take the area of a rectangle and return meaningful CAD objects. One also wants to describe new operators that return different types.

Stonebraker proposes facilities with which to register an ADT with the data manager and to define its data structure and associated procedures such as conversion routines, comparison routines, arithmetic operators, unary functions, and aggregate functions.

ADTs seem attractive for representing well-known types. The next step is to integrate the ADT representations. For example, integrate the data types transistor, rectangle, text, and line in order to define a new data type circuit_diagram. This integration is difficult when using database operations and notation. Specifically, it is difficult to use a relational query language to express the components and the relationships involved in circuit_diagram. ADTs are supposed to provide means for such integration. However, integration issues concerning ADTs in this context have yet to be examined. Type integration for type definition is complex even in the PL context. The circuit_diagram definition would require many parameters and a lot of code. The code is encapsulated in a generation procedure used to generate a new circuit_diagram instance.

The chapter proposes to extend a data manager by adding new operators and lower level types. One then uses a query language to construct new types from the operators and lower level types. However, since query languages have no abstraction facilities and no parameterized procedures, it is hard to define types, especially for complex objects.

An interesting question concerns the trade-off between having relational structure visible (so that relational query languages can be used) versus having operators that hide the relational structure. This is really an open question.

In the classical relational approach, having only simple fields available poses problems for complex objects. For complex objects, one has to define functions that return the object's characteristics. The results of these functions can be treated as field values for queries. This process requires a much richer query language environment, such as those proposed in PL (*e.g.,* use of functions and parameterized procedures). This is a problem of integration of PL and DB concepts, as addressed in Pascal/R or TAXIS. We should keep the benefits of query languages and extend them to support abstraction, parameterized functions, procedures, and more complex objects.

It is time for DB systems to support not only simple ADTs as proposed by Stonebraker, but also complex objects. To do this, well known database problems such as views must be addressed.

Computer science, in one sense, concerns the managing of complex issues that arise in computer systems. We should use ADTs in a relational framework and relations in ADT framework to deal with complex objects and to manage the complexity of real-world problems. These mechanisms must interface well. Compatibility of all objects in the system must be considered. The integration issues that arise in building these systems will clearly be the research challenge of the 80s.

Part IV

Perspectives from Programming Languages

13 The Functional Data Model and its Uses for Interaction with Databases

Peter Buneman and Rishiyur Nikhil
University of Pennsylvania

1. Introduction

During the last decade, much research has been done in the field of data abstraction techniques in programming languages (see the chapter by Shaw), and higher-level data models for databases [CODD70] [CHEN76] [SS77b]. It is thus not surprising that researchers have begun to attempt to integrate databases and programming languages (*i.e.*, by providing definitional and manipulative primitives for databases in the programming language that is consistent in philosophy with its existing data and control structures). The work in PASCAL/R (see the chapter by Mall, Reimer, and Schmidt) and PS-ALGOL [ACC82] are examples of such attempts made in the context of compiled, imperative (ALGOL-like) languages. This chapter describes our ideas on integrating databases into an interactive, applicative (Lisp-like) programming system.

Applicative and functional programming languages have recently received acclaim [BACK78] [BURG75] [BMS80] [TURN81a] as methods that greatly simplify the process of specifying complex programs. We shall present a simple functional data model and an implementation strategy for query languages that enables these programming techniques to be exploited for interactive database work. First, however, it seems appropriate to describe a larger problem, that of producing a good interactive programming system, for which the techniques developed in this chapter form a partial solution.

Lisp [MCCA62] is an example of an *applicative* language. In its pure form, the only control structure is the application of functions to arguments; and a Lisp program is no more than an expression built out of function applications. In APL [IVER79], a single expression can describe a highly involved computation. This is so because APL is endowed with a rich set of high-order functions that are especially well suited to mathematical problems. The formation of expressions in APL is an example of a *functional* style of programming. But these two widely used languages enjoy something else in common. Together with their programming environments, they are both extremely successful examples of experimental programming languages, languages that allow for the rapid and incremental development of programs that range from the simplest arithmetic computation to solutions of the most sophisticated problems in mathematics or artificial intelligence.

Now we would like to argue that such a language and programming environment is very much needed for database work. At present, there appears to be a dichotomy between "end-users," those who have a simple but limited query language at their disposal, and applications programmers, whose knowledge covers a programming language and a database system. Since the language and database system are frequently mismatched, this kind of applications programming is often the most difficult to learn. Why is it seemingly so difficult to provide a programming system for databases which, like Lisp and APL, combine the simplicity required by end-users and the power required by applications programmers?

In order to answer this question, let us list some of the advantages of these programming systems as they are seen by the users. A comprehensive list of requirements is found in [DT80].

Incrementality. Programs can be developed in very small pieces, and a very small subset of the language (such as the language of simple arithmetic) is all that is required to do elementary work. Thus the language provides immediate gratification for new users, and both the process of developing programs and learning the language are incremental.

Workspaces. All the programs and data relevant to a particular problem are logically encapsulated in a "workspace." Programs are developed by creating new objects in this workspace and the user does not have to switch to new agents (such as an editor or job control language) to do this.

Unstratified control.[1] Objects in the language, such as function definitions and structure declarations, can be manipulated in the language. The user can not only write, for example, his own editing routines, but can also embed workspace manipulation commands in his procedures. For database work, this would also imply access to, and manipulation of the schema, or "metadata."

---

[1] We are grateful to Saul Gorn for bringing this term to our attention.

Uniform structuring system. The language is based upon a simple set of generic types and functions (arrays and operators in APL, lists and recursion in Lisp).

Storage management. Programs may dynamically create new objects, and the user does not have to be concerned with the allocation and deallocation of storage for this purpose.

Some database query systems, notably those built on a relational database implementation, provide the user with some of these advantages. But none, to our knowledge, provide the user with the power or flexibility of the programming languages mentioned above. In fact it is a partial indictment of the state of the art of database technology that so many database applications are written in APL, a language whose data structures can hardly be used naturally to represent any of the current database models.[2]

In this chapter we will deal with some of the technical problems involved in developing a similar programming environment for databases. The particular problems we shall discuss in the following sections are: (a) a simple set of data structures and operators suitable for database work, (b) an implementation method that allows "large" objects, such as sets of records in a database, to be manipulated through function application rather than explicit control forms, and (c) an expressive yet convenient type system for such an environment. These do not provide a complete solution to the problem at hand, and there remain some outstanding obstacles to producing this "ideal" programming system, notably in dealing with update and metadata (unstratified control), and in the description of data models with "richer" semantics. These problems are discussed in the last section. Much of the technical material presented here is covered in detail in [BF79] [BFN82]; the purpose in describing it here is to show its relationship to other work in this area and to adopt a more speculative approach to the outstanding problems.

2. The Functional Data Model

It has been suggested in several papers [BF79] [HOUS77] [SHIP81] [SK77] that a variety of relationships among data could be simply represented through the mathematical notion of a function. The relation between a record class and a field, for example, is a function that maps the set of records in that class into the domain of the field. Thus,

[2] We understand that there is a marriage of convenience between IMS and APL.

rather than defining an EMPLOYEE record as having a SALARY field which is a NUMBER, SALARY is regarded as a function that maps EMPLOYEEs into NUMBERs. In this fashion, a single relation normally specified by

```
EMPLOYEE(NAME:STRING,SS#:NUM,FULLTIME:BOOL)
```

can be regarded as a set of functions

```
NAME:       EMPLOYEE -> STRING
SS#:        EMPLOYEE -> NUM
FULLTIME:   EMPLOYEE -> BOOL
```

The Codasyl set relationship is often called a "many-to-one" relationship, but it is nothing more than a function, and we could add to our database the functions

```
DEPT:        EMPLOYEE -> DEPARTMENT
DNAME:     DEPARTMENT -> STRING
```

where, in a Codasyl database, DEPT would refer to a set "owned by" DEPARTMENT and "owning" EMPLOYEE. Note that in the relational model, first normal form forbids domains to be nonprimitive types, such as EMPLOYEE and DEPARTMENT. The functional representation of the relational version would therefore be different (a department-number function would be introduced both for EMPLOYEE and DEPARTMENT), and this reflects the differing semantics of the relational and network representations of this database.

It is necessary to distinguish between the *data types,* such as EMPLOYEE and DEPARTMENT, and their *extents*, the set of EMPLOYEEs and set of DEPARTMENTs currently represented in the database. To do this we introduce the notation !EMPLOYEE, which we regard as a constant-valued function that returns a list of objects of type EMPLOYEE.

The functional data model, therefore, simply treats the database as a set of abstract data types, together with a set of (extensionally defined) functions on these types. There is no direct notion of record, aggregate, or tuple in the data model. This is consistent with our desire to define data types incrementally since it allows new database functions to be defined, and the schema to be extended, at any time. All that should be required is the definition of the range and domain of a new function, together with an initial value of the function (a set of ordered pairs). This version of the functional model is particularly simple compared to other versions of the same model [HOUS77] [SHIP81] [SK77]. In particular, it contains no notion of key or subtype [SK77], which are important in specifying, as opposed to querying, the database. These "semantic" refinements to the functional model are important; but they place constraints on updates and on the kinds of extensions to the schema that can be made. (Our simplified version has had the advantage of enabling us to build our system quickly over existing Codasyl and relational systems.)

Just as the relational algebra provides a set of operators that are well matched to the relational data model, it is desirable to produce a similarly natural set of operators for the functional model. Consider various ways of phrasing a very simple query to print the NAMEs of EMPLOYEEs:

```
findfirst EMPLOYEE                                    (a)
while not ENDOFCLASS do
   begin
      get EMPLOYEE;
      print NAME;
      findnext EMPLOYEE
   end

for each x in !EMPLOYEE, PRINT(NAME(x))               (b)

select NAME from !EMPLOYEE                            (c)
```

Of these three forms, the last two are eminently understandable: (b) is based upon the language Daplex [SHIP81] that is now being used in conjunction with Ada, and (c) closely resembles SEQUEL [CB74]. (a) is a rather unhappy attempt to represent a Codasyl traversal in a "structured" language, but is typical of programs in certain Codasyl "query" languages; it specifies the computation required in excruciating detail. (b) is much simpler, but still contains an explicit *for each* control structure and has to introduce an extra name "x" which may have to be declared earlier. On the other hand, (c) is an *applicative expression* and returns a result that, in terms of the relational model, is a one-column relation of character strings. Moreover, (a) and (b) are both *commands*, and construction of compound constructs (sequencing) involves the introduction of the additional notion of "states," and variables to hold such states between commands. We prefer instead to espouse the expression style (c), in which more complicated forms are created by simple functional composition. Further, applicative expressions are amenable to optimization by simple syntactic transformations: a fact that has been observed in connection with programming languages [BACK78] and query languages [SC75]. (The comparative semantic elegance of applicative expressions has been discussed in much more detail elsewhere [LAND66] [BACK78] [TURN81a].) Our problems are first to give a meaning to (c) in terms of the functional model, and second to devise an implementation that provides the efficiency of the program indicated by (a) and possibly (b).

Lisp has a solution to the first of these problems. If we regard !EMPLOYEE as a constant-valued function that returns a list of EMPLOYEEs, the Lisp expression for this query is

```
(MAPCAR NAME (!EMPLOYEE))
```

MAPCAR is a higher-order function or *functional.* It takes as one of its arguments a function—in this case, NAME —and applies it to each element of the list created by applying the function !EMPLOYEE. This indicates that the counterpart to the relational operators for the functional data model will be a set of functionals similar to MAPCAR of Lisp.

Using this idea, the authors and their colleagues have constructed a functional query language called FQL, based on a small set of functionals. We briefly review it here in order to make some general observations about query languages. A note about syntax: we are more concerned here with the functional nature of the language than its particular syntax. The admittedly austere syntax was inspired in part by Backus's FP language (because of its brevity and its amenability to algebraic manipulations that result in great optimizations [BACK78] [IMB81] [WADL81]). A more conventional, user-friendly syntax may easily be designed with the same operators.

Our simple query is expressed in FQL as

```
!EMPLOYEE.*NAME
```

which involves the use of two functionals, *extension* (*) and *composition* (.). Extension operates in a manner similar to Lisp's MAPCAR, but rather than being a two-argument function that takes a function and a list as arguments, it is a higher-order function that takes one argument that is a function (NAME) and produces another function (*NAME) that carries lists of EMPLOYEEs into lists of character STRINGs. For example:

```
*NAME: *EMPLOYEE -> *STRING
```

Note that the symbol "*" is doing double duty as a type operator in order to denote the data type of lists of things (*EMPLOYEE, *STRING) and as a functional operator (*NAME).

Composition (.) composes the functions !EMPLOYEE and *NAME, to produce a constant-valued function that returns a list of STRINGs. This is exactly what a database query is—a constant-valued function that produces some "printable" object such as a list of character strings. The reason for using the "reversed composition" notation is something of a mathematical idiosyncrasy, but it has two advantages in database work: the left-to-right order of composition follows the order of traversal of the functional arrows in the database schema, and the "." is nicely confused with the syntax of record selection in many conventional languages. Note that we have not created a list of EMPLOYEEs, but a function that, when applied, will return such a list. We shall elaborate on this in more detail later.

Some form of *restriction* operator is clearly needed. In FQL this is represented by "¦" and is a functional that takes a predicate (boolean valued function) as an argument, as in

```
!EMPLOYEE.¦FULLTIME.*NAME
```

FULLTIME is of type EMPLOYEE —> BOOLEAN. The restriction with FULLTIME, ¦FULLTIME, is a function that operates on a list of EMPLOYEEs to produce another (sub-) list of EMPLOYEEs. That is, it filters the original list to just those EMPLOYEEs who are fulltime. Thus the type of ¦FULLTIME is given by:

```
¦FULLTIME: *EMPLOYEE -> *EMPLOYEE
```

Note that restriction maps between lists of the same type but of (usually) different length, while extension maps between lists of (usually) different types but of the same length. Both preserve order.

A final functional, *construction*, needs to be introduced with another generic type constructor that forms tuples or aggregates. By [STRING, NUM] we denote the type of two-tuples whose first components are of type STRING and second components are of type NUM. This is much like a record type whose selectors are indicated by position rather than name. By [NAME, FULLTIME] we mean a function that applies NAME and FULLTIME to an EMPLOYEE argument and constructs the individual results into a tuple of type [STRING, BOOL]. For example:

```
!EMPLOYEE.*[NAME, SAL]
```

is a query that produces the names and salaries of all employees.

```
!EMPLOYEE.*[NAME, DEPT.DNAME]
```

produces the names and department names of all employees.

The details of FQL may be found in [BF79] [BFN82], and will not be elaborated upon here. There are, however, some general remarks that relate to query languages and to our desire to produce a "complete" interactive programming environment for databases.

We have concentrated so far on the use of functionals to combine database functions into queries, but they can be used equally well for performing arbitrary computations and for defining new functions. For example, [2, 2]. + is, if we regard the symbol "2" as a function that returns the value 2, a function that adds 2 and 2. This is certainly not the ideal syntax for this computation; however, some definitions are concisely expressed through the use of these combining forms:

```
AVERAGE = [/+,LENGTH].DIV
```

which is a compact definition of the average function in terms of /+ (add up a list), LENGTH (take its length), and DIV, divide two numbers. It is surprising that the designers of many query languages provide only for very limited forms of arithmetic, and even then usually only in the context of a database query.

The uniformity of the semantics of database functions, primitive functions, and user-defined functions demonstrates another advantage of the functional data model. Thus far we have indicated that database functions might be represented internally by an extensional definition (set of argument-value pairs). In fact, they may well be represented as computational rules, for example in a "log tables" database. They may involve a mixture of the two, as in a general rule together with extensionally defined exceptions. A more detailed discussion of this aspect may be found in [KOWA78] in the context of logic databases. We shall also explore, in Section 4, how this uniform semantics integrates cleanly the concept of "user-views" of the database.

By allowing recursion and providing the standard list-manipulation functions the power of pure Lisp is achieved. This is a form of typed Lisp. For example, CONS, whose generic type is:

```
CONS: [alpha,*alpha] -> *alpha
```

(where alpha is a type-variable) cannot construct lists of heterogeneous objects. Having the power of a recursive programming language again represents an improvement over the relational algebra in which constructing a transitive closure is impossible [AU79].

Though recursion is available, it is not an appropriate method either for the expression or implementation of traversals of large homogeneous collections of objects that are typical in databases. This is better expressed using the special operators. Recursion should be used only where the problem is inherently recursive,[3] as in

```
TOTAL_COST = [COST, SUBPARTS.*TOTAL_COST./+].+;
```

[3] To an advocate of functional programming, the unfettered use of recursion is almost as much of an anathema as the GOTO statement. In his recent thesis [MYER 81] Tom Myers has shown that a very large class of "inherently recursive" problems can be elegantly represented through the use of a very small set of tree-manipulating functionals.

which is a simple bill-of-materials processor to provide the total cost of a part from its cost to manufacture (COST: PART -> NUM) and the cost of its subparts (SUBPARTS: PART -> *PART).

There are two other aspects of this query formalism that deserve comment. One is that the language has no variables. This is not a requirement, and it can be shown [BFN81] [BURG75] [TURN79] that bound variables can be translated out of more traditional function definitions into expressions involving only constants, by using composition (.), tupling ([...]), and a few other functionals, called "combinators." Using this, we are currently building a more "friendly" query language not unlike an applicative subset of Daplex [SHIP81]. Lack of variables does appear as an important factor in implementation.

The second aspect of the formalism is that it allows only the construction of functions from other functions, and never explicitly creates or names data from the database. Compare, for example the two definitions:

```
EMPNAMES = select NAME from !EMPLOYEE
```

and

```
EMPNAMES = !EMPLOYEE.*NAME
```

Does the first of these define a function, whose result varies with changes in the EMPLOYEE relation, or does it create, once and for all, a set of names corresponding to the current status of the EMPLOYEE relation? The second definition uses composition of functions, and makes explicit the fact that we have only defined a function that is yet to be applied, at which time it will return a set of names. It is often useful to think of the constant-valued functions, such as !EMPLOYEE, as actually taking the whole database as an implicit argument. The usefulness of creating data, as opposed to functions, will be discussed later.

3. Implementations

It has been argued that an essential ingredient to producing a good experimental programming environment for databases is to have a language (the relational algebra and FQL are candidates) whose basic mode of interaction is the evaluation of an expression. While this is semantically very elegant, how is this to be implemented? The naive solution suggested by the relational algebra is straightforward: each relational operator of the (unadulterated) algebra creates a new relation, and these operators are implemented by having them physically create new relations. Unfortunately, for any database containing large relations, this will require substantial use of secondary storage and I/O. Implementations of the relational algebra occasionally get around this problem by "pipelining" the output of one operator to the input of another, a technique that was suggested in [SC75]. However, to achieve efficiency, the semantics of the operators are sometimes modified (*e.g.*, "relations" are allowed to contain duplicated tuples).

The other method of implementation is to translate the expression-based query into a conventional program in some iterative form that will run against the database system. There are several objections to this solution. One is that translation from a high-level query language into efficient code in a relatively low-level programming language is not at all straightforward, given that the translator has to take into account interactions with physical representations of the database on secondary storage. Also, if the target language is subsequently put through a preprocessor and compiler, as is common for many database management systems, the number of translation steps will make the execution of a "one-shot" query both time-consuming and inefficient, thus discouraging such use. Another problem, from the standpoint of an interactive programming environment, is that the user is too widely separated from the run-time execution of the program. Error messages that result from run-time errors must be translated into a form that is readily understood by the user of the high-level system. It is generally impossible to ensure that a translator will produce code that will not cause run-time errors, but even if it were, the process of examining the run-time state of a program is an invaluable debugging tool that should not be sacrificed. It is our opinion that such translation into a low-level, efficient, iterative language ought to be performed, if at all, via program transformation techniques, *after* it has already been debugged and well understood at a high level.

Although we appear to have dismissed the two most common strategies for implementing an expression-based query language, this is not quite the case. An attractive possibility is to extend the "pipelining" approach that has been suggested for the relational algebra. We can do this in one of two ways: either by emulating a "pipeline" machine or by physically constructing one. The relationship between such machines (commonly known as dataflow machines) and functional programming systems is the subject of considerable research. Later, we shall investigate the possibility of using dataflow concepts on a large scale, that of communicating databases on different computers; but first, let us examine how data flow ideas can be emulated in a very simple fashion, resulting in savings in I/O and secondary storage.

The idea that makes it possible to represent very large sequences of data objects in a fashion that makes them amenable to manipulation without the overhead of physically instantiating them originated with Landin [LAND65], who actually used the idea in the reverse direction: to represent iterative programs as operations on data objects. Rather than represent a list as a conventional pointer structure, it is represented as a *stream*, which is a two-component structure whose first component corresponds to the head of the list, and whose second component is a "promise" to create another stream that corresponds to the tail of the list. The promise corresponds to some kind of procedure that is only invoked when required, say, in order to print the list. Thus no promises are discharged until they are required, and this has led to the term "lazy evaluation" for this kind of interpretation. However, the precise definition of the promise is an important technical matter that can crucially effect efficiency.

A common method [BURG75] [FW76a] is to define the promise as a "closure" (function-argument pair) that, when evaluated, returns a stream. Since the stream itself contains a promise, this closure that generates the tail of the list is actually creating another closure that generates the tail of the tail of the list. As a result, the implementation must support functions that are capable of creating new functions, and embedding of functions in data structures. This is precisely what is needed for a functional language, for functionals themselves are functions that create new functions. Now suppose that in a conventional language the invocation of a function F were to create a new function G. The environment in which G is to run (the bindings of all variables global to G) is the environment that obtained when F created G. But unfortunately, in a normal implementation, this environment will disappear after the invocation of F is complete. The solution is to maintain this environment and attach it to G, so that G will have available a set of variable bindings when it, in turn, is invoked. The preservation of environments (usually performed by "spaghetti stacks") is a costly process and accounts for much of the inefficiency of this kind of evaluation (cf. FUNARGs in Lisp).

We noted before that our query formalism was variable-free. Since there are no bound variables, there are no bindings and hence no environments. We appear to have finessed the environment problem out of existence! This is not quite the case, and a brief summary of the implementation of FQL may be appropriate. A comprehensive account will be found in [BFN82]. A "promise" in FQL is implemented as a *suspension*. This is a tagged two component structure $\{U\,f\,a\}$ consisting of a function f and an argument a. The tag U (for *U*nevaluated) distinguishes this structure from other types of structure used in the implementation. The evaluation of a suspension, performed by the interpreter function EVAL, is achieved simply by applying f to a.

A *stream* is now defined as a two component structure {*S x u*} whose second component, *u*, is a suspension. The evaluation of *u* yields another stream {*S x' u'* }, the evaluation of *u'* yields {*S x'' u''* }, and so on. This stream therefore corresponds to the sequence of values *x, x',x''* ..., each of which may be a suspension. Unlike other implementations of lazy evaluators, there is no need for the suspension {*U f a*} to carry around an "environment"; it is a self-contained object. Each of the components *f* and *a* may, however be compound objects.

The internal representation of a *tuple* of objects is an *n*-component structure {*T x1 x2...xn*}. All internal functions have one argument, and multiple arguments are achieved by tupling them together. For example, the expression 2+3, just prior to the final evaluation, will be represented as

```
{U plus {T 2 3}}
```

where plus is the name of the internal function that adds two numbers.

Suppose we have an internal function EXTEND that takes a function *f* and stream *s* as arguments and produces, like MAPCAR of Lisp, the stream of values created by applying *f* to each member of *s*. That is, if *s* yields the values *x, x', x''* ..., the application of *f* to *s* should yield the values *f(x), f(x'), f(x'')*... We can represent the application of EXTEND by the simple rule:

```
{U EXTEND {T s f}} ->
    {S {U f x} {U EXTEND {T u f}}}
    where {S x u} = EVAL(s)
```

This rule, and a few others like it, form the basis for the code for function application.

Now consider the representation of an FQL function like *NAME. "*" is a functional that produces a result which is the function created by giving EXTEND only its function argument. This is often called the "partial application" of EXTEND to NAME. It is represented by a fourth, and final, internal structure, {F EXTEND {T NAME} }. This is a structure that describes a function. When at a later time this function is given a stream as argument, it will appear as

```
{U {F EXTEND {T NAME}} s}
```

which is then transformed by EVAL to

```
{U EXTEND {T s NAME}},
```

a form suitable for the application of EXTEND.

There is surprising uniformity among the low-level database access routines provided with database management systems. Codasyl, for example, may be thought of as providing two functions for the traversal of a record class: FINDFC (find-first-in-class), that takes the name of a class as argument and returns (a reference to) the first record in that class; and FINDNC (find-next-in class), that takes the class name and (a reference to) a record and returns (a reference to) the following record. The internal access method for the relational system Ingres [HSW75] is remarkably similar. This provides an extremely simple database interface for the implementation method we have sketched, for the stream of EMPLOYEEs produced by !EMPLOYEE is generated by successively applying the partial application {F FINDNC {T EMPLOYEE}} to a database reference to obtain a new database reference. It is a straightforward matter to turn this into a stream [BFN82].

To someone who has not studied lazy evaluation techniques, this method of interpretation may seem esoteric, and the reason for its description in a book on data models may appear tenuous. There are, however, a number of points that bear upon the construction of interpreters (and hence experimental programming environments) for databases.

Generality. Not only is the functional data model well suited to the representation of a variety of database management systems, but the implementation we have sketched is also well-matched to their internal subroutines. The method may be used to evaluate expressions in a more general language.

Efficiency. The removal of variables (and hence environments), whether or not it is syntactically suitable for database programs, has a marked effect on the efficiency of lazy evaluation schemes. Turner [TURN79] has devised a similar technique based on a different internal representation, and notes similar improvements in efficiency.

Compactness. The code for such an implementation is extremely compact, amounting to a few hundred lines of Pascal. This includes storage management and a number of special optimizations.

In short, if one is intending to build an interpreter for an expression-based database query language without resorting to a translator but keeping the storage efficiency of iterative programs, some form of lazy evaluation scheme seems essential.

Looking at implementations from a wider scope, it has been recognized [AGP78] [KL80a] that there is a very different form of implementation for functional programming systems on *dataflow* machines. The structure and semantics of an applicative expression strongly suggest a great potential for parallelism, and in fact the architecture of a multiprocessing machine can be made to correspond closely to this structure. The processing elements in such a system are usually considered to do rather simple processing tasks. However, the ideas apply equally well when the individual processors are more complicated, as in the case of two communicating (conventional) machines that each support a database.

Consider, for example, a database query that requires reference to both databases for its evaluation. In the first place, decomposition of a query across machines is easily represented in the functional notation. Suppose that a library database on machine A contains information on BOOKs and BORROWERs (represented by their names) and that an employee database on machine B contains information on DEPARTMENTs and EMPLOYEEs. A query issued on machine B is required to compute, for each department, the average number of books borrowed by its members, and print out a list of department names and averages.

In the functional model, the relevant functions are:

```
Machine A
  BORROWER: BOOK -> STRING    (The result is
                               the name of
                               the borrower)
Machine B
  DEPT:      EMPLOYEE   -> DEPARTMENT
  DNAME:     DEPARTMENT -> STRING
  NAME:      EMPLOYEE   -> STRING
```

The FQL query that provides the name of each department and the average number of books borrowed by its members is then

```
!DEPARTMENT.*[DNAME,
            ^DEPT.*NAME
                 .*(^BORROWER.LENGTH)
                 .AVERAGE                ]
```

Note, first of all, that nothing has been said about whether the databases are network or relational. In fact, the library database could be relational, and the employee database Codasyl. Equally important is that the entire sub-function

```
*(^BORROWER.LENGTH).AVERAGE
```

of type *STRING —> NUM, may be given to machine A. Thus for each sequence of names, machine A returns a number. This represents a drastic reduction in network traffic from the many situations where the remote machine (A) has inadequate processing power, and must therefore return the names, say, of all the borrowers and let the more powerful processor (B) do the counting and averaging. Our variable-free notation also facilitates this kind of decomposition.

We can view our simple two-machine network as a (very high level) "data flow" machine:

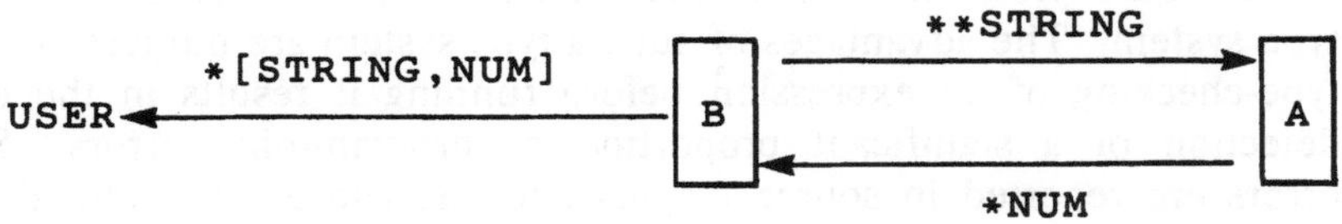

It is possible to imagine that the two machines are in "synchronous" communication for the purpose of resolving this query. B transmits to A a sequence of sequences of EMPLOYEE names produced by each application of ^DEPT.*NAME. A returns to B a sequence of averages. For each sequence of strings sent to A, B may simultaneously compute the department name while it is waiting for A to respond with a number. The output delivered to the user would therefore be simultaneous with the evaluation on two machines! Again, this technique of "synchronous" communication can result in considerable reduction in network traffic over the conventional techniques for distributing relational queries [HY79].

4. Type Systems

We have seen that the functional model treats a database as a collection of abstract data types, together with a collection of functions on these types. This is an environment rich in types, and it is important that our query language have a flexible, efficient and robust type system to support it. However, the applicative languages we have been quoting as paradigms (Lisp and APL) have very weak type systems. They provide few primitive types (numbers, character strings, . . .) and few structuring methods (s-expressions, arrays). Type-checking is done at run time at the very last moment, just before applying a primitive function to its arguments, by examining type-tags that are carried with each argument. While this is certainly type-safe (in the sense that type errors are always recognized), there are several problems with it. Reporting type errors at such a late stage may be pointless and does not, in general, lead to robust programs in which one can have much confidence (an airline clerk may well be baffled by an error message "CAR applied to a number"). Since there is no distinction between an abstract type (it exists only in the mind of the Lisp programmer) and its implementation as a data structure, there is no protection from spurious values that just happen to have the same structure. This also makes it difficult to relate type-error messages to the original query, because the effect of such type errors may only be felt at some later stage in the execution, in some relatively remote part of the program.

We would prefer instead a much more powerful, statically checked type system. The advantages of such a type system are numerous. The type-checking of an expression before running it results in the early detection of a significant proportion of programming errors. Such errors are reported in source language terms, and are pinpointed to a location in the immediate expression being checked. The static detection of type errors needs significantly less resources, and may thus be considerably cheaper than running the query to find them. If the type system has no loopholes, no type-checking need be done at run time, thereby speeding up the query and reducing storage requirements, because no type-tags need be carried around. Annotation of expressions with type declarations serves as a form of machine-checkable documentation, making queries easier to read and understand. If the type system supports the definition of new abstract data types, this serves as additional powerful tool for structuring programs, and provides the the capability of defining "user-views" of a database.

There are several difficulties involved in designing such a type system for the sort of language and incremental environment that we have been describing, and we shall discuss these in the context of our plans for FQL.

Firstly, we do not wish to sacrifice the *convenience* of the style of programming that Lisp and APL environments provide. This convenience arises principally from the extensive use of polymorphic and higher-order functions. A polymorphic function is one that may be used at an infinity of types, such as the function CONS. CONS has the polymorphic type

```
[alpha,*alpha] -> *alpha
```

where alpha is a type variable, and in different contexts CONS may operate on lists of numbers, lists of booleans, lists of lists of functions from numbers to booleans, and so on (*i.e.,* the type variable alpha may be instantiated by any type). This polymorphism is not limited to primitive functions. More complex functions inherit this polymorphism in a very natural way (*e.g.,* the expression *CONS inherits the the polymorphic type).

```
*[alpha,*alpha] -> **alpha
```

from the polymorphic types of its constituent functions CONS and EXTEND (whose type is (beta->gamma)->(*beta->*gamma)).

FQL has a robust yet convenient type system similar to that in the programming language ML [GMW79], based on a polymorphic type theory due to Milner [MILN78]. In FQL, expressions are written exactly as they have been described thus far. Type declarations are optional. However, a sophisticated but simple type-inferencing algorithm based on the unification computation deduces a type for every expression at compile time, and guarantees the absence of run time type errors. In fact no types are carried around or checked at run time.

Next, we would like the type system to support the definition of *abstract data types*. Again, ML provides a good model in this respect. An example of such a definition is:

```
type FRIEND <=> EMPLOYEE
  private
    IS_IN_CS: EMPLOYEE -> BOOLEAN
      = [DEPT,'CS'].EQ
  public
    !FRIEND:      -> *FRIEND
      = !EMPLOYEE.¦IS_IN_CS.*ABS_FRIEND
  public
    FRIEND_NAME: FRIEND -> STRING
      = REP_FRIEND.FIRSTNAME
  public
    ADVISING_DAY: FRIEND -> DAY
      = ....
end
```

Here FRIEND is a new abstract data type, represented as an EMPLOYEE. The "<=>" notation represents the isomorphism between an abstract value and its representation, and the two special functions

```
REP_FRIEND: FRIEND -> EMPLOYEE
ABS_FRIEND: EMPLOYEE -> FRIEND
```

map in the two directions of this isomorphism. They do not perform any actual computation, but they serve to make the type FRIEND distinct from the type EMPLOYEE. An attempt to use an EMPLOYEE as a FRIEND or vice-versa will be caught as a type error. These special functions are available *only* within the scope of this definition. A set of associated functions may also be defined (IS_IN_CS, !FRIEND, ...) and selectively exported outside the definition. (We give type declarations here only for readability. They may be automatically inferred from the function definitions.) Outside this type definition, these are the only primitive functions that may create or manipulate FRIENDs. (Of course, they may be combined into more complex functions.)

Such an abstract data type facility is a powerful tool for structuring programs, and this aspect has been widely discussed in the literature in the context of programming languages. In our database environment, it also provides a means to extend the database schema and create new user-views of an existing schema. We can regard the FRIEND type as a private view of the general EMPLOYEE database. We represented a FRIEND directly as an EMPLOYEE, and generated a list of friends (!FRIEND) by generating a restricted a list of EMPLOYEEs. One advantage is that functions on FRIEND values are kept consistent with updates in the underlying EMPLOYEE database. Instead, we could just as well have chosen to represent the list of FRIENDs as an extensionally defined list of [STRING,DAY] tuples, perhaps generated once and for all from the EMPLOYEE database, or with values that don't even exist in the EMPLOYEE database, with appropriately modified associated functions. We can also have functions on FRIENDs that do not correspond to any existing function on EMPLOYEEs (such as ADVISING_DAY). All this is transparent to any use outside the definition. The type FRIEND appears as just another type in the schema.

Though we showed a very simple example, it is fairly straightforward to extend this facility to handle recursive and parameterized abstract types. A richer system may also include the notion of subtypes and inheritance of functions, and axioms to express the semantics of types. There are several interesting proposals in the programming language Hope [BMS80] for such a system.

Finally, we want all this to be available in an *incremental* system, where functions and types may be defined and redefined incrementally. This raises problems in maintaining consistency in the type system, similar to the problems encountered in maintaining consistency in a conventional program with independently compiled modules. Dependencies between functions must be maintained in a dependency graph. When a function or a type is redefined, this dependency graph has to be analyzed to see which other functions are critically affected by this change and appropriate action has to be taken. These effects are reduced, and the analysis made easier by of the applicative nature of the language and the use of abstract data types.

5. Update and Metadata

Thus far we have examined formalisms for query and programming languages and associated implementation problems, but we have yet to look at the more general problems of programming environments. Our point of departure for this discussion is an apparent paradox. We have described what is technically regarded as a "powerful" programming language (in the sense that it can compute any recursive function), but it is incapable of update. To an applicative programmer a program consists of an expression to be evaluated in the context of a set of definitions, and if asked how this concept of a program takes care of database update, he may reply that an update is nothing more than a function that transforms one database into another. Such a view of update is correct but naive. It tells us nothing of the update mechanism itself, and logically identifies the database as the sequence of all updates that created it.

A pragmatic solution to the problem is to simply loosen our purely applicative framework and define a set of update primitives. Let us digress briefly, examining what such a set of primitives would look like, and then return to the more philosophical issue of reconciling such a set of primitives with the applicative programmer's view of the world.

Kershberg and his colleagues [HK81] have examined update semantics for a specific, and semantically rich, version of the functional model. The typical problem here is to ensure that the update does not violate a constraint on the function. For example, a function may be constrained to be bijective, as in the case of the functional relationship of a key (such as social security number) and its class (employee). In keeping with our desire to have "bulk" operators, we should have bulk update statements. For example, a modify command (it is no longer an expression) would take two arguments: the name of the function to be modified and a sequence of argument-value tuples that are to replace existing mappings, as in

```
MODIFY(SAL, !EMPLOYEE.¦FULLTIME.*[ID,SAL×1.05])
```

which is a command to give all full time employees a salary increase of 5%. In a similar vein, addition of new entities would entail supplying a list of new entities to a CREATE command, as in

```
CREATE_EMPLOYEE(READ)
```

where READ reads in a stream of [STRING,NUM,...] tuples corresponding to new EMPLOYEE names, salaries, *etc.*, from an input device. CREATE_EMPLOYEE would then update all the functions of the abstract type EMPLOYEE (!EMPLOYEE, NAME, SAL, ...) to include these additions. Deletion of entities, if it is required, can be accomplished by similar forms.

It should be emphasized that these are are minimal solutions to the update problem. They take little account of database semantics; they bear little relation to the semantics of the rest of the language; and there is no provision for "repair" (*e.g.*, of an error in a stream of update data).

Let us re-examine the problem of update from a more orthodox point of view. To an applicative programmer, a query (expression) will always produce the same result no matter how many times it is evaluated (*i.e.*, the expression and its environment form a closed system). If it is to produce a different result, he must "step out" of the closed system, manipulate the environment creating a new closed system, and re-evaluate the query in the new environment.

Traditionally (in Lisp and APL), there is always a single "current" environment which is changed by editing a function. Function names are always bound to a single, "most recent" definition. Similarly, in our database environment, one may imagine a simple editor that would display the structure of a database function (argument-result pairs, or expression to be computed) in a form convenient for editing.

In ML, however, there is a different concept of "environment." The environment is never modified, but continually *extended* during a session. When a function *F* is defined, it is permanently bound to the the current environment. If a definition for *F* is given again, a new function *F* is created which, because of the linear growth of the environment, hides the old *F*, which is still unchanged. For example, if we use the notation {*F*} to refer to *F* in its *previous* environment, our salary-update example may be expressed as

```
SAL = if FULLTIME then
        {SAL} × 1.05
      else
        {SAL}
```

Thus, a new function SAL is defined in terms of the old SAL, having the effect of giving all fulltime employees a 5% raise. One may think of the { ... } notation as a kind of "environment operator" similar to version numbers that are popular in many file systems. We would like to extend this notion to a formalism that gives more detailed control over environments.

Another implication of this highly speculative view of update is that old data never disappear. The function {SAL} is, internally at least, still available, and it is possible to recover the definition of SAL before the redefinition was made. It has been argued [AM81] that a database system in which one can "roll back" time is desirable, and this is very similar to the ability to visit previous environments. Such a system may indeed be well-suited to the advent of video-disk technology which offers the potential of immense, write-once-only storage. It is interesting to note that the ability to "backtrack" in the interactive development of a program is also of concern to the developers of programming systems (cf. the Interlisp "undo" command).

The discussion on updates and abstract data types showed examples of what we have termed "unstratified control" (*i.e.*, switching between manipulation of data, descriptions of data, and so on). To do this conveniently, it is also very useful to be able to query details about the environment. In FQL this is done in a manner analogous to many relational systems where the schema itself is stored in a relation. We provide abstract types and associated functions such as

```
!TYPES:                 -> *TYPE
TYPE_NAME:        TYPE  -> STRING
^TYPE_NAME:  STRING     -> TYPE
ASSOC_FNS:        TYPE  -> *FUNCTION
FN_NAME:   FUNCTION     -> STRING
^FN_NAME:      STRING   -> FUNCTION
FN_DEF:    FUNCTION     -> STRING
```

These may be combined in FQL expressions, as in

```
!TYPE.*[TYPE_NAME, ASSOC_FNS.*[FN_NAME,FN_DEF]]
```

which produces a listing of all types accompanied by the names and definitions of their associated functions.

6. Conclusion

In this chapter we have described how one can provide an interactive, Lisp-like environment for working with real databases. This involved representing the database within the functional data model, and providing a functional language with higher-order operators to compose queries. An implementation technique using lazy evaluation allows us to interpret this language compactly and efficiently. The simplicity of the data model and the interpreter have allowed us quickly to implement such a language (FQL) over existing Codasyl and relational databases.

We feel that the database environment demands a strong type system (though Lisp itself does not have one). We have shown how to provide such system while maintaining the convenience of interactive programming with polymorphic functions and without type declarations.

In our opinion, the functional approach provides a much more powerful, yet semantically simpler (and thus more intuitive) means to query a database than the imperative approach usually associated with databases and the mixed functional and imperative approach that is found in systems that embed the relational operators in an imperative programming language; however there still remains the need to deal adequately with the notion of update.

7. References

[AU79] [AM81] [AGP78] [ACC82] [BACK78] [BF79] [BFN82] [BFN81] [BM77] [BURG75] [BMS80] [CB74] [CHEN76] [CODA71] [CODD70] [DT80] [FW76a] [GMW79] [HM78] [HK81] [HSW75] [HY79] [HOUS77] [IMB81] [IVER79] [KL80a] [KOWA78] [LAND66] [LAND65] [MCCA62] [MILN78] [MYER81] [SHIP81] [SFL81] [SC75] [SS77b] [SK77] [TURN79] [TURN81a] [WALD81]

Discussion

Many ideas from applicative programming have found their way into data model and query language design. Functional data models (FDMs) simply treat the database as defined by abstract types, together with a set of functions on these types. Functional query languages, like FQL, are based on functional expressions. Instead of providing operators like the relational "join" and "select," however, they use functionals for function composition and function application, similar to, say, the "mapcar" functional in LISP. FDMs do not distinguish a functional view (think of functions instead of many to one relations) from a relational view (think of relations instead of Boolean-valued functions). Instead, they emphasize the applicative, expression-like style of querying over the imperative, command-like one.

Query Languages

The claim is that expressing queries in a functional style is significantly simpler than using conventional, say relational, query languages.

Michael Stonebraker: "We can all put up our favoured query language and then have a religious discussion about which is better. It seems to me that FQL is sort of the APL notion of a query language. What's the big deal?"

Rishiyur Nikhil: "Don't focus just on the language syntax. The main contribution is to have a nice applicative language, and then to implement it in an efficient way. I don't want FQL's syntax to distract us. Admittedly it is terse (APL-like?) but that is a red herring. The emphasis is more that the functional data model and the functional query language a) are intuitively easy to grasp and manipulate, and b) together with user defined functions provide an intergrated environment for programming in database contexts."

Updates in a Functional Data Model

A crucial issue with respect to functional languages is how to handle nonapplicative operations such as updates. A first approach is to treat updates as functions, mapping a database into a database. Conceptually, that may be sufficient; however, it doesn't illuminate very well what is meant by a database update.

Charles Rich: "What a heck of a frame problem!"

A second approach is to stay within the functional framework but introduce new special operators that modify a database via side effects.

A third approach is not to think of actually updating the environment, but to take a more monotonic approach and just extend it. This approach has the advantage (?) that one can always refer to past values.

The latter way of handling updates may totally destroy grouping of data on physical media. Clustering, however, is crucial to the efficiency of a database management system.

A more AI-oriented approach to the update problem would be to collect the environments into more complex viewpoints and to reason explicitly about them and the different situations they represent. In addition, one would like to distinguish two kinds of updates: one is changes, and the other one is simply additional information. Situations are changed only when someone has told a lie. The case of adding information can be handled more easily.

Charles Rich: "Except if you had a closed world assumption that every addition is nonmonotonic."

Carl Hewitt: "Which is one of the better arguments against the closed world assumption."

Michael Stonebraker: "Managing all the changes in the environment is more difficult than managing structured objects. For me it seems that using a functional representation makes life harder."

Rishiyur Nikhil: "The whole discussion on update was very speculative. In the paper we do not make any claims yet about update. FQL gives you a style of programming where you can think of infinite structures. From a database point of view this means that you can think you have a large amount of data at your disposal without having to pull them into core."

Query Optimization

That is, of course, exactly the way any relational database management system works. In fact, query optimization is exactly the process of trying to figure out the minimum of data that has to be pulled into core.

Michael Stonebraker: "What's worse is that in order to really optimize your formalization, your notation offers no advantage to query optimization. Basically, current relational systems do all the optimization you are doing plus some more. Maybe your notation even has a disadvantage. People from SYSTEM/R and others found it harder to optimize a block-structured notation because one has to 'flip around the scope' and that's harder than in a non-block-structured notation."

Rishiyur Nikhil: "I believe that because of their cleaner semantics, functional query languages offer far more promise for optimization through algebraic manipulation."

Implementation of Functional Query Languages

Two standard ways to implement an FQL-like query language are: first, to build up relations dynamically—which is not very efficient; second, to compile the applicative language into a lower level language that does deal with individual records, *etc.*

The FQL implementation avoids both ways. Basically, it represents lists as "streams," and maps streams into each other in the standard "lazy evaluation" sense of applicative programming. (A stream is essentially an actual element plus a promise to provide more elements.)

Rishiyur Nikhil: "There have been some measurements that compare an implementation technique such as ours, which is essentially a graph reduction technique (we have no variables!), with implementations that have environments (with expressions). The result was that the graph reduction technique leads to much faster implementations. The reason is basically that it implements an "outside-in" or "normal-order" implementation. The "outside-in" order is what gives us the lazy evaluation of sequences, crucial to handling large database sequences. This is difficult to implement efficiently if you have variables and environments, but because of its special sharing properties, is naturally implemented efficiently by the graph-reduction method."

Michael Stonebraker: "You cannot come up with a relationally complete language without variables. This follows from the fact that languages like SQUARE, which have been proven to be complete, could not do without variables."

Rishiyur Nikhil: "If you write a lambda-calculus expression with variables I can get these variables out into combinators. And I think that the set of combinators we use are specifically well tuned for big collections of data. (See the 1982 ACM Symposium on LISP and Functional Programming for more discussion of the relative efficiencies of combinators and closures.)"

David Israel: "Maybe. I just don't believe the claim in the abstract that combinators are better than closures.

It looks as if the FQL implementation technique is well suited for data flow machines since subexpressions can be evaluated on separate machines or simultaneously. That reduces, for example, network traffic and lends itself to distributed computing.

Functional Programming

It is generally agreed that functional programming was a good response to the state before Backus's paper. There are definitely too many "unnatural" assignments. On the other hand it is not more "natural" to make nearly everything functional. Functional programming is not appropriate for something that naturally has a state in it. It is true that the mathematics of functional programming are simpler, however, in order to achieve a "real task of interest," the complexity to be added to a purely functional program makes the approach much too complex.

Stephen Zilles: "Backus would make two more comments if asked:

1. He is interested in functional notation primarily because memories inhibit composition of things. There is no reasonable notion of putting two memories together and composing programs in nice ways. The notion of state is a barrier to composable units."

Carl Hewitt: "I disagree. I think state is not composed out of memories, it is composed of machines (objects or actors) — and those we can compose."

Stephen Zilles: "I do not agree with that: it's not easier to compose machines than it is to compose transactions on memories. The focus is that it is much easier to compose functions.

2. The other focus is mainly that we should come away from operations on individual objects and should proceed to operations on collections as a whole.

And I think that that was one of the intents of the paper and that it is extremely valid for all of the work we are concerned with."

Final question: What is the historical importance of distinguishing the imperative from the applicative style of programming? Answer: It means the separation of church and state.

14
Types in the Programming Language Ada

Bernd Krieg-Brueckner
Universitaet Bremen

ABSTRACT *Data types have played a key role in the design of the programming language Ada. Issues concerning the separation of logical properties, implementation and physical representation, the isolation of static and dynamic properties of data, the abstraction from and hiding of implementation details, and the parameterization of type definitions had to be addressed. The design motivations and specific solutions of Ada are presented and illustrated by numerous examples. An extension of Ada by concepts of formal specification is briefly sketched.*

1. Introduction

The Ada project [IKWL79] [IKWL80] [IKWL82] was started primarily to meet the needs of a specific user community. Due to financial constraints, the strict time schedule, the competitive nature of the project, and, in particular, the requirements catalogue [DoD79], the emphasis was on "language engineering" because it made the best possible use of the state-of-the-art in language design and compiler technology for a wide range of existing hardware. One would think that there is little room for research in such a situation. As it turned out, however, considerable development effort was needed to satisfy the detailed and seemingly conflicting requirements, and to consolidate existing solutions and research ideas from a variety of sources into a consistent overall design. New solutions to existing problems had to be found and to be discarded whenever they were in conflict with other solutions for

---

This work was partially supported by the Sonderforschungsbereich 49, Programmiertechnik, Technische Universitaet Muenchen.

related problems or for general requirements such as implementation efficiency, reliability, maintainability, or separate compilability of program portions.

Data types are central for any language design that aims to achieve a high degree of readability, maintainability, modularity, and, most of all, reliability. It forms the largest single part of the design of Ada, but is by no means isolated. Type definitions interact with the typing of expressions, the definition of parameters and the results of subprograms, overloading resolution for calls on subprograms that have the same name, hiding of information in packages for "abstract data types," (generic) program units to define new types as if they were "built-in," and the specification of the physical representation of data structures for systems implementation.

In this chapter, the data types of Ada and their design motivation are presented with particular concern for innovative aspects. An extension of these concepts to allow formal specification is sketched in Section 10.

2. Motivation

There are some basic goals that motivate the concern for types in the design of Ada.

Reliability. This is the overriding concern. Data objects should have well defined properties; the rules of the language should guarantee that these properties are maintained throughout the program and that an error indication is given in case of violation.

Maintainability. The user should be encouraged to state the properties of objects explicitly in the program text. Commonality of properties between several objects should be factorized into a single declaration, for example a type declaration, and referred to by name. If a property of these objects must be changed during program maintenance, only one declaration that states the common property is affected instead of each individual object declaration. As we shall see, an important distinction is made in Ada between static and dynamic properties.

Readability. The isolation of properties in the form of a declaration is a useful piece of information for any reader who tries to understand the original programmer's intent. Apart from this maintenance aspect, the language should provide good tools for data description and for structuring that will aid in program development.

Modularity. Types are regarded as the primary vehicle for communication of properties via interfaces. Modularization should lead to a separation of concerns between implementor and user of a type that embodies these properties, to the extent that implementation details can be hidden and therefore changed during maintenance without affecting the user. This becomes particularly important in the context of separate compilation, or, in more general terms, separate development of program portions.

Genericity. There should be ways to parameterize type definitions in order to avoid cumbersome repetition during program development, in much the same way that control constructs can be parameterized via subprograms (*i.e.,* functions or procedures). It should not only be possible to define types parameterized by objects, for example stacks that have arbitrary bounds, but also type schemas parameterized by other types, for example a schema of stacks of arbitrary component objects.

We shall see in the following sections how these goals are met in Ada.

3. Type Definitions

A type characterizes a *set of values* and a *set of operations* applicable to these values. All objects that can assume values must be declared. Because of the first two of the following typing rules, the type of an object is invariant during execution.

- Each object (*i.e.,* constant, variable, parameter) gets a unique type in its declaration.
- Any operation (*i.e.,* operator, function, procedure) must preserve the type of its parameter and yield a result of the specified type.
- Each type definition introduces a distinct type.

The third rule enforces a disjointness of types in Ada that is stronger than in most languages and deserves some discussion. Consider Figure 3.1. In many languages, such as Algol 68 [WMPK75] or several versions of Pascal [JW74], the types RATIONAL and DIAGRAM would be considered as equivalent types (cf. [WSH77]). For a detailed discussion of various possibilities for equivalence rules see [IBHK79]. Although the types have the same mathematical properties and are structurally similar, the decision in Ada was to keep them distinct.

The major reason for this rule is program development and maintainability. Two programmers working on a large program system should indicate the same intent explicitly by referring to the same type name. There should be no accidental equivalence of types during program maintenance (for example, by the deletion of a component of a large record), and no unintended equivalence that is only detected (and leads to an error) after such a change is made or when the program has been in use for a long time. Such language traps often lead to unmaintainable programs due to a fear of change. The rule is also simple to learn, simple to check by a reader or compiler, and it poses no extra problem for separate compilation, as an equivalence rule would.

```
type RATIONAL is
  record
    N, D: INTEGER;
  end record;

type DIAGRAM is
  record
    N, D: INTEGER;
  end record;

R1, R2: RATIONAL;
R3:     RATIONAL; -- R3 has the same type as R1 and R2
D:      DIAGRAM;  -- D  has a distinct type from R1
```

Figure 3.1 *Type Declarations with Distinct Type Definitions*

Since types are distinct, conversion must be explicit if it is allowed for types that have similar properties, for example for derived types as discussed in Section 5.

Explicit conversion emphasizes the mapping that is logically necessary although the implementation may be the same. This separation of concerns between *logical definition* and *implementation* is a sound principle since it allows an easy transition to a modified implementation. A similar separation occurs between *implementation* and *physical representation* in terms of bit patterns in words or bytes on a contemporary machine. Representation clauses are optional and do not influence the semantics of an Ada program. They may be vital in systems implementation, however, where explicit interfacing to peripheral hardware is required. The rule:

- one type — one representation

forces a disjointness between types that have distinct physical representations specified by the user.

The advantage of such a separation of concerns are evident: the user can concentrate on the correctness of the program with respect to the logical properties, and add/change a correct implementation or physical representation at a later stage of program development.

4. Classes of Types

Four major classes of types that are distinguished in Ada provide for the explicit structuring of data according to predefined rules (see Figure 4.1):

```
type MONTH_NAME is ( JAN, FEB, MAR, APR, MAY, JUN,
                     JUL, AUG, SEP, OCT, NOV, DEC );
     -- an enumeration type

type YEAR_NUMBER is range 1901 .. 2099;
type DAY_NUMBER  is range    1 .. 31;
     -- integer types

type REAL         is digits 9 range -1e15 .. 1e15;
     -- a floating point type

type DURATION     is delta 0.001 range -86_400.0 .. 86_400.0;
     -- a fixed point type

type LINE         is array ( 1 .. 128 ) of CHARACTER;
     -- an array type

type DATE is
  record
    YEAR:   YEAR_NUMBER;
    MONTH:  MONTH_NAME;
    DAY:    DAY_NUMBER;
  end record;
     -- a record type

type LINE_PTR is access LINE;
```

Figure 4.1 *Classes of Type Definitions*

1. *Scalar Types.* Values have no components. The set of values is definable by explicit *enumeration,* or by giving a range for *integer types* and an error bound for *floating point types* and *fixed point types* used in approximate computations. Enumeration and integer types are said to be *discrete types,* since every value has an immediate successor.

2. *Composite Types.* Values are aggregates of component values. For *array types,* components must be of the same type and can be indexed by values of a discrete type. For *record types,* components can be of distinct types and are selected by component identifiers. Record types can have variants as discussed in Section 7; component selection is safe. That is, the selector can only refer to a corresponding variant. Thus cartesian power and product, disjoint union, but

no undiscriminated union (as the record types without explicit tag field in PASCAL) exist for reasons of reliability.

Composition is arbitrary; that is, arrays of records of arrays are possible; recursive composition requires intermediate access types.

3. *Access Types.* Values provide access to other objects. All these objects must be of the same type and are allocated dynamically. There can be no "dangling references," since the collection of allocated objects has the same scope as the access type declaration, and each access type definition introduces a distinct collection.

4. *Private Types.* The structure of values is hidden from the user. Values can only be created and manipulated by user defined operations declared in the same package as the private type. See Section 8.

With each type definition, a set of values and their denotation is implicitly defined (literals for scalar types, aggregates for composite types), as well as a set of basic operations, some having a special attribute notation that provides a separate name space that is in no conflict with identifiers declared by the user. See Figure 4.2.

```
-- enumeration type declarations:

   type DAY is        ( MON, TUE, WED, THU, FRI, SAT, SUN );
   type PLANET is     ( SUN, MERCURY, VENUS, EARTH, MARS, JUPITER,
                        SATURN, URANUS, NEPTUNE, PLUTO );
   type CHARACTER is ( ..., 'A', 'B', ..., 'Z', '[', '\', ']', ... );

-- implicitly declared literals for values:

    MON   WED   SUN   JUPITER   'A'   '['

-- predefined operators:

    =   /=   <   <=   >   >=

-- attributes:

    DAY'FIRST           -- = MON
    CHARACTER'SUCC('A') -- = 'B'

-- resolution of overloaded literals by context:

    DAY'LAST = SUN              -- SUN of type DAY
    PLANET'PRED(MERCURY) = SUN -- SUN of type PLANET

-- explicit qualification:

    DAY'(SUN)
    CHARACTER'('A')
```

Figure 4.2 *Characteristics of Enumeration Types*

Enumeration literals can be identifiers or characters, thus character types are definable. The type CHARACTER is predefined to denote the ASCII characters. Literals can be overloaded, *i.e.*, the same literal can denote values in different types, with resolution by context. As an example, SUN can denote a DAY or a PLANET (at least from the classical Greek point of view). Different character types are distinguished in the same way.

5. Derived Types

To support the notion of strong typing further, several types can be *derived* from a common parent type. They are distinct types, but each inherits the same characteristics from the parent (see Figure 5.1). Conversion to and from the parent type is allowed but must be explicit. It is then possible to define special operations for the distinct derived types; these operations are not shared by the other types. For the types in Figure 5.1, we might want to define special printing operations for HEAD_LINEs or FOOT_LINEs although general line manipulation is the same. On the other hand, there is no danger of accidentally mixing the various kinds of lines, or to apply the special PRINT_HEADER operation to a TEXT_LINE, since the derived types are distinct.

The notation of derived type declarations can be seen as an abbreviation for an otherwise cumbersome duplication of text (or the instantiation of a common generic package; see Section 9). At the same time it preserves the strict separation between types and therefore aids reliability and maintainability. An analogy can be made to the separation of units in physics, which are disjoint although they have the same mathematical properties. Units can be simulated by derived types in Ada.

6. Static and Dynamic Propeties

In Ada, an important distinction is made between the *static properties* of objects, embodied in the notion of type, and *dynamic properties,* embodied in the notion of *constraint* and *subtype.* The property of an object or value to belong to one and only one of a number of types is a static property; that is, it can always be checked by inspection of the program text only, without knowledge of the input data. See Figure 6.1.

```
   type LINE is array ( 1 .. 128 ) of CHARACTER;

-- derived type declarations:

   type HEAD_LINE is new LINE;
   type TEXT_LINE is new LINE;
   type FOOT_LINE is new LINE;

   HEADER: HEAD_LINE; FOOTER: FOOT_LINE; L: LINE;

-- derived aggregates:

   ( 1 .. 128 => ' ' )
   ( 64 .. 65 => '1', 62 | 67 => '-', others => ' ' )

-- derived operators:

   =   /=   <   <=   >   >=   &

-- derived attributes:

   HEADER'LAST     -- = 128

-- derived operations for indexing, slicing:

   HEADER(64)    HEADER(1..10)

-- resolution of aggregates by context:

   HEADER := ( 64 .. 65 => '1',
               62 | 67 => '-', others => ' ' );
   FOOTER := ( others => ' ' );

-- resolution by explicit qualification:

   FOOT_LINE'('2', others => ' ' )

-- explicit conversion:

   L := LINE(FOOTER); FOOTER := FOOT_LINE(L);
```

Figure 5.1 *Characteristics of Derived Types*

Relative to the set of values of a given type, we can be more specific about the subset of values that an object, for example a variable, may assume during the execution of the program. This is possible in Ada by imposing an additional constraint on each object, for example that its value always lies in a specified range for scalar types. As we shall see, the notion of constraint is generalized to apply to the other classes of types as well. Such a dynamic property can also be given a name in a subtype declaration. The subtypes of a given type may overlap, thus a value of the base type may belong to several subtypes. In Figure 6.2, MON is of subtype WEEK_DAY and SCHOOL_DAY, and 'F' is a LETTER and a HEX.

```
-- constant declarations:

   PROBLEM_DAY: constant DAY := MON;
   OUR_PLANET:  constant PLANET := EARTH;
   MY_INITIAL:  constant CHARACTER := 'B'

-- variable declarations:

   TODAY:      DAY := TUE;
   TOMORROW:   DAY := DAY'SUCC(TODAY);
   NEXT_CHAR:  CHARACTER;

-- correct use:

   NEXT_CHAR := 'A';      -- assignment of value of same type
   PROBLEM_DAY /= SUN     -- comparison of values of same type
   TODAY < TOMORROW       -- application of operation with
                          -- corresponding actual parameter types

-- incorrect use:

   PROBLEM_DAY := TUE;    -- assignment to constant illegal
   NEXT_CHAR := PLUTO;    -- PLUTO is not of type CHARACTER
   TODAY + 2              -- operation "+" is not defined for type DAY
   DAY'LENGTH             -- attribute LENGTH is not defined for
                          -- enumeration type
```

Figure 6.1 *Correct and Incorrect Use of Static Properties*

It is clearly preferable to factorize constraints by introducing a subtype declaration. Instead of declaring many variables that have an explicit range constraint, such as L in Figure 6.2, it is better to abbreviate the corresponding property by declaring the subtype LETTER, and to use the name of the subtype in the respective declarations, such as for L1, L2. Presumably, subtype declarations will appear together at the beginning of a declarative part and will increase readability by introducing mnemonic names for dynamic properties. Factorization also increases maintainability. Only one declaration in the program has to be updated when a property needs change. Structured partitioning of the set of values of a type by subtypes declared relative to other subtypes allows additional checking for consistency. Consider the subtype HEX in Figure 6.2, defined by a further constraint on the subtype LETTER. A change during maintenance to

```
subtype HEX is LETTER range '0' .. 'F' ;
```

by someone who erroneously assumed HEX to stand for hexadecimal digits rather than letters, is reported as erroneous since the character '0' is not a LETTER.

```
-- explicit range constraints in object declarations:

   L: CHARACTER range 'A' .. 'Z';
   SEMINAR_DAY: DAY range TODAY .. TOMORROW;

-- range constraints in subtype declarations:

   subtype NATURAL    is INTEGER range 0 .. INTEGER'LAST;
   subtype POSITIVE   is INGETER range 1 .. INTEGER'LAST;
   subtype HOT_PLANET is PLANET range SUN .. PLANET'PRED(OUR_PLANET);
   subtype WEEK_DAY   is DAY range MON .. FRI;
   subtype SCHOOL_DAY is DAY range MON .. SAT;
   subtype LETTER     is CHARACTER range 'A' .. 'Z';
   subtype HEX        is LETTER range 'A' .. 'F';

-- implicit range constraints in object declarations:

   HOTTEST_PLANET: constant HOT_PLANET := SUN;
   L1, L2: LETTER;
   H: HEX;

-- correct use:

   L1 := L2;        -- same subtype
   L  := H;         __ range constraint always satisfied

-- potentially incorrect use:

   L  := '[';       -- '[' is not a LETTER; always incorrect
   H  := L;         -- value of L may be out of range
   READ(L);         -- input CHARACTER may not be a LETTER
```

Figure 6.2 *Correct and Incorrect Use of Dynamic Properties*

In general, checking of constraints can only be performed at execution time during the elaboration of declarations, the execution of assignments, and parameter passing. Clever compilers will often anticipate errors by a static analysis and report that the exception CONSTRAINT_ERROR will always be raised (for example, for the assingment of '[' to L in Figure 6.2). A much higher degree of readability is achieved as compared with other high level languages. At the same time, a lot of checking during execution can be avoided by inference on the basis of subtype information. In assignments, a check for the lower or upper bound of the value on the right hand side need not be made, if these bounds are included in the range of the left-hand side. See Figure 6.2. Similarly, if we declare:

```
LINE_POS: INTEGER range 1..128 ;
```

then LINE_POS can always be used as an index for an array of type LINE (see Figures 4.1 and 5.1) without any need for checking. Instead, violation of the constraint is checked upon assingment to LINE_POS when necessary.

The constraint information also can effectively be used by the compiler to increase storage economy. LINE_POS need only occupy 7 bits. Objects of a subtype of a record type that has variants need only the space corresponding to the variant, not the maximum necessary for any variant.

The distinction between types and subtypes, together with the strict rule of disjointness of types (see Section 3), clarifies and generalizes the important idea of the subrange type in Pascal whose semantics was not precisely defined (see [HABE73] [WSH77]).

It is only consequential to refine the idea of constraint further to be able to state properties even more precisely, allowing a formal specification of programs and a proof of correctness w.r.t. the specification. In Anna [KL80b] [KLHO82], an Ada program can be extended by formal comments, so-called annotations. For example, they can express all values of an object as EVEN or PRIME. See Figure 6.3 and Section 10.

```
subtype NATURAL  is INTEGER;
   --| where N: NATURAL  => N >= 0;
subtype POSITIVE is INGETER;
   --| where N: POSITIVE => N >= 1;
subtype EVEN     is INTEGER;
   --| where X: EVEN     => X mod 2 = 0;
subtype PRIME    is INTEGER;
   --| where P: PRIME    =>
           --| not exist N: NATURAL range 2 .. P-1 =>
           --|     P mod N = 0;
```

Figure 6.3 *Subtype Annotations in Anna*

7. Dynamic Type Parameters

So far we have only considered constraints and subtypes for scalar types. For a scalar object, the constraint, if any, is fixed in the object declaration. For a composite object, a constraint is conceptually like a *dynamic type parameter* (a "descriptor") that is carried along with each value during execution (see also Euclid [LHLM77]). A formal subprogram parameter of an array or record type may be unconstrained in its declaration and gets the constraint information from the actual parameter at each call, much like an additional implicit parameter. The constraint of the current value of an object can be inquired; therefore the computation can be made dependent on it.

This solution has not been chosen for scalar types. In general, the constraint of an actual scalar subprogram parameter is of no interest (with the possible exception of its accuracy constraint for which a different solution has been chosen). Anyway, the inefficiency of carrying along descriptive information with each scalar value is unacceptable.

The specific solutions for array, record, and access types are discussed below. The generalization for private types is described in Section 8.

7.1 Array Constraints

An array constraint determines the range of possible index values or, in other words, their lower and upper bounds. Array types can be defined as *unconstrained* or as a priori *constrained.* The array type LINE of Figure 4.1 is constrained (its indices are integers in the range 1 to 128), just as the integer type DAY_NUMBER is constraint a priory to the range 1 to 31. See also Figure 7.1.

Every array object is constrained. For variables or constants of an unconstrained type, a constraint must be given explicitly, or via a subtype, in the object declaration. For a constant it may be deduced from the value given in the declaration. Formal subprogram parameters of an unconstrained array type get their constraint from the actual parameter.

Such a solution is conventional in most high level languages (omission of dynamic arrays, parameters in particular, has been recognized as a mistake in the design of Pascal and has led to an upgrade in the International Standards Organization (ISO) standard). A minor novelty in Ada is the extension of the concept to formal *out* parameters of an unconstrained array type. Although a formal *out* parameter has no initial value, its constraint is nevertheless obtained from the actual parameter and can be used, for example, to determine the size of the required final value during its computation in the procedure. This facility is used effectively in the input output package for text files in Ada, where the procedure GET has an out parameter whose size determines the number of characters read. See Figure 7.1.

```
-- "a priori" constrained array type declarations:

   type LINE            is array ( INTEGER range 1 .. 128 ) of CHARACTER;
   type DAYS_PER_MONTH is array ( MONTH_NAME ) of DAY_NUMBER;

-- unconstrained array type declarations:

   type STRING is array ( POSITIVE range <> ) of CHARACTER;
   type MATRIX is array ( INTEGER range <>,
                          INTEGER range <> ) of real;

-- subtype declarations:

   subtype CARD_IMAGE      is STRING ( 1 .. 80 );
   subtype TEXT_IMAGE      is STRING ( 1 .. 72 );
   subtype NUMBER_IMAGE    is STRING ( 73 .. 80 );

   subtype GRID            is MATRIX ( -MAX..MAX, -MAX..MAX );
   subtype FOUR_BY_EIGHT is MATRIX ( 1..4, 1..8 );

-- object declarations:

   NORMAL_DAYS_PER_MONTH: constant DAYS_PER_MONTH
      := ( FEB => 28, APR | JUN | SEP | NOV => 30, others => 31 );
   NAME:   STRING ( 1..20 );     -- explicitly constrained
   SCREEN: GRID;                 -- implicitly constrained via subtype
   QUESTION: constant STRING := "Who likes to count characters?";
                           -- constrained by value to STRING ( 1..30 )

-- subprogram declarations:

   function "&" ( X,Y: STRING ) return STRING;
   procedure GET ( ITEM: out STRING );
   function "+" ( X,Y: MATRIX ) return MATRIX;

-- body with attributes referring to constraints of actual
-- parameters:

   function "&" ( X,Y: STRING ) return STRING is
      R: STRING ( 1..X'LENGTH + Y'LENGTH );
   begin
      R ( 1 .. X'LENGTH ) := X;
      R ( X'LENGTH + 1 .. R'LAST ) := Y;
      return R;
   end "&";
```

Figure 7.1 *Array Constraints*

7.2 Record Constraints

A record constraint restricts values to one subset chosen from a number of disjoint subsets. It consists of one or more discriminants. Their notation ("formal" discriminants in the record type declaration, actual discriminant values supplied in the constraint) emphasizes their nature as type parameters. Record types that have discriminants are analogous to unconstrained array types, record subtypes that have discriminant constraints are analogous to constrained array subtypes. As we see in Figure 7.2, "parameters" can be carried over from record objects to "dynamic" array component objects (but not vice-versa).

The component array VAL of SQUARE_MATRIX is partially constrained to have 1 as lower bounds, and is constrained to be square; that is, the upper bounds are the same in both dimensions. Disjoint union is possible via record types that have variants, one for each value of a discriminant. See PERSON in Figure 7.2.

There is one distinction in the kind of parameterization that is possible for array and record types. Record objects can be declared without a constraint, provided that the corresponding formal discriminants have default values, as in PERSON. Thus, P can assume arbitrary PERSONs as values. Note that assignment of a value of a distinct variant is safe, since a total value must always be assigned, the discriminants cannot be changed individually. Therefore, illegal access to a component in the wrong variant (or to a component whose value becomes undefined because of a change of variants as in Pascal) can always be checked and raises the exception CONSTRAINT_ERROR.

7.3 Access Constraints

Composite objects designated by access values must always be constrained upon allocation. Access objects can be unconstrained. For example IDENTIFIER in Figure 7.3 can designate an arbitrary allocated STRING; the constraint of the designated object can be different for distinct access values. However, an access object may also be constrained, such as CARD-PTR in Figure 7.3, and is then restricted to designate objects with this constraint only. The formulation of such indirect constraints is a marked increase in reliability; consider for example the discrimination into HUSBAND and WIFE rather than just SPOUSE.

```
   type GENDER is ( FEMALE, MALE );

   subtype INDEX is 0 .. MAX;    -- MAX is implementation defined

-- record type declarations with discriminants:

   type SQUARE_MATRIX ( LENGTH: NATURAL ) is
     record
       VAL: MATRIX ( 1..LENGTH, 1..LENGTH );
     end record;

   type TEXT ( MAXIMUM_LENGTH: INDEX ) is
     record
       POS:    INDEX := 0;
       VALUE: STRING( 1..MAXIMUM_LENGTH );
     end record;

-- record type with variant part; discriminant with default value:

   type PERSON ( SEX: GENDER := MALE ) is
     record
       BIRTH_DATE: DATE;
       case SEX is
         when FEMALE => CHILD_BIRTHS: NATURAL;
         when MALE => BEARDED: BOOLEAN;
       end case;
     end record;

-- subtype declarations:

   subtype TEN_BY_TEN is SQUARE_MATRIX(10);
   subtype NAME_SPACE is TEXT(30);
   subtype MAN   is PERSON(MALE);
   subtype WOMAN is PERSON(FEMALE);

-- object declarations:

   PLAY_BOARD: SQUARE_MATRIX(8);     -- explicitly constrained
   TEXT_BUFFER: TEXT(256);           -- explicitly constrained
   LESLIE: WOMAN := ( FEMALE, (1981,MARCH,13), 0 );
                                     -- implicitly constrained
   P: PERSON;                        -- unconstrained; initially MALE

-- safe change of variant:

   P := LESLIE;      -- discriminant can only be changed by total
                     -- assignment

-- safe component selection:

   P.SEX             -- always has a value; initially MALE
   P.BEARDED         -- raises CONSTRAINT_ERROR if P.SEX /= MALE
```

Figure 7.2   Record Constraints

```
-- access types referring to object types with constraints:

   type STRING_PTR is access STRING;

   type NEXT_OF_KIN ( SEX: GENDER );    -- incomplete type
                                        -- declaration, see below
   type RELATIVE is access NEXT_OF_KIN;
   type NEXT_OF_KIN ( SEX: GENDER ) is -- completion of recursive
                                        -- type declaration
     record
       NAME: STRING_PTR;
       MOTHER: RELATIVE(FEMALE);
       YOUNGER_SIBLING, OLDEST_CHILD: RELATIVE;
       case SEX is
         when FEMALE => HUSBAND: RELATIVE(MALE);
         when MALE =>   WIFE:    RELATIVE(FEMALE);
       end case;
     end record;

-- unconstrained object declarations:

   IDENTIFIER: STRING_PTR;
   NEW_BORN: RELATIVE;

-- constrained object declarations;

   CARD_PTR: STRING_PTR(1..80);
   LADY_LOVELACE: RELATIVE(FEMALE) := new NEXT_OF_KIN
      ( FEMALE, new STRING("ADA AUGUSTA"), LADY_BYRON,
        null, null, LORD_LOVELACE );
```

Figure 7.3 *Access Constraints*

8. Type Encapsulation

The notation of *type encapsulation,* based originally on the class concept of Simula 67 [DMN68], has widely stimulated research in the programming language area in the last decade. A type is defined jointly with the basic operations manipulating its values in an isolated piece of program text. This leads to a separation of concerns between user and implementor of a type who communicate via a common interface. Most importantly, the implementation of a type and the associated operations can be changed without affecting the user, as long as the interface is left untouched. Since the implementation is abstracted away from, encapsulated types are often called "abstract data types";

indeed, their properties can be formally specified in the interface before use or implementation have been defined. See Section 10.

In Ada, a *package* is used to encapsulate one or more types with associated operations and constants. The *visible part* contains the users interface (*i.e.*, all information about subprograms, their parameters, results, *etc.*, that is necessary to use the type and must therefore be visible). Details about the implementation are hidden, primarily in the *package body*, a separate piece of program text that can be separately compiled and may even be supplied in a later stage of top-down development. See Figure 8.1.

```
package RATIONAL_NUMBERS is    -- cf. [IWKL82], 9.6

  type RATIONAL is
    record
      NUMERATOR   : INTEGER;
      DENOMINATOR : POSITIVE;
    end record;

  function EQUAL(X,Y : RATIONAL) return BOOLEAN;

  function "/"  (X,Y : INTEGER)  return RATIONAL;
    -- to construct a rational number

  function "+"  (X,Y : RATIONAL) return RATIONAL;
  function "-"  (X,Y : RATIONAL) return RATIONAL;
  function "*"  (X,Y : RATIONAL) return RATIONAL;
  function "/"  (X,Y : RATIONAL) return RATIONAL;
end;

package body RATIONAL_NUMBERS is separate;
     -- separately compiled, not shown here
```

Figure 8.1 Encapsulation of Type and Associated Operations in a Package

In most cases it is desirable to hide the implementation not only of the operations but of the type as well. The type then is said to be *private*. Its complete declaration is given in the *private part* that acts as a compiler interface and is not accessible by the user.

This way, user defined types can be defined as if they were built into the language. Consider Figure 8.2. Since "*" is overloaded to denote multiplication of rational numbers as well as of rationals by integers, rational expressions can be written with the same notation as integer expressions, the constructor for *a* over *b* being *a/b*. The implementation is hidden. It can be changed to an implementation with arbitrary precision (for example using prime factorization), without affecting the visible part, and therefore the user. In contrast, the implementation of RATIONAL is exposed in Figure 8.1, and individual components of a

```
package RATIONAL_NUMBERS is

  type RATIONAL is private;
  function "/" ( NUMERATOR, DENOMINATOR: INTEGER ) return RATIONAL;
  function EQUAL ( X,Y: RATIONAL ) return BOOLEAN;
  function "+" ( X,Y: RATIONAL ) return RATIONAL;
  function "-" ( X,Y: RATIONAL ) return RATIONAL;
  function "*" ( X,Y: RATIONAL ) return RATIONAL;
  function "/" ( X,Y: RATIONAL ) return RATIONAL;

  function "*" ( R: RATIONAL; N: INTEGER ) return RATIONAL;
  function "*" ( N: INTEGER;  R: RATIONAL ) return RATIONAL;
  function "/" ( R: RATIONAL; N: INTEGER ) return RATIONAL;
private
  type RATIONAL is
    record
      N: INTEGER;
      D: POSITIVE;
    end record;
end RATIONAL_NUMBERS;

package body RATIONAL_NUMBERS is

  function "/" ( NUMERATOR, DENOMINATOR: INTEGER ) return RATIONAL is
  begin
    if     DENOMINATOR > 0 then
         return ( NUMERATOR, DENOMINATOR );
    elsif DENOMINATOR < 0 then
         return ( - NUMERATOR, - DENOMINATOR );
    else
         raise NUMERIC_ERROR;
    end if;
  end "/";

  function REDUCE ( R: RATIONAL ) return RATIONAL is
    G: POSITIVE := GCD(ABS(R.N),R.D);
  begin
    return ( R.N/G, R.D/G );
  end REDUCE;

  function EQUAL ( X,Y: RATIONAL ) return BOOLEAN is
  begin
    return REDUCE(X) = REDUCE(Y);
  end EQUAL;

-- and so on for the other operations

end RATIONAL_NUMBERS;
```

Figure 8.2 A Package with a Private Type

rational number can be changed. This is clearly undesirable, if not dangerous.

The equality operation is a special case. "=" cannot be overloaded in Ada; it has been provided by the function EQUAL. The user of the package RATIONAL_NUMBERS must be cautious and must use EQUAL, not "=", the identity on the implementation. This danger can be avoided by declaring RATIONAL as *limited private;* then equality and assignment are not available. Assignment can be provided via a procedure.

9. Static Type Parameters

We have seen in Section 7 how types can be parameterized by discrete values denoting bounds for arrays or discriminants for records. The notion of dynamic parameterization by discriminants carries over to private types. In other words, a type parameter can be made visible while the implementation is hidden. Compare the definition of a package for handling variable length strings with implementation defined maximum length as in [IKWL80] [IKWL82], and stacks of arbitrary size as in Figure 9.1.

One can go an important step further in Ada; types can be parameterized by other types and associated operations by means of a *generic package.* Figure 9.1 shows a generic package for stacks that have some conventional stack operations. ITEM, the type of components, is a generic parameter.

A generic package can be instantiated, as many times as necessary, to a (concrete) package by generic instantiation. A *generic instantiation* can always be performed at compile-time; it is a *static parameterization* since all relevant information is available in the program text and does not depend on execution data. Figure 9.1 shows a combination: the type STACK is statically parameterized by an arbitrary type (*e.g.,* RATIONAL), and a constraint defining the size (*e.g.,* N) can thereafter be given for declarations of stack objects to provide dynamic parameters (as discussed in Section 7.2).

Generic units allow the formulation of (packages of) operations over arbitrary types, provided that the necessary operations on these types are supplied as additional generic parameters. Figure 9.2 shows an iteration over a discrete domain whose elements are enumerated from FIRST to LAST by a successor operation SUCC.

```
-- declaration of a generic package:

   generic
     type ITEM is private;
   package STACK_OF is
     type STACK (SIZE: POSITIVE) is limited private;
     function PUSH (S: STACK; E: ITEM) return STACK;
     function POP  (S: STACK) return STACK;
     function TOP  (S: STACK) return ITEM;
     OVERFLOW, UNDERFLOW: exception;
   private
     -- the private part is implementation dependent;
     -- a particular implementation of STACK is given here
     type TABLE is array (POSITIVE range <>) of ITEM;
     type STACK (SIZE: POSITIVE) is
       record
         SPACE: TABLE(1..SIZE);
         INDEX: NATURAL := 0;
       end record;
  end STACK_OF;

-- generic instantiation ("static parameterization"):

   package STACK_RATIONAL is new STACK_OF(RATIONAL); use STACK_RATIC

-- declaration of a STACK object ("dynamic parameterization"):

   S: STACK(N);    -- N can be a variable
```

Figure 9.1 *Declaration and Instantiation of a Generic Package*

In an instantiation for a discrete type such as (a subtype of) an integer type, the actual parameters for FIRST, LAST, and SUCC can be omitted using the defaults indicated by the attributes on the actual domain type. In the instantiation for the type RELATIVE (see also Figure 7.3), explicit actual parameters yield the desired effect.

It is expected that the powerful generic facility in Ada will lead to a new style of programming, with an additional degree of *generic abstraction.* As for functional/procedural abstraction in subprograms, or data abstraction in packages, there is a separation of concerns between generic declaration, generic body (providing a generalized implementation correct with respect to the formal generic parameters) and generic instantiation in the user's program (correct with respect to the actual generic parameters and their association to the formal ones).

```
-- generic declaration:

   generic
     type DOMAIN is private;
     FIRST: DOMAIN := DOMAIN'FIRST;
     LAST:  DOMAIN := DOMAIN'LAST;
     with function SUCC ( X: DOMAIN ) return DOMAIN is DOMAIN'SUCC;
     with procedure ACTION ( X: DOMAIN );
   procedure FOR_ALL_DO;

-- body

   procedure FOR_ALL_DO is
     δ: DOMAIN := FIRST;
   begin
     while δ /= LAST loop
       ACTION(δ);
     end loop;
     ACTION(LAST);
   end FOR_ALL_DO;

-- instantiation with omission of default parameters:

   subtype RANGE_1_100 is INTEGER range 1 .. 100;
   procedure PRINT_SQUARE ( N: RANGE_1_100 ) is
   begin
     PUT(N*N);
   end PRINT_SQUARE;

   procedure PRINT_SQUARES_1_100 is
     new FOR_ALL_DO ( RANGE_1_100, ACTION => PRINT_SQUARE );
       -- defaults: RANGE_1_100'FIRST, RANGE_1_100'LAST,
       -- RANGE_1_100'SUCC

-- instantiation with explicit parameters:

   function NEXT_REMOVED ( R: RELATIVE ) return RELATIVE is
   begin
     if R = null then
       return null;
     elsif R.YOUNGER_SIBLING /= null then
       return R.YOUNGER_SIBLING;
     else
       return NEXT_REMOVED(R.MOTHER);
     end if;
   end NEXT_REMOVED;

   function NEXT ( R: RELATIVE ) return RELATIVE is
   begin
     if R.OLDEST_CHILD /= null then
       return R.OLDEST_CHILD;
     else
       return NEXT_REMOVED(R);
     end if;
   end NEXT;
```

Figure 9.2 *A Generic Procedure with Default Parameters*

```
procedure PRINT_COUPLE ( R: RELATIVE ) is
begin
  PUT(R.NAME);
  case R.SEX is
    when FEMALE => if R.HUSBAND /= null then
                      PUT("Wife of"); PUT(R.HUSBAND);
                   end if;
    when MALE =>   if R.WIFE /= null then
                      PUT("Husband of"); PUT(R.WIFE);
                   end if;
  end case;
end PRINT_COUPLE;

procedure PRINT_ALL_IN_THE_FAMILY is
  new FOR_ALL_DO ( RELATIVE, GRAND_GRAND_MA, null, NEXT,
                   PRINT_COUPLE ) ;
```

Figure 9.2 *A Generic Procedure with Default Parameters (Con't)*

10. Abstract Types in Anna

It was never a design goal for Ada to be able to formally specify or verify programs or to support formal program development, as for example for CIP-L [BBDG81a] [BBDG81b]. Extensions to Ada have been designed for this purpose in Anna, a language for ANNotating Ada programs (see [KL80b] [KLHO82]). These extensions appear as comments in Ada, but have a well defined syntax and semantics in Anna. Formal comments may be *virtual Ada text,* starting with --:, or *annotations,* starting with --|. For example, in Figure 10.1 the function LENGTH is introduced in virtual Ada text only for the purpose of using it in annotations.

The axioms complement the package specification in Ada to form a complete and unambiguous interface, the definition of an abstract data type in the algebraic sense. The subprogram annotations on PUSH, POP, and TOP define constraints on their domains. The functions, and the axioms, are only defined if the constraints are satisfied on the actual parameters, otherwise the annotations and the Ada program are inconsistent. Alternatively, it could have been specified that corresponding exceptions OVERFLOW, UNDERFLOW are raised. See Figure 9.1.

Concepts in Anna are adapted to and defined in terms of concepts of Ada. Many annotations are, for example, a generalization of the constraint concept in Ada. See Section 6 and Figures 6.2 and 6.3. The concepts of Anna are not restricted to the applicative language level of Ada. Constraints are mapped into assertions as statement annotations.

The theory of abstract data type specification essentially carries over to the procedural level in the form of axioms on package states. See Figure 10.2.

```
generic
  type ITEM is private;
package STACK_OF is
  type STACK (SIZE: POSITIVE) is limited private;
--: function LENGTH (S: STACK) return NATURAL;
    function PUSH (S: STACK; E: ITEM) return STACK;
    --| LENGTH(S) < S.SIZE;
    function POP  (S: STACK) return STACK;
    --| LENGTH(S) > 0;
    function TOP  (S: STACK) return ITEM;
    --| LENGTH(S) > 0;
--| axiom for all S: STACK; X: ITEM =>
--|       POP(PUSH(S,X)) = S,
--|       TOP(PUSH(S,X)) = X,
--|       LENGTH(STACK'INITIAL) = 0,
--|       LENGTH(PUSH(S,X)) = LENGTH(S) + 1;
end STACK_OF;
```

Figure 10.1 Algebraic Specification of an Ada Package in Anna

```
generic
  type ITEM is private;
  SIZE: POSITIVE;
package STACK_OF is
--: function LENGTH return NATURAL;
    function PUSH (E: in ITEM) return STACK;
    --| LENGTH < SIZE;
    function POP return STACK;
    --| LENGTH > 0;
    function TOP (E: out ITEM);
    --| LENGTH > 0;
--| axiom for all S: STACK'TYPE; X: ITEM =>
--|       S[PUSH(X);POP] = S,
--|       S[PUSH(X)].TOP'OUT(Y) = X,
--|       STACK'INITIAL.LENGTH = 0,
--|       S[PUSH(X)].LENGTH = S.LENGTH + 1;
end STACK_OF;
```

Figure 10.2 Specification of a Package in Anna Using Package States

The state S of the package state type STACK'TYPE, modified by the execution of the operation PUSH(X), then POP, is equivalent to the original state S. Thus, Anna is also suitable for specifying an object oriented programming approach in Ada.

11. Conclusion

Ada provides a framework to *represent* conceptual models of data in a form that is suitable for *efficient* execution of algorithms on these data using currently available machinery. Complemented by Anna, its conceptual expressibility is quite rich. Compare, for example, the chapter by Borgida, Mylopoulos, and Wong. Specialization of a class by introducing additional attributes for subclasses is represented in Ada by a record (or private) type with discriminants and one variant for each subclass (*i.e.,* subtype). Transactions can be similarly specialized by distinguishing the appropriate cases. Initial, final, and invariant conditions are represented directly by corresponding annotations in Anna and can be mapped into corresponding assertions in Ada. In general, it seems that methodologies of conceptual design can be transformed into program development methodologies in Ada and Anna in a fairly straightforward way.

12. References

[BBDG81a] [BBDG81b] [DMN68] [DoD79] [HABE73] [IKWL79] [IBHK79] [IKWL80] [IKWL82] [JW74] [KL80b] [KLHO82] [LHLM77] [WMPK75] [WSH77]

Discussion

Since types have played a key role in the design of Ada, the discussion concentrated on the strong and weak points of Ada's type concept.

Self-Describing Data

Problems like self-describing input data were of particular interest from the point of view of database and artificial intelligence. It seems that in Ada this kind of input requires a type that is more general than anything on the disk (for example, a "super variant" record type covering all the alternatives).

This solution, however, is not sufficient to write an interpreter for the Ada language in Ada. There is no way to write something like "eval" which takes an arbitrary Ada expression and returns a value. The problem is that one cannot anticipate the type of the result returned by "eval." In Ada, for example, there is nothing similar to CLU's type "any."

Mary Shaw: "I don't like that example. The problem it addresses is not so much the type structure of Ada but the fact that the basic semantic execution structure of the language is not an obvious data type in Ada. There is nothing like s-expressions."

Carl Hewitt: "I don't agree. The problem is the return value and it's a type issue. There is no problem with the input, it's the output that causes the problem. You have to give it a—disjoint!—type."

Stephen Zilles: "If you try to solve the problem by a variant record you have to update the variant with every type you add to the program. There is no way of writing "eval" once and using it with any other program. My opinion is that they wanted to be efficient and do everything at compile time. That's why they have wired things down and are no longer adaptive for I/O, or "eval," or database access, or more abstract modelling: anyplace where you want adaptive behaviour."

In defense of Ada's strong typing one should say that it fails only in strange cases. In 99% of regular use it does improve program reliability, maintainability, and readability.

Defaults

Another feature that is interesting from the point of view of AI and programming language is the way Ada deals with defaults. Unlike CLU and ALPHARD, one can specify default parameters and discriminants in a rather general way. In this respect Ada seems to be under the influence of the AI approach to defaults.

Formal Specifications

The Ironman requirements definition specifically precludes any formal specification as part of the Ada design activity. As a consequence, a function "specification" cannot be more than function name and types of parameters and result. ALPHARD, for example, did much more in this respect. That is where the ANNA activity fits in. ANNA is a language that is used for writing annotations to Ada programs that can be analyzed and verified.

Stephen Zilles: "I am curious about Ada as a conceptual modelling language!" (laughter!!)

Mary Shaw: "I think Ada was not intended for the problem domain of conceptual modelling; it is a programming language for 'here and now,' providing concepts that are well understood."

Stephen Zilles: "But it was proposed as a design language."

Rebuttal by Bernd Krieg-Brueckner: "Ada was never explicitly designed for "conceptual modelling" in the abstract sense, that is, for a high level design in a formal way. The intent to use Ada as a program design language (by at least one major manufacturer) must be understood pragmatically: compilers do not yet exist, and the use of Ada as a program design language that permits hand-translation to another language does not imply a firm commitment.

Ada, plus facilities for formal specification as embodied in ANNA, is a more complete basis for the representation of conceptual modelling decisions. Abstract data types can be specified formally, and interactions between data objects can be expressed in the form of (invariant) constraints. It remains to be seen how various conceptual modelling methodologies will be Adapted by or translated into Ada."

15
Data Selection, Sharing, and Access Control In a Relational Scenario

Manuel Mall and Joachim W. Schmidt
Universitaet Hamburg
Manuel Reimer
ETH Zurich

ABSTRACT *Fully fledged database systems have operational characteristics not commonly provided by programming language systems. Examples of this would be access and integrity control, failure recovery, data sharing, and concurrency management.*

This chapter discusses the way in which programming language constructs (such as data structures and their selection mechanisms, scope rules, procedures, modules, and variable import and passing mechanisms) can be utilized to support the above operational characteristics in the context of an integrated database programming environment.

1. Introduction

Integration of database models and programming languages is an area of research and development that has gained increasing interest during the last few years. One of the major reasons is that database (*i.e.*, data type) design and transaction (*i.e.*, program) development are two closely interrelated activities (see for example the chapters by Borgida *et al.*, Brodie and Ridjanovic, and King and McLeod). The relational approach to databases and PASCAL-like programming languages, both known for their well designed data structuring capabilities, have been proven to be a framework particularly suited to that integration effort.

This work was supported in part by the Deutsche Forschungsgemeinschaft (DFG), under grant Nr. Schm 450/2-1, Bonn, Federal Republic of Germany.

Early database programming languages concentrated on the integration at the algorithmic level (*i.e.*, they constructed an interface between the data model's algorithmic facilities for data definition and manipulation and the programming language's data structures and operators). This facilitated one homogeneous set of language constructs for data definition and operation.

However, database systems, in particular those based on the relational model, also contribute to the solution of nonalgorithmic (*i.e.*, operational) issues of data processing. Examples of these issues are access and integrity control, failure recovery, data sharing, and concurrency management.

This chapter discusses the way modern programming language concepts, such as data structures and their selection mechanisms, scope rules, procedures, modules, and variable import and passing mechanisms (*e.g.*, see the chapter by Shaw), can be utilized to support the above operational characteristics of database systems.

In Section 2, a short introduction to the relational approach presents relations as typed variables. Section 3 develops a selection mechanism by which parts of relation variables can be denoted. Sections 4 and 5 introduce and refine various mechanisms used to control access to relational variables. Some of the basic issues raised when relation variables are shared are discussed in Section 6. Those addressed are integrity control, error recovery, and concurrency management.

2. Relations as Typed Variables

It is now generally accepted that relations can be introduced as typed and named objects that can be imported into the scope of a database-processing environment [SCHM77] [CODD82] [BS82b]. The type determines a relation's time-invariant properties, such as its structure, additional value-dependent constraints, and a set of operations applicable to relations.

This section gives a short introduction to relation types and variables, and it closely follows the PASCAL/R approach [SM80].

2.1 Structural Aspects

Relations, according to Codd [CODD70], can be perceived as sets of record-structured elements. The record component types are restricted because they are not allowed to be of unbound cardinality, like file or relation.

Example 2.1 defines a relation, *schedule,* that associates identifying information about the lecturer, course, and room, and determines the time at which the lecture is scheduled.

```
var schedule: relation of
                record
                   enr : 1..99;
                   cnr : 1..99;
                  time : record
                            day  : (monday,...,friday);
                            hour : 0810..1820
                            end;
                  room : packed array [1..7] of char
                end;
```

Example 2.1 *Relation Declaration*

2.2 Integrity Constraints

The set property already guarantees that no two elements of a relation have the same value in all their components. A generalization of that condition leads to a class of integrity constraints that enforces the uniqueness of distinguished key components of relation elements.

Example 2.2 constrains the previously defined relation, *schedule,* by imposing the constraint that no two lectures can be scheduled at the same time in the same room. The keylist, *<time, room>*, determines that the following constraint in the class of key predicates has to be maintained:

```
all s1, s2 in schedule
((<s1.time, s1.room> = <s2.time, s2.room>) -> (s1 = s2))

var schedule: relation <time, room> of
                record
                   enr : 1..99;
                   cnr : 1..99;
                  time : record
                            day  : (monday,...,friday);
                            hour : 0810..1820
                            end;
                  room : packed array [1...7] of char
                end;
```

Example 2.2 *Relation Declaration with Key Constraint*

2.3 Operations on Relations

Two classes of operations are defined for relations: operations for the evaluation and operations for the alteration of relations.

Relations are evaluated through Boolean and relational expressions. PASCAL/R follows the relational calculus approach and provides existential and universal quantifiers. As a consequence, Boolean expressions of the power of first-order predicate calculus can be defined, and relational expressions can be formed in order to select relation elements fulfilling some first-order selection predicate. If types are compatible, records and elements selected from different relations can be converted into one relation (value).

The basic operation for relation alteration is the assignment (:=). Statements that insert (:+), delete (:-), and update (:&) elements in a left-hand-side relation variable based on a right-hand-side relation expression are equivalent to assignment statements that have extended right-hand-side relation expressions. For details of the syntax and semantics of PASCAL/R see [SM80] [LS80].

Example 2.3 sketches a PASCAL/R program that schedules a new lecture, provided the integrity constraints on the existence of the lecturer, course, and availability of lecturer and room are fulfilled.

3. Selection Mechanisms for Relations

Structured variables need not always be accessed in their entirety. Data structures, therefore, like arrays and records, provide denotations that designate selected parts of entire variables.

In this section, the notion of so-called selected (relation) variables introduced in [SM80] is extended to provide general access to selected parts of relations.

3.1 Relation Elements

The key constraint defined with relation types guarantees that in every relation variable there are no two elements that have the same key field values. Thus, every relation element can be denoted by the relation name, *rel,* followed by a selector that provides a list of key field values, *xk1, . . . , xkn.*

Hence, the lecture scheduled for Friday, 6 to 8 p.m., in the auditorium maximum is denoted by *schedule[<friday, 1820>, 'audimax'].*

```
      { declaration of university database }

type
   statustype = (student, technician, assistant, professor);
   nametype   = packed array [1..10] of char;
   titletype  = packed array [1..40] of char;
   roomtype   = packed array [1..7 ] of char;
   hourtype   = 0810..1820;
   yeartype   = 1900..1999;
   daytype    = (monday,tuesday,wednesday,thursday,friday);
   leveltype  = (freshman,sophomore,junior,senior);
   enumbertype= 1..99;
   cnumbertype= 1..99;
   timetype   = record
                   day  : daytype;
                   hour : hourtype
                end;

   erectype   = record
                   enr    : enumbertype;
                   name   : nametype;
                   status : statustype
                end;
   ereltype   = relation <enr> of erectype;

   prectype   = record
                   enr   : enumbertype;
                   year  : yeartype;
                   title : titletype
                end;
   preltype   = relation <enr,title> of prectype;

   crectype   = record
                   cnr   : cnumbertype;
                   level : leveltype;
                   title : titletype
                end;
   creltype   = relation <cnr> of crectype;

   srectype   = record
                   enr  : enumbertype;
                   cnr  : cnumbertype;
                  time : timetype;
                  room : roomtype
                end;
   sreltype   = relation <time,room> of srectype;

var university : database
                   employees : ereltype;
                   papers    : preltype;
                   courses   : creltype;
                   schedule  : sreltype
                end;

      { end of declaration of university databases }
```

Example 2.3 Declaration of and Operations on a Relational Database

```
var newlecture : srectype;
begin
  with university do ...
     newlecture := <...>;

     begin schedulelecture
       with newlecture do
         if not some e in employees ((e.enr = enr) and
                      (e.status in [assistant,professor])) then
           WriteLn ('unknown lecturer')
         else if not some c in courses (c.cnr = cnr) then
           WriteLn ('unknown course')
         else if some s in schedule
                      (<s.time,s.room> = <time,room>) then
           WriteLn ('room occupied')
         else if some s in schedule
                      (<s.time,s.enr> = <time,enr>) then
           WriteLn ('lecturer busy')
         else schedule :+ [newlecture]
     end schedulelecture;
     ...
end;
```

Example 2.3 Declaration of and Operations on a Relational Database (Cont'd)

The notion of selected variables supports a perception of relations close to that of arrays. The major difference lies in the fact that the value of a selected variable may be 'void,' indicating that there is no relation element having the key field values provided by the selector. The test to determine whether a selected variable is void consists of a comparison with the empty record constructor (*i.e., rel [<key value list>]* = <>). In fact, relations are often sparse (*i.e.*, most of their elements are void). For example, take the relation *papers,* declared by Example 2.3, which can hold an element for every combination of employee number (1..99) and title (40 character string). However, only a very small fraction of the up to ca.10 to the power of 75 elements will ever exist.

Further differences between relations and arrays become apparent when the operations on selected variables are discussed. The differences originate in the fact that selection of relations is content-oriented whereas indexing of arrays is address-based.

3.2 Generalized Selectors

The indexing mechanism of arrays actually provides more than one selector because an index value list may be truncated, thus denoting a subarray instead of an array element. Accordingly, a selector having a truncated key value list denotes a subrelation that has values in the element components that correspond to the leading components of the relation's key definition. For example, *schedule[<friday, 1820>]* denotes the lectures scheduled for Friday, 6 to 8 p.m., using a selector that provides only the first key component, *time*. A selected part of a relation variable will be called a selection of that relation.

Using the current notation, only a restricted class of selections can be denoted because a selector's key value list has to match the leading part of the relation's key component list. As a consequence, lectures scheduled at a given time can be denoted (*e.g.*, *schedule[<friday, 1820>]*); however, lectures scheduled in a given room (such as *schedule['audimax']*) cannot be denoted.

The notation of a **selector**, therefore, will be generalized to a first-class language construct that allows the definition of a broad class of selections on relation variables.

The definition of a specific selector introduces a selector name, binds the selector to a relation type, and provides a selection predicate. In addition, selectors may be parameterized. Take, for example, the key-oriented standard selector, *schedule[time]*. This selector is equivalent to the one introduced by the following selector definition:

```
selector on (time: timetype) for srel: sreltype;
begin each s in srel: s.time = time end;
```

This selector is applicable to every variable of type *sreltype*, and the two denotations, for example, *schedule[on (<friday, 1820>)]* and *schedule[<friday, 1820>]*, designate the same selection of the schedule relation. Accordingly,

```
selector in (room: roomtype) for srel: sreltype;
begin each s in srel: s.room = room end;
```

can be used to designate, for example, *schedule[in ('audimax')]*.

In its most general form a selector is based on an arbitrary selection predicate, *pred(. . .)*,

```
selector sp(...) for rel: reltype;
begin each r in rel: pred(r,...) end;
```

3.3 Operations on Selected Relations

Selected relations are variables. Consequently, each operation defined on a relation is applicable also to a selected relation.

In an expression, selected relations, *rel[sp(. . .)]*, can be replaced by the equivalent relational expressions, *[each r in rel: pred(r, . . .)]*, without changing the semantics of the expression.

The semantics of an assignment statement that has a selected relation on the left-hand-side requires more detailed discussion. In the simple case of assigning a record to a selected relation element, for example,

```
schedule[<friday,1820>,'audimax'] := newlecture;
```

the following two constraints are expected to hold:

```
1. [each s in schedule(post):
       <s.time,s.room> = <<friday,1820>,'audimax>] =
       [newlecture];

2. [each s in schedule(post):
       not (<s.time,s.room> = <<friday,1820>,'audimax'>)] =
       [each s in schedule(pre):
         not (<s.time,s.room> = <<friday,1820>,'audimax'>)];
```

The suffixes pre and post distinguish the values of the relation, *schedule*, before and after the assignment.

The above constraints are implemented by the subsequent statement which replaces the assignment to a selected relation element by an assignment to an entire relation variable. The assignment statement

```
schedule[<friday,1820>,'audimax'] := newlecture;
```

is equivalent to

```
with newlecture do
if <time,room> = <<friday,1820>,'audimax'>
then schedule := [each s in schedule:
                    not (<s.time,s.room> =
                         <<friday,1820>,'audimax'>),
                   newlecture]
else <exception> ;
```

Raising the exception means that the assignment does not fulfill constraints (1.) and (2.).

A generalized example uses the selector, *on(time)*, introduced above. The assignment statement

```
    schedule[on(<friday,1820>)] := latelectures;
```

reschedules the late Friday lectures. The variable, *latelecture*, is assumed to be of type *sreltype*.

According to the definition of the selector, *on(time)*, the above assignment is equivalent to:

```
if all l in latelectures(l.time = <friday,1820>)
then schedule := [each s in schedule:
                     not (s.time = <friday,1820>),
                   each l in latelectures: true]
else <exception> ;
```

It can be shown [SCHM82] that the above semantics extend to the case of general selectors, *sp(...)*. The statement

```
relk[sp(...)] := rex;
```

with

```
selector sp(...) for rel: relktype;
begin each r in rel: pred(r,...) end;
```

is equivalent to

```
if all x in rex( pred(x,...) )
then relk := rex'
else <p-exception> ;
```

with the relational expression

```
rex' = [each r in relk: not pred(r,...),
        each r in rex: true].
```

When using general selection predicates, however, it is not guaranteed that the modified right-hand-side relational expression, *rex'*, meets the key constraint defined on the left-hand-side relation, *relk*. Hence, the assignment statement

```
relk := rex';
```

may raise another exception.

The homogeneity of our approach is enhanced since key-constrained relations such as *relk* can be introduced by unconstrained (set-like) relations such as *rel*, which are accessed via a selected relation, *rel[sk]*. The selector, *sk*, is defined by:

```
selector sk  for rel: reltype;
begin each r in rel: keytest(r,rel) end;
```

with

```
function keytest(r: rectype;
                 rel: relation of rectype): Boolean;
begin
  keytest := all l in rel(l.key = r.key) -> (l = r)
end;
```

l.key and *r.key* denote the key components of *l* and *r*; in the case of composite keys, *k1,...,ki, l.key* and *r.key* have to be replaced by <*l.k1,...,l.ki*> and <*r.k1,...,r.ki*>.

The general case

```
relk[sp(...)] := rex;
```

is equivalent to

```
rel[sk][sp(...)] := rex;
```

and rewrites to

```
if all x in rex(pred(x,...))
then rel[sk] := rex'
else <p-exception> ;
```

and further

```
if all x in rex(pred(x,...))
then if all x' in rex'(keytest(x',rex'))
     then rel := rex'
     else <k-exception>
else <p-exception> ;
```

The modified relational expression, *rex'*, is given by:

```
[each r in rel: not pred(r,...),
each x in rex: true]
```

The following example assigns new lecturers to the employees relation:

```
employees[with_degree] := newlecturers;
```

using the

```
selector with_degree for erel: ereltype;
begin each e in erel:
      e.status in [assistant,professor] end;
```

The employees relation itself may be represented by:

```
var set_of_erecs: relation of erectype;
```

accessed via the

```
selector with_unique_enr
for eset: relation of erectype;
begin each e in eset: enrtest(e,eset) end;
```

with

```
function enrtest(e: erectype;
                 eset: relation of erectype): Boolean;
begin enrtest :=
      all s in eset((s.enr = e.enr) -> (s = e)) end;
```

The assignment statement

```
employees[with_degree] := newlecturers;
```

may be replaced by

```
set_of_erecs[with_unique_enr][with_degree] := newlecturers;
```

which is equivalent to

```
if all l in newlecturers
          (l.status in [assistant,professor])
then if all e in newemployees(enrtest(e,newemployees))
     then set_of_employees := newemployees
     else <k-exception>
else <p-exception> ;
```

For the purpose of brevity, *newemployees* is used to identify the relational expression

```
[each e in set_of_employees:
   not(e.status in [assistant,professor]),
 each l in newlecturers: true].
```

For the further generalization of selectors, one which also includes a discussion of insert, delete, and update operators on selected variables, see [SCHM82].

4. Access Control Mechanisms

There are basically two classes of mechanisms used to control the use of program objects such as constants, variables, types, and functions.

Since objects can be used only if their names are known, the first class of control mechanisms is given by the scope rules of the language. Scope rules regulate the visibility of names, and thus they determine the group of statements that are able to access a specific object. The second class of control mechanisms associates objects that are defined in different scopes. Associated objects can communicate through specific protocols commonly called parameter passing mechanisms.

In practice, adequate access control to data objects requires a combination of the two basic mechanisms.

4.1 Visibility Control

The sequence of statements in which an identifier is introduced and known with the same meaning is called 'the scope' of an identifier. A very general approach opens scopes in such a way that identifiers introduced in an enclosing scope are also known in the enclosed scopes. In other words, the set of identifiers known in a scope is the union of identifiers declared in that scope and in its enclosing ones.

Example 4.1 makes use of the 'open scope' approach typical of a wide class of programming languages (ALGOL, PL/1, PASCAL).

```
        { declaration of university database }

var
   newlecture : srectype;

begin
  with university do ...
    newlecture := < ... >;

    begin schedulelecture
      with newlecture do
        if not some e in [employees[enr]]
                 (e.status in [assistant,professor]) then
          WriteLn ('unknown lecturer')
        else if courses[cnr] = <> then
          WriteLn ('unknown course')
        else if not (schedule[time,room] = <>) then
          WriteLn ('room occupied')
        else if some s in schedule[time] (s.enr = enr) then
          WriteLn ('lecturer busy')
        else schedule[time,room] := newlecture
    end schedulelecture;
    ...
end;
```

Example 4.1 *Open Scope Approach*

In this approach a procedure can 'view very far,' up to the limit of the encompassing program, and, in addition, it can access all the objects imported by the program. In PASCAL/R, following PASCAL's 'open scope' approach, the entire database can be accessed by any program statement. Consequently, it requires costly program analysis to determine which relations are actually accessed within each scope.

Conversely, the 'closed scope' approach restricts the visibility of an identifier to the scope in which it is declared. Languages following this strict approach often provide, however, specific import and export clauses by which a 'trade of names' across scope boundaries can be explicitly established. Example 4.2 outlines this approach.

```
      { declaration of university database }

var
   newlecture : srectype;

begin
  with university do ...
    newlecture := < ... >;

    begin schedulelecture
      import newlecture;
      with newlecture do
        import employees, courses, schedule;
        { body schedulelecture }
    end schedulelecture;
    ...
end;
```

Example 4.2 *Closed Scope Approach with Import of Variables*

In the above example, only explicitly introduced names are known in a scope, either by declaration or import. Thus, access to named objects can be controlled quite strictly.

4.2 Parameter Passing Mechanisms

Parameter passing mechanisms establish communication between distinct objects declared in different scopes. Programming languages provide a great variety of protocols that regulate which way and at what time communication takes place. For example, take the 'by-reference' mechanism. Communication between a local variable (the formal parameter) and a global variable (the actual parameter) starts at procedure invocation time by initializing the former through the value of the latter. Communication ends after the last statement of the procedure has been executed. Meanwhile, every value alteration of the local variable is forwarded instantaneously to the global variable, and vice versa. The interaction between a procedure and its environment, established through 'by-reference' parameters, is very strong. It is very likely that a procedure that does not terminate correctly leaves its environment in an inconsistent state, and that an environment altered by a third party interferes adversely with the execution of a procedure. Access control via 'by-reference' parameter mechanisms is comparable to that of the 'open scope' approach to visibility control. Hence, the procedure shown in Example 4.3 should produce the same result as the statements of Example 2.3.

```
        { declaration of university database }

begin
  with university do ...

    procedure schedulelecture (employees: ereltype;
                               courses : creltype;
                               schedule : sreltype;
                               newlecture: srectype);
      with newlecture do
      { body schedulelecture }
    end schedulelecture;

    schedulelecture (employees, courses, schedule, < ... >);
    ...
end;
```

Example 4.3 *Closed Scope Approach with Passing of Parameters*

In one respect, however, mechanisms for parameter passing and variable import differ substantially. Parameter mechanisms are able to associate any two formal and actual parameters as long as their types are compatible, thus providing much flexibility in associating data with procedures. Import mechanisms, however, are restricted to the import of distinct variables only.

There are pros and cons for each solution. A procedure that removes, for example, the maximum value from a set of integers should be applicable to any such set, whereas the procedure given in Example 2.3 cancels a lecture and probably makes sense only for the one relation: *schedule.*

4.3 Combination of Mechanisms

When designing a sequence of statements, a programmer often has in mind a specific variable that alone fulfills the condition under which the execution of the statements is correct. This is particularly true regarding procedures designed for variables that have a semantic not completely covered by its type definition. Database applications are examples of this kind. The relation (*e.g.*, *employees*) holds a property not covered by its type since it represents all employees existing in the realm of an application. Other relations of type *ereltype* may not fulfill this condition.

Procedures, however, use data in different ways. There is input data that provides the basis for modifying other data, and control data that adapts a procedure within certain limits. Output data returns the redundant copies required for later processing, and status data reports the success or failure of a procedure execution. These kinds of data may be produced or requested through more than one data object defined in different scopes.

To cope adequately with the needs of nontrivial applications, data objects have to be introduced and controlled by a combination of mechanisms.

Example 4.4 reprograms the previous example using parameters and imported variables.

```
      { declaration of university database }

begin
  with university do ...

    procedure schedulelecture (newlecture: srectype);
      with newlecture do
        import employees, courses, schedule;
        { body schedulelecture }
    end schedulelecture;

    schedulelecture (< ... >);
    ...
end;
```

Example 4.4 *Closed Scope Approach with Import of Variables and Passing of Parameters*

5. Refinement of Access Control

In Section 4 access control mechanisms are discussed under a set of specific assumptions. For example, data objects are introduced into a scope as variables having unrestricted access rights (*i.e.*, with read and write access). Furthermore, it is assumed that only entire variables are imported. Finally, exchange of variables is restricted to scopes in which the importing variable is nested within the exporting one. In this section, these restrictions are released gradually, allowing a finer control of data access.

5.1 Access Rights

Variables are declared with the generic access capabilities of read and write. However, variables imported or locally declared in formal parameter positions need not always be accessed with their full generic capabilities.

```
        { declaration of university database }

begin
  with university do

    procedure schedulelecture (newlecture read: srectype);
      with newlecture do
        import employees read, courses read,
               schedule readwrite;
        { body schedulelecture }
    end schedulelecture;

    schedulelecture (< ... >);
    ...
end;
```

Example 5.1 *Definition of Access Rights*

In Example 5.1 access to variables is restricted to rights explicitly stated in the import clause and parameter declaration. Only one relation, *schedule,* is imported with 'readwrite' capability; the other variables are 'readonly.'

5.2 Access to Selected Variables

Data processed by a certain part of a program are often known to be stored in a certain part of a variable. This is particularly true with variables like relations that are used to hold all data on some application. For reasons similar to those used when partitioning 'lumps of operations' (*e.g.*, programs) into modules, 'lumps of data' (*e.g.*, relations) are partitioned into what was called selections in Section 3.

Example 5.2 rephrases the procedure *schedulelecture*, utilizing the generalized selectors of Subsection 3.2. In addition, it binds new identifiers to imported variables, and thus increases program readability. For example, *parallellectures* identifies the selection of the relation *schedule* that describes lectures parallel in time. Notice that *parallellectures* is imported with 'read' access only while the selected variable *slecture* has 'write' access only.

```
      { declaration of university database }

begin
  with university do ...

    selector with_degree for erel: ereltype;
    begin each e in erel: e.status in [assistant,professor]
    end;

    procedure schedulelecture (newlecture read: srectype);
      with newlecture do
        import lecturer = employees[with_degree][enr] read,
               course   = courses[cnr] read,
               parallellectures = schedule[time] read,
               slecture = schedule[time,room] write;
        if lecturer = <> then
          WriteLn ('unknown lecturer')
        else if course = <> then
          WriteLn ('unknown course')
        else if some l in parallellectures(l.room = room) then
          WriteLn ('room occupied')
        else if some l in paralllectures(l.enr = enr) then
          WriteLn ('lecturer busy')
        else slecture := newlecture
    end schedulelecture;

    schedulelecture (< ... >);
    ...
end;
```

Example 5.2 *Selector Definition and Binding of Variables*

5.3 Modularization of Scopes

In essence, two kinds of relationships between scopes can be established by the export and import of named objects.

The '*1:n — case*' relates a scope, *Si*, hierarchically to *n* scopes, *Si1, . . . ,Sin*. *Si* exports to the *Sij* and the *Sij* imports exclusively from *Si*. This case copes with applications in which one activity, *Ai*, is decomposed into subactivities, *Ai1, . . . ,Ain,* sharing the data provided by *Ai*.

In the '*n:m — case*' scopes can import from and export to more than one scope, and two scopes, *Si* and *Sj*, can become mutually related by exchanging data objects. The '*n:m — case*' includes, of course,

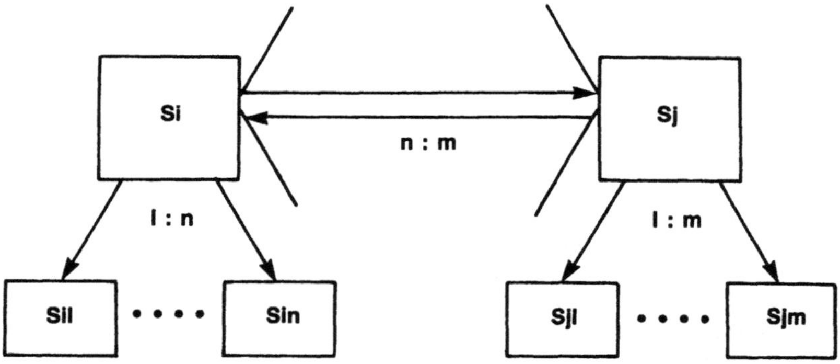

Figure 5.1 *Export/Import Relationships between Scopes*

1:n-relationships; from an access control point of view, however, the two cases should be treated separately.

In Example 5.3 the term **module** is used for scopes that can enter *n:m*-relationships, while procedures are restricted to *1:n*-relationships with modules. The compound activity dealing with lectures in general is concentrated in the one module, *scheduling,* and the two procedures, *schedulelecture* and *cancellecture*, represent specific subactivities within the scheduling activity.

The module, *scheduling,* imports the two relations, *employees* and *courses* 'readonly,' and the relation *schedule* 'readwrite' from the module *universitydatabase.* It exports the two procedures, *schedulelecture* and *cancellecture*, and the relation *schedule* 'readonly' to whatever module is interested in scheduling. Notice that the relation, *schedule,* is on the export and import list of the module, *scheduling.* It is exported 'readonly' under the assumption that any alteration is to be done through the exported procedures. It is imported with the 'readwrite' privilege allowing for the generic altering operations, :=, :+, :-, and :&.

6. Data Sharing

Scopes that import and export variables may become related because they share some of their data objects. Since every one of the related scopes is affected by an incorrect operation on one of the shared objects, data integrity control and failure recovery become increasingly important. These issues are of particular concern when shared data objects are accessed in parallel.

```
module universitydatabase;
  export employees readwrite, courses readwrite,
      schedule readwrite;

      { declaration of university relations }

end module universitydatabase;

module scheduling;
  from universitydatabase
  import employees read, courses read, schedule readwrite;

  export schedulelecture, cancellecture, schedule read;

  selector with_degree for erel: ereltype;
  begin each e in erel: e.status in [assistant,professor]
  end;

  procedure schedulelecture (newlecture read: srectype);
    with newlecture do
      import lecturer = employees[with_degree][enr] read,
             course    = courses[cnr] read,
             parallellectures = schedule[time] read,
             slecture = schedule[time,room] write;
      if lecturer = <> then
        WriteLn ('unknown lecturer')
      else if course = <> then
        WriteLn ('unknown course')
      else if some l in parallellectures (l.room = room) then
        WriteLn ('room occupied')
      else if some l in parallellectures (l.enr = enr) then
        WriteLn ('lecturer busy')
      else slecture := newlecture
    end schedulelecture;

  procedure cancellecture (lecturekey read: skeytype);
    with lecturekey do
      import clecture = schedule[time,room] readwrite;
      if clecture = <> then
        WriteLn ('unknown lecturer')
      else clecture := <>
  end cancellecture;
end module scheduling;

begin
  from scheduling
  import schedulelecture, cancellecture;

  schedulelecture (< ... >);
  ...
  cancellecture (< ... >);
  ...
end;
```

Example 5.3 Modules

6.1 Integrity Control

Integrity constraints on shared data objects can be divided into two broad categories.

The 'global or database constraints' have to be maintained for the lifetime of the database and must be controlled for the majority of importing procedures because any one may violate them. Typical candidates for this category are the constraints enforcing uniqueness of keys within relations and referential integrity across relations.

The 'local or application constraints' are the ones that may vary in time and may be affected only by a few procedures.

Our standard example, *schedulelecture,* shows constraints of both kinds. The existence test for the particular lecturer and course is a constraint of the first kind, while the test for whether lecturers are assistants or professors can be regarded as an application dependent constraint that may well change with time.

It is a common strategy to have the more general database constraints controlled by the exporting scope, and to maintain the application specific constraints within the importing scope.

Example 6.1 reprograms our standard application along these lines.

6.2 Failure Recovery

Application procedures, like *schedulelecture,* are expected to maintain all the application specific constraints. Furthermore, they are assumed to be correct in the sense that their execution produces values representing states of the application system to be described by the database. In other words, an application procedure is expected to be executed on a correct initial state and to produce a correct final state of the database—if it runs to completion. If not (*e.g.*, if an exception is raised due to an incorrect assignment to a selected variable or some other runtime event), the initial state has to be restored.

The term **transaction** is applied to distinguish 'application procedures' from other procedures, such as those used for program modularization in general.

Transactions are the units of database state transition and, consequently, the units of recovery if a transaction fails. Transaction recovery means, in essence, that in case of a failure the variables introduced from outside the transaction have to be set back to their initial values.

The semantics of parameter passing and variable import regarding transactions can be explained best by a 'value-result' mechanism. Local variables are used as shadows [LORI77] initialized by the value of the global variables. The transaction works exclusively on the local shadows, and the final values of the local variables are assigned to their

```
module universitydatabase;
  export employees read,
    consistent_schedule =
      schedule[consistent_with(employees,courses)] readwrite,
        ... ;

       { declaration of university relations }

  selector consistent_with(erel: ereltype; crel: creltype)
    for srel: sreltype;
  begin each s in srel: some e in erel (s.enr = e.enr) and
                        some c in crel (s.cnr = c.cnr)
  end;
end module universitydatabase;

module scheduling;
  from universitydatabase
  import lectures =
    consistent_schedule[related_to(employees[with_degree])]
    readwrite;

  export schedulelecture, cancellecture, lectures read;

  selector with_degree for erel: ereltype;
  begin each e in erel: e.status in [assistant,professor]
  end;

  selector related_to (erel: ereltype) for srel: sreltype;
  begin each s in srel: some e in erel (s.enr = e.enr) end;

  procedure schedulelecture (newlecture read: srectype);
    with newlecture do
      import parallellectures = lectures[time] read;
             slecture  = lectures[time,room] write;
      if some l in parallellectures (l.room = room) then
        WriteLn ('room occupied')
      else if some l in parallellectures (l.enr = enr) then
        WriteLn ('lecturer busy')
      else slecture := newlecture
  end schedulelecture;

  procedure cancellecture (lecturekey read: skeytype);
    with lecturekey do
      import clecture = lectures[time,room] readwrite;
      if clecture = <> then
        WriteLn ('unknown lecture')
      else clecture := <>
  end cancellecture;
end module scheduling;
```

Example 6.1 Modules, Database and Application Constraints

global counterparts, but not before the transaction has run to completion. Thus, a normal execution of a transaction is divided into three phases: initialization, read and compute, commit and return. In case of failure, the transaction is aborted without executing the third phase.

An implementation technique contrary to the one sketched above works directly on the global variables and maintains a protocol of altering operations. The protocol entries are used to undo the result of a failed transaction [GRAY78].

6.3 Concurrency Management

Transactions sharing data objects may be processed in parallel. From a semantic point of view concurrency does not change the picture substantially. Transactions now become units of recovery **and** concurrency, and the access rights to imported and passed data objects are interpreted as 'readsharable' and 'writeexclusive.' Sharable means that an access right for the same data object may be granted to several transactions in parallel. Exclusive means that, for the time an access right is granted to one transaction, access rights granted to other transactions refer to disjoint variables only. Two variables, *Di* and *Dj*, are defined to be disjoint if and only if there is no expression such that its assignment to one of the variables, say, *Di*, changes the value of the other, *Dj*. If variables are not disjoint they are said to overlap.

Variables introduced by separate declarations clearly do not overlap. According to our previous definitions, two variables selected from the same base relation overlap if and only if there is a (nonempty) expression that can be assigned to both variables without raising a selection exception. Hence, the disjointness test for two selected variables is essentially a test of whether two data spaces (*i.e.*, value sets), as defined by the relation's types and restricted by selection predicates, are disjoint. Depending on additional knowledge of transactions and data, these tests can follow different strategies.

6.3.1 Locking: The Pessimistic Approach

Requesting access rights may be a highly competitive process in the sense that nonsharable access to overlapping data is requested in parallel. Hence, in heavily loaded systems the pessimistic assumption has to be made than an access right requested by one transaction may already have been granted to another one. With the pessimistic approach, privileges are claimed and granted prior to accessing a data object for the first time and are held until completion of the final operation on that data object.

A common implementation technique employs locks on data objects to indicate which access rights have been currently granted. A data object need not necessarily be locked for the entire sequence of statements involved in a transaction execution. Narrowing the sequence of statements for which a data object is locked towards the minimal interval (as defined by the actual data access) has, however, its well known trade-offs. The advantage of a possible increase in concurrency is counterbalanced by the possibility of deadlocks due to incremental locking, and by rather complex recovery procedures if locks are released before a transaction terminates. Additional restrictions on locking protocols result from one of the fundamental theorems in transaction scheduling. It states, generally speaking, that concurrent transactions can be scheduled consistently only if the statement intervals for which the various data objects of a transaction are locked have at least one statement in common. In other words, for every execution of a transaction there must be a minimal statement interval during which all the locks requested by the transaction are held simultaneously. The resulting locking protocols are two-phase in the sense that no lock can be set after the first lock has been released [EGL76]. Example 6.2 shows our standard transaction augmented by a locking protocol. Additional details can be found in [RS81].

6.3.2 Optimistic Scheduling

For cases in which competition for exclusive access to overlapping data objects is low, the overhead of maintaining locks may not be justified. Instead, transactions may get permission to read shared objects without any scheduling effort and to assign their results to local shadows as described by the 'value-result' mechanism outlined above. In addition, any read access is recorded by entering the accessed variable into a readset, and any write access is noted by entering the right-hand-side expression into a writeset [KR81].

Before the local results finally are returned to their global counterparts, the transaction runs through a validation phase. This phase tests whether one of the competing transactions has returned a result so that one of the variables read by the transaction has been changed. If so, the transaction does not pass its validation test and is set back. Otherwise the final results are returned and the transaction terminates.

6.3.3 Compile-Time Knowledge on Data and Transactions

The two previously discussed scheduling strategies rely exclusively on runtime information and require costly runtime algorithms to test the disjointness of data objects. The notion of selected variables and the mechanisms for data import allow, on the other hand, a rather fine and sometimes early determination of access rights. For example, it is known at compile-time that the module, *scheduling,* requires read access only to that part of the *employees* relation selected by the selector, *with_degree.* As a consequence, any transaction requiring exclusive access to employees with no degree (*i.e.*, with status different from

```
module scheduling;
  from universitydatabase
  import lectures =
    consistent_schedule[related_to(employees[with_degree])]
    readwrite;

  export schedulelecture, cancellecture, lectures read;

  selector with_degree for erel: ereltype;
  begin each e in erel: e.status in [assistant,professor]
  end;

  selector related_to (erel: ereltype) for srel: sreltype;
  begin each s in srel: some e in erel (s.enr = e.enr) end;

  transaction schedulelecture (newlecture read: srectype);
    with newlecture do
      import parallellectures = lectures[time] read,
             slecture  = lectures[time,room] write;
      if { LOCK parallellectures SHARABLE }
        some l in parallellectures (l.room = room) then
        Message ('room occupied')
      else if some l in parallellectures (l.enr = enr) then
        Message ('lecturer busy')
      else { LOCK slecture EXCLUSIVE } slecture := newlecture
      { COMMIT Messages, slecture, RELEASE ALL LOCKS }
  end schedulelecture;

  transaction cancellecture (lecturekey read: skeytype);
    with lecturekey do
      import clecture = lectures[time,room] readwrite,
      if { LOCK clecture SHARABLE } clecture = <> then
        Message ('unknown lecture')
      else { LOCK clecture EXCLUSIVE } clecture := <>
      { COMMIT Messages, clecture, RELEASE ALL LOCKS }
  end cancellecture;

end module scheduling;
```

Example 6.2 Transactions with Locking Protocols

assistant or professor) can be executed in parallel. Knowledge of that kind can be used at compile-time to classify transactions and to simplify a transaction's locking protocol [BSR80].

Locking protocols also can be simplified if data are known to be accessed by each transaction in a predefined order [SK80a] [YANN82]. If the order is a hierarchy, specific tree protocols that are not two-phase and that allow for more concurrency can be used. Example 6.3 makes the hierarchic relationship between the relations *employees* and *papers* explicit by defining one relation that is not in first normal form.

```
var employees: relation <enr> of
                record
                   enr    : enumbertype;
                   name   : nametype;
                   status : statustype;
                   papers : relation <title> of
                                 record
                                   year  : yeartype;
                                   title : titletype
                                 end
                end;
```

Example 6.3 *Non-Normalized Relations*

7. Concluding Remarks

The approach to data selection, sharing, and access control taken in this chapter relies heavily on the notion of selected relation variables and, therefore, on first-order predicates. This observation supports the general statement that many issues in relational database modelling (*e.g.*, query language design [CODD71], semantic definition (chapter by Reiter), query optimization [JS82]) can be treated effectively in the framework of first-order theory. Tests for the disjunctness of (selected) relation variables as required for the correct execution of concurrent transactions imply disjunctness tests of predicates. For arbitrary complex predicates, the problem of testing their disjunctness may not be resolvable. It is, in fact, undecidable for general predicates of the first-order calculus.

The disjunctness of predicates over relations, however, is decidable even if it includes quantifiers, provided the value sets (*i.e.*, the range relations) are constant [KLEE71]. This can always be enforced by a read lock on the range relation associated with the quantified variable. The main problem in implementing disjunctness tests is that such a decision requires the inspection of the predicates, including the range relations. In the case of large range relations, the overhead for testing quantified predicates may be tremendous.

It must be concluded, therefore, that in practice, selection predicates have to be restricted [EGL76] [HR79]. Since selected variables involving complex predicates can always be extended to encompassing variables defined by less complex predicates, those restrictions can be hidden from the user, possibly at the expense of increased locking granules and decreased concurrency.

8. Acknowledgments

The authors are grateful to J. Koch, W. Lamersdorf, and P. Putfarken for their comments on earlier versions of this chapter.

9. References

[BSR80] [BS82b] [CODD70] [CODD71] [CODD82] [EGL76] [GRAY78] [HR79] [JS82] [KLEE71] [KR81] [LS80] [LORI77] [RS81] [SCHM77] [SCHM82] [SK80a] [SM80] [YANN82]

Discussion

In the database research community there seems to be general agreement that more powerful data modelling tools are needed. Essentially there are three different approaches.

1. Conceptual models are developed to capture more of the application semantics (see the chapters by Borgida, Mylopoulos, and Wong, by Brodie and Ridjanovic, and by King and McLeod).
2. Abstract specification techniques are adopted based on first order logic, algebra, denotational semantics, *etc.* (see the chapters by Israel and Brachman, by Levesque, and by Reiter).
3. Data models are extended by embedding them into programming languages.

This chapter follows the third approach. It is a continuation of earlier work on PASCAL/R, but is not tied exclusively to PASCAL or the relational model. Four of the major issues in data model and programming language integration discussed in this chapter are:

1. Relational model definition.
2. Selection mechanisms for relation variables.
3. Database access control.
4. A transaction concept for high level languages.

Relation Types

The most natural way to embed the relational model into a high level language is by a relation definition in the form of typed variables that are declared in or imported into the scope of an application program. A relation type has a value set that is the power set over the value set of a record type. The set elements are constrained by a predicate enforcing the uniqueness of values in distinguished record fields, called the key fields of the relation. Operators for defining relation-valued expressions or queries are first order calculus-like that have predicates for subset definition. An assignment operator and derived operators like insert, delete, and update provide for altering relations.

Selection Mechanisms

Defining relations as structured variables raises the question whether there are appropriate selection mechanisms for relations that allow the denotation of parts of relation variables. The content-oriented selection mechanism suggested allows one to fix, for example, "one slot" of some *n*-ary relation and to treat the result as a relation variable. Standard relational calculus or algebra does not provide this because it is intended to be a query language only, not a denotation for parts of relation variables.

Assignments to selected parts of relation variables raise issues similar to those of the view update problem in databases. In terms of predicate calculus, a database view can be considered as a derived formula. Modifying a view then means changing the ground set of axioms in order to make the derived formula true. Selected relations are, however, not as general as database views defined by the full power of a query language. A relation selector refers to one relation only (the one to be selected), and under these restrictions it does not involve other selectors such as projection. The compiler can always translate an assignment to a selected relation variable into the right sets of assignments to the base relation.

When one allows arbitrary selection predicates, however, the problem arises that after an assignment to a selected variable its value may not be equal to that of the right-hand-side expression of the assignment statement. This may occur when the right-hand-side expression interferes with the selector used to denote the left-hand-side variable. This problem is well known in programming languages from assignment to arrays, and the classic example is a row operation on a matrix. It may happen that while updating the row by multiplying it with one of the elements, the multiplier is changed in the process of doing the update.

Essentially, there are two solutions: one can assume this semantic to be the one intended, or one can select the multiplier first, hold it fixed, and then do the update. In terms of the proposed relation selection mechanisms, the first case means a "by-reference" mechanism for the selector's parameters, the second case has a "by value" semantics.

The above problem is also closely related to what is called the "aliasing problem." It arises when an operation that has independent parameters is applied to a set of overlapping variables. For verification, one must either be sure that this doesn't happen, or one has to reason separately about the overlap.

It seems as if there are three alternatives for selection that are currently being investigated in the realm of data abstraction:

- Classes and generalization hierarchies with time-varying class extensions and objects being instances of several classes.
- Types and subtype hierarchies as in this chapter.
- Types, variables, and subvariables selected by a fairly general, predicate-based selection mechanism.

Access Control

Programming languages accessing databases require several kinds of access control mechanisms delimiting the access rights within a scope. The chapter investigates three of them.

- Import and export declarations that regulate access to external variables by an otherwise closed scope.
- Parameter passing mechanisms that provide several alternatives for communication between data objects, external and local to the scopes.
- Read and write privileges that determine which way data objects may be accessed.

The scopes under consideration are procedures, modules, and programs.

Modules import relations, or selected parts thereof, that are required by their procedure entries in order to implement the high level operations defined on the database. Modules usually export relations with read access for query purposes, and they export procedures for relation alteration.

Transactions

Some of the procedures accessing a database have to fulfill the basic condition that their execution is quasi-atomic. This means that under any circumstance it is guaranteed that they either run to completion or they are not executed at all. These procedures are the units of database transition and are called transactions. In case of parallel database access, transactions are also the units of concurrency. This says, in essence, that during the execution of any two transactions, the relations read by one are not altered by the other, and vice versa.

In realistic applications, transactions may have additional properties such as long-lived transactions and transactions that are nested. There are many problems with these kinds of transactions that are not yet solved. One solution is not to coordinate transactions by such strict mechanisms as locking, but instead to allow transactions to store their results in new "virtual relations." This approach requires, of course, that the results are integrated later on.

The issue raised here is parallel to the one raised in programming languages, the distinction between sharing and copying. There are no good mechanisms for this distinction, and languages deal with it on an ad hoc basis in a number of ways. Examples are sharing of code or, at a lower level, definition of assignment to list structures. In programming languages the problem is not solved, but it is well recognized.

Deferring the commit of transactions raises issues similar to version control in software engineering, and to context control in programming languages. The big problem is what to do with the vast amounts of pending "commits." It is not a solution if, during the process of integrating the pending results of transactions, a message is issued saying "it doesn't work for the following list of reasons. . . . " Instead of waiting for the big clash, two alternatives are discussed. One solution is to teach transactions to communicate with each other while building up their results; the other solution is to commit inconsistent information and to add an extra language facility with which to express consistency over local alterations of a transaction. The latter solution requires some mechanism to collect transactions that are to be merged, and to capture what their intention was at the time the merger was made.

All strategies seem feasible for some classes of problems, and no one is perfect universally. The most one can expect in the short term is a set of useful programming language mechanisms that help to build up specific application areas. In this respect, there are no fundamentally new problems coming out of databases that have not been recognized in programming languages, except the difference in magnitude of data and transactions to be dealt with.

16
Types, Algebras, and Modelling

Stephen N. Zilles
IBM Research Laboratory

ABSTRACT *Programming languages, database systems, and artificial intelligence systems all have the notion that entities can be classified into* types. *As might be expected, however, the usage of the notion of type is not the same among or even within these areas. This chapter presents a view of type that is based on work in programming languages. This view is then used to indicate how the programming languages and database systems can be integrated to produce a more powerful modelling environment.*

1. Modelling

The major issue in modelling real and abstract aspects of the world is the choice of what to model and what properties of what is being modelled are to be realized in the model. These choices should be left to the modeller, but any system designed to aid the modelling process will naturally have facilities that make it easier to model some properties rather than others. So it is with computer systems that aid modelling, such as database systems and programming languages.

Database systems typically provide a relatively small set of representation structures that are to be used to represent all models. For example, relational database systems have tuples (a related collection of attribute-value pairs) and relations (sets of tuples with the same set of attributes in each tuple). Related structures are available in typical network and hierarchical database systems. The advantage of using a small number of structure types is that the data contained in the database can be accessed in a uniform manner with a relatively simple query language. The cost is that some aspects of the world may be modelled only with difficulty.

The above database structures make it simple to model the scalar properties of an entity, such as the age, salary, and department number of an employee. These simply become fields in the tuple or record representing the employee. Nonscalar properties, such as the names of the employee's children, become more difficult to model, especially where these properties are shared by several entities. Difficult questions begin to arise about what should be removed from the database when an entity is deleted from the model.

The bias in modelling via programming languages is different. If anything, programming languages are too prone to detail and to handling special cases. They frequently lack uniformity in their data representations so that it is not possible to easily formulate arbitrary information retrievals from the data representations used for a particular problem. The strength of programming languages is in their ability to represent operations on the entities being modelled; that is, they are best at capturing the behavioural aspects of a model.

Since the biases of database systems and programming languages are complementary, it is natural to consider a combination of the best features of each approach. This chapter will develop an outline of such a combination by first examining how the concept of the *type* of an entity can be used in modelling, particularly in programming languages. Then an overview of the main features of a possible integration of a programming language and a relational database system will be presented.

2. Types

At the Pingree Workshop on Data Abstraction, Databases, and Conceptual Modelling, Peter Deutsch [DEUT81] presented a very good abstract characterization of the term *type* as it is used by people in artificial intelligence, databases, and programming languages:

> A *type* is a precise characterization of structural or behavioural properties which a collection of entities (actual or potential) all share. An *instance* of a type is an entity which has the properties characteristic of the type.

As the definition of *instance* indicates, the term *type* will be used ambiguously to mean both the set of properties defining the type and the collection of entities that all have those properties.

This pair of definitions highlights the two most important aspects of an entity from the viewpoint of modelling it: (1) its *identity*, that which distinguishes this instance from all other instances; and (2) its *substance*, the properties that hold for the entity and can be discovered by investigation of the entity.

This is a very broad definition of the term *type* because there is no limit to the kinds of properties that may be used to characterize a given type. Properties might include membership in one or more sets or classes, the form of the representation of the entities, operations that are applicable to the entities, or any other attribute of the entity.

This definition sets a goal for the type notion used in any modelling system. The type system of an ideal modelling system would allow all the types implied in the definition to be expressed and distinguished. More frequently, however, this definition of type is too broad. By limiting the kinds of properties that can be used to define a type, more efficient implementations of the type notion can be achieved. For example, in programming languages, the properties that define a type usually are restricted to those that can be tested at compile time. This means that most type checking can be eliminated from the executable code with a consequent improvement in execution speed.

Whether a type is testable at compile time depends upon the language because the language determines the type calculus used to express new types in terms of other types, and it determines the rules for deciding when two types match. If the rules for matching can always be evaluated at compile time, then the class of types expressible in the type calculus for that language is a compile time testable class.

One of the major issues in the design of programming languages is the choice of a tradeoff between the expressiveness of the type calculus and the size of the subset of the expressible types that can be matched at compile time. The more expressive the type calculus, the larger the subset of types (as defined above) that can be expressed, but the more difficult it becomes to decide when two such types match.

In most modern programming languages, a compromise is made between doing all type checking at compile time and doing some type checking at run time. For example, in Ada [IKWL82], assignment from a variable of one type to a subtype of that type is allowed as long as the value being assigned belongs to the subtype. Since, in many cases, this constraint cannot be evaluated at compile time, run time checks are used to insure that the constraint is satisfied. The use of run time checks allows the expressiveness of the type calculus to be increased at the cost of a loss in performance when the run time checks must actually be made.

As the example of compile time testability shows, there is a structure to the collections of types that fit Deutsch's definition. Each *meta*class groups together all types that have certain properties, such as the class of types expressible in some language's type calculus, or the class of types for which an addition operation is defined on the instances of each type. This last class is itself a type which has as its instances the union of the instances of all the types that belong to the class. This kind of class will be discussed in more detail below.

For the remainder of the chapter, I will adopt a more restricted notion of type than the one proposed by Deutsch. This notion of type is strongly influenced by work on data abstraction in programming languages [LZ74] [LZ75] [ZILL80] [ZLT82]. In very abstract terms, the function of a programming language is to specify the order and operations that are applied to entities expressible in that language. This viewpoint holds whether the language is functional (and the ordering is specified by composing operations) or procedural (and the ordering is specified by composition plus sequencing statements). Thus, the action of applying an operation to one or more entities is central to modelling with programming languages.

Operations are used to construct new entities and to investigate the properties of existing ones. Yet, not all combinations of operations and entities are meaningful. Some combinations may make little or no sense; for example, there is no proper meaning to applying the POP_STACK operation to an INTEGER. Historically, the role of typing in programming languages has been to identify those instances for which a given operation application is defined; for example, the POP_STACK operation can be applied to instances of the type STACK. With this use of the notion of type, Deutsch's definition has been specialized so that the only properties that can be used to determine a type are the applicability or nonapplicability of one or more operations to the instances of the type.

This restricted definition of type still ignores a distinction found in most programming languages. Some operators, for example ADDition, are defined on several disjoint sets of instances, such as FIXED POINT NUMBERS and FLOATING POINT NUMBERS. Typically it is not possible to directly ADD a FIXED POINT NUMBER to a FLOATING POINT although usually it is possible to *convert* the FIXED POINT NUMBER to a FLOATING POINT NUMBER and then ADD. Hence the opera*tor* ADD is realized by two distinct ADD opera*tions*: one for FIXED POINT NUMBERS and one for FLOATING POINT NUMBERS. (In actual practice, other ADDition operations may be defined as well.) Thus, there is a distinction between the *generic* (or overloaded) operator ADD and the *specific* ADD operations that realize ADDition.

Specific operations exist in computer models because the computer is working with models of the entities, such as the NUMBERS, rather than with the entities themselves. For each model, a specific representation for the entity is chosen. The operations, such as ADD, act on these representations. Each operation becomes a function or procedure that is written to process the representation of the entities being modelled. Therefore, the applicability of a specific operation is limited to the representations of the entities for which it was designed. Because they are based on a particular choice of representation for the entities being modelled, types determined by the applicability of specific operations will be called *concrete types.*

It is not, however, the representations of the entities that are interesting in modelling, but the behaviour of the entities. It is the generic operator ADD that captures the notion of ADDition, independently of the particular representation of NUMBERS. The semantics of the generic operator are those of the entities being modelled, not those of a specific model. The set of entity instances for which an ADD operation is applicable then forms the *abstract type* NUMBERS which includes, as subsets, the concrete types for the particular representations of NUMBERS, such as fixed point and floating point.

This notion of an abstract type is slightly different than the one commonly used with abstract data types in programming languages (see the chapter by Shaw), and this is intentional. Rather than saying that a type (or in SIMULA 67 [DNM68] and SMALLTALK a class) consists of a set of entities together with a set of primitive operations on the entities, a type is once again just a set of entities, but a set to which certain operators are applicable. This is a subtle distinction. Its purpose is to emphasize that the operations applicable to a type need not be an integral part of the type representation as they are in SIMULA and SMALLTALK. Instead, a set of entities belongs to an abstract type if the requisite operations for that abstract type are defined (no matter where or how).

Some examples may help to clarify this point. Consider a SORT operator. For sorting to be defined there must be an ordering defined on the entities being sorted. It is not important that the ordering be built into the type definition, however. It would suffice that an ordering operation be definable in terms of other operations applicable to the entities. For example, one can consider the two element Boolean algebra to be ordered by the IMPLICATION operator. (Checking its truth table will show that IMPLICATION is equivalent to the LESS THAN OR EQUAL operator on two Boolean entities.) If the SORT operator required that the ordering be builtin with the type definition, then SORTING over the Boolean values would not be possible, but, by being able to identify or construct the ordering operation using procedure or function definitions, the set of Boolean entities is contained in the abstract type of sortable entities.

A set of entities may have more than one ordering operation, for example LESS THAN OR EQUAL and GREATER THAN OR EQUAL. By choosing one or the other of these operations as the ordering operation by which the set participates in the sortable type, one gets either ascending or descending sorts.

These examples show that a concrete type may be contained in many different abstract types and that these inclusions need not be prespecified. Inclusion in an abstract type depends solely on the existence of (and designation of) the requisite operations for the operators whose applicability define the abstract type. With this approach to type inclusion, it is not necessary to explicitly specify the inclusion relations, nor is it necessary to restrict one's self to a purely hierarchical, tree-oriented type structure. This observation is important to the type structure of Russell [DD80].

But more is needed than just the notion of types. Most programming is not done with a single type, but with a related collection of types. Operations are defined over several concrete types; for example, an operation for the SET MEMBERSHIP operator is defined over the concrete types for SETS, INSTANCES, and BOOLEANS. Operations may be used in combination only if they are defined over the same collection of concrete types. It is of little use to have a SET INSERTION operation for INTEGER SETS and a SET MEMBERSHIP operation for CHARACTER STRING SETS.

To have a structure that combines a particular collection of types with the operations upon those types, the notion of an algebra is introduced. An algebra combines a collection of types together with a family of operations upon those types. The operations do not belong to a type; they belong to the algebra (that is, that particular collection of types).

By viewing the model building blocks as algebras, we obtain more power to construct models from simple components and to adapt models to special circumstances. It is clear, for example, that the SORT operator mentioned above requires more than an ordering operation on the elements to be sorted. These elements must be stored in a structure that has ordered components so that the sorted result can be presented in order. If the sort is to occur in place, there must also be an EXCHANGE operation defined on the ordered structure. Therefore, SORT is defined over an algebra with the types ELEMENTS, STRUCTURES, INDEX_SET, BOOLEANS and the operations LESS THAN OR EQUAL, SELECT ELEMENT OF STRUCTURE, and CONSTRUCT STRUCTURE or EXCHANGE ELEMENTS IN STRUCTURE. Some of these operations may be primitive to a type and some may be defined for the purpose of using the SORT operator as above. From this viewpoint, the SORT operator takes two parameters: an instance of the structure to be sorted, and an algebra parameter which defines the requisite operations and the types that actually occur in that structure.

Providing a single algebra parameter is a great simplification over specifying separate operation and type parameters. It naturally insures the coherence of the entities passed to a generic operator. It also provides a natural framework for describing the class over which a given operator is generic. The class of algebras suitable as the parameter of a given generic operator can be given a formal characterization (for example, by using an equational definition of the class [TWW78] [ZLT82]). The formal characterization establishes the semantics of the operations required of the algebra parameter independently of any particular algebra that works. These semantics can be used to prove the correctness of the generic operator, which is then known to work correctly for any algebra satisfying the abstract semantics.

In summary, a programming language view of types has been presented that is concerned with the construction of general purpose, flexible modelling tools that allow reuse of component pieces. Taking a step backward in time, a type is once again defined as:

Type: A set of entities. Two types are equivalent if the sets are isomorphic.

The role of the behaviour of the entities in related types is taken over by the algebra. It is the algebra that defines the properties that must hold on operations of the types:

Algebra: A collection of types, together with a family of operations, such that the operations are closed within the types in the collection. In formal treatments, types are more often called *sorts.* Each operation has a name (which may be generic) and a functionality (that is, specifications for the types of its operands and result). Two algebras are equivalent if the component types are equivalent and the operations can be put in correspondence so that they behave the same way.

In addition to the abstract concepts above, programming languages introduce the notion of packaging a model in separate pieces or *modules.* This notion is particularly relevant in structuring the output of programming languages.

Module: An encapsulated implementation of (a) one or more types and/or (b) one or more procedures or functions. In the case of types, the module defines a representation for the elements of each of the types implemented in the module and procedures that implement each of the operations applicable to the types.

3. Data Abstraction and Database Models

In contrast to the viewpoint outlined above, the emphasis in most of the work on data models has been on providing a standard view of all data entities. The common database models have a standard representation format or structure for entities, the attributes of those entities, and the relationships among them. The model for a data entity is constructed from a relatively small set of standard modelling primitives.

For example, in the relational model, a model is constructed from domains and relations. With each model there is a standard set of operations, such as create_entity, update_entity, delete_entity, and find_entity, which are applicable to all data entities representable in that data model. Operations unique to a particular class of data entities are most often not explicitly identified. This approach is used because it is difficult, if not impossible, to predict all the queries that might be asked against the data. Providing a general purpose structure, plus a language for combining fragments of the total collection, allows for such unanticipated queries.

In many cases, the operations applicable to the entities being modelled translate quite directly into operations on the representation of those entities; for example, changing the value associated with a attribute of an entity is done with the database update operation. There are, however, cases where neither the representation nor the operations fit naturally into the data model. Consider, for example, the class of queue entities that have operations to add, remove, or rearrange the queue elements. Representing the queue requires choosing a representation for the elements and the way that the elements are ordered. In a relational model, the queue elements might be represented by tuples with a domain for an element identifier and domains for the element contents. The ordering might be represented by an extra ordering domain in the element tuple, or by a separate relation consisting of pairs of element identifiers that precede/succeed each other in the ordering. The operations on queues are not simple query language statements, but must be *programs* that take into account the ordering representation.

From the viewpoint of the queue, the form of the queue elements is specified as an external property of the queue, but the form chosen to represent the queue ordering is not to be externally visible and is of concern only to the realization of the queue operations. Thus, the above representations have two distinct portions: the representation of externally defined entities that occur in the entity being modelled, and the representation of the details of the model. In choosing a relational representation for queues, these two aspects of the representation get mixed up and both are exposed. The relational representation is not directly a model of the queue; it allows too many extraneous possible interactions. It becomes a model of the queue only when access to it is restricted to the applicable operations. The essence of this point is that representation is not modelling, and that the data model operations only sometimes model the operations applicable to the entity being modelled.

The database community recognizes that more than substance representation is needed to model an entity. This can be seen in work on data models [CODD79] [SS77a] [SS77b] where more declarative information is being captured in the model so that the standard operations on the data model, such as delete, will more accurately reflect the semantics of the entity being modelled. For example, when an entity is modelled by several "normalized" components, the normalization information is used to insure that all the components are deleted when the top level component is deleted. This approach increases the number of entities that have natural models in the data model, but it seems unreasonable to believe that, even with such semantic additions, any fixed set of data representations will give natural models for all entities.

Therefore, the most recent work on modelling with database systems has placed increased emphasis on capturing the behavioural semantics of what is being modelled as well as the representational or structural semantics. (See the chapters by Brodie and Ridjanovic and by King and McLeod and also [WONG81].) This work introduces operations on the data in the form of actions on the database.

4. Putting Data Abstractions in a Database

In the algebraic view of data espoused in this chapter, the operations of the algebra provide the only way to manipulate or investigate the entities being modelled. It is in this sense that the algebraic view of data give abstract data (or data abstractions). Since the database begins with a representational view, it is necessary to be able to encapsulate a representation to abstract it for some purpose. If the database is to be truly integrated with the programming language used to access it, the encapsulation should be uniform for all representations accessible through the programming language. The chapter by Stonebraker describes how programming language entities can be encapsulated and stored in the database. Rowe and Shoens [RS79] describe one approach to encapsulating relations to represent other abstract entities. Haskin and Lorie [HL82] deal with many of the systems issues in managing encapsulated relations. Yet there is still no clear integration of all these features into a coherent whole. Critical to such an integration is the notion of system service exits as described by Shaw and Wulf [SW80]. These provide ways to integrate user defined data to the builtin facilities of the system, such as locking, logging and recovery, indices, *etc.* Since most of the technology necessary to carry out the integration is now available I predict that we will see fully integrated systems in the very near future.

5. Acknowledgments

The views presented here were in part formed during discussions with Peter Lucas and Jim Thatcher and were further advanced by discussions with the participants of the Intervale, New Hampshire workshop.

6. References

[CODD79] [DD80] [DEUT81] [DMN68] [HL82] [IKWL82] [LZ74] [LZ75] [RS79] [SS77a] [SS77b] [SW80] [TWW78] [WONG81] [ZILL80] [ZLT82]

Part V

Concluding Remarks from Three Perspectives

17
An Artificial Intelligence Perspective

Carl Hewitt

I would like to address three issues: various aspects of generality, problem solving versus algorithmic systems, and communication.

First, let's consider several aspects of generality. What is the impact of increased generality on the basic nature of a system of partial and incremental notions? Although some people resort to the batch processing tradition to deal with these issues, new, practical technologies can be used. I will mention several system aspects that are candidates for the new technologies.

One aspect of generality concerns the contents of the system. Increasingly it seems useful for the database to contain knowledge about processes and procedures, including its own. This aids in creating reasonable interactions. To get real things done, a person needs knowledge of the pertinent processes in order to plan and to communicate with systems that have local functions and powers different from his own. For example, an actor's own personal database will have to negotiate with an airline reservation system in order to book a seat. Things become more complicated when we no longer have a single unified system.

A second aspect of generality is that systems are still far too low level. Even functional programming languages and languages like PL/1 or Ada are entirely inadequate in the long term. We should deal with the systems on the basis of interactions rather than on the basis of procedural commands. For example, we should deal directly with plans, goals, and constraints (*e.g.,* a plan using electronic fund transfer to finance a house). The whole idea is to raise the level at which we are dealing with these things and to suppress irrelevant details.

A third aspect of generality is problem solving. A tight, unified view of the world is inappropriate even for individual systems. We need to entertain multiple hypotheses and to pursue in parallel all effective user responses. In the house financing example, there may be different opinions within the system about the best financing strategy. AI systems cannot in general solve such problems themselves; their function is to collect data and be helpful. A simple objective for house financing would be for the system to go through mortgage proposals and to present reasonable alternatives.

AI deals with systems that lie somewhere in the spectrum between problem solving and algorithmic. For the most part AI does not produce completely algorithmic systems in which applications decide things themselves. Rather AI takes problems that are not well understood (hence require problem solving capability) and attempts to move them towards the algorithmic end of the spectrum. A procedure is more algorithmic to the extent that stronger properties can be proved about it. Problem solving may be done by the system or through interaction by the user. Interaction can be very helpful in presenting information for decision making. What can be represented initially in the machine is one's general way of doing a task. After gaining insight into the system by observing many cases, more procedural mechanisms can be constructed as is done in "programming by example."

Database design is a case in point. It is partly interactive and partly algorithmic. Database sizing is algorithmic whereas logical design is methodological. After one has experience and observes the effectiveness of the methods used, the design process can be made more algorithmic.

Problem solving is necessitated by the existence of anomalies. Anomalies pose big problems that will become worse in the future. We fill databases with conflicting statements about the complicated world in which we live and with nondeterministic, interactive procedures (*e.g.*, the house financing system may not produce a strategy). To make large databases general, procedures and real world knowledge must be added. Anomalies are going to be there. Knowledge cannot arbitrarily be divided into logical and analytical facts on the one hand, and illogical inferences, inaccuracies, and anomalies on the other. If we use predicate calculus to acquire precision, contradictions will arise since people describe things inconsistently. Current databases were not intended to handle anomalies. Whereas large amounts of data can be handled in databases, processing and inferencing over the data and dealing with anomalies is done outside the current database arena.

Some anomalies can be dealt with by means of exceptions. Exceptions are different from both inconsistent knowledge and improper definitions. Let's assume that our concept of "bird" includes feathers, wings, and so on. Something that does not fly but that has all these properties is classified as a bird even though it is partly inconsistent with this concept; it is an exception. Although a pigeon who has lost a wing violates the definition of a bird (*i.e.*, does not have two wings), it is still a bird.

Unlike the type concept in PL, the hypothesis concept in AI can be used to handle exceptions. Anything that satisfies the properties of a type can be hypothesized to be of that type. Every instance need not have all the properties in the frame. Thus the wounded pigeon can be hypothesized to be a bird that doesn't happen to fly. Hypotheses permit looser, more realistic descriptions. For example, a bird can be represented using several frames, such as biological bird, ground bird, air bird, *etc.* These categories are not logical definitions, they are approximate. Even here anomalies will arise. Satisfying the properties of a frame does not necessarily mean membership in the frame. This is the recognition problem. It is not a matter of truth. There are always anomalies. The purpose of these categories is to make approximate classifications for the purpose of conceptual modelling.

Anomalies can arise because of the source or point of view of the information. In the future, almost all data will come from end users. There will be a problem of defining and recognizing objects. We do not have good definitions even for natural objects such as houses. Currently databases require definitions. In business, we have practical definitions that are not definitions of houses, but they are abstractions that emphasize properties of interest for particular problems. In the house financing example, the bank's definition of house must agree sufficiently with the mortgage strategy system so that they can communicate.

People will not want to retrieve things exactly in the form in which they were put into the database. Databases will have to be able to draw reasonable conclusions that go beyond the logical implications of exactly what was put into the database. To handle anomalies, inference, and evolution, new information models will be required. Data will have to continually reorganize itself and alter itself in relation to new information.

The final issue concerns communication. There are two aspects of communication: subfield and subsystem communication. In subfields like AI, DB, and PL we have to find goals and rules of the game. Having established the subfields and means of communication we must construct subsystems to support the communication. These subsystems have to communicate with each other as well. Such communication poses many open problems for AI, DB, and PL. Communicating, autonomous subsystems are the way of the future.

18
A Database Perspective

Michael Stonebraker

PL researchers are like good craftsmen; they choose tools very carefully and are concerned with quality and esthetics. They are also somewhat parochial, refusing to deal with issues such as I/O and persistent objects that are of great real world concern. Although PL people claim to add new tools and features to their tool kit, it takes a long time for new ideas from other areas to be incorporated into their languages.

In the 70s, PL researchers introduced extendable types and languages. The major PL contribution of the 80s is likely to be in the area of programming environments. However, programming environments will require DBs for programs, among other things; and these are persistent objects. PL folks will have to get "databaseified."

AI researchers are contentious. They are very critical of the relational model because it doesn't deal with nulls and disjunctive information. There are many users of relational systems, and no one has ever objected very loudly to those properties. Although AI people stress the importance of inheritance, few database users ask for it. (Objection: Inheritance is a solution to many problems that users complain about most often, such as applications development.) AI researchers heatedly advance their paradigms (predicate logic, inheritance, *etc.*) as the solution to data base problems. As such, they are a little like missionaries.

AI researchers have a scope problem that differentiates them from the other researchers at this conference. While the scope of AI research is "the universe," other disciplines have much narrower scopes. A related AI problem is that there is no measure of success such as the ones that exist in the PL and DB communities. For example, a well defined method to prove the worth of a PL idea is to build a language processor for it and give it to the world to use. It is a measure of success if people immediately use the tool to solve its intended problem. AI may well remain contentious until it gains a success measure of its own. Moreover, I think it would be helpful if the AI community became more concerned with the transfer of their ideas to the real world rather than expecting others to perform that task.

I am struck by the non-DB view that DB researchers are considered a big success. From the inside it seems as though we muddle along like everybody else.

The AI researchers at this conference all ask the question "Where is the next leap of database functionality going to come from?" Hopefully, the next generation DBMSs should be noticeably better than the current ones. I would like to see DBMSs that deal much more intelligently with complex objects (*e.g.*, forms, maps, icons, *etc.*) and relationships (*e.g.*, generalization, inheritance, and associations). However, there is a problem with both complex objects and relationships in databases. The closure property of relational queries (the result of a query is a relation) is not satisfied for some queries on complex objects and generalization hierarchies. (Objection: Much more structure is required than relations give us.) The challenge of the next step in DBs is either to say that relations are not the answer and move to some new model, or to extend the relational model with some (yet to be defined) new features.

Real users' needs are a prime consideration to DB researchers. Real users know precisely what subsystems they want. They have data for which they want report writers, business graphics (charts, plots, *etc.*), form editors (to create new application oriented forms), and similar systems. The functions of these subsystems are known, for the most part. These subsystems must be treated like building blocks (*i.e.*, like high level objects). Users want an easy environment in which to switch between subsystems. Integration of these objects (subsystems) is a big challenge for the DB community.

19
A Programming Language Perspective

Stephen N. Zilles

My view is not restricted to classical programming languages. I am interested in formal languages that are used for manipulating things in general. I would like to argue that a language is a structure used for describing *combinations* of actions and objects. This definition includes Pascal as well as menu systems. The important notion underlying the definition is that of combination. Good language design is the process of combining features into an *integrated* whole. A good example is Pascal/R, which introduces the concept of relation into Pascal as a data type. Another example, ARGUS, adds the notion of a database transaction to CLU.

Integration implies that the result of combining operations and objects can itself be used in further combinations. (Mary Shaw: A system with this property is sometimes called a "calculus.") One example is a notion that took a while to get into programming languages, namely, that a procedure can be used as an argument to another procedure. Another example is the Plan Calculus in which two plans can be combined to form a plan suitable for further combination.

The study of programming languages has provided a *catalog of ideas* such as naming, scope rules, sequencing of structures and operations, notions of abstraction, *etc.* The ideas are fairly well worked out and can be added as new features to languages. An awareness of the catalog of ideas prompts investigations of how concepts fit into a given context. This awareness has led to discussions about the impact on a language of using relational data types as representations for newly introduced abstractions.

When adding a new construct to either a language, an AI system, or a DB system, two questions should be asked. First: How does the new construct fit with other constructs (all combinations)? Clean integration makes language and systems design really difficult. Caution is required. Tony Hoare suggested that one does not create new languages by combining a lot of new constructs. Experience with languages such as PL/1 and Ada have shown that one cannot predict what the interaction of many constructs is going to produce. Such languages have many weird interactions among the constructs and a lot of bumps and rough edges. It is far better to integrate a construct into an existing language. Then you can determine its effects on (and interactions with) other features. New languages should be designed from existing, proven features.

The second question is do new constructs being added compare with existing ideas. An example is how actions, transactions, and events in the work of Brodie and Ridjanovic, and in the work of King and McLeod, compare to the procedures in PLs. It is useful to determine what the differences are, and, in particular, why there are differences. Are the differences accidental or do they reflect different concepts? To answer these questions, we should use the catalog of ideas as a frame of reference.

I would like to mention three points to mark how far we have gone in the two years since the Pingree Park Workshop on Data Abstraction, Databases, and Conceptual Modelling was held.

We are still discussing the role of formal languages. First order logic (FOL) and equivalent formalisms should be used as they are in mathematics, namely, to deal with ambiguous concepts and ill-defined notions. Formal languages can be used to avoid arguments so that the concepts at hand can be emphasized. If we can communicate and understand each other there is no need to go back to FOL. FOL should be used as a tool.

Secondly, we are still arguing over the notion of type, and I expect we will for some time. A first step is to define a type as a predicate used to accumulate assertions about properties of similar things. A more interesting step is to consider classes of types. Seldom is a distinction made between an individual type (*e.g.,* an employee), and a class of types. Such confusion creates problems. One might create a meta level on top of the type predicate to define a collection of related predicates that have similar properties. Some of these properties can be evaluated at compile time or seldom require run time evaluation. Such predicate classes are important in strong typing in PLs. In DBs, types provide a uniform structure for representation. Those issues don't arise if one thinks of a type solely as a predicate. It is far better, though, to think of a type as a predicate rather than as an extension, a set of objects. However, extensions are useful in creating artificial types.

Finally, we have identified a number of important, unresolved concepts such as incomplete knowledge, abstract data types, and behavioural descriptions. From the PL viewpoint, these concepts must be understood and put into languages just as relations are being put into Pascal/R and transactions into ARGUS. Although concepts from other areas are interesting on their own, they are far more interesting when integrated with other features such as abstraction capabilities. It is a nontrivial process to make the resulting language uniform. It is easy to put a bump onto a language, and that has been done all too frequently.

References

[ABRI74]
Abrial, J. R., "Data Semantics," in J. W. Klimbie and K. L. Koffeman (eds.), *Data Management Systems,* North-Holland, Amsterdam, The Netherlands, 1974.

[ACC82]
Atkinson, M., K. Chisholm, and P. Cockshott, "PS-ALGOL: An ALGOL with a Persistent Heap," *SIGPLAN Notices,* Vol. 17, No. 7, July 1982.

[AGBB77]
Ambler, A. L., D. I. Good, J. C. Browne, W. F. Burger, R. M. Cohen, C. G. Hoch and R. E. Wells, "Gypsy: A Language for Specification and Implementation of Verifiable Programs," *SIGPLAN Notices,* Vol. 12, No. 3, March 1977, pp. 1-10.

[AGP78]
Arvind, (no initial), K. P. Gostelow, and W. Plouffe, "The (Preliminary) Id Report," Technical Report 114, Dept. of Information and Computer Science, Univ. of California, Irvine, 1978.

[AI80]
Artificial Intelligence, Special Issue on Non-Monotonic Logic, D. Bobrow (ed.), Vol. 13, Nos. 1 and 2, April 1980.

[AM81]
Ariav, G., and H. L. Morgan, "MDM: Handling the Time Dimension in Generalized DBMSs," Decision Sciences Working Paper 81-05-06, Wharton School, Univ. of Pennsylvania, 1981.

[ANSI75]
ANSI/X3/SPARC (Standards Planning and Requirements Committee), "Interim Report from the Study Group on Database Management Systems," *FDT* (Bulletin of ACM SIGMOD), Vol. 7, No. 2, 1975.

[AS81]
Attardi, G. and M. Simi, "Semantics of Inheritance and Attributions in the Description System Omega," *Proc. International Joint Conference on Artificial Intelligence*, Vancouver, B.C., Canada, August 1981.

[AU79]
Aho, A. V., and J. D. Ullman, "Universality of Data Retrieval Languages," *Proc. 6th ACM Symposium on Principles of Programming Languages,* 1979.

[AV80]
Apt, K. R., and Van Emden, M. H., "Contributions to the Theory of Logic Programming," Research Report CS-80-12, Dept. of Computer Science, Univ. of Waterloo, Waterloo, Ont., Canada, 1980.

[BACH77]
Bachman, C. W., "The Role Concept in Data Models," *Proc. 3rd International Conference on Very Large Databases,* Tokyo, Japan, 1977.

[BACK78]
Backus, J., "Can Programming be Liberated from the von Neumann Style?," *Communications of the ACM,* Vol. 21, No. 8 August 1978, pp. 613-641.

[BALZ81]
Balzer, R., "Transformational Implementation: An Example," *IEEE Transactions on Software Engineering,* Vol. SE-7, No. 1, January 1981.

[BARB82]
Barber, G. R., "Office Semantics," Ph.D. thesis, Massachusetts Institute of Technology, 1982.

[BARR80]
Barron, J. L., Dialogue Organization and Structure for Interactive Information Systems, Master's thesis, (CSRG Technical Report) Dept. of Computer Science, Univ. of Toronto, January 1980.

[BARS77]
Barstow, D. R., "Automatic Construction of Algorithms and Data Structures Using A Knowledge Base of Programming Rules," Stanford AIM-308, November 1977.

[BARW81]
Barwise, J., "Some Computational Aspects of Situation Semantics (Abstract)," Unpublished manuscript, 1981.

[BBC80]
Bernstein, P. A., B. T. Blaustein, and E. M. Clarke, "Fast Maintenance of Integrity Assertions Using Redundant Aggregate Data," *Proc. 6th International Conference on Very Large Databases,* Montreal, Que., Canada, October 1980.

[BBD77]
Bell, M. L., D. C. Bixler, and M. E. Dyer, "An Extendible Approach to Computer-Aided Software Requirements Engineering," *IEEE Transactions on Software Engineering*, Vol. SE-3, No. 1, January 1977.

[BBDG81a]
Bauer, F. L., M. Broy, W. Dosch, R. Gnatz, F. Geiselbrechtinger, W. Hesse, B. Krieg-Brueckner, A. Laut, T. A. Matzner, B. Moeller, H. Partsch, P. Pepper, K. Samelson, M. Wirsing, H. Woessner, "Report on a Wide Spectrum Language for Program Specification and Development" (tentative version), Institut fuer Informatik der TU

Muenchen, TUM-I8104, 1981; also in: *Lecture Notes in Comptuer Science,* Springer-Verlag, New York, 1981.

[BBDG81b]
Bauer, F. L., M. Broy, W. Dosch, R. Gnatz, B. Krieg-Brueckner, A. Laut, M. Luckmann, T. A. Matzner, B. Moeller, H. Partsch, P. Pepper, K. Samelson, R. Steinbrueggen, M. Wirsing, H. Woessner, "Programming in a Wide Spectrum Language: a Collection of Examples," *Science of Computer Programming* Vol. 1, 1981, pp. 73-114.

[BBG78]
Beeri, C., P. A. Bernstein, and N. Goodman, "A Sophisticate's Introduction to Database Normalization Theory," *Proc. 4th International Conference on Very Large Databases,* West Berlin, September 1978.

[BC75]
Bobrow, D., and A. Collins, (eds.), *Representation and Understanding,* Academic Press, New York, 1975.

[BD77]
Burstall, R. M., and J. L. Darlington, "A Transformation System for Developing Recursive Programs," *Journal of the ACM,* Vol. 24, No. 1, January 1977.

[BD81]
Barr, A., and J. Davidson, "Representation of Knowledge," in A. Barr and E. Feigenbaum (eds.), *Handbook of Artificial Intelligence,* William Kaufmann Inc., 1981.

[BDMN73]
Birtwistle, G. M., O.-J. Dahl, B. Myhrhaug, K. Nygaard, *Simula Begin,* Van Nostrand Reinhold, New York, 1973.

[BF79]
Buneman, O. P., and R. E. Frankel, "FQL—A Functional Query Language," *Proc. 1979 ACM SIGMOD International Conference on the Management of Data,* Boston, Mass., May 1979.

[BFN81]
Buneman, O. P., R. E. Frankel, and R. Nikhil, "A Practical Functional Programming System for Databases," *Proc. ACM Conference on Functional Programming and Archictecture,* New Hampshire, 1981.

[BFN82]
Buneman, O. P., R. E. Frankel, and R. Nikhil, "An Implementation Technique for Database Query Languages," *ACM Transactions on Database Systems,* Vol. 7, No. 2, June 1982.

[BG80a]
Bobrow, D. and Goldstein, I., "Representing Design Alternatives," *Proc. Society for Study of Artificial Intelligence and Simulation of Behavior Conference,* Amsterdam, The Netherlands, July 1980.

[BG80b]
Burstall, R. M., and J. A. Gougen, "The Semantics of CLEAR: A Specification Language," *Proc. Copenhagen Winter School on Abstract Software Specification,* Copenhagen, Denmark, 1980.

[BHR80]
Bayer, R., H. Heller, and A. Reiser, "Parallelism and Recovery in Database Systems," *ACM Transactions on Database Systems,* Vol. 5, No. 2, June 1980.

[BI82]
Borning, A.H., and D.H. Ingalls, "Multiple Inheritance in Smalltalk-80," *Proc. AAAI National Conference,* Pittsburgh, Penn., August 1982.

[BISK81]
Biskup, J., "Null Values in Data Base Relations," in [GM78].

[BJ78]
Bjorner, D., and C.B. Jones, *The Vienna Development Method,* Springer-Verlag, New York, 1978.

[BL82]
Brachman, R.J., and H. Levesque, "Competence in Knowledge Representation," *Proc. AAAI National Conference*, Pittsburgh, Penn., August 1982, pp. 189-192.

[BM76]
Basu, S., and J. Misra, "Some Classes of Naturally Provable Programs," *2nd International Conference on Software Engineering,* San Francisco, October 1976.

[BM77]
Buneman, O.P., and H.L. Morgan, "Alerting Techniques for Database Systems," *IEEE COMPSAC Conference,* Chicago, Ill., November 1977.

[BMS80]
Burstall, R.M., D.B. MacQueen, and D.T. Sanella, "HOPE: an Experimental Applicative Language," *Proc. Lisp Conference,* Stanford, Calif., 1980.

[BMW82]
Borgida, A.T., J. Mylopoulos, and H.K.T. Wong, "Methodological and Computer Aids for Interactive Information System Design," in H.J. Schneider and A. Wasserman (eds.), *Automated Tools for Information System Design — Proc. of IFIP Conference,* North-Holland, Amsterdam, The Netherlands, 1982.

[BOBR75]
Bobrow, D.G., "Dimensions of Representations," in [BC75].

[BOBR77]
Bobrow, D.G., "A Panel on Knowledge Representation," *Proc. 5th International Joint Conference on Artificial Intelligence,* Cambridge, Mass., August 1977.

[BORG81]
Borgida, A.T., "On the Definition of Specialization Hierarchies for Procedures," *Proc. 7th International Joint Conference on Artificial Intelligence,* Vancouver, B.C., Canada, August 1981.

[BORG82a]
Borgida, A. T., "Conceptual Modeling for Information System Development," *Proc. 1st AUC Conference on Databases,* Medellin, Colombia, August 1982.

[BORG82b]
Borgida, A. T., "Prospectus for Research on Flexible Information Systems," Dept. of Computer Science, Rutgers Univ., 1982.

[BOWL77]
Bowles, K. L., *Microcomputer Problem Solving Using Pascal,* Springer-Verlag, New York, 1977.

[BP80]
Barwise, J., and J. Perry, "The Situation Underground," unpublished manuscript, 1980.

[BP81a]
Barwise, J., and J. Perry, "Situations and Attitudes," *Journal of Philosophy,* Vol. 78, No. 11, October 1981, pp. 668-691.

[BP81b]
Barwise, J., and J. Perry, "Semantic Innocence and Uncompromising Situations," in P. A. French, T. E. Uehling, Jr., and H. K. Wettstein, (eds.), *The Foundations of Analytic Philosophy,* Midwest Studies in Philosophy, Vol. VI, Univ. of Minnesota Press, Minneapolis, 1981, pp. 387-404.

[BP81c]
Broy, M., and P. Pepper, "Program Development as a Formal Activity," *IEEE Transactions on Software Engineering,* Vol. SE-7, No. 1, January 1980.

[BPP76]
Bracchi, G., P. Paolini, and G. Pelagatti, "Binary Logical Associations in Data Modelling," in J. M. Nijssen (ed.), *Modelling in Database Management Systems* (Proc. IFIP TC2 Conference, Freudenstadt), North-Holland, Amsterdam, The Netherlands, 1976.

[BR70]
Buxton, J. N., and B. Randell (eds.), *Software Engineering Techniques,* NATO, 1970 (report on a conference sponsored by the NATO Science Committee, Rome, Italy, October 27-31, 1969).

[BRAC76]
Brachman, R. J., "A Structural Paradigm for Representing Knowledge," BBN Report No. 3605, Bolt, Beranek and Newman Inc., Cambridge, Mass., 1976.

[BRAC79]
Brachman, R. J., "On the Epistemological Status of Semantic Networks" in [FIND79], pp. 3-50.

[BRAC80a]
Brachman, R. J., "I Lied about the Trees," unpublished manuscript, 1980.

[BRAC80b]
Brachman, R. J., "An Introduction to KL-ONE," in R. J. Brachman, *et al.* (eds.), *Research in Natural Language Understanding, Annual Report (1 Sept. 78-31 Aug. 79),* Bolt, Beranek and Newman Inc., Cambridge, Mass., 1980, pp. 13-46.

[BRES72]
Bressan, A., *A General Interpreted Modal Calculus,* Yale Univ. Press, New Haven, Conn., 1972.

[BRIN75]
Brinch Hansen, P., "The Programming Language Concurrent Pascal," *IEEE Transactions on Software Engineering,* Vol. SE-1, No. 4, June 1975, pp. 199-207.

[BROD78]
Brodie, M. L., "Specification and Verification of Database Semantic Integrity," Ph.D. thesis (Computer Systems Research Group Technical Report No. 91), Univ. of Toronto, April 1978.

[BROD80a]
Brodie, M. L., "The Application of Data Types to Database Semantic Integrity," *Information Systems*, Vol. 5, No. 4, 1980.

[BROD80b]
Brodie, M. L., "Data Abstraction, Databases and Conceptual Modeling," *Proc. 6th International Conference on Very Large Databases,* Montreal, Que., Canada, October 1980.

[BROD80c]
"Data Quality in Information Systems," *Information & Management,* Vol. 3, 1980.

[BROD81a]
Brodie, M. L., "Association: A Database Abstraction for Semantic Modelling," *Proc. 2nd International Entity-Relationship Conference*, Washington, D.C., October 1981.

[BROD81b]
Brodie, M. L., "On Modelling Behavioural Semantics of Data," *Proc. 7th International Conference on Very Large Databases,* Cannes, France, September 1981.

[BROD82]
Brodie, M. L., "Axiomatic Definitions for Data Model Semantics," *Information Systems*, Vol. 7, No. 2, 1982.

[BROO75]
Brooks, F. P., Jr., *The Mythical Man-Month: Essays on Software Engineering,* Addison-Wesley, Reading, Mass., 1975.

[BROW73]
Brown, J. S., "Steps Towards Automatic Theory Formation," *Proc. International Joint Conference on Artificial Intelligence,* Palo Alto, Calif., August 1973.

[BROW80]
Browne, J. C., The Interaction of Operating Systems and Software Engineering," *Proc. IEEE,* Vol. 68, No. 9, September 1980.

[BRUC75]
Bruce, B., "Case Systems for Natural Language," *Artificial Intelligence,* Vol. 6, 1975, pp. 327-360.

[BS78]
Brodie, M. L., and J. W. Schmidt, "What is the Use of Abstract Data Types?," *Proc. 4th International Conference on Very Large Databases,* West Berlin, September 1978.

[BS79]
Bentley, J. L., and M. Shaw, "An Alphard Specification of a Correct and Efficient Transformation on Data Structures," *Proc. IEEE Conference on Specifications of Reliable Software,* April 1979, pp. 222-237.

[BS80]
Brachman, R. J., and B. Smith, Special Issue on Knowledge Representation, *SIGART Newsletter,* No. 50, February 1980.

[BS82a]
Bobrow, D. G., and M. J. Stefik, "Loops: An Object Oriented Programming System for Interlisp," Draft Report, Xerox PARK, 1982.

[BS82b]
Brodie, M. L., and J. W. Schmidt (eds.), "Final Report of the ANSI/X3/SPARC DBS-SG Relational Database Task Group," *SIGMOD Record,* Vol. 12, No. 4, July 1982.

[BS82c]
Brodie, M. L., and E. O. Silva, "Active and Passive Component Modelling: ACM/PCM," in [OSV82], pp. 41-91.

[BSD82]
Byrd, R. J., S. E. Smith, S. P. de Jong, "An Actor-Based Programming System," *SIGOA Conference on Office Information Systems,* June 1982.

[BSR80]
Bernstein, P. A., D. W. Shipman, and J. B. Rothnie, "Concurrency Control in a System for Distributed Databases (SDD-1), *ACM Transactions on Database Systems,* Vol. 5, No. 1, March 1980.

[BUNE79]
Bunemann, O. and E. Clemons, "Efficiently Monitoring Relational Databases," *ACM Transactions on Database Systems,* Vol 4., No. 3, September 1979.

[BURG75]
Burge, W. H., *Recursive Programming Techniques*, Addison-Wesley, Reading, Mass., 1975.

[BW77]
Bobrow, D., and T. Winograd, "An Overview of KRL, a Knowledge Representation Language," *Cognitive Science*, Vol. 1, No. 1, January 1977.

[BW81]
Borgida, A. T., and H. K. T. Wong, "Data Models and Data Manipulation Languages: Complimentary Semantics and Proof Theory," *Proc. 7th International Conference on Very Large Databases*, Cannes, France, September 1981, pp. 260-271.

[BYTE81]
Special Issue on Smalltalk, *BYTE*, August 1981.

[BZ81]
Brodie, M. L., and S. N. Zilles (eds.), *Proc. Workshop on Data Abstraction, Databases, and Conceptual Modelling, SIGART Newsletter*, No. 74, January 1981; *SIGMOD Record*, Vol. 11, No. 2, February 1981; *SIGPLAN Notices*, Vol. 16, No. 1, January 1981.

[CB74]
Chamberlin, D. D., and R. F. Boyce, "SEQUEL: a Structured English Query Language," *Proc. 1974 ACM SIGMOD International Conference on the Management of Data*, 1974.

[CBLL82]
Curry, G., L. Baer, D. Lipkie, B. Lee, "Traits: An Approach to Multiple-Inheritance Subclassing," *Proc. Conference on Office Information Systems, SIGOA Newsletter*, Vol. 3, Nos. 1 and 2, June 1982.

[CHAM75]
Chamberlin, D. D., *et. al.*, "Views, Authorization and Locking in a Relational Data Base System," *Proc. 1975 National Computer Conference*, Anaheim, Calif., May 1975.

[CHAM76]
Chamberlin, D. D., "Relational Database Management Systems," *Computing Surveys*, Vol. 8, No. 1, March 1976.

[CHEA81]
Cheatham, T. E., "Program Refinement by Transformation," *Proc. 5th International Conference on Software Engineering*, San Diego, Calif., March 1981.

[CHEN76]
Chen, P. P. S., "The Entity-Relationship Model: Toward a Unified View of Data," *ACM Transactions on Database Systems*, Vol. 1, No. 1, March 1976.

[CHEN78]
Chen, P. P. S., *The Entity-Relationship Approach to Logical Database Design*, Monograph No. 6, QED Information Sciences, Wellesley, Mass., 1978.

[CHIL77]
Childs, D. L., "Extended Set Theory," *Proc. 3rd International Conference on Very Large Databases,* Tokyo, Japan, October 1977.

[CHUR40]
Church, A., "A Formulation of the Simple Theory of Types," *Journal of Symbolic Logic,* Vol. 5, 1940, pp. 56-68.

[CHUR41]
Church, A., "The Calculi of Lambda-Conversion," *Annals of Mathematics Studies No. 6,* Princeton Univ. Press, 1941.

[CL73]
Chang, C. L., and R. C. T. Lee, *Symbolic Logic and Mechanical Theorem Proving,* Academic Press, New York, 1973.

[CLAR78]
Clark, K. L., "Negation as Failure," in [GM78].

[CLIN81]
Clinger, W. D., "Foundations of Actor Semantics," Technical Report MIT/AI/TR-633, MIT Laboratory for Artificial Intelligence, May 1981.

[CM79]
Carlson, E. and W. Metz, "A Design for Table-Driven Display Generation and Management Systems," Technical Report, IBM Research Laboratory, San Jose, Calif., 1979.

[CODA71]
CODASYL Data Base Task Group, April 1971 Report.

[CODD70]
Codd, E. F., "A Relational Model of Data for Large Shared Data Banks," *Communications of the ACM,* Vol. 13, No. 6, June 1970, pp. 377-387.

[CODD71]
Codd, E. F., "A Database Sublanguage Founded on the Relational Calculus," *Proc. SIGFIDET Workshop,* San Diego, Calif., 1971.

[CODD72]
Codd, E. F., "Relational Completeness of Database Sublanguages," in R. Rustin (ed.), *Data Base Systems,* Prentice-Hall, Englewood Cliffs, N.J., 1972.

[CODD79]
Codd, E. F., "Extending the Database Relational Model to Capture More Meaning," *ACM Transactions on Database Systems*, Vol. 4, No. 4, December 1979, pp. 397-434; IBM Research Report RJ2599, San Jose, Calif., August 1979.

[CODD82]
Codd, E. F., "Relational Database: A Practical Foundation for Productivity," *Communications of the ACM,* Vol. 25, No. 2, February 1982.

[COHE78]
Cohen, P.R., *On Knowing What to Say: Planning Speech Acts*, Ph.D. thesis (TR-118), Dept. of Computer Science, Univ. of Toronto, 1978.

[CWAM75]
Collins, A., E. Warnock, N. Aiello, and M. Miller, "Reasoning from Incomplete Knowledge," in [BC75].

[DATE81]
Date, C.J., *An Introduction to Database Systems,* 3rd ed., Addison-Wesley, Reading, Mass., 1981.

[DATE83]
Date, C.J., *An Introduction to Database Systems Volume II,* Addison-Wesley, Reading, Mass., 1983.

[DAVI58]
Davis, M., *Computability and Unsolvability,* McGraw-Hill, New York, 1958.

[DAVI77]
Davis, R., "Interactive Transfer of Expertise: Acquisition of New Inference Rules," *Proc. 5th International Joint Conference on Artificial Intelligence,* Cambridge, Mass., August 1977.

[DB82]
Dayal, U., and P.A. Bernstein, "On the Updatability of Network Views—Extending Relational View Theory to the Network Model," *Information Systems,* Vol. 7, No. 1, 1982.

[DD80]
Demers, A.J., and J.E. Donahue, "Data Types, Parameters, and Type Checking," *Proc. ACM Symposium on Principles of Programming Languages,* SIGACT and SIGPLAN, January 1980, pp. 12-23.

[DEJO80]
de Jong, S.P., "The System for Business Automation (SBA): a Unified Application Development System," *Proc. 1980 IFIP Congress,* Tokyo, Japan, 1980.

[DENN74]
Dennis, J.B., "First Version of a Data Flow Procedure Language," *Proc. Symposium on Programming,* Institut de Programmation, Univ. of Paris, Paris, France, April 1974, 241-271.

[DEUT81]
Deutsch, L.P., "In Summary of Workshop Session on Types," *Proc. Workshop on Data Abstraction, Databases, and Conceptual Modelling, SIGPLAN Notices,* Vol. 16, No. 1, January 1981, p. 49.

[DH72]
Dahl, O.-J., and C.A.R. Hoare, "Hierarchical Program Structures," in O.-J. Dahl, E.W. Dijkstra, and C.A.R. Hoare (eds.), *Structured Programming,* Academic Press, New York, 1972, pp. 175-220.

[DH73]
Duda, R. O., and P. E. Hart, *Pattern Classification and Scene Analysis,* Wiley-Interscience, New York, 1973.

[DIJK68]
Dijkstra, E. W., "Goto Statement Considered Harmful," *Communications of the ACM,* Vol. 11, No. 3, March 1968, pp. 147-148.

[DIJK72]
Dijkstra, E. W. "Notes on Structured Programming," in O.-J. Dahl, E. W. Dijkstra, and C. A. R. Hoare (eds.), *Structured Programming,* Academic Press, New York, 1972.

[DIJK76]
Dijkstra, E. W., *A Discipline of Programming*, Prentice-Hall, Englewood Cliffs, N.J., 1976.

[DISE77]
diSessa, A., "On Learnable Representations of Knowledge: A Meaning for the Computational Metaphor," Memo MIT/AIM-441, MIT Laboratory for Artificial Intelligence, September 1977.

[DK75]
Davis, R., and J. King, "An Overview of Production Systems," Memo AIM-271, Stanford Artificial Intelligence Laboratory, 1975.

[DK76]
DeRemer, F., and H. H. Kron, "Programming-in-the-Large vs. Programming-in-the-Small," *IEEE Transactions on Software Engineering,* Vol. SE-2, No. 2, June 1976, pp. 80-86.

[DMN68]
Dahl, O.-J., B. Myrhaug, and K. Nygaard, *Simula 67 Common Base Language,* Pub. S-22, Norwegian Computing Center, Oslo, 1968.

[DN66]
Dahl, O.-J., and K. Nygaard, "SIMULA — An ALGOL-Based Simulation Language," *Communications of the ACM,* Vol. 9, No. 9, September 1966, pp. 671-678.

[DoD78]
Department of Defense, *Steelman Requirements for High Order Computer Programming Languages,* June 1978.

[DoD79]
Department of Defense, *Revised Steelman Requirements for High Order Computer Programming Languages,* 1979.

[DoD80]
Department of Defense, *Requirements for Ada Programming Support Environments: Stoneman,* February 1980.

[DOYL80]
Doyle, J., "A Model for Deliberation, Action and Introspection," Technical Report MIT/AI/TR-581, MIT Laboratory for Artificial Intelligence, 1980.

[DR79]
Davis, A. M., and T. G. Rauscher, "Formal Techniques and Automatic Processing to Ensure Correctness in Requirements Specifications," *Proc. IEEE Conference on Specifications of Reliable Software,* IEEE Catalog No. 79 CH1401-9C, 1979, pp. 15-35.

[DT80]
Deutsch, L. P., and E. A. Taft, "Requirements for and Experimental Programming Environment," Xerox PARC Report CSL-80-10, 1980.

[DV77]
Davis, C. G., and C. R. Vick, "The Software Development System," *IEEE Transactions on Software Engineering,* Vol. SE-3, No. 1, January 1977.

[EARL71]
Earley, J., "Toward an Understanding of Data Structures," *Communications of the ACM,* Vol. 14, No. 10, October 1971, pp. 617-627.

[EGL76]
Eswaren, K. P., J. N. Gray, R. A. Lorie, and I. L. Traiger, "The Notions of Consistency and Predicate Locks in a Database System," *Communications of the ACM*, Vol. 19, No. 11, November 1976.

[ESWA76]
Eswaren, K. P., "Specifications, Implementations and Interactions of a Trigger Subsystem in an Integrated Database System," IBM Research Report RJ1820, San Jose, Calif., August 1976.

[FAHL79]
Fahlman, S. E., *NETL: A System for Representing and Using Real-World Knowledge*, MIT Press, 1979.

[FALK80]
Falkenberg, E. D., "Conceptualization of Data," *Infotech State-of-the-Art Report on Data Design,* Pergamon Infotech Limited, London, 1980.

[FAUS81]
Faust, G., "Semiautomatic Translation of COBOL into HIBOL," M.S. thesis (Technical Report MIT/LCS/TR-256), MIT Laboratory for Computer Science, March 1981.

[FEIG77]
Feigenbaum, E. A., "The Art of Artificial Intelligence: Themes and Case Studies of Knowledge Engineering," *Proc. 5th International Joint Conference on Artificial Intelligence,* Cambridge, Mass., August 1977.

[FIND79]
Findler, N. V., *Associative Networks: Representation and Use of Knowledge by Computer*, Academic Press, New York, 1979.

[FLOY67]
Floyd, R. W., "Assigning Meanings to Programs," in J. T. Schwartz (ed.), *Proc. Symposium in Applied Mathematics,* Vol. 19, American Mathematical Society, 1967, pp. 19-32.

[FN79]
Feiertag, R., and P. G. Neumann, "The Foundations of a Provably Secure Operating System (PSOS)," *Proc. National Computer Conference,* 1979, pp. 329-334.

[FOGG82]
Fogg, D., "Parser Support for Abstract Data Types in INGRES," Masters Report, Univ. of California, Berkeley, September 1982.

[FW76a]
Friedman, D. P., and D. S. Wise, "CONS Should Not Evaluate its Arguments," in *Automata, Languages, and Programming*, Edinburgh Univ. Press, Edinburgh, Scotland, 1976.

[FW76b]
Friedman, D. P., and D. S. Wise, "The Impact of Applicative Programming on Multiprocessing," *Proc. ACM International Conference on Parallel Processing,* 1976, pp. 263-272.

[GANE80]
Ganes, C. P., "Data Design in Structured System Analysis," in P. Freeman and A. I. Wasserman (eds.), *Tutorial on Software Design Techniques,* 1980.

[GBM82]
Greenspan, S., A. T. Borgida, and J. Mylopoulos, "Capturing More World Knowledge in the Requirements Specification," *Proc. 6th International Conference on Software Engineering,* Tokyo, Japan, 1982.

[GERH75]
Gerhart, S. L., "Knowledge About Programs: a Model and Case Study," *Proc. of International Conference on Reliable Software,* June 1975, pp. 88-95.

[GH78]
Guttag, J. V., and J. J. Horning, "The Algebraic Specification of Abstract Data Types," *Acta Informatica*, Vol. 10, 1978, pp. 27-52.

[GH80]
Guttag, J. V., and J. J. Horning, "Formal Specification as a Design Tool," *Proc. ACM Symposium on Principles of Programming Languages,* SIGACT and SIGPLAN, January 1980, pp. 251-261.

[GHM78]
Guttag, J. V., E. Horowitz, and D. R. Musser, "Abstract Data Types and Software Validation," *Communications of the ACM,* Vol. 21, No. 12, December 1978, pp. 1048-1064.

[GKB82]
Gustafsson, M. R., T. Karlsson, and Bubenko, J. A., Jr., "A Declarative Approach to Conceptual Information Modelling," in [OSV82], pp. 93-142.

[GM78]
Gallaire, H., and J. Minker (eds.), *Logic and Data Bases*, Plenum Press, New York, 1978.

[GM80]
Goodenough, J. B., and C. L. McGowan, "Software Quality Assurance: Testing and Validation," *Proc. IEEE,* Vol. 68, No. 9, September 1980.

[GMS77]
Geschke, C. M., J. H. Morris, Jr., and E. H. Satterthwaite, "Early Experience with Mesa," *Communications of the ACM,* Vol. 20, No. 8, August 1977, pp. 540-553.

[GMW79]
Gordon, M. J., A. J. Milner, and C. P. Wadsworth, "Edinburgh LCF," *Lecture Notes in Computer Science,* No. 78, Springer-Verlag, New York, 1979.

[GOLD73]
Goldberg, J., "Proceedings of a Symposium on the High Cost of Software," Technical Report, Stanford Research Institute, Stanford, Calif., September 1973.

[GOOD77]
Good, D. I., "Constructing Verified and Reliable Communications Processing Systems," *Software Engineering Notes,* Vol. 2, No. 5, October 1977, pp. 8-13.

[GP77]
Goldstein, I., and S. Papert, "Artificial Intelligence, Language, and the Study of Knowledge," *Cognitive Science,* Vol. 1, No. 1, 1977.

[GR77]
Goldstein, I., and R. B. Roberts, "NUDGE: A Knowledge-Based Scheduling Program," *Proc. 5th International Joint Conference on Artificial Intelligence,* Cambridge, Mass., August 1977.

[GRAY78]
Gray, J. N., "Notes on Data Base Operating Systems," *Proc. Advanced Course on Operating Systems,* Munich, West Germany, in *Lecture Notes in Computer Science,* No. 60, Springer-Verlag, New York, 1978.

[GREE69a]
Green, C., "The Application of Theorem Proving to Question-Answering Systems," Ph.D. thesis, Dept. of Electrical Engineering, Stanford Univ., 1969.

[GREE69b]
Green, C., "Theorem Proving by Resolution as a Basis for Question-Answering Systems," in D. Michie and B. Meltzer (eds.), *Machine Intelligence 4*, Edinburgh Univ. Press, Edinburgh, Scotland, 1969.

[GRIF76]
Griffiths, P., and B. Wade, "An Authorization Mechanism for a Relational Data Base System," *ACM Transactions on Database Systems,* Vol. 2, No. 3, September 1976.

[GTW78]
Goguen, J. A., J. W. Thatcher, and E. G. Wagner, "An Initial Algebra Approach to the Specification, Correctness, and Implementation of Abstract Data Types," in R. Yeh (ed.), *Current Trends in Programming Methodology,* Vol. IV, Prentice-Hall, Englewood Cliffs, N.J., 1978.

[GUAR78]
Guarino, L. R., "The Evolution of Abstraction in Programming Languages," Technical Report CMU-CS-78-120, Carnegie-Mellon Univ., May 1978.

[GUTT77]
Guttag, J. V., "Abstract Data Types and the Development of Data Structures," *Communications of the ACM,* Vol. 20, No. 6, June 1977, pp. 396-404.

[GUTT80]
Guttag, J. V., "Notes on Type Abstraction (Version 2)," *IEEE Transactions on Software Engineering,* Vol. SE-6, No. 1, January 1980, pp. 13-23.

[GW79]
Gerhart, S. L., and D. S. Wile, "Preliminary Report on the Delta Experiment: Specification and Verification of a Multiple-User File Updating Module," *Proc. IEEE Conference on Specifications of Reliable Software,* IEEE Catalog No. 79 CH1401-9C, 1979, pp. 198-211.

[GY76]
Gerhart, S. L., and L. Yelowitz, "Observations of Fallibility in Applications of Modern Programming Methodologies," *IEEE Transactions on Software Engineering,* Vol. SE-2, No. 5, September 1976, pp. 195-207.

[HABE73]
Habermann, A. N., "Critical Comments on the Programming Language Pascal," *Acta Informatica,* Vol. 3, 1973, pp. 47-57.

[HAL79]
Hewitt C., G. Attardi, and H. Lieberman, "Specifying and Proving Properties of Guardians for Distributed Systems," *Proc. Conference on Semantics of Concurrent Computation,* INRIA, Evian, France, July 1979.

[HARD80]
Hardgrave, W. T., "Positional Set Notation," internal report, National Bureau of Standards, February 1980.

[HAS80]
Hewitt, C., G. Attardi, and M. Simi, "Knowledge Embedding with a Description System," *Proc. 1st AAAI National Conference,* August 1980.

[HAYE74]
Hayes, P. J., "Some Problems and Non-Problems in Representation Theory," *Proc. AISB Summer Conference,* Essex Univ., Essex, Great Britian, 1974.

[HAYE77]
Hayes, P. J., "In Defense of Logic," *Proc. 5th International Joint Conference on Artificial Intelligence,* Cambridge, Mass., 1977, pp. 559-565.

[HAYE78]
Hayes, P. J., "The Ontology of Liquids," unpublished manuscript, 1978.

[HAYE79]
Hayes, P. J., "The Logic of Frames," in D. Metzing (ed.), *Frame Conceptions and Text Understanding,* Walter de Gruyter and Co., Berlin, 1979, pp. 46-61.

[HAZE76]
Hazen, A., "Expressive Completeness in Modal Language," *Journal of Philosophical Logic,* Vol. 5, 1976.

[HB77]
Hewitt, C., and H. Baker, "Laws for Communicating Parallel Processes," *Proc. 1977 IFIP Congress,* 1977.

[HBS73]
Hewitt, C., P. Bishop, and R. Steiger, "A Universal Modular ACTOR Formalism for Artificial Intelligence," *Proc. International Joint Conference on Artificial Intelligence,* Palo Alto, Calif., August 1973.

[HEND75]
Hendrix, G., "Expanding the Utility of Semantic Networks through Partitioning," *Proc. International Joint Conference on Artificial Intelligence,* Tbilisi, USSR, September 1975.

[HENI79]
Heninger, K. L., "Specifying Software Requirements for Complex Systems: New Techniques and Their Applications," *Proc. IEEE Conference on Specifications of Reliable Software,* IEEE Catalog No. 79 CH1401-9C, 1979, pp. 1-14.

[HENK50]
Henkin, L., "Completeness in the Theory of Types," *Journal of Symbolic Logic,* Vol. 15, 1950, pp. 81-91.

[HEWI69]
Hewitt, C. E., "PLANNER: A Language for Proving Theorems in Robots," *Proc. International Joint Conference on Artificial Intelligence,* Washington, D.C., May 1969.

[HEWI71]
Hewitt, C. E., "PLANNER: A Language for Proving Theorems in Robots," *Proc. International Joint Conference on Artificial Intelligence,* London, Great Britian, August 1971.

[HEWI72]
Hewitt, C. E., *Description and Theoretical Analysis (Using Schemata) of PLANNER: A Language for Proving Theorems and Manipulating Models in a Robot,* Ph.D. thesis, Dept. of Mathematics, MIT, 1972.

[HEWI75]
Hewitt, C. E., "How To Use What You Know," *Proc. International Joint Conference on Artificial Intelligence,* Tbilisi, USSR, August 1975.

[HEWI77]
Hewitt, C. E., "Viewing Control Structures as Patterns of Passing Messages," *Artificial Intelligence,* Vol. 8, 1977, pp. 323-364.

[HEWI80]
Hewitt, C. E., "The Apiary Network Architecture for Knowledgeable Systems," *Conference Record of the 1980 Lisp Conference,* Stanford Univ., Stanford, Calif., August 1980.

[HG74]
Hewitt, C. E., and I. Greiff, "Actor Semantics of PLANNER-73," Working Paper No. 81, MIT Laboratory for Artificial Intelligence, 1974.

[HINT62]
Hintikka, J., *Knowledge and Belief: An Introduction to the Logic of the Two Notions,* Cornell Univ. Press, 1962.

[HK81]
Hecht, M. S., and L. Kershberg, "Update Semantics for the Functional Data Model," Data Base Research Report No. 4, Bell Labs, Holmdell, N.J., 1981.

[HL82]
Haskin, R. L., and R. A. Lorie, "On Extending the Functions of a Relational Database System," *Proc. 1982 ACM SIGMOD International Conference on the Management of Data,* Orlando, Fla., 1982, pp. 207-212.

[HM75]
Hammer, M., and D. McLeod, "Semantic Integrity in a Relational Database System," *Proc. 1st International Conference on Very Large Databases,* Framingham, Mass., September 1975, pp. 25-47.

[HM76]
Hammer, M., and D. McLeod, "A Framework for Database Semantic Integrity," *Proc. 2nd International Conference on Software Engineering,* San Francisco, Calif., October 1976.

[HM78]
Hammer, M., and D. McLeod, "The Semantic Data Model: a Modelling Mechanism for Database Applications," *Proc. 1978 ACM SIGMOD International Conference on the Management of Data,* Austin, Texas, May-June 1978.

[HM81]
Hammer, M., and D. McLeod, "Database Description with SDM: A Semantic Database Model," *ACM Transactions on Database Systems,* Vol. 6, No. 3, September 1981.

[HOAR69]
Hoare, C. A. R., "An Axiomatic Basis for Computer Programming," *Communications of the ACM,* Vol. 12, October 1969, pp. 576-580, 583.

[HOAR72a]
Hoare, C. A. R., "Proof of Correctness of Data Representations," *Acta Informatica,* Vol. 1, No. 4, 1972, pp. 271-281.

[HOAR72b]
Hoare, C. A. R., "Notes on Data Structuring," in O.-J. Dahl, E. W. Dijkstra, and C. A. R. Hoare (eds.), *Structured Programming,* Academic Press, New York, 1972, pp. 83-174.

[HOAR78]
Hoare, C. A. R., "Communicating Sequential Processes," *Communications of the ACM,* Vol. 21, No. 8, August 1978.

[HOT76]
Hall, P., J. Owlett, and S. J. P. Todd, "Relations and Entities," in J. M. Nijssen (ed.), *Modelling in Database Management Systems,* Elsevier North-Holland, New York, 1976.

[HOUS77]
Housel, B. C., "A Unified Approach to Data Conversion," *Proc. 3rd International Conference on Very Large Databases,* Tokyo, Japan, 1977.

[HOWD79]
Howden, W. E., "An Analysis of Software Validation Techniques for Scientific Programs," Technical Report DM-171-IR, Dept. of Mathematics, Univ. of Victoria, Victoria, B.C., Canada, March 1979.

[HR79]
Hunt, H. B., and D. J. Rosenkrantz, "The Complexity of Testing Predicate Locks," *Proc. 1979 ACM SIGMOD International Conference on the Management of Data,* Boston, Mass., May 1979.

[HSW75]
Held, G., M. Stonebraker, and E. Wong, "INGRES: A Relational Database System," *Proc. AFIPS 1975 National Computer Conference,* Vol. 44, 1975.

[HW73]
Hoare, C. A. R., and N. Wirth, "An Axiomatic Definition of the Programming Language PASCAL," *Acta Informatica*, Vol. 2, No. 4, 1973, pp. 335-355.

[HWY79]
Housel, B. C., V. Waddle, and S. B. Yao, "The Functional Dependency Model for Logical Database Design," *Proc. 5th International Conference on Very Large Databases,* Rio de Janeiro, Brazil, October 1979.

[HY79]
Hevner, A. R., and S. B. Yao, "Query Processing in Distributed Database Systems," *IEEE Transactions on Software Engineering,* Vol. SE-5, No. 3, 1979.

[IBHK79]
Ichbiah, J. D., J. P. G. Barnes, J.-C. Heliard, B. Krieg-Brueckner, O. Roubine, and B. A. Wichmann, "Rationale for the Design of the Ada Programming Language," *SIGPLAN Notices,* Vol. 14, No. 6, Part B, 1979.

[IEEE79a]
IEEE Computer Society (eds.), *Workshop on Quantitative Software Models for Reliability, Complexity, and Cost: an Assessment of the State of the Art,* IEEE Catalog No. TH0067-9, 1979.

[IEEE79b]
IEEE Computer Society (eds.), *Proc. Conference on Specifications of Reliable Software,* IEEE Catalog No. 79 CH1401-9C, 1979.

[IKWL79]
Ichbiah, J. D., B. Krieg-Brueckner, B. A. Wichmann, H. F. Ledgard, J.-C. Heliard, J.-R. Abrial, J. P. G. Barnes, and O. Roubine, "Preliminary Ada Reference Manual," *SIGPLAN Notices,* Vol. 14, No. 6, Part A, 1979.

[IKWL80]
Ichbiah, J. D., B. Krieg-Brueckner, B. A. Wichmann, H. F. Ledgard, J.-C. Heliard, J.-R. Abrial, J. P. G. Barnes, M. Woodger, O. Roubine, P. N. Hilfinger, and R. Firth, *Reference Manual for the Ada Programming Language: Proposed Standard Document,* Department of Defense, US Government Printing Office 008-000-00354-8, July 1980; also in: *Lecture Notes in Computer Science,* No. 106, Springer-Verlag, New York, 1981.

[IKWL82]
Ichbiah, J. D., B. Krieg-Brueckner, B. A. Wichmann, H. F. Ledgard, J.-C. Heliard, J.-L. Gailly, J.-R. Abrial, J. P. G. Barnes, M. Woodger, O. Roubine, P. N. Hilfinger, and R. Firth, *Reference Manual for the Ada Programming Language,* Draft Revised MIL-STD 1815; Draft Proposed ANSI Standard Document for Editorial Review, US Department of Defense, Honeywell Inc., and Alsys, July 1982; also available from AdaTEC, ACM order no. 825820.

[IMB81]
Islam, N., T. J. Myers, and P. Broome, "A Simple Optimizer for FP-like Languages," *Proc. ACM Conference on Functional Programming and Architecture,* New Hampshire, 1981.

[INGA78]
Ingalls, D. H., "The Smalltalk-76 Programming System: Design and Implementation," *Conference Record of the Fifth Annual ACM Symposium on Programming Languages,* Tucson, Arizona, January 1978.

[IOS79]
International Organization for Standardization, *Draft Specification for the Computer Programming Language Pascal,* ISO/TC 97/SC 5 N, 1979.

[ISRA80]
Israel, D. J., "What's Wrong with Non-Monotonic Logic?," *Proc. 1st National Conference on Artifical Intelligence,* American Association for Artificial Intelligence, Stanford, Calif., 1980, pp. 99-101.

[ISRA82]
Israel, D. J., "On Interpreting Semantic Network Formalisms," *International Journal of Computer Mathematics,* (to appear in a special issue on Computational Linguistics edited by N. Cercone); also available as BBN Report No. 5117, Bolt, Beranek and Newman Inc., Cambridge, Mass., 1982.

[IVER79]
Iverson, K. E., "Operators," *ACM Transactions on Programming Languages and Systems,* Vol. 1, No. 2, 1979.

[JACO82]
Jacobs, B. E., "On Database Logic," *Journal of the ACM,* Vol. 29, No. 2, April 1982, pp. 310-332.

[JL76]
Jones, A. K., and B. H. Liskov, "An Access Control Facility for Programming Languages," MIT Computation Structures Group and Carnegie-Mellon Univ., MIT Memo 137, 1976.

[JS82]
Jarke, M., and J. W. Schmidt, "Query Processing Strategies in the Pascal/R Relational Database Management System," *Proc. 1982 ACM SIGMOD International Conference on the Management of Data,* Orlando, Fla., June 1982.

[JW74]
Jensen, K., and N. Wirth, *Pascal User Manual and Report,* Springer-Verlag, New York, 1974.

[KAHN79]
Kahn, K. M., "Creation of Computer Animation from Story Descriptions," Ph.D. thesis, MIT, 1979.

[KENT78]
Kent, W., *Data and Reality,* Elsevier North-Holland, New York, 1978.

[KH81]
Kornfeld, W. A., and Hewitt, C., "The Scientific Community Metaphor," *IEEE Transactions on Systems, Man, and Cybernetics,* Vol. SMC-11, No. 1, January 1981.

[KING82]
King, R., "A Semantics-Based Methodology for Database Design and Evolution," Ph.D. thesis (Technical Report), Computer Science Dept., Univ. of Southern California, October 1982.

[KL80a]
Keller, R. M., and G. Lindstrom, "Parallelism in Functional Programming through Applicative Loops," Technical Report, Univ. of Utah, 1980.

[KL80b]
Krieg-Brueckner, B., and D.C. Luckham, "Anna: Towards a Language for Annotating Ada Programs," *SIGPLAN Notices,* Vol. 15, No. 11, 1980, pp. 128-138.

[KLEE71]
Kleene, S.C., *Introduction to Metamathematics,* Elsevier North-Holland, New York, 1971.

[KLVO82]
Krieg-Brueckner, B., D.C. Luckham, F.W. von Henke, and O. Owe, *Anna: a Language for Annotating Ada Programs,* Springer-Verlag, New York (to appear).

[KM82a]
King, R., and D. McLeod, "Semantic Database Models," in S.B. Yao (ed.), *Principles of Database Design,* Prentice-Hall, Englewood Cliffs, N.J. (to appear).

[KM82b]
King, R., and D. McLeod, "The Event Database Specification Model," *Proc. Second International Conference on Databases: Improving Usability and Responsiveness,* Jerusalem, Israel, June 1982.

[KM82c]
King, R., and D. McLeod, "A Methodology and Tool for Database Life-Cycle Management," Technical Report, Computer Science Dept., Univ. of Southern California, November 1982 (submitted for publication).

[KNUT73]
Knuth, D.E., *The Art of Computer Programming, Vol. 1: Fundamental Algorithms,* Second edition, Addison-Wesley, Reading, Mass., 1973.

[KOLA82]
Kolata, G., "How Can Computers Get Common Sense?," *Science,* Vol. 217, No. 4566, September 24, 1982.

[KONO82]
Konolige, K., "Circumscriptive Ignorance," *Proc. AAAI National Conference,* Pittsburgh, Penn., August 1982.

[KORN82]
Kornfeld, W., "Concepts in Parallel Problem Solving," Ph.D. thesis, MIT, 1982.

[KOWA74]
Kowalski, R., "Predicate Logic as a Programming Language," *Proc. IFIP Congress,* 1974, pp. 569-574.

[KOWA78]
Kowalski, R., "Logic for Data Description," in [GM78].

[KOWA79]
Kowalski, R., *Logic for Problem Solving,* Elsevier North-Holland, New York, 1979.

[KP76]
Kernighan, B. W., and P. J. Plauger, *Software Tools,* Addison-Wesley, Reading, Mass., 1976.

[KR81]
Kung, H. T., and J. T. Robinson, "On Optimistic Methods for Concurrency Control," *ACM Transactions on Database Systems,* Vol. 6, No. 2, June 1981.

[KUHN67]
Kuhns, J. L., "Answering Questions by Computer—a Logical Study," Memorandum RM 2428 PR, Rand Corporation, Santa Monica, Calif., December 1967.

[LAND65]
Landin, P. J., "A Correspondence Between ALGOL 60 and Church's Lambda Notation," *Communications of the ACM,* Vol. 8, Nos. 2 and 3, 1965.

[LAND66]
Landin, P. J., "The Next 700 Programming Languages," *Communications of the ACM,* Vol. 9, No. 3, 1966.

[LENA77]
Lenat, D. B., "The Ubiquity of Discovery," *Proc. International Joint Conference on Artificial Intelligence,* Cambridge, Mass., August 1977.

[LEVE81a]
Levesque, H., "A Formal Treatment of Incomplete Knowledge Bases," Ph.D. thesis, Dept. of Computer Science, Univ. of Toronto, 1981; also available as Technical Report No. 3, Fairchild Laboratory for Artificial Intelligence Research, Palo Alto, Calif.

[LEVE81b]
Levesque, H., "The Interaction with Incomplete Knowledge Bases: a Formal Treatment," *Proc. International Joint Conference on Artificial Intelligence*, Univ. of British Columbia, Vancouver, B.C., Canada, 1981.

[LEVI77]
Levin, R., "Program Structures for Exceptional Condition Handling," Ph.D. thesis, Carnegie-Mellon Univ., June 1977.

[LEWI68]
Lewis, D., "Counterpart Theory and Quantified Modal Logic," *Journal of Philosophy,* Vol. 65, 1968, pp. 113-126.

[LGHL78]
London, R. L., J. V. Guttag, J. J. Horning, B. W. Lampson, J. G. Mitchell, and G. J. Popek, "Proof Rules for the Programming Language Euclid," *Acta Informatica,* Vol. 10, No. 1, 1978 pp. 1-26.

[LHLM77]
Lampson, B. W., J. J. Horning, R. L. London, J. G. Mitchell, and G. J. Popek, "Report on the Programming Language Euclid," *SIGPLAN Notices,* Vol. 12, No. 2, February 1977, pp. 1-79.

[LIEB81a]
Lieberman, H., "A Preview of Act-1," AI Memo No. 625, MIT Artificial Intelligence Laboratory, 1981.

[LIEB81b]
Lieberman, H., "Thinking About Lots of Things At Once Without Getting Confused: Parallelism in Act-1," AI Memo No. 626, MIT Artificial Intelligence Laboratory, 1981.

[LIPS78]
Lipski, W., Jr., "On Semantic Issues Connected with Incomplete Information Data Bases," PAS Report 325, Institute of Computer Science, Warsaw, Poland, 1978.

[LIPS79]
Lipski, W., Jr., "On Semantic Issues Connected with Incomplete Information Databases," *ACM Transactions on Database Systems,* Vol. 4, No. 3, September 1979, pp. 262-296.

[LISK77]
Liskov, B., *et al.,* "Abstraction Mechanisms in CLU," *Communications of the ACM,* Vol. 20, No. 8, August 1977, pp. 564-576.

[LM79]
Levesque, H., and J. Mylopoulos, "A Procedural Semantics for Semantic Networks," in [FIND79].

[LMW79]
Linger, R. C., H. D. Mills, and B. I. Witt, *Structured Programming Theory and Practice*, Addison-Wesley, Reading, Mass., 1979.

[LOCK79]
Lockmann, P. *et al.,* "Data Abstractions for Data Base Systems," *ACM Transactions on Database Systems,* Vol. 4, No. 1, March 1979.

[LOND75]
London, R. L., "A View of Program Verification," *Proc. International Conference on Reliable Software,* IEEE Computer Society, April 1975, pp. 534-545.

[LORI77]
Lorie, R. A., "Physical Integrity in a Large Segmented Database," *ACM Transactions on Database Systems,* Vol. 2, No. 1, March 1977.

[LS80]
Lamersdorf, W., and J. W. Schmidt, "Specification of Pascal/R," Report No. 73/74, Fachbereich Informatik, Univ. of Hamburg, July 1980.

[LSAS77]
Liskov B., A. Snyder, R. Atkinson, and C. Schaffert, "Abstraction Mechanism in CLU," *Communications of the ACM,* Vol. 20, No. 8, August 1977, pp. 564-576.

[LW76]
Lorie, R., and B. Wade, "The Compilation of a Very High Level Data Language," IBM Research Report RJ2008, San Jose, Calif., May 1977.

[LZ74]
Liskov, B., and S. Zilles, "Programming With Abstract Data Types," *SIGPLAN Notices,* Vol. 9, No. 4, April 1974, pp. 50-59.

[LZ75]
Liskov, B., and S. Zilles, "Specification Techniques for Data Abstractions," *IEEE Transactions on Software Engineering,* Vol. SE-1, No. 1, March 1975, pp. 7-19.

[LZ77]
Liskov, B., and S. Zilles, "An Introduction to Formal Specifications of Data Abstractions," in R. Yeh (ed.), *Current Trends in Programming Methodology, Vol. I,* Prentice-Hall, Englewood Cliffs, N.J., 1977.

[MANN74]
Manna, Z., *Mathematical Theory of Computation,* McGraw-Hill, New York, 1974.

[MBW78]
Mylopoulos, J., P. A. Bernstein, and H. K. T. Wong "A Preliminary Specification for TAXIS," Technical Report CCA-78-02, Computer Corporation of America, Cambridge, Mass., January 1978.

[MBW80]
Mylopoulos, J., P. A. Bernstein, and H. K. T. Wong, "A Language Facility for Designing Interactive Database-Intensive Applications," *ACM Transactions on Database Systems,* Vol. 5, No. 2, June 1980, pp. 185-207.

[MCAL80]
McAllester, D. A., "An Outlook on Truth Maintenance," Memo MIT/AIM-551, MIT Laboratory for Artificial Intelligence, August 1980.

[MCCA62]
McCarthy, J., *et al., LISP 1.5 Programmer's Manual,* MIT Press, Cambridge, Mass., 1962.

[MCCA80]
McCarthy, J., "Circumscription — A Form of Non-Monotonic Reasoning," *Artificial Intelligence,* Vol. 13, Nos. 1 and 2, April 1980, pp. 27-39.

[MCDE80]
McDermott, D., "Non-Monotonic Logic II: Non-Monotonic Modal Theories," Research Reort No. 174, Dept. of Computer Science, Yale Univ., February 1980.

[MCGE76]
McGee, W. C., "On User Criteria for Data Model Evaluation," *ACM Transactions on Database Systems,* Vol. 1, No. 4, December 1976.

[MD78]
McDermott, D., and J. Doyle, "Non-Monotonic Logic I," Memo MIT/AIM-486, MIT Laboratory for Artificial Intelligence, 1978.

[MEND64]
Mendelson, E., *Introduction to Mathematical Logic,* Van Nostrand, Princeton, N.J., 1964.

[MG77]
Miller, M. L., and I. Goldstein, "Problem Solving Grammars as Formal Tools for Intelligent CAI," *Proc. ACM,* 1977.

[MH69]
McCarthy, J., and P. Hayes, "Some Philosophical Problems from the Standpoint of Artificial Intelligence," in D. Michie and B. Meltzer (eds.), *Machine Intelligence 4,* Edinburgh Univ. Press, Edinburgh, Scotland, 1969.

[MILL76]
Millen, J. K., "Security Kernel Validation in Practice," *Communications of the ACM,* Vol. 19, No. 5, May 1976, pp. 243-250.

[MILL79]
Miller, E. (ed.), *Tutorial: Automated Tools for Software Engineering,* IEEE Computer Society, IEEE Catalog No. EHO 150-3, 1979.

[MILN78]
Milner, R., "A Theory of Type Polymorphism in Programming," *Journal of Computer and System Sciences,* Vol. 17, 1978, pp. 348-375.

[MINS75]
Minsky, M., "A Framework for Representing Knowledge," in P. Winston (ed.), *The Psychology of Computer Vision,* McGraw-Hill, New York, 1975, pp. 211-277.

[MISR78]
Misra, J., "Some Aspects of the Verification of Loop Computations," *IEEE Transactions on Software Engineering,* Vol. SE-4, No. 6, November 1978, pp. 478-485.

[MN74]
Moore, J. and A. Newell, "How can MERLIN Understand?," in L. Gregg (ed.), *Knowledge and Cognition,* Lawrence Erlbaum Associates, Hillsdale, N.J., 1974.

[MONT74]
Montague, R., "The Proper Treatment of Quantification in Ordinary English," in R. Thomason (ed.), *Formal Philosophy,* Yale Univ. Press, New Haven, 1974, pp. 247-270.

[MOOR77]
Moore, R., "Reasoning About Knowledge and Action," *Proc. 5th International Joint Conference on Artificial Intelligence,* Cambridge, Mass., August 1977.

[MOOR81]
Moore, R., "Reasoning about Knowledge and Action," Technical Note 191, Artificial Intelligence Center, SRI International, Menlo Park, 1980.

[MOOR82]
Moore, R.C., "The Role of Logic in Knowledge Representation and Commonsense Reasoning," *Proc. AAAI National Conference,* Pittsburgh, Penn., August 1982.

[MORR73a]
Morris, J.H., "Types Are Not Sets," *Proc. ACM Symposium on Principles of Programming Languages,* 1973, pp. 120-124.

[MORR73b]
Morris, J.H., "Protection in Programming Languages," *Communications of the ACM,* Vol. 16, January 1973, pp. 15-21.

[MP82]
Manola, F., and A. Pirotte, "CQLF—A Query Language for CODASYL-Type Databases," *Proc. 1982 ACM SIGMOD International Conference on the Management of Data,* Orlando, Fla., 1982.

[MPBR82]
Manola, F., A. Pirotte, B. Blaustein, and D.R. Ries, "Family of Data Model Specifications for DBMS (Database Management System) Standards," Computer Corporation of America, Cambridge, Mass., December 1982; NBS-GCR-82-419, available as NTIS Report PB83-163394.

[MS73]
McDermott, D., and G.J. Sussman, "The Conniver Reference Manual," Memo MIT/AIM-259A, MIT Laboratory for Artificial Intelligence, 1973.

[MS81]
McLeod, D., and J.M. Smith, "Abstraction in Databases," in [BZ81].

[MSHI78]
McCarthy, J., M. Sato, T. Hayashi, and S. Igarashi, "On the Model Theory of Knowledge," Memo AIM-312, Dept. of Computer Science, Stanford Univ., 1978.

[MW80]
Mylopoulos, J., and H. Wong, "Some Features of the TAXIS Data Model," *Proc. 6th International Conference on Very Large Databases,* Montreal, Que., Canada, October 1980.

[MYER81]
Myers, T.J., Ph.D. Dissertation, Univ. of Pennsylvania, 1981.

[MYLO81]
Mylopoulos, J., "An Overview of Knowledge Representation," in [BZ81].

[NEWE62]
Newell, A., "Some Problems of Basic Organization in Problem-Solving Programs," Memorandum RM-3283-PR, Rand Corporation, Santa Monica, Calif., December 1962.

[NEWE80]
Newell, A., "Physical Symbol Systems," *Cognitive Science,* Vol. 4, No. 2, April-June 1980, pp. 135-183.

[NEWE81]
Newell, A., "The Knowledge Level," *Proc. AAAI National Conference,* (presidential address) Stanford, Calif.; reprinted in *AI Magazine,* Vol. 2, No. 2, 1981.

[NG78]
Nicolas, J. M., and H. Gallaire, "Data Base: Theory vs. Interpretation," in [GM78].

[NILS71]
Nilsson, N., *Problem Solving Methods in Artificial Intelligence,* McGraw-Hill, Englewood Cliffs, N.J., 1971.

[NR69]
Naur, P., and B. Randell (eds.), *Software Engineering,* NATO, 1969 (report on a conference sponsored by the NATO Science Committee, Garmisch, West Germany, October 7-11, 1968).

[NS78]
Navathe, S. B., and M. Schkolnick, "View Representation in Logical Database Design," *Proc. 1978 ACM SIGMOD International Conference on the Management of Data,* Austin, Texas, May-June 1978.

[NY78]
Nicolas, J. M., and K. Yazdanian, "Integrity Checking in Deductive Databases," in [GM78].

[ONG82]
Ong, J., "Specification of an ADT Facility for a Relational Data Base System," Masters Report, Univ. of California, Berkeley, September 1982.

[ORGA76]
Organick, E. I. (chrm.), *Proc. of Conference on Data: Abstraction, Definition, and Structure, SIGPLAN Notices,* Vol. 11, No. 2, 1976.

[OSV82]
Olle, T. W., H. G. Sol, and A. A. Verjn-Stuart, *Information Systems Design Methodologies: A Comparative Review* (Proc. IFIP TC 8 Working Conference on Comparative Review of Information Systems Design Methodologies, Noordwijkerhout, Netherlands, May 1982), Elsevier North-Holland, Amsterdam, The Netherlands, 1982.

[OVER81]
Overmeyer, R., "A Time Expert for INGRES," M.S. thesis, Univ. of California, Berkeley, August 1981.

[PARN71]
Parnas, D. L., "Information Distribution Aspects of Design Methodology," *Proc. of IFIP Congress,* Booklet TA-3, 1971, pp. 26-30.

[PARN72a]
Parnas, D. L., "A Technique for Software Module Specification with Examples," *Communications of the ACM,* Vol. 15, May 1972, pp. 330-336.

[PARN72b]
Parnas, D. L., "On the Criteria to be Used in Decomposing Systems into Modules," *Communications of the ACM,* Vol. 15, No. 12, December 1972.

[PETE80]
Peters, L., "Software Design Engineering," *Proc. IEEE,* Vol. 68, No. 9, September 1980.

[POPL73]
Pople, H. E., "On the Mechanization of Abductive Logic," *Proc. International Joint Conference on Artificial Intelligence,* Palo Alto, Calif., August 1973.

[POWE82]
Powell, M., private communication.

[QUIL68]
Quillian, M. R. "Semantic Memory," in M. Minsky (ed.), *Semantic Information Processing,* MIT Press, 1968.

[RAMS79]
Ramshaw, L. H., "Formalizing the Analysis of Algorithms," Ph.D. thesis, Stanford Univ., 1979.

[RAPH71]
Raphael, B., "The Frame Problem in Problem-Solving systems," in N. V. Findler and B. Meltzer (eds.), *Artificial Intelligence and Heuristic Programming,* Edinburgh Univ. Press, Edinburgh, Scotland, 1971.

[RB82a]
Ridjanovic, D., and M. L. Brodie, "Semantic Data Model-Driven Design, Specification and Verification of Interactive Database Transactions," Computer Corporation of America, Cambridge, Mass., April 1982.

[RB82b]
Ridjanovic, D., and M. L. Brodie, "Defining Database Dynamics with Attribute Grammars," *Information Processing Letters,* Vol. 14, No. 3, May 1982.

[RB82c]
Ridjanovic, D., and M. L. Brodie, "Definition of Fundamental Concepts and Tools for Semantic Modelling of Data and Associated Operations," submitted for publication.

[RB82d]
Ridjanovic, D., and M. L. Brodie, "Disciplined Methodology for Database Transaction Design," submitted for publication.

[RB82e]
Ridjanovic, D., and M.L. Brodie, "Functional Specification and Implementation Verification of Database Transactions," submitted for publication.

[RB82f]
Ridjanovic, D., and M.L. Brodie, "Conceptual Modelling of Office Procedures," submitted for publication.

[RB83]
Ridjanovic, D., and M.L. Brodie, "Action and Transaction Skeletons: High Level Language Constructs for Database Transactions," *Proc. 1983 SIGPLAN Conference,* San Francisco, Calif., June 1983.

[REIT77]
Reiter, R., *An Approach to Deductive Question-Answering,* BBN Technical Report 3649, Bolt, Beranek and Newman, Inc., Cambridge, Mass., September 1977.

[REIT78a]
Reiter, R., "Deductive Question-Answering on Relational Databases," in [GM78], pp. 149-177.

[REIT78b]
Reiter, R., "On Closed World Data Bases," in [GM78], pp. 55-76.

[REIT78c]
Reiter, R., "On Reasoning by Default," *Proc. Second TINLAP Conference,* Urbana, Ill., July 1978, pp. 210-218.

[REIT80a]
Reiter, R., "Equality and Domain Closure in First Order Databases," *Journal of the ACM,* Vol. 27, No. 2, 1980, pp. 235-249.

[REIT80b]
Reiter, R., "Databases: A Logical Perspective," in [BZ80], pp. 174-176.

[REIT80c]
Reiter, R., "A Logic for Default Reasoning," *Artificial Intelligence,* Vol. 13, 1980, pp. 81-132.

[REIT81]
Reiter, R., "On Interacting Defaults," *Proc. International Joint Conference on Artificial Intelligence,* Vancouver, B.C., Canada, 1981.

[REIT82]
Reiter, R., "Circumscription Implies Predicate Completion (Sometimes)," *Proc. AAAI National Conference,* Pittsburgh, Penn., August 1982.

[REYN79]
Reynolds, J.C., "Reasoning About Arrays," *Communications of the ACM,* Vol. 22, No. 5, May 1979, pp. 290-298.

[RICH80]
Rich, C., "Inspection Methods in Programming," Ph.D. thesis (Technical Report MIT/AI/TR-604), MIT Laboratory for Artificial Intelligence, December 1980.

[RICH81]
Rich, C., "Multiple Points of View in Modeling Programs," *Proc. Workshop on Data Abstraction, Data Bases and Conceptual Modeling, SIGPLAN Notices,* Vol. 16, No. 1, January 1981, pp. 177-179.

[RICH82]
Rich, C., "Knowledge Representation Languages and Predicate Calculus: How to Have Your Cake and Eat it Too," *Proc. AAAI National Conference,* Pittsburgh, Penn., August 1982.

[ROSC75]
Rosch, E., "Cognitive Representations of Semantic Categories," *Journal of Experimental Psychology: General,* Vol. 104, 1975, pp. 192-233.

[ROSS77]
Ross, D.T., "Structured Analysis (SA): A Language for Communicating Ideas," *IEEE Transactions on Software Engineering,* Vol. SE-3, No. 1, January 1977.

[ROSS82]
Rosser, B.J., "Highlights of the History of the Lambda-Calculus," *Conference Record ACM Symposium on Lisp and Functional Programming,* Plymouth, Mass., August 1982.

[ROUS77]
Roussopoulos, N., "ADD: Algebraic Data Definition," *Proc. 6th Texas Conference on Computing Systems,* Austin, Texas, November 1977.

[ROUT79]
Routley, R., unpublished manuscript, 1980.

[ROWE82]
Rowe, L.A., *et al.,* "A Form Application Development System," *Proc. 1982 ACM SIGMOD International Conference on the Management of Data,* Orlando, Fla., June 1982.

[RS76]
Rich, C., and H.E. Shrobe, "Initial Report On A LISP Programmer's Apprentice," M.S. thesis (Technical Report MIT/AI/TR-354), MIT Laboratory for Artificial Intelligence, December 1976.

[RS79]
Rowe, L.A., and K.A. Schoens, "Data Abstraction, Views and Updates in RIGEL," *Proc. 1979 ACM SIGMOD International Conference on the Management of Data,* Boston, Mass., May 1979, pp. 71-81.

[RS81]
Reimer, M., and J.W. Schmidt, "Transaction Procedures with Relational Parameters," Report No. 45, Institut fuer Informatik, ETH Zurich, October 1981.

[RSW79]
Rich, C., H. E. Shrobe, and R. C. Waters, "An Overview of the Programmer's Apprentice," *Proc. 6th International Joint Conference on Artificial Intelligence,* Tokyo, Japan, August 1979.

[RSWS78]
Rich, C., H. E. Shrobe, R. C. Waters, G. J. Sussman, and C. E. Hewitt, "Programming Viewed as an Engineering Activity," NSF Proposal, (Memo MIT/AIM-459), MIT Laboratory for Artificial Intelligence, January 1978.

[RUTH73]
Ruth, G., "Analysis of Algorithm Implementations," Ph.D. thesis (MIT Project MAC Technical Report 130), 1973.

[SACE74]
Sacerdoti, E. D., "Planning in a Hierarchy of Abstraction Spaces," *Artificial Intelligence,* Vol. 5, No. 2, 1974, pp. 115-135.

[SC75]
Smith, J. M., and P. Y. Chang, "Optimizing the Performance of a Relational Algebra Database Interface," *Communications of the ACM,* Vol. 18, No. 10, 1975.

[SCHM77]
Schmidt, J. W., "Some High Level Language Constructs for Data of Type Relation," *ACM Transactions on Database Systems,* Vol. 2, No. 3, September 1977.

[SCHM78]
Schmidt, J. W., "Type Concepts for Database Definition," *Proc. International Conference on Data Bases,* Haifa, Israel, August 1978.

[SCHM82]
Schmidt, J. W., "Generalized Data Definition and Selection Mechanisms," Fachbereich Informatik, Univ. of Hamburg, 1982 (to appear).

[SCHU71]
Schuman, S. A. (ed.), *Proc. International Symposium on Extensible Languages, SIGPLAN Notices,* Vol. 6, No. 12, December 1971.

[SCHU76a]
Schubert, L. K., "Extending the Expressive Power of Semantic Networks," *Artificial Intelligence,* Vol. 7, No. 2, Summer 1976, pp. 163-198.

[SCHU76b]
Schuman, S. A., "On Generic Functions," in S. A. Schuman (ed.), *New Directions in Algorithmic Languages—1975,* IRIA, Le Chesnay, France, 1976, pp. 169-192.

[SCHW75]
Schwartz, J. T., "On Programming," Interim Report on the SETL Project, Courant Institute of Mathematical Sciences, New York Univ., June 1975.

[SCOT72]
Scott, D.S., "Lattice Theoretic Models for Various Type-free Calculi," *Proc. 4th International Congress on Logic, Methodology and the Philosophy of Science,* Bucharest, Hungary, 1972.

[SE74]
Stonebraker, M., and E. Wong, "Access Control in a Relational Data Base System by Query Modification," *Proc. ACM Annual Conference,* San Diego, Calif., November 1974.

[SFFH78]
Shaw, M., G. Feldman, R. Fitzgerald, P. Hilfinger, I. Kimura, R. London, J. Rosenberg, and W.A. Wulf, "Validating the Utility of Abstraction Techniques," *Proc. ACM National Conference,* December 1978, pp. 106-110.

[SFL81]
Smith, J.M., S. Fox, and T. Landers, "Reference Manual for ADAPLEX," Technical Report CCA-81-02, Computer Corporation of America, Cambridge, Mass., 1981.

[SGC79]
Schubert, L.K., R.G. Goebel, and N.J. Cercone, "The Structure and Organization of a Semantic Net for Comprehension and Inference," in [FIND79], pp. 121-175.

[SHAP79]
Shapiro, S., "The SNePs Semantic Network Processing System," in [FIND79].

[SHAW79]
Shaw, M., "A Formal System for Specifying and Verifying Program Performance," Technical Report CMU-CS-79-129, Carnegie-Mellon Univ., June 1979.

[SHIP81]
Shipman, D.W., "The Functional Data Model and the Data Language DAPLEX," *ACM Transactions on Database Systems,* Vol. 6, No. 1, March 1981.

[SHM77]
Szolovits, P., L. Hawkinson, and W.A. Martin, "An Overview of OWL, A Language for Knowledge Representation," Technical Memo MIT/LCS/TM-86, MIT Laboratory for Computer Science, 1977.

[SHRO79]
Shrobe, H.E., "Dependency Directed Reasoning for Complex Program Understanding," Ph.D. thesis (Technical Report MIT/AI/TR-503), MIT Laboratory for Artificial Intelligence, April 1979.

[SK77]
Sibley, E.H., and L. Kershberg, "Data Architecture and Data Model Considerations," *Proc. AFIPS National Computer Conference,* Dallas, Texas, 1977.

[SK80a]
Silberschatz, A., and Z. Kedem, "Consistency in Hierarchical Database Systems," *Journal of the ACM,* Vol. 27, No. 1, January 1980.

[SK80b]
Stonebraker, M., and K. Keller, "Embedding Hypothetical Data Bases and Expert Knowledge in a Data Manager," *Proc. 1980 ACM SIGMOD International Conference on the Management of Data,* Santa Monica, Calif., May 1980.

[SL79]
Su, S. Y. W., and D. H. Lo, "A Semantic Association Model for Conceptual Database Design," *Proc. International Conference on the Entity-Relationship Approach to Systems Analysis and Design,* Los Angeles, Calif., December 1979.

[SM72]
Sussman, G. J., and D. McDermott, "Why Conniving is Better Than Planning," Memo MIT/AIM-255A, MIT Laboratory for Artificial Intelligence, 1972.

[SM80]
Schmidt, J. W., and M. Mall, "Pascal/R Report," Report No. 66, Fachbereich Informatik, Univ. of Hamburg, January 1980.

[SMIT82]
Smith, B. C., "Reflection and Semantics in a Procedural Language," Technical Report MIT/LCS/TR-272, MIT Laboratory for Computer Science, May 1982.

[SOWA76]
Sowa, J. F., "Conceptual Structures for a Database Interface," *IBM Journal of Research and Development,* Vol. 20, No. 4, July 1976, pp. 336-357.

[SS75]
Schmid, H. A., and J. R. Swenson, "On the Semantics of the Relational Data Model," *Proc. 1975 ACM SIGMOD International Conference on the Management of Data,* San Jose, Calif., June 1975.

[SS77a]
Smith, J. M., and D. C. P. Smith, "Database Abstractions: Aggregation," *Communications of the ACM,* Vol. 20, No. 6, June 1977.

[SS77b]
Smith, J. M., and D. C. P. Smith, "Database Abstractions: Aggregation and Generalization," *ACM Transactions on Database Systems,* Vol. 2, No. 2, June 1977, pp. 105-133

[SS78a]
Smith, J. M., and D. C. P. Smith, "Principles of Conceptual Database Design," *Proc. NYU Symposium on Database Design,* New York, May 1978.

[SS78b]
Steele, G. L., Jr., and G. J. Sussman, "The Art of the Interpreter, or, The Modularity Complex (Parts Zero, One, and Two)," Memo MIT/AIM-453, MIT Laboratory for Artificial Intelligence, May 1978.

[SS78c]
Steele, G. L., Jr., G. J. Sussman, "The Revised Report on SCHEME: A Dialect of LISP," Memo MIT/AIM-452, MIT Laboratory for Artificial Intelligence, January 1978.

[SS79]
Smith, J. M., and D. C. P. Smith, "A Database Approach to Software Specification," Technical Report CCA-79-17, Computer Corporation of America, Cambridge, Mass., April 1979.

[STAN67]
Standish, T. A., "A Data Definition Facility for Programming Languages," Ph.D. thesis, Dept. of Computer Science, Carnegie-Mellon Univ., 1967.

[STEE78]
Steele, G. L., "Rabbit: A Compiler for Scheme (A Study in Compiler Optimization)," Technical Report MIT/AI/TR-474, MIT Laboratory for Artificial Intelligence, May 1978.

[STON75]
Stonebraker, M., "Implementation of Integrity Constraints and Views by Query Modification," *Proc. 1975 ACM SIGMOD International Conference on the Management of Data,* San Jose, Calif., June 1975.

[STON76]
Stonebraker, M., *et al.,* "The Design and Implementation of INGRES," *ACM Transactions on Database Systems,* Vol. 2, No. 3, September 1976.

[STON80]
Stonebraker, M., "Retrospection on a Database System," *ACM Transactions on Database Systems,* Vol. 5, No. 2, June 1980, pp. 225-240.

[STON82a]
Stonebraker, M., *et al.,* "Document Processing in a Relational Database System," Report M82/20, Electronic Research Laboratory, Univ. of California, Berkeley, June 1982.

[STON82b]
Stonebraker, M., *et al.,* "A Rules System for a Relational Database System," *Proc. 2nd International Conference on Databases,* Jerusalem, Israel, June 1982.

[SUNA78]
Sunagren, B., "Database Design in Theory and Practice," *Proc. 4th International Conference on Very Large Databases*, West Berlin, September 1978.

[SUSS75]
Sussman, G. J., *A Computer Model of Skill Acquisition,* MIT Press, 1975.

[SUSS78]
Sussman, G. J., "Slices at the Boundary Between Analysis and Synthesis," in J.-C. Latombe (ed.), *Artificial Intelligence and Pattern Recognition in Computer Aided Design,* Elsevier North-Holland, New York, 1978.

[SW80]
Shaw, M., and W. A. Wulf, "Toward Relaxing Assumptions in Languages and Their Implementations," *SIGPLAN Notices,* Vol. 15, No. 3, March 1980, pp. 45-61.

[SW82]
Schneider, H.-S., and A. I. Wasserman, *Automated Tools for Information Systems Design* (Proc. IFIP WG 8.1 Working Conference on Automated Tools for Information Systems Design and Development, New Orleans, La., January 1982), Elsevier North-Holland, New York, 1982.

[SWC70]
Sussman, G. J., T. Winograd, and E. Charniak, "MICRO-PLANNER Reference Manual," Memo MIT/AIM-203, MIT Laboratory for Artificial Intelligence, 1970.

[SWL77]
Shaw, M., W. A. Wulf, and R. L. London, "Abstraction and Verification in Alphard: Defining and Specifying Iteration and Generators," *Communications of the ACM,* Vol. 20, No. 8, August 1977.

[TARK56]
Tarski, A., *Logic, Semantics, Metamathematics,* Oxford Univ. Press, 1956.

[TF76]
Taylor, D. C., and R. L. Frank, "CODASYL Database Management Systems," *Computing Surveys,* Vol. 8, No. 1, March 1976.

[TF80]
Teorey, T. J., and J. P. Fry, "The Logical Record Access Approach to Database Design," *Computing Surveys,* Vol. 12, No. 2, June 1980.

[TH77]
Teichroew, D., and E. A. Hershey, "PSA/PSL: A Computer-Aided Technique for Structured Documentation and Analysis of Information Processing Systems," *IEEE Transactions on Software Engineering,* Vol. SE-3, No. 1, January 1977.

[THER82]
Theriault, D., "A Primer for the Act-1 Language," Memo MIT/AIM-672, MIT Laboratory for Artificial Intelligence, April 1982.

[TK78]
Tsichritzis, D., and A. Klug, "The ANSI/X3/SPARC DBMS Framework," *Information Systems,* Vol. 3, No. 4, 1978.

[TL76]
Tsichritzis, D., and F. Lochovsky, "Hierarchical Database Management: A Survey," *Computing Surveys,* Vol 8, No. 1, March 1976.

[TL82]
Tsichritzis, D., and F. Lochovsky, *Data Models,* Prentice-Hall, Englewood Cliffs, N.J., 1982.

[TSIC82]
Tsichritzis, D., "Form Management," *Communications of the ACM,* Vol. 25, No. 7, July 1982.

[TURI37]
Turing, A. M., "Computability and Lambda-Definability," *Journal of Symbolic Logic,* Vol. 2, 1937, pp. 153-163.

[TURN79]
Turner, D. A., "A New Implementation Technique for Applicative Languages," *Software—Practice & Experience,* Vol. 9, No.1, 1979.

[TURN81a]
Turner, D. A., "The Semantic Elegance of Applicative Languages," *Proc. ACM Conference on Functional Programming and Archictecture,* New Hampshire, 1981.

[TURN81b]
Turner, R., "Montague Semantics, Nominalization, and Scott's Domains," unpublished manuscript, 1981.

[TWW78]
Thatcher, J. W., E. G. Wagner, and J. B. Wright, "Data Type Specifications: Parameterization and Power of Specification Techniques," *Proc. SIGACT 10th Symposium on Theory of Computing,* May 1978, pp. 119-132.

[ULLM80]
Ullman, J. D., *Principles of Database Systems,* Computer Science Press, Potomac, Maryland, 1980.

[VASS79]
Vassiliou, Y., "Null Values in Database Management: A Denotational Semantics Approach," *Proc. 1979 ACM SIGMOD International Conference on Management of Data,* Boston, Mass., May 1979, pp. 162-169.

[VASS80]
Vassiliou, Y., "A Formal Treatment of Imperfect Information in Database Management," Ph.D. thesis, Dept. of Computer Science, Univ. of Toronto, 1980.

[VMPK75]
Van Wijngaarden, A., B. J. Maiuoux, J. E. L. Peck, C. H. A. Koster, C. M. Sintzoff, C. H. Lindsay, L. G. L. T. Meertens, and R. G. Fisker, "Revised Report on the Algorithmic Language Algol 68," *Acta Informatica,* Vol. 5, 1975, pp 1-236.

[WALD81]
Wadler, P., "Applicative Style Programming, Program Transformation and List Operators," *Proc. ACM Conference on Functional Programming and Architecture,* New Hampshire, 1981.

[WALK80]
Walker, A., "Time and Space in a Lattice of Universal Relations with Blank Entries," *XP1 Workshop on Relational Database Theory,* Stony Brook, N.Y., June-July 1980.

[WASS77]
Wasserman, A. I., "Procedure-Oriented Exception-Handling," Technical Report 27, Medical Information Science, Univ. of California, San Francisco, February 1977.

[WASS79]
Wasserman, A. I., "The Data Management Facilities of PLAIN," *Proc. 1979 ACM SIGMOD International Conference on the Management of Data,* Boston, Mass., May 1979.

[WATE78]
Waters, R. C., "Automatic Analysis of the Logical Structure of Programs," Ph.D. thesis (Technical Report MIT/AI/TR-492), MIT Laboratory for Artificial Intelligence, December 1978.

[WATE79]
Waters, R. C., "A Method for Analyzing Loop Programs," *IEEE Transactions on Software Engineering,* Vol. SE-5, No. 3, May 1979, pp. 237-247.

[WATE81]
Waters, R. C., "The Programmer's Apprentice: Knowledge Based Program Editing," *IEEE Transactions on Software Engineering,* Vol. SE-8, No. 1, January 1982.

[WB81]
Wirsing, M., and M. Broy, "An Analysis of Semantic Models for Algebraic Specifications," *International Summer School on the Theoretical Foundations of Programming Methodology,* Marktoberdorf, 1981.

[WE79]
Wiederhold, G., and R. El-Masri, "The Structural Model for Database Design," *Proc. International Conference on the Entity-Relationship Approach to Systems Analysis and Design,* Los Angeles, Calif., December 1979.

[WEYH80]
Weyhrauch, R. W., "Prolegomena to a Theory of Mechanized Formal Reasoning," *Artificial Intelligence,* Vol. 13, Nos. 1 and 2, April 1980, pp. 133-170.

[WH78]
Waterman, D. A., and F. Hayes-Roth (eds.), *Pattern-Directed Inference Systems,* Academic Press, New York, 1978.

[WILS75]
Wilson, M. L., "The Information Automata Approach to Design and Implementation of Computer-Based Systems," Technical Report FSD76-0093, IBM Federal Systems Division, Gaithersburg, Md., 1975.

[WINO72]
Winograd, T., *Understanding Natural Language,* Academic Press, New York, 1972.

[WINO73]
Winograd, T., "Breaking the Complexity Barrier (Again)," *Proc. SIGIR-SIGPLAN Interface Meeting,* November 1973.

[WINO75]
Winograd, T., "Frame Representation and the Declarative-Procedural Controversy," in [BC75].

[WIRS82]
Wirsing, M., "Structured Algebraic Specifications," *Proc. AFCET Symposium for Computer Science*, Paris, France, March 1982.

[WIRT71]
Wirth, N., "Program Development by Stepwise Refinement," *Communications of the ACM,* Vol. 14, No. 4, April 1971, pp. 221-227.

[WIRT73]
Wirth, N., *Systematic Programming, An Introduction,* Prentice-Hall, Englewood Cliffs, N.J., 1973.

[WIRT77]
Wirth, N., "Modula: A Language for Modular Programming," *Software—Practice & Experience,* Vol. 7, No. 1, January 1977, pp. 3-35.

[WKP80]
Walker, B. J., R. A. Kemmerer, and G. J. Popek, "Specification and Verificaton of the UCLA Security Kernel," *Communications of the ACM,* Vol. 23, No. 2, February 1980, pp. 118-131.

[WLGL78]
Wensley, J. H., L. Lamport, M. W. Green, K. N. Levitt, P. M. Melliar-Smith, R. E. Shostak, and C. B. Weinstock, "SIFT: Design and Analysis of a Fault-Tolerant Computer for Aircraft Control," *Proc. IEEE,* Vol. 66, No. 10, October 1978, pp. 1240-1255.

[WLS76]
Wulf, W. A., R. L. London, and M. Shaw, "An Introduction to the Construction and Verification of Alphard Programs," *IEEE Transactions on Software Engineering,* Vol. SE-2, No. 4, December 1976, pp. 253-265.

[WM77]
Wong, H. K. T., and J. Mylopoulos, "Two Views of Data Semantics: Data Models in Artificial Intelligence and Database Management," *INFOR,* Vol. 15, No. 3, 1977.

[WM81]
Weinreb, D., and D. Moon, "LISP Machine Manual," MIT Laboratory for Artificial Intelligence, March 1981.

[WONG81]
Wong, H. K. T., "Design and Verification of Interactive Information Systems Using TAXIS," Technical Report CSRG-129, CSRG, Univ. of Toronto, April 1981.

[WOOD75]
Woods, W. A., "What's in a Link: Foundations for Semantic Networks," in [BC75], pp. 35-82

[WPPD83]
Wirsing, M., P. Pepper, H. Partsch, W. Dosch, and M. Broy, "On Hierarchies of Abstract Data Types," *Acta Informatica,* 1983 (to appear).

[WS73]
Wulf, W. A., and M. Shaw, "Global Variables Considered Harmful," *SIGPLAN Notices,* Vol. 8, No. 2, February 1973, pp. 28-34.

[WSH77]
Welsh, J., M. J. Sneeringer, and C. A. R. Hoare, "Ambiguities and Insecurities in PASCAL," *Software—Practice & Experience,* Vol. 7, No. 6, 1977, pp. 685-696.

[WSHF81]
Wulf, W. A., M. Shaw, P. N. Hilfinger, and L. Flon, *Fundamental Structures of Computer Science,* Addison-Wesley, Reading, Mass., 1981.

[YANN82]
Yannakakis, M., "A Theory of Safe Locking Policies in Database Systems," *Journal of the ACM,* Vol. 29, No. 3, July 1982.

[YZ80]
Yeh, R. T., and P. Zave, "Specifying Software Requirements," *Proc. IEEE,* Vol. 68, No. 9, September 1980.

[ZANI77]
Zaniolo, C., "Relational Views in a Database System; Support for Queries," *Proc. IEEE Computer Applications and Software Conference,* Chicago, Ill., November 1977, pp. 267-275.

[ZILL80]
Zilles, S. N., "An Introduction to Data Algebras," in D. Bjoerner (ed.), *Abstract Software Specifications, Lecture Notes in Computer Science,* No. 86, Springer-Verlag, New York, 1980, pp. 248-272.

[ZISM78]
Zisman, M., "Use of Production Systems for Modelling Asynchronous Parallel Processes," in [WH78].

[ZLT82]
Zilles, S. N., P. Lucas, and J. W. Thatcher, "A Look at Algebraic Specification," submitted for publication.

Authors and Symposium Participants

Alex Borgida*†
46D Cedar Lane
Highland Park, NJ 08904

Ronald J. Brachman*
MS 30-888
Fairchild AI Lab
4001 Miranda Avenue
Palo Alto, CA 94304

Michael Brodie*†
Computer Corporation of America
Four Cambridge Center
Cambridge, MA 02142

Peter Buneman*
Moore School of Electrical Engineering
University of Pennsylvania
Philadelphia, PA 19104

Carl Hewitt*†
Artificial Intelligence Laboratory
Massachusetts Institute of Technology
545 Technology Square
Cambridge, MA 02139

David J. Israel*†
Bolt Beranek & Newman, Inc.
10 Moulton Street
Cambridge, MA 02238

Peter de Jong*†
Artificial Intelligence Laboratory
Massachusetts Institute of Technology
545 Technology Square
Cambridge, MA 02139

Roger King*†
Computer Science Department
University of Colorado
Campus Box 430
Boulder, CO 80309

Bernd Krieg-Brueckner*
FB 3 Mathematik und Informatik
Universitaet Bremen
Postfach 330440
2800 Bremen 33
Federal Republic of Germany

Winefried Lamersdorf‡
Fachbereich Informatik
Universitaet Hamburg
Schlueterstrasse 70
D-2000 Hamburg 13
Federal Republic of Germany

Hector Levesque*†
MS 30-888
Fairchild AI Lab
4001 Miranda Avenue
Palo Alto, CA 94304

* contributing author

† symposium participant

‡ assisted with recording and transcribing of symposium discussions

Manual Mall*
Fachbereich Informatik
Universitaet Hamburg
Schlueterstrasse 70
D-2000 Hamburg 13
Federal Republic of Germany

Dennis McLeod*†
Computer Science Department
SAL-200
University of Southern California
Los Angeles, CA 90007

John Mylopoulos*†
Department of Computer Science
University of Toronto
Toronto, Ontario
M5S 1A7
Canada

Rishyur Nikhil*†
Dept. of Computer and Information Science
University of Pennsylvania D2
Philadelphia, PA 19104

Michel Pilote‡
Department of Computer Science
University of Toronto
Toronto, Ontario
M5S 1A7
Canada

Manuel Reimer*†
Institut fur Informatik
ETH-Zentrum
CH-8092 Zuerich
Switzerland

Ray Reiter*†
Department of Computer Science
University of British Columbia
Vancouver, B. C.
V6T 1W5
Canada

Charles Rich*†
Artificial Intelligence Laboratory
Massachusetts Institute of Technology
545 Technology Square
Cambridge, MA 02139

Dzenan Ridjanovic*†‡
School of Management
271 19th Avenue South
University of Minnesota
Minneapolis, MN 55455

Joachim W. Schmidt*†
Fachbereich Informatik
Universität Frankfurt
Dantestr. 9
6000 Frankfurt
Federal Republic of Germany

Mary Shaw*†
Department of Computer Science
Carnegie-Mellon University
Pittsburgh, PA 15213

Michael Stonebraker*†
College of Engineering and Computer Science
M265 Cory Hall
University of California
Berkeley, CA 94720

Harry K. T. Wong*†
Bldg. 50-B, Room 3238
Lawrence Berkeley Lab
Berkeley, CA 94720

Stephen N. Zilles*†
IBM Research Division
K52/282
5600 Cottle Road
San Jose, CA 95193

Index

E

F

G

H

I

S

T

U

V

Relational Database Systems

Analysis and Comparison

Edited by **J. W. Schmidt** and **M. L. Brodie**

1983. xv, 618 pages, cloth
ISBN 3-540-12032-7

This book is the most comprehensive and detailed analysis of relational database technology to date. A detailed catalog of Relational Database Management System (RDBMS) features is presented and used to analyze fourteen of the most important existing RDBMS. All fourteen systems are compared, in a simple tabular form, with respect to their features. The book therefore gives a detailed analysis of the state-of-the-art in relational technology. In addition, the feature catalog provides a generic description of RDBMS that can be used to evaluate future RDBMS and DBMS in general.

MIX
Papier aus verantwortungsvollen Quellen
Paper from responsible sources
FSC® C105338

If you have any concerns about our products,
you can contact us on
ProductSafety@springernature.com

In case Publisher is established outside the EU,
the EU authorized representative is:
Springer Nature Customer Service Center GmbH
Europaplatz 3, 69115 Heidelberg, Germany

Printed by Libri Plureos GmbH
in Hamburg, Germany